Law in Urban Design
and Planning

LAW IN URBAN DESIGN AND PLANNING

The Invisible Web

Richard Tseng-yu Lai

 VAN NOSTRAND REINHOLD COMPANY
_____New York

Printed in the United States of America

Designed by Rosa Delia Vasquez

Van Nostrand Reinhold Company Inc.
115 Fifth Avenue
New York, New York 10003

Van Nostrand Reinhold Company Limited
Molly Millars Lane
Wokingham, Berkshire RG11 2PY, England

Van Nostrand Reinhold
480 La Trobe Street
Melbourne, Victoria 3000, Australia

Macmillan of Canada
Division of Canada Publishing Corporation
164 Commander Boulevard
Agincourt, Ontario M1S 3C7, Canada

16 15 14 13 12 11 10 9 8 7 6 5 4 3 2 1

Library of Congress Cataloging-in-Publication Data

Lai, Richard Tseng-yu, 1937–
    Law in urban design and planning.

    Bibliography: p.
    Includes index.
    1. City planning and redevelopment law—United
States. I. Title.
KF5729.L35 1987   346.7304'5   86-32436
ISBN 0-442-25885-2   347.30645

This book is dedicated to the memory of my father, Shih Chen Lai, who taught me how to write and to think; and to my mother, Hsiao-hsin Chang Lai, who made me who I am; and to my wife, Barbara, for her persevering support, patient understanding, and sustaining love; and to my sons, Valdrian and Alexander, who are teaching me the truly important things of life.

Contents

Preface

There are several facets to the conception and purpose of this book. First is to obtain a view of urban design and planning law, not through the disciplinary confines of a single profession, but from a broadly humanist vantage, or, in terms less ambitious and more current, from an interdisciplinary perspective. The second intent is to examine law as a historic, if sometimes indeliberate, determinant of urban form, and to study the present practice of planning law as well as its frequently overlooked but powerful potential as an instrument of purposeful urban design. Third is to suggest a definition of architectural and design professionalism that would construe law and other disciplines nontraditional to architecture as effective vehicles for advancing the values of design in society. However, because it is somewhat propositional in nature, this third facet is suggested only implicitly, so that the book may function with the objectivity, comprehensiveness, and detail necessary of any instructional text and substantive reference.

In pursuing this work, I have enjoyed the inspiration, encouragement, and guidance of many friends, in particular Robert Burrows, Martin T. Farris, John C. Keene, Barbara E. Lai, Morton J. Schussheim, and Myer R. Wolfe. I am also grateful to the departments of city planning of New York and San Francisco for their cooperation. I must also acknowledge my debt for the inspiration and aid of the many writers cited in the pages of this book, and I apologize for any inaccuracies or distortions that I may have committed in expressing their views. Last, I wish to thank my colleagues, peers, and students in architecture, planning, and law, for whom I write.

Introduction: The Invisible Web

Ideas and creations reflect cultural origin as much as individual genius. However myriad and diverse, a people's perceptions, beliefs, institutions, and creations are all woven into and cut from a common fabric that distinguishes their civilization from all others. Though apparently disparate in focus and discipline, the urban design and legal system that characterize a society are threads of the same cloth. The nature of law and the design of cities inherently reflect and contribute to the parent culture. As Churchill once said, "We shape our buildings and afterwards our buildings shape us."[1] In much the same way that architecture and man share a reciprocal relationship, so law and urban design exist in a cultural symbiosis, at once expressing and molding the very nature of social man and determining and reflecting each other as attributes of his civilization.

Simply defined, urban design is the composition of architectural form and open space in a community context. The elements of a city's architecture are its buildings, urban landscape, and service infrastructure just as form, structure, and internal space are elements of a building. Whether public or private in actual ownership, urban design comprises the architecture of an entire community that all citizens can enjoy and identify as their own. Like architecture, urban design reflects considerations of function, economics, and efficiency as well as aesthetic and cultural qualities.

[1]393 H. C. Deb. (5th ser.) 403 (1943). Cited by James B. Milner, "The Development Plan and Master Plans: Comparisons," in *Law and Land,* ed. Charles M. Haar (Cambridge: Harvard U. Press and M.I.T. Press, 1964), 60.

1

Though customarily construed in terms of elements traditionally associated with the environmental design professions, urban design reasonably
embraces all land-use considerations that affect the physical and aesthetic
character of the city. In addition to being involved in the composition and
control of urban form and open space, the urban designer should be vitally
concerned about a variety of related issues: the social and functional elements that lend life and vitality to the city; the conservation of landmarks
that enhance the quality of urban life; the purging of eyesores that detract
from it; the public regulations and economic incentives that either foster or
detract from design quality; indeed, the full spectrum of considerations that
influence or respond to the physical nature of cities.

This is not to suggest that urban design should be totally inclusive of
all city planning concerns. Whereas the early pioneers of urban design once
believed that their craft alone held the means and ends of all city planning,
today urban design is valued more as an essential part of the interdisciplinary approach necessary to plan for and deal with what Timothy J. Cartwright has labeled a "metaproblem,"[2] the immense complex of intertwined
and ever-changing issues—social, economic, political, technological, cultural, environmental, and design—that confront contemporary urban society.

Of all the planning disciplines, urban design is distinguished, even
among those also devoted to consideration of the physical elements of the
city, by its particular concern for the aesthetic quality of the city environment. Though most urban designers would be quick to point out—and quite
correctly—that aesthetics is not their sole concern, none would deny the
aesthetic aspect of design. In this regard, nothwithstanding its fundamental
association with comprehensive city planning, urban design also has a ge-
neric affiliation with architecture, the mother discipline of design, recognized for its capability in matters of man-made environmental aesthetics.

From a traditional perspective, urban design is a progeny and variation
of architecture, albeit at a generally greater scale and complexity. Like architecture, urban design is seen as project oriented, entailing construction
goals and direct expenditures of capital. It is undertaken under the mandate
of a unified entity that maintains full practical control over all considerations of design, development, and use, usually through ownership or contractual interest in the property intended for development. As in individual
building design, urban design seen in this way generally has definitive, end-
state objectives that can be attained in a relatively short term. This view is
not unlike the traditional concept of urban planning that is held by archi-

---

[2]Timothy J. Cartwright, "Problems, Solutions and Strategies: A Contribution to the
Theory and Practice of Planning," *Journal of the American Institute of Planners* 39 (May
1973): 183.

tects, embodied in the City Beautiful movement of the late nineteenth century or urban design practice under the federal Urban Renewal program of the mid twentieth century.[3]

A second perception of urban design derives more from an approach associated with public planning in a democracy, emphasizing the pluralistic nature and incremental process of urban development and the definition of long-term and, for the most part, more comprehensive and general public goals. While maintaining its creative roots in architecture, urban design from the public-policy perspective is the discipline within the field of city planning that is specifically concerned with the design and coordination of the physical future of an entire community. It is concerned with all development, public or private, and how such development can be administered by local government to forward the community's urban-design objectives.

New York urban designer Jonathan Barnett characterizes this second view of urban design as "designing cities without designing buildings."[4] Seen in this way, it is design without the expectation of immediate, concrete execution but with the definition and implementation of long-range policies that will lend design coherence and form to incremental private development. Given the private nature of land ownership and the piecemeal pattern of growth and redevelopment, this public-policy concept of urban design requires for its fulfillment some measure of centralized control so that private development can be coordinated and guided toward deliberate, meaningful design objectives.

By necessity as much as by conviction, this approach considers the client for urban design as a heterogeneous community of individual citizens, typically representing fragmented rather than unified views. Among those with particular interest in any given public plan or urban design scheme are the private owners of affected properties, many of whom have their own plans and intentions concerning the best use of their holdings that may well be at variance with the design objectives sought by the community and its governing body. Such conflict between public planning and private rights is a fundamental characteristic distinguishing urban design in the tradition of architecture from urban design as public policy.

An implicit requirement of the latter perspective is that the law on land development, city planning, and urban design be not only understood but creatively wielded by the urban designer, city planner, and public attorney as a deliberate instrument of design policy and implementation. Said Dallas

---

[3]42 U.S.C. 1450 *et seq.,* Slum Clearance and Urban Renewal, Pub. L. 560, 68 Stat. 622, Title III of the Housing Act of 1954, amending Title I of the Housing Act of 1949, Pub. L. 171 (81st. Cong.), 63 Stat. 413, 414.

[4]Jonathan Barnett, *An Introduction to Urban Design* (New York: Harper & Row, 1982), 55.

city attorney H. P. Kucera before a conference of planners and lawyers in
1960:

> Civic beautification cannot be done directly by law, but it may be done indi-
> rectly. The law can prevent or suppress certain things that are ugly by control-
> ling or regulating the same. The law can provide the warp so that the architect,
> engineer, planner or artist can use his talents in designing and arranging the
> woof to give the eye a pleasant reaction.[5]

For the designer of cities, knowledge of the nature of law should be as
essential as is knowledge of the nature of materials for the architect of
buildings. Only with an understanding of the essence of the law can the
urban designer create in terms of it and use it advantageously. For the
knowledgeable and skilled, the law can be an implement of design as much
as mortar and stone.

Whether at all acknowledged or consciously used, law has been a determinative factor in the design of cities from early history to the present day.
Like architecture and the city, it is integral to the very definition of civilization. In *Law in Economy and Society,* the German social analyst Max
Weber in 1925 defined the power of law as a basic structural element of
man's ecology:

> An order will be called law if it is externally guaranteed by the probability
> that coercion (physical or psychological), to bring about conformity or avenge
> violation, will be applied by a staff of people holding themselves specially
> ready for that purpose.[6]

The force of law remains whether that "order" is a social norm arrived at
through democratic process or authoritarian means. In the latter case, the
function of law is relatively simplistic, for in a monolithic society the controversy that characterizes conflict resolution in a democracy is minimal.
Indeed, according to the Marxist ideal, law would "wither away" in the
harmony of a classless society. In a pluralistic free-enterprise system, however, law is recognized as fundamental, for it defines and guarantees
through its coercive potential the norms for all social conduct, in land use
and development as in other areas of a free-market democracy. According
to Weber, a prerequisite of a modern economy is "a legal system the function of which is calculable in accordance with rational rules."[7] In a capitalist society, the importance of the state lies in its laws, which provide the

---

[5]H. P. Kucera, "The Legal Aspects of Aesthetics in Zoning," *Institute on Planning and
Zoning* 1 (1960): 45.

[6]Max Weber, *On Law in Economy and Society,* ed. and trans. Max Rheinstein (1925;
reprint, New York: Simon & Schuster, Clarion, 1954), 5.

[7]Ibid., 40.

social structure or predefined rules according to which the free market must function. Weber's thesis holds that a modern economic system cannot exist without the frame of a promptly and predictably functioning "statal" legal order, enforced and guaranteed by the strongest coercive power of government.[8] It is this coercive force of law that can be fashioned into a tool for affirmative urban design and planning.

In his classic definition of laissez-faire capitalism, the eighteenth-century English economist and philosopher Adam Smith suggested that a free-enterprise society is effectively guided by the "invisible hand" of the free market.[9] In more contemporary times, urban designer David A. Crane describes the urban infrastructure of public facilities as being a "capital web" that can be manipulated by the designer in determining the direction and form of urban development.[10] Accepting the premise that law is the structure by which society institutes and enforces its mores and practices, one might borrow concepts and terms from both Smith and Crane, and consider a society's system of law as constituting an "invisible web" to which urban development, as other social endeavors, must conform. Significantly, this invisible web is not immutable and can itself be woven by the astute urban designer into a conscious instrument of community design.

Creation of design is distinct from design control. Certainly the architect commands the virtuosity of artistic creativity, but it is the owner of property and not the architect who determines whether a design is to be successfully executed, abandoned, or corrupted. Though the owner can check his architect's efforts, he is not power omnipotent, for private property itself is subject to the constraints of law. Any applicant for a building permit can attest that zoning and other codes can specify requirements, exact expenditures, and exercise veto over an architect's design or even an owner's wishes. Robert M. Anderson writes:

> Most zoning ordinances are in some degree intended to affect the appearance of the community. Some influence the design of buildings, at least insofar as to dictate whether they shall be large or small, one story or two, tall or short, and residential or commercial. Others limit placement and shape by regulating yards, setback and size of lot. In concert, these regulations have been said to exert more influence upon the design of a building than the architect who draws the plans.[11]

Such is the compulsion of the invisible web, for just as building design—and by extension, urban design—are subject to proprietary rights, so

[8]Ibid., 39–40.

[9]Adam Smith, *An Inquiry into the Nature and Causes of the Wealth of Nations* (1776; reprint, Chicago: U. of Chicago Press, 1976), bk. 4, ch. 2, 477.

[10]David A. Crane, "The City Symbolic," *Journal of the American Institute of Planners* (Nov. 1960): 26, 285–86.

[11]Robert M. Anderson, "Architectural Controls," *Syracuse L. Rev.* 12 (1960–61): 26.

property rights are subject to the law. As Francis S. Philbrick observed, "Property is the creature and dependent of law."[12] Whereas design is subservient to the prerogatives of property, and property in turn is a product of law, law itself is determined by society. John E. Cribbet, quoting the early-nineteenth-century English jurist Jeremy Bentham as well as Francis S. Philbrick, writes:

> "Property and law are born together, and die together. Before laws were made there was no property; take away laws and property ceases." However, [Philbrick] recognized the vital truth that the law itself evolves only as it reflects the society it serves. In his opening paragraph, he noted: "The forces that change the law in other than trivial ways lie outside it. It is to other things than law, therefore, that your attention must primarily be called." Thus the pattern is complete: property is shaped by law, but law is shaped and controlled by society.[13]

It is interesting to reflect upon Churchill's remark on the relation between man and architecture in light of Cribbet's observation, for Churchill's comment that mankind is shaped by environment would complete a full circle of symbiosis. In the final analysis, all of social man's ideas and creations in any realm, whether urban design or law, are threads of a common weave.

Integral to this cultural tapestry is the singular effect that law exerts over urban development. If ideas and creations are indeed as attributable to cultural heritage and social environment as to individual genius, then it is appropriate that perceiving law as one determinant of urban design begins with an awareness of the origin and nature of the invisible web itself, as well as an appreciation of its demonstrated historic consequences on urban form.

Understanding the past is fundamental in contemplating the law. American case law itself derives from the practice of common law, which is based on past practice and precedent. Accordingly, in addition to providing a synopsis of the intertwined history of urban design and law, this book also emphasizes case law, beginning with the foundations of American constitutionalism, proceeding to the evolution of the law governing land zoning and city planning practice, and turning finally to consideration of more current issues and methods of aesthetic and design controls.

---

[12]Francis S. Philbrick, "Changing Conceptions of Property in Law," *U. of Pennsylvania L. Rev.* 86 (1938): 729.

[13]John E. Cribbet, "Changing Concepts of the Law of Land Use," *Iowa L. Rev.* 50 (1965): 245–46. Quoting Jeremy Bentham, *Theory of Legislation,* transl. R. Hildreth (London: Kegan Paul, Trench, Trubner and Co., 1911), 113, and Philbrick, "Changing Conceptions," 691.

The first part of the book traces the historic origins of the invisible web in England and the United States, observing the social and philosophical correlation between the law and the urban design of the two English-speaking cultures. Part 2 studies the constitutional foundations of American planning, focusing on principles articulated by economic philosopher Friedrich A. Hayek and those established by Oliver Wendell Holmes, justice of the United States Supreme Court. Part 2 traces the historic emergence of zoning under the police power, the predominant legal instrument for land planning in the United States to this day. Part 3 presents an introductory but critical summary of the organization and function of the contemporary system of land planning and development controls that has evolved through practice over the last half century. The section also includes a brief examination of some innovations attempted and various issues that have arisen during recent years.

Part 4 addresses considerations adjunct to urban design, specifically the regulation of such potential aesthetic nuisances as junkyards and outdoor advertising and the preservation of such urban amenities as historic and architectural landmarks. Part 5 analyzes the public regulation of aesthetic expression, as practiced by local communities in reviewing and regulating private architectural design. The section concludes with a study of comprehensive urban design controls being carried out in two American cities, New York and San Francisco. Part 6 examines aspects of other public authorities, such as eminent domain, compensable regulation, public subsidy, and tax policy, that offer potential new avenues for progressive urban design controls beyond the police power.

I am not a lawyer, but an urban-design architect and city planner whose goals in writing this book are twofold. The first objective is only implied: to achieve a humanistic or interdisciplinary perspective of the cultural correlation among urban design, city planning, and the law. I hope to offer an interdisciplinary introduction to law in urban design and planning to the professional and student urban designer and architect, and conversely, to acquaint the legal professional and law student with the values and concerns of urban design and city planning as they relate to the law.

My second aim is to extend beyond the normal purview and methodology of traditional architectural and urban design to perceive the law as a determinative factor in the form and design of cities: to recognize the law as a historic though ofttimes indeliberate and even accidental ordainer of city form, and to conceive the law as an effective and compelling public instrument for purposeful and reasoned urban design in the context of a pluralistic, free-enterprise society.

Concerning this second, more practical view, though much of the language used and perspectives adopted in the book are those of law, and legal citations are provided for purposes of reference and research, this work does not venture into technical consideration of planning controls as applied to specific issues of urban design. Such practical problem solving is the proper domain of the attorney expert in the practice of property and land development control law. There exist many fine texts on property and city planning law, as well as a number of provocative monographs, journal articles, and critiques on innovative techniques and new practices in urban planning and design law. These publications address specific considerations and applications of practical law regarding planning and design, and their focus is not duplicated here. The reader is also cautioned to appreciate the constantly evolving nature of the law, both legislative and case law, and to understand that in this book detail is included to substantiate longer-lasting principles and to indicate trends rather than to serve a journal function.

Urban designers have yet to realize and take full advantage of the potential of law as an urban-design control element. An exciting new frontier of urban design is being opened up in such cities as New York and San Francisco—urban design through public policy and regulation, or urban design in the comparatively new tradition of American city planning that recognizes the constraints to centralized determination and planning power that are posed by social pluralism and private rights guaranteed by the Constitution. Significantly, urban design through public policy and regulation assumes particular relevance when investment capital is lacking for public improvements at an urban scale. But to be effective in this emerging form of urban design demands of the designer new perceptions, skills, and training in the law.

Until the urban designer acquires at least a conceptual understanding of the law relevant to his subject and craft, he will be to city design like an architect ignorant of the logic of structures. As Supreme Court Justice William J. Brennan, Jr., once wrote: "After all, if a policeman must know the Constitution, then why not a planner?"[14] For that matter, why not an urban-design architect? Although he need not be a lawyer any more than he need be a structural engineer, understanding the invisible web is a working requitement of the public designer. It is such basic knowledge of legal considerations in urban design and planning that this book is in large part intended to impart.

More fundamental is for the urban designer to grasp the full social implications of not only the end artifacts of city building but of the implemental process as well. Only with such understanding can he seek appropriate social means to create city environments that are both a suitable habitat and a fitting expression of a free, pluralistic, and humane society. In combining the perceptions of law and design, it should be understood that whereas law by nature and intent strives for precision and clear articulation,

---

[14]San Diego Gas & Electric Co. v. City of San Diego, 450 U.S. 261 (1981), 661, note 26.

good urban design, like good architecture, defies precise definition. As Paul Goldberger, the *New York Times* architecture critic, has expressed it:

> Architecture has never been a question of formulas—like all kinds of design, the making of a great, or even a good building involves something special, something magical if you will, that cannot be put into words.[15]

Nonetheless, there is no incongruity to aspire to an interdisciplinary vantage, whereby the special insight and wisdom of the many writers cited—the historian, the philosopher, the city planner, the urban designer, the lawyer, and the court judge—are synthesized to appreciate and understand the law as a practical and historic determinant of urban design.

[15]Paul Goldberger, *United Airlines Mainliner,* May 1978, 63. Quoted by Clifford L. Weaver and Richard F. Babcock, *City Zoning: The Once and Future Frontier* (Chicago and Washington, D.C.: Planners Press, 1979), 302.

PART I

THE ORIGINS

Chapter 1

England: The Organic Society

The nature of any society is evident in every aspect of its culture. The religious beliefs, social institutions, language, art, and technology of a civilization all contribute to and draw from a symbiotic totality. A common cultural thread runs throughout the weave of any social fabric, both in history and in the present day.

Each facet of pre-Hellenic culture, for example, revealed the ancient Greek's characteristic preoccupation with comprehensive understanding. His magnificent obsession with finite definition was equally reflected in the anthropomorphic nature of his religion, the tangible quality of his art and architecture, his geometric description of abstract space, and even his idealized society as defined in Plato's *Republic*. In much the same way, the social formalism of Confucianism and the harmonious dichotomy of Taoism were embodied in every aspect of Chinese civilization, from the patriarchal order and scholarly foundations of Chinese society to the spatial

While annotated references to Rasmussen's *London: The Unique City* are minimal, research for this chapter draws heavily from Rasmussen's work. Much of the material on the development of London contained in this chapter condenses information found in chapters 2 through 6 of Rasmussen's book. The appendix chapter "Land and Building Speculation" of the 1967 edition is of particular interest as well. Researchers are also directed to *The Taking Issue* by Bosselman, Callies, and Banta, especially chapter 5 and the valuable footnote annotations throughout this governmental report. Other information on early land law in England is available in Cornelius J. Moynihan, *Introduction to the Law of Real Property,* and to Frederic William Maitland, *Domesday Book and Beyond.* All works cited above are listed in the bibliography.

essence and sequential hierarchy of its architecture, and from the mysticism and infinitude of the misty landscapes of the Sung dynasties to the passive strength of kung fu combat. By the same token, the nature of modern American culture is mirrored in such diverse aspects of contemporary society as the American's implicit faith in the free-enterprise system and his romantic identification with legendary frontier individualism, as well as in the leisure diversions and sociopsychological concerns of the modern American.

From this premise of cultural symbiosis a corollary can be drawn. Though a society's system of law may differ considerably in form and substance from the physical character and design of its cities, both invariably manifest some fundamental attribute and philosophical perspective particular to that society. In abstracting this common essence, one can better comprehend the diversities and complexities that compose a culture. To assume a single distinctive characteristic is perhaps to oversimplify, but often, as in the natural sciences, the greatest mysteries are unraveled by simple conceptions. What is the cultural essence shared by a society's urban design and system of law? How can considerations seemingly as disparate as urban form and law reflect a common characteristic? The answers to these questions are at the heart of these first two chapters that explore the cultural symbiosis between law and urban design in history.

Beyond the intellectual value of history is its practical application in refining one's perception of the present and future. Even the most worthy venture in urban design and planning must not be narrowly conceived but should be considered in the context of history and culture and in terms of its fundamental effect on society as a whole. To understand the full social implications of any undertaking—whether a goal in city planning, an objective in urban design, or an implemental process in zoning law—there can be no better teacher than history.

THE ORGANIC ESSENCE

Many aspects of contemporary American culture derive from England. Language may be the most apparent and even the most fundamental, but it is not the sole characteristic of the English heritage in the United States. Concepts of government and law as well as tastes in design and architecture survived the Revolution to contribute to the foundations of American civilization. To perceive the invisible web in contemporary America and its effect upon urban design, it is therefore appropriate to examine the origins that the American web shares with the development of English law and townscape, for the unique evolution of these two cultural attributes has bestowed upon English society an organic quality that distinguishes Anglo culture and its colonial derivatives from all others.

English Law

Two developments stand out in the emergence of English law, both occurring during the Middle Ages. The first was the evolution of English common law. Prior to the Norman Conquest, Saxon law was based largely upon local customs, but these customary laws, or *custumals,* were found inadequate and ill-suited to the establishment of a strong, centralized government that William the Conqueror required to rule his new kingdom. Therefore, to build a military administration for his island conquest and to ensure a loyal following, William assigned much of his domain to his Norman henchmen and delegated them authority to govern it.

With the kingdom divided administratively, justice became the purview of individual feudal lords. Disputes among the populace were settled by the local ruler presiding at his court, with decisions based largely on arguments, testimony, and evidence presented by the quarreling parties. In time, however, the number of cases brought to trial at each feudal administration became so overwhelming and complex as to require a professional judiciary at its own court. Gradually, a body of common law emerged incrementally through experience gained from numerous precedent decisions.

Although doctrines of permissible social conduct were never formally codified, decisions written by professional judges on individual cases were recorded as precedents to be respected and adhered to in adjudicating subsequent disputes. As in the past, when appeals from rulings by lesser nobility could be brought before an overlord, decisions made by lower courts of law could also be appealed to higher courts.

Because juries composed of laymen participated in the trial process, traditional social mores became part of the common law. Principles of law applicable to cases at trial emerged piecemeal through a continual empirical process of precedent and interpretation. Only when diverse and confused rulings caused technical entanglements or when the system of stare decisis thwarted the natural evolution of social norms was deliberate legislative reform necessary. This evolutionary and organic system of law reflected practical response to the immediate situation rather than adherence to preconceived principles of jurisprudence or government. As a consequence, the common law held no special awe for the dictates of a ruler, however rationally or benevolently conceived.

The second development that contributed to the singular English perspective on the law, and on property in particular, was the demise of feudalism and the ascension of private rights. The decline of feudal authority was significantly greater in Britain than elsewhere because internal rebellions forced the English Crown to accede early to laws promulgated initially by the nobility and later by the common people. These events forever distinguished the English relationship between the ruler and the ruled from the monarchies of continental Europe. Foremost in influence was the Magna Carta, which was forced upon King John in 1215 by barons aggrieved by "arbitrary infringements of personal liberty and rights of property."[1]

Before the Magna Carta was adopted, England practiced the feudal model inherited from William the Conqueror's native Normandy, whereby the king and his heirs claimed dominion over all territory. Under the system, only the king actually "owned" land. The landed nobility "held" freehold title to their estates on condition of fealty and an obligation to supply a specified quota of knights to defend the Crown. Such conditional tenure was most prevalent, although vassals of the king ranging from cooks to clergy were also awarded tenancy in land. Noblemen with large freehold estates would often subinfeudate or dispense subtenures through copyhold or leasehold to retainers pledged to their own service rather than to the king, thus further extending the feudal hierarchy and dispersing land tenure to a greater segment of society.

Beginning with the Magna Carta, control over land by the monarch began to diminish. Failure to obey royal demands for funds or military assistance no longer meant automatic forfeiture of rights in land held. Chapter 39 of the Magna Carta addressed one of the major complaints of the noble tenants against the Crown.

> No free man shall be taken, imprisoned, disseised, outlawed, banished, or in any way destroyed, nor will We proceed against or prosecute him, except by the lawful judgment of his peers and by the law of the land.[2]

The provisions of Chapter 47 further reduced the king's right to "afforest" large areas as his hunting preserves, an onerous practice since it deprived tenants of potentially profitable land for cultivation and other purposes. No longer could the king usurp land for his own ends or for the needs of the state.

Personal military service as a running covenant on the land likewise began to decline. Among its radical provisions, the Magna Carta allowed the heir of a holding conditional on martial allegiance to escape his military responsibilities by payment of a sum for each knight's service due. Seventy-five years later, the Statutes Quia Emptores permitted the transfer of land and accompanying military obligation without payment of penalty to the overlord. Thus martial allegiance as an encumbrance on real property in Britain lost its meaning. Even peasants managed to purchase their land in copyhold or otherwise evade their feudal responsibilities. Other statutes

---

[1]William S. Holdsworth, *A History of English Law* (1903; reprint, London: Methuen & Co., Sweet and Maxwell, 1966), vol. 2, 215.

[2]*Magna Carta, Text and Commentary,* ed. A. E. Dick Howard (Charlottesville: U. Press of Virginia, 1964), 43.

gradually eroded the vestiges of feudalism until eventually legislation abolished tenurial obligations in England altogether. With feudal service no longer a requirement of land tenure, the concept of active civic responsibility as a concomitant obligation of land ownership also diminished, the real property tax remaining as the sole vestige of that ancient duty.

With the demise of the feudal system in England, the power of the English monarchy gradually gave way to the rights of private property. The ascendancy of private rights culminated in the constitutional conflict of the seventeenth century that led to the Civil War of 1642–49 and the Revolution of 1688. In their native Scotland, the Stuart Kings had enjoyed a tradition of strong monarchical powers, unimpeded by English common law and the strictures of the Magna Carta. With the ascension of James Stuart to the English throne in 1603, Britain became torn by the issue of divine rights versus the prerogatives of Parliament. James's notion that the sovereign's power of proclamation was absolute was challenged by Sir Edward Coke, who championed the supremacy of common law, arguing that the courts had the right to interpret and enforce statutes, and that "the King cannot take any cause out of any courts and give judgment upon it himself."[3] Coke held the guarantees of the Magna Carta to be fundamental. The second of his *Institutes of the Laws of England* published in 1642 reiterated the Magna Carta.

> No man shall be disseised, that is, put out of seisen, or dispossessed for his free-hold (that is) lands, or livelihood, or of his liberties of free-domes, and free-customes, as belong to him by his free birthright, unless it be by the lawful judgment, that is, verdict of his equals (that is, men of his own condition) or by the law of the land (that is, so to speak, once and for all) by the due course and process of law.[4]

Coke's defense of property became the foundation of even stronger arguments later set forth in the eighteenth century by Sir William Blackstone, who declared in his *Commentaries on the Laws of England,*

> There is nothing which so generally strikes the imagination, and engages the affections of mankind, as the right of property; or that sole and despotic dominion which one man claims and exercises over the external things of the world, in total exclusion of the rights of any other individual in the universe.[5]

[3]Catherine Drinker Bowen, *The Lion and the Throne* (Boston: Little, Brown, Atlantic Monthly Press, 1956), 304. Citing Edward Coke, 12 *Reports* 64–65 (ed. 1738).

[4]Fred Bosselman, David Callies, and John Banta, *The Taking Issue* (Washington: USGPO, 1973), 78. Quoting Edward Coke, *The Second Part of the Institutes of the Laws of England* (1642; reprint, London: E. and R. Bronke, Bell-Yard, New Temple Bar, 1797), 46.

[5]William Blackstone, *Commentaries on the Laws of England* (1765–69; reprint, London: Dawsons, 1966), bk. 2, ch. 1, 2.

In contrast to the absolute reign of kings elsewhere, the rights of private property in England became established as the most liberal in Europe, free even from edicts issued by the king. From the feudal domination by the monarch, the rights of property evolved into absolute domination by the private landowner, his free use of property brooking interference by neither king nor government. Thus as in the empirical development of common law, so events in Britain's political history expanded the rights of private property to supersede even the power of Crown and state. Together with the rise of common law, the decline of centralized authority in England in relation to the developing rights of private property owners foreshadowed the government's inability during the later Renaissance to administer urban design.

The organic development of English common law is particularly revealing as a characteristic reflection of fundamental English thought. The principles of English empiricism as described by such philosophers as Locke, Berkeley, Hume, and Mill share an emphasis on experience and observation as the principal guides. The inherent influence of organic English empiricism is evident not only in the development of English law but in all aspects of native English culture. This inductive essence is also apparent in the precepts of Adam Smith's laissez-faire, wherein social order and benefit would arise organically from the natural functions of free-enterprise economics.

The Design of the English Village

Like English common law, the most native English urban form, the village, also evolved organically during the Middle Ages. The origins of most towns were based on matters of practicality rather than on any theoretical or abstract plan. A source of water such as a spring or river ford was usually the basis for the initial settlement. Some hamlets evolved along a roadside, while others clustered about a central green. A naturally defensible site was often a principal consideration, although less so on the island kingdom than on the Continent. The most typical aspect of the medieval village was its atypical form. Though some were founded on the planned, rectilinear forms of ancient Roman encampments, most grew organically in practical response to the geography of the site and the needs of the inhabitants.

Lacking the skill or need for accurate surveys, the original villagers constructed their communities along irregular lines. Each structure was distinct in its design and construction, reflecting the particular needs of occupants. For the same reason, of the ten thousand villages in Britain, no two evolved alike, since variations of site and function yielded an infinite variety of urban form and space. As Lewis Mumford wrote on the organic development of the medieval town:

> In organic planning, one thing leads to another, and what began as the seizure of an accidental advantage may prompt a strong element in a design, which

an a priori plan could not anticipate, and in all probability would overlook or rule out. Many of the surviving irregularities in medieval towns are due to streams that have been covered over, trees that were later cut down, old balks that once defined rural fields. Custom and property rights, once established in the form of lots, boundaries, permanent rights of way, are hard to efface.

> Organic planning does not begin with a preconceived goal: it moves from need to need, from opportunity to opportunity, in a series of adaptations that themselves become increasingly coherent and purposeful, so that they generate a complex, final design, hardly less unified than a pre-formed geometric pattern.[6]

Despite its apparent randomness, Mumford emphasized, organic planning nevertheless led to "deliberately unified and integrated design" embodying a "universal pattern . . . as if there were in fact a conscious theory that guided this town planning."[7]

As in English common law, organic development and empirical response to practicality were the essence of indigenous English community design. Other societies also evolved organic town forms during the Middle Ages. However, on the Continent, neither native philosophy nor law developed organically as in England but instead were based in part upon the traditions of classicism. During the Renaissance, continental society and law permitted the supersedure and even the obliteration of medieval urban forms by Renaissance designs. In contrast, the system of English law not only protected its medieval urban form, but actually resurrected the organic plan of London after the destruction of the capital city by fire at the height of the Renaissance.

CONTINENTAL EUROPE: THE A PRIORI SOCIETY

The quest for perfect definition of the unknown and abstract is a characteristic of classicism that has pervaded Western thought through the centuries, presaging the rationalist views of such influential continental philosophers as Descartes, Spinoza, Leibniz, and Kant. In contrast to the medieval trust in experience and observation characteristic of English empiricism, the rationalists held the belief that reason, independent of the senses, constitutes a superior source of knowledge.

Continental Law

On the Continent, this thirst for rational understanding and absolute definition became the basis for intellectual preconception, both in law and in city design. Whereas English common law is an organic product of em-

---

[6]Lewis Mumford, *The City in History* (New York: Harcourt, Brace & World, Harbinger, 1961), 302.
[7]Ibid., 302–3.

pirical development through the Middle Ages, continental societies trace their formal codes of civil law directly to Roman law and the canons of Catholicism, which itself originated in classical law. Since the Justinian Code, civil law has been conceived through the abstract philosophies of learned men, whose a priori concepts of ideal morality and justice took the form of written legal codes to govern social behavior. Continental concepts of government, from Plato's *Republic* to Marx's socialist state, have prescribed social institutions according to intellectual principles rather than empirical experience. Following the same premise, civil law has been based on deductive and rational preconceptions of society and behavior, unlike common law, which has evolved inductively through practice and observation. Despite the Reformation, even the civil codes of Protestant Europe derived from Catholic belief in absolute divine order and natural law.

Perhaps the definitive distinction between common law and civil law was made by Max Weber in his analysis *On Law in Economy and Society,* in which he categorized different legal theories as evolved through history.[8] The first type is inductive or "irrational" law, so labeled by Weber because it results from experience rather than from a priori principles. So-called irrational laws may derive from either formal or substantive processes. In the formal method, a principle comes about as a consequence of a formal event beyond the realm of reason, such as from prophecy, oracle, or trial by combat. In contrast, substantively irrational laws result from reactions to particular cases or circumstances, as exemplified by jury trial, a practice generally associated with common law. In this type of proceeding, laymen jurors with no formal background in the law are empowered to pass judgment based solely on the substance of factual evidence presented before the court.

The second type of law was labeled by Weber as "rational" because it is derived deductively through the application of preconceived rules. As with the irrational, this type of law can arise through either substantive or formal means. Substantively rational law is guided by ideological concepts outside of law itself, such as ethical, religious, or political principles. The second type of rational law can itself be extrinsically or logically derived. Rational laws conceived through extrinsically formal processes confirm significance to external factors perceivable by the senses. Those arrived at through logically formal means are a function of a completely intellectual process drawn from abstract legal concepts to produce a self-contained system of legal thought. This latter type of law, based on a completely internalized set of rationalizations, was believed by Weber to be the "most perfect" system of jurisprudence and the epitome of civil law.[9]

The basic principle behind this ideal of logically formal rationality is

[8]Max Weber, *On Law in Economy and Society,* ed. and trans. Max Rheinstein (1925; reprint, New York: Simon & Schuster, Clarion, 1954).
[9]Ibid., xliii.

that it is possible to derive legal decisions in each concrete "fact situation" through the application of abstract legal propositions by means of legal logic. The law that evolves must constitute or at least be considered a "gapless system" whereby every social action must be either an "application" or "execution" of these legal concepts. Actions that are not legally construed in rational terms were deemed by Weber to be legally irrelevant. Social actions that are not applications of the abstract legal propositions he considered "infringements" of such concepts.[10]

In contrast to this perfect expression of civil law and its highly intellectual theories, common law is generally seen as an essentially empirical system of resolving disputes ad hoc. It is perceived as a system with comparatively modest theoretical pretensions. Max Rheinstein, an editor and translator of Weber's thesis from the original German, associates common law with "substantive irrationality."[11] In *The Idea of Law,* Dennis Lloyd further suggests that common law is basically a pragmatic art that focuses on particular facts and individual circumstances as opposed to the assumption of civil law of an inherently logical and abstract system of legal doctrine. Whereas civil law is the concern of social and legal theoreticians such as professors and scholars, common law is a function administered by judges and lawyers, whom Lloyd contrasts as "men of the world."[12]

While civil law may aspire to Weber's logically formal rationality based on pure abstract thought, in practice it is actually more akin to substantive rationality, since reality is invariably prejudiced by ideological principles of a social, religious, political, or economic nature. Significantly, Rheinstein adds, "Substantively rational . . . is any law which a conqueror imposes upon a subject population as a means of maintaining and strengthening his rule."[13] Accordingly, an inherent characteristic of abstract, a priori rationalism, however idealistic, is the threat of authoritarian practice. The potential is demonstrably evident in reviewing the history of Marxism, which Rheinstein also relates to substantive rationality, insofar as the objective of Soviet law is to advance communist ideology. By the same reasoning, any social or legal system that is conducive to the implementation of rational urban planning and design is open to the danger of a wider-reaching system of social and economic dictatorship.

Continental Urban-Design Controls

Notwithstanding the organic genesis of urban form during the Middle Ages, regulations governing the practical aspects of building and community safety were not uncommon. Protection against fire was a major con-

---

[10]Ibid.
[11]Ibid.
[12]Dennis Lloyd, *The Idea of Law* (1964; reprint, Baltimore: Penguin, 1970), 223.
[13]Weber, *On Law,* xli.

cern. In medieval London, a disastrous conflagration in 1189 prompted the Lord Mayor, Henry Fitz-Elwyne, to enact the Assize of Buildings, a pioneer code that required the use of tile roofs and masonry party walls three feet thick and sixteen feet high to prevent the spread of fire. In 1212, thatched roofs in the city were ordered whitewashed to reduce their flammability. Later, in the fourteenth century, detailed regulations governing buildings required roofs to be covered with tile, lead, or stone. Laws likewise regulated other practical aspects of construction and public safety. In 1297, it was required that every property owner in London maintain the front of his house in good condition, that "low pentices" or penthouses be removed, and that pigsties adjacent to the street be prohibited. Similar laws safeguarding against fire and unsanitary conditions were also passed in cities on the Continent. During the Middle Ages and earlier, building regulations were characteristically initiated in reaction to the practical expediency of communal safety. As often as not, these laws were neither stringently enforced nor followed.

In contrast to the practical function of building law during the Middle Ages, the Renaissance saw continental law used to implement theoretical concepts of urban design. With its origins in classical and rationalist theory, continental civil law provided a logical and effective foundation to realize its philosophy in town planning: Renaissance design according to rational, a priori principles. As noted earlier, where civil law falls short of Weber's ideal of logically formal rationality, the result is often substantive rationality. The authoritarian nature of this latter form of civil law suited continental autocracies in carrying out rationally conceived goals in Renaissance urban design. Conversely, English substantively irrational common law, not based on legal rationalism, fostered town design in Britain that continued to retain the organic quality characteristic of the medieval period well into the Renaissance.

As the Middle Ages passed, urban design on the European mainland became increasingly subject to definitive laws guided by abstract concepts of reason and design. As early as 1262, the Italian city of Siena passed an ordinance governing the character and height of private structures facing the city's Piazza del Campo. Unlike previous laws motivated for practical reasons of public safety, this regulation was distinctive as a conscious effort to preserve the holistic, radial design of the piazza. Although chronologically belonging to the Middle Ages, the deliberate aesthetic order and unity of Siena's piazza heralded the early Renaissance in city design.

Three hundred years later, the machinery of papal absolutism and the ecclesiastical law of Catholicism lent themselves to true Renaissance city planning in one of the earliest and most monumental of urban renewal programs. After the collapse of the Roman Empire, Rome fell into a state of disrepair that was to last through the Middle Ages. It was not until 1585, when Sixtus V ascended to the papacy, that an earnest attempt was made to reconstruct Rome as a holy city with a formal design befitting the center of Christendom. With the help of his architect, Dominica Fontana, Sixtus conceived a far-reaching plan that would bring order and rationality to the city by creating a unifying urban geometry—a network of long, straight avenues that would cut through the irregular property lines of the existing settlement. The axes of these projected Renaissance perspectives were marked with great Egyptian stone obelisks removed from the remains of the Circus Maximus. At these locations were later developed several of the famous Baroque piazze that today grace the city. Sixtus's rule ended only five years after it began, but the autocratic power of the papacy under Catholic civil law ensured the completion of his ambitious concept by his successors.

Civil law finds its origins in the context of philosophical rationalism and centralized authority; hence the invisible web on the Continent was appropriate and conducive to the enforcement of reason and control in Renaissance urban design, as exemplified in Siena and Rome. As a philosophy, rationalism appeals strongly to the intellect for the high value it places on human reason and planning aforethought. However, by requiring unity in purpose and direction, it also fosters elitist decision making, which in turn can lead to autocratic administration capable of dictating human behavior as much as urban design. Indeed, rationally conceived utopias from Plato to Marx have achieved their goals only through popular submission to the prescribed order or through the threat of coercion.

In comparison, societies that rely on empirical processes for direction may appear vulnerable to disorganization, inefficiency, even chaos. The history of economic capitalism has shown, however, that pluralism, diversity, and competition are not only viable but eminently successful foundations for a social economy. Furthermore, in both economics and city planning, organic empiricism has an additional attribute that rationalist societies inherently lack: freedom of choice for the individual in the pursuit of independent goals and in the use of private property. That more vibrant and humane cities can be shown historically to be the result of such freedom is a lesson not to be forgotten by city planners and urban designers today.

The City of the Sun King

The contrast between law in urban design and planning in England and on the Continent can readily be seen in examining the disparate design effects of their divergent systems of law. In comparing the architecture and town planning of France, a civil law society, to that of England, governed by common law, consider first the difference in the design of royal residences and gardens, which reflect in microcosm their respective attitudes toward urban planning.

Nowhere is the rationality of Renaissance design and the absolute power of continental authority more evident than at Versailles, the immense palace of Louis XIV. The rigid and formal symmetry, the infinite size and scale, and the endless perspectives of manicured, geometric landscape all symbolize the dominance of man over nature, reason over chaos, and ruler over men: characteristics distinctive of Renaissance France. True, Versailles was not urban design in a community sense, but the massive channeling of public funds into an essentially personal project of urban scale was itself a testament to the absolute rule of the king's will. So total was the king's dominion over private rights that his advisors could justify heavy taxes to pay for this architectural extravagance by explaining that all property in France belonged to the sovereign by divine right anyway, and thus the king was only taxing his own holdings. As Louis XIV declared, *"L'état, c'est moi."*

The cultural pervasiveness of a priori rationalism in French Renaissance thought is further revealed in the writings of René Descartes, the philosopher and mathematician. The rationality of Cartesian geometry is fundamental and explicit in the monumental simplicity of the plan for Versailles. Descartes's disdain for empirical process extended to incremental and organic urban development, his own rationalist philosophy favoring deliberate planning and centralized design control. On architecture and planning, he wrote:

> There is very often less perfection in work composed of several portions, and carried out by the hand of various masters, than in those in which one individual alone has worked. Thus we see that buildings planned and carried out by one architect alone are usually more beautiful and better proportioned than those which many have tried to put in order and improve, making use of old walls which were built with other ends in view. In the same way also those ancient cities which, originally mere villages, have become in the process of time great towns, are usually badly constructed in comparison with those which are regularly laid out on a plain by a surveyor who is free to follow his own ideas.[14]

Having lost the divine right enjoyed by continental kings through such popularly imposed measures as the Magna Carta, the English monarchy never regained sufficient power to build a royal residence to match Versailles or the many other monumental palaces of absolutist Europe. In England, empirical practice prevailed in philosophy and behavior; the populace and private property owners held dominance in politics and economics. British kings retained political power only by courting the good will of the London merchants. Charles II, the English contemporary of Louis, longed

[14]René Descartes, "Discourse on the Method of Rightly Conducting the Reason," *The Philosophical Works of Descartes,* transl. E. S. Haldane and G. T. R. Ross (Cambridge: University Press, 1934), 87–88.

to construct a royal capital at Winchester to rival Versailles where he could rule without interference from Parliament and the London bourgeoisie. It is indicative of the relative impotence of the English monarchy that neither he nor his successors were ever to succeed. Several additions were made to Hampton Court, started by Thomas Cardinal Wolsey a century and a half earlier, but magnificent though this palace is, it is no competition to the sheer grandeur and scale of the Sun King's palace. Lewis Mumford writes that absolutism could afford civic monumentality, "lavishing money on costly public works of every kind. Democracies are often too stingy in spending money for public works, for its citizens feel that the money is theirs."[15]

The relative impotence of the English monarchy was also evident in the manner by which the English kings took possession of land. In 1540, when Henry VIII "afforested" the lands surrounding Hampton Court, he was able to do so only with the express approval of Parliament and by paying compensation to neighbors whose properties declined in value as a result of his action.

Haussmann's Paris

The differences between continental rationalism and English empiricism in town planning and law can also be seen in comparing the development and reconstruction of London with the reconstruction of Paris. The tale of these two cities reveals great dissimilarities, not only in the concepts of private property, law, and urban design, but in the essence of their philosophical traditions, one of which is a priori rationalism, the other organic empiricism.

In the mid nineteenth century, Napoleon III and his prefect of the Seine, Baron Georges-Eugène Haussmann, undertook a massive redesign of the French capital. Like Sixtus V before them in Rome, their aim was to transform the organic, winding contours of the old medieval town into the radiating geometry of a great neo-Renaissance city. This feat of centrally dictated, rational planning was made possible by the character of France's civil law society. To build the city's network of grand boulevards and infinite vistas, Haussmann did not hesitate to displace countless people and to expropriate and demolish fine historic works of architecture, houses, and other private properties. The plan was baldly insensitive to the needs of the masses, for its avowed purpose was to create a grandiose setting for the parade of triumphant armies and the promenade of the fashionable carriage trade rather than to advance any cause of social betterment. It has even been suggested that Paris was rebuilt along geometric lines for military

---

[15]Mumford, *City in History,* 197.

purposes, to allow the use of artillery and to deny potential revolutionaries an undivided field for street combat.[16]

There is some speculation that the contrast between the existing and the new was intentional in order to preserve the organic fiber of the old districts as an integral part of the city.[17] But it seems more likely that finances alone thwarted Haussmann's ambition to achieve absolute Cartesian perfection in his grand design. Though the Napoleonic Code permitted Paris to be transformed under the Second Empire as no other large city had ever been, staggering costs forced Haussmann to compromise his original, more ambitious scheme. According to Howard Saalman, who chronicled Haussmann's work, the boulevards built during the reconstruction are little more than "wardrobes," behind whose fashionable facades "the most appalling disorder lies concealed."[18] As land and buildings were swallowed up by boulevards and monuments, the remaining medieval quarters became even more congested for the lower-class inhabitants. In attempting to offset the taking of land, the administration permitted greater building heights and densities, thus only adding to the problem of overcrowding.

As Paul Spreiregen and others suggest, the government worked hand in pocket with entrepreneurs.[19] Many profited through increased property values and rents caused by overcrowding; others received overly generous compensation for condemnation or reaped windfall benefits as owners of property improved by a fashionable new avenue. Yet, according to Lewis Mumford, the greatest sacrifice for such rational "order and unity" was a social one: "a unified attitude toward life, the unified ownership of land, and the unified control of the architect and builder."[20]

THE PEOPLE'S LONDON

Though entrepreneurs and speculators took obvious advantage of the Paris reconstruction through the corruption of government officials, power essentially resided with the prefect. The plan for Paris was basically a monumental expression of imperial authority, conceived and executed by Haussmann on behalf of Louis Napoleon and under the aegis of civil law. In London, on the other hand, the real source of power behind the city's development and reconstruction was the middle class. More often than not, the English Crown was compelled to act on behalf of the mercantile populace rather than for its own aggrandizement. The history of London's growth is

[16]Arthur B. Gallion and Simon Eisner, *The Urban Pattern* (1950; reprint, New York: Van Nostrand, 1975), 83.

[17]Howard Saalman, *Haussmann: Paris Transformed* (NewYork: Braziller, 1971), 114.

[18]Ibid.

[19]Paul D. Spreiregen, *Urban Design: The Architecture of Towns and Cities* (NewYork: McGraw-Hill, 1965), 27.

[20]Mumford, *City in History*, 398.

marked not by centralized planning decisions, but by frequent instances wherein government catered to the will of the city's merchant society. Free enterprise was the guiding force, in the manner of Adam Smith's "invisible hand." Whereas the geometric order of Haussmann's neo-Renaissance Paris remains a grand symbol of centralized authority and rational planning under a civil code, the less unified and more organic urban form of London reflects its origins in pluralism and capital enterprise under English common law.

London under Elizabeth I

In the 1580s, the same decade in which Pope Sixtus V planned the Renaissance reconstruction of Rome, the government at Westminster was, by contrast, under the domination of the mercantile populace of London, which virtually controlled the English economy. Far from any ambitions to usurp private properties to redesign London, the monarchy was often manipulated by bourgeois merchants and craftsmen to further their own ends.

Under the reign of Elizabeth I, London began to grow rapidly, and the city's middle class became alarmed over the rising immigration of the poor from the surrounding countryside. In 1580, under pressure from the influential guilds, which were fearful of competition by recently arrived craftsmen, Queen Elizabeth issued a proclamation restricting development near and within the city. Enacted by Parliament in 1592, her decree had three major provisions: to prohibit "any new building of any house or tenement within three miles from any of the gates of the said city of London"; to restrict the construction of habitations "where no former house hath been known to have been"; and to forbid in any house "any more families than one only to be placed." Passed by the queen at the behest of established London residents and tradesmen, "by good and deliberate advice of her Council, and . . . by the considerate opinions of the lord mayor, alderman, and other grave, wise men in and about the city," all three restrictions were aimed at stemming immigration into London through measures strikingly similar to the exclusionary methods practiced by many American communities today.[21]

If enforced stringently through the years, the limitation on development within three miles of London would have created a broad agricultural green belt around the city, not unlike Ebenezer Howard's Garden City ideal of the twentieth century. It is intriguing to speculate that the Green Belt concept might have had its indeliberate origins in Elizabethan law and, though dormant, the idea had resided in the British psyche until Howard

---

[21]Steen Eiler Rasmussen, *London: The Unique City* (1934; reprint, Cambridge: M.I.T. Press, 1967), 68.

gave it definition. During the era before the Commonwealth, between 1602 and 1630, no fewer than fourteen proclamations were enacted in attempts to limit London's growth.

Though ostensibly enacted to rid London of unhealthy congestion and to provide open space, Queen Elizabeth's enactments on behalf of middle-class interests were not without other social consequences. Many immigrants were crowded into existing common quarters within the city, and the provisions forbidding the taking in of lodgers and the rental of a house to more than one family only exacerbated their plight by virtually banning tenement housing within their means. Other rulings were passed to discourage population density and not coincidentally to expel the alien and poor. A law of 1588 applicable to smaller, unincorporated towns required that each house have "fower [four] acres of Grownde at the least . . . to be contynuablie occupied & manured."[22] Again similar to contemporary minimum lot-size restrictions aimed at exclusion, this regulation served established, wealthy interests in the name of environmental protection. From the vantage of design, one might again speculate that these Elizabethan edicts on housing may have helped fashion the habitual preference for single-family, detached housing that distinguishes Anglo-Saxon cultures from most others.

The English were not unaware of Renaissance efforts on the Continent aimed toward unified urban design. During this period, there were attempts to include aesthetic considerations in building regulations despite the incompatibility of such controls with English tradition. In *The Taking Issue,* Fred Bosselman, David Callies, and John Banta note that in the early 1600s:

> These royal proclamations seemed to be concerned with aesthetics as well as safety. For example, the 1604 Proclamation decreed no new houses were to be built in London or within nine miles thereof, " . . . except all the utter wals and windowes thereof, and the fore-front of the same, be made wholly of bricke, or bricke and stone." And the 1620 Proclamation established rules for the number and height of stories, size of windows, and so forth.[23]

However, the authors amended these observations in a footnote that betrays the typical English attitude toward such controls: "These royal building regulations were for the most part ignored, as there simply was not a sufficiently-interested body charged with their enforcement."[24]

Of course, it would be presumptuous to attribute design to legislation alone, especially since law itself is but a sanctioned social norm and, as

[22]Ibid., 72.
[23]Bosselman, Callies, and Banta, *The Taking Issue,* 67.
[24]Ibid.

such, only a reflection of the parent culture. Nevertheless, if enforced diligently, even an unreasoned and oppressive law can be a compelling force for establishing a social habit or a design norm. Moreover, a law may have an unintentional but considerable effect as an incidental or accidental consequence to the principal purpose of an enactment. Unlike the redesign of Rome, it is doubtful that the queen had any reasoned intent to influence designed urban form toward a green-belt concept or to promulgate detached single-family housing as a practice. The avowed aim of the Elizabethan laws was only to prevent unhealthy overcrowding, although a hidden purpose was also the exclusion of aliens and the protection of the city's craftsmen and merchants from immigrant competition. In *London: The Unique City,* a prime source on the history of the city's growth, Steen Eiler Rasmussen noted:

> Elizabethan proclamations and enactments have a note of their own. They are not orders of an absolute monarch, but rather the thoughtful advice and admonitions of a judicious and prudent householder. They are always very full of reasoning and common sense, written for the common people, to make them understand that it is to their advantage that the acts have been passed. Even if the actual regulations in which they result are generally an expression of the wishes of certain of the upper classes, the explanations which accompany them are generally destined for the people.[25]

It was scarcely surprising that the rich could be exempted from certain building regulations upon payment of a fee to the Crown. With the English emphasis on free enterprise, danger lay not in the imposition of oppressive design goals dictated by an authoritarian ruler with little regard for private property rights, but rather in inequity. While the English monarch had to defer to the interests of the people, the distribution of social benefit was hardly uniform, for the Crown catered principally to the will of the propertied and politically influential.

Obvious differences distinguish Haussmann's redesign of Paris from the Elizabethan edicts affecting London's development. The rebuilding of the French capital followed a preconceived design initiated under central authority, with entrepreneurs taking advantage only where possible. Queen Elizabeth, on the other hand, never initiated planning but acted principally as the tool of the wealthy merchants and craftsmen of London. In other words, whereas the French followed a rational plan conceived by a central governmental authority to achieve an abstract design ideal, Elizabeth I had no real plan but was responding pragmatically to middle-class pressure in order to retain what little power the English Crown possessed. The pattern of development of the French and English capital cities thus seems remark-

[25]Rasmussen, *London,* 71.

ably consistent with the organization of their respective systems of civil and common law.[26]

London under Charles II

At the height of the Renaissance, when Louis XIV was building his new capital at Versailles, the people of London would tolerate no such royal monument that implied absolutist domination, much less pay for it. Nor would they stand for any grand design that would disrupt their city as Sixtus V's plan had altered Rome. The shields of English common law and property rights well served their resolve. Even when calamity offered the greatest opportunity for the total redesign of London, traditional English regard for private property deterred centralized planning by the Crown.

The Great Fire that broke out on September 6, 1666, reduced London to ashes. Yet when reconstructed, the new city virtually followed original building lines, thus retaining the basic form of the medieval town. It was not that Charles II did not want a Renaissance design for the capital, but that he lacked the power, under English law, to exercise the necessary planning authority, despite the devastation.

Within a few days after the holocaust, several designs for the rebuilding of London were submitted to the king, including one proposed by the architect Sir Christopher Wren. Many believe that Wren's plan might have made London the most beautiful city in Europe. An admirer of the fashionable Renaissance designs being built on the Continent, Wren submitted a baroque plan that was both monumental and sensible. His scheme called for the city to be laid out in a rectangular grid crossed by radiating, fan-

---

[26]Regional land-use patterns in England were also influenced by the early practice of farming on open commons. Commons were lands belonging to a manorial lord, on which yeomen or "commoners" were permitted to farm or graze livestock. An individual's "common rights" were often in land scattered in various locations, with the result that much time was spent by the farmer journeying from one site to another. Worse was the problem of "surcharge," or over-grazing of common pastureland or "wastes," since there was no limitation on the number of livestock that each commoner could raise on land shared with others. Following the War of the Roses, however, the lords found wool to be more profitable than tillage and began to enclose much of their land for sheep herding. Commoners made vigorous attempts to preserve their rights, but with the loss of population caused by the plague of the fourteenth century, the farming of commons began to decline. The Statute of Merton in 1239, the Gateway Case of 1603, and several Parliamentary Enclosure Acts, including that of 1845, all contributed to the demise by permitting the enclosure and consolidation of former common land. A statute of 1555 even used national defense as an excuse to enclose land near the Scottish border. Some of the lands were enclosed to create private hunting preserves or parks for the nobility. Later, these one-time commons began to form prototypical green belts around London and other cities. In 1965, the Commons Registration Act placed one-and-one-half million acres in England and Wales under public management, creating a generous national reserve of open space. See Rutherford H. Platt, "Feudal Origins of Open Space Law," *Land-Use Controls Quarterly* 4, no. 4 (1970): 27.

shaped diagonals, fashioned after Giuseppe Valadier's Piazza del Popolo in Rome. Like the other proposals, Wren's plan basically ignored the original random layout of streets and properties that characterized the medieval urban form.

King Charles would have liked nothing better than to construct a monumental capital city to match or diminish the works of the French king. However, his awareness that the treasury was depleted as a result of the plague and the fire, and that he had neither the authority nor the financial resources to expropriate or rearrange private properties to the requirements of any of the plans, led him to discard all the proposed plans, albeit with reluctance. Whereas the absolutist rulers of Rome and Paris could demolish inhabited buildings to carry out a grand scheme, the English king could not violate even wasted land for a royal design. For a brief time, Charles II entertained hopes of pursuing Wren's plan, but he was ultimately persuaded by the Lord Mayor and other representatives of London that the scheme was infeasible. Even more than the rest of England, mercantile London was financially and politically independent; as in Queen Elizabeth's day, the populace had to be appeased by the government at Whitehall, which still needed the support of the city's middle class. In the end, the king had little choice but to profess an unwillingness to violate the sacred rights of private property and to allow Londoners to reconstruct essentially along original site lines. His proclamation of September 13, 1666, promised that rights of possession that existed before the disaster would be respected.[27]

He did, however, impose an injunction on reconstruction until proper legislation could be enacted by Parliament. The purpose of his mandate was basically to ensure that rebuilding would not recreate the conditions that led to the plague and the fire. The king's order, far less than a declaration of a grand design in the continental style, was reminiscent of edicts issued earlier by Elizabeth I. Its tone was not of command but rather of counsel and reasoned persuasion that the rule was in the best interests of the community.

The fire and plague of the year preceding were most certainly the result of the wretched physical condition of medieval London. Before the fire,

---

[27]Among the redevelopment plans submitted to the king was a proposal by a Captain Valentine Knight. Instead of a graphic plan, Knight presented a description that suggested that the devastated area be divided into long, narrow blocks, which could then be efficiently subdivided into building lots. In an elaborate scheme to finance the rebuilding, Knight proposed that each developer pay an annual subscription to the Crown in proportion to his land holdings, the proceeds going to subsidize the army and navy. Later, a Colonel Birch made a similarly radical proposal that all owners of property ravaged by the Great Fire should consolidate their individual public domain to permit centralized planning. Both these proposals, which were seen to aggrandize the powers of the king, were rejected. Charles even had the hapless Knight arrested for daring to suggest a scheme so subversive of private rights in property.

and especially within the boundaries of the old city walls, properties had been small, haphazard, and crowded, with flammable, corbelled, half-timber structures four or five floors high. All air and light had been cut off to the narrow, winding streets, which often flowed with refuse and sewage. Inadequate tenements had been packed with several households sharing common quarters, in violation of Elizabeth's forgotten edicts. The streets had been so congested with vendors and stalls that pedestrian and horse-drawn traffic could scarcely move. However destructive, the fire eradicated this blight and offered opportunity for reform.

The measures Charles called for in his proclamation were to prevent such dangerous and unsanitary conditions from recurring. He asked that rebuilding be only of brick or stone, that common nuisance activities such as brewing be segregated, and that streets provide easier access, especially to the waters of the Thames. The king appointed a committee, including Wren among its members, to make a study of conditions and properties in London prior to the fire and to draft regulations governing reconstruction. In 1667, six months after the conflagration, Parliament passed an act for the rebuilding of London. The legislation included rules modeled after the precepts suggested by King Charles in his proclamation. The enactment did not propose any intellectually rationalized, overall scheme laid down by decree, but specified practical standards to be adhered to by individual landowners in reconstructing their properties. Fred Bosselman, David Callies, and John Banta summarized some of the provisions as follows:

> [The Act] divided all new housing in London into four classes, with separate regulations governing each. Uniform roof lines were required in many areas, and the Act required all houses on "high" streets to have front balconies, "four feet broad, with rails and bars of iron, of equal distance from the ground," with pavements in front "of good and sufficient flat stone." The ground floor was required to be not less than six nor more than eighteen inches above street level, and no bulks, jetties, windows, posts, seats, "or anything of like sort" was to be made to extend "beyond the ancient foundation of houses." . . .[28]

Although broad streets seemed a logical solution to alleviate the congestion of the original city, and though wide thoroughfares were also in keeping with the Renaissance style of the day, the members of the committee astutely realized that a general widening of streets would only exacerbate the potential of overcrowding in the area left for the building—a situation largely ignored or overlooked by Baron Haussmann in his later redesign of Paris. The draftsmen of the resolution prudently elected to permit the heights of buildings to vary in relation to the width of the adjacent

---

[28]Bosselman, Callies, and Banta, *The Taking Issue,* 68.

street, with taller structures allowed along broader arterials but with lower edifices stipulated along narrower streets so that sufficient light would not be obstructed in either case.

A significant and far-reaching aspect of the new law also initiated in the king's proclamation was the balance struck between the power of the sovereign to impose strict measures to protect the community's welfare and the right of the landowner to control his own possession. While the king's proclamation guaranteed that the rights of ownership existing prior to the fire were to remain, the government could exercise the sovereign's power of eminent domain to condemn private holdings where physical changes had to be made for the benefit of the community. An impartial jury would assess the value of the property seized, and the government was then obligated to reimburse the owner the amount specified. As other properties stood to appreciate in worth as a result of public works undertaken in their vicinity, the owners of these properties were conversely obliged to return to the public the equivalent of the rise in value of their holdings. The expropriation of private land for community use and the concomitant public recapture of betterment values was not a new concept of law, having been instituted as early as 1480 by Pope Sixtus IV for the construction and improvement of roads in Rome.

Despite these advances in public planning controls, even the use of eminent domain remained ad hoc rather than for the furtherance of a preconceived, overall plan. The new law consisted principally of pragmatic, "don't-do" police regulations to ensure public safety and did not project any initiative design for positive planning. London redeveloped essentially along the random lines of the old medieval city, albeit with wider streets and Renaissance building styles. Thus, the organic medieval form of London was restored because the invisible web of English law placed greater social value on individual property rights than on centralized planning ideals, however rational or benevolent. In contrast, the rulers of Paris passed eleven laws between 1548 and 1789 that limited settlement to within the city's successive walls. Referring to the first effort by Henry II to contain the development of Paris for reasons of defense as well as to exclude commercial competition as in London, Rasmussen observes:

> The absolute French king fixed a limit for the town; in England, on the contrary, the legislation allows the rebuilding of what already exists, but not more than that. The first conception rests upon an abstract idea as to the right form of a city, the other simply legalizes what has already taken place. It gives a true picture of the judicial ideas of the two countries. English law is always based upon precedent and practice, and the laws therefore do not form a coherent, logical system but one organically developed out of the life of the people.[29]

[29]Rasmussen, *London,* 75.

Implicit is the contrasting relationship between the empirical origin and nature of English concepts of law, property, and urban development and the rationalism and unified authority evident in continental civil law and Renaissance city design. Law is thus a precursor of form in urban design.

London under Free Enterprise

As much as the character of English city design owes to private property rights and common law, its debt to free enterprise is even greater. With the English heritage of landed aristocracy and commercial free enterprise, it seemed inevitable that British city building would grow from an amalgamation of both patricianism and profit. Indeed, much of London west of the original medieval site was developed through the commercial undertakings of the upper class. The quality of these developments was enhanced by many aristocratic entrepreneurs' sense of noblesse oblige, which dictated certain codes of propriety and social responsibility—a legacy of the long defunct feudal system.

Among the most interesting aspects of English urban development from a legal standpoint has been the private, speculative development of leasehold land and the use of the private convenant or contract as a means for design control. During the eighteenth century, large tracts of developable land in England were held almost exclusively in freehold or copyhold by nobility whose forebears had been granted the land by the Crown. In Britain there existed no mortgage system that could make large amounts of capital available to entrepreneurs. As a consequence, development of land acquired through leasehold became commonplace. The townhouses of the Circus and Royal Crescent, built by John Wood and son at the fashionable hot-springs resort of Bath, and the Adelphi, the six-story residential complex constructed by Robert Adam and his brothers in London, were typical speculative projects developed on land obtained through ninety-nine-year lease agreements. The practice of speculative, commercial development of residences on leasehold land and the use of the private, restrictive convenant contributed fundamentally to the design character of the pleasant, tree-filled squares that are so much a part of London today.[30]

---

[30]To the American observer, a peculiarity of the seemingly public squares of Bloomsbury is their siting on private leasehold land. Development of leasehold land is not unknown in the United States, but it is not used to any great extent or advantage. Baltimore is the only city in which leased land is common. In New York City, Rockefeller Center was developed on land leased from Columbia University. Planning historian John W. Reps has remarked on the opportunities lost when American cities sold rather than leased their public lands, in "Historical Perspective on Urban Land Policy," Lecture, *Forum on Modernizing Urban Land Policy,* April 13, 1972, Washington, D.C.: Resources for the Future, Inc. Nonetheless, in releasing state-owned land at the urban fringes of Phoenix and Tucson for private development, the state of Arizona is even now typically selling rather than leasing this resource. In financial terms alone, American city governments could have been wealthy today had their lands been

The forerunner of the residential London squares was Covent Garden Piazza, which was originally part of a monastic orchard and produce garden given to the first Earl of Bedford after the Protestant Reformation. In 1630, Francis Russell, the fourth Earl of Bedford, decided to take financial advantage of the high demand for dwellings in London. He engaged the architect Inigo Jones to develop the property, which had come to be used as a produce market, into townhomes for the purpose of commercial profit. The result was a series of Renaissance-style townhouses clustered about a central square facing the Doric portico of St. Paul's Chapel. The beauty and commercial success of the project notwithstanding, the noise and bedlam of the persistent and increasingly popular produce market eventually led to the decline of the residential function and the replacement of the square and many of the houses by permanent market structures. Although the piazza at Covent Garden did not survive, its initial success prompted the commercial development of several other private residential squares, among which were Bloomsbury, Soho, Grosvenor, Berkeley, and St. James.

After the Great Fire, development spread west of the old city to the open land of the urban fringe owned by the Russell family, the earls of Bedford. Toward the end of the eighteenth century, the then Duke of Bedford decided to subdivide for commercial development a 112-acre estate in the area now known as Bloomsbury. His plan consisted of a series of squares of varying shapes and proportions, each with a central garden surrounded by narrow lots to be leased for the building of residences. One of the first projects was Bedford Square, completed about 1780. It is uncertain whether the building program was devised by the Bedford estate or a farsighted developer who had secured a long-term lease. In any event, as Rasmussen notes, the resulting rowhouses are so pleasantly matched in exterior appearance that it is apparent that they were constructed either under a unified plan or a lease agreement that specified uniformity, even though the interior of each dwelling varied to accommodate the individual needs and preferences of the lessee.

Notably, the covenants accompanying the leasehold contracts have effectively determined the tenancy, the exterior design, the maintenance of the property, and ultimately the character of Bloomsbury to this day. Initially, each lot was leased for a period of ninety-nine years, after which the property, including the building erected upon it by the lessee, reverted to the Bedford estate. Each property was then leased again, with terms adjusted individually, so that tenants who would contribute considerable improvements to their leasehold would be granted longer lease periods than tenants who would not. Characteristically, the policy of the Bedford estate has been

leased rather than sold when the option was still available. Furthermore, as the management of the English squares illustrates, the continuing ability to control and unify urban design through lease agreements is an outstanding advantage for city planning and design.

conservative; short-term speculative gains have been foregone in favor of maintaining financial stability. Leases have been deliberately managed to expire at different times, so that periodic fluctuations in the economy would not adversely affect the overall financial status of the properties. While long-term profitability has always been a primary motive, this approach has not been taken because of expediency but instead reflects the aristocratic roots of the estate, whose upper-class sense of social responsibility has precluded any tendency to cupidity.

The regulations imposed by the lease agreements have been quite strict, prohibiting any use that would disrupt the residential quality of the area, such as commercial activities or signboards. Conspicuously, no obligations bind the estate itself. It has no maintenance standards it must meet; it can lease or sell properties whose agreements have expired for more lucrative uses, even those that may be totally incompatible with the existing homes. In practice, however, the estate has maintained the trust not to change the character of its holdings. Thus, as a consequence of a blend of private entrepreneurship and noblesse oblige, and with the use of leasehold and covenant, the design character of the Bloomsbury squares has not been drastically altered since their inception two hundred years ago.

Some squares in London retain names like Russell or Bedford, recalling the fee ownership of these properties. At one time, fences marked them as private terrain, but in 1893, an act of Parliament called for the removal of many of these barriers, thus obscuring the line between public and private domain. Since the origin of London squares at Covent Garden, the primary incentive behind their gentle landscapes and simple domestic charm has been capitalism rather than self-conscious, altruistic urban design. To attract residential tenants for commercial profit, the character and scale of the squares was made informal and personal. Their simplicity and unpretentiousness offer soft and personal contrast to the grandiosity of the urban spaces of Paris, which originated as monuments to French autocracy and rationalism. In these London squares, the practical empiricism innate in both Adam Smith's invisible hand of free enterprise and the invisible web of English common law on property and contracts has been joined with British feudal traditions of aristocratic responsibility of private ownership. Together these practices have created a unified public environment that stands to this day as a distinctive part of London. Rasmussen notes that it is in domestic architecture, the physical fabric of daily life, in which the English excel. The London squares, built for profit, are an exemplary strand of that fine weave.

London under the Regency

Another part of London that stands as an elegant symbol of English traditions and empiricism in urban development is Regent Street. Begun in 1813 by John Nash for the prince regent (later George IV), Regent Street was planned as a ceremonial way connecting the regent's residence at Carlton House with the new Regent's Park to the north. Nash's original intentions were for a long, axial design to match the powerful and unyielding Renaissance splendor of the Rue de Rivoli constructed earlier in Paris by the architects Percier and Fontaine for the emperor Bonaparte. But whereas the construction of the monolithic French boulevard followed the geometry of the straight line unswervingly, with respect for neither existing buildings nor private properties, Regent Street was to become less a monument to royal planning ambitions and more a graceful design reflection of the English supremacy of private rights in property.

Under English law, even the prince regent lacked the authority to cut a straight swath through existing private properties as had Napoleon's architects in building the French ceremonial way. Nash's final plan was ultimately carried out in segments, taking pragmatic, ad hoc advantage of existing private developments, such as Robert Adam's design of Portland Place,[31] and necessarily deviating at several points to avoid disturbing private properties, in much the same way, as Lewis Mumford described, that a medieval village road might bend to avoid a house or to preserve a tree. This approach proved fortunate, for the modulating curvatures of the resultant thoroughfare around Lord Foley's house and All Souls Church at Portland Place, and along the Quadrant at Picadilly Circus, contributed to the rich, visual sequence of Regent Street its most subtle and graceful passages.

The adaptive quality of design in response to restrictions imposed by private property lent to English city development a gentle, more humane quality that was absent in the totalitarian, geometric planning on the Continent. As any sensitive architect knows, the challenges of a difficult site can often result in a more interesting design than an abstract design on a blank field without constraints. Similarly, physical restrictions on design resulting from limited ability to manipulate individual properties can lead to ingenuity and diversity in city planning that simplistic "bulldozer" authority often cannot achieve. Likewise, reasonable constraints imposed by law can compel urban design to have a more adaptive, softer quality than what might

---

[31]The law of contracts played a unique role in the earlier design of Portland Place. To take economic advantage of the expansion of London, the Duke of Portland wanted to develop his property at the north end of the city. Earlier, however, he had contracted with his neighbor, Lord Foley, not to block the view from the Foley mansion northward to the countryside. He engaged as his architects the developers of the Adelphi, Robert Adam and his brothers, who submitted a scheme that evaded the agreement by following the letter of the contract but no more. Portland's development built up the land around Foley House on three sides, leaving only a broad avenue, Portland Place, running directly north from the house to what would later be Regent's Park. Foley's view northward was thus preserved as the contract required, even though the panoramic view had been virtually destroyed. The resulting avenue, lined with rowhouses designed by Adam, was integrated into the design of Regent Street, which Nash curved around the Foley House to connect with Portland Place.

result if legal obstacles were completely absent. It can be further maintained that private development has generally been more inclined than government to create at the scale of the individual rather than at the monolithic scale of the state.

In *The Road to Serfdom*, Friedrich A. Hayek points out that the degree to which government can plan is inversely proportional to individual freedom.[32] This relationship determines the fundamental nature of a society and is reflected not only in the prevailing system of law but also in urban form. As an elemental part of the social fabric, the invisible web of law is also a structural determinant of city design. The formal civil law of Europe gave autocratic rulers power to initiate great plans, a power that cast their capitals in the holistic geometry of rationalism. The common law of England, though empirical, was comparably influential, but in a different manner. Because the incremental urban development resulting from free enterprise and pluralistic determination was protected, the organic form of the medieval village became the characteristic quality of English city design. Urban design, no less than law, can be seen as a reflection of freedom—or lack of it—within a society.

This is a lesson from history that should not be lost on American urban designers, even as some urban-design theorists today still cling to the influence of latter-day rationalists like Le Corbusier, whose vision of modernist city design continued in the controlled, geometric tradition of the great continental plans of the past. Only since the 1960s, beginning with the writings of such critics as Lewis Mumford and Jane Jacobs, has there been a renewed appreciation of the humanity and organic design of incremental, empirical urban development as the more fitting urban design idiom for a free, pluralistic society in both social process and physical form.

[32]Friedrich A. Hayek, *The Road to Serfdom* (Chicago: U. of Chicago Press, 1944), 76.

Chapter 2

America: The Pragmatic Society

From Britain, the United States has inherited many social mores and practices. The contributions of English tradition are basic: the system of common law (or case law, as its modern progeny is called in America); the ethic of free enterprise; and the concept of private property. In this chapter, we will focus initially on English thinking at the time of the American Revolution, as these precepts formed the mold from which many American values have been cast. The discussion will subsequently turn to American thought itself, for as the nation matured, American culture gradually acquired its own character. Though fundamental in its influence, the heritage of Britain is but one element of many that have combined to create a singular national culture. In addition, the character of the United States has drawn not only from diverse national and ethnic origins but also from its own experience; each culture becomes unique by virtue of its history.

   To ascertain the effect of law on American urban form, three causes may be considered that together have made the American phenomenon distinctive. The first cause, the concepts of private property and democratic free enterprise, stems from English tradition, as already discussed. The second is the American land: an unprecedented abundance of good, virgin earth that offered opportunity to all. The third is constitutional law, a uniquely American concept drawn in part from European history. The implication of the first two factors on American attitudes toward government, liberty, and land development is the subject of this chapter. The chapter immediately following will turn to the third element of constitutional law.

LAND, PROPERTY, AND LAISSEZ-FAIRE

Scarcity of land resources in the Old World often led to conflict and domination within a society, and aggression and colonization without. In Britain as elsewhere in Europe, under the ancient practice of feudalism, land had been bequeathed only to those who could claim descendancy from titled or landed forebears. Self-determination, much less ownership of land, was beyond the worldly aspirations of the masses. To the common people who migrated to America, the New World surely must have seemed a godsend, for abundant land offered not only livelihood but even ownership and wealth to those with the capacity and perseverance to force the earth to yield its riches. The Protestant ethic of the pilgrims fostered the idea that an individual's capability and will determined his fortune. This belief found sustenance and strength in the American earth, for individual enterprise could flourish peacefully only amidst such affluence of exploitable resources as the colonies possessed. Thus, from a seed in English tradition, the ideals of individuality and self-sufficiency took root in America. From the resourcefulness necessary for pioneer survival, individual independence of character developed into a fierce national ethic and the philosophical foundation of American constitutional law. This concept of law is the special attribute of the invisible web in America, which in turn has determined the particular form of the nation's urban environment.

The seemingly infinite expanse of territory gave rise in America to a new breed of landowners whose claim of property rights was based not on feudal legacy as in Europe, but on their own determination, ability, and toil, free from interference by government. Property, they believed, was a sacred right. Attempts by the English king to compromise this right ultimately led them to proclaim in 1776 their Declaration of Independence. Indeed, justification for their cause could be found in the writings of the philosophers and jurists of Britain itself.

Foremost among these influential English men of letters was John Locke. His repudiation of the divine rights of kings is seen by some to have motivated the democratic and egalitarian spirit behind the English Revolution of 1688. Locke held, in *The Second Treatise of Civil Government,* that the maintenance of private property is the essential basis of society and government.

> The great and chief end, therefore, of men's uniting into commonwealths, and putting themselves under government, is the preservation of their property . . .
>
> The supreme power cannot take from any man any part of his property without his own consent. For the preservation of property being the end of government, and that for which men enter into society, it necessarily supposes and requires that the people should have property, without which they must

be supposed to lose that by entering into society, which was the end for which they entered into it; too gross an absurdity for any man to own.[1]

[American revolutionaries came to regard Locke's assertion of private property as an ordained right under divine natural law as the raison d'être of society and government./His thesis helped promulgate the influential Puritan belief that the earth's riches are to be harvested and that hard work will be rewarded with personal fulfillment in spirit and in body.[Max Weber, in *The Protestant Ethic and the Spirit of Capitalism,* asserted that the Puritan's divine call to labor and duty is the philosophical basis of modern capitalism.[2]]

The principle of capitalism was first defined by Adam Smith in *The Wealth of Nations*, his classic work on laissez-faire. His description of free enterprise appeared a direct application of empirical thinking to economic process. According to his theory, order and benefit would be determined through organic, pluralistic experience rather than centralized planning.

> Every individual is continually exerting himself to find out the most advantageous employment for whatever capital he can command. It is his own advantage, indeed, and not that of the society, which he has in view. But the study of his own advantage, naturally, or rather necessarily, leads him to prefer that employment which is most advantageous to the society. . . .
>
> By directing that industry in such a manner as its produce may be of the greatest value, he intends only his own gain, and his is in this, as in many other cases, led by an invisible hand to promote an end which was no part of his intention. Nor is it always the worse for the society that it was no part of it. By pursuing his own interest he frequently promotes that of the society more effectually than when he really intends to promote it.[3]

[*The Wealth of Nations* was published in 1776, the same year as the beginning of the American Republic.] Clearly, Smith's precepts, like Locke's, were not lost on America; the teachings of both men underscored the founding fathers' belief that society as a whole would stand to benefit from their personal gain. Commenting on the influence of such English intellectuals on American land-use law, professor John E. Cribbet begins with a quotation by Arnold Toynbee,

> "Two conceptions are woven into every argument of *The Wealth of Nations*— the belief in the supreme value of individual liberty, and the conviction that

---

[1]John Locke, *The Second Treatise of Civil Government,* ed. J. W. Gough (1690; reprint, Oxford: Basil Blackwell, 1948), 62, 69.

[2]Max Weber, *The Protestant Ethic and the Spirit of Capitalism,* transl. Talcott Parsons (1904; reprint, New York: Scribner's, 1958).

[3]Adam Smith, *An Inquiry into the Nature and Causes of the Wealth of Nations* (1776; reprint, Chicago: U. of Chicago Press, 1976), bk. 4, ch. 2, 474, 477–78.

man's self-love is God's providence, that the individual in pursuing his own interest is promoting the welfare of all." These concepts meshed perfectly with Locke's ideas on property and further cemented the rights' side of ownership. Property was an individual right to be protected, not regulated, by the state. Duties there might be but they were minimal and could be handled by the *ad hoc* processes of common law. Translated to the use of land, this meant the individual could develop it as he pleased and the public welfare would be served by the collective results of the individual's freedom of action.[4]

[Implicit is the assumption on which the theory of American land-use law is founded: that the basis of American freedom and capital enterprise is the right of private property, to which governmental controls and planning are anathematic.]

The influence of English philosophers on America's first leaders was fundamental, for the United States Constitution institutionalized the empirical free market as the basis of the nation's economic system. Indeed, capitalist advocacy may have had a more direct bearing on the drafting of the Constitution than some would admit. According to the historian Charles Beard, the creators of the Constitution, while ostensibly engaging in civic altruism, were also promoting their own economic self-interest as property owners. In *An Economic Interpretation of the Constitution of the United States*, Beard reasoned:

> Suppose, on the other hand, that substantially all of the merchants, money lenders, security holders, manufacturers, shippers, capitalists, and financiers and their professional associates are to be found on one side in support of the Constitution and that substantially all or the major portion of the opposition came from the non-slaveholding farmers and the debtors . . . would it not be pretty conclusively demonstrated that our fundamental law was not the product of an abstraction known as "the whole people," but of a group of economic interests which must have expected beneficial results from its adoption?[5]

Beard's thesis has been damned as heretical by those who would rather perceive the founding fathers more as saints than practical and far-sighted politicians and businessmen. Nevertheless, his research into the circumstances surrounding the drafting of the Constitution was substantial. There can be little dispute that the enactment indeed laid the foundation for the development of the United States as a capitalist society.

The ethic of capitalism is also implicit in Sir William Blackstone's de-

[4]Arnold Toynbee, *Lectures on the Industrial Revolution of the Eighteenth Century in England* (London: Longman's Green, 1908), 148. Quoted in John E. Cribbet, "Changing Concepts in the Law of Land Use," *Iowa L. Rev.* 50 (1965): 249.

[5]Charles A. Beard, *An Economic Interpretation of the Constitution of the United States* (1913; reprint, New York: Macmillan, 1960), 17.

fense of property rights. His concept of private property as the "sole and despotic dominion" of the owner is unequivocal.

> So great moreover is the regard of the law for private property, that it will not authorize the least violation of it; no, not even for the general good of the whole community. If a new road, for instance, were to be made through the grounds of a private person, it might perhaps be extensively beneficial to the public; but the law permits no man, or set of men, to do this without consent of the owner of the land. In vain may it be urged, that the good of the individual ought to yield to that of the community; for it would be dangerous to allow any private man, or even any public tribunal, to be the judge of this common good, and to decide whether it be expedient or no. Besides, the public good is in nothing more essentially interested, than in the protection of every individual's private rights, as modelled by the municipal law.[6]

Blackstone offered the same premise as Adam Smith in his concept of laissez-faire: that private prosperity is at the heart of public benefit. Blackstone's impact on American thinking at the time of the revolution is beyond doubt. Write Fred Bosselman, David Callies, and John Banta:

> Edmund Burke, in his famous speech to Parliament on Conciliation with America, said, "I hear that they have sold nearly as many of Blackstone's Commentaries in America as in England." . . . As early as 1759, John Adams of Massachusetts, later President of the United States, wrote about a favorable impression those lectures had made upon him. Literally thousands of copies of *Commentaries* themselves were available by the time of the revolution itself. It is thus no wonder that, according to one of Blackstone's biographers, when the Constitutional Convention met in 1787, "most of the members of that body were familiar with, and they were no doubt greatly influenced by, Blackstone's analysis of the English governmental system."[7]

Another English concept current during the birth of the American republic was Jeremy Bentham's idea of social utilitarianism. This theory advocated "maximizing" human happiness by assessing the aggregate of pleasure and pain in a society and endeavoring "the greatest happiness of the greatest number."[8] Like Adam Smith, Bentham believed that society as a whole benefited when the individual prospered. Accordingly, the utility of law could be evaluated by weighing its benefits to the individual. Prop-

---

[6]William Blackstone, *Commentaries on the Laws of England* (1765–69; reprint, London: Dawsons, 1966), bk. 1, ch. 1, 135.

[7]Fred Bosselman, David Callies, and John Banta, *The Taking Issue* (Washington, D.C.: USGPO, 1973), 90–91.

[8]Jeremy Bentham, *An Introduction to the Principles of Morals and Legislation,* eds. J. H. Burns and H. L. A. Hart (1780; reprint, London: U. of London, Athlone, 1973), 12–13.

erty, while not the absolute dominion of the owner, as Blackstone had claimed, was nevertheless the basis of an individual's expectation of advantage and hence the proper creation of law and deserving of its protection. "The social utility of private use," John Cribbet comments, "was the justification for private property, and anything more than minimal interference by the state was dangerous."[9] Although it has been argued that Bentham's theory of social utilitarianism never influenced American thought as did Blackstone's simplistic legal dogma, Cribbet credits Bentham with contributing to the American institution of laissez-faire no less than did Locke, Blackstone, or Smith.

The sanctity of private possession in nineteenth-century society was extreme; in Britain, as Dennis Lloyd notes, "the hanging of small children being regarded as a lesser evil than any threat to property that their depredations might lead to."[10] This excessive emphasis on private property, which led on the one hand to the assertions of Locke and Blackstone and on the other to the hanging of young thieves, should be seen in the context of the battle between the monarchy versus the rights of Parliament and of the people. As attorney Rutherford H. Platt points out, the concern of both Locke and Blackstone was to prevent the monarchical tyranny that had brought about the English Civil War and the Revolution of the seventeenth century. He observes,

> Their intent was to justify the accession of Parliament to the powers of sovereignty which the Stuarts so reluctantly yielded. It is ironic then that arguments intended to curb the tyranny of a monarch might be turned to justify the tyranny of a landlord.[11]

Thus, the pendulum swung from the extreme of sovereign power to rebellion on behalf of private property. In their renunciation of the Crown, American revolutionaries saw only the threat of centralized public power. Alluding to Beard's thesis, Cribbet writes,

> It has been frequently stated that the framers of the Constitution of the United States understood liberty as having to do primarily with property rights. . . . Property rights, as both natural and individual, fitted America like a glove. Land was cheap, if not actually free, and the loose economic conditions gave maximum opportunity for the self-made man of property.[12]

Echoing Francis Philbrick, Cribbet points out, "Cheap land had as one of its consequences that of stimulating and universalizing acquisitive instincts

---

[9]Cribbet, "Changing Concepts," 250.

[10]Dennis Lloyd, *The Idea of Law* (1964; reprint, Baltimore: Penguin, 1970), 245.

[11]Rutherford H. Platt, "Feudal Origins of Open Space Law," *Land-Use Controls Quarterly* 4, no. 4 (1970): 37.

[12]Cribbett, "Changing Concepts," 250–51.

and respect for property rights."[13] [Land as real property became the prime commodity of American capitalism.]

The tenets of laissez-faire, a basis of American economy and society, can also be traced to the ideas of the nineteenth-century English philosopher Herbert Spencer. An associate of Charles Darwin, Spencer originated the phrase "survival of the fittest." His theory of society, published in *Social Statics,* applied the Darwinian concept of biological evolution to the human condition, thus lending philosophic justification to the callous social pragmatism that characterized this period:

> It seems hard that a labourer incapacitated by sickness from competing with his stronger fellows, should have to bear the resulting privations. It seems hard that widows and orphans should be left to struggle for life or death. Nevertheless, when regarded not separately, but in connection with the interests of universal humanity, these harsh fatalities are seen to be full of the highest beneficence—the same beneficence which brings to early graves the children of diseased parents, and singles out the low-spirited, the intemperate, and the debilitated as the victims of an epidemic.[14]

Spencer provided the rationale behind the capitalist robber barons who flourished in the United States at the turn of the century. Citing historian Richard Hofstadter's *Social Darwinism in American Thought,* Seymour Toll writes:

> As the argument went, Spencer offered them a perfect rationalization for the brutal competition out of which they gathered their riches and power. They survived and prospered because they were the fittest in the struggle. Success was the practical demonstration of Spencer's theory.[15]

Andrew Carnegie, the steel tycoon, said in praise of his English friend, "Few men have wished to know another man more strongly than I to know Herbert Spencer, for seldom has one been more deeply indebted than I to him and to Darwin."[16] In explaining his father's success in business, John D. Rockefeller, Jr., echoed the same sentiment:

> The growth of a large business is merely a survival of the fittest. . . . The American Beauty rose can be produced in the splendor and fragrance which brings cheer to its beholder only by sacrificing the early buds which grow up

[13]Francis S. Philbrick, "Changing Conceptions of Property in Law," *U. of Pennsylvania L. Rev.* 86 (1938): 723. Quoted in Cribbet, "Changing Concepts," 250–51.

[14]Herbert Spencer, *Social Statics* (London: Chapman, 1851), 323.

[15]Seymour I. Toll, *Zoned American* (New York: Grossman, 1969), 14. Research material for this chapter has been drawn liberally from this source.

[16]Andrew Carnegie, *Autobiography* (New York: Houghton Mifflin, 1920), 338. Cited by Toll, *Zoned American,* 14.

around it. This is not an evil tendency in business. It is merely the working out of a law of nature and a law of God.[17]

This Spencerian pragmatism was accepted, not only in the circles of capitalist monopoly, but as an ethic in American life. Seymour Toll quotes William Howard Taft, the only man to have served both as President and Chief Justice:

> The tendency in my own case, and I think in that of most graduates of my time, was toward the *laissez faire* doctrine that the least interference by legislation with the operation of natural laws was, in the end, the best for the public; that the only proper object of legislation was to free the pathway of commerce and opportunity from the effect of everything but competition and enlightened selfishness; and that being done, the Government had discharged all of its proper functions.[18]

Beyond Spencer, the entrepreneur could find vindication for the priority of practical consequences in formal American thought as easily as in success itself. The native philosophy of pragmatism emphasizes the primacy of actual experience and outcome over rationalized and theoretical principles. William James, the leader of this school, stated that the pragmatist

> turns away from abstraction and insufficiency, from verbal solutions, from bad *a priori* reasons, from fixed principles, closed systems, and pretended absolutes and origins. He turns towards concreteness and adequacy, towards facts, towards action, and towards power.[19]

To the practical man of action, nothing is more concrete and adequate than private fortune and power. Significantly, the *Encyclopaedia Britannica* holds that "pragmatism is a continuation of critical Empiricism," the philosophical premise of English thought, exposing again the heritage of British philosophy in America.[20]

In 1905, a case reached the United States Supreme Court involving a New York State labor reform law that provided that no employee be required or permitted to work in bakeries more than sixty hours a week or ten hours a day. The act was an effort to outlaw the dangerously unhealthful sweatshop working conditions typical of that period. However, in *Lochner v. New York,* the Supreme Court struck down the New York regulation on

---

[17]William J. Ghent, *Our Benevolent Feudalism* (New York: Macmillan, 1902), 29. Cited by Toll, *Zoned American,* 14.

[18]Alpheus Thomas Mason, *William Howard Taft: Chief Justice* (New York: Simon & Schuster, 1964), 50. Cited by Toll, *Zoned American,* 17.

[19]William James, *Pragmatism* (Cambridge: Harvard U. Press, 1975), 31.

[20]*Encyclopaedia Britannica* 14 (15th ed., 1980), 940.

the basis that "there is no reasonable ground, on the score of health, for interfering with the liberty of the person or the right of free contract . . ."[21] Writing the dissenting opinion, Oliver Wendell Holmes observed, "This case is decided upon on economic theory which a large part of the country does not entertain. . . . The Fourteenth Amendment does not enact Mr. Herbert Spencer's Social Statics."[22] However, even Holmes had admitted of Spencer, "I doubt if any writer of English except Darwin has done so much to affect our whole way of thinking about the universe."[23] The mainstream of American thought favored, as it still does today, the promise of pragmatic free enterprise. The proper role of government, according to the *Lochner* majority, is the protection of the competitive market, not its impediment through regulation.]

Like labor in the *Lochner* case, land in America has also been regarded as a capital commodity, best free from public interference. Traditional American values have always championed free enterprise and private property, planning and regulation by government being suspect as contrary to the national code. However, some critics of this philosophy have echoed the British economic historian Richard Tawney's assertion that the unbridled pragmatism of the entrepreneur has too often led to depredations for the sake of profit.[24] Indeed, the age of American big business was soon followed by an era of social reform. Still, the fundamental ethic that has persevered to this day in America is that the first function of government in protecting individual liberty is the enhancement of private opportunity. Law is perceived as the handmaiden, not the mistress, of free enterprise. Implicit in this view is Adam Smith's belief that the community benefits from individual prosperity.

THE DESIGN OF CAPITALIST EXPEDIENCY

Urged on by the exigency of capitalist profit, Americans came to regard their bounty in land less as a resource for life than as a means for gainful speculation. Expediency rather than design emerged as the standard for land and city planning. Lewis Mumford observes, "Urban land, too, now became a mere commodity, like labor: its market value expressed its only value."[25] Ease of measurement and subdivision became the criteria for land planning. Since rectangular lots required less effort on the part of the

[21]198 U.S. 45 (1905), reporter summary.

[22]Ibid., 75.

[23]Oliver Wendell Holmes, *Holmes-Pollock Letters,* ed. Mark D. Howe (1941; reprint, Cambridge: Harvard U. Press, 1961), 58. Letter dated July 2, 1895.

[24]Richard H. Tawney, *The Acquisitive Society* (New York: Harcourt, Brace, 1920).

[25]Lewis Mumford, *The City in History* (New York: Harcourt, Brace & World, Harbinger, 1961), 422.

surveyor, the lawyer, and the speculator to describe, divide, and sell, the rectangular plot multiplied became the gridiron framework of the American city. Mumford writes,

> With a T-square and a triangle . . . the municipal engineer could, without the slightest training as either an architect or a sociologist, "plan" a metropolis, with its standard lots, its standard blocks, its standard street widths, in short, with its standardized, comparable, and replaceable parts.[26]

The commercial compulsion led to the laying out of blocks and streets as abstract units for subdivision and sale without regard for environmental or social considerations. In America, the "country of the most unbridled capitalism," as Max Rheinstein described it,[27] the subdivided city-for-sale seemed a natural outgrowth. From border to border and from sea to sea, the gridiron spread rampant throughout the country, stamping out the pattern of virtually all communities from farm settlements to metropolises. Writes planner Hans Blumenfeld,

> So the contemporary American city has, in fact, been designed not by a Master Plan but by the forces of the real estate market—good old Adam Smith's "Invisible Hand," the hand of Mammon.[28]

The gridiron, of course, did not originate from speculative expediency. In its simplicity, the pattern was among the town designs employed by the ancient civilizations of Egypt, Mesopotamia, and China. The rectilinear shape that was the logical choice for colonization in New World settlements, such as Savannah and Philadelphia, had also been the plan of the Greek colonial towns and Roman military camps that later evolved into the major cities of Europe. Even though ill-adapted to irregular topography, the rectangle provided a simple formula that allowed colonists to bring spatial order to a settlement quickly without spending time exploring the peculiarities of each particular site. It seemed a natural and historically proven choice for early community settlements in the New World.

The proliferation of the gridiron in America, however, had no reason other than its convenience for the subdivision of land. With real property the prerogative of only the privileged few in feudal Europe, a fundamental raison d'être of the new nation was the promise of land ownership for all. Hence, the founding fathers felt that a simple method of survey to distribute land efficiently to the people was not inappropriate. Design conse-

---

[26]Ibid.

[27]Max Weber, *On Law in Economy and Society,* ed. and trans. Max Rheinstein (1925; reprint, New York: Simon & Schuster, Clarion, 1954), xxv.

[28]Hans Blumenfeld, "The Role of Design," *Journal of the American Institute of Planners* 33 (Sept. 1967): 307.

quences of the survey system were not a consideration. In 1785, the Continental Congress passed *An Ordinance for Ascertaining the Mode of Disposing of Lands in the Western Territory,* which institutionalized the gridiron plan as the basis of man-made geography in America.[29] Never in history has the invisible web of law had such explicit, far-reaching, and long-lasting impact on urban form and environmental design. The law stipulated a scheme of mapping federal lands west of the original states, whereby virtually the entire country was laid out as a gridiron of rectangular parcels and townships.

> The territory coded by individual States to the United States, which has been purchased of the Indian inhabitants, shall be disposed of in the following manner . . . The Surveyors . . . shall proceed to divide the said territory into townships of six miles square, by lines running due north and south, and other crossing these at right angles, as near as may be . . . The first line, running north and south as aforesaid, shall begin on the Ohio river, at a point that shall be found to be due north from the western termination of a line which has been run as the southern boundary of the State of Pennsylvania; and the first running east and west shall begin at the same point, and shall extend throughout the whole territory. . . . [30]

Thus much of the United States was divided into a gigantic grid. Even townships were subdivided for sale:

> The plats of the townships respectively, shall be marked by subdivisions into lots of one mile square, or 640 acres . . . The Board of Treasury shall transmit a copy of the original plats . . . to the Commissioners of the loan office of the several states, who . . . shall proceed to sell the townships or fractional parts of townships, at public vendue . . . Provided, that none of the lands within the said territory to be sold under the price of one dollar the acre.[31]

The entire physical expanse of the new nation was viewed by the lawmakers as a Brobdingnagian cake to be mapped, divided, and ultimately carved up for sale in the most efficient manner possible.

Lawyer Donald Hagman noted that the land conveyance system was also economically significant to the government. At one time, over 40 percent of federal revenues were derived from land sales. Speculation on land was given impetus by easy sales on credit and by minimum 640-acre purchases. Land was the cheapest and most readily available financial asset of the new government. In lieu of money, military service was rewarded by "land warrants." Some social provisions were made in platting the land;

---

[29]28 J. Cont. Cong. 375 (1785).
[30]Ibid.
[31]Ibid.

notably, 640 acres of each township were reserved for schools. In the main, however, social and design factors were not considerations. The physical impact of this survey system on the environment is still evident today. As Hagman noted,

> The basic grid system was followed in the planning of roads, farms and subdivisions. Roads therefore went up hills rather than around them, and farm boundaries required cultivation up hills resulting in unnecessary soil erosion.[32]

It seems ironic that Thomas Jefferson, the great humanist of American history, played an instrumental role in the drafting of the bill that would turn the gridiron into the cliche of the American planned environment. As an accomplished amateur architect and student of classical design, he was doubtless aware of the Hippodamian Greek colonial city, the first example of urban grid design. Like his colleagues, however, Jefferson failed to foresee the far-reaching consequences of the law, which proliferated rectangular geometry without design. The numbing uniformity of the grid, its insensitivity to land forms, and the inefficiency and visual monotony that it eventually visited on urban America are now the legacies of planning through expediency. Noting the effect of the survey system, John Reps, the noted urban historian, writes:

> Today, as one flies over the last mountain ridges from the east, one sees stretching ahead to the horizon a vast checkerboard of fields and roads. With military precision, modified only on occasion by some severe topographic break, or some earlier system of land distribution, this rectangular grid persists to the shores of the Pacific. America thus lives on a giant gridiron imposed on the natural landscape by the early surveyors carrying out the mandate of the Continental Congress expressed in the Land Ordinance of 1785.[33]

Rectilinear section lines grew into rural roads with gridiron-shaped towns springing up at their intersections. The speculator's instinct for the easiest method to survey and subdivide land became the basis of all city planning. Later, federal legislation further reinforced the gridiron pattern for the majority of American cities. Reps comments,

> Perhaps the rectangular survey pattern for the west was the only system that could have resulted in speedy settlement and the capture of a continent for the new nation, but its results in city planning were dullness and mediocrity.[34]

[32]Donald G. Hagman, *Urban Planning and Land Development Control Law* (St. Paul: West, 1971), 26.

[33]John W. Reps, *The Making of Urban America* (Princeton, N.J.: Princeton U. Press, 1965), 216–17.

[34]Ibid., 217.

Perhaps the needs of both capitalism and colonization encouraged rectangular gridiron planning in urban land development, and the ordinance of 1785 did not so much mandate a norm on society as it conformed to one. Nevertheless, the legal institution of an expedient planning solution obliterated even reasonable deviation. City sites possessing distinctive natural topographies of hills, valleys, shorelines, and rivers were obliged to submit to the unyielding gridiron. The absolute adherence to one type of land layout was neither organic, as was English planning, nor rational, as was the idealized geometry characteristic of French design. Indeed the blind geometric dogma of the gridiron plan eluded both the rationale of laissez-faire and the organic functionalism of the colonial frontier. Ironically, through its uncontrolled excesses in proliferating the gridiron as the physical norm of urban America, the ordinance of 1785 vividly demonstrates the compelling if sometimes unreasoning force of the invisible web of law over environmental design.

Certainly some early towns along the East Coast were deliberately and thoughtfully planned according to the gridiron scheme. The influence of some of these, such as the Philadelphia of William Penn and Thomas Holme and the Savannah of James Olgethorpe, may have created prototypes for others to follow. Yet most gridiron cities resulted from less than sensitive considerations. The Commissioners' Plan of New York City of 1811, for instance, converted the island of Manhattan north of Washington Square into an endless sea of rectangles in the belief that "a city is to be composed principally of the habitations of men, and that strait sided, and right angled houses are the most cheap to build, and the most convenient to live in."[35] Chicago's origins were even less considered, the city having been laid out in 1830 as part of a survey to enable a speculative real estate transaction.

By no other system but the gridiron could land be "surveyed," subdivided, described in deed, and auctioned off so easily without "planners" even having to leave the land office. Even the hills of San Francisco, which more naturally favor contour development, conformed to the abstract two-dimensional blanket of a gridiron plot devised on a speculator's map. It was sheer fortune that such callous pragmatism combined with the natural beauty of the Golden Gate site to confer upon San Francisco a distinctive character of peculiarly steep streets and magnificent vistas unlike any other city in the world.[36]

[35]William Bridges, "Commissioner's Remarks," *Map of the City of New York and Island of Manhattan* (1811), 24. Quoted in Reps, *Urban America,* 297.

[36]Actually, the gridiron plan of downtown San Francisco is bifurcated along Market Street. North of Market is the "Jeffersonian" grid following the standard north-south, east-west orientation; south of Market is the older "Spanish" grid running at a 45 degree angle from the north-south axis in accordance with Spanish colonial law. City and County of San Francisco, Department of City Planning, *The Downtown Plan* (1983), 98.

Most communities were not so lucky and succumbed to the monotonous uniformity of the rectangular imprint. Frontier capitalism in land, enforced by public law and promoted in private practice, thus removed any trace of thoughtful urban design during the era of westward expansion. Wrote Morris Birkbeck: "Gain! Gain! Gain! is the beginning, the middle and the end, the *alpha* and *omega* of the founders of American towns."[37]

Oddly enough, the design of America's capital city stands as the most prominent exception to the rule of the speculator's grid. It is no coincidence that the designer of Washington was a Frenchman, Major Pierre Charles L'Enfant, for despite America's cultural origins in England, France was a valued ally in the new nation's struggle against British colonial rule. Following L'Enfant's concept, the plan of Washington displayed the same radiating Cartesian geometry that Haussmann would impose upon Paris. The formal and grandiose design for the American city was motivated by the desire for an impressive new capital that would reflect the ambition of the young nation. Nevertheless, by the time L'Enfant's proposal for Washington was devised, the authoritarian Renaissance planning idiom had already lost favor in Europe. Furthermore, as John Reps points out:

> It was . . . ironic that the new nation which boasted so loudly of its democracy and freedom should have employed for its capital city the plan forms that were the very symbols of autocratic rule and aristocratic elegance.[38]

Jefferson was likely aware of this incongruity, for his voluminous writings on the plan of the capital city contain no praise for L'Enfant's design. Jefferson was not averse to the expression of democratic ideals in the classic idiom in architecture, as his own designs for Monticello and the University of Virginia attest, but apparently he realized the symbolism of neoclassicism to be un-American when applied at the scale of city design. In 1790, while L'Enfant was working on the plan, Jefferson even submitted a memorandum sketch showing a rectilinear gridiron scheme for the capital, but his suggestion met with derision from L'Enfant. Of course, L'Enfant's plan was accomplished without the oppressive authoritarian measures later used by Haussmann. Unlike Paris, which was already an existing city, Washing-

[37]Morris Birkbeck, *Notes on a Journey in America* (1817; reprint, Ann Arbor: University Microfilms, 1966), 66. Cited by Reps, *Urban America*, 349.

Another standard also helped promote the gridiron plan. In the mid nineteenth century, the railroads used a stock map for the speculative development of towns on company land along their tracks. Typically, street and lot sizes were standardized, and even street names were made identical, with numbered streets running in one direction at a right angle to arboreal-named streets like Chestnut, Oak, and Walnut laid out along the other.

[38]John W. Reps, *Town Planning in Frontier America* (1965; reprint, Princeton, N.J.: Princeton U. Press, 1971), 323.

ton was planned on virgin land, and few if any developed properties were disturbed, even though land was acquired from private owners.

The design of the capital city was a departure from the norm in American urban planning, in its inception as in its design. Washington was created as an ideological symbol, whether appropriate or not. In contrast, most American cities find their form in the expediency of the gridiron division of land as a commodity, a basis not altogether unfitting for cities of a society dedicated to capitalism and the freedom of private property.

THE CAPITALIST TRADITION AND THE QUIET REVOLUTION IN LAND-USE CONTROL

Abundance of land on the American continent engendered an attitude in the new nation, not only toward land, but toward freedom itself. Whereas the European feudal concept of land tenancy entailed concomitant social obligations commensurate with property and social rank, the territorial wealth of the United States voided these responsibilities and gave new credence to the "sole and despotic dominion" that Blackstone argued was the power of private property. A manner of western frontier law based on rugged individualism and unrestrained free enterprise became the national norm. These qualities assumed the sanctity of God-ordained natural law and became at once the basis and the guaranteed values of the Constitution. Even today, particularly in the less densely settled parts of the country where the dilemmas and interdependencies of urbanization are less apparent, conservative belief still emphasizes the ideals of competition and freedom from governmental interference. Critics of this entrepreneurial ethic claim that a consequence of unrepressed individualism, coupled with an absence of a feudal sense of duty, is a propensity for selfishness and social irresponsibility. Certainly, increased individual freedom on one hand diminishes on the other the ability of society to plan and enforce goals for the common good. Nevertheless, today as in the past, ultimate trust in America is invested not in government but still in Adam Smith's thesis that the individual can best advance his own interests and that collectively such independent enterprise best serves society as a whole.

The history of free enterprise's effects on real property amply illustrates the equivocal nature of capitalism in terms of social benefit. In England, as Rasmussen pointed out, examples of sensitive urban design, such as the Circus and Royal Crescent at Bath and the Squares of Bloomsbury, owe their existence to the incentive of capitalism combined with noblesse oblige. The same is true of many outstanding urban developments today. Speculation that furthers new construction actively adds value, not only to the immediate property, but to adjacent areas as well, thereby giving substance to Smith's capitalist maxim. However, Rasmussen also points to the deleterious side of capitalism by contrasting such productive development against idle speculation on vacant land and older existing buildings.[39] Unlike investments in constructive development, land speculation is a social parasite, for it withholds land and underdeveloped property from full productive use, cashing in on the commodity only when market pressures and improvements on neighboring property have increased the value of all adjacent real estate. Such speculation contributes nothing and serves only to depress other values; it encourages vacant, deteriorated, and underdeveloped properties, promotes urban sprawl by forcing development to "leapfrog" potentially useful properties, and generally retards healthy urban growth.

It is ironic that contemporary tax law in America has actually served to provide incentives for idle speculation. Despite efforts as early as economist Henry George's advocacy of a "single tax" on land value in the nineteenth century, the prevalent method of local property tax assessment largely overlooks the "unearned increment" of increased site value caused by community growth and development.[40] One inadvertent consequence of this policy was to penalize constructive improvements undertaken by the owner himself. Before their reform in 1986, income tax laws further added to the inequity by conferring advantageous lower rates on profits realized from speculative capital gains due to appreciation of property values than on income earned from constructive enterprise. (See chapter 13.)

Speculation was not always regarded benignly in America. During the early colonial period, the Dutch brought with them an intolerance of land speculation apparently bred in their own land-scarce nation. Settlers in New Amsterdam were granted land by the colonial government, but when some chose to speculate rather than develop on their parcels, Director General Peter Stuyvesant and his council passed a decree in 1647 that "they must erect on their lots good and convenient houses within nine months . . . or in default thereof such unimproved lots shall fall back to the patroon or Landlord."[41]

Modern American attitudes toward independent ownership and opportunity find their wellspring in England. There, despite traditional British respect for private property, early law shared the Dutch abhorrence of the destructive consequences of land speculation. One of the legal provisions passed after the Great Fire of London is as follows:

> If the owner has not built a house on his site within three years after the Fire, it would become the property of the town, which must pay full compensation

[39]Steen Eiler Rasmussen, *London: The Unique City* (1934; reprint, Cambridge: M.I.T. Press, 1967), 410–411.

[40]Henry George, *Progress and Poverty* (1879; reprint, New York: Robert Schalkenbach Foundation, 1966), 433 ff.

[41]Reps, *Town Planning,* 188.

according to the valuation made, and has then the right to sell it to others who do wish to build. Behind this lies the idea that land can never be considered as entirely private property. By right the land belongs to the community and a private individual may acquire the use of it, but if it lies without being made any use of, then he loses his right to it and must make it over to others. On the other hand, he who has been able to make his land productive, acquires a special right over it of which he cannot well be deprived.[42]

Government usurpation of private property that serves no community good strikes at the very heart of idle land speculation. In contemporary America, however, such a law would contravene the national ethic and would appear inconceivable. The capital commodity most fundamental in the history of Tawney's "acquisitive society"—and the most hoarded—has been speculative real property. The pragmatic land market and the illusion of endless land resources have promoted inefficient use and waste, seemingly without penalty.

Fortunately, speculation was not the only factor in the history of American land development. The Homestead Act[43] propagated the best values of private enterprise and stewardship. Passed in 1862, the act initiated the unprecedented policy of transferring frontier territory from the public domain to private citizens. One hundred and sixty acres were provided free of charge to individuals on the condition of settlement and active use. In their effort to better their own fortunes, the homesteaders who took advantage of this law brought civilization to the undeveloped regions of the nation.

The Homestead Act and later laws promoting and subsidizing owner occupancy took full advantage of the natural incentive for individuals to maintain property that they own and use actively. The strong motivation for stewardship of privately held property as opposed to state mandate to achieve communal ends is the chief argument advanced by advocates of free enterprise. Certainly there is ample proof of the validity of this theory in the material achievements of American society. However, its practice has also spawned less fortunate consequences that have required mitigation. Success, for instance, cannot be rewarded by monopolistic exclusion of the rights of other members of society. A finite resource such as land cannot be regarded solely as an individual's means to private gain, for its use can adversely affect the lives and properties of others. As society becomes more crowded and interdependent, perceptions must change. In their aptly named publication, *The Quiet Revolution in Land Use Control,* Fred Bosselman and David Callies point out that the concept of land has indeed been shifting. No longer is land considered simply as a commodity; it is also being perceived as a social resource.

---

[42]Rasmussen, *London,* 120–21.

[43]*An Act to Secure Homesteads to Actual Settlers on the Public Domain,* 37th Cong., Sess. 2, Ch. 75 (1862), 12 Stat. 392.

> "Land" means something quite different to us now than it meant to our
> grandfather's generation . . . Basically we are drawing away from the 19th
> century idea that land's only function is to enable its owner to make
> money.[44]

They balance the growing view held by conservationists against the traditional view of the entrepreneur.

> Conservationists describe the changing attitude toward land by saying that
> land should be considered a *resource* rather than a *commodity*. But while this
> correctly indicates the direction of the change, it ignores the crucial impor-
> tance of our constitutional right to own land and to buy and sell it freely. It
> is essential that land be treated as *both* a resource and a commodity. The right
> to move throughout the country and buy and sell land in the process is an
> essential element in the mobility and flexibility our society needs to adjust to
> the rapid changes of our times. Conservationists who view land only as a
> resource are ignoring the social and economic impact that would come with
> any massive restrictions on the free alienability of land. But land speculators
> who view land only as a commodity are ignoring the growing public realiza-
> tion that our finite supply of land can no longer be dealt with in the freewheel-
> ing ways of our frontier heritage.[45]

The United States was founded on the principle of individual liberty,
and unquestionably the corollary of free economic enterprise is the prime
impetus of this country's success. Capitalism is an established American
norm with proven merits. Nevertheless, perceiving real estate only in economic terms does not acknowledge the primary function of land as the environment for life. The imperfect conditions of American cities testify that
Adam Smith's free market has failed to design an urban environment worthy of the aspirations of American society. Of course, utopian perfection
cannot be expected of any system. An absolutist government may be able
to impose rational order, but it can no more promise paradise than capitalism can. In any case, totalitarianism is too high a price for a democracy to
pay for physical efficiency and beauty.

On the other hand, the ethic of unregulated rights in land as a speculative commodity makes even moderate measures to improve the living environment difficult. In pursuit of easy profits, uncontrolled speculation on
underdeveloped urban land has fostered the ugly and inefficient uses—the
dilapidated buildings, the gutted lots, the junkyards—that form the blight
of the American city. The notion that land is in endless supply at the metropolitan periphery has likewise contributed to the practice of virtually aban-
doning the deteriorated areas around the city core. Thoughtless speculation

---

[44]Fred Bosselman and David Callies, *The Quiet Revolution in Land Use Control* (Washington, D.C.: USGPO, 1971), 314.
[45]Ibid., 315–16.

and leapfrog development have pushed urban sprawl further and further into the hinterland of the "disposable" city, usurping valuable farmland and irreplaceable open space for inefficient land uses while relegating the inner city to increasing decay. Not only are environmental aesthetics affected but other aspects of urban life, such as transportation, energy, waste of resources, and health-endangering pollution. To achieve the quality of life that community design offers, a compromise between laissez-faire capitalism in land and government regulation must be attained without forsaking the basic economic system of the country. Quoting one of the nation's most revered leaders, Arthur Gallion and Simon Eisner write:

> In the absence of concerted willingness or ability on the part of those who own urban property to check disintegration, it falls to the lot of the public through the instrument of government. ["The legitimate object of government," said Abraham Lincoln, "is to do for a community of people whatever they need to have done but cannot do at all or cannot do so well for themselves in their separate and individual capacities."[46]]

Even Sir Edward Coke believed that regulation "extends to the public benefit . . . for this is the public, and every one hath benefit by it."[47]

It is now apparent that land in the United States is not limitless and cannot be wasted in a shortsighted quest for individual wealth. Given the social and market inclinations toward megalopolitan aggregation and the inability of democratic government to plan authoritatively, densities in much of urban America are now as high as any in the Old World. In less populous regions of the country, prime open space and productive agricultural land that feed the spiritual and material needs of the people are being swallowed up by unrelenting and wasteful urban sprawl. The era of colonial expediency is past, and future efforts must be diverted instead to achieve the higher quality of community life that America can doubtless afford if it so desires. The shift of goals necessitates a reexamination of practices and mores that served past aims. Democratic individuality and free enterprise are not to be sacrificed but changing conditions demand that these values be made compatible with increasing community needs. As even John Locke wrote of property:

> As much as any one can make use of to any advantage of life before it spoils, so much he may by his labour fix a property in; whatever is beyond this is more than his share, and belongs to others. Nothing was made by God for men to spoil or destroy.[48]

---

[46]Arthur B. Gallion and Simon Eisner, *The Urban Pattern* (1950; reprint, New York: Van Nostrand, 1975), 354.

[47]Edward Coke, "The Case of the King's Prerogative in Saltpetre," 12, *Reports*, 12–13, 77 E.R. 1295 (1606). Quoted in Bosselman, Callies, and Banta, *The Taking Issue*, 76.

[48]Locke, *Second Treatise*, 17. Quoted in Cribbet, "Changing Concepts," 248.

PART II

UNDER THE CONSTITUTION

Chapter 3

Doctrine and Certainty versus Fact and Flexibility

In America, the distinctive pattern of the invisible web of law is attributable to several sources: the economic philosophy of capitalism, the modern system of case law, and above all the American invention of constitutionalism. This latter attribute contrasts the American law of planning with its English precursor.

The empiricism of English common law is consistent with British government, which is characterized in its authority by flexibility. No written constitution limits British parliamentary power, nor is there provision for judicial review of governmental action. Britain's government is less restrained by formally codified limitations on its authority than by a traditional sense of propriety. The realism and prudence behind the acts of Elizabeth I and Charles II testify to the discretion exercised even by early English rulers. Though Britain is no longer a monarchy except in name, some feel that the Crown still serves as moral assurance against excessive usurpation of power by any political party, since government remains in theory under royalty's benevolent aegis. The trust that the British invest in their government has by and large been deserved; indeed, its integrity still serves as a model for others. In a historic instance where this trust was violated, rebellion ensued, and England lost her American colonies.

As a result of their disenchantment with discretionary governmental authority under the British, the American revolutionaries constructed a written Constitution that defined the system by which the new nation would be governed. This document was soon amended with a set of guarantees that spelled out the limits of governmental power. Although codified and strongly identified with God-ordained natural law, the original amendments comprising the Bill of Rights must be differentiated from the more elaborate codes of European civil law. The catholic codes of Europe sought to define the ideal society deductively after the rationalists' conception of what a model society should be and how ideal justice should function, whereas the Bill of Rights harbors no such rationalist intentions. Following English tradition, American social patterns are instead derived organically through empirical experience. The Bill of Rights serves only to institutionalize and guarantee the freedom of the individual against government manipulation, whether in the use of land or any other activity where personal liberties or property rights might be compromised. Whereas European civil law endeavors to balance both governmental and individual freedoms to achieve and maintain a rational idea of how society should function, American constitutional law presumes individual liberties as fundamental and places restrictions on government to ensure that these independent prerogatives shall not be subordinated.

By so doing, American law and government became distinct from their English forebears. English practice allows freedom for both the individual and government, with no classified limitations of consequence to restrict the discretionary freedom of either. Just as behavioral patterns have gained social sanction through the empirical development of common law, so have organization and authority in British government evolved organically through the "unwritten constitution" of past practice. Thus, unlike American public authority, which must observe constitutional restrictions, British planning bureaucracy is free to exercise considerable discretion in its actions, constrained only by its sense of propriety and political reality. The American system places no such trust in administrative discretion. By codifying the guaranteed rights of the individual against government interference, the Bill of Rights effectively limits discretionary authority in American government to plan.

HAYEK'S CONSTITUTIONAL PREDETERMINATION

During the rise of Nazi Germany, Friedrich A. Hayek wrote *The Road to Serfdom,* for which he would win the Nobel Prize in economics some thirty years later. He describes in fundamental terms the boundaries of social planning under law:

> Nothing distinguishes more clearly conditions in a free country from those in a country under arbitrary government than the observance in the former of the great principles known as the Rule of Law. Stripped of all technicalities, this means that government in all its actions is bound by rules fixed and announced beforehand—rules which make it possible to foresee with *fair certainty* [emphasis added] how the authority will use its coercive powers in given

circumstances and to plan one's individual affairs on the basis of this knowledge.[1]

Hayek assumes the basic tenet of free enterprise—that individual determination is both moral and beneficial for society. Though he counsels principally against the excesses of unfettered government, he also seems to recognize that the pragmatism of laissez-faire can lead to undesirable extremes. Spencerian survival has as its corollary the tyranny of the weak by the strong—hardly an improvement over tyranny by government. If such unfortunate consequences of laissez-faire are to be avoided, whether in commercial monopoly or in the exploitation of labor or land, then the excesses of pragmatism that seek selfish gain without regard to social consequence must be contained. Hayek's principal thrust is simply that public restraints cannot be at the whim of government but must be predetermined under the Rule of Law. This predetermination is the essence of American constitutionalism. Certainly every regulation governing commerce or land use diminishes individual freedom to some degree, but if laws are preestablished and clear, then individual enterprise is free to be conducted within the known restrictions with assurance that the coercive power of government shall not be applied arbitrarily. The idea is succinctly expressed by Frederic W. Maitland, the legal historian: "Known general laws, however bad, interfere less with freedom than decisions based on no previously known rule."[2]

In describing the difference between the Rule of Law and arbitrary government, Hayek explains two paradigms as follows:

> Under the first the government confines itself to fixing rules determining the conditions under which the available resources may be used, leaving to the individuals the decision for what ends they are to be used. Under the second the government directs the use of the means of production to particular ends. The first type of rules can be made in advance, in the shape of formal rules which do not aim at the wants and needs of particular people. They are intended to be merely instrumental in the pursuit of people's various individual ends.[3]

The first of these examples, the Rule of Law, or constitutionalism as Americans understand it, is the principle that constrains governmental action in the United States. According to this idea, government cannot exercise ad hoc discretionary controls over private behavior, enterprise, or property; its sanctions can be applied only insofar as the Constitution permits. Stated

---

[1]Friedrich A. Hayek, *The Road to Serfdom* (1944; reprint, Chicago: U. of Chicago Press, 1960), 72. Research material for this chapter has been drawn liberally from this source.

[2]Frederic W. Maitland, *Collected Papers,* ed. H.A.L. Fisher (1911, Cambridge U. Press, reprint, Buffalo, N.Y.: Hein, 1981), vol. 1, 81.

[3]Hayek, *Road to Serfdom,* 73.

another way, whether in economics or land use, the pragmatism of laissez-faire is free to function, limited only by predetermined rules, not by the discretion of fallible government.

Not all analysts agree with Hayek's thesis of the Rule of Law, however. Some advise that Hayek's views should be considered only in light of his reputation today as an apostle of political conservatism and an advocate of an economy free of governmental control.[4] Others point to the practical need for government to exercise discretion in administration. One of Hayek's most prominent critics is Kenneth Culp Davis, an American authority on administrative law. In a 1969 essay entitled *Discretionary Justice,* Davis finds pure interpretations of the Rule of Law "extravagant" and assails Hayek's idea taken to its extreme as "an absurdity." He observes,

> Every governmental and legal system in world history has involved both rules and discretion. No government has ever been a government of laws and not of men in the sense of eliminating all discretionary power. Every government has always been a government of laws and of men. A close look at the meaning of Aristotle, the first user of the phrase "government of laws and not of men," shows quite clearly that he did not mean that governments could exist without discretionary power.[5]

While arguing the practical need for discretion in government, Davis also admits that such discretion must be "confined, structured, and checked."[6] He suggests that moderation can be best achieved, not through fixed standards, but through fair administrative procedures that include open plans, policy statements, and rules, as well as open precedents, findings, and reasons. On police actions, he writes,

> The system is atrociously unsound under which an individual policeman has unguided discretionary power to weigh social values in an individual case and make a final decision as to governmental policy for that case, despite a statute to the contrary, without review by any other authority, without recording the facts he finds, without stating reasons, and without relating one case to another.[7]

Critical as he is of what he considers extravagant reliance on the Rule of Law, Davis himself is, to an extent, guilty of imputing that extreme posi-

---

[4]See, e.g., Lawrence Minard, "Wave of the Past? Or Wave of the Future?" *Forbes,* October 1, 1979, 45.

[5]Kenneth Culp Davis, *Discretionary Justice* (Westport, C.T.: Greenwood, 1969), 17, 28, 32.

[6]Ibid., 26.

[7]Ibid., 88.

tion to those emphasizing a conceptual ideal that he himself recognizes. Hayek need not be interpreted as advocating unyielding rigidity in government, precluding even reasonable flexibility. He warns only of the dangers of discretionary administration without predetermined rules. "Fair certainty" is as necessary an element of a free society as reasonable discretion, whether its assurance is by "rules fixed and announced beforehand," as Hayek suggests, or by administrative procedures using open plans, policy statements, rules, and precedents (not unlike the common law), as Davis also advocates. It is entirely likely, in fact, that Hayek was not referring specifically to constitutional law as the requisite for predictability, but rather to the common law, since after escaping from Hitler's Germany, much of his writing was done in Britain, not in the United States.

As even Davis concedes, the preoccupation of jurisprudence has been with the Rule of Law rather than with the exercise of discretion, a fact that underlines the importance of the former. Davis goes so far as to quote William O. Douglas, a Supreme Court Justice hardly known for his conservative construction of the Constitution.

> Mr. Justice Douglas has declared: "Law has reached its finest moments when it has freed man from the unlimited discretion of some ruler, some civil or military official, some bureaucrat. Where discretion is absolute, man has always suffered. . . . Absolute discretion . . . is more destructive of freedom than any of man's other inventions." In another opinion, Mr. Justice Douglas has said: "Absolute discretion, like corruption, marks the beginning of the end of liberty."[8]

As part of his idea of fair certainty as an essence of freedom, Hayek shares the understanding of Max Weber that a prerequisite of a modern economic system is a legal system that is calculable and predictable. Weber emphasized this requirement of capitalism in several of his works on law and economy. In *The Protestant Ethic and the Spirit of Capitalism,* for example, he wrote of the essential parts of capitalism:

> Among those of undoubted importance are the rational structures of law and of administration. For modern rational capitalism has need, not only of the technical means of production, but of a calculable legal system and of administration in terms of formal rules. Without it adventurous and speculative trading capitalism and all sorts of politically determined capitalisms are possible, but no rational enterprise under individual initiative, with fixed capital and certainty of calculations.[9]

[8]*United States v. Wunderlich,* 342 U.S. 98 (1951), 101, and *New York v. United States,* 342 U.S. 882 (1951), 884. Both quoted in Davis, *Discretionary Justice,* 152.

[9]Max Weber, *The Protestant Ethic and the Spirit of Capitalism,* trans. Talcott Parsons (1904; reprint, New York: Scribner's, 1958), 25.

Predictability in the state's coercive power of law is essential to a free capitalist economy. Following the precepts of free enterprise, the private sector must be able to determine its own objectives and plan its own actions. According to this premise, in the use of capital resources, including real property, it is not the proper role for government to decide on social goals or to plan for the people. Rather, the function of government and law in a free society is only to establish predetermined principles that apply to general circumstances so that the private sector may pursue its own ends, assured with foreknowledge of society's restrictions, or what Hayek terms the Rule of the Road.[10] If government endeavors to deliberate between individual merits and needs of different people or to plan to meet specific situations, then its actions become ad hoc and unpredictable, thus impeding the private individual's ability to judge and even infringing on his freedom of choice. From this view, certainly arbitrary action by government is antithetical to individual freedom. Hayek writes,

> The state should confine itself to establishing rules applying to general types of situations and should allow the individuals freedom in everything which depends on the circumstances of time and place, because only the individuals concerned in each instance can fully know these circumstances and adapt their actions to them. If the individuals are to be able to use their knowledge effectively in making plans, they must be able to predict actions of the state which may affect these plans. But if the actions of the state are to be predictable, they must be determined by rules fixed independently of the concrete circumstances which can be neither foreseen nor taken into account beforehand: and the particular effects of such actions will be unpredictable. If, on the other hand, the state were to direct the individual's actions so as to achieve particular ends, its action would have to be decided on the basis of the full circumstances of the moment and would therefore be unpredictable. Hence the familiar fact that the more the state "plans," the more difficult planning becomes for the individual.[11]

Hayek continues with the observation that discretion in government is the tool of dictatorship; once the effects can be foreseen when a law is made, the law becomes the lawgiver's instrument, by which he can serve his own ends.[12]

The principle of the Rule of Law is recognized in all modern free societies. In England, where strong adherence to the doctrine of common law essentially substitutes for constitutionalism, the Franks Committee on Administrative Tribunals and Enquiries noted in its 1957 report:

> The rule of law stands for the view that decisions should be made by the application of known principles of laws. In general such decisions will be

[10]Hayek, *Road to Serfdom,* 74.
[11]Ibid., 75–76.
[12]Ibid., 77.

predictable, and the citizen will know where he is. On the other hand there is what is arbitrary. A decision may be made without principle, without any rules. It is therefore unpredictable, the antithesis of a decision taken in accordance with the rule of law.[13]

With a strong tradition in common law, the doctrine of precedents is more stringently observed in Britain than in the United States, with the result that British courts are less inclined than their American counterparts to overturn precedent. While this observance of common law doctrine has resulted in a predictability not unlike that afforded by American constitutionalism, courts in Britain are also much more reluctant to interfere with the administrative judgment of government than in America.

The comparative implications for public planning are significant. On the Continent, codified civil law is inherently conducive to a planned society in terms of rationalist predetermination. In England, the empirical system of common law has evolved doctrines that at once ensure the Rule of Law and permit considerable administrative discretion in the pursuit of public planning objectives. The American approach contrasts with both English and European practice. By placing restrictions on governmental power and discretion, the Constitution effectively places limits on public planning and urban design authority.

The Early Years

During the colonial era in America, land-use regulations were based mainly on practical considerations. The settlers' newly found freedom of private land ownership was tempered by the realization that everyone's survival and welfare depended upon a measure of community cooperation and regulation. For example, several laws passed in Virginia and New Amsterdam during the mid seventeenth century governed the cultivation of land to ensure that certain crops necessary for the community, such as grain, corn, peas, and flax, would not be slighted by individual eagerness to grow more profitable crops, such as tobacco. A Virginia law likewise regulated tobacco cultivation to prevent ruin of valuable farmland through overplanting.

In the cities, regulations not unlike those existing in England were enacted to protect public health and safety. Several laws passed in Boston in the seventeenth century required buildings to be of masonry with roofs of slate or tile, the penalty for noncompliance being a fine equal to twice the worth of the construction itself. Measures concerning structural stability and the provision of firewalls were also common. In Philadelphia, codes

[13]Committee on Administrative Tribunals and Enquiries, *Report* (The Franks Report) (London: HMSO, 1957), Cmnd. 218.

determined the construction and width of party walls. Other laws governed land use rather than construction. In Boston and New York City, statutes prohibited or restricted the location of noxious activities, such as slaughterhouses.

In *The Taking Issue*, Fred Bosselman, David Callies, and John Banta write that ordinances ostensibly concerning public health sometimes extended to aesthetic considerations.[14] In New Amsterdam, for instance, surveyors hired to keep roads free of hog pens and privies were also charged to prevent the construction of unsightly buildings and fences. In Philadelphia, a health ordinance enacted in 1700 had decidedly urban design objectives.

> Every owner or inhabitant of any and every house in Philadelphia, Newcastle and Chester shall plant one or more tree or trees, viz., pines, unbearing mulberries, water poplars, lime or other shady and wholesome trees before the door of his, her or their house and houses, not exceeding eight feet from the front of the house, and preserving the same, to the end that the said town may be well shaded from the violence of the sun in the heat of summer and thereby be rendered more healthy.[15]

The founding of the Republic and the institution of the Bill of Rights subjected all governmental regulations on private property to the test of constitutionality—a test unprecedented in either the common law of England or the civil law of Europe. Whether the power of government to enforce community planning and design goals was paramount or whether the free prerogatives of private property were to prevail became questions to be decided based on the interpretation of the written Constitution. A federal judiciary was established to interpret this ultimate law, with the United States Supreme Court serving as the final forum for appeals. Similar state judicial systems were set up to rule on questions regarding the constitution of each state. As arbiters of the Constitution, the courts in America began to assume a role of power and responsibility unequaled in the effect of the invisible web of law on society and on patterns of urban development.

Initially, the courts wielded their new power cautiously, for there were no common-law precedents by which to judge the concept of constitutionality. The majority of cases on land use were state decisions concerning police-power measures to control hazardous conditions in urban areas. An example of such a case was *Respublica v. Philip Urbin Duquet*,[16] decided in 1799. In this dispute, the Pennsylvania Supreme Court found constitutional

---

[14]Fred Bosselman, David Callies, and John Banta, *The Taking Issue* (Washington, D.C.: USGPO, 1973). Research material for this chapter has been drawn liberally from this source.

[15]2 Pa. Stat. 66, Ch. 53. Quoted by Bosselman, Callies, and Banta, *The Taking Issue*, 84.

[16]2 Yeates 493, 7 Pa. Rpts. 493 (1799).

legislation that enabled the mayor, aldermen, and common council of Philadelphia to pass ordinances "to prevent any person or persons, from erecting or causing to be erected, any wooden mansion house, shop, ware house, store, carriage house, or stable, within such part of the city of Philadelphia . . . 'as they may judge proper.' "[17] The remedial intent of the ordinance was not unlike the practical measures imposed by Charles II more than a century earlier in England.

As in Europe, much of American land-use controls prior to planning stemmed from practical efforts to control, prevent, or remove nuisances through the police power. Even William Blackstone, the author of the "sole and despotic dominion" concept of private property, had acknowledged the necessity to curtail private activity, however lawful, if it became a source of danger or nuisance to others, whether to a neighboring property owner or to the general public.

> If a man builds a house so close to mine that his roof overhangs my roof, and throws the water off his roof upon mine, this is a nusance, for which an action will lie. Likewise to erect a house or other building so near to mine, that it stops up my antient lights and windows, is a nusance of a similar nature. . . . Also, if a person keeps his hogs, or other noisome animals, so near the house of another, that the stench of them incommodes him and makes the air unwholesome, this is an injurious nusance, as it tends to deprive him of the use and benefit of his house. A like injury is, if one's neighbor sets up and exercises any offensive trade; as a tanner's, a tallowchandler's, or the like: for though these are lawful and necessary trades, yet they should be exercised in remote places . . . [18]

Several cases in New York City during the 1820s concerned the authority of the municipality to forbid interment of the dead in certain areas. In *Brick Presbyterian Church v. the City of New York,* the land had indeed been conveyed by the city specifically for the location of a church and cemetery.[19] The court emphasized in its decision the fact that the dynamics of urban growth compelled recision of rights previously granted.

> Sixty years ago, when the lease was made, the premises were beyond the inhabited part of the city. They were a common, and bounded on one side by a vineyard. Now they are in the very heart of the city. When the defendants covenanted that the lessees might enjoy the premises for the purposes of burying their dead, it never entered into the contemplation of either party that the health of the city might require the suspension or the abolition of that right.[20]

[17]Ibid., 501.
[18]William Blackstone, *Commentaries on the Laws of England* (1765–69; reprint, London: Dawsons, 1966), bk. 3, ch. 13, 216–17.
[19]5 Cowen 538, 8 N.Y. Com. L. Rpts. 5 (1826), 538.
[20]Ibid., 540.

In 1853, the Massachusetts court ruled in *Commonwealth v. Alger* that a statute forbidding the construction of wharves beyond certain boundaries within Boston Harbor was a constitutional exercise of the police power.[21] As in the *Brick* case, the land had been conveyed by the state for the very purpose undertaken by the plaintiff, albeit the grant had taken place two centuries earlier. Wrote Chief Justice Lemuel Shaw:

> We think it is a settled principle, growing out of the nature of well-ordered civil society, that every holder of property, however absolute and unqualified may be his title, holds it under the implied liability that his use of it may be so regulated, that it shall not be injurious to the equal enjoyment of others having an equal right to the enjoyment of their property, nor injurious to the rights of the community.[22]

The prerogative of the public to restrain the nuisance of "an injurious private use" was justified in Shaw's view by the ancient common-law dictum enunciated by Sir Edward Coke, *sic utere tuo ut alienum non laedes,* that the free use of property did not extend freedom to cause damage or nuisance to others.[23] Shaw took pains to distinguish between two public authorities: the police power, which does not constitute a taking of property rights requiring compensation; and the power of eminent domain, which does. According to Shaw, the police power could be properly exercised to forbid a private and otherwise lawful land use that posed a hazard or nuisance to the public even though the restriction would diminish the value of the property.

> This is very different from the right of eminent domain, the right of a government to take and appropriate private property to public use, whenever the public exigency requires it; which can be done only on condition of providing a reasonable compensation therefore. The power we allude to is rather the police power . . . Nor does the prohibition of such noxious use of property, a prohibition imposed because such use would be injurious to the public, although it may diminish the profits of the owner, make it an appropriation to a public use, so as to entitle the owner to compensation.[24]

The power of the sovereign to take private property for public use through condemnation is commonly accepted as ancient doctrine, but this authority is explicitly limited by the "taking clause" of the Fifth Amendment to the Constitution: "nor shall private property be taken for public use, without just compensation." In the United States, until the 1920s, the

---

[21]7 Cushing 53, 61 Mass. 53 (1853).
[22]Ibid., 84–85.
[23]Edward Coke, 9, *Reports* 59 (1658).
[24]Note 21, 85–86.

distinction drawn by Shaw between public regulation and public taking was the prevailing construction. This attitude was summarized by Theodore Sedgwick in his 1857 treatise on constitutional law: "It seems to be settled that, to entitle the owner to protection under this clause, the property must be actually taken in the physical sense of the word . . . [25] Bosselman, Callies, and Banta also note that "the great majority of the cases held that only actual physical appropriation or divesting of title constituted a taking . . .[26] This early belief gave great flexibility to the police power, for it implied that regulation could extend to the very threshold of expropriation without offending the Constitution.

The attitude of the state courts toward the police power was evident also in the consensus of federal court decisions. The idea that police-power regulation was unrelated to public taking was enunciated in 1887 by the Supreme Court in *Mugler v. Kansas*. The opinion of the Court was written by Justice John Marshall Harlan.

> The present case must be governed by principles that do not involve the power of eminent domain, in the exercise of which property may not be taken for public use without compensation. A prohibition simply upon the use of property for purposes that are declared, by valid legislation, to be injurious to the health, morals, or safety of the community, cannot, in any just sense, be deemed a taking or an appropriation of property for the public benefit. Such legislation does not disturb the owner in the control or use of his property for lawful purposes, nor restrict his right to dispose of it, but is only a declaration by the State that its use by any one, for certain forbidden purposes, is prejudicial to the public interests.[27]

The *Mugler* decision upheld a state prohibition against the manufacture and sale of intoxicating liquor, even though the regulation had the effect of stripping a brewery of all value. Bosselman, Callies, and Banta comment on the decision,

> In Harlan's view the difference between a police power regulation upon property use and a public taking of property was not a difference of degree, but a difference in kind. His opinion explicitly stated that a prohibition upon the use of property designed to protect the public health and safety could never be deemed a taking because such a prohibition did not affect an individual's title to his property, nor did it result in governmental use of private property. Rather, the sole purpose of such a regulation was to declare that a particular property use was forbidden because it was injurious to the community. The

[25]Theodore Sedgwick, *A Treatise on the Rules which Govern the Interpretation and Construction of Statutory and Constitutional Law* (1857; Baker Voorhis, reprint, Littleton, C.O.: Rothman 1980), 456-57.

[26]Bosselman, Callies, and Banta, *The Taking Issue,* 106.

[27]123 U.S. 623 (1887), 668-69.

test, therefore, would be whether the regulation had a rational relationship to the public welfare.

The *Mugler* opinion established as a constitutional principle the doctrine that police power regulations do not constitute compensable takings, but where the government action permanently appropriated the owner's property compensation was required even if the government's purpose was to abate a nuisance.[28]

The distinction made by Harlan between the police-power regulation and public taking was given further legitimacy when it was echoed by Professor Ernst Freund of the University of Chicago School of Law in his 1904 treatise *The Police Power,* which was regarded for many years as the definitive work on the subject. "The state," wrote Freund, "takes property by eminent domain because it is useful to the public, and under the police power because it is harmful.[29] Again, the difference between regulation and public taking was seen as absolute.

Mugler set the precedent for many subsequent court decisions enforcing the cessation of existing land uses that had become public nuisances. Several of the so-called nuisance cases were Supreme Court rulings occurring between 1915 and 1920. One of these, *Hadacheck v. Sebastian,*[30] upheld a Los Angeles municipal ordinance enjoining the operation of a brickyard, even though the yard had existed previous to city annexation and to residential development around it, and despite the claim that the regulation would cause a reduction in value of the property from $800,000 to only $60,000. Another decision upheld the removal of a livery stable from a commercial area;[31] one allowed the prohibition of signs from a residential district;[32] and yet another upheld the exclusion of oil storage within 300 feet of dwellings.[33] Over time, the doctrine of nuisance law evolved through these cases became the foundation of the law on land-use planning, aesthetics, and urban design. As lawyer H. P. Kucera observed in 1960, "Aesthetic considerations in zoning are nothing more than the legal evolution and growth of the concept of the nuisance."[34]

THE HOLMES DOCTRINE

The relationship between police power and property rights established in these cases was substantially altered in 1922 by the most influential of

---

[28]Bosselman, Callies, and Banta, *The Taking Issue,* 120.

[29]Ernst Freund, *The Police Power* (Chicago: Callaghan, 1904), 546–47.

[30]239 U.S. 394 (1915).

[31]*Reinman v. Little Rock,* 237 U.S. 171 (1915).

[32]*Cusack Co. v. City of Chicago,* 242 U.S. 526 (1917).

[33]*Pierce Oil Corp. v. City of Hope,* 248 U.S. 498 (1919).

[34]H. P. Kucera, "The Legal Aspects of Aesthetics in Zoning," *Institute on Planning and Zoning* 1 (1960): 21.

Supreme Court decisions affecting land use to that time. During the late nineteenth century, much of the land in the anthracite region of Pennsylvania was owned by coal companies, and in order to build, it was usually necessary to purchase property from them. Typically the deeds contained provisions that retained the mineral rights for the coal company and waived any future claims by purchasers against the company for damages caused by subsidence due to mining. By the first decade of the new century, however, just such subsidence had become widespread in Scranton, Wilkes-Barre, and several other communities in the region. To forestall the menace, in 1921 the state passed into law the Kohler Act, prohibiting mining that would cause damage to buildings, roads, and other structures within certain municipalities.

Shortly after its enactment, Mr. and Mrs. H. J. Mahon were notified by the Pennsylvania Coal Company that their residence in the town of Pittston would soon be subject to subsidence due to mining operations beneath the land. The coal company made clear that, under the conditions of the original deed on the Mahon property, it reserved the right to continue mining excavations without liability for damage or injury resulting from surface subsidence. Mahon, an attorney, immediately filed for an injunction under the Kohler Act to enjoin the coal company permanently from operations under his house. He and his wife were joined in their suit by several parties, notably the state of Pennsylvania and the city of Scranton as amici curiae. The Pennsylvania court ruled in favor of the plaintiffs, upholding the authority of the act. In response, the coal company appealed to the United States Supreme Court.

The case of *Pennsylvania Coal Company v. Mahon* pitted two of the greatest minds ever to serve the high court against each other.[35] Louis Brandeis assumed a judicially conservative attitude, holding in essence that the court's past rulings on *Mugler* and subsequent nuisance cases should govern, an argument leading somewhat paradoxically to the rather liberal conclusion that the state's police authority embodied in the Kohler Act should be upheld. Oliver Wendell Holmes took the contrary position: that precedent doctrine should not apply and that the rights of the coal company should be maintained. He reached this conclusion by placing emphasis, not on past court decisions, but on his perception of the facts and circumstances surrounding the case. As the majority opinion, Holmes's view prevailed, thereby establishing a new perspective of the relationship between the public's police power and the private rights of property.

The coal company's appeal was based on arguments that the Kohler Act would impair the validity of contracts and would result in the taking of property without just compensation. Holmes's opinion focused principally on the latter issue. He began by recognizing the legitimacy of the police power but quickly emphasized the need for its limitation.

[35] 260 U.S. 393 (1922).

Government hardly could go on if to some extent values incident to property could not be diminished without paying for every such change in the general law. As long recognized, some values are enjoyed under an implied limitation and must yield to the police power. But obviously the implied limitation must have its limits, or the contract and due process clauses are gone. One fact for consideration in determining such limits is the extent of the diminution. When it reaches a certain magnitude, in most if not in all cases there must be an exercise of eminent domain and compensation to sustain the act. So the question depends upon the particular facts.[36]

Holmes observed: "This is the case of a single private house. . . . The damage is not common or public. . . . On the other hand the extent of the taking is great."[37] The benefit of the regulation, Holmes believed, should be weighed against the loss in value caused by the restriction.

The general rule at least is, that while property may be regulated to a certain extent, if regulation goes too far it will be recognized as a taking. . . . As we already have said, this is a question of degree—and therefore cannot be disposed of by general propositions.[38]

Implicit was Holmes's rejection of Harlan's earlier distinction in the *Mugler* case between the police power and public taking. The difference, according to Holmes, was a matter of degree and not of kind. This understanding was first evident in Holmes's opinions thirty-three years earlier, in *Rideout v. Knox,*[39] which he wrote as a judge on the Massachusetts Supreme Judicial Court. In *Pennsylvania Coal,* however, Holmes was speaking for the highest court in the land.

In his dissent, Brandeis maintained the court's earlier stand in *Mugler.* From this position, the essential test for the constitutionality of a police-power regulation was whether it had a rational and appropriate relationship to the public welfare. Accordingly, since the prohibition of mining had been "obviously enacted for a public purpose" to secure public safety,[40] the restriction constituted a valid exercise of the police power. As for Holmes's assertion that the line between regulation and taking is "a question of degree," Brandeis argued that "values are relative," returning to the rationale expressed in *Mugler* that regulation and taking are different in kind.[41] In Brandeis's view, what was at issue was not a single dwelling, nor the validity of a private contract, nor the value of the property rights restricted, but the principle of whether the legislature could exercise the police power in order

[36]Ibid., 413.
[37]Ibid., 413–14.
[38]Ibid., 415–16.
[39]148 Mass. 368 (1889).
[40]Note 35, 422.
[41]Ibid., 419.

to protect the safety of the public in general without making compensation. Brandeis noted that "coal in place is land; and the right of the owner to use his land is not absolute."[42]

The positions taken by the two justices differed fundamentally. Brandeis agreed with general principles set in precedent cases that police-power "restriction imposed to protect the public health, safety or morals from dangers threatened is not a taking," and that compensation is unnecessary where "the property so restricted remains in the possession of its owner."[43] Holmes, on the other hand, held that "general propositions" could not apply and that determination of the line between the police power and compensable regulation must consider instead "the extent of diminution" of property values, which necessarily depends on "particular facts."[44]

This approach by Holmes is seen by Bosselman, Callies, and Banta as establishing the now commonly accepted principle that any police-power regulation over private land use is subject to a constitutional "balancing test."[45] According to this thesis, it is not enough to demonstrate the public purpose and reasonableness of a regulation. Instead, the value of the regulation to the public must also be weighed against the loss in value to the owner caused by the restriction. Failure of a regulation to meet the test causes it to be construed as a taking, for which compensation is required under the Fifth Amendment.

On an immediate and practical level, the decision upholding the claim of the coal company reinforced and even extended the conservative notion of the inviolability of private property, for it seemed to leave little room to justify the use of the police power to abate a nuisance. As the authors of *The Taking Issue* asked: "What could be a greater nuisance than having your land collapse underneath your house?"[46] Though Holmes saw *Pennsylvania Coal* as a "case of a single private house," he also went on to say that "a source of damage to such a house is not a public nuisance even if similar damage is inflicted on others in different places. The damage is not common or public."[47] What circumstances then constitute enough of a menace to the public health and safety to warrant a police-power restriction? Indeed, if Holmes's finding of fact is seen as a governing paradigm, might not the concept of private property return to the age of Blackstone? The language used in *Pennsylvania Coal* is strikingly similar to that of the eighteenth-century champion of private property. Wrote Holmes: "A strong public desire to improve the public condition is not enough to warrant achieving the desire by a shorter cut than the constitutional way of paying

---

[42]Ibid., 417.
[43]Ibid.
[44]Ibid. 415, 416.
[45]Bosselman, Callies, and Banta, *The Taking Issue,* 139.
[46]Ibid., 258.
[47]Note 35, 413.

for the change."[48] This argument is almost identical to Blackstone's charge that the law holds private property so sacrosanct that it will not allow the slightest violation of it, even for the good of the whole community.

On a higher level, however, the furtherance of the rights of property was achieved in *Pennsylvania Coal* only through a liberal interpretation of the taking clause. This free construction of the Fifth Amendment has set a longer-lasting if "hidden" doctrine whose effect has been more equivocal than the more apparent principle delimiting the police power. By its very nature, the constitutional test suggested by Holmes requires judicial discretion in admitting and weighing "particular facts" to determine "a question of degree." Holmes never construed his findings of fact in the immediate case to be an exemplification. Quite on the contrary, his principal admonition was to consider the particular facts governing each individual circumstance. Thus, his opinion provided no general standard by which future courts could ascertain the "certain magnitude" at which public regulation evolves by "degree" into public taking.

Indeed, only six years after the case, the Supreme Court held in *Miller v. Schoene*[49] that a Virginia statute providing for the removal of cedar trees infected with cedar rust to be within the authority of the police power. The fungus disease was not harmful to cedars but posed a threat to apple trees in nearby orchards. The Court made no reference to *Pennsylvania Coal* nor to any standard for the police power. It is certainly arguable that the prevention of subsidence beneath occupied houses is no less pertinent to public safety than the protection of apple trees. Thus while confirming the widely observed doctrine for courts to conduct the constitutional balancing test, the *Pennsylvania Coal* decision left open the question of just where "regulation goes too far." That determination essentially was left to the judiciary in each individual case.

The potential of Holmes's opinion to establish a definitive standard to guide judicial discretion in land-use matters was also clouded by another issue. The grant to Mahon and other holders of surface rights included a contractual waiver of liability claims against the coal company. Holmes made several references to this contract in his opinion, but it is unclear how much this condition influenced his finding. It has been pointed out, for example, that people in the area had little choice but to buy land from the coal company in order to build their homes, and hence they were effectively compelled to accept any terms that the company set forth.

In view of his eloquent dissent in favor of labor reform in *Lochner v. New York,*[50] it seems somewhat of an anomaly for Holmes to have placed commercial property interests above public protection in *Pennsylvania*

[48]Ibid., 416.
[49]276 U.S. 272 (1928).
[50]198 U.S. 45 (1905).

Coal. Indeed, his usual respect for the police power and legislative determination has been compared with that of Harlan, who wrote the *Mugler* decision. As evidenced in *Lochner,* Holmes customarily practiced judicial restraint in applying constitutional due-process restrictions on legislative experiments in social reform. His usual approach was to follow a strict construction of the Constitution and to base judgment on the essence of the public purpose and the reasonableness of the regulation. In *Pennsylvania Coal,* however, Holmes departed from this conservative judicial practice and extended the Fifth Amendment prohibition against uncompensated taking to include police-power regulation of land use.

In many ways, the decision in *Pennsylvania Coal* reflected its place in time. As Bosselman, Callies, and Banta note: "It is worth remembering that when U.S. constitutional doctrine on the taking issue was formulated during the late Nineteenth and early Twentieth Centuries, land was regarded as unlimited and its use not ordinarily of concern to society."[51] Against the perceived expansion of the police power in such preceding cases as *Mugler* and *Hadacheck,* the decision resurrected and upheld the deep-rooted American belief in private property, fundamental to the nation's tradition of free enterprise. The particular social implications in the case of local government attempting to protect small homeowners from the actions of a large corporation have been lost in history. What remains relevant is the powerful precedent that the case offered to succeeding claims against public regulation. *Pennsylvania Coal* is undoubtedly important in its own right, but it has been made even more so by the numerous courts that have subsequently chosen to cite its findings to support their own arguments. The significance of the case was also magnified by its timing, for in the decade following the decision the foundations were laid for present land-use and planning law.

Although the balancing test initiated by Holmes in *Pennsylvania Coal* cast a shadow of doubt and uncertainty on the issue of land use and public controls, its empirical approach seems more logical than does adherence to a strict doctrine based on precedent, especially since the doctrine at that time supported the police power. However, considering Hayek's proposition that fair certainty in law is the private sector's greatest protection against arbitrary use of governmental authority, it is ironic that by the last quarter of this century, the uncertainty in outcome inherent in discretionary judgment has begun once again to erode the ability of private property to withstand public regulation.

From a philosophical standpoint, Holmes's denial of "general propositions" in this landmark not only depreciated constitutional standards as a basis for judgment, but it also rejected the abstract, rationalist logic commonly associated with judicial interpretation of codes like the Constitution. By turning to "particular facts" and circumstances, Holmes assumed an

[51]Bosselman, Callies, and Banta, *The Taking Issue,* 253.

approach usually identified with the empiricism of common law in which experience and evidence are primary. In this regard, his reasoning approximates Weber's concept of "substantive irrationality," wherein judgment is "influenced by concrete factors of the particular case" and by the exercise of discretion.[52] As Kenneth Davis points out, "Exercising discretion may be a part of finding facts and applying law, and finding facts may be a part of exercising discretion."[53]

For Holmes to take this approach and for Brandeis to advocate adherence to principles set by precedent doctrine was somewhat of a reversal for both men. As a lawyer, Brandeis had made such compelling use of factual evidence that the "Brandeis brief"[54] was credited for attaching new significance to the role of evidence in constitutional litigation. On the other hand, as Bosselman, Callies, and Banta write: "Holmes constantly professed a good-natured impatience with Brandeis's preoccupation with the facts, preferring to think cases could be decided by reliance on basic principles."[55] His decision in *Pennsylvania Coal,* however, belies this general assessment.

The judgment has had further implications for the courts, not only in technical considerations of the law, but also in terms of the judiciary's role in planning practice. The American courts are empowered to overrule governmental determination on the basis of constitutional oversight. In *Pennsylvania Coal,* however, intervention was based less on constitutional standards than on discretionary review of specific circumstances. Thus the decision effectively subordinated legislative determination to the discretionary judgment of the judiciary and set an example for the judiciary's subsequent activism and power in matters of land-use control and public planning. By forming judgments more on ad hoc discretion than on a strict construction of preestablished principles, the judiciary in effect increased its own power; for power, as Hayek infers, lies in just such exercise.

The power of the American judiciary is unique, contrasting with England and Europe, where planning bureaucracies are invested with a discretionary capability that the courts in this country have usurped, even if unwittingly. Barring a constitutional change—a long and uncertain political process—the judiciary can virtually supersede the determination of legislators and planning experts, checked only by superiors within its own hierarchy. Indeed, in recent years, some courts have effectively initiated affirmative actions through their rulings, both in land-use and social planning.

Dennis Lloyd, as quoted earlier, suggested that common law is made essentially by judges who are practical "men of the world," as distinct from

[52]Max Weber, *On Law in Economy and Society,* ed. and trans. Max Rheinstein (1925; reprint, New York: Simon & Schuster, Clarion, 1954), 63.

[53]Davis, *Discretionary Justice,* 5.

[54]Alpheus Thomas Mason, *Brandeis: A Free Man's Life* (New York: Viking, 1946), 248–52.

[55]Bosselman, Callies, and Banta, *The Taking Issue,* 244.

the scholars and theoreticians who determine doctrines of civil law. However, with their interpretative monopoly over constitutional intent, and with appointment of life tenure to the highest judicial ranks, it can be questioned seriously whether judges in America are truly "men of the world," or whether they assume the oracular status of Weber's "legal *honoratiores*."[56] As a result of adjudication, some judges have become credible experts in the field of land-use planning. Though acquired acumen may be creditable, it may nonetheless be questioned whether judicial decisions should be based essentially on substantive constitutional issues, not on discretion achieved in light of a particular case's facts where other disciplinary professionals might be better qualified to judge.

The control that the American judicial system exerts over city planning is that of the invisible web. A corollary is that this power is matched proportionally by the influence of those schooled in the law, for no planner, urban designer, or other member of society is as trained to engineer and manipulate the weave of the web and its effect on urban design and planning as is the legal professional, whatever his background—or lack of it—in the field of planning.

[56]Weber, *On Law,* 52.

Chapter 4

Spinning the Zoning Web

By the 1920s, the era of *Pennsylvania Coal,*[1] the social cost of the Industrial Revolution had become all too clear. The earlier *Lochner v. New York*[2] decision had granted Herbert Spencer legitimacy and had translated his philosophy of Social Darwinism into cruel reality. For the working class, the city had evolved into a veritable jungle. Child labor, sweatshop exploitation, slum tenements, and dangerously overcrowded and filthy conditions seemed endemic to urban life. Gradually, however, the deplorable conditions of both European and American cities touched social consciences and fostered movement toward reform. Socialists, including the Fabians in Britain and Eugene V. Debs in the United States, gained popularity, as did muckraking writers like Lincoln Steffans and Upton Sinclair. The effects of capitalism on the poor became a common target of criticism. Wrote Richard H. Tawney of the capitalistic ethic in his classic reform work, *The Acquisitive Society:*

> It assures men that there are no ends other than their ends, no law other than their desires, no limit other than that which they think advisable. Thus it makes the individual the center of his own universe, and dissolves moral principles into a choice of expediences. And it immensely simplifies the problems of social life in complex communities. For it relieves them of the necessity of discriminating between different types of economic activity and different sources of wealth, between enterprise and avarice, energy and unscrupulous greed, property which is legitimate and property which is theft, the just enjoyment of fruits of labor and the idle parasitism of birth or fortune, because it treats all economic activities as standing upon the same level, and suggests that excess of defects, waste or superfluity, require no conscious effort of

[1]*Pennsylvania Coal Company v. Mahon*, 260 U.S. 393 (1922).
[2]*Lochner v. New York*, 198 U.S. 45 (1905).

80

the social will to avert them, but are corrected almost automatically by the mechanical play of economic forces.[3]

In the city, the movement toward reform fused the socialist's aim of attaining a more humane society with the planner's vision of creating a more livable environment. Reform leaders enthusiastically supported planning, which they saw as a means to mitigate the harsh social and physical conditions of cities. In New York City, their drive focused in part on ways to manage development. In a rather incongruous but not illogical alliance, the reformers were joined in their efforts to implement planning controls by their apparent antagonists, the capitalists and merchants whose homes and businesses epitomized the wealth of the city.

During the late nineteenth century, several such wealthy New Yorkers as Andrew Carnegie, the Vanderbilts, and the Astors built large and resplendent new mansions along Manhattan's upper Fifth Avenue. The residential exclusivity of these grand homes was not long to last, however, for they were soon followed by the relocation of the very stores that the rich themselves patronized. "Millionaires' Row" on Fifth Avenue was quickly invaded by such fashionable retail department stores as Lord and Taylor, Arnold Constable, and W. J. Sloane. But even then, further change was brewing. By the 1910s, the proprietors of these expensive carriage-trade stores along the avenue found their own establishments threatened by an even greater "menace"—the seemingly inexorable northward migration of the garment industry from lower Manhattan. In *Zoned American,* author and lawyer Seymour I. Toll describes the battle of successive invasion and exclusion in New York as the epitome of Spencer's Social Darwinism, with "garment manufacturers fighting retail merchants fighting wealthy residents."[4] Land-use controls, if not planning, became a prime weapon in this war. To thwart the intrusion of the garment factories and the immigrant hordes that these sweatshops employed, the merchants and residents of Fifth Avenue, like the guildsmen and mercantile class of Elizabethan London some four centuries earlier, joined to prevail upon the government to enact laws to safeguard their urban enclave from invasion by the immigrant poor. The instrument used for this exclusion was zoning, which the city formally adopted by resolution in 1916.

THE CONTINENTAL CONTRIBUTION

The utilization of this land-use control was somewhat an anomaly. Whereas the heritage of America derives largely from Britain and from a

---

[3]Richard H. Tawney, *The Acquisitive Society* (New York: Harcourt, Brace, 1920), 30–31.

[4]Seymour I. Toll, *Zoned American* (New York: Grossman, 1969), 110.

strong tradition of individual freedom, zoning was adopted from perhaps the most authoritarian of European cultures of the late nineteenth century. "Zoning," wrote historians George and Christiane Collins, " . . . was virtually an invention of the Germans."[5] Toll explains: "In his surging optimism, the American reformer also had a great love affair with the German city. The infatuation with zoning was an essential part of it, for Germany was the culture in which he first saw zoning fully developed."[6]

Men prominent in the early days of American city planning commonly made reference to the German initiative. Frederick Law Olmsted, Jr., son of the great landscape architect, discussed the success that the German methods had achieved in managing planned growth in Hamburg. "One of the most fundamentally important features of recent city planning in Europe," he said in an address before the first National Conference on City Planning, "has been the system of differentiated building regulations . . . to give each district as nearly as possible just what it wants, to protect it from deterioration at the hands of a selfish minority, and to give stability to its real estate values."[7] Edward M. Bassett, a leading pioneer of zoning in the United States, also had traveled in Europe and was quite familiar with German planning techniques. Other advocates, like the wealthy owners of property along Fifth Avenue, supported adoption of the control device for reasons of economic self-interest. The main incentive behind Henry Morgenthau's corroboration, for instance, was the protection that zoning afforded his substantial investments in real estate.[8]

The reform proponents of zoning were not unaware of the incongruity of importing this German control technique to America. Toll cites Frederic C. Howe, a leader in the movement, as describing Germany as "an autocratic caste-controlled country" where obedience was inbred.[9] Toll makes the contrast between the "blindly subservient personality" of the German people at the time and the "national character of unruly freedom" to be found in America.[10]

> In a culture like Germany's, public controls have tended to beget obedience. In an American setting, the tendencies have run in the opposite direction, especially at a time like the early twentieth century when the ghost of Herbert Spencer haunted the houses of government.[11]

[5]George R. Collins and Christiane C. Collins, *Camillo Sitte and the Birth of Modern City Planning* (New York: Random House, 1965), 21.

[6]Toll, *Zoned American*, 128-29.

[7]Frederick Law Olmstead, Jr., "The Scope and Results of City Planning in Europe," *Hearing Before the Committee on the District of Columbia*, Sen. doc. no. 422, 61st. Cong., 2nd. Sess. (March 11, 1910), 69. Cited by Toll, *Zoned American*, 129.

[8]Toll, *Zoned American*, 124-25.

[9]Frederic C. Howe, "In Defence of the American City," *Scribner's* 51 (April 1912), 485. Quoted by Toll, *Zoned American*, 130.

[10]Toll, *Zoned American*, 130.

[11]Ibid.

The adoption of the police power as the basis for land-development administration signaled a fundamental divergence of American planning controls from the British. By the mid twentieth century, public regulation and planning of private development in England became formally based on the concept of compensation, with government obliged to pay owners for development interest in their property. America, with a culture of expanding diversity beyond Britain alone, was not constrained to follow. Of course, there also existed a pragmatic and compelling reason for adoption of the German scheme: its apparent economy, for with a basis in the police power, zoning seemed to exact no evident public expenditure.

Potentially, however, the social cost of the police power indiscriminately used can be the most elemental of all, particularly for a free-enterprise society. Ernst Freund, author of *The Police Power*[12] who was himself raised and educated in Germany, warned in the early 1900s to distinguish between the cultures of Germany and the United States. Toll, writing on Freund's understanding of German authoritarianism, said:

> Freund carried the police power out of the sovereign hands of American government and back into eighteenth-century continental Europe. There the sovereign, a powerful monarch or petty prince, exercised the police power. He had the power to lay down the style and the detail of city building, especially in capital cities.[13]

The manifestations of this absolutist authority were evident in continental urban design. Continued Toll:

> In the late twenties the results were still apparent in German cities like Mannheim, Darmstadt, Karlsruhe, Potsdam, and Dresden, and in French cities like Nancy and areas of Paris. All of this was evidence of benevolent despotism.[14]

The influence of German planners like Reinhard Baumeister, Joseph Stubben, and Werner Hegemann was not insignificant during the infancy of American city planning and zoning. Even the American inclination toward administrative decentralization had an unlikely antecedent in Prussian municipal practice. Toll attributes decentralization of authority in Germany to a Prussian baron, Heinrich Friedrich Karl Stein, who managed to persuade Wilhelm III that towns should operate independently within the state. His reason was not to further democratic representation, as was the American motive, but to take advantage of more efficient local authority.[15] Interest-

---

[12]Ernst Freund, *The Police Power* (Chicago: Callaghan, 1904).
[13]Toll, *Zoned American*, 265.
[14]Ibid.
[15]Ibid., 132.

ingly, it has been largely forgotten that American zoning had its roots in Germany, no doubt because of the enmity caused by the subsequent world wars and the consequential tendency to disavow the German legacy.

Zoning of course was not the only alien idea to take root in the United States. Foreign concepts of urban design also contributed fundamentally to the genesis of the modern planning profession in America. During this period, theory and practice in city planning were dominated by and large by the design professions. Architects and landscape designers captured the public imagination with the idea that their physical design values could overcome the social depravities as well as the ugliness brought about by industrialization.

Foremost among these design visionaries was Daniel Burnham, the eminent beaux-arts architect and leading force behind Chicago's impressive, neoclassical Columbian Exposition of 1893. The City Beautiful was Burnham's inspired goal. "Make no little plans;" he exhorted, "they have no magic to stir men's blood . . . "[16] Though a formulative influence on American city planning, Burnham nevertheless championed an anachronistic style of design foreign to the nation's heritage, in view of its English legacy as well as its native soil. While Louis Sullivan was laying the foundations of an indigenous American architecture through his iconoclastic merging of traditional motifs with expressive raw materials, and at a time when Ebenezer Howard was searching in England for salvation from the industrial city through his radical concept of urban green belts and satellite garden villages, the City Beautiful movement turned instead to France for inspiration. Architects trained at the École des Beaux-Arts in Paris brought to America the giant rationalist symmetries that were to resurrect L'Enfant's neo-Renaissance scheme for Washington and transfigure—with varying degrees of success—other American cities previously laid out only by the land agent's survey.

One lasting contribution during this period did have its origin in an English idiom, however. Through his great public parks, Frederick Law Olmsted, Sr., introduced to the nation's cities the romantic naturalism of the English garden, but at a scale to match and integrate with the ambitious continental schemes of Daniel Burnham. Despite the symbolic incongruity of the neo-Renaissance City Beautiful with American traditions, the movement's ideals swept the nation. Grand geometric design became the fashionable planning goal for all cities to attain. The movement's basic assumption of physical design as the panacea for all urban woes became the underlying premise of city planning during planning's incipient years as a profession and for many decades thereafter.

---

[16]Charles Moore, *Daniel H. Burnham, Architect, Planner of Cities* (Boston: Houghton Mifflin, 1921), vol. 2, 147.

THE STANDARD ACTS AND THE CASE OF EUCLID V. AMBLER

Two events occurred in the 1920s that had profound consequences on the design of the invisible web and its effect on American planning. One was the formulation and widespread adoption of zoning legislation; the other was a Supreme Court ruling on zoning's constitutionality.

After its inception in New York, the concept of zoning gained immediate popularity as an effective tool with which municipalities could control growth. Significantly, it caught the attention of then Commerce Secretary Herbert Hoover, who had a particular interest in housing and the protection of residential neighborhoods from industrial encroachment. Hoover shared the conservative belief of most Republicans at the time that most governmental functions work best at a local rather than at a higher level. In 1921, he appointed an Advisory Committee on Zoning with a membership composed largely of men active in the urban reform movement, including several who had participated in the New York effort. Within a year, the committee drafted the Standard State Zoning Enabling Act (SZEA),[17] a suggested model code which, upon adoption by state legislatures, would authorize towns and cities in their jurisdiction to zone under the police power. Significantly, in a reflection of Hoover's conservatism, the choice of whether to zone would be left a local option.

Published in 1924, the SZEA was widely distributed. In less than a year, about one fourth of the states had passed a zoning enabling act; and by the end of the 1930s, every state had some form of legislation that gave their municipalities the option to zone. Also widely copied by the states was the Standard City Planning Enabling Act (SPEA),[18] printed in 1928. Most legislatures did not alter the substance of these model codes to any degree, and to this day the SZEA and SPEA remain the basis of land-use controls in the preponderance of states, with the notable exception of Hawaii.

Concurrent with the formulation of the Standard Acts, a small Ohio town at the eastern outskirts of Cleveland came into national prominence as the testing ground for the constitutionality of zoning. Like many residential communities, the village of Euclid wished to preserve its pleasant, rural character by restricting the expansion of industry from its metropolitan neighbor to the west. In 1922, the same year as the *Pennsylvania Coal* decision, and under the authority of new enabling legislation from the state, the town passed an ordinance placing the entire village under zoning regulation.

Land uses in Euclid were divided into six classes, ranging from various

[17]U.S. Department of Commerce, *Standard State Zoning Enabling Act* (1922, revised 1926; reprinted in *A Model Land Development Code, Tentative Draft No. 1,* Philadelphia: American Law Institute, 1968), 210–21.

[18]U.S. Department of Commerce, *Standard City Planning Enabling Act* (1928; reprinted in *A Model Land Development Code, Tentative Draft No. 1,* Philadelphia: American Law Institute, 1968), 222–71.

levels of residential density to generally unrestricted use for purposes to include manufacturing and industrial operations. Among properties affected by the ordinance were sixty-eight acres of land assembled by the Ambler Realty Company on speculation for resale or development as factory sites. According to the claim of the real estate company, the zoning of its property for other than its intended purposes reduced the investment value of its holdings from ten thousand to twenty-five hundred dollars per acre.[19] Ambler filed suit in United States District Court, claiming that the ordinance deprived it of property without due process as guaranteed by the Fourteenth Amendment.[20]

Judge David Courtney Westenhaver upheld the realty company's claim and struck down the village's zoning ordinance. He repeated Holmes's arguments on behalf of property rights in *Pennsylvania Coal* and cited the Supreme Court: "There can be no conception of property aside from its control and use, and upon its use depends its value."[21] Westenhaver knew, however, that because of public interest in zoning, his would not be the last word, and commented at the outset of his opinion that the case was "obviously destined to go higher."[22]

Euclid's appeal to the Supreme Court evoked the national implications of the case. The village's brief contained frequent references to the national planning movement, the New York effort, Hoover's Committee, and the Standard Act, noting that "the Euclid Ordinance is almost an exact duplicate of the New York City Zoning Ordinance, except as to local names and locations."[23] Interest in the case was intense, and collaboration on behalf of the village included participation by the founders of the American zoning movement, including such lawyers as James F. Metzenbaum, Alfred Bettman, and Edward M. Bassett.

In late 1926, the Supreme Court ruled on *Village of Euclid v. Ambler Realty Company.*[24] It found zoning to be constitutionally sound. Justice George Sutherland wrote the opinion of the court, joined by five of the other justices, including both Holmes and Brandeis.

> The ordinance now under review, and all similar laws and regulations, must find their justification in some aspect of the police power, asserted for the public welfare. The line which in this field separates the legitimate from the

[19]Toll, *Zoned American*, 217.

[20]*Ambler Realty Co. v. Village of Euclid, Ohio*, 297 F. 307 (1924).

[21]Ibid., 313. Citing, e.g., *Cleveland, Cincinnati, Chicago and St. Louis Railway Co. v. Backus*, 154 U.S. 439 (1894), 445.

[22]Ibid., 308.

[23]*Village of Euclid v. Ambler Realty Co.*, "Brief on Behalf of Appellants," 96. Quoted by Toll, *Zoned American*, 231.

[24]*Village of Euclid v. Ambler Realty Co.*, 272 U.S. 365 (1926).

illegitimate assumption of power is not capable of precise delimitation. It varies with circumstances and conditions. A regulatory zoning ordinance, which could be clearly valid as applied to the great cities, might be clearly invalid as applied to rural communities. In solving doubts, the maxim *sic utere tuo ut alienum non laedas* [use your own property in such a manner as not to injure that of another], which lies at the foundation of so much of the common law of nuisances, ordinarily will furnish a fairly helpful clue. And the law of nuisances, likewise, may be consulted, not for the purpose of controlling, but for the helpful aid of its analogies in the process of ascertaining the scope of, the power. Thus the question whether the power exists to forbid the erection of a building of a particular kind or for a particular use, like the question whether a particular thing is a nuisance, is to be determined, not by an abstract consideration of the building or of the thing considered apart, but by considering it in connection with the circumstances and the locality. A nuisance may be merely a right thing in the wrong place,—like a pig in the parlor instead of the barnyard. If the validity of the legislative classification for zoning purposes be fairly debatable, the legislative judgment must be allowed to control.[25]

Following Holmes's example in *Pennsylvania Coal* four years earlier, Sutherland relied on discretionary judicial review of the particular "circumstances and conditions" surrounding the case. He also noted that when the validity of a regulation is debatable, legislative determination is to prevail.

In giving sanction to zoning, the court allowed that prevention of land-use relationships that would result in potential nuisances constitutes legitimate grounds for the exercise of the police power. This use of the police power as a preventive remedy rather than a corrective one was a significant expansion of its applicability. In spite of nuisance cases prior to *Euclid,* including *Mugler,*[26] *Hadacheck,*[27] and *Pennsylvania Coal,* there had been no previous inference of the fact that predetermination of permissible land uses would not only prevent nuisances but could also circumvent unnecessary losses to proprietors of extant activities that might later be enjoined.

Save for Brandeis and Holmes, most of the justices that voted for zoning in *Euclid* had conservative leanings. Although zoning as an extension of the police power probably went against the better instincts of these men, one of its greatest attractions to them was apparently the protection it offered to residential values by segregating one land use from another. Toll quotes a current article in the Chicago *Journal of Commerce,* "The Justices do their work in Washington. Most of them live within the city limits. As

---

[25]Ibid., 387–88.
[26]*Mugler v. Kansas,* 123 U.S. 623 (1887).
[27]*Hadacheck v. Sebastian, Chief of Police of the City of Los Angeles,* 239 U.S. 394 (1915).

they hold office for life, they regard the place of work as their permanent home. Many of them own homes within the city. And Washington has zoning . . . and Washington is benefited by zoning."[28]

It was precisely such segregation that concerned Judge Westenhaver of the trial court. Though his decision in *Euclid* was eventually overruled by the high court, his opinion exhibited an astute and almost prophetic recognition of one of zoning's most critical deficiencies. Looking beyond zoning's effect on property values, his fundamental objection to zoning was its segregative and exclusionary consequences.

> The plain truth is that the true object of the ordinance in question is to place all the property in an undeveloped area of 16 square miles in a strait-jacket. The purpose to be accomplished is to regulate the mode of living of persons who may hereafter inhabit it. In the last analysis, the result to be accomplished is to classify the population and segregate them according to their income or situation in life. The true reason why some persons live in a mansion and others in a shack, why some live in a two-family dwelling and others in an apartment, or why some live in a well-kept apartment and others in a tenement, is primarily economic. It is a matter of income and wealth, plus the labor and difficulty of procuring adequate domestic service. Aside from contributing to these results and furthering such class tendencies, the ordinance has also an esthetic purpose; that is to say, to make this village develop into a city along lines now conceived by the village council to be attractive and beautiful. . . . Whether these purposes and objects would justify the taking of plaintiff's property as and for a public use need not be considered. It is sufficient to say that, in our opinion, and as applied to plaintiff's property, it may not be done without compensation under the guise and exercising of the police power.[29]

Half a century later, Westenhaver's concern was manifested as one of the great issues of contemporary planning, particularly in consideration of the ability of each region, under the autonomy provided by the Standard Acts, to exclude unwanted land-use elements.

Following the *Euclid* victory, zoning became widespread as the governing bodies of towns and cities across the country felt they had a free hand to manage land development. Within two years, the Supreme Court felt obliged to issue a caveat on the use of this police power. In Cambridge, Massachusetts, a situation arose wherein the private sale of a parcel of land for industrial purposes was voided as a result of a city restriction permitting only residential use of the property. In *Nectow v. City of Cambridge,*[30] the

---

[28]*Literary Digest,* "Now We Can Zone Our Cities," 91, no. 11 (Dec. 11, 1926), 14. Quoted by Toll, *Zoned American,* 253.

[29]Note 20, 316.

[30]277 U.S. 183 (1928).

Supreme Court found that the public need to zone in this case was not essential and hence constituted a denial of the owner's rights under the Fourteenth Amendment. It reaffirmed the limitation decreed in *Euclid* that zoning must have substantial relation to the public health, safety, or general welfare—the classic grounds for constitutional exercise of the police power.

After *Euclid* and *Nectow,* the Supreme Court did not rule directly on land planning for a quarter of a century. However, the effects of these two cases and of *Pennsylvania Coal* were to influence the direction of lower court decisions on land use and to define the practice of urban planning to the present day.

CONSTITUTIONAL CERTAINTY AND THE POLICE POWER

The authority that forms the legal basis of zoning under the Standard Enabling Acts is the police power. The reach of this power is defined in law by notions of "public necessity"[31] and "reasonableness,"[32] but these terms are themselves so abstract as to elude any definitive measure. In scope, the authority has traditionally been confined to the requirements of "public health, safety, and morals."[33] However, these justifications have been expanded incrementally, not only through broadened interpretation, but also through explicit additions to encompass a wide spectrum of public concerns. By the time of the *Euclid* case, the Supreme Court was breaking no new ground in citing the more general term "public welfare"[34] as part of zoning's rationale. F. Stuart Chapin, Jr., summarizes the contemporary planner's understanding of the "public interest," which he construes as grounds for the police power:

> For planning purposes, a more advanced concept of the public interest is warranted, one which builds on the legal tests but which seeks forward-looking guideposts taken directly from the social currents of the times. In land use planning, the purposes usually identified with the public interest are five: health, safety, convenience, economy, and amenity. Morals come into play in some aspects of land use planning but play a relatively less important role. "Economy" may be identified with prosperity, and perhaps, by a stretch of

---

[31]See, e.g., *Alabama Public Service Commission v. Crow,* 22 So. 2nd 721 (Ala., 1945). "The word 'necessity' (in the context of a Certificate of Public Convenience and Necessity) is not used in the Statute in the sense of being essential or absolutely indispensible but merely that Certificate is reasonably necessary for public good" (p. 724).

[32]In *Reinman v. Little Rock,* 237 U.S. 171 (1915), the Supreme Court noted that the police power falls under the constitutional requirements of due process and equal protection and that it be "not . . . clearly unreasonable or arbitrary" (p. 177).

[33]See, e.g., *Euclid v. Ambler,* note 24, 395.

[34]Ibid., 387.

the imagination, "amenity" may be associated with comfort in the legal definitions of public interest.[35]

Certainly, as a society expands in size, density, and complexity, the potential for conflict rises, increasing public interest in broadening the scope and furthering the reach of governmental authority. Principles set by Holmes in the *Pennsylvania Coal* case, once considered a revolutionary precedent but now widely regarded as a thoroughly accepted or "black letter"[36] law, are now being questioned as too restrictive of government's ability to protect the public interest. In recent years, the quest for expanded means to achieve public ends has been embodied in the search for greater administrative flexibility in planning and zoning controls.

The ultimate limitation in the United States of the police power lies in the Constitution. Hayek's analysis of the Rule of Law applies to all government conduct under this document as well as to zoning, since this planning tool is no more than a derivative of the public's policing authority. According to Hayek, it is a premise of the Rule of Law that unpredictability in public authority is at the heart of tyranny.[37] Such unpredictability is epitomized by the exercise of ad hoc administrative discretion in wielding the coercive powers of government. Under this concept of the Constitution, the police-power regulation of land use can be legally enforced only insofar as it is predictable and certain in its enforcement, and on condition that administrative discretion is guided by established standards. This assurance against possible arbitrary use of governmental power is both a requirement and justification of the predetermination in land-use controls that zoning offers. Harvard law professor Charles M. Haar has called the amendable comprehensive zoning plan an "impermanent constitution,"[38] in that it enables a property owner or land developer to foresee with reasonable certainty the direction of governmental reaction to his private initiatives. He writes,

> If the plan is regarded not as the vest-pocket tool of the planning commission, but as a broad statement to be adopted by the most representative municipal body—the local legislature—then the plan becomes a law through such adoption. A unique type of law, it should be noted, in that it purports to bind future legislatures when they enact implementary materials. So far as impact is concerned, the law purports to control the enactment of other laws (the so-

---

[35]F. Stuart Chapin, Jr., *Urban Land Use Planning* (Urbana: U. of Illinois Press, 1965), 41.

[36]Fred Bosselman, David Callies, and John Banta, *The Taking Issue* (Washington, D.C.: USGPO, 1973), 138.

[37]Friedrich A. Hayek, *The Road to Serfdom* (1944; reprint, Chicago: U. of Chicago Press, 1960), 72.

[38]Charles M. Haar, "The Master Plan: An Impermanent Constitution," *Law and Contemporary Problems* 20, no. 3 (1955): 353.

called implementary legislation) solely. It thus has the cardinal characteristic of a constitution.[39]

While drawing a likeness between a comprehensive plan and a constitution, Haar also points out that a plan is nonetheless "impermanent" in that it is more subject to change: "But unlike [a constitution, a comprehensive plan] is subject to amendatory procedures not significantly different from the course followed in enacting ordinary legislation."[40]

Haar also assigns the characteristic of reasonable certainty to a master plan and to its effect on private property interests. In the same vein, law professor Allison Dunham writes:

> Bentham tells us that property is nothing more than the expectation of deriving a certain advantage from a thing which the law allows us. . . . If the property is the established expectations which the law gives an owner, then as long as the owner is not commanded to use his property in a particular way and is secured some freedom of choice as to its use, it cannot be said that government restriction on land use has in it any denial of private property.[41]

Dunham echoes Hayek's admonition that government is free to lay down reasonable restrictions as long as the limitations of permissible social behavior are clearly preestablished without regard to the individual case. Dunham continues,

> I might add that as far as private property is concerned . . . the important thing is that it be adopted without knowledge of any particular case of land use; that it be definite enough so that it can be objectively determined whether administrative action conforms to it or not; and that it be adhered to when government action is taken. . . . The problem of liberty or freedom in relation to planning is the inability of a property owner to anticipate the restraints which are to be placed upon him.[42]

Predictability in governmental response to a land development proposal is clearly important to the developer, but stability in extant zoning is just as critical to owners of neighboring properties whose values or accustomed life-styles may be jeopardized by the development of unanticipated activities nearby. Public assurance of certainty in the restriction of designated urban districts to specified types of private land use was indeed one of the principal attractions of German planning administration to early pro-

---

[39]Ibid., 375.

[40]Ibid.

[41]Allison Dunham, "Property, City Planning, and Liberty," in *Law and Land,* ed. Charles M. Haar (Cambridge: Harvard U. Press and M.I.T. Press, 1964), 30.

[42]Ibid., 34, 39.

ponents of zoning in America. In his advocacy of zoning at the first National Conference on City Planning in 1910, Frederick Law Olmsted, Jr., said:

> We are all familiar with cases of the marked depreciation of property, especially of residential property, and of the forced breaking up of pleasant home neighborhoods, by the introduction of objectionable features on one or two lots. . . . One selfish or short-sighted lot owner can ruin a neighborhood.
>
> Now, one of the purposes in view in the system of district building regulations which forms a feature of recent city planning in Europe is to give to every lot owner in each district in the city a fair degree of assurance as to the kind of thing which may be done and which may not be done in the way of building and of commerical and industrial occupations in the vicinity of his lot.[43]

While zoning may deprive some land of full use and potential worth, its promise of certainty has generally been considered a compensating and balancing attribute.

If Hayek's thesis is to be strictly observed, then planning controls must necessarily be governed by the requirement for administrative discretion to be delimited by explicit, preestablished standards. This principle was vividly illustrated in the 1957 case of *Rockhill v. Township of Chesterfield*.[44] With the intent of preserving its rural character, the township of Chesterfield, New Jersey, passed an ordinance that in essence zoned its area of jurisdiction for "normal agricultural uses" and residential uses only, with the proviso that "certain uses may be permitted and certain modification of requirements may be made in accordance with the special provisions" of the ordinance. The provisions for special uses declared: "In view of the rural characteristics of the Township, it is deemed desirable to permit certain structures and uses but only after investigation has shown that such structures and uses will be beneficial to the general development." The ordinance specified, "In order to assure that such structures and uses meet all requirements and standards, all applications for zoning permits shall be referred to the Planning Board for review . . . "[45] By this measure, the township virtually subjected all development except residential and farm use to discretionary approval or disapproval by the planning board.

The New Jersey Supreme Court echoed the thoughts of Hayek in its rejection of such discretionary administration.

> The scheme of the ordinance is the negation of zoning. It overrides the basic concept of use zoning by districts, that is to say, territorial division according

[43]Olmsted, "City Planning in Europe."
[44]128 A. 2d 473 (N.J., 1957).
[45]Ibid., 475.

to the character of the lands and structures and their peculiar use suitability and a comprehensive regulatory plan to advance the general good within the prescribed range of the police power. The local design . . . [uses] terms hardly adequate to channel local administrative discretion but, at all events, making for the "piecemeal" and "spot" zoning alien to the constitutional and statutory principle of land use zoning by districts and comprehensive planning for the fulfillment of the declared policy. The fault is elementary and vital; the rule of the ordinance is *ultra vires* [beyond the scope of the enabling act] and void.

Reserving the use of the whole of the municipal area for "normal agricultural" and residence uses, and then providing for all manner of "special uses" . . . placed according to local discretion without regard to districts, ruled by vague and illusive criteria, is indeed the antithesis of zoning. It makes for arbitrary and discriminatory interference with the basic right of private property, in no real sense concerned with the essential common welfare. The statute . . . provides for regulation by districts and for exceptions and variances from the prescribed land uses under given conditions. The course taken here would flout this essential concept of district zoning according to a comprehensive plan designed to fulfill the declared statutory policy. Comprehensive zoning means an orderly and coordinate system of community development according to socio-economic needs. . . .

Zoning and planning are not identical in concept. Zoning is a separation of the municipality into districts for the most appropriate use of the land, by general rules according to a comprehensive plan for the common good in matters within the domain of the police power. And, though the landowner does not have a vested right to a particular zone classification, one of the essential purposes of zoning regulation is the stabilization of property uses. Investments are made in lands and structures on the faith of district use control having some degree of permanency, a well considered plan that will stand until changing conditions dictate otherwise. Such is the nature of use zoning by districts according to a comprehensive plan. The regulations here are in contravention of the principle.[46]

The need for a comprehensive plan as defined by the court seemed all but to preclude any unzoned planning. However, this unequivocal and strict construction in *Rockhill* does not always apply. A contrasting attitude had been adopted about six years earlier in Connecticut. The high court of that state had before it two situations within a year of each other that seemed virtually identical in their circumstances. In *Bartram v. Zoning Commission of City of Bridgeport*,[47] a determination by a zoning commission was upheld; in *Kuehne v. Town Council of Town of East Hartford*,[48] on the other hand, the position of the council was rejected. The court referred to its *Bartram* decision in its opinion on *Kuehne:*

[46]Ibid., 478–80.
[47]68 A. 2d 308 (Conn., 1949).
[48]72 A. 2d 474 (Conn., 1950).

> In *Bartram v. Zoning Commission,* we recently had before us an appeal from the granting by a zoning commission of an application to change a lot in Bridgeport even smaller than the tract here in question from a residence to a business zone, and we sustained the action of the commission. . . . It appeared in that case that the change was granted by the commission *in pursuance of a policy* [emphasis added] to encourage decentralization of business in the city and to that end to permit neighborhood stores in outlying districts. . . . In the case before us, it is obvious that the council looked no further than the benefit which might accrue to Langlois and those who resided in the vicinity of his property, and that they gave no consideration to the larger question as to the effect the change would have upon the general plan of zoning in the community.[49]

The deciding factor in the court's determination of validity in the *Bartram* case was the government's apparent adherence to a predictable zoning policy, which was not manifest in *Kuehne.* Evidently the Bridgeport commission's declaration of policy was enough to satisfy the court's understanding of the Rule of Law.

Even in New Jersey, the apparently strict interpretation of the comprehensive plan in *Rockhill* proved to be not absolute. In April 1957, a scant three months after it issued the decision asserting that zoning must conform to a comprehensive plan, the New Jersey Supreme Court observed in *Kozesnik v. Montgomery Township*[50] that a plan need not be a document separate from the zoning ordinance that gives it effect. The court's opinion stated,

> Without venturing an exact definition, it may be said for present purposes that "plan" connotes an integrated product of a rational process and "comprehensive" requires something beyond a piecemeal approach, both to be revealed by the ordinance considered in relation to the physical facts and the purposes authorized by [statute]. Such being the requirements of a comprehensive plan, no reason is perceived why we should infer the Legislature intended by necessary implication that the comprehensive plan be portrayed in some physical form outside the ordinance itself. A plan may readily be revealed in an end-product—here the zoning ordinance—and no more is required by the statute.[51]

Evolution in Oregon

Despite an apparent trend among courts to permit greater discretion and flexibility on the part of planning authorities, in 1973 the Oregon Supreme Court, in *Fasano v. Board of County Commissioners of Washington*

[49]Ibid., 478.
[50]131 A. 2d 1 (N.J., 1957).
[51]Ibid., 7–8.

County,[52] underscored the importance of administering zoning "in accordance with a comprehensive plan."[53] The facts of the case revolved about a challenge brought by neighboring homeowners against a change in zoning of a tract of land from single-family residential use to a classification that permitted construction of a mobile-home park. In considering the case, the court distinguished between local legislative acts establishing general policies without regard to any specific piece of property and activities that are administrative, quasi-judicial, or judicial in nature. Whereas the former can be attacked only on constitutional grounds for arbitrary abuse of authority, the court found that the latter should properly be subject to judicial scrutiny. Said the court,

> Because the action of the commission in this instance is an exercise of judicial authority, the burden of proof should be placed, as is usual in judicial proceedings, upon the one seeking change. The more drastic the change, the greater will be the burden of showing that it is in conformance with the comprehensive plan as implemented by the ordinance, that there is a public need for the kind of change in question, and that the need is best met by the proposal under consideration. As the degree of change increases, the burden of showing that the potential impact upon the area in question was carefully considered and weighed will also increase. If other areas have previously been designated for the particular type of development, it must be shown why it is necessary to introduce it into an area not previously contemplated and why the property owners there should bear the burden of the departure.[54]

The court also demonstrated a view of the relationship between the comprehensive plan and the zoning ordinance contrary to the position held earlier by the New Jersey court in *Kozesnik.* Though it saw the plan and zoning ordinance as "closely related" and "both . . . intended to be parts of a single integrated procedure for land use control," the Oregon court distinguished the comprehensive plan as a document separate from the zoning ordinance. "The plan embodies policy determinations and guiding principles; the zoning ordinances provide the detailed means of giving effect to those principles."[55]

The *Fasano* ruling on the indefeasibility of the comprehensive plan was reasserted with even greater vigor two years later by the same court in *Baker v. City of Milwaukie.*[56] It said,

[52]507 P. 2d 23 (Ore., 1973).
[53]*Model Code, Tentative Draft No. 1,* 214–15.
[54]Note 52, 29.
[55]Ibid., 27.
[56]533 p. 2d 772 (Ore., 1975).

In summary, we conclude that a comprehensive plan is the controlling land use planning instrument for a city. Upon passage of a comprehensive plan a city assumes a responsibility to effectuate that plan and conform prior conflicting zoning ordinances to it. We further hold that the zoning decisions of a city must be in accord with that plan and a zoning ordinance which allows a more intensive use than that prescribed in the plan must fail.[57]

The Oregon court was not unaware of the implications of its stand. It concluded its decision in *Fasano* thus:

By treating the exercise of authority by the commission in this case as the exercise of judicial rather than of legislative authority and thus enlarging the scope of review on appeal, and by placing the burden of the above level of proof upon the one seeking change, we may lay the court open to criticism by legal scholars who think it desirable that planning authorities be vested with the ability to adjust more freely to changed conditions.[58]

Reaction to the court's decisive endorsement of conservative planning was strong enough that in 1976, one year after the *Baker* case, the court found it necessary to modify its stand. In *Green v. Hayward,*[59] the court observed:

If the opinion of the Court of Appeals reflects or creates an understanding that our decision in *Baker v. Milwaukie* was intended to hold that a local government's zoning map must coincide in detail with the map portion of the comprehensive plan, that misunderstanding should be corrected. . . .

There is as yet no agreement within the planning profession as to the form which a good comprehensive plan should take. . . .

In light of the freedom given local governments, both in the past and for the future, to design the form of their comprehensive plans, we refrain from statements of general application about how such plans are to be read or interpreted. The relationship between the text and the maps within a particular plan must be determined from the plan document itself, considered as a whole.

In the present case, the Plan itself tells us that neither the text nor the illustrative diagram was intended to provide advance answers to the kinds of questions involved in this case. We conclude that in the 1990 Plan, the plan map or diagram was intended to illustrate what the text calls the "broad allocation" of land within the area shown, but not to put a limit on the permissible uses of each and every tract within that area. In order to determine whether a particular zoning decision is in compliance with the Plan, we must look to other portions of the Plan in addition to the diagram.[60]

[57]Ibid., 779.
[58]Note 52, 29–30.
[59]552 P. 2d 815 (Ore., 1976).
[60]Ibid., 817–19.

In 1979, the Oregon court amended its position still further. Pointing to intervening changes in legislative and case law, the court, in *Neuberger v. City of Portland,*[61] allowed that "a comparison of the characteristics of the site under consideration with other property which is available for the proposed use may well be relevant in determining whether particular requirements of the comprehensive plan . . . or other applicable standards have or have not been met."[62] The court cited the governing municipal code as distinguishing "between zone changes initiated by the planning commission or the city council on the one hand, and changes initiated by petition of the owners of that affected property on the other."[63] The latter it reasoned to be quasi-judicial in nature. The question of whether a specific land-use decision is legislative or quasi-judicial must necessarily take into consideration a number of factors, such as whether "a particular action by a local government is directed at a relatively small number of identifiable persons" and whether "that action also involves the application of existing policy to a specific factual setting."[64]

Zoning and the Ballot Box

In 1976, the case of *City of Eastlake v. Forest City Enterprises, Inc.*[65] brought to question still another issue. In considering the legitimacy of a referendum held in an Ohio town denying a zoning change to permit construction of an apartment building, the Supreme Court was faced with the question of whether zoning and rezoning are legislative (and hence subject to the political referendum) or administrative (and thus within the executive purview of the administration). The court chose to accept the premise of the Ohio Supreme Court that zoning and rezoning are legislative functions; but in doing so, it also reversed the state court's decision to reject the referendum process as a means to determine zoning matters. The court's decision to uphold the referendum process seemed at first blush to subject virtually all planning and zoning to voter approval. However, in his dissent from the majority, Justice John Paul Stevens shed appropriate light on the issue. Stevens pointed out that, notwithstanding the Ohio finding that zoning is a legislative function, other courts have concluded otherwise. In addition to *Fasano,* he quoted the Washington court in *Fleming v. City of Tacoma.*[66]

> Zoning decisions may be either administrative or legislative depending on the nature of the act. . . .

[61]603 P. 2d 771 (Ore., 1979).
[62]Ibid., 779.
[63]Ibid., 775.
[64]Ibid.
[65]426 U.S. 668 (1976).
[66]502 P. 2d 327 (Wash., 1972).

Generally, when a municipal legislative body enacts a comprehensive plan and zoning code it acts in a policy making capacity. But in amending a zoning code, or reclassifying land thereunder, the same body, in effect, makes an adjudication between the rights sought by the proponents and those claimed by the opponents of the zoning change. The parties whose interests are affected are readily identifiable. Although important questions of public policy may permeate a zoning amendment, the decision has a far greater impact on one group of citizens than on the public generally.[67]

From this it can be surmised that zoning ordinances that result from a process of public policy formulation of a general, comprehensive nature without regard to any specific properties should be viewed as legislative and be accorded a presumption of validity by the courts. Being legislative, however, adoption of such major planning policies is subject to the political process, including referenda (by which legislative acts are brought before the voters) and initiatives (issues brought before the electorate by petition). In contrast, rezoning that is requested by property owners or developers regarding specific parcels of land is essentially administrative or adjudicatory in nature, notwithstanding action by the legislature. In such rezoning, the legislature acts administratively in execution of existing policy or sits in a quasi-judicial capacity to arbitrate the zoning reclassification. While acting in this administrative or adjudicatory capacity, the legislature should not have its determination subject to the referendum and initiative processes but rather subject only to court review.

It should be cautioned, of course, that Stevens's opinion in *Eastlake* was only a minority opinion and that courts are generally more inclined to conform to majority rather than dissenting opinions from the high bench. For instance, although it did not specifically mention the *Eastlake* decision, a majority of the California Supreme Court, in weighing the validity of a voter initiative restricting growth in *Associated Home Builders of the Greater Eastbay, Inc. v. City of Livermore,*[68] found no fault with the premise that zoning can be determined by the ballot box. Instead, its principal reservation regarding the ordinance focused, interestingly enough, on the initiative's failure to take regional considerations into account and "the interests of nonresidents who are not represented in the city legislative body and cannot vote on a city initiative."[69] The *Livermore* case reaffirmed the same court's approval of zoning enactments by the electorate in 1974 in *San Diego Contractors Association v. City Council of the City of San Diego,*[70] a case preceding the *Eastlake* ruling.

---

[67]Ibid., 331. Citing note 65, 684–85.
[68]557 P. 2d 473 (Cal., 1976).
[69]Ibid., 487.
[70]529 P. 2d 570 (Cal., 1974).

In 1980, the California Supreme Court ruled, in *Arnel Development Company v. City of Costa Mesa,*[71] that, regardless of the size of the parcel affected, all rezoning acts in California are legislative rather than adjudicative, and hence subject to voter initiatives and referenda. The case concerned a fifty-acre property upon which a developer proposed to construct mostly multifamily housing units but that was rezoned by initiative action, together with several acres of adjoining land, for single-family homes only. In spite of this judgment, it is interesting to note that when the case was retransferred to the lower court of appeals,[72] that court reached back to the *Livermore* opinion to strike down the enactment on the grounds that the initiative had, as in *Livermore,* failed to "effect a reasonable accommodation of the competing interests on a regional basis and [was] therefore not a valid exercise of the police power."[73]

Thus it is apparent that, notwithstanding the California doctrine of considering all rezoning as legislative acts subject to popular vote, the state judiciary will not condone exclusion through the ballot box. Indeed, all dissenting opinions in the California cases cited seemed to argue for even stronger rulings against exclusion, either by direct censure or by disallowing local initiatives that would invariably further parochial, exclusionary interests.

The concealed potential of exclusion is not always recognized or addressed by other state courts. For instance, in grappling with the question of whether zoning is a legislative function subject to voter action, the Colorado court, in *Margolis v. District Court in and for the County of Arapahoe,*[74] chose not to address the problem at all. In the 1981 case, which consolidated consideration of three separate zoning enactments by three separate Colorado municipalities, the acts of the governing bodies in each instance were challenged by voters opposed to development. In ruling zoning and rezoning to be legislative in character and hence subject to popular initiative and referendum, the court demonstrated its awareness of the precedent cases in California. But while citing those decisions to buttress its position, it ignored the issue of exclusion that the California opinions also took pains to consider.[75]

It is plain from reviewing these cases that even the Constitution cannot ensure absolute certainty, since judicial perception of its provisions regarding planning, zoning, and voter legislation in particular can and does vary.

---

[71]620 P. 2d 565 (Cal., 1980).

[72]178 Cal. Rptr. 723 (App., 1981).

[73]Ibid., 729.

[74]638 P. 2d 297 (Colo., 1981).

[75]For further discussion on exclusion, see chapter 6. See also Gregory Longhini and Vivian Kahn, "Ballot Box Zoning," *Planning* (May 1985), p. 11, on zoning and rezoning through popular initiatives and referenda.

As Kenneth Davis, the author of *Discretionary Justice,* would be quick to point out, a degree of flexibility is not necessarily a failing, for law would ill serve if it were totally insensitive and irresponsive to changing social norms. Thus it is only realistic for the law to offer no more than a functional perception of reasonable "fair certainty" or predictability. If the constitutional lessons suggested by Hayek are to be heeded, however, then the social evolution of law cannot violate popular faith in the stability and impartiality of the institution.

THE SHADOW OF PENNSYLVANIA COAL

There is an ambiguity in the constitutional requirements for public control of private land use. On one hand is the admonition by Hayek that public regulation, as exemplified by Euclidean zoning as a police power, must be certain and predictable in order to conform to the constitutional Rule of Law. On the other is the suggestion made by Justice Holmes in *Pennsylvania Coal* that the constitutionality of a police-power measure depends on the "particular facts" of an issue and can be determined only by an empirical test to ascertain whether the regulation has passed the "certain magnitude" at which a police-power restriction turns into a regulatory taking. Since the determination of this "question of degree" is necessarily a discretionary one, uncertainty becomes intrinsic. Both aspects of this dichotomous requirement for land-use controls have applied historically and still do. Logically, however, the combination of a certainty with an uncertainty results only in the latter.

The most immediate and apparent consequence of *Pennsylvania Coal* was the powerful argument that the case provided for subsequent claims of private property rights against police-power regulation. Of even greater significance, however, was the "hidden" doctrine of factual consideration established by the Court. Beyond its instant effect on public regulation, Holmes's rejection of the previous strict construction of *Mugler* also implied a diminution of the concept of constitutional precedent as the basis for court decisions. The outcome of the case resulted from a weighing of "particular facts" in discretionary judgment. With this empirical process as doctrine, the police power began to rely less on constitutional precedents such as *Mugler* for support and began to depend more on the strength of factual evidence to substantiate the public interest. Concomitantly, since *Pennsylvania Coal* failed to provide any definitive criterion to guide judicial discretion, the element of uncertainty inherent in any trial was greatly increased.

Despite the evident defeat dealt the police power, *Pennsylvania Coal* was far from a lasting setback since the decision was limited by its own factual reasoning to the immediate situation. The shift of constitutional litigation from strict doctrine based on precedent to the empirical approach has proven to be the more durable consequence. A reasonable corollary that can be drawn from Hayek's hypothesis is that the uncertainty inherent in such discretion as the judgment employed would eventually magnify the public authority. As Holmes correctly (and critically) observed in his opinion, "When this seemingly absolute protection is found to be qualified by the police power, the natural tendency of human nature is to extend the qualification more and more until at last private property disappears."[76] It is an ironic illustration of his commentary that the incremental if not invariable trend of Supreme Court decisions since *Pennsylvania Coal* was gradually to reverse the tenor of that decision from a position favoring the rights of private property to attitudes more sympathetic to the demands of the public welfare. Only four years after the ruling, the Court was persuaded to uphold the police power of zoning in another landmark case, *Euclid v. Ambler.*

Even after a hiatus of half a century in the high Court's involvement in matters of police-power control of private land, more recent decisions have seemed to resume the general trend of acceding to the public interest. Equally significant is the conspicuous reluctance of the Court either to use or establish firm constitutional doctrine as in *Mugler,* preferring the empirical flexibility demonstrated by Holmes in *Pennsylvania Coal.*

The modern Court's attitude is exemplified by its reasoning in the case of *Goldblatt v. Town of Hempstead.*[77] Events leading to litigation in this 1962 case took place on Long Island, New York. Goldblatt owned a thirty-eight-acre tract there on which his company had excavated sand and gravel since 1927. Mining had continued after the operation had reached below the water table, and eventually half the land was covered by water averaging over twenty feet in depth. Though the property had originally been located in a rural setting, expansion of the town gradually surrounded the site with over two thousand homes and four public schools serving some forty-five hundred students. In late 1958, the town passed an ordinance prohibiting such excavations below the water table. Although the regulation voided the beneficial use of the property, the Supreme Court reached a unanimous verdict, agreeing with the New York Court of Appeals that the ordinance was a valid exercise of the police power. The Court cited *Pennsylvania Coal,* implicitly concurring with Holmes's principle that a regulation is subject to a weighing test to determine whether it constitutes a taking. Significantly, however, the opinion went on to note the absence of a standard: "There is no set formula to determine where regulation ends and taking begins. Although a comparison of values before and after is relevant, it is by no means conclusive."[78] The Court continued to maintain the principle established by

[76]Note 1, 415.
[77]369 U.S. 590 (1962).
[78]Ibid., 594.

Holmes for discretionary judgment on the extent of police-power regulation while specifically rejecting any inference that a standard measure has ever been set by the Court. It declared: "Except for the substitution of the familiar standard of 'reasonableness,' this Court has generally refrained from announcing any specific criteria."[79] Thus, though the judgment in *Goldblatt* to uphold the police power seemed contrary to the majority decision in *Pennsylvania Coal,* the Holmes principle of exercising judicial discretion to determine the extent to which the police power can lawfully be exerted was again affirmed—and with it the uncertainty inherent in such ad hoc judgments.

The general approach of the Court was also evidenced in its decision in *Penn Central Transportation Co. v. New York City.*[80] The conclusions of this 1978 case hold special importance for contemporary urban design and for the preservation of architectural landmarks in particular, and will be discussed further in following chapters. Of greater relevance, however, was its confirmation of the Court's empirical approach to constitutional judgment, even though the weight of empirical arguments in the case resulted in a conclusion different from that reached by Holmes in *Pennsylvania Coal.* In essence, the *Penn Central* decision upheld a state court ruling that New York City's landmarks preservation commission could lawfully prevent the corporate owner of Grand Central Terminal, earlier designated an architectural landmark, from constructing a 55-story office building over the station. Citing such decisions as *Goldblatt,* the Court said,

> [This court] has been unable to develop any "set formula" for determining when "justice and fairness" require that economic injuries caused by public action be compensated by the government, rather than remain disproportionately concentrated on a few persons. Indeed, we have frequently observed that whether a particular restriction will be rendered invalid by the government's failure to pay for losses proximately caused by it depends largely "upon the particular circumstances (in that) case."[81]

The Court itemized as factors in its deliberation "the economic impact of the regulation" on "investment-backed expectations" and "the character of the governmental action," which it admitted as "essentially ad hoc, factual inquiries."[82] Thus, while the Court upheld the police power as it had in *Mugler,* the decision was based not on doctrine but "particular facts."

Still another Supreme Court ruling in 1980 continued the trend of empirical reasoning in support of the public position. The case of *Agins v.*

---

[79]Ibid.

[80]438 U.S. 104 (1978).

[81]Ibid., 124. Quoting *United States v. Central Eureka Mining Co.,* 357 U.S. 155 (1968), 168.

[82]Ibid.

City of Tiburon[83] concerned a zoning ordinance passed by the governing body of an affluent San Francisco Bay residential community that restricted development of a five-acre residential tract to no more than five single-family houses. The Court affirmed the determination of the California court that the regulation did not constitute a taking, notwithstanding the owner's claim for monetary damages under inverse condemnation to compensate for the alleged taking. (For further discussion of *inverse condemnation,* see chapter 12.) The Court did not cite *Pennsylvania Coal,* no doubt because the apparent finding of the earlier Court was contrary to its own. Nonetheless, the legacy of Holmes's balancing test was apparent in its comment: "Although no precise rule determines when property has been taken, the question necessarily requires a weighing of private and public interests."[84]

It is interesting to note that the decision affirmed in *Agins* was a finding of the California Supreme Court. As late as 1971 UCLA law professor Donald G. Hagman was moved to comment that "the California Court will sustain regulations that no or few courts in the country will sustain."[85] He was not referring to *Agins,* of course, but to California court decisions of the 1950s and 1960s upholding comparatively stringent regulations that deprived much or virtually all value from private land. By 1980, however, that sort of restriction—though neither universal nor certain—was no longer confined to California.

As to be expected, the attitude held by the Supreme Court in the cited cases was reflected in decisions by lower federal courts. A notable example is the 1979 case of *Haas v. City and County of San Francisco.*[86] The case concerned a city ordinance that lowered the allowable building height on a lot newly purchased by the appellant for the construction of a 300-foot high-rise building to permit a structure only 40 feet high. Despite the appellant's claim of a loss in value from his cost of almost $2 million to only $100,000, the federal appeals court upheld the new restriction, citing such Supreme Court precedents as *Goldblatt, Penn Central,* and even *Hadacheck v. Sebastian,* one of the so-called nuisance cases predating *Pennsylvania Coal* and *Euclid* that upheld the police power.

An early indication that the federal courts did not support the government imperative absolutely on matters of public authority and private property was the case of *Kaiser Aetna v. United States.*[87] The events surrounding this case occurred in Hawaii less than two years after the *Penn Central* case.

---

[83]447 U.S. 255 (1980).

[84]Ibid., 261.

[85]Donald G. Hagman, *Urban Planning and Land Development Control Law* (St. Paul: West, 1971), 213. Citing *Lockhard v. City of Los Angeles,* 202 P. 2d 38 (Cal., 1949); *McCarthy v. City of Manhattan Beach,* 264 P. 2d 932 (Cal., 1953); *Consolidated Rock Products Company v. City of Los Angeles,* 370 P. 2d 342 (Cal., 1962).

[86]605 F. 2d 1117 (1979).

[87]444 U.S. 164 (1979).

At issue was the status of a marina developed by Kaiser Aetna through the dredging and filling of Kuapa Pond, a shallow lagoon separated by a narrow beach from Maunalua Bay and the Pacific Ocean. Under ancient Hawaiian law, the pond had always been considered private property. However, when the lagoon was converted to a marina and connected to the bay, the federal appeals court ruled that the property became subject to the "nagivational servitude" of the federal government with the public acquiring right of access.[88] In reviewing the case, the Supreme Court reversed the lower court's decision, holding that the right of public access could be acquired only through eminent domain with payment of compensation. Significantly, the majority quoted extensively from *Pennsylvania Coal* to justify its stand.

Both *Kaiser Aetna* and *Penn Central* were 6–3 decisions, with the same six justices consistently and evenly split in favor of either the public authority or private rights, and with the remaining three casting the "swing votes." The *Agins* decision, on the other hand, was a unanimous decision, with Justice Lewis F. Powell, Jr., who voted with the swing factor in the other cases, writing the court opinion. Another Supreme Court decision in 1981, *San Diego Gas & Electric Co. v. City of San Diego,*[89] found the Court split 5–4 in support of a city zoning ordinance that the utility company claimed would amount to a taking without just compensation. While concurring with the majority—largely on the basis of a technicality—Justice William H. Rehnquist nonetheless noted that he "would have little difficulty in agreeing with much of what is said in the dissenting opinion."[90] Notably, the writer of that dissent, Justice William J. Brennan, Jr., is generally considered to be Rehnquist's opposite in terms of political philosophy. Commented law professor (and attorney for Agins) Gideon Kanner on *San Diego Gas & Electric,*

> The coin came down, and it landed on its edge—again. The U. S. Supreme Court evidently means to adhere to its decisional pattern—or, more accurately, nonpattern—of the past half century. Substantive resolution of taking issue controversies remains banished to the outer reaches of ad hoc, case-by-case adjudication, with the court taking (or making) every opportunity to avoid a decision on the merits.[91]

It would be folly, of course, to attempt to second guess the Supreme Court, particularly in consideration of the modern Court's apparent preference for deciding empirically on the "particular facts" and its seeming reluctance to furnish clear principles to settle the question of just how far

[88]Ibid., 169.
[89]450 U.S. 621 (1981).
[90]Ibid., 633–34.
[91]Gideon Kanner, "Comment," *Land Use Law & Zoning Digest* 33, no. 5 (1981): 8.

police-power regulation of private land use can reach without becoming a taking requiring compensation. In 1985, lawyers, planners, and developers alike looked forward to some definitive resolution by the Court in the case of *Williamson County Regional Planning Commission v. Hamilton Bank of Johnson City.*[92] However, in throwing out an award made by a lower court of $350,000 to a Tennessee housing developer to compensate for allegedly unreasonable land-use restrictions, the Court effectively evaded the larger issue. Its action, it explained, was taken because the developer's claim was "premature,"[93] because not all possible grounds for variance appeals had been exhausted, and because no final determination had been made as to how the regulations would be applied to the property at hand.

The element of "ripeness"[94] found wanting in *Hamilton Bank* had also been a factor in both the *Agins* case and *San Diego Gas & Electric.* In the first case, the Court noted that no approval for development had actually been sought;[95] in the latter, no "'final judgements or decrees' of a state court"[96] had been made to warrant jurisdiction by the high Court. Professor Kanner, lamenting the outcome of these three Supreme Court cases and the apparent reluctance of the justices to provide a clear articulation of the boundary between police-power zoning and regulatory taking, asked: "Why do they take these cases? This is the third time in a row."[97]

In its seeming preference for discretionary consideration of each individual circumstance, it may be that the Court has not been evading the issue as much as it has simply been reflecting the prevailing social tendency to eschew such rigidity as associated with stare decisis and rationalist dogma in favor of a more empirical and flexible approach to practical problem solving. Arguably, contemporary American jurisprudence in practice has few intellectual pretensions at establishing far-reaching, abstract doctrine. Constitutional law notwithstanding, at least since Holmes's consideration of "particular facts" in *Pennsylvania Coal,* even the Supreme Court seems inclined, as in these cases, to practice what Max Weber termed "substantive irrationality," or judgments based on reaction to the "concrete factors of the particular case,"[98] unencumbered by intellectual dogma. It is interesting to note that, whatever their individual leanings on matters concerning public authority and the rights of private property, seven of the eight justices participating in deliberations on *Hamilton Bank* agreed not to consider the basic merits of the case because of lack of "ripeness."

[92]_____ U.S. _____ (1985), 105 S. Ct. 3108.

[93]Ibid., 3124.

[94]Ibid., 3117.

[95]Note 83, 257.

[96]Note 89, 633.

[97]Kanner, quoted in Steven Wermiel, "Supreme Court Puts off Zoning Question for 'Another Day' Causing Confusion," *Wall Street Journal,* July 1, 1985, 36.

[98]Max Weber, *On Law in Economy and Society,* ed. and trans. Max Rheinstein (1925; reprint, New York: Simon & Schuster, Clarion, 1954), 63.

More recently, in June 1986, in *MacDonald, Sommer & Frates v. Yolo County,*[99] the high Court had yet another opportunity to resolve the issue of regulatory taking and again ducked the issue. The appellants in this California case alleged that improper zoning of a property intended for residential development and denial of subdivision approval and extension of roads and service utilities had deprived them of any beneficial use of their land. The property had been classified as "agricultural reserve" despite the claim of unsuitableness of the land for farming, in part because the state had earlier removed the topsoil under threat of condemnation to provide fill for a highway. The Court cited *Agins, San Diego Gas & Electric,* and *Hamilton Bank* in referring to the issue of ripeness. It held that the decisions of the lower courts left "open the possibility that some development will be permitted, and thus again [leaving the Court] in doubt regarding the antecedent question whether appellant's property [had] been taken."[100]

The resolution—or nonresolution—of the issue in *MacDonald* resulted from a narrow 5–4 vote. Conceivably, the modern Court's perspective on the question of regulatory taking may become more ideologically acute as the Court evolves away from its stance in the 1950s and 1960s as a politically liberal tribunal under Chief Justice Earl Warren to one that has had less political definition but a growing conservative tendency under Chief Justice Warren E. Burger, and now to a court with a potentially conservative political agenda through the appointments of justices by President Reagan. (The propensity of judges to harbor conservative or liberal *political* points of view is distinguished from their attitude toward either conservative or liberal *judicial* approaches to constitutional interpretation and adherence to the doctrine of stare decisis. Whereas political conservatism in America is usually identified with traditional values dating to the founding of the Republic, political liberalism is generally perceived as being more pragmatic and progressive. There is no necessary correlation between political and judicial ideology; a politically liberal judge can be judicially conservative or vice versa. Whether to advance a politically conservative goal or to fulfill a politically liberal agenda, a judicially conservative judge would be less inclined to overturn precedent and more prone to interpret the Constitution strictly, whereas a judicially liberal judge would exhibit the opposite tendency in jurisprudence.)

Reagan, certainly the most conservative president to serve in many years, nominated Associate Justice William Rehnquist in June 1986 to replace the retiring Warren Burger as Chief Justice and Circuit Judge Antonin Scalia to fill Rehnquist's seat. Both men, who have since been confirmed by Congress and appointed to the Court, have demonstrated political conservatism in their past decisions. Notably, two of the leading political liber-

---

[99]_____ U.S. _____ (1986), 54 U.S.L.W. 4782.
[100]Ibid., 4785.

als on the Supreme Court, Justices William Brennan and Thurgood Marshall, are aged and are apparently waiting for President Reagan to conclude his second term before retiring from the Court, presumably in hopes that the next president will appoint more liberal replacements for them. As these changes in the composition of the Court occur, it may assume a more definitive position on these and other issues.

Without a conclusive resolution of the question of regulatory taking by the Court, local governing bodies are still inclined to push the limits of their authority. Nevertheless, many local planning officials are nervous even as they explore the furthest extent of the police power, for as Holmes warned, "if regulation goes too far it will be recognized as a taking."[101] Recent application of federal civil rights and antitrust laws to the land-use planning activities of local government and the threat of heavy monetary damage awards under these laws against local communities have also emerged as a new area of concern for public planners and will be the subject of discussion in the following chapter.

Even should some future case produce guidelines governing the exercise of the police power in land-use planning, considering the empiricism of the present Court and the resulting unpredictability of its actions, it would seem imprudent indeed to regard any doctrine as sure and immune from reversal. A disciple of Friedrich Hayek who strictly construes his master's teaching would be driven to despair, others to frustration and confusion.

Uncertainty is further exacerbated by yet another factor. With the exception of the federal appellate decision in *Haas*, all the cases cited here are adjudications of the Supreme Court. Though high-Court rulings are undeniably the most powerful and influential, they are not absolutely binding in all situations. Beyond the federal systems, the states have their own courts and their own laws. This diversity of jurisdiction and the capacity of courts to exercise empirical discretion as a result of Holmes's initiative have increased the uncertainty surrounding the issue.

Pennsylvania Coal established a difficult but nonetheless quintessential doctrine that has haunted all subsequent deliberations on land-use controls. It has been a test with no definitive criterion; and since that case, neither has the case-law process yielded a substantive consensus. After an exhaustive study of the "mass of decisions" that have emanated from both state and federal courts on land-use controls since the *Pennsylvania Coal* case, Fred Bosselman, David Callies, and John Banta concluded in 1973 that the state of the current law is indeed "chaotic." In *The Taking Issue*, they maintain that this opinion is shared by many other experts.

> After the 20's [the Supreme Court] left the state and lower federal courts with a general principle for making decisions—the balancing test in *Pennsylvania*

---

[101]Note 1, 415.

Coal—and few examples of its application. Since that time the courts have applied that test to a wide variety of fact situations. . . .

As this wealth of cases has piled up legal scholars have searched for some pattern that would provide guidelines to predict the outcome of future cases. Most of the scholars who have made the attempt have concluded that the search was not too rewarding.

Professor Arvo Van Alstyne, whose exhaustive analysis of the taking cases is one of the most recent, concludes that "judicial opinions rejecting constitutional attacks . . . seldom provide reliable guides to the relevant substantive standards. . . . " while "decisions invalidating land use controls are often equally devoid of helpful explanatory data. . . . " Professor Allison Dunham of the University of Chicago Law School has characterized the cases as "a crazy-quilt pattern of Supreme Court Doctrine" and concludes that "it is not surprising that there are floundering and differences among judges and among generations of judges."[102]

Bosselman, Callies, and Banta cite law professors Joseph Sax and Frank Michelman as sharing the same basic observation that no clear principles have been satisfactorily derived from court decisions on the issue. The authors conclude:

The taking clause has bedeviled some of our brightest and most lucid legal scholars. A number of excellent articles have appeared in our legal periodicals over the past ten years. We were impressed with the profound logic by which each author attempted to make sense out of the confused body of cases—at least until we read the next article in which a new author convincingly demolished the logic of his predecessor and expounded a new and even more convincing system of analysis.

We eventually came away with a sense of frustration, convinced that the world did not need one more analytically good, true and beautiful solution to the taking problem. Holmes' own observation that experience, not logic, governed the law, seemed most appropriate here.[103]

Variables in time and judicial ideology have both contributed to the lack of uniform and enduring perception. A half century after Holmes's decision in *Pennsylvania Coal,* Fred Bosselman and David Callies, in their 1971 report *The Quiet Revolution in Land Use Control,* suggest in the title of their work that social change has indeed evolved more liberal attitudes. "Circumstances are different today,"[104] they maintain in *The Taking Issue.*

---

[102]Bosselman, Callies, and Banta, *The Taking Issue,* 195. Quoting Arvo Van Alstyne, "Taking or Damaging by Police Power: The Search for Inverse Condemnation Criteria," *So. Cal. L. Rev.* 44 (1971), 14; and Allison Dunham, "*Griggs v. Allegheny County* in Perspective: Thirty Years of Supreme Court Expropriation Law," *Sup. Ct. Rev.* (1962), 105.

[103]Bosselman, Callies, and Banta, *The Taking Issue,* 324.

[104]Ibid., 253.

They argue that Holmes's reasoning in favor of the private property rights of the coal company in that famous case can be criticized as being "historically unsound, logically unnecessary, and environmentally disastrous."[105] With the opinion that "it is not too late to recognize that Justice Brandeis was right,"[106] the writers urge reexamination of the precedent that Holmes's landmark ruling established. But since the "quiet revolution" of the early 1970s, public attention to environmental concerns has perhaps diminished, and the entreaties of environmentalists today may fall on deafer ears.

While time may vary attitudes, differences can also exist among court jurisdictions. Not surprisingly, courts that find for the private owner still tend to cite *Pennsylvania Coal* with approval. Those that decide for the police power invariably attempt diverse means to rationalize or to overcome the logic of the case without appearing to denigrate Holmes's opinion. Some seek gaps or nuances in Holmes's reasoning to disqualify his precedent as it applies to their decision; others try to use the "particular facts" of their case at bar to distinguish the situation before them; still others try to ignore the precedent of the case altogether while nonetheless deciding on the facts as Holmes had suggested. To those outside the legal profession, the sometime compulsion of courts to contort their reasoning in order to accommodate conflicting precedents brings to question the entire logic of stare decisis. Certainly on the issue of public control versus private rights in property, arguments on both sides can be overwhelmingly convincing, as the opinions on the *Pennsylvania Coal* case itself attest.

The impact of *Pennsylvania Coal Company v. Mahon* on subsequent land-use cases, including other rulings by the Supreme Court, has been substantial, not only because of the compelling intellectual force of the decision but because the decision was handed down during the birth of zoning. Although "hidden" and largely unrecognized, the doctrine that it established—that of supporting the exercise of judicial discretion in ascertaining the line between public regulation and taking of property rights in each case—has become a principle with long-term implications. Though the court's immediate finding for private property rights over the public interest has been a powerful precedent, it has been neither as enduring nor as influential as the doctrine, established by Holmes, of considering the "particular facts" at hand. The more lasting principle was summarized by the Supreme Court in *Nebbia v. New York,* eleven years after the case:

> The Fifth Amendment . . . and the Fourteenth . . . do not prohibit governmental regulation for the public welfare. They merely condition the exertion

---

[105]Ibid., 238. Much of the research for this chapter is based on material taken from *Zoned American* by Seymour I. Toll, and *The Taking Issue,* by Fred Bosselman, David Callies, and John Banta.

[106]Bosselman, Callies, and Banta, *The Taking Issue,* 253.

of the admitted power, by securing that the end shall be accomplished by methods consistent with due process. And the guaranty of due process, as has often been held, demands only that the law shall not be unreasonable, arbitrary or capricious, and that the means selected shall have a real and substantial relation to the object sought to be attained. It results that a regulation valid for one sort of business, or in given circumstances, may be invalid for another sort, or for the same business under other circumstances, because the reasonableness of each regulation depends upon the relevant facts.[107]

LATE DEVELOPMENTS

After vacillating over procedural technicalities in a series of land-use cases over some six years, the Supreme Court, on June 9, 1987, handed down what may be a definitive ruling on the issue of public land-use regulation versus the rights of private-property owners. In *First English Evangelical Lutheran Church of Glendale v. County of Los Angeles,*[108] the Court held that a property owner is entitled to compensation, under the taking clause of the Fifth Amendment, should a land-use regulation deprive the owner of all reasonable use of his or her property, even on a temporary basis. Writing for the 6–3 majority, Chief Justice William H. Rehnquist said,

> The value of a leasehold interest in property for a period of years may be substantial, and the burden on the property owner in extinguishing such an interest for a period of years may be great indeed. Where this burden results from governmental action that amounted to a taking, the Just Compensation Clause of the Fifth Amendment requires that the government pay the landowner for the value of the use of the land during this period. . . . Invalidation of the ordinance or its successor ordinance after this period of time, though converting the taking into a "temporary" one, is not a sufficient remedy to meet the demands of the Just Compensation Clause.[109]

The Court ruling reversed a decision by the California courts, which had upheld an interim flood-control ordinance, enacted in 1979, that prohibited any building alongside a creek where the Lutheran church had once operated a campground retreat and recreational area for handicapped children. The regulation had been adopted after a forest fire had denuded the hills upstream from the twenty-one-acre church property and a flood had destroyed the campground's buildings and had taken several lives. The church did not challenge the validity of the ordinance but rather sought compensation for the denial of "all use" of its property.

---

[107]291 U.S. 502 (1933). 525.
[108]_____ U.S. _____ (1987), 55 U.S.L.W. 4781.
[109]*Ibid.,* 4785–86.

By allowing the church to initiate inverse-condemnation proceedings, by which a landowner can recover damages on the claim that a regulation had effectively acted to condemn or "take" his or her property rights, the Supreme Court upset the California court's 1979 ruling in *Agins v. Tiburon* (which it had supported at the time) that an aggrieved property owner could not maintain an inverse-condemnation suit based on a regulatory taking, and that the only remedy lay in invalidating the ordinance. The Court noted, however, that its decision did not mean that "normal delays in obtaining building permits, changes in zoning ordinances, variances, and the like"[110] would be considered grounds for damages.

A vigorous dissent was mounted by Justice John Paul Stevens, who was joined by justices Harry A. Blackmun and Sandra Day O'Connor. Stevens asserted, among other things, that the Court erred "in concluding that it is the Taking Clause, rather than the Due Process Clause, which is the primary constraint on the use of unfair and dilatory procedures in the land use area."[111] He said: "Regulatory programs constantly affect property values in countless ways, and only the most extreme regulations can constitute takings."[112] In conclusion, Stevens warned,

> The policy implications of today's decision are obvious and, I fear, far reaching. Cautious local officials and land-use planners may avoid taking any action that might later be challenged and thus give rise to a damage action. Much important regulation will never be enacted, even perhaps in the health and safety area. Were this result mandated by the Constitution, these serious implications would have to be ignored. But the loose cannon the Court fires today is not only unattached to the Constitution, but it also takes aim at a long line of precedents in the regulatory takings area. It would be the better part of valor simply to decide the case at hand instead of igniting the kind of litigation explosion that this decision will undoubtedly touch off.[113]

The *First English Evangelical Lutheran Church* case will clearly have a dampening effect on aggressive attempts to impose land-use controls, including flood-plain regulation, historic preservation, and urban design, especially since the decision exposes regulating governments to liability claims for the period during which a regulation is in effect, should the restriction be later found invalid by the courts. Because of the decision, planners will likely be more constrained in attempting innovative regulatory programs, such as the urban design plan being implemented in San Francisco.[114] Following the lead of the Supreme Court, courts may be less in-

---

[110]*Ibid.*, 4786.
[111]*Ibid.*
[112]*Ibid.*, 4788.
[113]*Ibid.*, 4791–92.
[114]David W. Dunlap, "Ruling May Dampen Ardor of Local Planners," *New York Times*, June 10, 1987.

clined in the future to approve regulations that might cause a diminution
of the value of property, such as the lowering of allowable building heights
upheld in *Haas v. City and County of San Francisco.* Arguably, however,
the restriction in *First English Evangelical Lutheran Church* had deprived
the owner of "all use" of the property, not just a diminution in value.

Subscribers to a "cyclical" theory in the waxing and waning of public
authority in relation to private rights in property might compare *First English Evangelical Lutheran Church* to *Pennsylvania Coal,* for the similarity
of the two in their affirmation of private property rights is evident. Certainly the Supreme Court's position in the 1979 *Penn Central* case in favor
of public regulation (in which Chief Justice Rehnquist cast a dissenting
vote) is at the opposite phase of the cycle.

After the apparent indecision in the *San Diego Gas & Electric, Hamilton Bank,* and *MacDonald* cases, land developers jubilant at the outcome
of *First English Evangelical Lutheran Church* are hailing the case as the
most important landmark since *Euclid v. Ambler.* As Justice Stevens pre-
dicts, there will likely be an explosion of damage suits brought by developers who feel wronged by public land-use regulations. On the other hand,
despite the example set by this latest case, law professor Gideon Kanner
points out, a "procedural muddle" remains: how far must a landowner go
in seeking development permits, in applying to state agencies for compensation, and in filing suit in state courts, all as prerequisites to going to federal
court?[115] Moreover, the "certain magnitude" at which regulation becomes
unreasonable has yet to be determined and landowners may have to prove
deprivation for "all use" of their land to merit compensation.

As these cases flood the courts, the Supreme Court itself will be under
increasing pressure to resolve the myriad questions left unanswered—and
even created—by its 1987 decision. Then, just as the Court in 1928 found
it necessary to moderate and define the limits of zoning regulation upheld
in *Euclid* by its ruling in *Nectow,* the modern Court may be required to give
fuller definition to its intent in *First English Evangelical Lutheran Church.*
It may be that the Court will establish doctrine by defining regulatory taking in absolute terms. More likely, however, decisions will continue to be
reached on a case-by-case basis, in light of the "particular facts." Even
while ruling for the property owner in this latest case, the Court majority
limited their holdings to the facts presented. In this age of information systems and data analysis, judges are far more likely than in Holmes's day to
eschew rigid doctrine in favor of empirical, factual consideration.

Since its reinvolvement in the 1960s in questions of the constitutionality
of local land-use regulation, the Supreme Court has opened a Pandora's
box of issues, both constitutional and procedural, that it now cannot easily

---

[115]Steven Wermiel, "Justices Find For Landowners in Zoning Case," *Wall Street Journal,* June 10, 1987.

close. The social implications of these questions are more urgent than ever as urban functions, employment, traffic, and densities continue to migrate from the traditional center cities into the one-time residential suburbs, changing the pattern and quality of community life. In an earlier day, the outcome of *First English Evangelical Lutheran Church* might have assumed the mantle of doctrine. However, notwithstanding its landmark characteristic, this case may today do no more than reflect the Court's response to an instant situation or indicate the direction of the present Court's predilections, rather than establish a truly definitive resolution of the taking issue.

PART III

THE TANGLED WEB

Chapter 5

The Flawed Weave of Planning, Zoning, and Building Codes

The years after the *Euclid v. Ambler*[1] decision saw the substantive adoption of the Standard Zoning and Planning Enabling Acts[2] as the legal foundation of planning throughout the continental United States. The most significant consequence of the invisible web woven by these model acts has been Euclidean zoning, so named with dual reference to the geometric division of land and to the Ohio town that took the concept before the Supreme Court. The idea that planning could be made fixed and certain beforehand is inherent to Euclidean zoning; the notion grew out of the physically oriented view that dominated the formulative years of modern American planning. Drawing from the legacy of the City Beautiful movement, the word "plan" was then understood largely in the architectural context of a "diagram" rather than in the word's alternate meaning of "future intention"— a broader connotation that has since emerged and even prevailed. To the drafters of the Standard Acts of the 1920s, a city plan could be embodied in a zoning map just as a work of architecture could be described in a blueprint. Like a blueprint, the zoning map defined a predetermined, physical end state that would be essentially permanent and need little administrative discretion in implementation. Hayek's value of certainty is implicit in this approach.

[1]272 U.S. 365 (1926).

[2]U.S. Department of Commerce, *Standard State Zoning Enabling Act* (1922, revised 1926), and *Standard City Planning Enabling Act* (1928), both reprinted in *A Model Land Development Code, Tentative Draft No. 1* (Philadelphia American Law Institute, 1968), 210–71.

117

Over the years zoning has undergone the test of practical application. It has been a history not without failings, owing partly to shortcomings of the original model acts but also to failures in legislative and administrative implementation, changing circumstances, and evolving perceptions of planning itself. Some fifty years after wide adoption of the acts, the American Law Institute embarked on a comprehensive review of planning and zoning practice that culminated in a suggested model for legislative reform. In one of the many preliminary commentaries leading to the *Model Land Development Code,* a reporter wrote of the Standard Acts,

> At the root of the entire system . . . lies a concept of land use control which has proved to be of variance with reality. . . . Under this concept, the local legislative body was supposed to establish regulations governing development which would look to an end state for the community, perhaps twenty or thirty years into the future. The regulations would be so detailed that development would be permitted to occur thereunder automatically—without the intervention of further official discretion. A review of the provisions of the SZEA, leads to an inescapable conclusion: the draftsmen had a static rather than a dynamic concept of land use control. If there is anything to be learned from the history of zoning to date, it is that development tends to occur more through a series of modifications in the preestablished rules than through an automatic satisfaction of them.[3]

Although the acts specified that zoning "regulations shall be made in accordance with a comprehensive plan,"[4] actual practice has fallen short of the professed intent. The focus of the original acts was almost exclusively on the public control of private land development through the police power. Even the structural elements of the physical city mentioned in the acts, including "transportation, water, sewerage, schools, parks, and other public requirements,"[5] were not considered integrally with the zoning of land. Social, economic, and environmental aspects of urban growth were given only nominal attention or simply ignored. However, in the 1920s the analytical methodology of the social sciences had yet to mature, and this contribution to planning theory had to await a later day.

With popular emphasis on zoning as a means to protect residential values, especially in the suburbs, the goals of true comprehensiveness were largely overlooked. Indeed, many have construed land-use zoning to be synonymous with planning, even though zoning has always been intended as a tool to implement planning. Charles M. Haar makes the distinction as follows:

[3]*Model Code, Tentative Draft No. 1,* 196.
[4]Ibid., 214–15.
[5]Ibid., 215.

To the city planner, the relation of the master plan to such regulatory ordinances is simple and clear. The plan is a long-term general guide for the development of the city; the regulatory laws are tools to bring the plan's goals into realization. Warnings have constantly emanated from the planners that the two must be confused. "Instead of being itself the city plan, for which unfortunately it is often mistaken," says one of the early standard works in the field, "zoning is but one of the devices for giving effect to it." To select another example, in an unpublished note to his model County Planning Enabling Act, [Alfred] Bettman wrote:

"There has been some discussion as to whether the zoning plan is to be conceived of as a part of the master plan. But when the arguments are analyzed, there will be found to be some confusion as the difference between the planning and the execution. The zoning ordinance is, of course, execution and the planning precedes it. . . . It may be that to some extent a land classification and utilization program, and a zoning plan are synonymous. But the mention of both is desirable so as to make perfectly clear that the zoning plan is a part of a precising of the plan for land classification and utilization."[6]

Writing on planning controls in New York, the first American city to adopt zoning in 1916, urban designer Jonathan Barnett observes:

City planning courses teach that zoning regulations represent the means for implementing master plans; but the first New York City zoning resolution predates the establishment of the New York City Planning Commission by twenty-two years, and the publication of the city's first comprehensive plan by fifty-three years. The experience of other American cities has been similar, showing that zoning first, planning afterwards, is the usual sequence.[7]

The confusion was foreshadowed by the fact that the Standard Planning Act was issued a full six years after the Standard Zoning Act. Following this lead, many states did not enact legislation to enable their municipalities to plan until many years after they had passed legislation authorizing zoning. Arizona, for instance, did not pass planning legislation until 1973, some fifty years after it had enabled zoning.

Ironically, the end-state ideal implicit in the traditional concept of the comprehensive plan limits the plan's usefulness, since its rigidity invites deviations that can dilute or destroy the original planning intent. Writes Richard F. Babcock of the long-range plan and its administration: "Once

---

[6]Charles M. Haar, "The Master Plan: An Impermanent Constitution," *Law and Contemporary Problems* 20 (1955): 362. Quoting Ladislas Segoe et al., *Local Planning Administration* (Chicago: International City Managers' Assoc., 1941), 44; and Alfred Bettman, "A Model County Planning Enabling Act," note 14, *National Resources Committee Archives,* box 159.

[7]Jonathan Barnett, *An Introduction to Urban Design* (New York: Harper & Row, 1982), 61.

drawn, such a "plan" was tacked on a wall and was forgotten while the local plan commission and city council went about the pressing business of acting upon innumerable requests for changes in the zoning map."[8] Notwithstanding the widespread idea, upheld in *Fasano*,[9] that rezoning must conform to and be consistent with a comprehensive plan, the zoning map embodying the end-state plan has, since its inception, been under constant pressure to be flexible in meeting changing circumstances.

From a practical standpoint, planning policy can hardly be tied to a long-term preconception that does not take into account either the unpredictability of future circumstance or the political nature of governmental decision making in response to events as they unfold. Richard Babcock and Clifford Weaver note that flexibility is even more necessary in an urban context than in the suburbs, where much of zoning practice and development take place:

> City planning for a city must have resiliency and a capacity to react to opportunity when and where it emerges out of the existing reality. The idea of a long-term plan, or of a zoning ordinance to implement it, is for a major city, both unreasonable and unrealistic.[10]

They quote Robert Rider's observation of an abortive attempt to introduce policy planning to Honolulu city government:

> Policy cannot fit into the formula of the general plan. It is as specific or as general as the problem warrants. Policies cannot be neatly programmed or divided into nine subject areas or, as required by the charter, reviewed at least every five years. They tended to be made in a piecemeal manner and limited to specific issues.[11]

Long-term a priori planning is necessarily ignorant of future realities. While an established plan may be used as an argument by those who agree with its assumptions and ends, it can also be regarded as an anachronistic impediment to reasoned if ad hoc responses to circumstances as they evolve. Furthermore, those in political power may well consider commitment to a plan, especially one conceived under a previous incumbency, as a hindrance to their own discretionary, decision-making prerogatives. As Weaver and Babcock comment on zoning and discretion:

---

[8]Richard F. Babcock, "Zoning," in *The Practice of Local Government Planning*, ed. Frank S. So et al. (Washington, D.C.: International City Management Assoc., 1979), 419.

[9]*Fasano v. Board of Commissioners of Washington County*, 507 P. 2d 23 (Ore., 1973).

[10]Clifford L. Weaver and Richard F. Babcock, *City Zoning: The Once and Future Frontier* (Chicago and Washington, D.C.: Planners Press, 1979), 264.

[11]Ibid. Quoting Robert W. Rider, "Transition from Land Use to Policy Planning: Lessons Learned," *Journal of the American Institute of Planners* 44 (January 1978): 32.

Were we to choose two great lessons to be learned . . . they would be, first, that nothing is so important to a successful scheme of land use regulation as discretion in its administration and, second, that nothing is more subject to destructive abuse than that administrative discretion.[12]

PLANNING AND ZONING ADMINISTRATION

Under Euclidean zoning, a local jurisdiction is divided into districts, within which all private development on land is restricted by the police power to certain designated types. Typically, residential, commercial, industrial, and agricultural activities are segregated from one another, and usually each functional type is categorized again into different classes to reflect density or intensity of use. Residential districts, for instance, normally differentiate between land set aside for multifamily apartment buildings and areas designated for single-family detached housing. Minimum lot size per dwelling is often regulated, and sometimes building area.[13] Structural height and setback from property lines as well as provisions for on-site parking are also usually subject to zoning regulations.[14] Early codes were generally "cumulative" in that residences were allowed in commercial and industrial zones, and commercial uses in industrial areas, but not vice versa. However, more recent codes have favored "exclusivity" to ensure that an industrial district would not be mixed with residential land use that might later force curtailment of the original zoned use.

Following the rule of the Standard Acts, planning is administered at the municipal or county government level with functions ordinarily divided among three bodies: the local legislature, the planning commission, and the board of adjustment. The first of these institutions, typically the city council or county board, has two principal responsibilities in planning. One is the adoption of a plan by formal resolution as a broad statement of long-range public policy toward future development. The other is the enactment of the zoning ordinance and map to give specific, legal enforcement to the plan. In addition, it is the duty of the legislature to appoint the memberships of the planning commission and board of adjustment. Following normal civil practice, meetings of the legislature and its appointed boards must be open for public hearing and comment.

---

[12]Weaver and Babcock, *City Zoning,* 257.

[13]Minimum lot size: see, e.g., *Clemons v. City of Los Angeles,* 222 P. 2d 439 (Cal., 1950). Even in cases in which minimum lot-size zoning has been held unconstitutional as applied, courts have consistently recognized the general validity of lot-size regulation. See, e.g., *Appeal of Kit-Mar Builders, Inc.,* 268 A. 2d 765 (Pa., 1970), 766. Regulation of building area: see, e.g., *Lionshead Lake, Inc., v. Township of Wayne,* 89 A. 2d 693 (N.J., 1952). But also see, e.g., *Appeal of Medinger,* 104 A. 2d. 118 (Pa. 1954).

[14]Building height regulation: *Welch v. Swasey,* 214 U.S. 91 (1909); building setback: *Gorieb v. Fox,* 274 U.S. 603 (1927).

The function of the second body, the planning commission, is to formulate and recommend planning policy to the legislature, generally in the form of amendments to the existing comprehensive plan and the zoning ordinance and map. In most jurisdictions of any size, the administrative functions of research, analysis, and design that lead to a plan recommendation are performed by a permanent staff of planning professionals organized into a department of planning under the aegis of the commission, although sometimes some of the work is done by engaged private consultants. Under the process suggested by the Standard Acts, the commission and its staff are charged with responsibility for comprehensive planning, subdivision regulations and approvals, and the control of land for future streets through official mapping. The acts also provided for the establishment of a separate planning commission with regional purview, but this provision has been largely overlooked by state legislatures.

The board of adjustment, the third branch of planning administration, is alternately known as the board of variance or the board of zoning appeals. This body assumes the responsibility of determining at open hearings whether relief should be granted from the zoning ordinance. Under the Standard Acts, relief may be allowed by the board, without legislative action in an appeal, from staff interpretation of the zoning ordinance or where a variance or special exception is warranted. Unlike the functions of the other two bodies, the task of the board is not intended to be one of policy but rather one of redress.

Significantly, neither the planning commission nor the board of adjustment was originally designed for truly discretionary ad hoc planning administration. The original acts essentially saw the plan and zoning maps as permanent documents that would be largely self-executing. The administrative function was provided purely as a judicial "safety valve"[15] to safeguard against claims of unconstitutionality, not as a vehicle to modify the plan in any substantial way.

Experience, however, has proven the assumption of preordained planning to be unrealistic. The end-state plan, thought viable for upward of twenty years, has been found insubstantial in the face of rapid and unpredictable change. In its place has arisen new theories of "continuous" planning, emphasizing responsiveness to change through information compilation, data analysis, and policy evaluation of issues encompassing socioeconomic as well as design and environmental considerations. Practice has correspondingly become more responsive to changing conditions, with plans subject to annual review and comprehensive revision every five to ten years. Alterations of the plan and zoning map, originally conceived as rarities, are now considered routine.

[15]*Model Code, Tentative Draft No. 1,* 197.

The flexibility that now exists has been achieved in spite of rather than because of the Standard Acts. Without anticipating that flexibility would ever become a problem, the drafters of the original acts failed to allow for the problems and opportunities created by unforeseen circumstances. A notable weakness was the lack of an authority capable of determining with expertness and consistency the effect of privately initiated development modifications on the total plan. Nor was there provision for an administrative mechanism by which significant proposals made by private developers could be conveniently incorporated into the plan itself. To overcome this lack of discretionary authority, local planning administrations have subjected a continuing number of innovative control techniques to court tests, with the result that the original enabling statutes have been incrementally adapted for greater flexibility. In addition, the enabling acts themselves have been amended by the states to the same end. However, while such legitimate flexibility is desirable, practice has shown that all too often planning and zoning controls have been distorted, not so much in knowledgeable attempts to overcome inadequate enabling authority, but through ignorance or in deference to political pressure. Such abuses have not only been injurious to planning efforts but have often violated constitutional principles.

ZONING VARIATIONS AND THE BOARD OF ADJUSTMENT

The problem is epitomized by the practice of the board of adjustment, whose shortcomings have been amply documented in innumerable critiques by both lawyers and planners. Although the board's administration of variances and special exceptions requires discretion in review of individual circumstances, these devices were intended only to address specific and unusual cases not amenable to the broad generalizations of the plan. As noted in the *Harvard Law Review:* "Zoning theory assumes that land development can be regulated by ordinances. The elements of discretion present in most zoning codes—provisions for variances and special exceptions—were designed for only rare use."[16]

A variance allows relaxation of the zoning code where strict enforcement would result in an unusual and "unnecessary hardship."[17] It can refer to either the physical aspects of a proposed structure—for example, building area, height, bulk, setback, or parking provisions—or it may concern the use of the building within a zone. Over the years, the legal definition of the qualifying term "unnecessary hardship" has been relatively well established by the courts. The hardship must derive from the specific circum-

[16]*Harvard L. Rev.,* "Administrative Discretion in Zoning," 82 (1969), 668–69.
[17]*Model Code, Tentative Draft No. 1,* 219.

stances of the property in question, such as its dimensions or topography, that would prevent the owner from obtaining a fair and reasonable return on his investment. It cannot be construed in financial terms alone in order to create greater profit. The hardship must concern the property itself and not the personal situation of the owner; nor can it be self-inflicted. Any alleged hardship must affect the particular property in such a manner as to be discriminatory. A complaint against a restriction common to other properties within the district would be grounds for the planning commission and legislators to consider amending the zoning ordinance itself, rather than adopt a variance from the law. Properly issued, the variance must conform to the planned character of the neighborhood so as not to be detrimental to nearby property values or otherwise be harmful to the public health, safety, and welfare. Thus the variance was visualized as a specific adjustment from the ordinance where rigid adherence would result in individual and "unnecessary hardship."

Besides the variance, the board of adjustment can also grant a special exception or one of its related variations, such as the special-use permit or the conditional use. Frequently confused with variances, special exceptions are uses that are allowable within a district provided certain conditions are met to the satisfaction of the board. The idea behind the special exception is that uses that are normally objectionable within a district can be rendered unobjectionable if certain provisions are made. Where requirements of special exceptions are predetermined and specific, the likelihood is that the ordinance will be found valid by the courts. On-site parking, for instance, is a common special-exception request. If specific requirements are met, such uses as churches may be permitted as exceptions within residential zones. If, however, the conditions are too general or vague, then the ordinance is more likely to encounter the same difficulties as the "special use" provision that was voided in the *Rockhill*[18] case.

Neither the variance nor the special-exception use was intended as an instrument to achieve broad flexibility. They were designed to deal only with specific situations in which the sweeping generality of the predetermined and broad planning policy would be unsuited. As conceived by the Standard Acts, neither device administered by the board of adjustment should violate the intent or integrity of the plan as determined by the legislature and the planning commission.

Unfortunately, various studies have shown that the exercise of discretion by the board has been much less controlled. In the conclusion of a well-known study conducted in 1962 on the administration of a board of adjustment in Kentucky, Jesse Dukeminier, Jr., and Clyde L. Stapleton made a summation that is disturbingly applicable to a majority of boards.

[18]*Rockhill v. Chesterfield Township,* 128 A. 2d 473 (N.J., 1957).

In any system of *ad hoc* decision-making serious problems of equal protection of the law arise. As indicated above, the Board has to a very large extent shifted to an *ad hoc* system of variance granting. Whatever one may say about the legality of the Board's action in failing to follow standards laid down by the enabling act, the ordinance, and the courts, justice could still be dispensed if the Board promulgated standards of its own making or articulated in each case the substantive factors it considered critical. But it has done neither. The public and the petitioners are not candidly told in advance of a case what factors really move the Board, nor are they told afterwards. To be blunt, why the Board behaves as it does is anyone's guess and anyone's rumor.[19]

Under the management (or mismanagement) of the board of adjustment, a perverse manner of flexibility has resulted, whereby the stability and predictability of preestablished zoning has been compromised with no compensating advantage in the quality of planning. One critic of the board believes that half of all variance decisions are "probably illegal usurpations of power."[20] Another wrote: "If the courts really superintended their issuance, upwards from ninety percent of the variances granted would probably be found invalid."[21] Commenting that "zoning boards tend to ignore both the law and expert advice,"[22] Minnesota law professor David P. Bryden summarizes the perception of several commentators as follows:

> Critics contend that . . . the boards have usurped legislative prerogatives, undermined public confidence in zoning, deceived persons who buy land without knowing about nearby variances, denied equal treatment to applicants, permitted destruction of neighborhoods, subverted comprehensive plans, and endangered our democratic institutions.[23]

The central problem of board misrule has been the piecemeal destruction of Haar's "impermanent constitution," the comprehensive plan, and the violation of Hayek's Rule of Law. Dukeminier and Stapleton observe,

> The board was originally conceived as a device to avoid constitutional problems which might be raised when broad, general regulations imposed an unusually severe hardship upon an individual landowner because of the uniqueness of his lot. The board was not instituted to achieve flexibility. Variances were

---

[19]Jesse Dukeminier, Jr., and Clyde L. Stapleton, "The Zoning Board of Adjustment: A Case Study of Misrule," *Kentucky L. Jour.* 50 (1962): 30.

[20]Walter H. Blucher, "Is Zoning Wagging the Dog?" In *Planning 1955* (Chicago: American Society of Planning Officials, 1956): 100.

[21]Donald G. Hagman, *Urban Planning and Land Development Control Law* (St. Paul: West, 1971), 197.

[22]David P. Bryden, "The Impact of Variances: A Study of Statewide Zoning," *Minn. L. Rev.* 61 (1977): 775.

[23]Ibid., 773.

not to be granted merely because the proposed use did not involve a substantial departure from the comprehensive plan nor injuriously affect the adjoining land. Unnecessary hardship, not insubstantial harm, is theoretically the touchstone of the board's jurisdiction.

According to traditional zoning theory, a board of adjustment, unlike a planning commission, does not make broad planning policy. It makes policy only interstitially, as courts make policy, by deciding individual cases within a framework of laws and regulations constructed by others. Operating in a quasi-judicial capacity, the board is not at large to decide cases by its own notions of desirable land use or its personal preferences respecting land use policies.[24]

The board of adjustments, like the planning commission, was designed by the drafters of the Standard Acts to be composed of unpaid lay citizens appointed by the legislature for overlapping terms on the presumption that it would thus be free of any special interests. The competence of the board so constituted to meet its charge has, however, been open to question. Their civic-minded intentions notwithstanding, most boards of adjustment members are, after all, part-time amateurs wrestling with formidable issues that demand high professionalism in planning practice, administrative procedure, and legal judgment. More often than not, board members lack the planner's expertise in zoning and the professional judge's concern for constitutional due process and equal protection. As noted in the *Harvard Law Review* article,

> In most cities, amateurs must do the professionals' job of analyzing the foreseeable impact of new construction. Confronted by complex plans or by an unusual use, lay members of an appeal board may have to rely on representations of the applicant or his architect in determining the project's effect on the community. The city's planning department might solve this problem by cooperating closely with the appeal board, but such coordination does not always occur. Where the city planning department does furnish advice, the zoning board may give it little weight.[25]

The advice of professional staff planners is frequently discounted, particularly if the recommendation is for denial, no doubt because it is usually easier to accede to a request than to deny it unless opposition is voiced. A study made in Boston during 1965–66 showed that the appeal board granted 72 percent of appeals that the Boston Redevelopment Authority would have withheld.[26] Another investigation by the *California Law Review* of variance

---

[24]Dukeminier and Stapleton, "Board of Adjustment," 321–22.
[25]*Harvard L. Rev.* "Administrative Discretion," 674.
[26]Ibid.

administration of Alameda County, California, indicated that staff recommendations were rejected in 208 of 332 cases examined: "Significantly, in each instance the staff had recommended disapproval of the application because the applicant had not demonstrated circumstances or hardship justifying a variance."[27] Dukeminier and Stapleton's study in Kentucky had similar findings: "Of 102 requests for variances, the staff recommended denying 75. The board denied 26. . . . [However, when] the staff recommended granting 25 requests for variances, the Board granted 23 of these requests."[28] Often the granting of variances is warranted neither by circumstance nor by law. The *California Law Review* study reported that "although 284 variances were granted during the year, in only fifteen cases does the record appear to contain substantive evidence of special circumstances and hardship sufficient to warrant a variance."[29] Syracuse law professor Robert M. Anderson writes, "An examination of 200 decisions in which the courts reviewed board of appeals decisions granting or denying application for use variances discloses that 65% of variances granted by boards were reversed by the courts. Only 25% of the board denials were reversed."[30]

The tendency of the board to rely on biased opinion rather than professional staff advice is doubtless caused by its own makeup. Notwithstanding the attempt of the Standards Acts to divorce the board from special interests, the quasi-judicial nature of its function has made the institution exceptionally subject to influence, attracting membership in particular from local real-estate and development-related business people. Dukeminier and Stapleton's study in Kentucky dealt with a board of typical composition,

> of two lawyers, two businessmen, an architect and a real estate dealer. Quite naturally most of these men moved freely among, and had business connections with, persons in the building industry and property-owning citizens at large. One does not take the veil or the robe when he goes on a board of adjustment. He is not retired from the business world, as judges are. . . . Board members who have the same general perspectives as the litigants who appear before them simply cannot meet one afternoon a month and for one session slough off all their identifications with the business community and the propertied class acquired over the twenty-nine days. For good psychological reasons they cannot see themselves as impartial officials enforcing an impartial law.[31]

[27]Thomas B. Donovan, "Zoning: Variance Administration in Alameda County," *Cal. L. Rev.* 50 (1962), 108.

[28]Dukeminier and Stapleton, "Board of Adjustment," 329.

[29]Donovan, "Variance Administration," 107.

[30]Robert M. Anderson, "The Board of Zoning Appeals—Villain or Victim?" *Syracuse L. Rev.* 13 (1962), 365.

[31]Dukeminier and Stapleton, "Board of Adjustment," 335.

While boards of adjustment often ignore the advice of professionals on the planning staff, the *Harvard Law Review* study also indicates that the boards frequently succumb to local political influence: "Although planning department recommendations do little to sway appeal board decisions, local private pressure has proved highly effective."[32] The study cites several regional studies that compare the outcome of variance appeals where opposition existed, to those appeals where there was none. In Philadelphia, 77 percent of appeals were granted when there was no protest, but only 24 percent were allowed when there was opposition. In Boston, 81 percent of all unopposed appeals were allowed compared with 60 percent of protested appeals. In their Kentucky study, Dukeminier and Stapleton found 85 percent of variance appeals were approved when no opposition existed, compared to a 63 percent approval rate of appeals faced with opposition. They write, "On one hand, protestants may present facts and arguments of which a board is unaware. But mere opposition in and by itself is only indirectly relevant to the question of individual hardship, which is what the Board is supposed to be deciding in variance cases."[33]

Although public hearings are a cornerstone of democratic process, such forums on variance applications also permit the intrusion of political influence into a decision that should theoretically be a result of technical and legal determination. The Harvard investigators conclude: "It seems likely that such protesters serve more as an unprincipled check upon the equally unprincipled granting of variances and exceptions than as an accurate guide for policy judgement."[34] Doubtless the public hearing process reinforces the bias of the board's own composition to favor local political interests over petitioners from outside the community. Babcock finds that variances have served less as a safety valve than as a device used either to grant or deny favors, thus opening up the constitutional question of equal protection.[35]

However subject to vagary, the impact of boards of adjustment on planning and land use is tremendous. The *Harvard Law Review* article points to the enormous number of cases in which a staff's decision that a proposal would violate the zoning ordinance is appealed by the building-permit applicant. In 1955, over 2,500 of 9,000 applications for permits in Philadelphia were appealed; in Boston, 52 percent of permits issued for dwelling units were brought before the board. Many of the appeals resulted in the issuance of building permits. Eighty-one percent of all variance requests in Boston were granted, and 85 percent in Cambridge, Massachu-

[32]*Harvard L. Rev.*, "Administrative Discretion," 675.
[33]Dukeminier and Stapleton, "Board of Adjustment," 328–29.
[34]*Harvard L. Rev.*, "Administrative Discretion," 675.
[35]Richard F. Babcock, *The Zoning Game* (Madison: U. of Wisconsin Press, 1966), 7.

setts. In Austin, Texas, 67 percent of appeals were successful; in Milwaukee, 74 percent were approved.[36]

The Standard Acts, based on the governing premise of local autonomy, did not provide for review of board decisions by higher regional planning administrations. The responsibility of adjudicating further arguments on land-use matters was effectively relegated to the judiciary. However, of the literal thousands of land-use permits disputed each year, only a few actually end up before the courts. Litigation is a last resort, even at the trial level. Legal battles are invariably expensive, drawn-out, and uncertain in outcome. Not all developers or protestants can afford the time and financial cost exacted. Nor do all development projects warrant legal confrontation where some other kind of settlement or compromise is available as a remedy, even at the expense of some perceived principle. Even success is shadowed by the possibility of appeal. In practice, therefore, most decisions regarding land use are settled administratively, presumably—but rarely—on standards set by legislative or trial law.

Aside from problems of equity caused by deficiencies in its administration of due process and equal protection, the preponderant problem caused by the board from the planning viewpoint is that its free issuance of variances has tended to dilute and even negate the intent of the plan. This problem was pointed out as early as 1941 by planner Hugh R. Pomeroy:

> Every improperly granted special permit, every adjustment, which is in effect an instance of spot zoning, is a leak in the zoning ordinance. And it doesn't take very many such leaks to exhaust the strength of the zoning plan. Even if the excess densities, or the fudging on yard and area requirements or, mayhap, the change of use, permitted by improper actions of the board of appeals do not greatly affect the broad land use and density pattern (if any) of the master plan, they do start a disintegration of the zoning plan, and they do undermine confidence in its integrity.[37]

In the same vein, University of Pennsylvania law professor Jan Z. Krasnowiecki has commented informally to the author that "planning" in Philadelphia has indeed been carried out by the city's board of adjustment rather than its planning commission. The *Harvard Law Review* article likewise concurs that "the zoning boards of appeal have become vest pocket planning agencies."[38] The result of such ad hoc "planning" by the board has amounted to control without policy, rendering flexibility both illegal and meaningless. With mismanagement of its charge, the board has effec-

[36]*Harvard L. Rev.,* "Administrative Discretion," 673.

[37]Hugh R. Pomeroy, "Losing the Effectiveness of Zoning through Leakage," *Planning and Civic Comment* (Oct. 1941): 8–9.

[38]*Harvard L. Rev.,* "Administrative Discretion," 673.

tively destroyed the stability of Haar's "impermanent constitution" of planning, not to mention Hayek's ideal of constitutional certainty.

But is the local board of adjustment indeed a villain, or is it simply caught in the invisible web of the Standard Acts? However much individual boards may be faulted in their operation, much of the blame lies in their inherent character and composition, both directly attributable to the Standard Acts. Even the decidedly critical report by Dukeminier and Stapleton concludes that, though the board is guilty of misdeeds, its arrogation of power has been largely caused by a "power vacuum" within a system that lacks legitimate flexibility.

> Under Euclidean zoning no body legally has power to make individual discriminations in the context of a given locale based on rational planning considerations, and to permit development accordingly. The board of adjustment, under pressure from applicant after applicant, has assumed this power.[39]

Certainly some of the problems generally ascribed to the board are a result of the three-way division of planning authority within a local jurisdiction, a fragmentation of responsibility and power characteristic of the system's origins under the acts. With lack of internal coordination on planning matters, it has not been unknown for legal conflicts to erupt even within an administration.

A 1972 case brought before an Illinois appellate court illustrates such a confrontation, with a city council involved in direct litigation against its own zoning board of appeals. The case of *Reichard v. Zoning Board of Appeals of the City of Park Ridge*[40] centered around the board's approval of the construction of an 88-foot-high office building in a district with a 40-foot building height zoning limitation. The court ruled the board's action void, noting that the power of a city to challenge a decision by its own zoning board was implicit in the state's municipal code.

In New York, as in several other states, municipalities have the express statutory authority to seek court review of actions by their own boards of zoning appeals. Referring to an article in the state's Civil Practice Act that makes explicit provision for judicial review, one reference on New York law states, "Generally, a municipality may bring an Article 78 proceeding to review a decision of its board of zoning appeals. This has been held in the case of a city, a village, a town board, and a town officer,"[41] Use of such

---

[39]Dukeminier and Stapleton, "Board of Adjustment," 345, 349.

[40]290 N.E. 2d 349 (Ill. App., 1972).

[41]12 *New York Jurisprudence 2d* 396, Sect. 361 (1981). Citing Civil Practice Law and Rules *et seq.* (McKinney).

court proceedings by municipalities against their own appeals boards is not uncommon, the reference citing several such instances as documentation.

In New York City, a charter amendment has gone a step beyond the provisions of Article 78 by allowing administrative review of any determination by the city's Board of Standards and Appeals prior to any court action. The 1977 charter amendment allows the city's governing Board of Estimate authority to make "an administrative determination as to whether the decision of the board of standards and appeals under each of the specific requirements of the zoning resolution was supported by substantial evidence before the board of standards and appeals."[42] Enacted as a remedy to the problem of having the appeals board effectively bypass the city's planning policies, the amendment permits appeals to the Board of Estimate to be initiated by either the planning commission or the community affected by the zoning board's actions.

San Francisco has taken an even firmer approach to the problem. The actions of the zoning administrator and the Board of Permit Appeals are tightly circumscribed by a provision in the city and county planning code that explicitly prohibits any variance that would effectively result in a zoning reclassification or a deviation from any land-use, sign, or building height and bulk regulation applicable to a district. As will be explored in chapter 11, the city planning code adopted by San Francisco is generally regarded as the most stringent of any zoning ordinance enacted by a major city in this country.

Richard Babcock summarizes as follows the lack of coordination and confusion caused by divided and amateur administrative authority under the model suggested by the Standard Acts:

> The irony lies in the fact that the mantle of authority has been draped over an administrative system which has an aboriginal ethical code, possesses no cohesive body of principles, is multiform in its methods for handling complaints and is composed of constantly proliferating and unconnected units.[43]

Uninformed administration of zoning by a multitude of local agencies and, indeed, less than knowledgeable oversight by some courts have effectively contributed to the evolution of zoning practices with no legislative foundation and with little consistency or coherence. Since the 1960s, however, when many of the critical studies of boards of adjustment were made, the profession of planning has grown in capability and stature. The acceptance of public planners as land-use specialists combined with the mounting tech-

[42]City of New York Charter, 1976, Sect. 668c.
[43]Richard F. Babcock, "The Unhappy State of Zoning Administration in Illinois," *U. of Chicago L. Rev.* 26 (1959), 538.

nical complexity and scope of urban planning seem at last to be persuading board members and other elected and appointed local government officials that the counsel of professionals should be heeded over the entreaties of private parties, and that objective finding of unusual and unnecessary hardship must remain the legitimate criteria for zoning variance. With time and knowledge, the problems caused by board administration may well diminish.

PLANNING FLEXIBILITY AND THE PLANNING COMMISSION

The opening general statement of the Standard City Planning Enabling Act enumerates three responsibilities assigned the local planning commission: the making of the city plan, the regulation of subdivisions, and the control of buildings in planned streets through official mapping. A fourth function, that of regional planning, was recommended by the act for assignment to a separate regional planning commission. Just as the use of the variance and special exception has deviated from original intent under the administration of the board of adjustment, so have the functions of the planning commission evolved through practice since their conception in the 1920s.

Because the Standard Acts were based on the assumption that planning and zoning would remain essentially static and undergo only infrequent modification, there seemed little need for the planning commission to be invested with discretionary authority. It was believed by the drafters of the original acts that the variance and special exception administered by the board of adjustment would provide all the fine tuning that planning and zoning would require. Given the Standard Acts as the traditional basis, any departure from conventional zoning practice must still assume as fundamental the original tenet of reasonable certainty, a criterion deeply rooted in the end-state origins of planning as well as in rule of constitutional law.

The traditional doctrine holding the comprehensive plan as indefeasible was restated by the Oregon court in 1973 in *Fasano v. Board of Commissioners of Washington County* and reiterated again by the same court two years later in *Baker v. City of Milwaukie.*[44] Subsequently, however, in *Neuberger v. City of Portland,* the same court has drawn a distinction between planning amendments that define broadly applicable policy, which should be accorded the presumption of validity allowed legislative acts, and planning actions that are more narrowly aimed, which are thus quasi-judicial or administrative in nature and properly subject to more rigorous judicial scrutiny.[45]

Nothwithstanding such modification, the *Fasano* doctrine that regula-

[44]533 P. 2d 772 (Ore., 1975).
[45]603 P. 2d 771 (Ore., 1979).

tions shall be "in conformance with the comprehensive plan"[46] underscores once more the principle that planning enactments must avoid the pitfall of "spot zoning." This term, though often used generically with regard to many improper zoning practices, refers specifically to the singling out of small parcels of land for individual treatment that would benefit only a small minority rather than the general public interest. It was a finding of this kind of discrimination that moved the Connecticut court in the *Kuehne* case[47] to rule the contested amendment invalid. For similar reasons, the "special use" provision in the Chesterfield ordinance was also found illegal in *Rockhill,* the New Jersey court holding the classification too vague and inadequate "to channel local administrative discretion."[48]

A related doctrine is that zoning classifications must be general and not confined to only one use. This rule, like the prohibition against spot zoning, limits the ability of public planners to undertake specific design of private land use. For instance, an attempt by the city of Mount Vernon, New York, to rezone a private parcel of land adjacent to the railroad station in a highly developed business area to "Designed Parking District" was ruled invalid in the 1954 judgment *Vernon Park Realty v. City of Mount Vernon.*[49] The owner intended to use the property to develop a shopping center, even though the land had been used for several years as a parking lot. This principle was summarized by the Kentucky court in 1960 in *Pierson Trapp Company v. Peak:*

> Nowhere in the field of zoning law do we find any indication that the zoning authority may establish a zone or district that is limited to only one particular use. Our concept of the legitimate scope of the zoning power does not extend it to the point of embracing the power to restrict the use of property other than to reasonable general classification.[50]

Another section of the Standard Zoning Act provides that "all such regulations shall be uniform for each class or kind of buildings throughout each district."[51] This provision prohibits the imposition of special conditions on individual properties. By the same token, it generally forbids the practice of "contract zoning" whereby a quid pro quo agreement between a planning agency and an applicant results in a breach of the uniformity clause. The Maryland court ruled in *Baylis v. City of Baltimore,*[52] a typical case, that the rezoning of a lot from residential to commercial upon agree-

[46]Note 9, 29.
[47]*Kuehne v. Town Council of Town of East Hartford, 72 A. 2d 474.* (Conn., 1950).
[48]Note 18, 479.
[49]121 N.E. 2d 517 (N.Y., 1954).
[50]340 S.W. 2d 456 (Ky., 1960), 459.
[51]*Model Code, Tentative Draft No. 1,* 214.
[52]148 A. 2d 429 (Md., 1959).

ment by the owner to use the property only for a funeral parlor was invalid. Besides finding the action disruptive of the basic plan, the court also admonished that a municipality cannot contract away its future right to exercise the police power. Even where there is no commitment by government, such conditions may still be questionable as an improper impediment to the exercise of the police power. The court also distinguished rezoning by the city council from special exceptions granted by the board of zoning appeals.

Despite this general doctrine against contractual zoning agreements, some courts, since the 1959 *Baylis* decision, have approved the use of private covenants to secure approval for a specific development. For example, the New York court in the 1960 case *Church v. Town of Islip*[53] and the Massachusetts court in the 1962 case *Sylvania Electric Products, Inc., v. City of Newton*[54] both permitted rezoning of residential land on condition that deed restrictions make the proposed business and light manufacturing uses compatible with adjacent residential areas.

In discussing the function of the planning amendment, the American Law Institute's commentary in its *Model Code* minimizes some of the legal arguments that limit planning flexibility. It advocates instead reexamination of the basis of the Standard Acts: "The real objection is that an activity which ought to be carried on at the public control level has been driven underground. It has been driven underground because the end state concept of public control is incapable of accommodating reality."[55] The implication is that fundamental legislative reform of planning controls is needed both to permit rational and purposeful flexibility and to stem abuses of discretion under the guise of flexible administration.

Subdivision Regulation

One area in which the Standard Acts allowed greater flexibility is the control of subdivisions. According to the ALI Model Code reporters, the Standard Acts actually provided the planning commission with considerable discretionary authority to control subdivision developments, but preoccupation with end-state planning led to the abrogation of this flexibility by most state legislatures. The reporters observe,

> It would not be fair to the draftsmen of the SZEA to say that they overlooked the dynamic aspects of land use control entirely. . . . Indeed, there is language in . . . the Standard City Planning Enabling Act which can be read to have authorized delegation to the planning commission of a power to decide not

[53]168 N.E. 2d 680 (N.Y., 1960).
[54]183 N.E. 2d 118 (Mass., 1962).
[55]*Model Code, Tentative Draft No. 1,* 198.

only planning questions but also questions of land use, height, area, and bulk.
. . . The provision reads:

"The commision shall have the power to agree with the applicant upon use, height, area or bulk requirements or restrictions governing buildings and premises within the subdivision, provided such requirements or restrictions do not authorize the violation of the then effective zoning ordinances of the municipality."

Unfortunately, this provision was lost in an Act whose concern with planning lay in the direction of preserving the integrity of the street pattern and of preventing interference with public improvements. . . . As a result, it was unlikely that any state legislature would realize the significance of that provision. Indeed, the pattern of development prevailing in the twenties and early thirties (largely grid and lot by lot) was not calculated to alert anyone to the fallacy of the end state concept of land use control. Of the jurisdictions that adopted parts of the SPEA, only eight included the above provision.[56]

The reporters note that so little significance was attached to the provision that New Jersey, which had originally enacted an analogous law drafted by Edward Bassett in 1925, repealed it in 1953 despite growing awareness of the need for flexibility in planning administration.

The authority of local jurisdictions to approve or disapprove subdivision plans also includes the power to exact conditions from a developer in order to ensure that a proposed subdivision project will conform to the planning standards of the community. Planning commissions commonly require developers to dedicate streets and utility lines to avoid having the burden of providing such facilities fall upon the public. Leading cases confirm the validity of this requirement, construing dedication to be a reasonable condition for the privilege of subdividing. The general rule was summarized in 1960 by the Illinois court in *Rosen v. Village of Downers Grove,* which made specific reference to a 1949 California court judgment:

The distinction between permissible and forbidden requirements is suggested in *Ayres v. City Council of City of Los Angeles,* which indicates that the municipality may require the developer to provide the streets which are required by the activity within the subdivision but can not require him to provide a major thoroughfare, the need for which stems from the total activity of the community.[57]

In an echo of Holmes in *Pennsylvania Coal,*[58] the California court observed in *Ayres:* "Questions of reasonableness and necessity depends on matter of fact. They are not abstract ideas or theories. . . . It is no defense

[56]Ibid., 199–200.
[57]167 N.E. 2d 230 (Ill., 1960), 234. Citing 207 P. 2d 1 (Cal., 1949).
[58] *Pennsylvania Coal Company v. Mahon,* 260 U.S. 393 (1922).

to the conditions imposed . . . that their fulfillment will incidentally also benefit the city as a whole."[59]

The matter of street and infrastructure dedication within a subdivision is fairly well settled, but whether the cost of communitywide facilities can be exacted from a developer is less certain. A 1961 Illinois case, *Pioneer Trust and Savings Bank v. Village of Mount Prospect*,[60] held invalid a community's stipulation that a developer of a 250-unit subdivision dedicate a site for an elementary school and playground. The court reasoned that the cost of providing school facilities that serve the entire community should be paid by the community as a whole, not be shifted to one developer. Since that case, however, some courts have become more sympathetic toward dedication, or a fee in lieu of dedication, as a condition for development. For example, in the 1974 case of *City of Mesa v. Home Builders Association of Central Arizona, Inc.*,[61] the Arizona court found a "residential development tax" of $150 for each new dwelling unit to be proper. It dismissed the argument that the levy would result in double taxation, even though the expense would presumably be passed on to the purchaser, who would also be liable for ad valorem taxes on the property. Significantly, the court, only a year earlier in *Home Builders Association of Central Arizona, Inc. v. Riddel,* held a "park and recreation facility tax" levied by Tempe, a city immediately adjacent to Mesa, to be invalid. The court said, "We cannot presume that the special taxes collected under the ordinance will be used for neighborhood park land at a location so as to specially enhance the value of the taxpayers' property as opposed to benefits diffused throughout the City."[62] Apparently the city of Mesa learned from the experience of its sister community and refrained from specifying the purpose of its levy when imposing its "residential development tax."

Regardless of the law on subdivision dedication requirements, practical considerations tend to favor the public planning agency. Since most developers acquire land through loan arrangements that require payment of interest, they are under financial pressure to obtain building permission as quickly as possible. Any protestation against dedication requirements, even without litigation, could mean expensive delays that could outweigh the cost of meeting the demands of the governing body.

In the late 1960s, Ramapo, an outlying suburb of New York City, attempted an innovative strategy to integrate the provision and scheduling of public facilities and infrastructure with subdivision controls. Neither the planning of community capital improvements nor the timing of land-use controls were subjects of the original Standard Acts. To cope with unprec-

[59]207 P. 2d 1 (Cal., 1949), 7.
[60]176 N.E. 2d 799 (Ill., 1961).
[61]523 P. 2d 57 (Ariz., 1974).
[62]510 P. 2d. 376 (Ariz., 1973), 379.

edented population growth and rampant development, especially of single-family detached houses, the Ramapo town board in 1969 adopted an extensive master plan, the most notable element of which was an eighteen-year capital improvements program and budget that indicated when various municipal services and facilities would be provided in different parts of the community.

These improvements included roads, sanitary sewers, drainage systems, and firehouses, as well as public park, recreational, and school facilities. Each facility or service was designated to have a certain point value to be awarded when the improvement was installed according to the capital program. As each site accumulated 15 points, it would become eligible to receive a special permit for development. The permit would become a vested right at a specific time within the eighteen-year life of the program, even if the budgeted improvements had not actually been realized. If a developer wished to accelerate the date for his permit to mature, he could do so by furnishing improvements to the requisite number of points at his own expense. In 1972, in *Golden v. Planning Board of the Town of Ramapo,* a majority of the New York Court of Appeals held this scheme of "timing controls" for "phased growth" to be constitutional, sweeping aside suggestions that the ordinance was exclusionary in nature and an "unsupportable extrapolation from existing enabling acts," as argued by the minority.[63]

Court approval of the scheme notwithstanding, the Ramapo town board decided to abandon the point system eleven years after it won the *Golden* case. The plan had been based on the assumption that planned community services and facilities would be forthcoming, but with the loss of expected federal funds and voter reluctance to approve bond issues to support the entrance of newcomers, public improvements failed to keep up with new development. Though the plan had been lauded as a rational program to control and accommodate growth rather than to prohibit it, developments were delayed with no compensating advantage in terms of public improvements. Also, by the mid 1970s, the federal courts had approved alternate methods by which communities could control development without making a commitment to phased growth or to provide services.[64] Though innovative and well conceived, the Ramapo plan could not be sustained.

Official Mapping

In addition to subdivision regulation, the planning commission is also authorized in many states to practice official mapping. This device permits

[63]285 N.E. 2d 291 (N.Y., 1972), 303, 304–5, 309.
[64]See, e.g., *Construction Industry Association of Sonoma County v. City of Petaluma,* 522 F. 2d 897 (1975), and *Agins v. City of Tiburon,* 447 U.S. 255 (1980).

a locality to reserve private land, sometimes even beyond its borders, in anticipation of future public acquisition for such improvements as streets and sometimes parks and other community facilities. At issue is the cost of the reservation restriction as well as the question of whether the public is liable to reimburse an owner for improvements to the reserved areas subsequent to mapping.

The most widely adopted method of land reservation follows the official mapping technique outlined in 1926 by Edward Bassett and Frank B. Williams in their *Model Laws for Planning Cities, Counties and States*[65] rather than the SPEA, since the latter provisions for reservation were, in the words of law professor Donald Hagman, "too expensive."[66] The SPEA scheme stipulated that compensation is to be paid by the public for the period of reservation in addition to the costs of condemnation at the time of actual taking, except for improvements made by the owner despite the reservation. In contrast, under the Bassett-Williams model, which is based on the police power, no permits are to be issued in areas designated for public improvements in an adopted official map unless it can be shown that the reservation would not allow a fair return, whereupon a "variance" would be permitted to the extent of relieving the hardship. Generally, a restriction is considered valid without compensation unless the owner can show that he cannot make reasonable use of his property without infringing on the mapped portion of the land. Citing the New York court's affirmation of an official mapping law in *Headley v. City of Rochester,*[67] Jan Krasnowiecki and James C. N. Paul point out that the provision that an owner is entitled to expect his property to "yield a fair return" to be the "shock absorber" that has enhanced the constitutionality of official mapping despite the restriction placed on private property.[68] Said the *Headley* court:

> So long as the owners of parcels of land which lie partly in the bed of streets shown on such a map are free to place permanent buildings in the bed of a proposed street and to provide private ways and approaches which have no relation to the proposed system of public streets, the integrity of the plan may be destroyed by the haphazard or even malicious development of one parcel or tract to the injury of other owners who may have developed their own tracts in a manner which conforms to the general map or plan.[69]

[65]Edward M. Bassett and Frank B. Williams, *Model Laws for Planning Cities, Counties and States,* 17, vii, Harvard City Planning Studies (1935). See Joseph C. Kucirek and J. H. Beuscher, "Wisconsin's Official Map Law," *Wisconsin L. Rev.* (March 1957): 176.

[66]Hagman, *Urban Planning,* 270.

[67]5 N.E. 2d 198 (N.Y., 1936).

[68]Jan Z. Krasnowiecki and James C. N. Paul, "The Preservation of Open Space in Metropolitan Areas," *U. of Pennsylvania L. Rev.* 110 (1961), 185.

[69]Note 67, 199.

In the best Holmesian tradition, discretionary court finding of reasonableness is the essential determinant of the validity of official mapping authority. Two cases in Pennsylvania and Wisconsin illustrate this principle. In 1951, the Pennsylvania court ruled in *Miller v. City of Beaver Falls*[70] that a statute authorizing uncompensated public reservation of private land for a period of three years was unconstitutional. Six years later, however, in *State ex rel. Miller v. Manders,*[71] the Wisconsin court upheld an official mapping law, taking particular note of a provision that a board can refuse a permit "where the applicant will not be substantially damaged by placing his building outside the mapped street, highway or parkway."[72] Said the court of the "fair return" requirement in the law: "Without such a saving clause it is extremely doubtful if an official map statute would be constitutional."[73]

Amortization of Nonconforming Uses

One obstacle to flexible rezoning of an area with existing development is the disposition of uses and structures not conforming to the new zoning requirements. The question has been debated since zoning began but now seems largely resolved with the general acceptance of a process known as amortization, or the gradual phasing out of previously existing, nonconforming land uses. Perhaps the leading case concerning amortization is the 1954 California appellate decision of *City of Los Angeles v. Gage.*[74] Since 1930, Gage had operated a plumbing supply business from a residential building in a zone permitting the activity. In 1946, the city rezoned the area for residential use only, designating Gage's shop as a nonconforming use and requiring its discontinuance within five years. In upholding the ordinance, the court noted the reasonableness of the amortization period in consideration of the relatively small loss and inconvenience to be endured. The court's reasoning seemed replete with the discretionary and factual consideration urged by Holmes in *Pennsylvania Coal* concerning the particular situation of each property use amortized.

The administration of amortization depends heavily on just such circumstantial concern. The period of amortization is not the sole factor. Others include an accounting of the actual character of the neighborhood in relation to the new zoning, the length of time of prior use of the property, and the possible benefit to the owner of enjoying a monopoly of an other-

[70]82 A. 2d 34 (Pa., 1951).
[71]86 N.W. 2d 469 (Wisc., 1957).
[72]Ibid., 472. Citing Wisc. Stat. Ann., Sect. 62.23 (6)(d).
[73]Ibid., 473.
[74]274 P. 2d 34 (Cal. App., 1954).

wise prohibited activity during the period of amortization. Prime considerations are the cost of the building, the expense of relocation, and the normal
useful life remaining in the investment. A distinction is usually drawn between a nonconforming *structure* and a nonconforming *use* in that a newly
acquired building of a specific and inflexible utilitarian design would call
for a much longer amortization period than would a building long under
the same ownership that can easily be converted to accommodate a use
permitted under the new zoning. In the *Gage* case, not only had the owner
derived use from the property for some twenty years, but the building itself
was a conforming structure despite its nonconforming use. The idea of amortization seems a repudiation of any claim of vested right in zoning, but
ultimately the principal criterion must be the discretionary standard of reasonableness.

The concept of amortization is now generally well accepted. In a 1981
case, *Metromedia, Inc. v. City of San Diego,*[75] the Supreme Court, while
finding a city ban on outdoor advertising signs to be unconstitutional on
other grounds, voiced no specific objection to the idea of removing nonconforming signs after a period of amortization. However, acceptance is not
universal. For instance, the Arizona Supreme Court decided in a 1978 case,
City of Scottsdale v. Scottsdale Associated Merchants, Inc.,[76] that state law
provides public purchase or condemnation with compensation to the property owner as the only legal means of eliminating nonconforming uses, not
amortization.

Building Height, Setback, and Bulk

Besides provisions explicitly outlined by the Standard Acts, other regulatory practices have gained such acceptance that they are now regarded as
traditional. Restrictions governing building height, bulk, and setback from
property lines predate the Standards Acts to the nation's first zoning resolution was passed in New York City in 1916, and have their roots in ancient nuisance law. Even Blackstone, it may be recalled, argued that buildings that overhang and throw water on neighboring structures or stop up
"antient lights and windows" are nuisances "for which an action will lie."[77]

With land in the city center always at a premium, the twentieth-century
advent of high-rise building technology made more urgent the need for
measures to check the economic incentive to fill building sites to the lot-line
edge with ever-higher and -larger structures. Nowhere was the problem
more acute than in New York City, where the profit motive in land develop-

---

[75]453 U.S. 490 (1981).

[76]583 P. 2d 891 (Ariz., 1978).

[77]William Blackstone, *Commentaries on the Laws of England* (1765-69; reprint, London: Dawsons, 1966), bk. 3, ch. 13, 216-17.

ment created not only a lofty realm of tall and massive skyscrapers but also an underworld of streets and smaller structures robbed of sunlight and fresh air. Seymour Toll, noting the consequences caused by the construction in 1915 of the 42-story Equitable Building, whose full 540-foot height covered the entire lot from property line to property line, recounts:

> Practically all of the surrounding owners got reductions in their assessed valuations when they proved a loss of rents because of the light and air stolen by the massive new building. Its noon shadow enveloped some six times its own area. Stretching almost a fifth of a mile, it cut off direct sunlight from the Broadway fronts of buildings as tall as twenty-one stories. The darkened area extended some four blocks to the north.[78]

Within the first quarter of the century, the urge to derive maximum economic use of valuable urban land transformed parts of lower Manhattan into dark canyons of masonry and concrete. Eventually, widespread dismay at the urban environment created by the proliferation of looming structures began to mount. Even the president of the construction company that was responsible for the Equitable and several other New York skyscrapers was to moved to admit,

> Socially, the gigantic buildings are, to my way of thinking, quite wrong. It should be obvious that it would be utterly impossible to cover the island of Manhattan with tall buildings, even to the extent of 30 or 40 percent of its area. The streets could not take care of the traffic of such buildings. The water supply would be inadequate, and the sewers too. The sidewalks would become a solid mass of suffocating humanity. . . . All these things add up to something which convinces me that no city ever was meant to contain the buildings of fabulous size, of fifty, sixty or seventy stories and more, that have been attached like monstrous parasites to the veins and arteries of New York. Those who create such buildings, in my opinion, are taking an unfair advantage of their neighbors, of their fellow property owners, of their fellow citizens.[79]

Popular sentiment against the architectural behemoths was also reflected in the response of the judiciary. In 1909, in *Welch v. Swasey,* the Supreme Court upheld a police-power regulation limiting building height in Boston; in 1927, in *Gorieb v. Fox,* it acted again in support of a Roanoke, Virginia, ordinance requiring buildings to be set back from property lines. With these decisions by the high Court, the legal foundation was laid for modern height and bulk regulations.

---

[78]Seymour I. Toll, *Zoned American* (New York: Grossman, 1969), 71.
[79]Louis J. Horowitz and Boyden Sparkes, "The Towers of New York," *Saturday Evening Post,* March 28, 1936, 49–50. Cited by Toll, *Zoned American,* 71–72.

In New York City, the consequences of height and bulk restrictions are a strikingly visual manifestation of the invisible web of law on urban design.[80] To preserve light and air in the vicinity of new construction, the 1916 zoning law specified for each district a maximum building height allowable at the property line in relation to street width. Structures that exceeded this height were regulated to set back successively a certain distance as they rise. At a specified point, the buildings were allowed to rise uninterrupted, provided each resulting tower covered no more than 25 percent of the lot area. As a consequence of the regulatory envelope created about each building site by this setback rule, much of New York City is still dominated by a peculiar skyline of pyramidal "wedding-cake" buildings whose form has been determined more by the dictates of the setback regulation and the expedient of profit than by architectural design.

In 1961, as part of a comprehensive revision of the city's zoning resolution, a regulatory device known as the sky-exposure plane (SEP) was introduced, replacing the setback rule with an angle-of-slope description of the maximum physical boundaries allowed for high-rise structures. The 25 percent limitation on tower construction was also modified to permit 40 percent coverage of the site. To monitor structural size, restrictions were placed limiting the floor-area ratio (FAR) of buildings to a specified multiple by which interior floor space can lawfully exceed the area of the lot. A maximum allowable FAR of 10, for instance, permits the construction of a multilevel building with an interior floor space ten times the area of the lot, regardless of whether the structure is tall and slender, occupying only a small portion of the site, or short and squat, covering the full 40 percent lot area allowable for tower construction. The most controversial part of the 1961 resolution permitted relaxation of these restrictions to encourage developers to incorporate certain design amenities, such as plaza setbacks, at their building sites. (See chapter 11 for a more detailed discussion of these zoning incentives.)

In most communities, building height, bulk, and setback are controlled by regulations not unlike those found in the New York City zoning code. Houses too must normally conform to height limitations and are usually required to be surrounded by minimum front, back, and side yards. Recently, however, some communities are allowing and even encouraging "zero lot line" development in order to permit more efficient use of building sites, to reduce walking distances, and to maximize urban land use.[81]

---

[80]For a concise, illustrated history on New York City zoning in relation to building height, setback, and bulk, see *Midtown Development,* City Planning Dept., New York City (1981), 62–65, and *Midtown Zoning,* City Planning Dept., New York City (1982), 18–20, 86–89. The preceding two paragraphs of text were derived largely from these sources.

[81]Welford Sanders, *Zero Lot Line Development,* Planning Advisory Service Report no. 367 (Chicago and Washington, D.C.: American Planning Association, 1982).

Indeed, in some New York City districts where urban design policy seeks to encourage shopping-arcade development and continuity in retail-store frontage along streets, zoning actually promotes shopping and restaurant access at the "build-to" line, the converse of the plaza setback concept advocated in the 1961 resolution.

BUILDING AND HOUSING CODES

In addition to planning and zoning controls under the Standard Acts, the police power also ensures standards of safety and health in buildings. Such regulations are as old as the law itself. In the eighteenth century B.C., Article 229 of the Hammurabian Code declared that if a building caves in and kills the son of the owner, the life of the builder's son would be forfeit.[82] In Rome the collapse of an amphitheater in A.D. 27 that caused death and injury to fifty thousand people resulted in the passage of laws to ensure the safety of such public buildings. But unlike the eye-for-an-eye vengeance exacted by the earlier Mesopotamian law, the only punishment dealt the architect of an unsafe building was banishment. In 1189 a calamitous fire in London led to the enactment of the Assize of Buildings requiring tile roofs and masonry firewalls to minimize the spread of fire. In America, the Dutch city of New Amsterdam passed a law in 1648 prohibiting wood or plastered chimneys because of their flammability. However sensible, early building laws were not always well regarded: the English Building Act of 1774 was so unpopular that it became known as the "Black Act."[83] None of the laws, however, was as demanding as the custom practiced among Polynesians of placing a live slave under each corner post of a building to ensure its proper support. Today, the law merely requires that architects, engineers, builders, and specialty tradesmen be examined and registered to verify their competence to engage in building design and construction.

Modern Building Codes

The police power also imposes direct restrictions on the design and construction of buildings to guard against the threat of fire or structural failure and to maintain adequate sanitary standards. These controls take the form of building codes that specify allowable materials and techniques in construction, dictate minimum standards of performance under fire and structural stress, and determine circulation and spatial requirements—even

[82]Dennis Lloyd, *The Idea of Law* (1964; reprint, Baltimore: Penguin, 1970), 347–48; and Richard L. Sanderson, *Codes and Code Administration* (Chicago: Building Officials Conference of America, 1969), 5.

[83]Lewis Mumford, *The City in History* (New York: Harcourt, Brace & World, Harbinger, 1961), 409.

to the extent of stipulating maximum egress distances to building exits and minimum window sizes. Virtually any practicing architect can attest to the constraints of building-code regulations that can force modification or even abandonment of creative building designs. Purposeful regulations to ensure health and safety are undeniably necessary, but all too often written codes effectively disallow sound building practices and products, are administered arbitrarily by local building officials with inadequate expertise, and are imposed unilaterally without proper recourse for appeal.

Although code adoption has traditionally been a local prerogative, three construction code associations have maintained regional spheres of influence in promulgating their standards. The Building Officials and Code Administrators International's *Basic Building Code*[84] is widely adopted in the Northeast United States and parts of the Midwest; the West largely follows the *Uniform Building Code*[85] of the International Conference of Building Officials; and in the South, the most commonly used set of model construction regulations is the *Southern Standard Building Code*[86] distributed by the Southern Building Code Congress. A fourth model code, the *National Building Code,*[87] is issued by the American Insurance Association as its standard for underwriting against losses due to fire. Additional specialty codes govern the design and installation of electrical, mechanical, plumbing, heating and cooling equipment, and elevators, as well as testing standards for such construction materials as steel, concrete, and masonry.

Great though the effect of building codes on the design of individual buildings may be, this impact is overshadowed by the larger influence of such laws on the building industry as a whole and on community development. While most states enable the regulation of building construction and often make reference to the model codes, code adoption is typically left to local determination. As a result, many localities have developed their own building ordinances by modifying and amending existing model codes. Larger cities with adequate budget resources and professional staffs have even drafted their own building regulations, typically to cover high-rise construction not adequately addressed by the model codes. As a consequence, a lack of conformity in building cases is pervasive.

The reasons for this lack of uniformity are diverse, with varying degrees of justifiability. Variations in climatic and seismic conditions call for reasonable regional modifications, but such adjustments are typically included in the model codes. In addition, there is a tendency for each locality

[84]Building Officials and Code Administrators, International, *Basic Building Code* (Chicago: BOCA, revised periodically).

[85]International Conference of Building Officials, *Uniform Building Code* (Whittier, C.A.: ICBO, 1985).

[86]Southern Building Code Congress, *Southern Standard Building Code* (Birmingham, A.L.: SBCC, revised periodically).

[87]American Insurance Association, *National Building Code* (New York: AInA, 1976).

to pass the most conservative regulations resulting from their own experiences, although this practice frequently produces unduly restrictive design requirements.

Even seemingly sensible restrictions can result in dubious consequences when imposed locally. In response to the energy crisis of the 1970s, the mountain resort community of Aspen, Colorado, amended the countywide enforcement of the *Uniform Building Code* to require such energy-conserving measures as double-pane thermal glazing and heavier construction to accommodate additional roof and wall insulation. While the regulation has doubtlessly resulted in some energy savings, it has also added to the already high cost of housing in the area. This high cost has caused the exclusion of many moderate-income workers from local housing, which in turn contributes to the energy-consuming practice of daily worker commutation from beyond the county.

More significantly, parochial economic interests have sometimes been influential in mandating the use of specific local building products or local trade techniques, effectively excluding the use of suitable, more competitive construction methods and building materials and components from outside the area. In one city, drywall construction was prevented by the local plastering trade; in another city, the use of plastic pipes was opposed by plumbers.[88] Some communities have acquired distinctive visual design characteristics through compulsory idiosyncrasies in their construction regulations that favor certain local industries. Such code patronage of local building industries has no real bearing on safety or health considerations and can add needlessly to construction costs and time.

The wide variation among local building codes is a primary obstacle to innovation and more efficient methods of housing production. A 1982 report to the Congress by the National Institute of Building Science said,

> A multitude of codes and regulations makes it difficult to introduce innovation which conforms to all requirements, and variation in local approval of new products creates uncertainty about their acceptance. Some States have statewide building codes but local control predominates, and while almost all jurisdictions base their codes upon one of several model codes . . . communities often make enough changes to destroy uniformity among jurisdictions.[89]

The exclusion affects not only builders and producers of more efficient and economic construction materials, but ultimately consumers, particularly

[88]Advisory Commission on Intergovernmental Relations, *Building Codes: A Program for Intergovernmental Reform* (Washington, D.C.: USGPO, 1966), 6–7.

[89]National Institute of Building Sciences, *Greater Use of Innovative Building Materials and Construction Techniques Could Reduce Housing Costs* (Washington, D.C.: U.S. General Acounting Office 1982), 10. See also National Institute of Building Sciences, *A Study of the Regulations and Codes Impacting the Building Process* (1979).

those who are able to afford housing in a community only if more efficient construction methods and products are not prohibited by code.

In a 1965 case, *Kingsberry Homes Corporation v. Gwinnett County, Georgia,*[90] a federal district court enjoined enforcement of an unreasonably restrictive local building code that effectively disallowed prefabricated housing, even though the product met or exceeded such minimum standards as set by the Federal Housing Administration, the Veterans Administration, and the Southern Standard Building Code, the basis of the county's own building code. Two years later, the same district court reaffirmed its position in *Boise Cascade Corporation v. Gwinnett County, Georgia;*[91] again, the court prohibited the county from excluding manufactured homes equivalent to houses constructed on site. As a result of these and other cases, it is now well settled under law that local regulations cannot stand in the way of economical construction products or techniques derived from reasonable innovations.

Even at a national level, political pressure has been exerted by construction trade and product interests to prevent code approval of competitive building methods and materials. In its 1968 report, *Building the American City,* the National Commission on Urban Problems summarized its findings on construction codes,

> Problems of building codes and other necessary product approvals plague both the home manufacturers and the makers of preassembled components. In far too many jurisdictions, various preassemblies are rejected outright. In others, inspection methods effectively exclude them. If electrical connections are installed inside preassembled panels, for example, they are subject to the possible demand of building inspectors, who often represent either local craft or building interests, that they be taken out and locally installed or that a panel be removed to permit inspection at the site. Costly delays and alterations can result. . . .
>
> Perhaps even more significant, though not precisely measurable, is the deterrent effect of existing code restraints on the development of new preassembled components and houses. Investors are understandably reluctant to expend large amounts on research and development when they fear that even technically successful innovations will not be allowed to reach the potential market.[92]

The obstacles caused by building codes pose a serious handicap to the efficiency of building construction, which in America lags far behind other countries, particularly Europe, in the industrialization of housing produc-

[90]248 F. Supp. 765 (1965).

[91]272 F. Supp. 847 (1967).

[92]National Commission on Urban Problems (Douglas Commission), *Building the American City* (Washington, D.C.: USGPO, 1968), 437.

tion. Write Charles G. Field and Steven R. Rivkin in their 1975 analysis, *The Building Code Burden,*

> An industrialized housing producer . . . is highly dependent upon demand within the effective transport radius of his plant, and any factor that bars entry to a market and thereby diminishes the effective market area is a highly significant problem.
>
> Local building code regulation has exactly that effect. By reason of prohibitive code provisions, cumbersome approval procedures, fragmentation of the overall market area into hundreds of uniquely defined submarkets, building codes and their regulation have constituted one of the foremost barriers to innovation and industrialization.[93]

The Advisory Commission on Intergovernmental Relations, in its 1966 report *Building Codes: A Program For Intergovernmental Reform,* commented:

> The mere existence of more than 5,000 different local codes presents a formidable barrier to the development of a broadly based building industry. Under such circumstances, it is difficult for any building organization or manufacturer of building products to take advantage of the economics of mass production that have contributed so significantly to other sectors of our economy. . . .
>
> The problem is not that local codes necessarily prohibit prefabricated homes, but that differences in local codes prevent their general use.[94]

Again, those ultimately hurt by the practice of fragmented local codes are consumers, particularly those requiring low-cost housing. Field and Rivkin note that "should the existing building code pattern continue, there can be little reason to expect substantial contributions from industrialized production in meeting our lower-income housing production needs."[95]

Despite the common finding of numerous studies that the diversity of local building regulations are at the root of serious problems for the construction industry, basic code reform has been limited. Study organizations such as the National Conference of States on Building Codes and Standards and the National Institute of Building Sciences have been created to seek greater standardization of building codes. In 1971, the model code associations coordinated efforts to produce a joint code, the *One and Two Family Dwelling Code.*[96] Cooperation by the model code groups through the Coun-

---

[93]Charles G. Field and Steven R. Rivkin, *The Building Code Burden* (Lexington, M.A.: Heath, 1975), 32.

[94]Advisory Commission on Intergovernmental Relations, *Building Codes,* 1, 4.

[95]Field and Rivkin, *Building Code Burden,* 99.

[96]Council of American Building Officials, *One and Two Family Dwelling Code: Under the Nationally Recognized Model Codes* (Homewood, I.L.: BOCA, 1983).

cil of American Building Officials and its Board for the Coordination of Model Codes has allowed the federal Department of Housing and Urban Development (HUD) to depend more on locally adopted codes based on standardized models to set construction criteria qualifying houses for federal mortgage insurance. Instead of its own *Minimum Property Standards for One and Two Family Dwellings,*[97] which has become regarded as the industry standard for suburban home construction. However, HUD continues to use its own *Minimum Property Standards for Multifamily Housing*[98] as a guide for construction of federally financed, multi-unit housing.

The federal government has moved to set national construction standards for the manufacturing of mobile homes. In 1974, it effectively preempted state authorities by passing the National Mobile Home Construction and Safety Standards Act,[99] which established federal criteria governing mobile-home fabrication. In addition to mobile homes, construction standards to ensure the health and safety of the workplace are enforced through the federal police power under the provisions of the Occupational Safety and Health Act of 1970.[100]

Still the road to satisfactory reform is long. Industrialization in construction has the potential of becoming a major factor in the design of the built environment, yet the invisible web of building codes, their diversity, and administration are effective deterrents to industrialization. There should be no doubt that the architectural and engineering design professions are competent to devise systems of prefabricated buildings and concepts of site planning that would provide the quality, beauty, and diversity conducive to a humane and safe building environment. The economy and efficiency possible through standardization and mass production could place these ideals in housing within the economic reach of more citizens and so alter the physical character of entire communities. To accomplish this end, the unnecessary obstacles posed by the tangled web of building codes must first be overcome.

Housing Codes

Closely related to police-power regulation of building construction are codes that specify minimum standards for the occupancy, sanitary require-

---

[97]U.S. Department of Housing and Urban Development, *Minimum Property Standards for One and Two Family Dwellings* (Washington, D.C.: USGPO, 1982).

[98]U.S. Department of Housing and Urban Development, *Minimum Property Standards for Multifamily Housing* (Washington, D.C.: USGPO, 1979).

[99]42 U.S.C. 5401 *et seq.,* National Mobile Home Construction and Safety Standards Act of 1974, Pub. L. 93-383, 88 Stat. 700.

[100]29 U.S.C. 651 *et seq.,* Occupational Safety and Health Act of 1970, Pub. L. 91-596, 84 Stat. 1590. See also, Peter S. Hopf, *Designer's Guide to OSHA* (New York: McGraw-Hill, 1975).

ments, maintenance, and construction of housing. Since the poor have invariably been the principal victims of substandard housing conditions, the adherence of low-income rental housing to health and safety standards has been the main object of regulation. In America, as in Europe, social concern for the condition of low-income housing arose during the era of reform following the Industrial Revolution, leading in this country to such landmarks in housing legislation as New York's Tenement Housing Act of 1901 and the publication of Lawrence Veiller's *A Model Housing Law*[101] in 1914. The laws have directly influenced the design of low- and moderate-income, multifamily housing as well as the physical character of urban residential districts.

Although the area had relatively low-rise buildings, population densities in the Lower East Side of New York in 1900 reached one thousand persons per acre, the highest recorded density in world history. Despite the city's first housing law, passed in 1867 to prevent the worst abuses, tenements built and owned for profit were characterized by deplorable crowding of occupants and excessive coverage of building lots.

Typical was the "railroad" plan, which permitted a tenement house to span across the full width of the lot and cover 90 percent of the site with neither side yard nor setback. Lots were commonly 25 feet wide and 100 feet deep. The plan described buildings six or seven floors high with four apartments on each level. Rooms were in tandem, like railroad cars, and had no exterior side walls, so that only the front room of each floor received daylight and ventilation. Privies were located in the rear yard. In 1879, as the result of a competition, the railroad plan was superseded by the "dumbbell" or "double-decker" plan. This "model" plan was a slight improvement. It included two common water closets on each floor and introduced a narrow light shaft along the side wall. However, these shafts scarcely allowed adequate light and air to rooms located on lower levels. In 1899, the Charity Organization Society held another competition, which resulted in the Tenement House Act of 1901 and in the abolishment of the dumbbell plan. Under the new law, housing requirements were patterned after the winning design, which reduced land coverage to 70 percent and increased lot widths to 50 feet. The wider site allowed interior courts to provide light and air to rooms and improved apartment floor plans. In addition, each apartment had its own toilet facilities. Despite their subsequent prohibition, many tenements of the railroad and dumbbell type still exist. It seems ironic that the inferior dumbbell plan had been promulgated in good faith and had even won a prize in design. The 1901 New Law remained in effect in New York without major revision until 1929, when it was replaced by the city's Multiple Dwelling Law.

The design influence of building and housing codes was by no means restricted to the United States. During the early years of the century,

[101]Lawrence Veiller, *A Model Housing Law* (New York: Russell Sage Foundation, 1914).

housing-construction regulations were also enacted in Germany, the Nether-
lands, and Sweden. In England, the dwellings resulting from government
regulations even came to be known as "by-law houses." Building regulations also contributed to the distinctive style of construction in Paris under
the Third Republic. To compensate for land usurped by Haussmann's
grand avenues, a law passed in 1902 allowed unprecedented densities in the
land remaining. Heights were limited only by a function of street widths,
with a consequence that structures with more than seven floors were permitted. Roofs were designed after the style of the Renaissance architect Fran-
çois Mansart to allow for additional habitable space in the attic. As a result,
higher buildings than ever before were constructed along the narrow streets
of the medieval city. Earlier regulations passed in 1884 stipulated minimum
interior courtyards, but the law of 1902 reduced these open spaces to mere
air shafts, each measuring less than ten feet square. Motivated by commercial interests to maximize the economic return on urban real property, the
law permitted extreme building densities and population crowding through
much of the city.

In the contemporary United States, the "urban crisis" of the 1960s
brought the problem of low-income housing to the attention of the federal
government. The government's prior involvement in housing policy was
typified by the operation of the Federal Housing Administration, which
was formed during the Depression to provide financing assistance for home
construction and ownership. In the mid 1960s, the agency's essentially narrow focus on middle-class housing and suburban development turned to the
broader issue of housing for all citizens, particularly the urban poor. It was
during this time that the Department of Housing and Urban Development
was created with the charge of administering a plethora of housing assistance programs for the purpose of providing housing from the low- and
moderate-income segments of the population. Among the programs established was the Federal Code Enforcement Program authorized in 1965. This
authority provided grants as much as three fourths of the cost of programs
to bring dilapidated housing up to code requirements.

The government during this period was also active in housing research
and prototype development. In 1968 national studies were published, including a report by the President's Committee on Urban Housing entitled
A Decent Home,[102] as well as the report of the National Commission on
Urban Problems. But, as with so many studies, the commissions' recommendations resulted more in platitudinous professions of concern than in
truly substantive action. Operation Breakthrough, a demonstration program authorized in the same year to promote industrialization of the housing industry and to remove impediments to the marketing of prefabricated

---

[102]The President's Committee on Urban Housing (Kaiser Committee), *A Decent Home*
(Washington, D.C.: USGPO, 1968).

housing and housing components, likewise concluded with few lasting benefits. As with basic building code reform, real progress to improve the regulatory climate for efficient production of sound, well-designed, economical housing has not been great. In addition, federal involvement in housing issues has diminished significantly since the 1960s, reflecting both a change in administrative ideology as well as changes in the national economy and in public priorities.

As the national committees implied in their 1968 reports, the complexity of housing problems are such that even the best intentions of professionals in housing policy and design have ended in only partial successes and even in failure. The issue is clearly beyond the limited scope of this discussion on police-power regulation; it will be considered again in the last chapter on public subsidies.

The invisible web of building and housing codes, like planning and zoning law, is undeniably flawed, its imperfections creating patterns of dubious consequence in the design of the city and its physical and social components. If the planner and architect are truly to determine the pattern of the built urban environment, they must participate with knowledge and vigor in the design and reform of this invisible web that affects so much of urban design and planning.

Chapter 6

Issues and Innovations: A Synopsis

In the years since widespread adoption of the principles set forth in the Standard Acts, issues in zoning practice have arisen that have induced changes in zoning and zoning administration. (See chapter 5 for a discussion of the acts and their effects.) The origins of some issues can be traced to characteristics intrinsic in the system itself, while others have come about for reasons external to zoning.

In this chapter, a selection of these issues and changes will be examined in five sections: the first exploring innovations toward greater flexibility in the administration of land-use planning and zoning, including planned unit development, performance zoning and environmental impact assessment, and transfer of development rights; the second dealing with laws regarding access to direct sunlight for solar-energy use; the third discussing parochialism and regionalism in land-use planning, including social exclusion and legislative efforts at reform; the fourth treating the comprehensive reform of the system of land-use controls derived from the Standard Acts; and the fifth section covering recent developments regarding federal civil rights and antitrust laws in relation to land-use regulation.

INNOVATIONS TOWARD FLEXIBILITY

As modern planning evolved from its end-state premise in the City Beautiful movement to new interdisciplinary theories in "continuous" planning, city planners have sought to gain legitimacy for innovative methods of control that allow greater discretion and flexibility in the regulation

152

of land use and development than were permissible under the original Standard Acts. A primary objective in selecting flexibility in "ad hocmanship"[1] or the "wait-and-see"[2] approach to planning administration is to obtain the ability to react to changing circumstances and opportunities in urban and suburban land development.

Planned Unit Development

Perhaps the most widely accepted innovation toward flexible administration is planned unit development (PUD), a technique that permits the public planner and the developer of large-scale projects to cooperate to override the constraints of segregated land use and predetermined "cookie-cutter" development traditionally associated with zoning. Essentially, PUD is a method of flexible land subdivision that permits the use of newer design concepts, such as integration of varied types of land uses, cluster development, and communal open space. It is closely related to a concept of control known as "floating zones," an earlier method of zoning flexibility that experienced only marginal acceptance.

The term "floating zone" derives from the idea of a land-use zone "floating" over designated sections of a planning jurisdiction until the fulfillment of certain conditions permits it to settle at a particular location. In practice, an ordinance is passed specifying the criteria for development, as for multifamily housing, without making reference to any particular parcel of land. When a landowner applies for permission to develop his property and the public planning body determines that the proposed development meets the stipulated requirements, a second ordinance is then enacted as an amendment to the zoning map, and the property under consideration is rezoned to permit construction. Although this technique gives developers and government freedom to work together to achieve more flexible patterns in urban design, floating zones have frequently been opposed by neighboring property owners protesting the destruction of perceived stability in pre-established zoning. Undeniably, the flexibility inherent in floating zones erodes some of the certainty attached to both traditional zoning and Hayek's ideal of administrative predictability and places greater demand on the discretionary judgment of the judiciary as well as the planning administration.

The legal history of floating zones and planned unit development can be seen in the evolution of several leading cases that took place in the state of Pennsylvania. In 1960, in *Eves v. Zoning Board of Adjustment of Lower*

---

[1]John W. Reps, "Requiem for Zoning," in *Planning 1964* (Chicago: American Society of Planning Officials, 1965), 62.

[2]National Commission on Urban Problems (Douglas Commission), *Building the American City* (Washington, D.C.: USGPO, 1968), 206.

Gynedd Township,[3] the Pennsylvania Supreme Court found invalid a floating-zone scheme of "flexible selective zoning" that would have permitted an industrial use to be located in an area previously zoned for residences only. The court concluded that "there was no orderly plan of particular land use for the community," and that "the development itself would become the plan, which is manifestly the antithesis of zoning 'in accordance with a comprehensive plan.'"[4] Despite certain provisions the township had made to safeguard the residential character of the area, the court found the concept to carry "evils akin to 'spot zoning'."[5]

Three years after this case, the same court made an apparent reversal. In *Donahue v. Zoning Board of Adjustment of Whitemarsh Township*, it ruled that two ordinances, one authorizing a residential "apartment house district" with specific criteria but no specific location, and the other rezoning a strip of land from "'A' residential" to the new classification at the owner's request, did not constitute "an unlawful floating zone."[6] The court took pains to distinguish this case from *Eves*. Apparently, one factor was that the time period between ordinances in *Donahue* was only six weeks, while in *Eves* the interval was about eight months. Perhaps of greater relevance was that the later opinion was written by Samuel J. Roberts, a judge who was not present on the court during the *Eves* decision, but who assumed a central position in the court's subsequent activities on land-use controls and planning.

In 1968, again with the active participation of Judge Roberts, the Pennsylvania Supreme Court approved the practice of planned unit development. The case of *Cheney v. Village 2 at New Hope*[7] concerned an early application of the PUD technique to a new development proposed for the town of New Hope, a resort community with historic roots located in rural Bucks County up the Delaware River from Philadelphia. As in the *Donahue* case, at issue in the case was the passage of two ordinances, one enabling PUD and the other amending the zoning map to rezone a large tract of land from low-density residential to the new classification. Both ordinances were passed on the same day following some six months of negotiation between the developer and the New Hope planning commission. Under the town ordinance establishing PUD, such diverse land uses as single-family attached or detached housing, apartments, hotels, restaurants, theatres, churches, offices, art galleries, parks, swimming pools, golf courses, and even ski slopes could all be integrated within a development.

Planned unit development is now a widely accepted method of land

---

[3]164 A. 2d 7 (Pa., 1960).
[4]Ibid., 8, 11.
[5]Ibid., 11.
[6]194 A. 2d 610 (Pa., 1963), 611.
[7]241 A. 2d 81 (Pa., 1968).

development. Scrupulous administration by public planning agencies has generally allayed early fears that mixed use and clustered density would be detrimental to neighboring interests. On the contrary, the flexibility of PUD has allowed greater diversity and interest in subdivision design as well as more efficient use of both land and infrastructure. Indeed, many communities actually provide incentives, such as increased overall development densities, to encourage PUD design. Today it is generally recognized that the flexibility made possible through PUD has had wide benefits for developers and communities alike, allowing new forms of suburban and community development to be realized. Flexibility in approving various forms of development beyond the "cookie-cutter" norm has, of course, demanded greater thought, responsibility, and professionalism of all concerned, particularly of the public planner charged with the exercise of discretion in administering planned unit development.

Performance Zoning and Environment Impact Assessments

Another recent development in land-use regulation, also intended to increase flexibility, is the use of performance standards in place of conventional use classifications in zoning. Technical improvements in methods to abate the noxious consequences of development, particularly of noise, odors, and pollutants resulting from industrial activity, as well as advances in standard measurement of such pollution, have led to the idea that building permission can be based on performance in controlling a potential problem rather than on the type of use itself. The willingness of an industrial developer to install equipment to reduce air pollution, for example, might qualify his proposed development to be constructed in a zone where it would otherwise be prohibited. Although this method of control seems largely applicable to industrial developments, proponents of performance zoning suggest a wider applicability, with performance variables concerning such considerations as density, site capacity, and ratios of open space, floor area, and impervious surface coverage.[8] Where variables can be subject to precise standards and measurement, flexibility is possible with a minimum of administrative discretion. However, when considerations are complex or difficult to quantify, the administration of performance standards may well be beyond the technical expertise of planning and zoning officials, particularly in smaller jurisdictions.

A related method of control calls for the prior technical assessment of the impact proposed development projects will have on the environment. Such consideration is the primary control provision of the National Envi-

[8]Lane Kendig, *Performance Zoning* (Washington, D.C.: American Planning Association, 1980).

ronmental Policy Act of 1969,[9] which requires a scrupulous and unbiased environmental impact statement (EIS) to be submitted before any major federal project is undertaken, describing in comprehensive detail all possible consequences of the proposal on the environment. Similar environmental impact assessments are also mandatory in several states as a requisite for development permission.

In its 1972 decision *Friends of Mammoth v. Board of Supervisors of Mono County,* the California Supreme Court found that that state's 1970 Environmental Quality Act[10] applies to private as well as public projects. Under the act, any application for development must be accompanied by an environmental impact report. The statement must include a careful accounting of any unavoidable or irreversible adverse consequences that could affect the environment, as well as consideration of alternatives to the proposal and mitigation measures that might be undertaken. As the court observed,

> The impact report must be specially prepared in written form before the governmental entity makes its decision. This will give members of the public and other concerned parties an opportunity to provide input both in the making of the report and in the ultimate governmental decision based, in part, on that report.[11]

The regulation, enforced through the police power, has given planning authorities in California substantial leverage to ensure that any development within the state will not adversely affect the surrounding natural or human environment.

Although their application is generally construed in terms of protecting the natural environment, environmental impact assessments have also been an effective basis for development control in the context of urban design. In its 1978 decision *Polygon Corporation v. City of Seattle,* the Washington Supreme Court found that the State Environmental Policy Act of 1971 conferred upon the city discretionary authority to deny development permission for the construction of a thirteen-story condominium project on grounds that the building design would result in adverse environmental impact primarily of an aesthetic nature.[12] Rezoning of the multiple-residential, high-density zone was not at issue, for the developer was not prevented from full use of the zoned area. The EIS even suggested alternative configurations of multifamily design that would have a less adverse effect on the environment. The specific design proposal was, however, considered to be

---

[9]42 U.S.C. 4321 *et seq.,* Pub. L. 91–190, 83 Stat. 852.
[10]Cal. Pub. Res. Code, Sect. 21000 *et seq.,* Sect. 21100.
[11]502 P. 2d 1049 (Cal., 1972), 1059.
[12]578 P. 2d 1309 (1978). Quoting Rev. Code of Wash. 43–21 C.

totally out of scale with neighboring structures, interfering with views from several directions as well as from a nearby park. It was found furthermore that the projected design would cast a shadow over surrounding properties and would cause an increase in traffic and noise.

Using an environmental impact statement to control urban design is by no means isolated to this case. In other states with strong requirements for environmental impact assessments, such as California, planning authorities have made use of the environmental impact report requirement to control urban design in much the same manner.

Transfer of Development Rights

Another innovation in controls derives from regulations governing the economic incentive to maximize the use of developable land. The idea of transfer of development rights (TDR) can be seen as early as 1943 in the writings of the renowned architect Eliel Saarinen. In his book, *The City,* Saarinen observed that the value of land is not intrinsic to the property itself but is rather in its use. He suggested that the right to this use need not be tied to a particular plot but could be effectively transferred from a site where overbuilding is a problem to another location in need of development, thus benefiting both places.[13] Some twenty years later, a New York developer, David Lloyd, made a similar suggestion: If a community refuses to permit development at a certain location, owners of property there should be permitted to sell their development rights to others who own land at a location where additional development density is not objectionable.[14] In the early 1970s, this idea was systematized by lawyer John J. Costonis as a means to preserve landmark buildings in Chicago located in areas under pressure for more intensive redevelopment.[15] The concept has broader application than to historic preservation alone, as in the protection of privately held scenic resources and as an urban design tool.

In the case of a historic or architectural landmark, the burden of a police-power regulation prohibiting the owner from demolishing or otherwise changing the external appearance of the building can be lessened—and the restriction made more constitutionally palatable—by permitting the transfer of potential development rights, usually defined in terms of allowable floor area or air rights, to a second location. The New York City TDR ordinance, for example, allows the owners of a regulated landmark building to transfer the "development rights to unbuilt but allowable floor area"

[13]Eliel Saarinen, *The City* (Cambridge: M.I.T. Press, 1943), 235.

[14]Richard F. Babcock, "Zoning," in *The Practice of Local Government Planning,* ed. Frank. S. So et al. (Washington, D.C.: International City Management Assoc., 1979), 437.

[15]John J. Costonis, "The Chicago Plan: Incentive Zoning and the Preservation of Urban Landmarks," *Harvard L. Rev.* 85 (1972), 574.

from the landmark site to contiguous lots. At one time, transfers could be made only to immediately adjacent lots, but this restriction has been relaxed gradually to permit transfers to lots separated by streets or intersections and now to lots linked to the landmark site by contiguous lots in common ownership. A rule limiting the allowable increase of a floor-area ratio at a recipient lot to 20 percent was also lifted in high-density commercial areas to enable a landmark owner to exhaust his surplus developable air rights at one location.

In an effort to increase the flexibility of such transfers still further, Costonis suggests in his Chicago Plan that "development rights transfer districts" be established encompassing areas of the city where landmarks are located.[16] The owner of a restricted landmark would be entitled to transfer his property's surplus development rights to other sites in the same district or possibly to other designated areas. Should an owner refuse the transfer option, the city could then acquire the property's unused development rights in addition to a "preservation restriction" through either negotiation or eminent domain. The cost of such preservation acquisitions would be covered by a municipal "development rights bank," which would be funded in turn by the sale of similarly acquired development rights to developers wishing to increase allowable building floor areas elsewhere. Transfers would be accompanied by such considerations as property tax adjustments and limitations on the maximum development allowable at recipient lots.

Since its provision in New York City law, the legitimacy of transfer of development rights has been widely studied and debated, but the question of whether the process can lawfully constitute full compensation for land-use restrictions beyond the police power has yet to be determined conclusively. In its 1978 ruling *Penn Central Transportation Co. v. City of New York,* the Supreme Court upheld a landmark restriction prohibiting construction of a high-rise office building above New York's Grand Central Terminal in a design that would have substantially altered the exterior appearance of that historic railroad station. The Court gave tacit recognition to TDR as mitigating the regulatory burden of landmark designation but chose not to rule specifically on its viability as just compensation:

> To the extent appellants have been denied the right to build above the Terminal, it is not literally accurate to say that they have been denied all use of even those pre-existing air rights. Their ability to use these rights has not been abrogated; they are made transferable to at least eight parcels in the vicinity of the Terminal, one or two of which have been found suitable for the construction of new office buildings. Although appellants and others have argued that New York City's transferable development-rights program is far

[16]Ibid., 590–91.

from ideal, at least in the case of the Terminal, the rights afforded are valuable. While these rights may well not have constituted "just compensation" if a "taking" had occurred, the rights nevertheless undoubtedly mitigate whatever financial burdens the law has imposed on appellants and, for that reason, are to be taken into account in considering the impact of regulation.[17]

The Supreme Court ruling in *Penn Central* upheld the New York Court of Appeals decision in the case. Two years earlier, however, in *Fred F. French Investing Company, Inc. v. City of New York,* the same state high court found an application of development rights transfer to be invalid. The case concerned an attempt by the governing body of New York City to rezone two private parks attached to a Manhattan residential complex as parks open to the public. To compensate the owner, the amendment provided that the developable air rights severed from the property be made transferable to other locations in midtown Manhattan. In voiding the city scheme, the court pointed out that no lot in which the plaintiff company had interest had been identified as a potential recipient of the severed development rights.

> In an attempt to preserve the rights they were severed from the real property and made transferable to another section of mid-Manhattan in the city, but not to any particular parcel or place. There was thus created floating development rights utterly unusable until they could be attached to some accommodating real property, available by happenstance of prior ownership, or by grant, purchase, or devise, and subject to the contingent approvals of administrative agencies. In such case, the development rights, disembodied abstractions of man's ingenuity, float in a limbo until restored to reality by reattachment to tangible real property.[18]

The court also distinguished the amendment from Costonis's Chicago Plan, noting that the Chicago Plan provided for a municipal "development bank" from which "the owner of the granting parcel may be allowed just compensation for his development rights instantly and in money."[19] Said the court of the New York City scheme,

> By compelling the owner to enter an unpredictable real estate market to find a suitable receiving lot for the rights, or a purchaser who would then share the same interest in using additional development rights, the amendment renders uncertain and thus severely impairs the value of the development rights before they were severed.[20]

[17]438 U.S. 104 (1978), 137.
[18]350 N.E. 2d 381 (N.Y., 1976), 387–88.
[19]Ibid., 388.
[20]Ibid.

The value of development rights and the efficacy of their transfer has been borne out in a practical way since the court cases by the sale of 75,000 square feet of air rights above Grand Central Terminal to a high-rise development across the street. The use of TDR has also been gaining considerable interest, not only in cities like New York for purposes of landmark preservation and urban design but also to conserve natural environments threatened by development.

The concept still raises a question with substantive legal and planning implications. If the original restriction limiting development density at the recipient site was imposed truly for the sake of public necessity, as required of the police power, the inference would be that any additional FAR allowance would be excessive and detrimental to the public interest. How, then, can additional density resulting from transferred development rights be justified at the second site, particularly when the public benefit actually accrues at a landmark site located elsewhere? In fact, it can be argued that undesirably large building sizes and excessive population densities have been the result of increasing floor-area ratios beyond original allowances. As Roberta Brandes Gratz comments on the New York preservation law allowing TDR:

> Landmarks preservation, long the bane of the real estate mogul's existence, is now a favorite tool for what one critic calls "architectural bribery"—demanding extras for preserving a landmark. Faced with a scarcity of good development parcels, builders seek out landmarks that can accommodate a new tower next door, made spectacularly larger by adding the landmark's air rights to the new building.[21]

An increase resulting from air-rights transfer can, moreover, be offered in addition to bonus floor-area ratios as an incentive for the development contribution of design amenities, thereby resulting in still larger buildings.

Beyond planned unit development and transfer of development rights, there have been other innovative proposals to improve upon police-power methods of land-use control. In a 1978 study entitled *Windfalls for Wipeouts*,[22] law professor Donald G. Hagman and economist Dean J. Misczynski suggested one of the most intriguing of these ideas, which in essence would be the taxing of windfall land-value increases created by public planning actions to compensate for losses in value caused by similar public activities elsewhere. Deriving in principle from the constitutional problem of public taking of private-property values as a result of planning restrictions,

[21]Roberta Brandes Gratz, "New York's Zoning Predicament," *Planning* 45, no. 12 (Dec. 1979), 26.
[22]Donald G. Hagman and Dean J. Misczynski, eds., *Windfalls for Wipeouts: Land Value Capture and Compensation* (Chicago and Washington, D.C.: Planners Press, 1978).

the proposed system of loss mitigation would permit planning regulations to exceed the normal boundaries of the police power.

The concept of public recapture of benefits arising from government activities borrows heavily from the idea of a levy on "betterment" initially conceived in British planning. Clifford L. Weaver and Richard F. Babcock criticize the scheme, pointing to problems experienced in the British system.[23] Even a relatively modest application of the Hagman-Misczynski concept, they feel, would be overly complex and would pose virtually insurmountable political problems in educating a public reluctant to have some new experiment in public control and taxation thrust upon it. Moreover, they point out, in urban planning practice—as distinguished from the planning of outlying land—property values may be reduced but are rarely subject to total wipeout that would need compensation beyond provisions already available through such devices as the transfer of development rights. Unfortunately, with the untimely death of Professor Hagman not long after his study was published, the idea has lost its most dedicated proponent.

SOLAR ACCESS FOR ENERGY GENERATION

As discussed earlier, zoning originated in part from building-height regulations intended to preserve accessibility of neighboring properties to the sun. In the 1970s, a half century after this genesis, interest in controlling building height and siting was renewed when declining resources in fossil fuels prompted development of alternative methods of energy generation. Solar collectors are among the recently devised means for obtaining alternative sources of energy. Because these collectors require direct exposure to the sun in order to function, and because solar energy systems have normally been located on the building rooftops, the question has been raised of whether the owner of a building with a solar energy unit can prevent a neighbor from undertaking construction or even cultivating vegetation that would block access of his collectors to direct sunlight.

While generating energy from sunlight may be relatively new, the legal issue of solar access can be traced back to the traditional problem of building height and setback regulation. According to Sir Edward Coke's proclamation *cujus est solum ejus est usque ad coelum*[24] (he who owns the land also owns upward even to heaven), a landowner possesses an unabridged right to use his property as he wishes, without regard to whether his development blocks sunlight from adjacent land. However, despite this ancient

[23]Clifford L. Weaver and Richard F. Babcock, *City Zoning: The Once and Future Frontier* (Chicago and Washington, D.C.: Planners Press, 1979).

[24]Edward Coke, *The First Part of the Institutes of the Laws of England, or A Commentary upon Littleton* (1628; reprint, London: Clarke, Saunders and Benning, Maxwell, Sweet, 1832), bk. 1, ch. 1, sect. 1–4a.

claim, English common law gradually evolved a contrary and more lasting precept known as the Doctrine of Ancient Lights. Following the doctrine, obstruction by a neighbor of one's "ancient lights," or sunlight that has radiated unimpeded upon one's property for a period of time, constitutes grounds for legal action against the neighbor. Application of this common-law principle originally required proof of uninterrupted use of the light since "immemorial antiquity,"[25] or testimony verifying continual use from "time immemorial, or time whereof the memory of man runneth not to the contrary."[26] An 1832 act of Parliament set twenty years as the length of time needed for the vesting of rights; in 1959 this period was extended to twenty-seven years.[27] Application of the 1959 Rights of Light Act requires the existence of an actual building with an opening designed specifically for the admission of light, as well as actual use of the admitted light and a substantial and unreasonable obstruction by the adjoining development.

Until a reversal by the Wisconsin court in 1982, the trend of American case law appeared to reject prescriptive sunlight easements as an infringement on the rights of neighboring landowners to develop their properties fully. At issue is whether owners of adjoining land may be enjoined from erecting otherwise lawful structures that would prevent sunlight from striking another's property directly. As early as 1838, in the case of *Parker & Edgarton v. Foote,* a New York Supreme Court judge wrote in repudiation of the English rule,

> There is, I think, no principle upon which the modern English doctrine on the subject of lights can be supported. It is an anomaly in the law. It may do well enough in England; . . . But it cannot be applied in the growing cities and villages of this country, without working the most mischievous consequences. It has never, I think, been deemed a part of our law. Nor do I find that it has been adopted in any of the states.[28]

Over the years, this early conclusion has been held steadfastly in American courts. In 1911, a California appeals court said: "The courts of the United States are practically unanimous that the English doctrine does not apply here, and that the right to light and air cannot be acquired by prescription or adverse user."[29] In 1939, the Delaware court reiterated: "The old general rule [of ancient lights] . . . is not suitable to the conditions of

---

[25]Richard R. Powell, *Powell on Real Property* (1949; reprint, with Patrick J. Rohan, New York: Matthew Bender, 1981), vol. 3, sect. 413, 34–129.

[26]The Prescription Act, 1832, 2 and 3 Wm. 4, Ch. 71.

[27]The Rights of Light Act, 1959, 7 and 8 Eliz. 2, Ch. 56.

[28]19 Wendell 309 (N.Y., 1838), 318.

[29]*Yuba Consol, Goldfields v. Hilton,* 116 P. 712 (Cal. App., 1911), 714.

a new growing and populous country, which contains many large cities and towns, where buildings are often necessarily erected on small lots."[30]

In 1959, this position was again expressed in *Fontainebleau Hotel Corp. v. Forty-five Twenty-five, Inc.,* perhaps the best-known precedent supporting the traditional American viewpoint to this time. The case involved two competing Florida resort hotels, the Fontainebleau and the Eden Roc, located adjacent to each other along the shoreline of Miami Beach. The dispute arose when the owners of the Fontainebleau began construction, at the northern boundary of their property, of a fourteen-story addition that threatened to shadow the cabana, swimming pool, and sunbathing areas of the Eden Roc during the afternoons of the winter tourist season. Alleging that the construction was "actuated by malice and ill will," the owners of the Eden Roc won a temporary injunction enjoining work on the addition on grounds that the building "would interfere with the easements of light and air enjoyed by plaintiff and its predecessors in title for more than twenty years"[31]—an argument echoing the historic English Doctrine of Ancient Lights. This position was rejected by the appeals court, which said: "No American decision has been cited, and independent research has revealed none, in which it has been held that—in the absence of some contractual or statutory obligation—a landowner has a legal right to the free flow of light and air across the adjoining land of his neighbor."[32] Referring to the earlier cases, the court observed, "The English doctrine of 'ancient lights' has been unanimously repudiated in this country."[33] In the absence of a contractual or statutory obligation, adjoining landowners can, by this ruling, build as they wish as long as the construction is within the law, even though the development may injure another by cutting off light and air or interfering with a view across the adjacent land, and notwithstanding a possible finding that the construction "may have been erected partly for spite."[34]

The implicit rule derived from these cases is that solar easements over adjacent land cannot be assumed where the use of the neighboring property is otherwise lawful. Accordingly, the burden of ensuring solar access must be shouldered by the owner of the solar-energy apparatus and cannot be shifted to his neighbors. The rule is not far removed from a caveat issued

[30]*Lynch v. Hill,* 6 A. 2d 614 (Del. Ch. Ct., 1939), 618.
[31]114 So. 2d 357 (Fla. App., 1959), 358.
[32]Ibid., 359.
[33]Ibid.
[34]Ibid. But also see *Sundowner, Inc. v. King,* 509 P. 2d 785 (Idaho, 1973), affirming lower court order partially abating a motel owner's billboard structure that largely obscured a competitor's motel and restricted passage of light and air to its rooms. The decision was based on a finding that the billboard served no useful purpose and that its erection was motivated by spite.

by Blackstone in eighteenth-century Britain. While confirming the English Doctrine of Ancient Lights, he cautioned,

> To erect a house or other building so near to mine, that it stops up my ancient lights and windows, is a nuisance. . . . But in this latter case it is necessary that the windows be ancient, that is, have subsisted there out of mind; otherwise there is no injury done. For he hath as much right to build a new edifice upon his ground, as I have upon mine: Since every man may do what he pleases upon the upright or perpendicular of his own soil; and it was my folly to build so near another's ground.[35]

In 1982 the Wisconsin court made a notable reversal of this position in the case of *Prah v. Maretti*.[36] Unlike the previous cases that considered solar access for uses other than energy generation, *Prah* focused specifically on access to the sun for the purpose of energy. This decision to accord inviolable solar access to a newly constructed residential solar-energy system exceeded even the English doctrine prescribed in the 1959 Rights of Light Act, which requires a period of twenty-seven years for investment of interest.

Glenn Prah was the first in a subdivision to build his house, which included a solar system with rooftop collectors to supply energy for heat and hot water. Subsequently, Richard Maretti also applied for a permit to construct his house on the lot immediately adjacent to and south of Prah's residence. Although Maretti's proposed construction conformed to all applicable codes, Prah objected that the proposed development would shadow his solar collectors, reducing their efficiency and possibly damaging the system. He requested Maretti to move his proposed house further from the common property line, but no agreement was reached. When the city of Muskego and the subdivision's architectural control committee issued him a building permit, Maretti began construction, whereupon Prah filed for an injunction to prevent the proposed building. Initially, the circuit court denied Prah's petition; but when this decision was appealed before the Wisconsin Supreme Court, the judgment was reversed and remanded in favor of ensuring Prah solar access.

In supporting Prah's claim, the court reviewed three reasons that American courts had previously rejected claims of solar-access rights. First, it noted that the right of landowners to use their property as they wished, as long as they caused no physical damage to a neighbor, had been jealously guarded. Second, the court said that sunlight had been previously valued only for aesthetic enjoyment or as illumination, and therefore loss of sun-

[35]William Blackstone, *Commentaries on the Laws of England* (1765–69; reprint, London: Dawsons, 1966), bk. 3, ch. 13, 216–17.
[36]321 N.W. 2d 182 (Wisc., 1982).

light was at most a personal annoyance and of little if any social consequence. Third, it wrote that society then had a significant interest in not restricting or impeding land development.

Rejecting these reasons as reflecting "factual circumstances and social priorities that are now obsolete,"[37] the court proceeded to refute each argument. Citing the *Euclid*[38] case, it first observed that society has increasingly regulated the private use of land for the general welfare. Second, it pointed out that sunlight has, in recent years, taken on a new significance beyond aesthetics and illumination as a source of energy, and that solar access is now important both to the landowner who invests in solar collectors and to society, which has an interest in developing alternative sources of energy. Third, it found that the policy of favoring unhindered private development in an expanding economy is no longer in harmony with social realities. Not incidentally, these views were held not only by the court but also by federal authorities, who advocated them in an amicus curiae brief submitted by the Land and Natural Resources Division of the Department of Justice. It is not unlikely that the court was influenced by the demonstrated federal interest.

In a lengthy dissent, Justice William G. Callow defended the traditional arguments rejected by the majority. He also pointed out the distinction between grounds for a private nuisance claim and cases like *Euclid* that support regulation of private land use in the interests of the public health, safety, morals, or welfare: "While the majority's policy arguments may be directed to a cause for action for public nuisance, we are presented with a private nuisance cause which I believe is distinguishable in this regard."[39] Callow then went on to cite recently enacted state legislation in Wisconsin enabling local governments to adopt procedures for guaranteeing access to sunlight, a consideration all but ignored by the majority except in a footnote. Callow stated,

> I would submit that any policy decisions in this area are best left for the legislature. "What is 'desirable' or 'advisable' or 'ought to be' is a question of policy, not a question of fact. What is 'necessary' or what is 'in the best interest' is not a fact and its determination by the judiciary is an exercise of legislative power when each involves political considerations." (Litigation is a slow, costly, and uncertain method of reform.) . . .
>
> This court's intrusion into an area where legislative action is being taken is unwarranted, and it may undermine a legislative scheme for orderly development not yet fully operational. . . .
>
> Under the majority decision, in a municipality which does not enact the ordinance, a common law cause of action for nuisance exists without any defined rights.[40]

---

[37]Ibid., 189.
[38]*Village of Euclid v. Ambler Realty Co.,* 272 U.S. 365 (1926).
[39]Note 36, 195.
[40]Ibid. Quoting *Town of Beloit v. City of Beloit,* 155 N.W. 2d 633 (Wisc., 1968), 199.

Certainly the route of protecting solar access through legislative regulation could more easily follow Hayek's precepts by providing all parties a full measure of certainty, while the route of private nuisance litigation would not. Whereas predetermined solar-access rules could advise all landowners and developers what to expect in terms of their solar-access rights and of any restrictions necessary to protect the access rights of others prior to building or purchasing, the option of litigation would leave these issues in limbo until a dispute arose. Callow also pointed out that the majority's failure to address the question of need for notice could perpetrate a "vicious cycle" whereby subsequent purchasers of land would not be informed of the legal impediment on the use of a property if it adjoins a development using solar collectors.

Although a policy of encouraging solar-energy use is undoubtedly meritorious and deserving of priority, the majority decision can be faulted on two counts in assuming that policy as a basis for a judicial finding. First, concerning the claim of a private nuisance, it can be fairly said that Prah had failed to take reasonable precautions to protect his solar system, "an unusually sensitive use," against *any* development of the adjacent property to the south, especially considering that his neighbor's proposed construction "conform[ed] to existing deed restrictions and local ordinances" and otherwise had "no 'peculiar nature'" associated with more traditional nuisance activities.[41] If his solar system was so dependent on direct exposure to the sun, surely Prah was remiss in not having the foresight to plan and locate his system to ensure himself absolute solar access in the event that the adjacent property was developed. As Justice Callow noted,

> Mr. Prah could have avoided this litigation by building his own home in the center of his lot instead of only ten feet from the Maretti lot line and/or by purchasing the adjoining lot for his own protection. Mr. Maretti has already moved the proposed location of his home over an additional ten feet to accommodate Mr. Prah's solar collector, and he testified that moving the home any further would interfere with his view of the lake on which the property faces.[42]

Second, and of greater social significance, is the fact that the court's disregard of current state legislative action on the issue of solar access undermined the effectiveness of that legislation. The court's decision substituted ad hoc judicial determination for a more orderly legislative process toward a reasoned and defined public policy of protecting solar access. It was not as if the state of Wisconsin had made no legislative move toward ensuring solar access rights. However admirable the majority's concern for

[41]Ibid., 197, 184, 198.
[42]Ibid., 199.

solar energy utilization, its ruling in *Prah* was a poor one that unnecessarily imposed judicial over legislative determination. As for the federal government's involvement as amicus curiae, the same observation is applicable. Callow said, in regard to federal interest in protecting solar access, "I note that the federal government supports the plaintiff's position in the instant case. If solar energy is in the national interest, federal legislation should be enacted."[43] Certainly, legislated rules would prevent the "mischievous consequences to property owners," warned against in the *Parker & Edgarton v. Foote* case that would result if unimpeded access to sunlight were granted primacy over all other considerations of land use, especially if restrictions were not defined.

Other courts would best serve the ends of solar energy development as well as their judicial charge if they confined their jurisdiction to judging on the constitutional integrity of solar-access legislation, instead of attempting to impose social policy, as did the Wisconsin court. There is no doubt that legislatures have moved toward public policies regarding solar access and solar energy. Wisconsin is not alone in passing solar legislation; it is only one of a vast majority of states that has adopted legislation to promote solar energy development and, in some instances, to ensure solar access. Indeed, under the Carter administration, federal incentives were created to encourage energy conservation and development of alternative sources of energy, including solar.

It is in public legislation rather than private litigation that the problem of solar access can best be solved. As in any aspect of land-use control, the test will ultimately take place at the local level. Several local communities have already taken steps. Some have adopted requirements for solar orientation and access in their subdivision regulations, and others have allowed density bonuses or other favorable considerations for individual projects or planned unit developments designed to take advantage of solar energy. A few have actually required specific utilization of solar energy. Among larger cities, Albuquerque, New Mexico, has been a leader in enacting a comprehensive solar access regulation. Los Angeles has likewise been experimenting with an innovative method of protecting solar access through a "solar envelope" concept developed by Ralph L. Knowles, a professor of architecture at the University of Southern California. Following the precepts of Hayek, legislative zoning requirements for solar access should be well defined beforehand so that developers will not unknowingly find themselves in violation of the law after the fact, a predicament not unlike that suffered in the early nuisance cases prior to *Euclid* as well as by Maretti.

Where localities have sought to prevent the installation of residential solar systems through zoning enforcement, the direction of recent decisions has supported the interests of solar-energy development. In the 1978 New

[43]Ibid., 197.

York case *D'Aurio v. Board of Zoning Appeals of Town of Colonie, Albany County*,[44] for example, a county court upheld the board's refusal to issue a variance from a zoning ordinance requiring a fifty-foot front-yard setback. The variance had been requested by owners of a solar heating system so that their unit could operate more effectively. However, a year later, another New York county court ruled in *Katz v. Bodkin* that a town zoning board's refusal to grant a variance to enable the installation of a domestic solar hot-water system, which would have exceeded the town's 10 percent area limitation on exposed, roof-mounted mechanical equipment, to be "arbitrary and capricious and in violation of law."[45] While the direction of these decisions is encouraging for solar-energy development, a local mandate for solar energy use may be undesirable, since it could effect the exclusion of those unable to afford the substantial initial investment needed to install such an energy-generating system.

Obviously, the court in *Prah v. Maretti* will not have the last say on solar access, and the question of whether building height, bulk, and setback can be restricted to ensure solar access for energy generation will continue to be raised. It would be best for all concerned if predictability were a requirement of any sanctioned regulation.

PAROCHIALISM IN PLANNING

The most overlooked provision of the Standard Acts is the suggestion for a separate commission for regional planning with responsibility and power reaching across jurisdictional boundaries. The distinction drawn between regional authority and state delegation of power to local jurisdictions was doubtless a very deliberate policy decision on the part of the drafters of the acts, for it allowed the states the option of virtually ignoring the regional planning issue. The choice of decentralizing planning and zoning authority is a clear reflection of the conservative leanings of the drafters of the Standard Acts.

Decentralization of public authority has historic roots in America. During the nation's infancy, a pioneer's survival depended first on self-reliance and then on the immediate community, hardly ever on distant government. The practical heritage of the American pioneer meshed perfectly with the philosophical legacy of Smith, Blackstone, and Spencer. Accordingly, the primary duty of public institutions was to protect individual rights, a function seen as best served by smaller units of local government, which presumably could be more responsive to the individual's will than

---

[44]401 N.Y.S. 2d 425 (Sup., 1978).

[45]Index. no. 3312/79, Sup. Ct., Westchester Cty., N.Y. (May 15, 1979). 1 Solar L. Rptr. 495 (1979), 502. See also 428 N.Y.S. 2d 1009 (1979).

could a central authority whose size and power could pose a greater threat to individual determination than an aid to it.

Born under British colonial rule and confirmed during the age of westward expansion, distrust of remote authority persists in America today. Though modern methods of communication have virtually overcome the former barrier of distance, the traditions and prerogatives of local self-government are still jealously guarded. As its very name implies, the United States is based on a federated rather than a centralized system of government. All public authority originates with the states, except for power expressly delegated by the Constitution to the federal government or assigned by individual state legislatures to their creature municipalities. Consistent with this tradition of decentralized authority, the Standard Acts allowed the adoption of any land-use control to be a state and local option with no national standard for enforcement.

Parochialism in planning administration is a peculiarity of the American system. Even in Britain, the wellspring of the American ethic of self-government, contemporary planning is determined according to a linear hierarchy. Local decisions must conform to regional objectives, and regional plans are based, in turn, on national priorities. Appeals against planning orders in Britain are directed to successively higher levels of regional administration. This executive authority is seldom challenged to any serious degree, and British courts are, moreover, inclined to defer to administrative discretion. In contrast, Americans are generally suspicious of government, and legal challenges to the constitutionality of administrative and even legislative orders are commonplace.

Curiously, the distrust that Americans have of government, and of the bureaucracy in particular, has generally been balanced by their implicit confidence in the judiciary. Once appeals have run their course, legal judgments are usually accepted. However, by directing appeals from local planning decisions to the courts instead of to higher regional planning administrations, American practice magnifies the planning effect of the legal system's invisible web. Furthermore, under the tradition of decentralized authority, any opportunity for administrative planning at a regional scale is all but precluded.

In the absence of effective legislative authority, regional planning practice has evolved largely through judge-made case law. One of the most often cited early opinions by a state supreme court concerning regional planning is the 1949 New Jersey decision in *Duffcon Concrete Products, Inc. v. Borough of Cresskill:*

> What may be the most appropriate use of any particular property depends not only on all the conditions, physical, economic and social, prevailing within the municipality and its needs, present and reasonably prospective, but also on the nature of the entire region in which the municipality is located

and the use to which the land in that region has been or may be put most advantageously. The effective development of a region should not and cannot be made to depend upon the adventitious location of municipal boundaries, often prescribed decades or even centuries ago, and based in many instances on considerations of geography, of commerce, or of politics that are no longer significant with respect to zoning.[46]

In this case, the court upheld the exclusion of a cement factory—in today's parlance, a "locally unwanted land use," or LULU—from a residential suburb. Five years later, the same community appeared before the court in *Borough of Cresskill v. Borough of Dumont,* a suit alleging regionally incompatible zoning by a neighboring suburb. The borough of Dumont had decided to rezone a property to permit construction of a shopping center, despite the fact that the land was immediately contiguous to residential areas in Cresskill and two other adjacent communities. The court affirmed a lower ruling that the rezoning was invalid since it was "not in accordance with a comprehensive plan considered in an intercommunity sense."[47] The court commented that the roads bordering the two boroughs "are not Chinese walls," and for a community not to consider the rights of citizens of another "would be to make a fetish out of invisible municipal boundary lines and a mockery of the principles of zoning."[48] Of course, however, courts in other states are under no obligation to follow the principles and admonitions set by the New Jersey court in this case.

Twenty years after *Cresskill,* the New York Court of Appeals faced a similar situation in *Town of Bedford v. Village of Mount Kisco* and came to the opposite conclusion. When Mount Kisco rezoned to permit a six-story, multifamily housing project on land virtually surrounded by one-acre, single-family homes located in the adjoining town of Bedford, the neighboring community filed suit. The court made its ruling for Mount Kisco, considering only the validity of the village's ten-year-old plan and virtually ignoring the interjurisdictional issue. In contrast, the court's dissent took a regional stance, pointing out that a special county regulation, section 452, required that if planning and zoning actions affect properties in neighboring jurisdictions, then their views must be heard. "In the absence of more effective tools to facilitate sensible regional growth," the dissenting judge wrote, "the courts should and are bound to view section 452 as a mandate for equitable resolution of zoning disputes between adjoining municipalities."[49]

The lack of regional planning can create other forms of intermunicipal disputes. In the 1962 Arizona case *City of Scottsdale v. Municipal of the*

[46]64 A. 2d 347 (N.J., 1949), 349–50.
[47]104 A. 2d 441 (N.J., 1954), 444.
[48]Ibid., 445, 446.
[49]306 N.E. 2d 155 (N.Y., 1973), 162.

City of Tempe, the issue was whether one municipality's sewage disposal plant, operating within another city's territorial boundaries, should be subject to the latter's zoning. The case was decided in favor of the city owning the sewage plant, leading the dissenting judge to pose a situation "where City A will locate a sewage disposal plant within the limits of City B, which in turn will retaliate by locating its sewage disposal plant within the limits of City A's borders, and so ad infinitum."[50]

Another form of intercity competition unique to the West is again illustrated in Arizona. Until its modification in 1980, a long-standing provision in state law[51] allowed municipalities to annex contiguous territory by presenting a petition signed by the owners of one half in *value* of the property. A city could thus reserve a large area of unincorporated territory simply by enlisting the cooperation of just one large landowner and by running the equivalent of his acreage in a long, narrow band to encompass a larger parcel. This practice of "strip annexation" has resulted in the crazy-quilt creation of "county islands," or county land completely encircled within a municipality. The process not only prevented other municipalities from annexing land across the strip, but denied property owners and residents of land surrounded by the strip any voice in their situation.

Social Exclusion

The most far-reaching and controversial aspect of parochialism in planning and land-use law is the issue of social exclusion. Such exclusion not only raises questions concerning planning practice and policy, but also raises sociological issues of a magnitude that can only be touched upon in the general scope of this chapter.

Exclusion is an inherent, even a fundamental, attribute of virtually all land-use controls. In zoning, land uses are classified and separated, ostensibly by function, type, and density. However, since different segments of society are invariably associated with each classification, either through residence or occupation, social and economic segregation invariably follows. Sometimes social exclusion is accepted as an unintentional or unavoidable consequence. Historically, however, the motive of social exclusion and the goals of planning are inextricably intertwined. Though unavowed, the exclusion of aliens from London was a basic intent of the early planning proclamations of Elizabeth Tudor, who acted principally at the behest of the guilds whose members felt threatened economically by an increasing influx of cheap immigrant labor. Likewise, land-use controls and zoning in America had their genesis as a means to bar Chinese laundries, and thus Chinese,

---

[50]368 P. 2d 637 (Ariz., 1962), 644.
[51]Ariz. Rev. Stat., Sect. 9–471, amended with Sects. 9–471 (G)–(J), Ariz. Laws 1980, Ch. 226, Sect. 1.

from San Francisco and to exclude the garment industry, and their immigrant European workers, from the more fashionable districts of New York City. More recently, blacks and Hispanics have been the particular targets of racially discriminatory exclusion. The history of zoning since *Euclid* can be chronicled in large part through its use by suburban communities to thwart the intrusion of newcomers and development that threaten unwanted social change.

Though the law now makes explicit racism difficult to enforce through the police power, social segregation has been kept alive through more surreptitious means. Zoning remains a viable tool, since such routine practices as the successive separation of mobile homes from multifamily housing from large-lot, single-family homes implies a division of income categories; and income stratification has in turn distinct social and racial overtones.

In his opinion in the *Euclid* case, federal District Court Judge Westenhaver correctly identified social and economic segregation as an invariable consequence of zoning.[52] Furthermore, in violation of the intention of the Supreme Court decision in that case, some communities have gone beyond zoning's implicit intent of confining "undesirable" elements to certain areas within their jurisdiction. With court approval, they have sometimes been able to exclude certain land uses altogether. In *Euclid,* the high Court found that the village had "determined, not that industrial development shall cease at its boundaries, but that the course of such development shall proceed within definitely fixed lines."[53] In *Duffcon,* however, the New Jersey court felt that regional considerations made the total exclusion of industry from a residential community a reasonable exercise of the borough's zoning power.

While it may be unreasonable to require every community to provide for all conceivable land uses, where a certain "undesirable" development serves a regional purpose—whether it is noxious industry, low-income housing, a low-tax-yielding business, or an activity that uses much federal or municipal revenue, such as a public school—one locality's unwillingness to assume a reasonable proportion of the unwanted land use can place undue burdens on neighboring communities. The practice of local autonomy has resulted in interjurisdictional conflict, as each suburban community erects land-use barriers to protect its social and economic self-interest not only against nuisance activities, outsiders, minority groups, and the poor, but even against increases in middle-class population that might threaten its preferred status quo.

For nearly fifty years after the landmark zoning decisions of the 1920s, the federal courts virtually withdrew from consideration of the police power as applied to planning, relegating the question of exclusion largely to state

---

[52]*Ambler Realty Co. v. Village of Euclid,* 297 F. 307 (1924), 316.
[53]Note 38, 389.

court determination. During this lengthy federal absence, leading state court decisions, notably in Pennsylvania and New Jersey, have been generally sympathetic to the need for a regional perspective on the issue of exclusion. In effect, case law from the states evolved to fill the void left by legislative emphasis on local control. However, with the newly constituted Supreme Court that emerged in the 1970s—six of the nine justices have been appointed since 1970—federal reluctance to intervene in land-use and urban-planning law shifted dramatically to active involvement. Significantly, the federal attitude has been in marked contrast to the position established earlier by the state courts.

Although the federal judiciary has invariably ruled against exclusion where racial discrimination is overt, it has been more receptive to regulations imposed by communities to protect the local environment, even though the restrictions may effect exclusion in numerical and economic terms. Several Supreme Court decisions confirm this position. In *Agins v. City of Tiburon,*[54] the high Court approved ordinances enacted by the exclusive San Francisco suburb of Tiburon rezoning a five-acre plot acquired for residential development to permit no more than five single-family homes. In another instance, the Court refused to hear appeals from a developers' association protesting restrictions imposed by the city of Petaluma that limited residential development to about one half of market demand.[55] The Court apparently dismissed the trial court's opinion that a grave decline and deterioration of the regional housing stock, affecting lower-income groups and population mobility in particular, would result if other developing communities in the metropolitan region were to respond by erecting their own legal barricades against immigration.[56] On the grounds of protecting "family values," the Court also upheld an ordinance passed by the village of Belle Terre, New York, that prohibited the occupancy of one-family dwellings by more than two unrelated persons. The regulation was effectively aimed at prohibiting a communal home maintained by a group of students of a nearby Long Island university.[57]

An even more contentious dimension to the problem of exclusion arose in the 1976 case of *City of Eastlake v. Forest City Enterprises, Inc.*[58] In its decision, the Supreme Court affirmed the power of a local electorate to act as its own legislature in determining zoning questions. Despite the likelihood that the voters of most established suburban communities would be generally suspicious of any change in local land use—and almost invariably

[54]447 U.S. 255 (1980).
[55]*Construction Industry Association of Sonoma County v. City of Petaluma,* 522 F. 2d 897 (1975). *Cert.* den., 424 U.S. 934 (1976).
[56]*Construction Industry Association of Sonoma County v. City of Petaluma,* 375 F. Supp. 574 (1974).
[57]*Village of Belle Terre v. Boraas,* 416 U.S. 1 (1974).
[58]426 U.S. 668 (1976).

would be opposed to the introduction of low-income housing in particular—the Court has refused to question the motives of an electorate acting on an issue as long as racial discrimination is not made explicit. In spite of the exclusionary effect of a local referendum barring low-cost public housing, the Court in the 1971 case *James v. Valtierra* maintained that "provisions for referendums demonstrate devotion to democracy, not to bias, discrimination, or prejudice."[59]

The problem is made even more difficult by yet another holding of the Court that "racially discriminatory intent" and not just "ultimate effect" must be proven by victims of exclusion.[60] Also, in an explicit denial of the regional view, the high Court has denied litigational standing to protestants who do not live in the excluding community.[61]

While some state courts have ruled in conformance with the Supreme Court and upheld the referendum and initiative processes in zoning despite the probable exclusionary impact of locally held elections, other state courts have sought to address the issue on their own terms. Although the California court has concurred with the Supreme Court's position in *Eastlake* that zoning is a legislative act subject to the ballot, state courts in California have not hesitated to censure zoning by popular vote when regional considerations and exclusionary effects have not been taken into account. As the California Supreme Court stated in 1976, in *Associated Home Builders of the Greater Eastbay, Inc. v. City of Livermore,*

> Municipalities are not isolated islands remote from the needs and problems of the area in which they are located; thus an ordinance, superficially reasonable from the limited viewpoint of the municipality, may be disclosed as unreasonable when viewed from a larger perspective.[62]

Like other courts condemning parochial and exclusionary interests in local zoning, the California judiciary has been apt to cite *National Land and Investment Company v. Kohn,* a landmark decision passed in Pennsylvania in 1965. In the case, the Pennsylvania Supreme Court rejected a township's attempt to restrict development largely to residential four-acre minimum lots, arguing the regional view against exclusion:

---

[59]402 U.S. 137 (1971), 141.

[60]*Village of Arlington v. Metropolitan Housing Development Corp.,* 429 U.S. 252 (1977). But see decision on remand requiring village under the Fair Housing Act of the Civil Rights Act of 1968 to refrain from policies that effectively foreclose construction of low-cost housing. 558 F. 2d 1283 (1977), *cert. den.,* 434 U.S. 1025 (1978).

[61]*Warth v. Seldin,* 422 U.S. 490 (1975).

[62]557 P. 2d 473 (Cal., 1976), 487.

The township's brief raises (but, unfortunately, does not attempt to answer) the interesting issue of the township's responsibility to those who do not yet live in the township but who are part, or may become part, of the population expansion of the suburbs. Four acre zoning represents Easttown's position that it does not desire to accommodate those who are pressing for admittance to the township unless such admittance will not create any additional burdens upon governmental functions and services. The question posed is whether the township can stand in the way of the natural forces which send our growing population into hitherto undeveloped areas in search of a comfortable place to live. We have concluded not. A zoning ordinance whose primary purpose is to prevent the entrance of newcomers in order to avoid future burdens, economic or otherwise, upon the administration of public services and facilities can not be held valid.[63]

The position of state courts counter to the federal judicial stance on the question of regional responsibility in local zoning was established by a somewhat later landmark passed by the New Jersey Supreme Court in 1975. In *Southern Burlington County N.A.A.C.P. v. Township of Mount Laurel,* the court denounced exclusion under any guise and required local communities to assume a "fair share" of regional responsibility for low and moderate income housing, noting that

> It is fundamental and not to be forgotten that the zoning power is a police power of the state and the local authority is acting only as a delegate of that power and is restricted in the same manner as is the state. So, when regulation does have a substantial external impact, the welfare of the state's citizens beyond the borders of the particular municipality cannot be disregarded and must be recognized and served.[64]

Scholars of planning and planning law have generally been critical of those federal decisions that condone local exclusion at the expense of regional considerations. Some have attributed the actions of the federal judiciary to inexperience, pointing to the long abstention of the federal courts from land-use zoning litigation. In his dissent in *Eastlake,* Supreme Court Justice John Paul Stevens acknowledged the greater experience of state courts on planning and zoning matters: "Although this Court has decided only a handful of zoning cases, literally thousands of zoning disputes have been resolved by state courts."[65] The late Professor Hagman was much more critical of the federal courts. Commenting on the Court's decision to uphold Belle Terre's exclusionary ordinance, he wrote,

[63]215 A. 2d 597 (Pa., 1965), 612.
[64]336 A. 2d 713 (N.J., 1975), 734, 726.
[65]Note 58, 683.

> There is only one way to develop a coherent body of land-use control case law: ignore the decisions of federal courts. As a general rule, the decisions of federal courts on land-use controls are aberrant, berserk, unknowledgeable, and unpredictable. *Belle Terre* illustrates the general rule. The Court did not know what it was doing.[66]

(It should be fairly stated that Professor Hagman apparently thought equally poorly of the Pennsylvania court, despite its early leadership in assuming a regional view. He also wrote: "As a general rule, federal cases on land-use controls are berserk. They are relatives to the Pennsylvania cases.")[67]

As the New Jersey and California decisions illustrate, state courts are not reticent about asserting their independence from the federal judiciary. Babcock observes,

> One of the intriguing aspects of the American federal system is that state courts may and, indeed, do interpret provisions in state constitutions which are identical to provisions in the United States Constitution in a contrary manner to construction by the United States Supreme Court.[68]

Mount Laurel is the epitome of this state-court independence, for in its decision, the New Jersey court evaded any possible reversal of its decision in a federal court by basing its judgment solely on New Jersey law and the state constitution, "the requirements of which may be more demanding than those of the federal Constitution."[69]

Even apparently conscientious local planning can be motivated by exclusion or be suspect of exclusionary intent. One former planning-commission member in Aspen, Colorado, a fashionable Rocky Mountain resort town, has complained that the present planning staff of his community has been so involved in environmental concerns that planning administration in the area has become effectively exclusionary. Burdensome local design review processes and extraordinarily restrictive local code requirements imposed for such ostensibly worthy purposes as energy conservation can so limit building production that housing becomes affordable only for the wealthy. Writing on Marin County, California, the home county of the town of Tiburon that figured in the *Agins* case, planning professor Bernard J. Frieden comments,

[66]Donald G. Hagman, "Reporter's Comments on *Village of Belle Terre v. Boraas*," *Land Use Law & Zoning Digest* 26, no. 6 (1974), 3.

[67]Donald G. Hagman, "Comment," *Land Use Law & Zoning Digest* 26, no. 7 (1974), 10.

[68]Richard F. Babcock, *"Eastlake v. Forest City Enterprises,"* *Land Use Law & Zoning Digest* 28, no. 8 (1976), 4.

[69]*Southern Burlington County N.A.A.C.P. v. Township of Mount Laurel,* 336 A. 2d 713 (N.J., 1975). See also *"Mount Laurel II,"* 456 A. 2d 390 (N.J., 1983), and *Oakwood at Madison, Inc. v. Township of Madison,* 371 A. 2d (N.J., 1977).

> Marin County . . . is the best place to look for an understanding of what it means to stop suburban growth in the name of environmental protection. It means closing the gates to people who may want to move in and, where possible, even to people who may want to visit; turning to state and federal governments for help in paying the costs of exclusivity; and maintaining a tone of moral righteousness while providing a better living environment for the established residents.[70]

As discussed earlier, part of the reason for the high cost of real estate and the unavailability of housing in many growth areas of the West is the overly stringent administration of planning and zoning, whether deliberately exclusionary or not.

Exclusion is a complex and divisive issue that can split normal ideological alliances. Builders and developers are frequently opposed by local real estate interests. Homeowners wishing to preserve and enhance their property values are pitted against potential home buyers hoping to become part of the same community. Civil-rights groups pushing for open housing are often opposed by local environmental interests. Some residents of retirement communities, such as Sun City and Youngtown, Arizona—typically grandparents themselves—have sought outright age-discriminate zoning to bar the entry of families with young children (much like their own progeny), both to forestall potential "nuisances" and to avoid paying school taxes. Sometimes those who normally might advocate free market determination turn to public regulation, while others who might normally seek public protection in legislative control find themselves in favor of open market determination. Even local planners have become alienated from their professional colleagues who maintain a more regional view. Much of the blame for these divisions can be reasonably traced to the parochialism inherent in the Standard Acts.

Considering the early history of land-use controls and the exclusionary origins of zoning itself, it can be fairly maintained that zoning and exclusion have always been converse sides of the same coin. Even without exclusionary intent, zoning—and virtually any other type of community planning and design control, for that matter—implies some form of exclusion. There are communities that unquestionably employ land planning as a cover for exclusion, at best to preserve long-held and worthy values, at worst to advance thoughtless self-interests. The issue deserves greater attention than this brief synopsis affords. Public planners, including urban designers, must be constantly aware that the controls they devise and administer— even for the best ends—have an inherent tendency to exclude. They must not permit their obligation to their client locality to obscure their profes-

---

[70]Bernard J. Frieden, *The Environmental Protection Hustle* (Cambridge: M.I.T. Press, 1979), 37.

sional responsibility for the regional community as a whole, and must strive to mitigate, or at least to recognize, this dark side of planning. As the Pennsylvania court said in the *National Land* case: "Zoning is a means by which a governmental body can plan for the future—it may not be used as a means to deny the future."[71]

The test of a just and humane society is not whether the majority rules, for even communist oligarchies today are wont to call themselves democratic republics and, notwithstanding the absence of truly free elections, can probably claim broad support from the majority in many cases. Rather, the test is whether the rights of the unpopular and disenfranchised are not sacrificed to the "public interest" and the "community good." In the delicate balance in which American freedom and democracy reside, the protection of these individual rights from the unjust demands of the majority is an essential duty of the courts. For if one man can be made to suffer at the hands of an electorate and under the sanction of the courts, so then might any other.

Legislative Regional Reforms

Although traditional zoning practice according to the Standard Acts has defied change, there have been attempts to establish substantive regional planning authority. Some regional and metropolitan associations have been formed voluntarily; of these, the greatest success has usually been enjoyed by agencies focused on a specific problem or issue, in which mutual cooperation is of obvious benefit for all. One such regional association is the Port Authority of New York and New Jersey, a bi-state cooperative agency coordinating port and transportation facilities at the interstices of the two states.

Another association that has had notable success in managing an exceptionally broad spectrum of regional responsibilities is the Metropolitan Council of Minneapolis-St. Paul, whose jurisdiction encompasses the Twin Cities' entire seven-county area. Growing out of cooperative associations initiated for such purposes as operating airports and managing sanitary districts, the council now serves under state mandate and its membership is appointed by the governor. Its planning authority has expanded to include housing, transportation, airports, water resources, waste management, recreational open space, health care, aging, criminal justice, and cable communications. The council is invested with taxing as well as planning powers and possesses approval authority over capital programs for municipal-waste management and transit. In addition to reviewing authority over the plans of local municipalities, counties, and special districts, the council is also empowered to review any "proposed matter" to determine whether it is of

[71]*National Land and Investment Company v. Kohn,* 215 A. 2d 597 (Pa., 1965), 610.

"metropolitan significance."[72] The apparent paradigm of the Twin Cities Council is, however, the exception rather than the rule, since parochial interests have generally been destructive of attempts at metropolitan government.

More often than not, of all the issues facing metropolitan or regional government, land use is among the most controversial, since smaller jurisdictions, especially in the suburbs, frequently perceive regional decisions on land use and population distribution as benefiting big-city interests, not their own. The most comprehensive effort at fundamental change in regional planning is embodied in *A Model Land Development Code*. The prototypal legislative reform is the result of the American Law Institute's study of land-use planning controls completed in 1975, in which the issue of regional planning was a primary consideration. The approach of the *Model Code* is summarized as follows:

> The Code follows the principle that policy should be established at the state level but the enforcement of that policy should be handled by the local Land Development Agencies in deciding particular cases, subject to appeal to a State Land Adjudicatory Board on the record made before the local Land Development Agency. Thus the state legislature and the State Land Planning Agency determine policies, the local Land Development Agencies administer them in conjunction with local policies, and the State Land Adjudicatory Board exercises an appellate function.[73]

The commentary cites several instances in which reform of land-use regulation has granted increased "new powers for state or regional agencies."[74] Most notable is land-development controls in Hawaii, where the model of the Standard Acts was rejected in 1961 in favor of returning substantial power to plan and regulate land development to state government.[75] Land in Hawaii is divided into four zoning classifications: urban, rural, agricultural, and conservation. Counties are able to designate allowable uses within some zones but under the general regulation of the state land-use commission.

In 1972, California voters adopted the Coastal Zone Conservation Act, which subjects all development with a thousand yards of the coast to regulation by regional authorities, thus effectively preempting local control. Of even wider regional significance in the state is a requirement that every city and county have a general plan addressing several elements: land use, circulation, housing, conservation, open space, noise, and safety (including seis-

[72]Minn. Stat. Ann., Sect. 473. 173.

[73]American Law Institute, *A Model Land Development Code: Complete Text and Commentary* (Philadelphia: American Law Institute, 1976), 253.

[74]Ibid., 252.

[75]Ibid., 249. Citing Haw. Rev. Stat., Sect. 205 (1968).

mic safety), the guidelines for which are prepared in detail by state agencies. In the 1981 decision *Camp v. Mendocino County Board of Supervisors,*[76] a state appellate court upheld the state's authority to ensure that local plans be consistent with state guidelines, thus providing effective regional oversight over local planning.

In addition to Hawaii and California, the reporters for the *Model Code* also cite increased regional planning authority in the states of Vermont, Wisconsin, Massachusetts, and Florida. However, despite these reforms, it has been asserted that states adopting comprehensive planning legislation have been "for the most part, exotic,"[77] and that major states, such as New York, Pennsylvania, Michigan, and Illinois, have not passed significant comprehensive planning legislation. While holding this view, Clifford Weaver and Richard Babcock nonetheless point out that state legislative attempts to address particular problems involving land use have been considerably more successful. They write,

> By the end of 1975, 13 states had adopted legislation requiring local governments to adopt land use plans, 10 had legislation mandating the adoption of local subdivision controls, and six also required the adoption of local zoning regulations. More than requiring local action, however, states have been preempting local action and taking over direct control of specific areas of land use regulation. Between 1969 and 1975, over 20 states adopted legislation giving a state regulatory agency power to approve or disapprove power plant and transmission line sites; six states had adopted controls over siting of developments of regional impact, and five states were directly regulating the siting of surface mines. Twenty-four states had adopted legislation giving the state control over areas of "critical concern."[78]

At the national level, initiatives toward regional planning have followed the American tradition of limiting federal participation to optional and indirect financial incentives rather than to direct action under the police power. Typical of such federal involvement are the federal Coastal Zone Management Act of 1972,[79] under whose auspices state coastal management programs such as that in California have received funding, and the highly successful 701 program, which provided federal financial assistance to encourage local communities to plan. Originally enacted under Section 701 of the Housing Act of 1954, the 701 program evolved from aid only to small communities to a 1964 amendment allowing aid also to urban counties regardless of population, provided the planning was coordinated with metro-

[76]176 Cal. Rptr. 620 (App., 1981).
[77]Weaver and Babcock, *City Zoning,* 245.
[78]Ibid., 246.
[79]16 U.S.C. 1451, Coastal Zone Management Act of 1972, Pub. L. 92–583, 86 Stat. 1280.

politan-wide programs of comprehensive planning. Unfortunately, Section 701 was repealed by the Reagan administration in 1981.

The formation of Metropolitan Councils of Governments under the provisions of the 1954 Housing Act and the Model Cities Act of 1966[80] established, for any given interjurisdictional area, a body representative of local governments but capable of functioning as a metropolitan or regional "clearinghouse" for development review. Pursuant to the Intergovernmental Cooperation Act of 1968, Circular A-95 of the federal Office of Management and Budget enabled such clearinghouses to review applications for some one hundred federal aid programs to determine that proposed projects complied with area-wide plans and to identify possible interjurisdictional problems and opportunities. The effectiveness of this review process was mixed, however, because of variations in enforcement among the intergovernmental councils whose constituent localities participate only on a voluntary basis. In any event, under the Reagan administration, which has been unsympathetic to governmental regulation in general and opposed to other than local planning controls in particular, the process has been discontinued.

The most ambitious federal effort to encourage regional planning experienced an abortive start. In the early 1970s, Representative Morris K. Udall of Arizona introduced legislation that would have provided grants-in-aid to states instituting direct state involvement in land planning. The bill called for the development of regional planning guidelines and state review of local decisions having regional impact but, in recognition of the strong sentiment for local control, it continued to permit state delegation of authority to local governments. Though the legislation would have exerted federal influence over land development as never before contemplated, the federal involvement would not have been mandatory; its role would have been to provide an economic inducement to encourage coordination of local planning with state guidance and review. Despite passage of the Senate version, which was sponsored by Henry M. Jackson of Washington state, the House bill failed after President Nixon withdrew his earlier support, in apparent response to conservative sentiment opposed to the idea of regional controls and federal involvement.[81]

Although the fervor of environmental consciousness experienced during the early 1970s has perhaps leveled off in recent years, the awareness instilled at that time has left its mark, not only in state planning legislation but in the administration of federal agencies and programs that now customarily require consideration of the policy effect of federal activity on land and land use.

---

[80]42 U.S.C. 3301, 3334, Demonstration Cities and Metropolitan Development Act of 1966, Pub. L. 89-754, 80 Stat. 1255, 1262.

[81]Land Use Planning Act of 1974, 93rd Cong., 2nd Sess., H.R. 10294.

COMPREHENSIVE REFORMS

Allowing active state and regional participation in planning is but one reform outlined in the ALI *Model Code*. Other shortcomings experienced in the history of zoning and identified by scholarly critiques of the established system of development controls are also addressed.

To enhance flexibility in planning, the *Model Code* provides greater administrative discretion in land-use controls. This move is seen by several observers as an adaptation of planning practice in Britain, where the administrative branch of government has traditionally enjoyed greater trust and authority than in America. In particular, the code includes provisions for government regulation of private property through the acquisition of interest and payment of compensation to the property owner—a concept that is standard in British controls but uncommon in the United States. Allison Dunham and Fred P. Bosselman, the chief and associate reporters of the code, deny any intent to emulate the British.[82] However, in attempting to overcome constitutional limitations in police-power flexibility in public controls over private property, and given the similarity in British and American social traditions, it is not unnatural that any attempt in American law to achieve greater discretion in controls should tread the same path that the British have already explored.

In lieu of present practice, which involves the administration of an array of regulatory means—zoning, subdivision controls, variances, and special exceptions—the ALI *Model Code* provides only two basic classifications, the "general development permit" and the "special development permit." The former allows "development for which a permit will be granted as of right of compliance with the terms of the ordinance."[83] If preestablished standards are met, a general development permit would be issued in much the same manner that a building permit is now granted when zoning requirements are met. The greatest change in the *Model Code* is the emphasis on administrative discretion, which is made possible by the second device, the special development permit. This permit is granted "only after exercise of discretion of an administrative agency in accordance with the criteria of this code and any additional criteria provided for in the ordinance."[84] Flexibility in land-use control is extended through permits that may be issued with conditions attached. Special development permits allow the same options now covered by variances, special exceptions, planned unit development, and other means, but the administration of these controls is consolidated under the proposed code.

---

[82]Allison Dunham and Fred P. Bosselman, "The Reporters' Reply," *Land-Use Controls Ann.* (1971) 113–14.
[83]*Model Code: Complete Text,* sect. 2–101 (2)(a), 30.
[84]Ibid., sect. 2–101 (2)(b), 30.

The integration of flexibility as an intrinsic aspect of the *Model Code* is an attempt to overcome the "static, end-state concept of land-use control"[85] implicit in the Standard Acts. Jeremiah D. O'Leary, Jr., notes the supplanting of the end-state premise of urban planning associated with the City Beautiful movement with controls based on more contemporary social-science theories of continuous planning. He writes,

> The ALI Model Land Development Code signals the demise of old-time utopian planning. In place of the crumbling edifice of the architect-planner we have the social scientist's modular masterpiece, just right for the fragmented incrementalists we have become. No one should be surprised that the authors of the Code took the approach they did.[86]

One of the most notable reforms suggested by the *Model Code* is the unification of local planning administration, which is presently divided among several bodies: the legislature, planning commission, board of adjustment, and staff—and with de facto participation by the judiciary. In place of this split authority, the code suggests a single Land Development Agency, the composition of which is deliberately left general: "the local governing body or any committee, commission, board or officer of the local government."[87] This wording in the code would allow planning professionals virtually to take over the responsibility and authority now held by the planning commission. In addition to its advisory and regulatory functions, the agency would also be able to exercise a degree of appellate authority in its issuance of special permits, thus obviating the need for the board of adjustment. By consolidating the various planning and zoning functions in one professional body under the aegis of the local elected legislature, the authors expect that many of the problems associated with the present system would be reduced.

Judicial review under the *Model Code* is also specifically provided for. Daniel R. Mandelker notes, however, that the code would shift much of the review process from the judiciary to an administrative agency by the delegation of substantive review power.

> My expectation is that the Code's extensive conversion to an administrative process will have the effect of narrowing the scope of judicial review over what we now consider zoning decisions. I predict that the scope of judicial review of most decisions will at least be no broader than the review now afforded variances and special exceptions. It is even more likely that the scope

[85]American Law Institute, *A Model Land Development Code: Tentative Draft No. 1* (Philadelphia: American Law Institute, 1968), 196.

[86]Jeremiah D. O'Leary, Jr., "On Being an Incrementalist during a Revolution," *Land-Use Controls Ann.*, (1971), 43.

[87]*Model Code: Complete Text*, sect. 2-301(1), 71.

of court review will come to be comparable to the review of legislative zoning changes enjoying the presumption of constitutionality.[88]

Mandelker further believes that direct attacks on the constitutionality of controls would be discouraged by the exhaustion principle, whereby a complainant would be unable to challenge the constitutionality of a land-control ordinance until he has exhausted all administrative appeal remedies provided for in the ordinance itself. The developer, it is thought, would hesitate to embark on the time-consuming and costly route of appeals, sensing a reluctance of the judiciary to interfere with defined administrative functions. Mandelker concludes,

> In brief, the impact of the total ALI structure will be to shift the emphasis in land development controls to an administrative process, with opportunities for judicial intervention decreasing as control procedures improve and as state agencies hopefully exercise a positive influence on the setting of standards and criteria.[89]

If Mandelker is correct in his analysis, the resemblance of the judicial function under the proposed code to the British reliance on executive control is very evident.

David Heeter and Frank Bangs summarize the proposed change in local development controls in terms of four provisions.[90] First, the administration of development controls would be vested in a single administrative agency, and the local legislature would be discouraged from involvement in individual development decisions. Second, although the conventional zoning mechanism would be retained, emphasis would be placed on more flexible control techniques that permit greater administrative discretion. Third, the adoption of a land-development plan would be made a prerequisite for most development control powers. Finally, the constitutional limitations of controls derived from the police power would be overcome by public acquisition of land and through the payment of compensation.

While few analysts of zoning practice would fault the thrust of reform, some have sounded cautionary notes. Among others, Weaver and Babcock warn that reform cannot assume that "'correct' zoning decisions depend merely upon a disinterested assessment of objective facts," a premise that they attribute especially to reforms that suggest "professionalization" as the solution to the problems and abuses that plague planning and zoning. They write: "Having all the facts may be helpful to guide policy, but it

---

[88]Daniel R. Mandelker, "Judicial Review of Land Development Controls under the ALI Model Code," *Land-Use Controls Ann.* (1971), 101, 103.

[89]Ibid., 104.

[90]David Heeter and Frank Bangs, "Local Planning and Development Control: One Bad Apple Spoils the Barrel," *Land-Use Controls Ann.* (1971), 28.

cannot make policy." Policy, they point out, is a political question to be decided in the political arena. The reality is that "local zoning issues and decisions are a sui generis combination of policy, politics, fact, and emotion." Reform should not seek "to eliminate 'politics' from the process or even to eliminate illegitimate and illegal influence from the process. None of those is fully possible."[91] As they note from an Oregon appellate decision, "In our system and tradition, political process means democratic process."[92] They write,

> The combined need to retain discretion while eliminating red tape and providing certainty is beginning to force urban officials to accept procedural reform as a way of assuring the development community that the city is prepared to deal quickly and fairly with any legitimate proposal. The acceptance of such reforms also serves to quiet the neighborhoods, which want assurance that zoning discretion is not just a cover to zoning abuse. . . .
>
> There is nothing glamorous or exciting about drafting 150 pages of zoning ordinance provisions designed to assure that discretion is exercised openly, honestly, fairly, and in a way that allows both applicant and objector to influence and understand the ultimate decision. We are convinced, however, that the conscientious implementation of such mundane procedural reforms will do more to rationalize local land use regulation than a book full of revolutionary ideas or a shelf full of multi-colored master plans.[93]

This recommendation by Weaver and Babcock that reform of planning regulation should focus on ensuring the fair and proper exercise of discretionary authority is not conceptually different from admonitions made by Kenneth Culp Davis that strict adherence to definitive standards of administrative procedure should be the cornerstone of reform.[94] In any event, legislative response to more ambitious, comprehensive reform has been predictably slow in terms of adoption.

CIVIL RIGHTS AND ANTITRUST

In addition to innovations and issues arising from planning practice, new areas of legal concern have emerged since 1978. In that year, the Supreme Court held that where there is a police-power violation of individual rights guaranteed by the Constitution, local governing bodies and their officials can be sued for monetary damages under the provisions of federal civil rights legislation. The Court in the same year also found municipalities

---

[91]Weaver and Babcock, *City Zoning*, 271–73.

[92]*Anderson v. Peden,* 569 P. 2d 633 (Ore. App., 1977), 640. Quoted in Weaver and Babcock, *City Zoning*, 260.

[93]Weaver and Babcock, *City Zoning*, 272–73.

[94]Kenneth Culp Davis, *Discretionary Justice* (Westport, C.T.: Greenwood, 1969).

subject to federal antitrust laws, which permit awards of trebled damages to injured parties. The effect of these rulings on public planning has been considerable, not least because of the intimidating threat of heavy monetary judgments against units and officials of local government.

Civil Rights

The Civil Rights Act of 1871, known as Section 1983 of the federal statutes,[95] prohibits "persons" acting "under color of law" from infringing upon individual rights guaranteed by the Constitution. In *Monell v. Department of Social Services of the City of New York,*[96] a 1978 case dealing with a city policy of compelling pregnant employees to take unpaid leaves of absence, the Supreme Court concluded that local governing bodies fall within the definition of "persons" under the law. According to the decision, where a civil rights violation exists, the offending municipality can be subject not only to declaratory and injunctive rulings but can also be required to pay monetary damages to the injured party. Two years after *Monell,* in *Owen v. City of Independence,*[97] a case arising from the improper firing of a city's chief of police, the high Court widened municipal exposure to adverse civil rights judgments by rejecting the city's contention that it enjoyed governmental immunity based upon "good faith."

Cases subsequent to *Monell* and *Owen* have lessened municipal vulnerability to civil rights actions somewhat. Notably, in *City of Oklahoma City v. Tuttle,* a 1985 case concerning the shooting death of a citizen by a police officer, the Supreme Court decided that a municipality is not liable for a civil rights violation unless the action is shown to be the result of "an existing, unconstitutional municipal policy."[98] However, in 1986, in *Pembaur v. City of Cincinnati,*[99] the Court found a municipality liable if a single decision by an authorized policymaker violates a constitutionally protected right, in this case a county prosecutor instructing police officers to make a forcible entry without a search warrant. To follow this line of reasoning, where a land-use restriction can be shown to deprive landowners of any beneficial use of their property, a municipality and its officials could conceivably be subject to civil rights liability under Section 1983.

Since *Monell,* the number of civil rights suits against units of local government has multiplied substantially, and the question of governmental liability for infractions of Section 1983 incurred in the exercise of land-use regulation still remains an open issue.

---

[95]42 U.S.C. 1983, 17 Stat. 13 (42nd Cong., Sess. I, Ch. 22) (1871).
[96]436 U.S. 658 (1978).
[97]445 U.S. 622 (1980).
[98]____U.S.____(1985), 105 S. Ct. 2427, 2436.
[99]____U.S.____(1986), 54 U.S.L.W. 4289.

Antitrust

The history of municipal liability under federal antitrust laws is not unlike that of municipal liability under civil rights legislation. The Sherman Antitrust Act of 1890[100] and the Clayton Antitrust Act of 1914,[101] which prohibit any contract, combination, or conspiracy leading to a monopoly of trade or commerce, have been proclaimed by the Supreme Court as "the Magna Carta of free enterprise."[102] In the past, the acts have been construed as applying only to the anticompetitive activities of private commerce rather than of government. This interpretation was largely derived from a 1943 case, *Parker v. Brown*,[103] in which the Supreme Court, noting the sovereignty of the states in the American system of federalism, ruled that the Sherman Act does not bind the conduct of a state acting through legislation.

In 1978, in *City of Lafayette v. Louisiana Power & Light Co.*,[104] a private investor-owned utility company claimed that municipal public utilities had conspired to eliminate competition in violation of federal antitrust laws. Although the city contended that it was immune from antitrust liability on the premise that the "state action" doctrine derived from *Parker* exempted municipal acts conducted pursuant to state legislation, the Supreme Court ruled that in the absence of an overriding state policy, municipalities are indeed subject to antitrust regulations, since they themselves are not sovereign. This viewpoint was confirmed again by the Court in 1982 in *Community Communications Co., Inc. v. City of Boulder.* In this case, the city of Boulder was sued by a television cable company objecting to a moratorium that prohibited it from installing new cable while other companies were invited to enter the market. The Court said that without a "clear articulation and affirmative expression" of specific state policy, a city cannot assume exemption from antitrust actions.[105]

Until its reversal by a federal district court in early 1986, a 1984 decision, *Unity Ventures v. County of Lake*,[106] seemed a realization of the worst fears of local officials regarding antitrust actions. The case was brought about by the refusal of officials of Lake County and the Village of Grayslake, Illinois, to grant a developer permission to connect a proposed subdivision outside the village limits to a public sewer system. The court found the defendants were not immune from antitrust actions, thereby upholding a jury award of damages to the plaintiff of $19 million, half under Section

[100]15 U.S.C. 1–7, 26 Stat. 209 (51st. Cong., Sess. I, Ch. 647) (1890).
[101]15 U.S.C. 12–27, 38 Stat. 730, Pub. L. 212 (63rd Cong., Sess. 2, Ch. 323) (1914).
[102]*United States v. Topco Associates, Inc.*, 405 U.S. 596 (1971), 610.
[103]317 U.S. 341 (1943).
[104]435 U.S. 389 (1978).
[105]455 U.S. 40 (1982), 54–56.
[106]C.C.H. 1984–1 Trade Case 65, 883.

1983 and half under antitrust laws. The latter amount was trebled under the law, resulting in a total damages award of $38 million. In the 1984 decision, the possibility was left open that local officials named in the suit could be held personally liable. Twenty-seven months later, much to the relief of planning officials, the decision was overturned.[107]

Predictably, the outcome of *Lafayette, Community Communications,* and the initial decision in *Unity Ventures* caused great consternation among municipal officials. As a consequence, considerable pressure was brought upon Congress, which in the intervening period between the 1984 court decision on *Unity Ventures* and its reversal in 1986, passed the Local Government Antitrust Act of 1984.[108] The act disallowed the levying of monetary damages against local government and officials in an antitrust action. Although the act was not retroactive and thus did not negate the 1984 *Unity Ventures* decision, it is nonetheless likely that the congressional action influenced the court in 1986 to reverse its earlier decision. The case is notable as one whose decision created such political furor that it prompted congressional action, which in turn may have influenced the same court to reverse its original decision. One commentator labeled the first judgment "The Case that Roared."[109]

In early 1985, the Supreme Court, in *Town of Hallie v. City of Eau Claire,* further clarified the extent of local government exemption from antitrust regulation. The Court recognized the immunity of local government when an action is taken that is "pursuant to a clearly articulated state policy to replace competition . . . with regulation."[110] As in *Unity Ventures,* the *Hallie* case involved the monopoly of sewage-treatment facilities; unlike the earlier suit, however, the plaintiffs in the case were four unincorporated townships protesting the city's requirement that sewer-treatment services be tied to sewage collection and transportation on the condition that the area(s) served be annexed to the city by referendum election.

The issues of civil rights and antitrust exemplify the fluid nature of land-use controls. Planning law has evolved and progressed in several areas: flexibility in planning regulation to foster sound, creative development and satisfy the private entrepreneur as well as the community as a whole; a reasonable, just reconciliation between legitimate local interests and increasingly pressing regional concerns; and thoughtful accommodation of new technologies that promise greater efficiency in the use of environmental resources. In a pluralist democracy like the United States, the resolution lies not in ideological absolutes but in a dynamic tension between opposing

---

[107]631 F. Supp. 181 (1986).
[108]Pub. L. 98-544, 98 Stat. 2750 (1984).
[109]Eric Damien Kelly, "Q & A: Municipal Liability," *Planning* 51 (Feb. 1985), 17–18.
[110]____U.S.____(1985), 105 S. Ct. 1713, 1721.

ideas and viewpoints, between what is perceived to be the public interest and the private goals of individuals. As champions of the values of foresight and community, public planners must participate in legislative and adversary law, for only through vigorous advocacy of diverse beliefs by those having conviction of purpose can this society continue to survive and flourish.

LATE DEVELOPMENTS

On June 2, 1986, in *Corrigan v. City of Scottsdale*,[111] the Arizona Supreme Court ruled that a landowner is entitled to monetary damages for a temporary taking of property caused by a zoning ordinance that is later found to be invalid. The court confirmed a lower court ruling that the transfer of density credits from one portion of the owner's 4,800-acre parcel to another, in order to conserve a scenic mountainous area in its natural state, was insufficient compensation and amounted to an unconstitutional taking of property.[112] The case preceded by one year the case of *First English Evangelical Lutheran Church of Glendale v. County of Los Angeles,* in which the Supreme Court took a similar position as the Arizona court. This latter case is discussed in the *Late Developments* section of chapter 4.

[111]720 P. 2d 513 (Ariz., 1986).
[112]720 P. 2d 528 (Ariz. App., 1985).

PART IV

THE BEAUTY WEB

Chapter 7

Billboards, Junkyards, and Aesthetic Regulation

In his analysis of land-use law in the United States, John E. Cribbet attributed its theoretical basis to four English writers of the eighteenth century: John Locke, William Blackstone, Adam Smith, and Jeremy Bentham.[1] The ideas spun by these men can be traced in the weave of the Constitution and have proven to be the philosophical warp and woof of the American social fabric, even to this day.

Given their precepts of individual freedom, private property, and of laissez-faire—fundamental to American tradition—it is hardly surprising that the aesthetic quality of the nation's cities should be so subject to market determination. In areas where ineffectual land-use regulation has given way to market forces, there is, unfortunately, ample visual evidence that the price of laissez-faire has almost invariably been waste and squalor in land use.

However, the tradition of free enterprise notwithstanding, social concern and more circumspect values are also a part of the national heritage and occupy a fundamental place in American thought. The belief that the welfare of the community must take precedence over individual concerns was indeed strongly advocated by Jeremy Bentham. Generally recognized as an intellectual soulmate of Adam Smith but a critic of William Blackstone, Bentham's theory of social "utility" shared in some fundamental perspec-

---

[1]John E. Cribbet, "Changing Concepts in the Law of Land Use," *Iowa L. Rev.* 50 (1965), 247–51.

tives with the outlook of the others, but it more closely linked the interests of the individual with those of society.[2]

Bentham believed that property is not a God-ordained and inalienable natural right as suggested by Locke, but rather a creature of law. He wrote: "Before laws were made there was no property; take away laws, and property ceases."[3] From his viewpoint, individual rights in property are subordinate to the interests of the community. Nonetheless, Bentham also subscribed to Smith's thesis that social interests are best served through individual enterprise, thereby leading to the idea that the social utility of any law should be measured by its benefit to the individual. On one hand, the imperative of Bentham's principle of utility is to maximize the benefit or happiness for the greatest number of people. "The only object of government," he wrote, "ought to be the greatest possible happiness of the community."[4] On the other hand, he equated community benefit with benefit to the individual: "That which is conformable to the utility, or the interest of a community, is what tends to augment the total sum of the happiness of the individuals that compose it."[5] Property-rights scholar Francis S. Philbrick observes a parallel between the attitudes of Bentham and Adam Smith toward property rights, laissez-faire, and "the concurrence of individual and social interests."[6] However, in the balance between individual and community interests, Bentham expresses the reciprocal advantage to the individual stemming from community benefit more explicitly:

> The law cannot create rights [including rights of property] except by creating corresponding obligations. It cannot create rights and obligations without creating offenses. It cannot command nor forbid without restraining the liberty of individuals.
>
> It appears, then, that the citizen cannot acquire rights except by sacrificing a part of his liberty. But even under a bad government there is no proportion between the acquisition and the sacrifice. Government approaches to perfection in proportion as the sacrifice is less and the acquisition more.[7]

In a 1974 case upholding a police-power restriction on billboard advertising, *Westfield Motor Sales Co. v. Town of Westfield,* New Jersey Judge Harold A. Ackerman reflected Bentham's thesis: "Embodied within the theory of police power is a concept of 'utilitarianism,' a theory balanc-

---

[2]Jeremy Bentham, *Theory of Legislation,* trans. R. Hildreth (London: Kegan Paul, Trench, Trubner and Co., 1911), 2.

[3]Ibid., 113.

[4]Ibid., 95.

[5]Ibid., 2.

[6]Francis S. Philbrick, "Changing Conceptions of Property in Law," *U. of Pennsylvania L. Rev.* 86 (1938), 712.

[7]Bentham, *Theory of Legislation,* 95.

ing individual rights against the general welfare of the community."[8] Undeniably, regulations furthering urban aesthetics restrict the free use of property. Following Bentham's theory, however, the community good that arises
from a restriction serves in the end to benefit property owners also, including the individual owner suffering immediately from the regulation. From
one perspective, the danger is an incremental erosion of individual rights;
from another viewpoint, however, the benefit of an urban community's
aesthetic and design qualities resulting from a restriction serves the best
interests, including economic, not only of the whole community but also of
the individuals, including property owners, who compose it. As Bentham
commented: "The community is a fictitious body, composed of the individual persons who are considered as constituting as it were its members. The
interest of the community then is, what?—the sum of the interests of the
several members who compose it."[9]

The issue of weighing individual against community utility and benefit
is complex and contentious, but, as Jesse Dukeminier observed in his classic
analysis:

> If we want our children to grow up in pleasant purlieus, we must give up
> something of the freedom of the individual to use his land as he chooses. This
> is inherent in the concept of land planning by community officials.[10]

The objective, as Dukeminier was quick to caution, is not easily achieved.
Following the judgment of Oliver Wendell Holmes in *Pennsylvania Coal,*[11]
in each individual case a balance between the public interest and private
rights must be struck. The issue is especially relevant in consideration of
urban aesthetics and design. As New York Court of Appeals Judge John
Van Voorhis noted in 1963 in an oft-quoted dissent:

> Aesthetic considerations, in a certain sense, underlie all zoning, usually in
> combination with other factors with which they are interwoven. Lot area,
> setback and height restrictions, for example, are based essentially on aesthetic
> factors.[12]

Indeed, many courts have shared the perception of New Jersey Judge Ackerman that "all planning and zoning is essentially aesthetic in nature."[13]

---

[8]324 A. 2d 113 (N.J. Sup'r., 1974), 120.

[9]Jeremy Bentham, *Collected Works: An Introduction to the Principles of Morals and
Legislation,* ed. J. H. Burns and H. L. A. Hart (London: U. of London, Athlone Press,
1970), 12.

[10]J. J. Dukeminier, Jr., "Zoning for Aesthetic Objectives: A Reappraisal," *Law and
Contemporary Problems* 20 (1955), 236.

[11]*Pennsylvania Coal Company v. Mahon,* 260 U.S. 393 (1922).

[12]*People v. Stover,* 191 N.E. 2d 272 (N.Y., 1963), 277.

[13]Note 8, 120.

Despite this frequent observation, judicial acceptance of aesthetics as a basis for the police power is more equivocal. Whether the public in pursuit of urban beauty can lawfully compel the sacrifice of private property rights is a question answerable only through Holmes's weighing test. An unavoidable consequence of this empirical test, it may be recalled, is uncertainty, a quality significantly magnified by the ethereal nature of aesthetics. In 1930, when the law governing public nuisances was fairly well established with regard to sound and smell, Benjamin N. Cardozo wrote, in *People v. Rubenfeld:* "One of the unsettled questions of the law is the extent to which the concept of nuisance may be enlarged by legislation so as to give protection to sensibilities that are merely cultural or aesthetic."[14]

Though some aspects of the question of aesthetic regulation have met some resolution since Cardozo's tenure on the New York bench, other issues remain. As Emory University law professor William H. Agnor summarized in a 1962 commentary:

> In the Euclid case the "general welfare" has clearly been added to the "public health, safety and morals" as a basis for the exercise of the police power in the area of zoning regulations. The concept of the general welfare has been enlarged gradually to include many new considerations. Such terms as public convenience, comfort, and prosperity become linked with the general welfare. Property values and economic considerations begin to appear. Our problem has to do with the admittance of aesthetics to this group, or when will aesthetics be admitted to "full partnership with health, morals and safety?"[15]

Agnor's article quotes John Forrest Dillon's treatise on *Municipal Corporations* fifty years previous, "The law on this point is undergoing development, and perhaps cannot be said to be conclusively settled as to the extent of the police power."[16] It is perhaps the nature of aesthetics that this observation seems as applicable today as it was then.

The history of police-power regulation of aesthetics in American planning in this century can be divided into three general periods. During the early years, aesthetic controls were generally regarded as an invalid exercise of the police power. The middle years saw controls rationalized as being for other, more traditional, purposes of police-power regulations, even where the true motivation may have been primarily aesthetic. Even today, this practice has not been entirely discarded. The final period, which still contin-

---

[14]*People v. Rubenfeld,* 172 N.E. 485 (N.Y., 1930), 487.

[15]William H. Agnor, "Beauty Begins a Comeback: Aesthetic Considerations in Zoning," *Journal of Public Law* 11 (1962), 264. Citing Paul Sayre, "Aesthetics and Property Values: Does Zoning Promote the Public Welfare?" *American Bar Assoc. Journal* 35 (1949), 471.

[16]Agnor, "Beauty Begins a Comeback," 264–65. Citing John Forrest Dillon, *Commentaries on the Law of Municipal Corporations* (Boston: Little, Brown, 1911), 5th ed., vol. 2, 1058–59.

ues, is witnessing aesthetics gaining legitimacy in itself as a basis for police-power regulation, notwithstanding recent consideration of First Amendment guarantees of freedom of expression. Also, as seen earlier, in some states, the requirement for developers to report the anticipated environmental impact of their proposed projects can effectively function as a means for aesthetic regulation.[17] While trends are evident, the history is by no means without overlaps and reversals. Nor has the issue been isolated from changes in social and legal perceptions.

BILLBOARDS AND JUNKYARDS

Consideration of aesthetics as justification for the police power began during the 1900s when the automobile was just becoming a part of American life. With plentiful resources in petroleum and an open landscape beckoning, a steadily increasing portion of the populace took to the newly constructed roadways in pursuit of profit and pleasure. Television had not yet made its debut, and the newly emergent advertising industry seized advantage of the outdoor urban and roadside environment as a cheap and ubiquitous medium to huckster its clients' wares. During this period, thousands of outdoor advertising signboards were built in the cities and along the highways of the nation. As the age of the automobile matured, the waste of a society bent on industrial production also spawned the automobile and industrial salvage yard. Ugliness spread throughout industrialized America. With preservation of the aesthetic quality of the public outdoors at stake, the issues of environmental aesthetics, billboard advertising, and junkyards became the subject of vigorous litigation.

During the early years, judicial response to regulatory attempts to curb the tide of billboards and junkyards held to the traditional doctrine of public noninterference into the private use of land. This attitude was epitomized in a 1905 New Jersey court decision concerning the regulation of billboards, *City of Passaic v. Patterson Bill Posting, Advertising & Sign Painting Co.*

> No case has been cited, nor are we aware of any case which holds that a man may be deprived of his property because his tastes are not those of his neighbors. Aesthetic considerations are a matter of luxury and indulgence rather than of necessity, and it is necessity alone which justifies the exercise of police power to take private property without compensation.[18]

This judicial approach to sign regulation was matched by a similar hands-off attitude toward junkyards. In a typical case, *Lane v. City of Concord,* the New Hampshire court found in 1901 that a lot strewn with rubbish

---

[17]See, e.g., *Polygon Corporation v. City of Seattle,* 578 P. 2d 1309 (1978).
[18]62 A. 267 (N.J., 1905), 268.

was not an actionable nuisance because "it is apparently well settled that the unsightly condition of one's premises does not of itself afford a right of action to a more aesthetic adjoining owner." [19] Blackstone and laissez-faire were being well observed.

However, as the threat of visual blight became increasingly apparent, public pressure for controls increased and court attitudes began to change. The beginning years evolved into the second stage—judicial rationalization to forestall further aesthetic depredations. The most quoted opinion that displayed this view was *St. Louis Gunning Advertising Co. v. City of St. Louis*, a decision reached by the Missouri court in 1911.

> The signboards and billboards upon which this class of advertisements are displayed are constant menaces to the public safety and welfare of the city; they endanger the public health, promote immorality, constitute hiding places and retreats for criminals and all classes of miscreants. They are also inartistic and unsightly. In cases of fire they often cause their spread and constitute barriers against their extinction; and in cases of high wind, their temporary character, frail structure and broad surface, render them liable to be blown down and to fall upon and injure those who may happen to be in their vicinity. The evidence shows and common observation teaches us that the ground in the rear thereof is being constantly used as privies and dumping grounds for all kinds of waste and deleterious matters, and thereby creating public nuisances and jeopardizing public health; the evidence also shows that behind these obstructions the lowest form of prostitution and other acts of immorality are frequently carried on, almost under public gaze; they offer shelter and concealment for the criminal while lying in wait for his victim; and last, but not least, they obstruct the light, sunshine, and air, which are so conducive to health and comfort.[20]

During this period, the courts turned to almost any and every ostensible reason to rule for aesthetic controls without facing the issue of whether aesthetics alone warranted the exercise of the police power. Even the Supreme Court employed this charade in *Thomas Cusack Company v. City of Chicago*.[21] In this 1917 case, the high Court upheld an ordinance limiting the size of billboards in a residential area, finding that "fires had been started in the accumulation of combustible material which gathered about such billboards; that offensive and insanitary accumulations are habitually found about them, and that they afford a convenient concealment and shield for immoral practices, and for loiterers and criminals."[22] The prevalent approach was summarized by the New York court in 1932 in *Perlmutter v. Greene:* "Beauty may not be queen, but she is not an outcast beyond

[19]49 A. 687 (N.H., 1901), 689.
[20]137 S.W. 929 (Mo., 1911), 942.
[21]242 U.S. 526 (1917).
[22]Note 21, 529.

the pale of protection or respect. She may at least shelter herself under the wing of safety, morality, or decency."[23]

The question of aesthetics as a justification for police-power intervention was a subject of much deliberation and produced great uncertainty during this time. As a Wisconsin court noted in 1923 in *State ex rel. Carter v. Harper:*

> It seems to us that aesthetic considerations are relative in their nature. With the passing of time, social standards conform to new ideals. As a race, our sensibilities are becoming more refined, and that which formerly did not offend cannot now be endured. That which the common law did not condemn as a nuisance is now frequently outlawed as such by the written law. This is not because the subject outlawed is of a different nature, but because our sensibilities have become more refined and our ideals more exacting. Nauseous smells have always come under the ban of the law, but ugly sights and discordant surroundings may be just as distressing to keener sensibilities. The rights of property should not be sacrificed to the pleasure of an ultra-aesthetic taste. But whether they should be permitted to plague the average or dominant human sensibilities well may be pondered.[24]

In 1930, Charles Light, Jr., wrote:

> The concept that the police power is limited strictly to the protection of the public health, safety, morals is outgrown. But the power is so vast and its exercise so fraught with possibilities of abuse, that those courts which conceive it dynamically cling to the terms of the past while giving them enlarged meaning. Progress lies along the path of realism, when each exercise of power shall be furnished its own well-fitted verbal raiment unhidden by the venerable cloak fashioned of safety and health and morals.[25]

Pondering the question thirty years later, William Agnor observed that, notwithstanding the expanding scope of the police power, the half-century-old idea still persists that beauty alone cannot justify police exercise, even though aesthetics may be the true if veiled motive for a regulation. Quoting the 1948 Missouri decision in *City of St. Louis v. Friedman,* he reflected the earlier attitude:

> It seems to be recognized here that aesthetic considerations may influence use regulations and even be the real motivating factor, as long as aesthetics can be assigned a secondary role and the exercise of the police power justified under other considerations. "Esthetic values alone are not a sufficient basis

---

[23]182 N.E. 5 (N.Y., 1932), 6.
[24]196 N.W. 451 (Wisc., 1923), 455.
[25]Charles P. Light, Jr., "Aesthetics in Zoning," *Minn. L. Rev.* 14 (1930), 123.

for classifications, but are entitled to some weight where other reasons for
the exercise of the power are present."[26]

Agnor's view is still shared by many contemporary courts and commentators on the law. As late as 1965, the Pennsylvania court in *Norate
Corporation, Inc. v. Zoning Board of Adjustment of Upper Moreland
Township*[27] quoted with approval the list of justifiable causes for police
power regulations of billboards specified in Eugene McQuillin's classic
treatise on *Municipal Corporations:*

> Specifically, billboard ordinances and regulations, where reasonable, are jus-
> tified under the police power for any or all of the following reasons: (1) bill-
> boards being temporary structures are liable to be blown down and thus injure
> pedestrians; (2) they gather refuse and paper which may tend to spread con-
> flagrations; (3) they are used as dumping places for dirt, filth and refuse, and
> as public privies; (4) they serve as hiding places for criminals; and (5) they are
> put to use by disorderly persons for immoral purposes.[28]

A 1964 commentary observes,

> Traditionally, the opinions have refused to face up to the aesthetic questions
> posed by the cases. It is clear enough in the great majority of zoning decisions
> that one of the predominating purposes of zoning legislation is the mainte-
> nance or improvement of community appearance. But traditionally the courts
> have exercised remarkable powers of imagination to find legislative concern
> limited to matters of light, air, traffic control and sewage disposal, even where
> the aesthetic impact of the decision must be obvious.[29]

Although courts have continued to this day to cling to the "safe" practice of approving police-power controls for ostensibly nonaesthetic reasons,
others have rejected such rationalization. In 1935 in *General Outdoor Advertising Co. v. Department of Public Works,* the Massachusetts court
quoted a master in concurrence with his finding of evidence that,

> In some isolated cases, certain signs and billboards in this Commonwealth
> have been used as screens to commit nuisances, hide law breakers, and facil-
> itate immoral practices. Around some few filth has been allowed to collect,
> and some have shut out light and air from dwelling places. In and around

---

[26]Agnor, "Beauty Begins a Comeback," 270. Quoting 216 S. W. 2d 475 (Mo., 1948),
478.

[27]207 A. 2d 890 (Pa., 1965), p. 894.

[28]Eugene McQuillin, *The Law of Municipal Corporations* (1904; reprint, Willmette, I.L.:
Callaghan, 1981), vol. 7, sect. 24–380, 297.

[29]*Northwestern U. L. Rev.,* "Aesthetic Control of Land Use: A House Built Upon the
Sand?" 59, no. 3 (1964), 373.

others, rubbish and combustible materials have been allowed to collect, which to some degree tends to create a fire hazard. Those instances were all so rare, compared with the total number of signs and billboards in existence, that I am unable to find upon the evidence that signs and billboards, in general, as erected and maintained in this Commonwealth, have screened nuisances, or created a danger to public health or morals, or facilitated immoral practices, or afforded a shelter for criminals, or created or increased the danger of fire, or hindered firemen in their work.[30]

Refusing such arguments, the court declared in forthright fashion,

Grandeur and beauty of scenery contribute highly important factors to the public welfare of a state. To preserve such landscapes from defacement promotes the public welfare and is a public purpose. . . . It is, in our opinion, within the reasonable scope of the police power to preserve from destruction the scenic beauties bestowed on the commonwealth by nature in conjunction with the promotion of safety of travel on the public ways and the protection of travellers from the intrusion of unwelcome advertising. . . .

Even if the rules and regulations of billboards and other advertising devices did not rest upon the safety of public travel and the promotion of the comfort of travellers by exclusion of undesired intrusion, we think that the preservation of scenic beauty and places of historical interest would be a sufficient support for them. Considerations of taste and fitness may be a proper basis for action in granting and in denying permits for locations for advertising devices.[31]

The court's position was strengthened by specific provision in the Massachusetts constitution for regulation of outdoor advertising.

Rejection of sham arguments by one state court did not necessarily mean full acceptance of an aesthetic basis for the police power, however. In the 1944 case of *Murphy, Inc. v. Town of Westport,*[32] the willingness of a lower Connecticut court judge to face the issue directly was not shared by the state's supreme court. The trial court found a zoning ordinance prohibiting billboards to be "illegally discriminative," since there were "no provisions as to size, construction or site designed to insure the safety of the public.[33] Remarking, "Of course this is nonsense," the judge declared,

Billboard regulation is within the police power, regardless of whether one relies on the reasons to which the courts still cling or on those which are

---

[30]193 N.E. 799 (Mass., 1935), 809.
[31]Ibid., 816.
[32]40 A. 2d 177 (Conn., 1944).
[33]Dukeminier, "Zoning for Aesthetic Objectives," 221. Citing *Murphy, Inc. v. West-port,* Record, vol. A-201, 11.

treated like step-children, but which, at least to my satisfaction, furnish the hidden impelling motive for modern legal thought.[34]

The judge said in comment,

> The earlier attitude appears to have been that billboard regulation was simon-pure aesthetic regulation and as such was condemned. Adverse public opinion against unsightly signs along highways quite probably had much to do in the rapid change of legal thought. This public opinion was not concerned with thoughts of safety, morals or welfare. It was occasioned by the disfigurement of the landscape and by the marring of the beauty of Nature. Yet the courts, somewhat sophistically, it seems to me, with many protestations against the use of aesthetic standards, urged with rather fantastic reasoning that what previously had no relationship to public safety had now developed into a public menace which an enlightened community not only had a right to regulate but, indeed, would be almost wayward in failing to control.[35]

While making these observations, the lower court nevertheless rejected claims that the order was related to public health and safety. On appeal, however, this conclusion was overturned by the Connecticut Supreme Court, which invoked the earlier method of rationalization:

> In the earlier cases, courts apparently did not realize as clearly as they do now, as the result of facts found upon various trials, that billboards may be a source of danger to travelers upon highways through insecure construction, that accumulations of debris behind and around them may increase fire hazards and produce unsanitary conditions, that they may obstruct the view of operators of automobiles on the highway and may distract their attention from their driving, that behind them nuisances and immoral acts are often committed, and that they may serve as places of concealment for the criminal. . . . As far as the record shows, the trial court did not have before it any adequate basis of facts upon which to determine that the invalidity of the provisions of the ordinance in question had been established.[36]

While the Connecticut high court was more liberal than the trial court in upholding public regulation of aesthetics, it was not particularly progressive in its reasoning, reverting as it did to the same traditional arguments used decades earlier.

Certainly much of the rationale used in early opinions following *St. Louis Gunning* would seem far-fetched if used today, even if not then. Construction codes can ensure the structural safety of sign boards, to render their absolute prohibition unnecessary. If physical danger were a real threat,

[34]Ibid., *Murphy, Inc. v. Westport.*
[35]Ibid., 16.
[36]Note 32, 178, 182.

then nothing less than a total ban would seem in order. In describing regulations proscribing overhanging signs along the fashionable East Side of New York City, Dukeminier observes that the intent of such restrictions must be aesthetic and not for public safety, "for if signs hanging from the best stores in town are really unsafe, reason demands that shabby ones hanging from stores in a low-price district also be prohibited."[37]

Along roadways, the public safety argument for sign regulations is strengthened by the visual distraction of motorists caused by advertising, particularly by illuminated signs. In 1961, in *New York State Thruway Authority v. Ashley Motor Courts, Inc.,*[38] the prohibition of signs along a highway was upheld for the purposes of providing maximum visibility, preventing unreasonable distraction of motorists, and ensuring that the effectiveness of traffic lights, signals, and signs not be compromised. The preservation and enhancement of the natural scenic beauty and the aesthetic features of the thruway system were considered equally with the promotion of the safety, comfort, and well-being of the motoring public. The New York court made the additional observation that the value of advertising signs derives from the location of the public highway in the first place, and that this betterment value could be properly withdrawn by the public without payment of compensation.

One law review commentator presupposes that "almost all billboards are aesthetic evils,"[39] pointing out that this supposition is implicit in the Federal Highway Beautification Act of 1965.[40] It might be noted parenthetically that this act, though originally intended as an incentive to encourage states and localities to control outdoor advertising signs along highways by threatening loss of federal funds, has instead been highly criticized as actually impeding billboard removal by stipulating payment of compensation to the owners rather than authorizing use of police-power regulation and amortization. Indeed, several states have statutes governing advertising signs along roadways or adjacent to other facilities that are in fact considerably more stringent than the federal law, in that they regulate and prohibit billboard advertising through the police power.

Notwithstanding the apparent assumption that outdoor advertising is inherently offensive, this premise is not universally held. In *Learning from Las Vegas,* for example, the noted architectural theorists Robert Venturi, Denise Scott Brown, and Steven Izenour perceive billboard and advertising

---

[37]Dukeminier, "Zoning for Aesthetic Objectives," 223.

[38]176 N.E. 2d 566 (N.Y., 1961).

[39]"Beyond the Eye of the Beholder: Aesthetics and Objectivity," *Michigan L. Rev.* 71 (1973), 1449.

[40]23 U.S.C. 131, 136, 319, Highway Beautification Act of 1965, Pub. L. 89–285, 79 Stat. 1028.

displays as valuable components of urban design worthy of emulation.[41] Certainly such vibrant, neon-luminescent urban centers as New York City's Times Square and London's Picadilly Circus give credibility to their argument. This attitude leads Colorado law professor Stephen F. Williams to ponder,

> But what of sign owners who allege a conscious aesthetic viewpoint that sign-studded landscapes are preferable to natural ones? Because a pecuniary interest so patently motivates most sign owners, courts may be skeptical of such claims. One sign owner in a million, however, might persuade a court that he had a conscious intent to improve upon the landscape or cityscape. As against such a sign owner, the government's purely aesthetic interest seems substantially related to the suppression of expression.[42]

Nevertheless, the view of Venturi and his associates is shared by some in planning law. In a 1968 article, "Can Billboards Be Beautiful?", Fred Bosselman poses the question and suggests that billboards may eventually win social acceptability "as aesthetic assets which, if well done and in the right place, can amuse us, keep drivers awake, and add interest to the environment."[43] This view is arguable, especially since there is no feasible method of control that can distinguish between well-done and poor displays. Bosselman adds the proviso, however, that he does not believe that "the sign industry will succeed in achieving these goals unless it is willing to accept the fact that the public wants a large share of the country free from any signs at all."[44]

As with billboards, judicial attitudes toward regulation of junkyards and automobile wrecking yards have gradually evolved since *Lane v. City of Concord* toward an explicit recognition of aesthetics as a basis for controls. However, even as late as 1943, state and local legislation regulating junkyards in Vermont were invalidated by the state supreme court in *Vermont Salvage Corporation v. Village of St. Johnsbury*[45] on the traditional argument that aesthetics alone does not justify use of the police power. With the advent of Euclidean zoning, of course, such aesthetic nuisances could be effectively segregated from other activities; for example, the prohibition of an automobile salvage business from an industrial district was specifically upheld by the Missouri court in *City of St. Louis v. Friedman*. As with

---

[41]Robert Venturi, Denise Scott Brown, and Steven Izenour, *Learning from Las Vegas* (Cambridge: M.I.T. Press, 1972).

[42]Stephen F. Williams, "Subjectivity, Expression, and Privacy: Problems of Aesthetic Regulation," *Minnesota L. Rev.* 62 (1977), 42.

[43]Fred P. Bosselman, "Regulation of Signs in the Post-McLuhan Age, Or—Can Billboards be Beautiful?" *Land Use Control Q.* 2, no. 3 (1968), 14.

[44]Ibid., 19.

[45]34 A. 2d 188 (Vt., 1943).

billboards, initial court approval of junkyard controls was characterized by judicial reluctance to legitimize beauty as the justification. Most courts preferred instead to invoke the classic purposes of public health and safety and to relegate aesthetic considerations to a secondary, supportive role.

In some instances, cases concerned with the fencing of junkyards distinguished specifically between the function of ensuring public safety and the provision of an aesthetic screen. In 1956, in *City of Shreveport v. Brock,* a regulation requiring junkyards to be fenced was upheld by the Louisiana court on the grounds that the

> Ordinance was adopted primarily as a safety measure to protect passersby from the dangers inherent in the dismantling and/or storage of wrecked and junked automobiles on the streets and sidewalks of the city, and also to protect children who are naturally attracted to such "nuisances," and it was only secondarily and incidentally to protect property values in the neighborhood and for aesthetic considerations—by screening the unsightly scene of junked cars from view.[46]

The court quoted an earlier state decision in saying that "considerations of taste and beauty may also enter in, and not be out of place."[47]

Three years later, in *People v. Dickenson,* a California appellate court held an ordinance requiring the fencing in of automobile wrecking yards to be in the interest of public safety; but it ruled invalid a requirement that the fence be a solid, visual barrier, since "the provision that has for its purpose the aesthetic one of regulating unsightly things must be held to an unreasonable interference with the right to carry on a lawful and legitimate business."[48] Although the West Virginia court in the 1960 case of *Farley v. Graney*[49] ruled a statute governing junkyards unreasonable as applied, it upheld the public right to regulate with the qualification that aesthetics alone could not be the controlling factor. Two years later, in a somewhat different twist, the Arkansas Supreme Court held in *Bachman v. State*[50] that a statute prohibiting automobile graveyards within one-half mile of paved highways was unreasonable and unrelated to its intended purpose of protecting travelers from "unsightly" views, since it afforded the owner no opportunity to save his business by erecting a high wall, fence, or other visual obstruction around the junkyard operation.

Aesthetics received one of its greatest boosts as a substantive basis for police-power regulation in 1965. In *Oregon City v. Hartke,*[51] the Oregon

[46]89 So. 2d 156 (La., 1956), 158.
[47]Ibid., 157. Quoting *State ex rel. Civello v. City of New Orleans,* 97 So. 440 (1923), 444.
[48]343 P. 2d 809 (Cal. App. Dept., Sup'r., 1959), 810.
[49]119 S.E. 2d 833 (W. Va., 1960).
[50]359 S.W. 2d 815 (Ark., 1962).
[51]400 P. 2d 255 (Ore., 1965).

Supreme Court upheld an ordinance totally banning automobile junkyards from within a municipality's boundaries on primarily aesthetic grounds. The court acknowledged the belief that land-use restrictions designed solely to improve the appearance of a community do not tend to promote public health, safety, morals, or general welfare, but commented:

> However, there is a growing judicial recognition of the power of a city to impose zoning restrictions which can be justified solely upon the ground that they will tend to prevent or minimize discordant and unsightly surroundings. This change in attitude is a reflection of the refinement of our tastes and the growing appreciation of cultural values in a maturing society. The change may be ascribed more directly to the judicial expansion of the police power to include within the concept of "general welfare" the enhancement of the citizen's cultural life.[52]

The *Hartke* decision is considered by many to represent the first sweeping use of the police power to enforce the abolition of a nuisance on solely aesthetic grounds. The judgment ushered in the third stage of development of judicial aesthetic attitudes and gave true credence to a comment made in 1940 by a lower New York court in *Preferred Tires, Inc. v. Village of Hempstead:*

> For years the courts have strained to sustain the validity of regulatory or prohibitory ordinances of this character upon the basis of the public safety. They decided that aesthetic considerations could afford no basis for sustaining such legislation. . . . But the views of the public change in the passing of years. What was deemed wrong in the past is looked upon very often today as eminently proper. What was looked upon as unreasonable in the past is very often considered perfectly reasonable today. Among the changes which have come in the viewpoint of the public is the idea that our cities and villages should be beautiful and the creation of such beauty tends to the happiness, contentment, comfort, prosperity and general welfare of our citizens.[53]

Even earlier, in 1937, in *Mid-State Advertising Corporation v. Bond,* a dissenting New York high court judge had written in opposition to the majority decision to void a billboard restriction: "Circumstances, surrounding conditions, changed social attitudes, newly-acquired knowledge, do not alter the Constitution, but they do alter our view of what is reasonable."[54]

The *Hartke* case was followed by similar decisions regarding outdoor advertising signs. In 1967, for example, the New York Court of Appeals in *Cromwell v. Ferrier*[55] upheld a township zoning ordinance that prohibited

[52]Ibid., 261.
[53]19 N.Y.S. 2d 374 (Sup., 1940), 377.
[54]8 N.E. 2d 286 (N.Y., 1937), 288.
[55]225 N.E. 2d 749 (N.Y., 1967).

the proprietor of a roadside diner and service station from erecting a nonaccessory sign on the opposite side of the highway. The court noted the gradual acceptance of "esthetic enhancement" as a "primary, if not . . . exclusive objective" of regulation so long as aesthetics is "related if only generally to the economic and cultural setting of the regulating community."[56] Later that same year, the Hawaii Supreme Court in *State v. Diamond Motors, Inc.*[57] cited the state constitution in sustaining a regulation governing advertising signs. It even admonished the city for not having argued that aesthetics alone is a valid basis for exercise of the police authority.

In 1974, a New Jersey court in *Westfield Motor Sales Co. v. Town of Westfield* took the final step. It not only held zoning for aesthetic purposes to be within the scope of the police power, but it also said that such action need not be clothed in the legal raiment of traditional, nonaesthetic rationalizations:

> This court today holds that it is now appropriate to permit a municipality, under proper safeguard, to legally deal with the problem without subterfuge. Zoning for aesthetic purposes is an idea whose time has come; it is not outside the scope of the police power.[58]

The court pointed out that "all planning and zoning is essentially aesthetic in nature," and in a reflection of Bentham and Holmes, it found that the police power embodies "a theory of balancing individual interests against the general welfare of the community."[59]

The history of judicial treatment of junkyard regulations by the North Carolina court is particularly revealing of the trend toward legal acceptance of aesthetics as a sole basis for regulation. In 1959, in *State v. Brown,*[60] the court found that a state statute requiring the visual screening of scrapped automobile parts and other refuse in the proximity of a hard-surfaced highway had been enacted solely for the purpose of making highways more attractive, in violation of the then-prevailing rule that aesthetics alone constituted insufficient grounds for such regulation. In 1972, in *State v. Vestal,*[61] it again invalidated a junkyard screening ordinance, this time because of the vagueness of the regulation in specifying the placement of the fence. Since the state had not advanced aesthetics as grounds for the regulation, the court refused to judge on the issue. Nevertheless, it did note "the growing body of authority in other jurisdictions to the effect that the police

[56]Ibid., 753.
[57]429 P. 2d 825 (Haw., 1967).
[58]Note 8, 119.
[59]Ibid., 120.
[60]108 S.E. 2d 74 (N.C., 1959).
[61]189 S.E. 2d 152 (N.C., 1972).

power may be broad enough to include reasonable regulation of property use for aesthetic reasons only."[62]

Ten years later, in 1982, the court confronted the question directly in *State v. Jones,*[63] a case also concerning a junkyard regulatory ordinance. It cited a 1980 study made by Samuel Bufford[64] that found that of all the states, a majority of sixteen state jurisdictions, including the District of Columbia, authorized regulations based on aesthetics alone. Bufford's study also identified nine states, including North Carolina, that prohibited regulations based solely on aesthetics; sixteen states where the issue was still an open question; and ten states with no reported cases regarding aesthetic regulation. Tracing the record of its own decisions since *Brown* and recent actions by other courts in Utah, Michigan, Tennessee, and Montana approving aesthetics as a basis for regulation, the North Carolina court said,

> In light of our 1972 perception in *Vestal* that the trend was growing toward allowing such regulation, the continued shift such that the trend now represents the new majority, and our general agreement with the views expressed in the recent cases above cited, we expressly overrule our previous cases to the extent that they prohibited regulation based upon aesthetic consideration alone. . . . The test focuses on the reasonableness of the regulation by determining whether the aesthetic purpose to which the regulation is reasonably related outweighs the burdens imposed on the private property owner by the regulation. We therefore hold that reasonable regulation based on aesthetic considerations may constitute a valid basis for the exercise of the police power depending on the facts and circumstances of each case.[65]

Again, extension of the police power was predicated on Holmes's balancing test of particular facts and circumstances.

To withstand charges of confiscatory effect, regulations requiring removal of existing outdoor advertising displays have frequently included provisions for amortization. As discussed earlier, this process enables the owner of an existing nonconforming property to recapture his investment over a specified period of time after enactment of a regulation. The length of time permitted is usually determined by such considerations as the amount of the investment and the period of time during which the property has already served its economic purpose. Amortization of billboards is generally feasible because of their relatively low capital investment. On the other hand, signs existing prior to a prohibition are usually considered nonconforming structures, thereby qualifying for somewhat longer amortiza-

---

[62]Ibid., 157.

[63]290 S.E. 2d 675 (N.C., 1982).

[64]Samuel Bufford, "Beyond the Eye of the Beholder: A New Majority of Jurisdictions Authorize Aesthetic Regulation," *U. of Missouri at Kansas City L. Rev.* 48 (1980), 125.

[65]Note 63, 681.

tion time than do nonconforming uses that can be converted to another function. Also, sign ordinances often distinguish between accessory and nonaccessory displays. Typically, regulations governing accessory signs, which are used to identify or advertise on-site activities, are more lenient than those regarding off-site, non-accessory signs, which are used for purely promotional purposes.

FREEDOM OF EXPRESSION

Beginning in the late 1970s a factor not previously considered to any great extent was entered into the weighing of billboard regulations: the freedom of expression provision of the federal Constitution. During this most recent phase of regulation, several cases concerning various forms of commercial advertising have reached the Supreme Court. Among the decisions were *Virginia State Board of Pharmacy v. Virginia Citizens Consumer Council*[66] in 1976 concerning the advertising of contraceptives; *Bates v. State Bar of Arizona*[67] in 1977 and *Ohralik v. Ohio State Bar Association*[68] in 1978, both on the advertising and promotion of legal services; and *Central Hudson Gas & Electric Corp. v. Public Service Commission of New York*[69] in 1980 on advertising by public utility companies. A common focus of these cases was the free-speech guarantee of the First Amendment as well as provisions of the Fourteenth. Although none of the cases concerned outdoor advertising as such, the interpretation of the First Amendment provision for free speech established by these decisions influenced subsequent judicial consideration of billboard regulations.

Many billboard cases during this period involved participation by the federal courts. In 1978 the Supreme Court dismissed an appeal of a 1977 New York state decision in *Suffolk Outdoor Advertising Co., Inc. v. Hulse.*[70] The case involved an ordinance enacted by the town of Southampton that prohibited the erection of all nonaccessory billboards and required the removal of all such existing signs from the community. Accessory displays were not affected. To ameliorate the effects of the ban, the ordinance provided for the establishment of public information centers where approved directional signs for businesses could be located. The regulation also allowed an amortization period of three years and further permitted extensions of time if an owner could show the period provided to be unreasonable as applied. The New York Court of Appeals approved the regulation, holding that aesthetics constituted a valid basis for exercise of

[66]425 U.S. 748 (1976).
[67]433 U.S. 350 (1977).
[68]436 U.S. 447 (1978).
[69]447 U.S. 557 (1980).
[70]373 N.E. 2d 263 (N.Y., 1977), App. Dismissed, 439 U.S. 808 (1978).

the police power and that the restriction did not infringe the right of free speech under the First Amendment. According to the decision, the regulation did not control the content of the speech appearing on billboards but regulated only the "place and manner" in which billboards could be maintained.

Notwithstanding the Supreme Court's refusal to hear the appeal of this case, a 1980 legislative attempt to ban billboards throughout the state of Maine was found by a federal appeals court in *John Donnelly & Sons v. Campbell*[71] to violate the First Amendment. The statute preamble listed three justifications for the prohibition: the protection of the state's landscape as a natural resource, the enhancement of the tourist industry, and the public interest in highway safety. Like the Southampton ordinance, the Maine statute allowed certain exemptions from the prohibition and provided for strictly controlled "official business directional signs" furnished by the advertiser but erected by the state to inform on "route and distance." The court quoted the *Virginia Pharmacy Board* case in declaring that "time, place, and manner" restrictions must not restrict the content of regulated speech and must "leave open ample alternative channels for communication of the information." Beyond these considerations, it focused in particular on one point: "Not only must these restrictions serve a 'sufficiently strong' or 'significant governmental interest,' they must significantly serve that interest. . . . In other words, the regulation must be no more restrictive than reasonably necessary to serve the governmental interest."[72]

The federal appeals court considered the reasons advanced by the state for the prohibition consecutively. Concerning the claim of highway safety, it questioned the connection between means and ends, noting that there was no reason to believe that signs permitted by the statute would be less distracting than signs prohibited. The court was considerably more sympathetic toward the public interest in preserving the state's natural beauty and the related purpose of enhancement of the tourist industry. It considered but dismissed the notion that the bill was impermissibly overinclusive in that some locations, less attractive to start with, would suffer less than others would from billboards. It was also unmoved by the suggestion that the state's aesthetic argument was diminished by the statute's allowance for on-premise signs. Concerning the commercial speech character of most advertising, the court found that the statute directly related to legitimate public interests and was no more restrictive than necessary. The fatal flaw, according to the majority opinion, was that the statute treated noncommercial or ideological speech more harshly than it did commercial speech. Ideological speech, it pointed out, is more dependent on outdoor advertising,

[71]639 F. 2d 6 (1980).
[72]Ibid., 8.

since noncommercial interests are less able to afford the cost of more expensive means of advertising.

In a concurring opinion, Judge Raymond J. Pettine shared the majority's sympathy toward the public interest in preserving and improving the beauty of the state's landscape, but he was more concerned about the effect of the statute's effective ban on an entire medium of communication. Alluding to the possibility that, under the court's ruling, the state could successfully revise the statute simply by applying the restriction to commercial advertising only, Pettine concluded, "In my view . . . Maine could not save this statute by limiting its application to commercial speech."[73]

In 1981, the Supreme Court summarily affirmed the *Donnelly* decision[74] and also involved itself in plenary consideration of billboard regulations in the case of *Metromedia, Inc. v. City of San Diego.*[75] Many of the issues dealt with in *Suffolk* and *Donnelly* were examined again by the high Court. The case is remarkable in the intensity of argument between the majority led by Justice Byron R. White, the concurrence of Justice William J. Brennan, Jr., and the dissenting opinions of Chief Justice Warren E. Burger and Justice John Paul Stevens. In his own dissent, Justice William H. Rehnquist characterized the decision as "a virtual Tower of Babel, from which no definitive principles can be clearly drawn."[76]

In its 6–3 decision, the tribunal reversed a decision by the California Supreme Court[77] that approved a sweeping prohibition of outdoor advertising signs by the city of San Diego. The stated purpose of the regulation was "to eliminate hazards to pedestrians and motorists brought about by distracting sign displays" and "to preserve and improve the appearance of the City."[78] The ordinance provided two kinds of exceptions from the general prohibition. One was to allow on-site or accessory signs identifying the owner or occupant of the premises or advertising goods produced or services rendered at the site; the other listed twelve specific categories of permissible displays, not to include commercial advertising.

The majority laid down the basis of its opinion by distinguishing between commercial and noncommercial speech. In considering the former, it cited such previous decisions as *Virginia Pharmacy Board, Bates,* and *Ohralik* and then focused on the essence of one case:

> Finally, in *Central Hudson Gas & Electric Corp. v. Public Service Comm'n,*
> we held: "The Constitution . . . accords a lesser protection to commercial

[73]Ibid., 24.
[74]*Campbell v. John Donnelly & Sons.* Aff'd., 453 U.S. 916 (1981).
[75]453 U.S. 490 (1981).
[76]Ibid., 569.
[77]610 P. 2d 407 (1980).
[78]Note 75, 493.

speech than to other constitutionally guaranteed expression. The protection available for a particular commercial expression turns on the nature both of the expression and of the governmental interests served by its regulation.'' We then adopted a four-part test for determining the validity of government restrictions on commercial speech as distinguished from more fully protected speech. (1) The First Amendment protects commercial speech only if that speech concerns lawful activity and is not misleading. A restriction on otherwise protected commercial speech is valid only if it (2) seeks to implement a substantial governmental interest, (3) directly advances that interest, and (4) reaches no farther than necessary to accomplish the given objective.[79]

In applying these precedent rules the Court found, ''In sum, insofar as it regulates commercial speech the San Diego ordinance meets the constitutional requirements of *Central Hudson*.'' In the next breath, however, it said: ''It does not follow, however, that San Diego's general ban on signs carrying noncommercial advertising is also valid under the First and Fourteenth Amendments.''[80] In amplifying its reservation and ultimate disapproval of the effect of the ordinance on noncommercial speech, the Court said,

> As indicated above, our recent commercial speech cases have consistently accorded noncommercial speech a greater degree of protection than commercial speech. San Diego effectively inverts this judgement by affording a greater degree of protection to commercial than to noncommercial speech. There is a broad exception for onsite commercial advertisements, but there is no similar exception for noncommercial speech. The use of onsite billboards to carry commercial messages related to the commercial use of the premises is freely permitted, but the use of otherwise identical billboards to carry noncommercial messages is generally prohibited. The city does not explain how or why noncommercial billboards located in places where commercial billboards are permitted would be more threatening to safe driving or would detract more from the beauty of the city. Insofar as the city tolerates billboards at all, it cannot choose to limit their content to commercial messages; the city may not conclude that the communication of commercial information concerning goods and services connected with a particular site is of greater value than the communication of noncommercial messages.[81]

The Court distinguished the San Diego ordinance from the Southampton regulation that it had approved two years earlier in the *Suffolk* case. It pointed out that the New York rule ''did not sweep within its scope the broad range of noncommercial speech admittedly prohibited by the San Diego ordinance''[82] and further provided for the establishment of public

[79]Ibid., 507.
[80]Ibid., 512–13.
[81]Ibid.
[82]Ibid., 499.

information centers where approved directional signs for business could be located. The Court also rejected the suggestion that the San Diego ordinance was a reasonable time, place, and manner restriction.

While concurring with the final judgment of the Court, Justice Brennan nonetheless disagreed with much of the majority's reasoning. In a separate opinion, Brennan quoted an annotation of the Court decision:

> Believing that "a total prohibition of outdoor advertising is not before us," the plurality does not decide "whether such a ban would be consistent with the First Amendment." Instead, it concludes that San Diego may ban all billboards containing commercial speech messages without violating the First Amendment, thereby sending the signal to municipalities that bifurcated billboard regulations prohibiting commercial messages but allowing noncommercial messages would pass constitutional muster. I write separately because I believe this case in effect presents the total ban question, and because I believe the plurality's bifurcated approach itself raises serious First Amendment problems and relies on a distinction between commercial and noncommercial speech unanticipated by our prior cases.[83]

Brennan voiced doubt as to whether the city's asserted interest in aesthetics was sufficiently substantial in the commercial and industrial areas to warrant the prohibition. Additionally, he questioned the majority's basic assumption that the exception for on-site advertising would be limited to only commercial speech. He pointed out that if an occupant of a premise is noncommercial in nature, the substance of the identifying sign would likely also be noncommercial. His main concern, however, seemed to stem from the majority's differentiation between commercial and noncommercial speech.

> I have no doubt that those who seek to convey commercial messages will engage in the most imaginative of exercises to place themselves within the safe haven of noncommercial speech, while at the same time conveying their commercial message. Encouraging such behavior can only make the job of city officials—who already are inclined to ban billboards—that much more difficult and potentially intrusive upon legitimate noncommercial expression.[84]

The three separate dissent opinions were in common agreement on the right of the community to protect environmental beauty. Chief Justice Warren Burger in particular entered into a rather heated exchange with the majority on the decision. Among other flaws in the ruling, according to Burger, was that the majority opinion left communities with

> a choice between two equally unsatisfactory alternatives: (a) banning all signs of any kind whatsoever, or (b) permitting all "noncommercial signs," no mat-

[83]Ibid., 521–22.
[84]Ibid., 540.

ter how numerous, how large, how damaging to the environment, or how dangerous to motorists and pedestrians.[85]

Justice Rehnquist felt it sufficient to cite only one past decision of the court to support the ordinance: *Berman v. Parker,*[86] a 1954 landmark decision that has been widely held as sanctioning broad public authority for aesthetic purposes. He disagreed with Brennan's belief that some areas already despoiled by commercial and industrial development would benefit only negligibly from a ban on billboards, reasoning that such areas should not be prevented from improvement. Justice Stevens alluded to what he considered the error of the majority in effectively restricting noncommercial speech more than commercial. His assessment was that the Court had concluded "somewhat ironically" that the ordinance was "an unconstitutional abridgement of speech because it does not abridge enough speech."[87]

Despite Rehnquist's reference to the judicial proceedings in the case as a "judicial clangor,"[88] it seems that reasonable inferences could be drawn from the decision. As several of the separate opinions pointed out, although the immediate outcome of the *Metromedia* case was to void the San Diego billboard ordinance, the decision seemed virtually to invite the possibility of a revised regulation that might be found constitutional. Not only were the options identified, if ruefully, by the chief justice as still possible, but the majority also had kind words for the New York rule that it had previously approved in *Suffolk.* Furthermore, in their various opinions, none of the justices seemed opposed to the principle that aesthetic conditions can be of sufficient public interest to warrant police-power regulations.

As it happened, when the case was reconsidered on remand in the following year, the California court decided that deletion of the offending provision was an unsatisfactory solution.

> Although [the United States Supreme Court] said that the ordinance could be saved by severance or a limiting construction, confining its prohibition to commercial signs, such a prohibition would be inconsistent with the language and original intent of the ordinance. It would, moreover, leave the city with an ordinance different than it intended, one less effective in achieving the city's goals, and one which would invite constitutional difficulties in distinguishing between commercial and noncommercial signs.[89]

So saying, the California court rejected the ordinance as invalid, despite its approval in 1980 of the entire ordinance and despite the dissenting argu-

[85]Ibid., 564.
[86]348 U.S. 26 (1954).
[87]Note 75, 540.
[88]Ibid., 570.
[89]*Metromedia, Inc., v. City of San Diego,* 649 P. 2d 902 (Cal., 1982), 909.

ment of one of its judges that "the choice between alternative, constitutionally permissible regulatory schemes is . . . a policy matter for the city, not this court."[90]

In 1984, four years after its *Metromedia* decision, the Supreme Court once again sat en banc to consider the legality of a municipal ban on the posting of signs. In *Members of the City Council of the City of Los Angeles v. Taxpayers for Vincent,*[91] however, the prohibition was against signs posted on public property only and did not concern signs or billboards placed on private property. Writing for the majority, Justice Stevens found the Los Angeles ordinance to be constitutional.

> [W]e accept the City's position that it may decide that the esthetic interest in avoiding "visual clutter" justifies a removal of signs creating or increasing that clutter. . . . As recognized in *Metromedia,* if the city has a sufficient basis for believing that billboards are traffic hazards and are unattractive, "then obviously the most direct and perhaps the only effective approach to solving the problems they create is to prohibit them." As is true of billboards, the esthetic interests that are implicated by temporary signs are presumptively at work in all parts of the city, including those where appellees posted their signs, and there is no basis in the record in this case upon which to rebut that presumption. These interests are both psychological and economic. The character of the environment affects the quality of life and the value of property in both residential and commercial areas. We hold that on this record these interests are sufficiently substantial to justify this content neutral, impartially administered prohibition against the posting of appellees' temporary signs on public property and that such an application of the ordinance does not create an unacceptable threat to the "profound national commitment to the principle that debate on public issues should be uninhibited, robust, and wide-open."[92]

In the *Vincent* case, the signs at issue were placards promoting a candidate for political office, but the order affected all signs posted on public property in general.

A dissent was voiced by Justice Brennan and joined by Justices Thurgood Marshall and Harry A. Blackmun. Brennan pointed out the inadequacy of alternative channels of communication, such as the posting of signs on private property—particularly in instances where the message may be generally unpopular—or the distribution of handbills, a means of communication that, he asserted, can reach only a limited audience. Though agreeing that aesthetics is a valid area of governmental responsibility, Brennan expressed concern for freedom of expression.

[90]Ibid., 911–12.
[91]466 U.S. 789 (1984).
[92]Ibid., 816–17. Quoting note 75, 508; and *New York Times v. Sullivan,* 376 U.S. 254 (1964), 270.

As I have said, improvement and preservation of the aesthetic environment
are often legitimate and important governmental functions. But because the
implementation of these functions creates special dangers to our First Amendment freedoms, there is a need for more stringent judicial scrutiny than the
Court seems willing to exercise.[93]

Notably, the Court during the same term also denied *certiorari* to an
appeal by a billboard company against a ruling by the Arkansas Supreme
Court. The denial let stand the state's 1983 ruling in *Donrey Communications Company, Inc. v. City of Fayetteville*,[94] which upheld municipal
ordinances limiting the size and location of billboards and providing a four-
year amortization period for nonconforming signs.

In light of the *Vincent* decision, and even in consideration of the somewhat muddied outcome of *Metromedia,* the general direction since the turn
of the century seems apparent. Over the years, judicial opinion has gradually evolved from outright rejection of any aesthetic controls to acceptance
of rationalized reasons for regulation to final recognition of forthright aesthetic controls. Samuel Bufford, whose 1980 article on the trend toward
judicial acceptance of aesthetics as a sole basis for regulation was cited by
the North Carolina high court in *State v. Jones,* offers this summary,

> The trend is clear: The authorization of regulation based solely on aesthetic
> considerations is an idea whose time has come. This trend further suggests
> that the sixteen states where the question is open and the ten with no reported
> decisions are much more likely to accept aesthetic regulation, if forced to face
> the issue, than to reject it. One may confidently predict that in the vast major-
> ity of American jurisdictions a court faced with the issue of validity of aes-
> thetic regulation today would approve it. In fact, this trend is sufficiently
> strong to cast doubt on the continuing vitality of the standing precedents in
> the remaining nine states that disapprove aesthetic regulation, particularly
> since these positions in some cases are based on ancient precedents. Thus, if
> beauty has not become queen, neither is she any longer a pauper in American
> law, always needing the help of other interests to entitle her to protection.[95]

The record since Bufford's publication has indeed shown his prediction
to have been correct. As the North Carolina court indicated in 1982, other
courts including itself have changed their stance from rejecting to accepting
aesthetics as a basis for the police power. Bufford's findings in 1980 showed
that a shift had taken place since the publishing of an appraisal only seven
years earlier in the *Michigan Law Review,* which had concluded, "While
aesthetic legislation has gained substantial support in recent years, only a

---

[93]Note 91, 828.
[94]660 S.W. 2d 900 (Ark., 1983), *cert.* den., 466 U.S. 959 (1984).
[95]Bufford, "Beyond the Eye of the Beholder," 166.

minority, although an increasing minority, of states will uphold it even where other interests are not served as well."[96]

Whether the legal basis for controls is aesthetics in itself or some related rationale, practical public regulation of environmental aesthetics in terms of billboards and junkyards is a reality in an increasing number of jurisdictions. As the Michigan article notes, "Currently, aesthetic controls are usually upheld in practice, if not on aesthetic grounds alone."[97] Some courts are cautious in accepting aesthetics alone as the sole reason for regulation, and with justification. Undeniably, others are lacking in sufficient knowledge of the issues in aesthetic regulation. Ultimately, a community's success in gaining court approval for aesthetic regulation of billboards and junkyards can fairly hinge on its administration's ability to gauge prevailing judicial attitudes, on its grasp of state law, and on its skill in legislative draftsmanship.

[96]*Michigan L. Rev.,* "Beyond the Eye of the Beholder: Aesthetics," 1442. Even now, however, there is no unanimity on this point. For example, Linda Pinkerton finds jurisdictions accepting aesthetics alone as a legitimate basis for billboard regulations still to be "a distinct minority." Pinkerton, "Aesthetics and the Single Building Landmark," *Tulsa L. J.* 15 (1980), 619.

[97]*Michigan L. Rev.* "Beyond the Eye of the Beholder: Aesthetics," 1463.

Chapter 8

Urban Resource Preservation and Adaptive Reuse

Closely associated with the values and purposes of urban design and planning are the practices of urban resource preservation and renewal. The importance of conserving buildings and districts of historical and architectural significance in planning a well-designed and vigorous city is now so imbued in the ethics of planning and design as to be axiomatic. The protection of a city's physical assets, whether historic buildings like the Alamo in San Antonio, or architectural masterpieces such as Frank Lloyd Wright's Robie House in Chicago, or entire districts like the Vieux Carre in New Orleans, can be well justified on sound urban design and planning principles as well as on historical grounds.

The cultural and regional differences that once created the rich diversity of historic architectural styles distinguished not only among national idioms of city design, as between London and Paris, but varied regionally within nations. The individual identity of older American cities—New Orleans, Boston, and San Francisco—is largely attributable to their historic buildings and original urban fabric. As techniques in architectural design become more universal, however, and as industrialized processes and materials in building construction become more standardized, the cultural and historical design characteristics that lend individuality to a city become blurred. The result is often a dreary sameness in the urban imagery of communities with neither a visible past nor a perceptible, individual distinction.

Preservation can also be argued for other reasons beyond the protection of old environs and the enhancement of their special charm or aesthetic quality. Maintaining a community's cultural heritage, encouraging the civic pride that historic and creative buildings can engender, and conserving irreplaceable urban artifacts as resources for the education of future generations are all purposes of indisputable public concern. Economics adds another reason; landmark and historic-district preservation can stabilize or increase neighboring property values and promote the attractiveness of the city for tourism and economic growth.

Nevertheless, especially in rapidly developing urban areas, old buildings and districts have all too frequently been razed to make way for new design and construction. Half of the buildings listed in the Historic American Buildings Survey, begun in the 1930s by the federal government, have since been either demolished or damaged beyond repair.[1] Gone forever are such masterworks as Henry Hobson Richardson's Marshall Field Wholesale Store and the Schiller Building by Adler and Sullivan in Chicago. In New York City, McKim, Meade and White's Pennsylvania Station has been replaced by the new Madison Square Garden. In Philadelphia, the National Park Service demolished Frank Furness's masterwork, the Provident Life and Trust Company Building. Frank Lloyd Wright's Midway Gardens in Chicago fell before the wrecker's ball as a result of Prohibition; his Larkin Building in Buffalo, New York, was destroyed and replaced by a parking lot. Some communities have realized too late that expedient development has been allowed to destroy not only important social and economic resources but indeed the vital identities of their cities.

Communities that have the foresight and will to pursue preservation can, however, find ample precedents in the law to support their cause. As Kenneth K. Kyle, Jr., observed in a 1976 compilation of cases on historic preservation, "There should be no doubt now that preserving historic areas by zoning regulations and restrictions is a valid exercise of the police power."[2] Even where preservation per se has not been granted as a justification for police-power intervention, like aesthetics, its practical end can usually be accomplished on some other basis.

As early as 1896, preservation was sanctioned by the Supreme Court in *United States v. Gettysburg Electric Railway Company*.[3] That case, concerning the public acquisition of the historic Civil War battlefield at Gettysburg, involved the power of eminent domain, however, not the police power. In 1924, zoning as a police-power exercise was first instituted in Charleston, South Carolina, to preserve historic property in private ownership. Since that time, numerous other communities across the country have adopted similar measures under the police power for historic preservation.

[1]John V. Conti, "Preserving the Past," *Wall Street Journal,* August 10, 1970, 1.

[2]Kenneth K. Krye, Jr., "Historic Preservation Cases: A Collection," *Wake Forest L. Rev.* 12 (1976), 242.

[3]160 U.S. 668 (1896).

HISTORIC DISTRICTS

The first major city to follow Charleston's initiative was New Orleans in 1925. Subsequently, this historic Louisiana city has gained fame in preservation law through a series of court battles over an ordinance enforcing the preservation of the Vieux Carre, the historic quarter of the city encompassing the original French and Spanish settlement that dates to the early eighteenth century.

In 1936, the Louisiana state legislature passed a constitutional amendment enabling New Orleans to take certain measures to preserve the appearance of this historic district.[4] To protect the "quaint and distinctive character of the Vieux Carre" and "those buildings having architectural and historic worth," the amendment authorized the council to create a Vieux Carre commission with power to review all applications for building permits in the quarter, including additions, alterations, signs, and new construction. In 1941, the adopted ordinance came before the Louisiana Supreme Court in *City of New Orleans v. Pergament,* a case in which the owner of a gasoline station in the district was charged with violating the ordinance by displaying a large advertising sign on his property without the commission's permission. The owner argued that his station was a modern structure having no architectural or historic worth. In upholding the regulation, the court pointed to the architectural and historic context of the entire district and to the dual purposes of culture and commerce.

> The purpose of the ordinance is not only to preserve the old buildings themselves, but to preserve the antiquity of the whole French and Spanish quarter, the tout ensemble, so to speak, by defending this relic against iconoclasm or vandalism. Preventing or prohibiting eyesores in such a locality is within the police power and within the scope of this municipal ordinance. The preservation of the Vieux Carre as it was originally is a benefit to the inhabitants of New Orleans generally, not only for the sentimental value of this show place but for its commercial value as well, because it attracts tourists and conventions to the city, and is in fact a justification for the slogan, America's most interesting city.[5]

Except for a specific instance in 1957 when the commission was found guilty of discriminatory enforcement,[6] the Vieux Carre ordinance has stood up well in court. Shortly before the *Pergament* case, it had been upheld in *City of New Orleans v. Impastato;*[7] after *Pergament,* it was upheld again in 1953 in *City of New Orleans v. Levy*[8] and again in both 1970 and 1975

---

[4]La. Const. 1921, Art. 14, Sect. 22A (1936).
[5]5 So. 2d 129 (La., 1941), 131.
[6]*City of New Orleans v. Levy,* 98 So. 2d 210 (La., 1957).
[7]3 So. 2d 559 (La., 1941).
[8]64 So. 2d 798 (La., 1953).

in *Maher v. City of New Orleans.* The *Maher* case concerning the city's refusal to permit a structure known as the Victorian Cottage to be demolished and replaced by a seven-unit apartment complex is of special significance, for unlike the other cases that were decided by the Louisiana court, the plaintiff's position was argued through both the state[9] and federal[10] court systems. The case was complicated by the fact that the demolition had initially been approved by the commission, which was then overruled by the New Orleans city council on appeal by local preservation groups. The final judgment upholding the council's action was issued by the federal circuit court and allowed to stand by the Supreme Court.[11]

The integrity of the Vieux Carre law—and of the entire district—was underscored, again against the will of the commission, in a 1964 case, *Vieux Carre Property Owners & Associates, Inc. v. City of New Orleans.*[12] In 1946 the city had amended the original ordinance, exempting from control specific commercial and industrial areas at the periphery of the district. However, owners of properties within the quarter that were not exempted contested the amendments, charging that selective nonenforcement would be discriminatory and would erode the value of other properties within the Vieux Carre. The Louisiana Supreme Court agreed with the plaintiffs, noting that the city had no authority to alter its constitutional charge to preserve the entire district. Ironically, much of the periphery of the Vieux Carre has since succumbed to large-scale, high-rise development, showing that no law can fully substitute for a lack of will on the part of local administrative bodies.

Massachusetts also gained an early reputation for the preservation of historic resources. In 1955, the legislature of that state requested the state supreme court's judgment on the constitutionality of proposed legislation to preserve the historic areas of Nantucket Island and the Beacon Hill district of Boston. In a pair of separate advisory pronouncements, both entitled *Opinion of the Justices to the Senate,*[13] the Massachusetts court affirmed the use of the police power as applied in the acts for historic preservation. The opinion on the Nantucket act upheld the power of a local historic-district commission "to pass upon the appropriateness of exterior architectural features of buildings and structures hereafter to be erected, reconstructed, altered or restored . . . wherever such exterior features are

---

[9]235 So. 2d 402 (1970).

[10]516 F. 2d 1051 (1975).

[11]*Cert.* den., 426 U.S. 905 (1976).

[12]167 So. 2d 367 (La. 1964). See also *State ex rel. Phillips v. Board of Zoning Adjustments of City of New Orleans,* 197 So. 2d 916 (La. App., 1967), disallowing issuance of a variance in the Vieux Carre district as violative of the ordinance.

[13]128 N.E. 2d 557 (Mass., 1955) (Nantucket), 128 N.E. 2d 563 (Mass., 1955) (Beacon Hill).

subject to public view from a public street or way.''[14] It saw as valid the purpose of the act to promote the general welfare

> through the preservation and protection of historic buildings, places and districts of historic interest; through the development of an appropriate setting for these buildings, places and districts; and through the benefits resulting to the economy of Nantucket in developing and maintaining its vacation-travel industry through the promotion of these historic associations.[15]

As in New Orleans, the maintenance and enhancement of the local tourist industry was cited as an essential justification for controls.

In later state legislation, the essence of the Nantucket and Beacon Hill bills was adapted to enable other communities to establish historic districts upon meeting prerequisite conditions and with the recommendation of the state historical commission. Like the earlier acts, the enabling legislation provides that the local historic district commission

> shall consider, among other things, the historic and architectural value and significance of the site, building or structure, the general design, arrangement, texture, material and color of the features involved, and the relation of such features to similar features of buildings and structures in the surrounding area. In the case of new construction or additions to existing buildings or structures the commission shall consider the appropriateness of the size and shape of the building or structure both in relation to the land area upon which the building or structure is situated and to buildings and structures in the vicinity, and the commission may in appropriate cases impose dimensional and set-back requirements in addition to those required by applicable ordinance or by-law.[16]

The statute specifically prohibits, however, "any recommendation or requirement except for the purpose of preventing developments incongruous to the surroundings and of the historic district," or considering "interior arrangements or architectural features not subject to public view."[17]

The enabling act is similar to the earlier Nantucket statute in its provision that no building within a historic district may be razed or removed unless the owner obtains permission from the local commission, which can reject an application where it deems "removal . . . would be detrimental to the public interest."[18] This provision, not unlike the demolition litigated in *Maher,* epitomizes the extent to which the police power may intervene into

---

[14]128 N.E. 2d 557 (Mass., 1955), 559.
[15]Ibid., 558–59.
[16]Mass Gen. Laws Ann., Ch. 40C, Sect. 7 (West, 1979).
[17]Ibid.
[18]Note 14. Citing note 16, sect. 5.

the use of private property. A historic structure, however valuable from a cultural viewpoint, may well be functionally obsolete or inefficient as a land use and incapable of returning an income commensurate with the owner's investment. Restricting its removal and replacement by a more profitable land use may render it a white elephant, with the owner suffering the financial consequences. The Massachusetts Supreme Court was not unaware of the potential for inequity, and while approving the general purposes of the act, it warned that "peculiar hardship and remoteness from the legitimate purposes of the act, would be unconstitutional applications of it."[19]

For preservation to be effective, it is not sufficient to restrict demolitions and alterations. Affirmative action is required to forestall "demolition by neglect," the owner's deliberate foregoing of necessary repairs and allowing the property to deteriorate to such a state that mandatory conformance to preservation standards would appear unreasonable. An anti-neglect provision in the New Orleans ordinance[20] was considered in *Maher* and was upheld by the federal circuit court as within the police power. The court pointed out that similar out-of-pocket expenditures for such items as fire sprinklers, emergency exits and lights, plumbing, and sewage disposal facilities are reasonably required in the interests of safety and health. The court reasoned that where the purpose is legitimate and the means reasonable in its specific application, such affirmative requirements can be enforced without constituting a taking.

In communities where tourism is a major industry, opposition to strong preservation regulations is tempered by popular realization that the charm of the historic setting is a prime economic asset that, as in Nantucket, "constitutes a substantial part of the appeal which has enabled it to build up its summer vacation business."[21] Following this economic reasoning, communities less dependent on tourism than Nantucket or New Orleans might find preservation controls more vulnerable to attack. However, as preservation gains greater legitimacy on its own merits, the necessity of relying on tourism as a justification diminishes.

In 1964, the New Hampshire court in *Town of Deering ex rel. Bittenbender v. Tibbetts* upheld a prohibition on building within a quarter mile of the town common, giving such nonspecific grounds for the police power as the promotion of "the general economy, welfare, and prosperity" of the community. Although the historic nature of the area was a principal consideration, no historical district as such was created; and while enhancement of property values was mentioned as a justification for controls, tourism was not. Instead the purpose of the Deering regulation, as well as the standard for enforcement, turned about the maintenance of "the urban

[19]Note 14, 562.
[20]New Orleans, La., Code Ch. 65, Ord. 14, 538 (1937), Sect. 65-36, 37.
[21]Note 14, 562.

atmosphere of the town"[22]—a descriptive term implying aesthetic and urban design values as much as preservation.

At least two court decisions beyond the New Orleans cases have affirmed that the design context or tout ensemble of a historic district can be maintained by requiring redevelopment to adhere to certain design criteria. In *City of Santa Fe v. Gamble-Skogmo, Inc.,*[23] the New Mexico court in 1964 upheld a historic zoning ordinance regulating the size and shape of windows. This minute-detail requirement was one of many architectural considerations regulated by the ordinance in order to ensure harmony with the "Old Santa Fe Style" of the district. Nine years later, in *Bohannan v. City of San Diego,*[24] a California appeals court likewise ruled that a preservation ordinance regulating signs and architectural design in a historic district for the purpose of maintaining an atmosphere reminiscent of "Old San Diego prior to 1871" was valid.

As preservation becomes increasingly accepted as a worthy community value and even a prudent and economic undertaking, more cities are incorporating landmark and historic district conservation in their general land-use and urban-design plans. To cite a famous example, an essential part of San Francisco's downtown urban design plan, which was adopted into code in 1985, is a section on conservation that establishes several conservation districts overlayed over conventional, functional zoning. The plan and ordinance list some 250 outstanding historic buildings for mandatory preservation and provide regulations governing about two hundred others that contribute to the traditional design context of the downtown. Designation of these historic resources resulted from a survey that made an inventory and ranking of the nearly two thousand buildings in the downtown area in terms of their historic and architectural significance. To compensate for preservation restrictions, the plan provides for the transfer of development rights from preservation sites to designated growth districts of the city.

Despite the generally sympathetic judicial attitude toward historic preservation, law professor George Lefcoe warns, preservation cannot be assumed to be an infallible rationale for design controls:

> The ready legitimacy of historic districts and the obvious appeal for many towns of reviving an imagined past has led to the formation of historic districts in places with no uniform or coherent style. These efforts often stifle architectural invention and preserve nothing so much as a pipe dream a community has evolved about its own past. Although supportive of authentic historic preservation, courts have not sanctioned architectural control on a historic model that never existed.[25]

[22]202 A. 2d 232 (N.H., 1964), 234–35.
[23]389 P. 2d 13 (N.M., 1964).
[24]106 Cal. Rptr. 333 (App., 1973).
[25]American Institute of Architects, *Design Review Boards: A Handbook for Communities* (Washington, D.C.: A.I.A., 1974), 13.

A requirement for new buildings to be in harmony with existing structures may fail to meet a substantive test in the context of the setting. Lefcoe cites the 1959 New Jersey case of *Hankins v. Borough of Rockleigh,* in which a prohibition against flat-roofed buildings that required houses to be of an "early American, or of other architectural style conforming with the existing residential architecture and with the rural surroundings in the Borough" was found "clearly and palpably unreasonable in the light of the actual physical development of the municipality"[26] which included many exceptions to the flat-roof rule.

Also, a requirement that new developments harmonize with the design of existing historic buildings must not be interpreted too stringently. In the 1961 Rhode Island case of *Hayes v. Smith,* a local historic commission had found a brick structure proposed as an addition to connect an existing church with an existing parish house, both with clapboard exteriors, to be incompatible and denied permission for constructions. The zoning board of review, in considering the rejection on appeal, noted that the addition proposed was indeed "quite dissimilar in materials and design from the buildings that it will join." Nevertheless, it overruled the commission's determination, believing that "the Historic Zone Commission took a view of the ordinance too restrictive to be in line with its intent or to be in the public interest." When the historic commission petitioned the decision of the review board to the state supreme court, it quoted the board's acknowledgment that "a more compatible architectural solution is desirable and possible."[27] The court, in finding for the review board, said,

> The language of the board relied on by petitioners inferentially acknowledges the general compatibility of the proposed design with the architecture of existing structures. The board, we think, was cognizant of its jurisdictional limitations and refrained from imposing its judgment or that of the commission in substitution for the plans submitted by the church in determining whether the plans met the test of compatibility. Compatibility, in the sense that it is used in the ordinance, in the last analysis necessarily involves a question of judgment and, subject only to review by this court, the judgment of the board on the issue of compatibility is final. The decision of the board in the instant cause, when read in its entirety, demonstrates that the board, while agreeing with the finding of the commission that the proposed plans lacked similarity, found nevertheless that they were compatible, even if not so compatible as the commission deemed advisable.[28]

ISOLATED URBAN LANDMARKS

The cases cited thus far are examples of historic-district preservation, but district preservation differs somewhat from preservation of single build-

[26]150 A. 2d 63 (N.J. Sup'r., 1959), 64, 66.
[27]167 A. 2d 546 (R.I., 1961), 548.
[28]Ibid., 550.

ing landmarks. District regulations attempt to maintain the design integrity of an entire area and work more or less evenly on all buildings or structures in the vicinity. The burden of regulations is shared by all properties in the area; by the same token, the advantages of preservation zoning, such as the continuity and attractiveness of the neighborhood and the enhancement of property values, also accrue to all properties in the vicinity as a mutual and reciprocal benefit. Where a designated landmark stands alone without a district, however, these advantages are not as apparent.

The situation of just such an isolated landmark was considered by the United States Supreme Court in 1978 in *Penn Central Transportation Co. v. New York City,*[29] a case discussed in chapter 6 with regard to transfer of development rights. At issue was the fate of Grand Central Terminal, the famous beaux-arts railroad station located at Park Avenue and Forty-Second Street. Its facade forms the focus of the avenue to the south; on the opposite face, the terminal looks across to the Pan Am Building, whose tall silhouette looms high over both the terminal and the original Grand Central Tower facing Park Avenue to the north. In 1967, pursuant to New York City's landmark preservation law,[30] the terminal was designated a landmark by the city's landmarks preservations commission. Not long thereafter, Penn Central, the owners of the building, entered an agreement to construct a high-rise office tower over the terminal and engaged the famous Bauhaus architect, Marcel Breuer, as the designer. Breuer proposed two alternative solutions: the first scheme consisted of a 55-story tower cantilevered over the terminal; the second suggested demolition of the south facade of the terminal and the construction of a 53-story building over it. After conducting four days of hearings, at which over eighty witnesses testified, the landmarks commission rejected both schemes. Of the first proposal, it said, "To balance a 55-story office tower above a flamboyant Beaux-Arts facade seems nothing more than an aesthetic joke."[31] It rejected arguments that the Pan Am Building, built in 1963 and only 375 feet away, had already destroyed the silhouette of the south facade and that an additional tower could do no further damage and might even provide a better background. Of the second scheme, the commission said: "To protect a Landmark, one does not tear it down. To perpetuate its architectural features, one does not strip them off."[32] Penn Central filed suit, asserting that the commission's action constituted a taking of private property without just compensation. The trial court agreed with the complaint, but its decision was overruled in subsequent reviews by the appellate and high courts of the state judiciary. The Supreme Court affirmed the New York ruling.

[29]438 U.S. 104 (1978).
[30]New York, N.Y., Admin. Code, Ch. 8-A, Sect. 205–1.0 *et seq.*, (1976).
[31]Note 29, 117–18.
[32]Ibid., 117.

In a 1970 law review comment predating the case, Grace Blumberg referred to the New York landmarks law as a "non-zoning use of the police power"[33] based on the constitutional validity of a comprehensive municipal policy as upheld in the Connecticut case of *Bartram v. Zoning Commission of City of Bridgeport.*[34] The Supreme Court in *Penn Central* implicitly agreed with this analysis.

> In contrast to discriminatory zoning, which is the antithesis of land-use control as part of some comprehensive plan, the New York City law embodies a comprehensive plan to preserve structures of historic or aesthetic interest wherever they might be found in the city, and as noted, over 400 landmarks and 31 historic districts have been designated pursuant to this plan.[35]

The Court cited several reasons advanced by the New York Court of Appeals in supporting the regulation, three of which are as follows:

(1) the landmark regulation permitted the same use as had been made of the Terminal for more than half a century;
(2) the appellants had failed to show that they could not earn a reasonable return on their investment in the Terminal itself;
(3) even if the Terminal proper could never operate at a reasonable profit, some of the income from Penn Central's extensive real estate holdings in the area, which includes hotels and office buildings, must realistically be imputed to the Terminal.[36]

Justice William H. Rehnquist disagreed, pointing out that in district zoning any decrease in the value of a property will

> more than likely be at least partially offset by an increase in value which flows from similar restrictions as to use on neighboring properties. All property owners in a designated area are placed under the same restrictions, not only for the benefit of the municipality as a whole but also for the common benefit of one another. In the words of Mr. Justice Holmes, speaking for the Court in *Pennsylvania Coal Co. v. Mahon,* there is "an average reciprocity of advantage."
>
> Where a relatively few individual buildings, all separated from one another, are singled out and treated differently from surrounding buildings, no such reciprocity exists.[37]

Notwithstanding this argument, the restriction was upheld.

---

[33]Grace Blumberg, "Legal Methods of Historic Preservation," *Buffalo L. Rev.* 19 (1970), 620.
[34]68 A. 2d 308 (Conn., 1949).
[35]Note 29, 132.
[36]Ibid., 121.
[37]Ibid., 139–40. Citing 260 U.S. 393 (1922), 415.

MITIGATING THE BURDEN OF LANDMARK STATUS

As in any zoning regulation, a basic principle behind police-power enforcement of historic preservation is that, whereas a beneficial use must be afforded the owner of a restricted property to allow a reasonable return on his investment, where a regulation has a rational relationship to a legitimate public end, there is no requirement of government that the owner be vested full economic advantage of the property. As the federal appeals court said in *Maher:* "The Supreme Court [has] repeatedly made clear that an ordinance within the police power does not become an unconstitutional taking merely because, as a result of its operation, property does not achieve its maximum economic potential."[38] Holmes's balancing test must be applied to the particular facts of each case, but there have been ample precedents that affirm this principle.

Frequently, the burden of having the value of one's property diminished because of its designation as a landmark is mitigated by tax relief. The 1921 Louisiana state constitutional amendment authorizing preservation of the Vieux Carre, for instance, allows tax-exempt status for regulated properties. The New York City landmarks law provides for restrictions to be lifted if a tax-paying owner of a designated landmark cannot realize a reasonable return on his investment and if no suitable alternative plans, including tax exemption or remission, can be formulated by the city. However, where the owner of a landmark property already enjoys a tax-exempt status, the New York law has run into trouble with the courts, since the tax rebate offers no benefit to those who are not liable for taxes in any case. In 1974, for example, in *Lutheran Church of America v. City of New York,*[39] the city lost in its efforts to prevent demolition of a landmark building owned by a tax-exempt religious organization. Earlier, the New York law had been upheld in the 1966 case *Manhattan Club v. Landmarks Preservation Commission,*[40] but in that litigation, the property owner did not qualify as a tax-exempt organization.

In addition to offering tax abatements, the New York law addresses a wide variety of preservation concerns. In Grace Blumberg's words, it is a "lengthy, comprehensive law containing a variety of legal tools," with its legal purpose based on "every reason ever advanced for historic preservation."[41] Beyond the police power, the act's many provisions include the ability of the city to acquire "protective interest" in private property through negotiation or condemnation. Such compensated controls include

a right or interest in or title to an improvement parcel or any part thereof, including but not limited to, fee title and scenic or other easements, the acqui-

[38]Note 10, 1065.
[39]316 N.E. 2d 305 (N.Y., 1974).
[40]273 N.Y.S. 2d 848 (Sup., 1966).
[41]Blumberg, "Legal Methods," 631.

sition of which by the city is determined by the commission to be necessary and appropriate for the effectuation of the purposes of this chapter.[42]

Another provision used in New York City to ease any economic loss caused by a property's landmark status is the transfer of development rights. It may be recalled from chapter 6 that the technique was, in fact, suggested by John Costonis specifically as a means for landmark preservation in Chicago.[43] To mitigate the effects of proscription against demolition of a landmark building, the New York law permits the owner to transfer the unbuilt but authorized floor area under zoning from the landmark site to a proximate lot in the same ownership.[44] The TDR provision has seen much use in New York. Indeed, as mentioned previously, some critics have contended that the device has been used too extensively, to the degree that ostensible preservation has become employed to enable development at the receiving lot to be of a higher density than appropriate. Reform of the provisions regulating TDR has been enacted to minimize such misuse.

PRESERVATION LEGISLATION

Although preservation of architectural and historic landmarks had a belated start in an America engrossed in expansion and new development, it now enjoys wide support. Over the past fifty years, all the states and over five hundred municipalities have enacted laws encouraging or requiring preservation of buildings and sites of historical or architectural significance. As already discussed, in cities such as New York and San Francisco, preservation laws have been vigorously applied. Even such recent designs as Gordon Bunshaft's Lever House is under the protection of New York City's landmarks law as an archetype of the International Style's high-rise office tower design.

Federal initiatives have been a primary motivation in passage of preservation legislation, particularly in the 1930s, when the Historic American Buildings and Sites Surveys were begun, and the Historic Sites Act of 1935 was passed, which declared historic preservation as national policy and consolidated federal preservation activities within the National Park Service. The year 1949 saw the founding of the National Trust for Historic Preservation, which has been instrumental in encouraging and coordinating on a national basis state and local efforts in preservation and preservation legislation.

[42]New York, N.Y., Admin. Code, Ch. 8-A, Sect. 207-1.0b.

[43]John J. Costonis, "The Chicago Plan: Incentive Zoning and the Preservation of Urban Landmarks," *Harvard L. Rev.* 85 (1972), 574.

[44]New York, N.Y., Zoning Resolution (1982), Art. VII, Ch. 4, Sect. 74.79 ff.; and Art VIII, Ch. 1, Sects. 81.211–213, 81.747.

In 1966, Congress passed the National Preservation Act authorizing the Secretary of Interior to maintain a national register of districts, sites, buildings, structures, and objects of historical, architectural, archeological, and cultural significance. Under the act, any federal or federally assisted undertaking must take into account the effect on landmark items included in the National Register and to provide the Advisory Council on Historic Preservation with an opportunity to comment. The provision is similar to the requirement of the 1969 National Environmental Policy Act discussed in chapter 6, which calls for an environmental impact statement to be filed before any federal action is begun that may significantly affect the "human environment," a term considered broad enough to include historic areas and structures.

The Historic Preservation Act Amendments of 1980 gave state and local governments more authority and funding to carry out historic preservation programs and also provided a loan insurance program to stimulate private initiatives in preservation. In 1981, federal tax incentives established five years previous allowing amortized deduction of expenses incurred in rehabilitating historic structures were supplanted by tax credits that provided even greater economic incentive for historic rehabilitation. These tax credits, which will be discussed further in chapter 13, resulted in a spectacular increase in the restoration and remodeling of older buildings through the early 1980s.

ADAPTIVE REUSE

Designating a building as a landmark under the police power cannot, of course, deprive the owner of all use and value of his property. Accordingly, most preservation laws impose no special restrictions, beyond normal zoning regulations, on the interior use of buildings. The New York City law is typical in its concern for the exterior appearance of buildings only; the Massachusetts law specifically refrains from restricting interior arrangements or building features not subject to public view. Thus in most cases, the owner of a historic building is free to convert the interior of the structure to serve a more utilitarian and economic purpose than the obsolescent, original function. Some preservationists decry this alteration of historic buildings as violative or at least misrepresentative of the past.

Accurate restoration, preservation, and maintenance of historic buildings in keeping with their original functions intact are, however, expensive undertakings usually requiring outright acquisition by public agencies or generously endowed private preservation groups. Independence Hall in Philadelphia, for instance, is maintained as a National Historical Park by the federal government; the Alamo in San Antonio is similarly preserved as a historical monument by the state of Texas; and the original English settlement of Williamsburg, Virginia, has been restored and kept open for visitors by Colonial Williamsburg, a Rockefeller-endowed private corporation.

Such full sponsorship, whether public or private, is costly and obviously beyond any obligation that the police power can constitutionally impose upon an unwilling owner. In any case, even if possible, a policy of retaining all landmarks as museum pieces would be questionable. As an alternative, adaptation of older structures to serve contemporary functions has advantages that are particularly attractive from the standpoint of urban center rejuvenation and design. Not only can adaptive reuse derive maximum economic return from otherwise functionally obsolete structures, but it also can reintroduce such buildings into the urban fabric of contemporary society, giving them a functional life and vitality that is ordinarily denied buildings preserved as museum artifacts.

It can also be argued that old buildings, even those with little original architectural or historic value as landmarks, have proven to be invaluable assets in the creation of specialty retail centers by lending a cultural character and charm that is difficult to match in an urban design employing only new construction. The conversion in 1964 of an old factory in San Francisco to a retail and restaurant center by the architectural firm of Wurster, Bernardi, and Emmons and landscape architect Lawrence Halprin has, for instance, given the city one of its most popular urban spaces, Ghirardelli Square. Similarly successful is the adaptive reuse in 1976 of the old Quincy Market in Boston by the development company of master builder James Rouse with architect Benjamin Thompson in the creation of Faneuil Hall Marketplace.

The great success of such projects has made it a virtual truism that good urban design should make the most of existing old buildings at the city center, even of nondescript and ordinary structures such as abandoned or absolescent factories, warehouses, railway depots, and wharf facilities. John Costonis cites Walter C. Kidney's study of eclecticism in American architecture as supporting his observation that old buildings and historic styles are popular because they are "sources of associations that go back for generations or centuries, offering the fullest play for imagination, fantasy, and specious romanticism."[45] Such old buildings, "freighted with historical associations that every cultured person was familiar with"[46] project a sense of comfort and social continuity that no modern style can achieve. Adaptive reuse that incorporates preservation with urban design has not only added to the attractiveness and vitality of the city center for resident and tourist alike; it has proven to be invariably profitable financially as

[45]John J. Costonis, "Law and Aesthetics: A Critique and a Reformulation of the Dilemmas," *Michigan L. Rev.* 80 (1982), 427.

[46]Ibid. Quoting Walter C. Kidney, *The Architecture of Choice: Eclecticism in America 1880–1930* (New York: Braziller, 1974), 2.

well. Obviously, both adaptive remodeling and reuse and true restoration and preservation serve valuable if different functions.

ISSUES IN PRESERVATION

Given the "metaproblematic"[47] nature of urban issues, however, even the practice of preservation and reuse is not without flaws and controversies. In preserving the Vieux Carre of New Orleans—in what amounts to an adaptive reuse of an entire historical district as an entertainment and tourist center—much of the original context of the area has been distorted by the dominance of bars and burlesque houses that now constitute an essential part of the local economy. Notwithstanding the long-held reputation of the quarter as a red-light district, for the preservation purist, the maintenance of this aspect of the district must seem a compromise at best.

Another problem is that in recent years selective preservation of the exterior of historic buildings without regard to their interior function has developed into an extreme. In "facadism," the exterior facade is preserved only as a veneer applique on an entirely new, larger, and more profitable structure; as a 1985 issue of *Newsweek* notes: "More often than not, facadism is ugly."[48] The article points to such examples as the development of a modern high-rise building behind the Red Lion row of nineteenth-century townhouses in Washington, D.C., and the construction of a modern shopping center behind the facade of the Zion Commercial Mercantile Institution built in Salt Lake City in 1876. The writers question the use of facades as "empty masks," noting that, "a 19th-century house does not look comfortable wearing a skyscraper as a hat."[49] In even more colorful terms, William Whitehill observed in a 1966 report on historic preservation that adaptive renovations of historic structures can result in buildings projecting "a Queen Anne front and a Mary Ann behind."[50]

The values of preservation can also be taken to extremes. While applauding "the preservation ethic," urban designer Jonathan Barnett describes the absurdity of "the preservation neurosis, which constructs a rationale for preserving everything." He cites an example in New York City in which

[47]Timothy J. Cartwright, "Problems, Solutions and Strategies: A Contribution to the Theory and Practice of Planning," *Journal of the American Institute of Planners* 39, no. 3 (May 1973), 183.

[48]Mark Stevens et al. "Putting on a Good Face, Saving Old Facades Is a Controversial Compromise," *Newsweek* 106, no. 14 (Sept. 30, 1985), 76-77.

[49]Ibid.

[50]Walter M. Whitehill, "The Right of Cities to Be Beautiful," in *With Heritage so Rich,* Special Committee on Historic Preservation, U.S. Conference of Mayors (New York: Random House, 1966), 53.

the historians for the National Park Service were with difficulty dissuaded from putting the parking lot at Riis Park on the National Register of Historic Places. The reason: At the time it was built it was rumored to be the largest parking lot in the world.[51]

John Costonis points out that preservation has been used by "no-change constituencies" (preservationists, environmentalists, and neighborhood groups opposed to change) as a tool to protect "cultural stability and identity" (or the status quo of the area as embodied in the "existing resource" to be preserved) from disruptive displacement and the development of an unwanted "new entrant." "Change constituencies" (developers, potential new residents, or other land tenants who would benefit from admission into the area) charge that since "the standards of most preservation ordinances are so vague that, literally read, they qualify almost any building or neighborhood as a landmark or historic district," preservation has in fact been exploited as a means for exclusion, with preservation commissions usurping power that should rightfully be exercised by land-use planning authorities.[52]

Jane Jacobs on Old Buildings

Ironically enough, one of the greatest problems associated with the preservation ethic and also with urban design stems from what might be considered a planning success. For generations, planners concerned about revitalization of the declining city center have lamented the shift of the middle class away from the city in favor of the newness and spaciousness of the residential suburb. Reversal of the tendency of this educated and economically powerful segment of the population to abandon the central city for suburbia was seen as vital in order for the city to survive as a socially healthy and economically viable population center.

One of the best known and most influential theses adopting this view was written in 1961 by journalist Jane Jacobs, *The Death and Life of Great American Cities*. Jacobs pointed out that a principal cause for the social and physical decay of the urban core was the growing lack of "diversity" in the population, function, and physical plant of the city center. She saw the causes for this decay in essentially physical terms and enumerated several conditions as indispensible in regenerating this needed diversity. She wrote: "Minglings of old buildings, with consequent minglings of living

---

[51]Jonathan Barnett, *An Introduction to Urban Design* (New York: Harper & Row, 1982), 53.

[52]Costonis, "Law and Aesthetics," 382 ff., 364.

costs and tastes, are essential to get diversity and stability in residential populations, as well as diversity in enterprise."[53]

Primary among her required conditions for revitalization was that an urban district must have a "fairly close-grained" mix of buildings that vary in age and condition, "including a good proportion of old ones so that they vary in the economic yield they must produce."[54] By old buildings, Jacobs meant "not museum-piece old buildings, not old buildings in an excellent and expensive state of rehabilitation—although these make fine ingredients—but also a good lot of plain, ordinary, low-value old buildings, including some rundown old buildings."[55]

She argued that only proven high-profit or highly subsidized enterprises can afford the costs of new construction. By necessity, these are limited to well-established, standardized, corporate operations such as chain stores, chain restaurants, and banks. Neighborhood bars, ethnic restaurants, good bookstores, and antique shops that give an area life, diversity, and interest cannot afford to own or rent high-cost quarters. Likewise, she reasoned, well-established, subsidized concert halls and art museums might afford imposing new buildings, but studios and galleries that feed the arts must begin in old buildings:

> As for really new ideas of any kind—no matter how ultimately profitable or otherwise successful some of them might prove to be—there is no leeway for such chancy trial, error and experimentation in the high-overhead economy of new construction. Old ideas can sometimes use new buildings. New ideas must use old buildings.[56]

In effect, Jacob identified a singular, economic function for the old, preserved urban structures that cannot be duplicated by new construction.

Gentrification

Whether Jacobs and her allies in planning were decisively persuasive in their beliefs, or whether other forces, including such incentives as tax benefits, home purchase and rehabilitation loans, and sometimes urban homesteading subsidies, were more determinative, the idea of returning to the urban center began to appeal to segments of the middle-class population. Gradually, it became quite fashionable, especially among young, well-educated professionals with no or few children, to reclaim and rehabilitate the old urban neighborhoods that their class had once abandoned. With

[53]Jane Jacobs, *The Death and Life of Great American Cities* (New York: Random House, 1961), 194.
[54]Ibid., 150.
[55]Ibid., 187.
[56]Ibid., 188.

them, these people brought renewed affluence as well as practical preservation and reuse to entire districts once dilapidated and in need of repair and reconstruction.

This "gentrification," or reestablishment of the middle-class "gentry" in homesteads in the middle of the city, is now a documented phenomenon in many older urban areas. In a 1980 article, Philip L. Clay notes: "The gentrified neighborhoods are more likely to be located on higher elevations, near water or public open space, or near areas of historic interest. Many of them are historic districts."[57] Such gentrified districts as Georgetown in Washington, D.C., and Society Hill in Philadelphia are now famous among preservationists for their renewed respectability and quality of restoration and reuse of historical areas that had once deteriorated into slums.

Residential districts are not the only areas experiencing building renovation and reuse. In New York City, it has become quite popular to convert loft spaces formerly used for industrial purposes into urban dwellings. In a material manifestation of another of Jacob's urban theories, many such conversions have combined the workplace with the home. Such mixing of uses was a common practice in ages before zoning and has been especially popular in New York among artists using lofts as joint living-work quarters. In some manufacturing districts of the city, so many lofts have been recycled—sometimes in violation of existing building and zoning codes—that the city has been obliged to pass regulations specifically to govern such conversions. The purpose is not only to safeguard residential occupants but also to prevent forced eviction of commercial and industrial tenants and to ensure at fair market prices an adequate supply of loft space for garment manufacturing, meat processing, printing, and other economically important industrial activities threatened with displacement by building uses able to afford higher land rents.[58]

Though the values of preservations are well served by gentrification, the problem of displacement can be substantial, particularly in a social context. The poor who migrated to old, decaying neighborhoods have in the process of renewal been frequently displaced by the return of the well-to-do. Although Jacobs had emphasized the necessity of diversity in social and economic backgrounds and had advocated a close-grained variation in building values to accommodate a broad spectrum of area inhabitants and enterprises, the realities of the marketplace have not always allowed such diversity and variation. Without public controls and subsidies, successful district renovation and reoccupation of buildings by the middle class result in the appreciation of real estate values throughout the area. Such rises in

[57]Philip L. Clay, "The Rediscovery of City Neighborhoods: Reinvestment by Long-time Residents and Newcomers," in *Back to the City: Issues in Neighborhood Renovation,* ed. Shirley Bradway Laska and Daphne Spain (New York: Pergamon, 1980), 21–22.

[58]New York, N.Y. Zoning Resolution (1982), Art. VII, Ch. 4, Sect. 74.78, Art. IV, Ch. 2, Sects. 42.01, 42.14D, Ch. 3, Sect. 43.17–171.

values in turn encourages reinvestment and prompts owners to raise rents, effectively driving out poor tenants already occupying the premises.

Resentment against middle-class gentrification by the poor suffering displacement can be demonstrable. In their book, *City Zoning: The Once and Future Frontier*, Clifford L. Weaver and Richard F. Babcock quote from a "fact sheet" prepared by a black community group opposed to the establishment of a historical preservation district in their neighborhood. The sheet cites in ironic tones three urban areas widely acclaimed by preservationists as showpieces of historic district renewal:

> Preservation districts were established in three other places across the country. These places have received national notoriety. They are: Society Hill, Philadelphia; College Hill, Providence, Rhode Island; and Georgetown, Washington, D.C. In all three of these places "black folk" removal has been the result.[59]

Weaver and Babcock note a graffito scrawled on a building in a largely black district of Rochester, New York, that reads, "Up the wall to Whitey's historic district."[60]

The subject of gentrification and the question of whether the phenomenon should be actively encouraged through public policy are controversial. Writing on the twin processes of urban abandonment and gentrification in New York City, Peter Marcuse, professor of planning at Columbia University, summarizes the argument against gentrification as follows:

> Gentrification attracts higher-income households from other areas in the city, reducing demand elsewhere and increasing tendencies to abandonment, and displaces lower-income people, likewise increasing pressures on housing and rents. Both abandonment and gentrification are directly linked to changes in the economy of the city, which have dramatically increased the economic polarization of the population. A vicious circle is created in which the poor are continuously under pressure of displacement and the well-to-do continuously seek to wall themselves in within gentrified neighborhoods. Far from being a cure for abandonment, gentrification worsens it. Both gentrification and abandonment have caused a high level of displacement in New York City. Public policies have contributed to this result, but are also capable of countering it.[61]

Conversely, other studies have disputed the severity of the adverse effects caused by privately sponsored area renovation. A 1984 study by the

---

[59]Clifford L. Weaver and Richard F. Babcock, *City Zoning: The Once and Future Frontier* (Chicago and Washington, D.C.: Planners Press, 1979), 42.

[60]Ibid.

[61]Peter Marcuse, "Abandonment, Gentrification, and Displacement: The Linkages in New York City," in *Gentrification of the City,* ed. Neil Smith and Peter Williams (Boston: Allen & Unwin, 1986), 154.

New York Department of City Planning on "Private Investment and Neighborhood Change" in New York between 1970 and 1980 concluded that gentrification has had a generally "positive influence" on the areas renovated. Reported the *Times,*

> The study concluded that the gentrification of these areas had improved housing conditions, sharply reduced deterioration, strengthened their commercial districts and increased the city's tax base.

As for displacement, the newspaper continued,

> It also found that, despite an influx of new, younger and more affluent residents, the areas' populations remained relatively stable in age, income, and racial and ethnic makeup.
>
>   The private investment in housing—which involved buying townhouses for personal use, cooperative and condominium conversions and the renovation of multifamily dwellings into higher-priced rentals—did force some poor residents to move, the report found. But it asserted that gentrification was not the sole, and perhaps not even the primary, cause of displacement. In some cases, it was the opposite of gentrification—continuing decay of the housing stock—that pushed poorer people out of their homes.[62]

As gentrification demonstrates, preservation planning, like all aspects of urban planning, must take into full account all effects of its actions. However sensible and worthy historic preservation may be as a value and an undertaking, like urban design, it cannot be conducted in isolation of all other considerations, whether the rights and welfare of residents or the rights and interests of the owner of a landmark property.

   Costonis emphasizes that preservation should not be presumed a preordained virtue. He cites such notable authorities as Lewis Mumford and Kevin Lynch: Mumford regards the city as the "best organ of memory man has yet created," but cautions that "the city itself, as a living environment, must not be condemned to serve the specialized purposes of the museum." Lynch recognizes the mnemonic quality of the environment but warns against preservation that might "encapsulate some image of the past . . . that may in time prove to be mythical or irrelevant (because) preservation is not simply the saving of old things but the maintaining of a response to those things." In suggesting cultural stability as a rationale for preservation and aesthetic regulation, Costonis writes,

> A community's decision to preserve is not preordained but is a self-defining political and cultural choice whose validity must ultimately rest on its compatibility with shared community values.[63]

   [62]Lee A. Daniels, "City Finds Gentrification Beneficial," *New York Times* March 23, 1984, 41.
   [63]Costonis, "Law and Aesthetics," 430–31.

Notwithstanding Costonis's caveat, preservation has gained stature over the years, not only for its cultural benefit but for its economic utility. As preservation continues to be seen as a task worthy of public participation, its legitimacy grows as a substantive basis for police-power regulation. As Holmes correctly foresaw in *Pennsylvania Coal,* the police power has indeed expanded over the years to encompass a wider concept of the public welfare. There is no better example of this broadening of government involvement than in the growing popular interest in urban landmarks and historic districts and in the expanding role of the police power to enforce their preservation.

PART V

THE CONUNDRUM OF DESIGN REGULATION

Chapter 9

The Basis for Design Regulation

Just as the first quarter of the twentieth century saw the development and acceptance of zoning as a planning tool of local government, the closing quarter is witnessing the gradual acceptance of local governmental authority in wielding the police power for more definitive ends in design. Conception of the police power in the interest of public necessity and public health, safety, and morals has gradually expanded to embrace consideration of public welfare, economy, and even convenience. Not least, the idea of beauty has gained ever-increasing legitimacy as grounds for police-power regulation. The objective need not be limited to such purposes as the purging of eyesores like billboards and junkyards or the preservation of historic and architectural landmarks. It can extend to the design control of private development to ensure conformity to community preferences in architecture and to enforce public goals in urban design.

Possibly the most influential case in this regard is the 1954 landmark of *Berman v. Parker,* in which the Supreme Court gave its unanimous approval for the conduct of urban renewal in the nation's capital city. At issue in the case was the constitutionality of an act empowering the local urban-renewal agency to acquire and assemble private real property through the process of eminent domain in order to implement a comprehensive, area-wide slum clearance and urban redevelopment plan. The Court's decision was a ringing endorsement of beauty as a valid public purpose:

> The concept of the public welfare is broad and inclusive. The values it represents are spiritual as well as physical, aesthetic as well as monetary. It is within

the power of the legislature to determine that the community should be beautiful as well as healthy, spacious as well as clean, well-balanced as well as care-
fully patrolled. In the present case, the Congress and its authorized agencies
have made determinations that take into account a wide variety of values. It
is not for us to reappraise them. If those who govern the District of Columbia
decide that the Nation's Capital should be beautiful as well as sanitary, there
is nothing in the Fifth Amendment that stands in the way.[1]

Berman was a notable case tinged with irony. Not since the 1928 *Nectow*[2] case had the Supreme Court ruled on any issue directly related to urban planning, and another decade would pass before the federal court system would join the state judiciaries in active consideration of planning
matters. From a planning standpoint, the decision cleared the way for "integrated plans for redevelopment,"[3] a well-intended concept of urban renewal at the time that has since been largely discredited for its promotion
of a rationalized, end-state urban design ideal with insufficient regard for
the existing community. From a legal standpoint, *Berman* has been widely
cited by subsequent courts and commentators as the ultimate verification
of aesthetics as a proper concern of government. Such interpretations have
frequently extended beyond the decision's original context of eminent domain and the Fifth Amendment, stretching the decision to apply to police-
power enforcement of aesthetic objectives. Noted Robert A. Bergs one year
after the case, "Even where it is accepted that *Berman v. Parker* stands for
the emancipation of aesthetics, there will be much room in which to dispute
whether the new rule is to be applied by the police power or by eminent
domain."[4] Notwithstanding such reservations, it is indisputable that many
court decisions since the *Berman* case have, in fact, justified police-power
regulation of aesthetics by referring to this high Court decision.

Besides *Berman*, several other Supreme Court decisions can be cited in
general support of aesthetic regulation and urban design. One such case is
City of Los Angeles v. Taxpayers for Vincent,[5] a 1984 decision that upheld
a municipal ordinance prohibiting the posting of signs on public property
to avoid "visual clutter" in the city. In the 1974 case, *Village of Belle Terre
v. Boraas*,[6] the Court upheld the right of a community to maintain its village
character by restricting dwelling types to the one-family variety. The Court
decisions in both *Belle Terre* and *Berman* were written by William O. Douglas, a justice known for his politically liberal views, although judges of vary-

[1]*Berman v. Parker*, 348 U.S. 26 (1954), 33.

[2]*Nectow v. City of Cambridge*, 277 U.S. 183 (1928).

[3]Note 1, 35.

[4]Robert A. Bergs, "Aesthetics as a Justification for the Exercise of the Police Power or
Eminent Domain," *George Washington L. Rev.* 23 (1955), 750.

[5]466 U.S. 789 (1984).

[6]416 U.S. 1 (1974).

ing political persuasions have also strongly supported aesthetic regulation as a legitimate police-power function of local government, perhaps for different reasons. In fact, most of the justices who voted to uphold the Los Angeles ban against posted signs in *Vincent* are generally regarded as conservatives.

Long before involvement of the Supreme Court, state courts had also sanctioned the imposition of the police power for aesthetic purposes, even beyond consideration of billboards, junkyards, and landmark preservation. In the 1923 case of *State ex rel. Civello v. City of New Orleans,* an ordinance excluding a retail grocery store from a residential district was upheld on largely aesthetic grounds, which the Louisiana court found related to the general public welfare.

> If by the term "aesthetic considerations" is meant a regard merely for outward appearances, for good taste in the matter of the beauty of the neighborhood itself, we do not observe any substantial reason for saying that such a consideration is not a matter of general welfare. The beauty of a fashionable residence neighborhood in a city is for the comfort and happiness of the residents, and it sustains in a general way the value of property in the neighborhood. It is therefore as much a matter of general welfare as is any other condition that fosters comfort or happiness, and consequent values generally of the property in the neighborhood. Why should not the police power avail, as well to suppress or prevent a nuisance committed by offending the sense of sight, as to suppress or prevent a nuisance committed by offending the sense of hearing, or the olfactory nerves? An eyesore in a neighborhood of residences might be as much a public nuisance, and as ruinous to property values in the neighborhood generally, as a disagreeable noise, or odor, or a menace to safety or health. The difference is not in principle, but only in degree.[7]

SEEKING A BASIS

Municipal zoning officials have been wont to justify community regulation of architecture and urban design on the grounds of public welfare. Jesse Dukeminier, for one, has associated aesthetics with a diversity of values beyond its own intrinsic worth, from power, wealth, and community health to patriotism. He wrote,

> Zoning regulations may, and often do, integrate aesthetics with a number of other community objectives, but it needs to be repeatedly emphasized that a healthful, safe and efficient community environment is not enough. More thought must be given to appearances if communities are to be really desirable places in which to live. Edmund Burke—no wild-eyed radical—said many

---

[7]97 So. 440 (La., 1923), 444.

years ago, "To make us love our country, our country ought to be lovely."
It is still so today.[8]

Dukeminier's argument of patriotism is shared by Bergs, who referred to a
theme suggested in the Supreme Court decision in *United States v. Gettysburg Electric Railway Company.* In the case, the Court supported the public
acquisition of the Civil War battlefield at Gettysburg as a national monument. Bergs argued,

> If a person has grown up in an attractive and well-ordered community, rather
> than an ugly, blighted one, certainly his affection for home—his neighbor-
> hood—his town, his state and nation—will be the stronger. Certainly he will
> rise to its defense more quickly and more wholeheartedly.[9]

Psychological Arguments

A somewhat more substantive argument that has been increasingly
used to justify aesthetic regulation is the adverse psychological effects of
ugliness, particularly in conjunction with other deleterious urban conditions
such as congestion, noise, and pollution. In 1915, the high court of the
Philippines, then still under American jurisdiction, ruled in *Churchill and
Tait v. Rafferty* to uphold an ordinance compelling the removal of billboards:

> Without entering into the realm of psychology, we think it quite demonstrable
> that sight is as valuable to a human being as any of his other senses, and that
> the proper ministration to this sense conduces as much to his contentment as
> the care bestowed upon the senses of hearing or smell, and probably as much
> as both together. Objects may be offensive to the eye as well as to the nose
> or ear.[10]

The effect of environmental aesthetics on public health, especially on
psychological well-being, has gained increasing recognition over the years.
In 1941, the American Public Health Association observed, "It is obvious
that matters of taste cannot be crystallized in quantitative terms, but the
desire for beauty is a fundamental urge whose satisfaction is essential to
healthy living in the full sense of the term."[11] In 1954, architect Richard
Neutra suggested that the practical utility of environmental beauty could be
proved in terms of mental health and physiology:

---

[8]J.J. Dukeminier, Jr., "Zoning for Aesthetic Objectives: A Reappraisal," *Law and Contemporary Problems* 20 (1955), 225.

[9]Bergs, "Aesthetics as Justification," 744. Quoting 160 U.S. 668 (1896).

[10]32 P.I. 580 (1915), 608.

[11]American Public Health Association, *Housing for Health* (Lancaster, P.A.: Science
Press, 1941), 205.

The increase, for example, in cardiac diseases and collapses has been explained by nervous strain. The brain physiologist observes this strain under the term of "arrhythmic innervation." He has minutely tabulated laboratory proofs of the damage and disaster that the daily stimuli of urban life hold in store for us. . . .

If there is such a dualism and duplicity of "utility" and "beauty," beauty surely comes out second best, and no art commission will help it much. But to raise children in psychologically satisfactory surroundings and not have them warped by sensorial privations, by confusion and irritations to the eye or the ear or the nose, to have them look out on a green surface, or into green foliage, or play in the shade of trees . . . all this is quite practical.[12]

The following year, Robert J. Albertson further urged in a paper on governmental administration that scientific study of the psychological effect of community aesthetics would justify its regulation.[13] Dukeminier wrote in agreement of the need for communities to be "emotionally satisfactory," noting that "when the inner life of an individual is out of balance, anxiety occurs, expressing itself in a number of socially destructive ways."[14] Dukeminier's article noted Neutra's viewpoint and the need for psychological investigations on the effect of the physical environment on personality, but he also pointed out that he was "unable to find any good study of this problem and my colleagues in sociology and psychology tell me none has been made."[15]

A decade later, in the 1960s, this void of empirical evidence was filled by numerous psychological studies substantiating the relationship between environment and mental well-being. One of the best-known early works in this area was *The Hidden Dimension,* in which psychologist Edward T. Hall described experiments in which mice evidenced a high incidence of deviant psychiatric behavior after being subjected to simulated urban conditions. Hall wrote,

The implosion of the world population into cities everywhere is creating a series of destructive behavior sinks more lethal than the hydrogen bomb. Man is faced with a chain reaction and practically no knowledge of the structure of the cultural atoms producing it. If what is known about animals when they are crowded or moved to an unfamiliar biotope is at all relevant to mankind, we are now facing some terrible consequences in our urban sinks.[16]

---

[12]Richard Neutra, "'Practical' Cities Must Not Be Full of Irritations," *American City* 69, no. 4 (Apr. 1954), 122–23.
[13]Robert J. Albertson, *Zoning for Aesthetics,* Master's thesis, University of Pennsylvania, 1955.
[14]Dukeminier, "Zoning for Aesthetic Objectives," 231.
[15]Ibid.
[16]Edward T. Hall, *The Hidden Dimension* (New York: Doubleday, 1966), 155.

Hall was joined in his concern by Lewis Herber, who wrote in *Crisis In Our Cities,*

> [The ears of the city dweller] are assailed by continual noise; his senses are blighted by the drabness of the urban development; his job tends to become increasingly sedentary, reducing the use of his muscles. Although these day-to-day insults to the human body and nervous system do not necessarily result in a sudden, acute illness, taken together there seems to be little doubt that they are very harmful. In fact a large mass of statistical information on respiratory disorders, cancer, heart disease, and mental illness establishes all too convincingly that we are steadily approaching a crisis in the field of urban public health.[17]

Hall explicitly related the physical environment to psychological health, asserting that

> To solve formidable urban problems, there is the need not only for the usual coterie of experts—city planners, architects, engineers of all types, economists, law-enforcement specialists, traffic and transportation experts, educators, lawyers, social workers, and political scientists—but a number of new experts. Psychologists, anthropologists, and ethologists are seldom, if ever, prominently featured as permanent members of city planning departments but they should be.[18]

The social significance of environmental psychology is now so well established that virtually every legal commentary concerning community aesthetics makes reference to some psychological study. A 1970 article by Charles J. Wilcox is typical in the author's finding that: "The quality of urban life is affected by physical surroundings. People are oppressed and depressed by drabness and lack of visual relief, and studies have shown that congestion is injurious to physical and mental health."[19] This commonly-held view has also influenced the courts. In 1972, for example, a Michigan appellate court upheld a sign ordinance in *Sun Oil Company v. City of Madison Heights,* stating: "The modern trend is to recognize that a community's aesthetic well-being can contribute to urban man's psychological and emotional stability."[20]

Economic Arguments

Beyond psychology and public health, an even stronger argument for aesthetic regulation can be made from economic considerations, especially

[17]Lewis Herber, *Crisis in our Cities* (Englewood Cliffs, N.J.: Prentice-Hall, 1965), 2.
[18]Hall, *Hidden Dimension,* 158.
[19]Charles J. Wilcox, "Aesthetic Considerations in Land Use Planning," *Albany L. Rev.* 35 (1970), 134–35. Citing Herber, *Crisis in our Cities.*
[20]199 N.W. 2d 525 (Mich. App., 1972), 529.

in areas where the effects of poor aesthetic conditions can be more readily subject to quantifiable assessment. In addition to the control of billboards and other visual nuisances, the economic argument has been particularly effective as a justification for the regulation of architectural design. In 1941, for example, the Florida court in *City of Miami Beach v. Ocean & Inland Co.* found the protection of the area's tourist industry to be the primary grounds for architectural restrictions that precluded general businesses from an area reserved for resort hotels. The court said, "It is difficult to see how the success of Miami Beach could continue if its aesthetic appeal were ignored because the beauty of the community is a distinct lure to the winter traveler."[21]

In cases where tourism or other similar income-producing activity can be affected by environmental appearance, aesthetics is of economic concern because of factors external to the property itself. The fact that Miami Beach, Nantucket, or New Orleans rely on their beauty to attract visitors and generate income exemplifies a relationship between economics and aesthetic quality that is essentially extrinsic in nature. Economic gain is realized from an external activity that is dependent on the attractiveness of a property or an environment of which the property is a part.

Another perspective also involves consideration of economics, but of economic value intrinsic to property itself. The more beautiful and desirable a property, the greater its inherent financial value, regardless of such external factors as tourism. Thus, a lot with a scenic view or one that is surrounded by other attractively developed and well-maintained properties has greater intrinsic value than a lot with no view, surrounded by ugly land uses. Wrote Dukeminier,

> Now it seems fairly clear that among the basic values of our communities, and of any society aboriginal or civilized, is beauty. Men are continuously engaged in its creation, pursuit, and possession; beauty, like wealth, is an object of strong human desire. Men may use a beautiful object which they possess or control as a basis for increasing their power or wealth or for effecting a desired distribution of any one or all of the other basic values of the community, and, conversely, men may use power and wealth in an attempt to produce a beautiful object or a use of land which is aesthetically satisfying. It is solely because of man's irrepressible aesthetic demands, for instance, that land with a view has always been more valuable for residential purposes than land without . . . [22]

Regulation of architectural design has been based on economic arguments, both of an extrinsic and intrinsic nature. Virtually all arguments supporting historic preservation, whether in New Orleans, Nantucket, or New York City, have advanced the rationale of protecting the extrinsic value

[21]3 So. 2d 364 (Fla., 1941), 367.
[22]Dukeminier, "Zoning for Aesthetic Objectives," 224–25.

of the local tourist economy. While extrinsic and intrinsic values are closely associated, this discussion will focus on economic arguments based on intrinsic values, or the component of speculative property values generally attributable to beauty.

If the value of a property is enhanced by the beauty of its surroundings, a development that is considered ugly or at variance with the design context of neighboring structures can depress the value of properties around it. In considering this, it has been suggested that a legal analogy exists between proximate land values and the value of oil-pool reserves beneath ground. In the 1928 case of *Marrs v. City of Oxford,* a federal court in Kansas affirmed the idea that underground oil is a common interest assignable to all owners of land over the pool. The court drew a comparison between oil reserves and urban land values. It pointed out that oil is a fugacious asset that flows from one area to another without regard to property lines, so that any pumping by one owner would affect an asset shared by all. In the same way, urban land values are also fugacious; any action on the part of one property owner can affect the holdings of other area landowners. Thus, the erection of an ugly building by one owner in a neighborhood is a legitimate concern of other landowners in the vicinity. Said the court in *Marrs,* "The stabilizing of property values, and giving some assurance to the public that, if property is purchased in a residential district, its value as such will be preserved, is probably the most cogent reason back of zoning ordinances."[23]

This sort of reasoning was implicit in the Wisconsin court decision in *State ex rel. Saveland Park Holding Corp. v. Wieland.* In this 1955 case, the state supreme court agreed with a trial court that a suburban community could properly deny an applicant permission to erect a residence if the community building board found the "architectural appeal of the proposed structure . . . so at variance with that of structures already constructed, or being constructed, 'as to cause a substantial depreciation in the property values' in the immediate neighborhood."[24] The court cited *Berman* to support its conclusion, but whether *Berman* is an appropriate precedent in regard to a police-power restriction on design is open to question.

Nonetheless, the relationship between aesthetics and property values brought out in *Saveland Park* is seen by several legal observers as a substantial one. As Daniel R. Mandelker and Roger A. Cunningham write, "To the extent that architectural control ordinances are based on the protection of property values rationale, the justification for governmental restriction of the freedom of architectural expression is strengthened."[25]

[23]24 F. 2d 541 (1928), 548.
[24]69 N.W. 2d 217 (Wisc., 1955), 222.
[25]Daniel R. Mandelker and Roger A. Cunningham, *Planning and Control of Land Development* (Indianapolis: Bobbs-Merrill, 1979), 920.

The *Columbia Law Review* was more specific in suggesting property values as a practical measure to determine the limits of aesthetic regulation. In a 1964 article, it said,

> Accurate knowledge of the correlation of aesthetics with property values could enable the courts to determine which aesthetically motivated legislation actually furthers the general welfare. More importantly, courts could use this correlation to define practical limits beyond which aesthetic considerations may not control.[26]

Citing this statement with approval, H. Rutherford Turnbull, III, notes: "Economic considerations, by their very nature, are concrete. Aesthetic ones are ephemeral. Judicial treatment of the former is customary. Judicial consideration of the latter is hesitant and halting and never particularly well reasoned."[27] Turnbull favors economics in general and property values in particular as the principal standards for aesthetic regulation.

Others, however, are more equivocal in accepting property values as a primary reason for justifying design regulation. Professor Frank Michelman of Harvard Law School, for instance, feels that to consider economics as the basic rationale for controls is to evade the real issue of aesthetics as the fundamental motivation. He argues that changes in property values are more a barometer of public reaction to aesthetic impacts than a valid primary factor and cause for controls. He writes,

> What appears to be an aesthetically aimed regulation is often upheld because it "protects property values," and therefore need not depend for its validity on its curbing a "merely aesthetic" nuisance. It should be clearly understood that this is escapist reasoning that evades the real issues.
>
> The effect on market value, after all, is derivative or symptomatic—not primary or of the essence. If the activities curbed by the regulation would otherwise make the surrounding property less valuable, it must be because those activities would radiate some kind of undesirable impact.
>
> If that impact is received and felt through visual sensibility, then the "economic" interest in question simply masks what has been referred to above as an "aesthetic" interest. In other words, without the aesthetic nuisance, there would be no market devaluation.[28]

Put in another way, Michelman seems to be suggesting that economics is little more than a rationalization, not unlike the rationalizations seen in the early days of billboard regulation.

---

[26]*Columbia L. Rev.* "Zoning, Aesthetics, and the First Amendment," 64 (1964), 90.

[27]H. Rutherford Turnbull III, "Aesthetic Zoning," *Wake Forest L. Rev.* 7(1971), 251.

[28]Frank Michelman, "Toward a Practical Standard for Aesthetic Regulation," *Prac. Lawyer* 15 (Feb. 1969), 37.

Stephen F. Williams picks up on a consideration broached by Michelman:

> A design that offends widely shared aesthetic viewpoints may depress the property values of neighboring houses. It would be unfair to say that such a property value change, if it can be proven, should have no bearing on how the state's interest is classified. After all, neighbors of a house of exceptionally unpopular design may not only suffer as captive viewers, but they may also suffer the pecuniary loss inflicted upon them through the reaction of others to the offending design. Although the harm inflicted is exclusively the *result* of popular reaction to a form of expression, the government interest in protecting innocent parties against pecuniary loss seems more tolerable than an interest solely in protecting the feelings of hostile members of the population.[29]

Williams notes that courtroom predictions of a projected design's possible adverse effects on neighboring property values is conjecture rather than scientifically obtained evidence. He cites Turnbull's reference to an unreported county court decision in Virginia, *Eustice v. Binford*.[30] In the case, testimony of three real estate appraisers on how surrounding values would be affected if a controversial house design were allowed to be completed resulted in contradictory appraisals: a decrease in values; no change; and an anticipated increase.

For the same reasons, law professor George Lefcoe agrees with Michelman that economics is a poor basis for design regulation. He argues,

> There is a practical difficulty in trying to bind the ethereal concept of "beauty" to what appears to be the hard rock data of "property values." It is nearly impossible to know whether a glass house located in a neighborhood of traditional homes will actually lower values.[31]

Even advocates of the use of economic values as a standard for aesthetic controls admit to procedural difficulties, such as the need for prior determination of the economic effect a design will have on neighboring property. Turnbull writes,

> In cases of aesthetic zoning . . . the question of valuation precedes the question of the legitimacy of the regulation. That is to say, there should be a determination concerning the effect of the proposed action by the property before the right to act is permitted or denied. This need for prior determina-

---

[29]Stephen F. Williams, "Subjectivity, Expression, and Privacy: Problems of Aesthetic Regulation," *Minnesota L. Rev.* 62 (November 1977), 26.

[30]Cir. Ct. of Arlington Cty., Va., Chancery no. 19497 (Sept. 24, 1969).

[31]American Institute of Architects, *Design Review Boards: A Handbook for Communities* (Washington, D.C.: A.I.A., 1974), 36.

tion may require the owner . . . to make a prior determination almost at the same time the costs of hiring an architect to design the structure are incurred. This is practically impossible, as no land appraiser, much less the usual property owner, can make the determination *in vacuuo*.[32]

Mandelker and Cunningham summarize the issue of considering architectural controls in light of the somewhat antagonistic ends of free expression and protection of existing property values as follows:

> In any event, when architectural control ordinances are challenged on the First Amendment grounds, justification of the restriction of the freedom of architectural expression will surely require more substantial evidence that the proscribed architectural styles have adverse effects on property values than has hitherto been required when architectural controls have been challenged on due process grounds. And ordinances which give local officials broad discretion to determine whether or not a particular design will adversely affect property values may constitute an invalid prior restraint on freedom of expression, even if the discretion is exercised by an architectural review board composed largely of architects.[33]

Such problems, however, have not diminished what has virtually become a traditional reliance of the courts on economic justifications. Despite the reasoning that economics is somewhat a make-weight argument, from a realistic standpoint, any lawyer arguing on behalf of community design controls would be incautious not to include economics as a primary justification for regulations. It can be convincingly maintained that the economic consequence of a building's appearance on neighboring properties is a valid public concern, and as a practical matter, the effect of a design on economic values is still a subject that can be addressed somewhat more readily by the courts than the aesthetic issue. As the New Jersey court said in a 1964 case,

> There are areas in which aesthetics and economics coalesce, areas in which a discordant sight is as hard an economic fact as an annoying odor or sound. We refer not to some sensitive or exquisite preference but to concepts of congruity held so widely that they are inseparable from the enjoyment and hence the value of property.[34]

Although unquestionably more sophisticated and relevant to the societal effects of environmental aesthetics, modern arguments based on economic and psychological considerations are, in a sense, an extension of indirect and ostensible justifications for aesthetic control that were advanced in

---

[32]Turnbull, "Aesthetic Zoning," 246.
[33]Mandelker and Cunningham, *Planning and Land Development*, 921.
[34]*United Advertising Corp. v. Borough of Metuchen*, 198 A 2d 447 (N.J., 1964), 449.

such turn-of-the-century cases as *St. Louis Gunning*.[35] And, although some scholars question the appropriateness of economic and psychological grounds for aesthetic regulation, the working judiciary still seems to favor these practical arguments. In upholding regulations restricting the "visual clutter" caused by signs posted on public property, the Supreme Court in the *Vincent* case, said: "[Aesthetic] interests are both psychological and economic. The character of the environment affects the quality of life and the value of property in both residential and commercial areas."[36]

Seeking a New Premise

In a 1982 article, law professor John J. Costonis tried to look beyond the usual justifications for aesthetic regulation to a reformulation of the questions involved. He suggests that the traditional basis for controls has been tied to a "visual beauty rationale" supported by three "defective" and "outmoded" premises of aesthetic analysis that have influenced legal thinking to this time. Costonis identifies the premises as sensory, emphasizing "the sensory dimension of human response over its intellectual, emotional, and cultural aspects"; formalistic, based on "an object's formal visual qualities—color, line, proportion, and the like"; and semantic, "determined by the feature viewed as if it existed in isolation from the context in which it is experienced."[37] Rejecting these premises for design regulation as fallacies "vulnerable to legal attack," Costonis suggests in their stead a "cultural stability hypothesis that views controversies about 'beauty' as surrogates for disagreements about environmental change itself." Focusing on the threat perceived by individuals and groups "to their personal and social identity and, hence, to cultural stability," the purpose of aesthetic regulation, according to Costonis, "is to regulate the pace and character of environmental change in a manner that precludes or mitigates damage to their identity, a constancy no less critical to social stability than biological constants are to the human body's physiological equilibrium."[38]

In spite of recent attempts to seek more meaningful rationales for aesthetic regulation—or perhaps even as measured by the propensity to cling to traditional rationalizations—the tendency today is increasingly to recognize consideration of aesthetics as valid grounds for police-power regulation on its own merits. Simply stated, the fundamental criterion for a community contemplating design regulation is to demonstrate substantively and conclusively an overriding and imperative public necessity for such use of the po-

---

[35]*St. Louis Gunning Advertising Co. v. City of St. Louis,* 137 S.W. 929 (Mo., 1911).
[36]446 U.S. 789 (1984), 817.
[37]John J. Costonis, "Law and Aesthetics: A Critique and a Reformulation of the Dilemmas," *Michigan L. Rev.* 80 (1982), 396–97.
[38]Ibid., 419–20.

lice power that would outweigh the constitutional prerogatives of private property and free expression in a Holmesian balancing test conducted by the judiciary.

THE FIRST AMENDMENT EXAMINED

Public control of architectural design differs from the regulation of junkyards and billboards. The ugliness of junkyards is generally not disputed; much of outdoor advertising is also considered offensive from an aesthetic viewpoint, except in exceptional instances or according to the most esoteric of tastes. In contrast, architecture is universally acknowledged as a major art form, and a work of architecture is usually considered to represent a designer's deliberate effort at artistic expression.

As with junkyard and billboard regulation, courts in the early part of the century maintained a hands-off policy toward regulation of aesthetic considerations in architecture. The typical attitude was displayed by the Ohio court in the 1925 case *City of Youngstown v. Kahn Bros. Bldg. Co.* The case concerned the construction of a three-story apartment house in a district reserved for single- or two-family residences under two-and-one-half stories high.

> Authorities in general agree as to the essentials of a public health program, while the public view as to what is necessary for aesthetic progress greatly varies. Certain legislatures might consider that it was more important to cultivate a taste for jazz than for Beethoven, and for posters than for Rembrandt, and for limericks than for Keats. Successive city councils might never agree as to what the public needs from an aesthetic standpoint, and this fact makes the aesthetic standpoint entirely impractical as a standard for use restrictions upon property. The world would be at continual seesaw if aesthetic considerations were permitted to govern the use of the police power.[39]

In the half century since this case was decided, however, court perception of aesthetic regulation has become more flexible, undoubtedly influenced by the empirical "balancing" test first demonstrated by Holmes in *Pennsylvania Coal* between the perceived loss of private rights and the exigency of the public interest. It has also been influenced by new consideration of the applicability of the First Amendment to architectural design expression. Stephen Williams writes,

> Even if aesthetic expression is entitled to first amendment protection, many regulations that have an impact on such expression will survive judicial scrutiny. An important key to any regulation's fate is the court's classification of the underlying government interest. Where the interest that the government

[39]148 N.E. 842 (Ohio, 1925), 844.

seeks to further by a regulation is related to the suppression of expression, only exceptional circumstances will save it. The rankest example of such an interest is popular or official aversion to the content of the forbidden expression. By contrast, where legislation appears to be genuinely based on a government interest unrelated to the suppression of free expression, the court is likely to rely on a "balancing" operation.[40]

Attempts by communities to control artistic expression in architecture through the police power are believed by most legal scholars to raise the issue of the First Amendment; that is, whether the regulation in question violates the constitutional guarantees of the property owner and the architect. In an article entitled "Architecture, Aesthetic Zoning, and the First Amendment," Bruce Rubin points out that architecture has long been regarded as an art form. He also notes that judges have recognized that artistic expression deserves the protection of the First Amendment and quotes Justice Douglas in a 1961 dissent opinion in *Poe v. Ullman:* "The actor on stage or screen, the artist whose creation is in oil or clay or marble, the poet whose reading public may be practically nonexistent, the musician and his musical scores . . . are beneficiaries of freedom of expression."[41] Rubin believes that this same freedom should extend to architects as well: "An architect—or the builder of a house working through an architect—uses brick as a painter uses canvas or a writer uses words to express his notions of beauty and comfort, as well as many of his social values."[42]

Williams shares Rubin's view and writes: "Like artistic expression generally, architecture is often a conscious attempt to make a meaningful aesthetic statement. It is this effort at artistic expression that makes it worthy of first amendment protection."[43] He cites not only such venerable writers on architecture as Sigfried Giedion, John Ruskin, and Viollet-le-Duc as substantiating this view, but even Plato.

However, there has yet to be specific Supreme Court determination of the applicability of the First Amendment to the protection of artistic expression in architecture. Notwithstanding the role of the Supreme Court as final arbiter of the Constitution and despite numerous decisions regarding the First Amendment in particular, the Court has never ruled specifically on the question of public regulation of architectural design. Hence, its attitude toward freedom of artistic expression in architecture must be extrapolated from its opinions on other applications of the First Amendment, on issues seemingly unrelated to architecture and public regulation of design. Accordingly, the following discussion will examine the question of freedom

[40]Williams, "Problems of Aesthetic Regulation," 24–25.
[41]Bruce A. Rubin, "Architecture, Aesthetic Zoning, and the First Amendment," *Stanford L. Rev.* 28 (1975), 182. Citing 367 U.S. 497 (1981), 514.
[42]Rubin, "Architecture, Aesthetic Zoning," 185.
[43]Williams, "Problems of Aesthetic Regulation," 22.

of expression under the First Amendment from a broad perspective. Chapter 10 will focus more specifically on community regulation of architectural design through the police power.

Freedom of Speech

The weighing of the public interest against First Amendment rights opens consideration of design controls to a plethora of precedent cases from the Supreme Court. Some of these decisions, such as *Vincent,* were discussed in chapter 7 with regard to billboard regulation and free speech in advertising. At least until 1986, these decisions have yielded a mixed history with no definitive doctrine, upholding regulation in one instance and finding for free expression in the next.

Earlier, in the 1948 case of *Terminiello v. Chicago,*[44] the Court found the fact that a speaker had caused a hostile and turbulent crowd to congregate outside a meeting hall to be inadequate grounds for his arrest. Similarly, in the 1969 case of *Tinker v. Des Moines Independent Community School District,*[45] it decided that the suspension of students wearing black armbands in quiet protest of the war in Vietnam was a breach of their constitutional rights. A year and a half later, in *Cohen v. California,* the Court reversed the state's conviction of a draft protestor on a charge of disturbing the peace for wearing a jacket bearing the expletive, "Fuck the Draft." The state's contention that it could legitimately protect the privacy of unwilling or unsuspecting viewers was rejected by the Court, which reasoned that those offended "could effectively avoid further bombardment of their sensibilities simply by averting their eyes."[46] In 1977, in *Linmark Associates, Inc. v. Township of Willingboro,*[47] the Court struck down on First Amendment grounds a local ordinance prohibiting the posting of "for sale" or "sold" signs on homes. The measure had been enacted largely to forestall "panic selling" of homes and "white flight" caused by increasing immigration of nonwhite residents, although aesthetic considerations were presented as a reason for the ban. In these cases and in others, the public interest represented was deemed insufficient to override First Amendment considerations.

There have also been high Court decisions on the opposite side of the ledger. For example, in 1969, in *Rowan v. United States Post Office Department,* the Court upheld a prohibition against the mailing of unsolicited advertising material considered offensive by the recipient. In regard to free expression, the Court said: "That we are often 'captives' outside the sanc-

[44]337 U.S. 1 (1948).
[45]393 U.S. 503 (1969).
[46]403 U.S. 15 (1971), 21.
[47]431 U.S. 85 (1977).

tuary of the home and subject to objectionable speech and other sound does not mean we must be captives everywhere."[48] The idea of the public being a "captive audience" to unwanted expression had appeared earlier in two cases, both of which involved the issue of expression aboard public transit vehicles. The term "captive audience" was first used in the Supreme Court by Justice Douglas in his dissent opinion in one of these cases, the 1952 case *Public Utilities Commission of the District of Columbia v. Pollak*.[49] In this case, the majority held that the amplification of radio programs aboard streetcars and buses was not detrimental to the public welfare, despite the protest of some passengers. Twenty-two years later, in *Lehman v. City of Shaker Heights*,[50] the Court cited Douglas's *Pollak* dissent in upholding the refusal of a city transit system to permit the purchase of car card advertising space by a candidate for political office. In another case, *United States v. O'Brien*,[51] the Court ruled in 1978 that the public interest in maintaining a draft registration system was sufficient grounds to deny the appellant of his right to free expression in the public burning of his draft registration card.

Sex Depiction and the First Amendment

Several other Supreme Court rulings on freedom of expression concern the public depiction of nudity and sex. Some also involved land-use regulation. In 1975, in *Erznoznik v. City of Jacksonville*, the Court was faced with the problem of determining the constitutionality of a city ordinance that prohibited the operator of a drive-in movie theater from showing films containing scenes of nudity. The ordinance specifically referred to exhibits "visible from any public street or public place,"[52] and evidence was introduced that the screen in question could be seen from two adjacent public streets and also from a nearby church parking lot. The Court saw the dispute as "pitting the First Amendment rights of speakers against the privacy rights of those who may be unwilling viewers or auditors."[53] Ruling in favor of the theater operator, the majority quoted both the *Rowan* and *Cohen* cases:

> The plain, if at times disquieting, truth is that in our pluralistic society, constantly proliferating new and ingenious forms of expression, "we are inescapably captive audiences for many purposes." Much that we encounter offends our aesthetic, if not our political and moral, sensibilities. Neverthe-

[48]397 U.S. 728 (1970), 738.
[49]343 U.S. 451 (1952).
[50]418 U.S. 298 (1974).
[51]391 U.S. 367 (1978).
[52]422 U.S. 205 (1975), 207.
[53]Ibid., 208.

less, the Constitution does not permit government to decide which types of otherwise protected speech are sufficiently offensive to require protection for the unwilling listener or viewer. Rather, absent the narrow circumstances described above, the burden normally falls upon the viewer to "avoid further bombardment of [his] sensibilities simply by averting [his] eyes."[54]

The Court dismissed the contention that the public would be held a captive audience. Borrowing a phrase from an earlier decision, the Court said: "In short, the screen of a drive-in theater is not 'so obtrusive as to make it impossible for an unwilling individual to avoid exposure to it.'"[55] The Court brushed aside oral arguments claiming that nudity on a drive-in motion picture screen would distract passing motorists, thus slowing traffic flow and increasing the likelihood of accidents. It also pointed out that, in any event, the ordinance applied to motion picture screens visible from public places as well as public streets, thus indicating that the purpose of the ordinance was not traffic regulation.

Although *Erznoznik* concerned the exhibition of motion pictures displaying nudity, the drive-in theater involved was not alleged to have been an "adult entertainment" theater specializing in X-rated films. Concerning such theaters, the Supreme Court has been more inclined to support community regulation, if not a complete ban. In the 1976 case of *Young, Mayor of Detroit, v. American Mini Theatres, Inc.,* and ten years later in *City of Renton v. Playtime Theatres, Inc.,* the Court upheld regulations governing the location of establishments displaying sexually explicit films.

The first case concerned zoning ordinances adopted by the city of Detroit that required theaters displaying sex films not be located within 500 feet of a residential area or within 1,000 feet of any two other "regulated uses," including such establishments as adult bookstores, cabarets, bars, pawnshops, pool halls, public lodging houses, secondhand stores, and shoeshine parlors. The regulations mandating the dispersal of such businesses were enacted as amendments to an "anti skid-row ordinance" passed earlier in an effort to prevent the deterioration of city neighborhoods. Brushing aside arguments based on the First Amendment and the equal-protection clause of the Fourteenth, the Court overturned a lower ruling and upheld the restriction, saying,

The city's general zoning laws require all motion picture theaters to satisfy certain locational as well as other requirements; we have no doubt that the municipality may control the location of theaters as well as the location of other commercial establishments, either by confining them to a certain specified commercial zones or by requiring that they be dispersed throughout the city. The mere fact that the commercial exploitation of material protected by

[54]Ibid., 210–11.
[55]Ibid., 212. Quoting *Redrup v. New York,* 386 U.S. 767 (1967), 769.

the First Amendment is subject to zoning and other licensing requirements is not a sufficient reason for invalidating these ordinances.[56]

The *Playtime Theatres* case concerned a zoning ordinance enacted by Renton, a small suburb of Seattle, that prohibited adult movie theaters from locating within 1,000 feet of any residential zone, dwelling, church, park, or school. The law effectively allowed the municipality to banish such theaters from the city's business and residential areas to unprofitable and hence unviable locations. The Court found that "content-neutral" restrictions that prescribe only "time, place, and manner regulations are acceptable so long as they are designed to serve a substantial governmental interest and do not unreasonably limit alternative avenues of communication."[57]

In an observation that could have relevance to design controls that relate aesthetics to such considerations as the psychological and economic welfare of a community, the Court noted with approval that the ordinance was "aimed not at the *content* of the films shown at 'adult motion picture theatres,' but rather at the *secondary effects* of such theatres on the surrounding community."[58] This reasoning could also be used in support of design controls that are not aimed at design but on the design's secondary effect on the value of neighboring properties and the psychological well-being of the surrounding community. However, the problems remain of proving such effect in a substantive way and, more fundamentally, of avoiding the propensity to indulge in illegitimate restrictions against expression that are masked behind rationalizations, however persuasive.

In considering *American Mini Theatres,* it might be noted that the strategy used in Detroit of dispersing adult entertainment and sex-related businesses to prevent development of a skid-row district is the diametric opposite of the control technique used in Boston, where authorities have confined such businesses to a specific, concentrated sector of the center city, the so-called combat zone. The outcome of the *American Mini Theatres* and *Renton* cases provides municipalities a substantial legal basis to implement either form of zoning control to regulate sex-oriented entertainment.

The issue of free expression and community control of adult entertainment was also the subject of Supreme Court deliberations in the 1981 case of *Schad v. Borough of Mount Ephraim.*[59] A New Jersey suburb in Camden county near the cities of Camden and Philadelphia, Mount Ephraim prohibited, on commercial land, all activities not included in a detailed list of permitted uses. Notably absent from the list was any provision for live entertainment. The appellants, operators of a store selling adult books,

[56]427 U.S. 50 (1976), 62.
[57]____ U.S. ____ (1986), 54 U.S.L.W. 4160, 4161.
[58]Ibid., 4162.
[59]452 U.S. 61 (1981).

magazines, and films, had obtained licenses that allowed installation of coin-operated devices that enabled customers to sit in a booth and watch an adult film. Subsequently, an additional coin-operated mechanism was also introduced to the store permitting the viewing of a live dancer, usually nude, performing behind a glass panel. Convicted for violating the zoning ordinance, the store owners appealed to the Supreme Court, alleging that the prohibition of all live entertainment, including nude dancing, amounted to a denial of their rights of free expression, guaranteed by the First and Fourteenth Amendments. The Court agreed with their argument and voided the ordinance.

The majority opinion, written by Justice White, first addressed the Mount Ephraim's exclusion of all live entertainment, whether musical and dramatic works or nude dancing. It said, "Nor may an entertainment program be prohibited solely because it displays the nude human figure. 'Nudity alone' does not place otherwise protected material outside the mantle of the First Amendment."[60] Referring to what it termed as the "overbroad" nature of the ordinance, the Court ruled: "Because appellants' claims are rooted in the First Amendment, they are entitled to rely on the impact of the ordinance on the expressive activities of others as well as their own."[61] While recognizing the essential need and broad power of local government to zone and control land use, the Court stressed that the power is "not infinite and unchallengeable."[62] In emphasizing the constitutional limits of zoning, it noted:

> Where property interests are adversely affected by zoning, the courts generally have emphasized the breadth of municipal power to control land use and have sustained the regulation if it is rationally related to legitimate state concerns and does not deprive the owner of economically viable use of his property. But an ordinance may fail even under that limited standard of review.
>
> Beyond that, as is true of other ordinances, when a zoning law infringes upon a protected liberty, it must be narrowly drawn and must further a sufficiently substantial government interest.[63]

This latter point was underscored by Justice Harry A. Blackmun in a concurring opinion: "I would not expect the citizens of Philadelphia to be under any obligation to provide me with access to theaters and bookstores simply because Mount Ephraim previously had acted to ban these forms of 'entertainment.'"[64] Blackmun also expanded on a point made in White's majority opinion concerning the balancing of a community's power to zone with the rights ensured by the First Amendment.

[60]Ibid., 66.
[61]Ibid.
[62]Ibid., 68.
[63]Ibid.
[64]Ibid., 78.

I would emphasize that the presumption of validity that traditionally attends a local government's exercise of its zoning powers carries little, if any, weight where the zoning regulation trenches on rights of expression protected under the First Amendment. In order for a reviewing court to determine whether a zoning restriction that impinges on free speech is "narrowly drawn [to] further a sufficiently substantial governmental interest," the zoning authority must be prepared to articulate, and support, a reasoned and significant basis for its decision.[65]

Quoting Justice Powell, Jr.'s, concurring opinion in the *Young* case, Blackmun wrote, "After today's decision, it should be clear that where protected First Amendment interests are at stake, zoning regulations have no such 'talismanic immunity from constitutional challenge.'"[66]

In the *Schad* case, as in the others, the public interest in the regulation was weighed against the individual's constitutional rights. Williams notes that this balancing operation is "an impossible intellectual process, that of 'weighing' elements for which no common unit of measurement exists." While noting some of the variables involved, he adds that, "the less courts are called upon to 'balance,' the more first amendment guarantees are likely to be insulated from the vagaries of the judges' preferences."[67]

Laundry Lines and Visual Clutter

One of the most interesting and best-known cases concerning the First Amendment in relation to public aesthetics was decided not by the Supreme Court but by the New York Court of Appeals in 1963. The events leading up to the case of *People v. Stover* took place in the suburb of Rye, near New York City. In 1956, as a protest against high property taxes, Marion and Webster Stover, who resided in a large, two-and-a-half story house in a pleasant built-up residential neighborhood of the town, hung a clothesline laden with old clothes and rags across their front yard. During each of the subsequent five years, another line was added as a continuing protest. In 1961, after the Stovers's front yard was traversed by six clotheslines, the city passed an ordinance prohibiting the hanging of clothes in yards abutting a street. Permits for the use of such clotheslines were obtainable and granted to all applicants pleading practical difficulty except for the Stovers, whose application was denied on the grounds that they had sufficient other property available for the hanging of clothes. Since they persisted in keeping the lines strung across their corner location, they were convicted of violating the ordinance.

[65]Ibid., 77.
[66]Ibid.
[67]Williams, "Problems of Aesthetic Regulation," 25, footnote 88.

In reviewing the lower court decision, the state high court rejected the Stovers's argument that the ordinance was an unconstitutional infringement of free speech and a deprivation of property without due process. It sustained the regulation "as an attempt to preserve the residential appearance of the city" and as a proscription against "conduct which offends sensibilities and tends to debase the community and reduce real estate values."[68] The ordinance, it maintained, imposed "no arbitrary or capricious standard of beauty or conformity upon the community." Rather, the court compared the ordinance to similar police-power restrictions banning offenses to the senses of hearing and smell and upheld it as simply proscribing "conduct which is unnecessarily offensive to the visual sensibilities of the average person."[69] As for Stovers's argument of freedom of speech, the court concluded,

> The ordinance and its prohibition bear "no necessary relationship" to the dissemination of ideas or opinion and, accordingly, the defendants were not privileged to violate it by choosing to express their views in the altogether bizarre manner which they did. It is obvious that the value of their "protest" lay not in its message but in its offensiveness.[70]

In a dissent that has been quoted as much as the majority opinion, Judge Van Voorhis wrote,

> [If the Stovers] can be told where to hang their clothes in their yards, these items would be but a small step beyond the present holding, or to prescribe what architectural designs should be adopted so as to harmonize with the designs of the neighbors. To direct by ordinance that all buildings erected in a certain area should be one-story ranch houses would scarcely go beyond the present ruling as a question of power, or to lay down the law that they should be all of the same color, or of different colors, or that each should be of one or two or more color tones as might suit the aesthetic predilections of the city councillors or zoning boards of appeal.
>
> This ordinance is unrelated to the public safety, health, morals or welfare except insofar as it compels conformity to what the neighbors like to look at. Zoning, important as it is within limits, is too rapidly becoming a legalized device to prevent property owners from doing whatever their neighbors dislike. Protection of minority rights is as essential to democracy as majority vote. . . . Even where the use of property is bizarre, unsuitable, or obstreperous, it is not to be curtailed in the absence of overriding reason of public policy. . . .
>
> It was once said of a famous lady of history that she had so much taste,

68191 N.E. 2d 272 (N.Y., 1963), 274.
69Ibid., 276.
70Ibid., 277.

and all of it so bad. Individual taste, good or bad, should ordinarily be let alone by government.[71]

Van Voorhis was alone in his dissent. The majority believed that freedom of speech must be considered not only in terms of content but in the form of expression, and that these two aspects must be distinguished. The court maintained that while the right to hold and propagate ideas cannot be abridged, freedom of speech does not extend to a right to create a public annoyance. The majority quoted a Supreme Court decision that said, "a person could not exercise [his freedom of speech] by taking his stand in the middle of a crowded street, contrary to traffic regulations, and maintain his position to the stoppage of all traffic. . . ."[72] It is interesting to speculate whether the case might have assumed a different character had the Stovers alleged their "nonverbal expression" to be a work of art having radically new aesthetic value rather than a political protest against taxes.

The Supreme Court was faced with a somewhat related issue in the 1984 *Vincent* case, which concerned the legality of a Los Angeles ordinance forbidding the posting of signs on public property. Again, as in *Stover,* it was the dissent that addressed the issue more directly. Writing for the minority was Justice William J. Brennan, Jr.

> Of course, all would agree that the improvement and preservation of the aesthetic environment are important governmental functions, and that some restrictions on speech may be necessary to carry out these functions. But a governmental interest in aesthetics cannot be regarded as sufficiently compelling to justify a restriction of speech based on an assertion that the content of the speech is, in itself, aesthetically displeasing. Because aesthetic judgments are so subjective, however, it is too easy for government to enact restrictions on speech for just such illegitimate reasons and to evade effective judicial review by asserting that the restriction is aimed at some displeasing aspect of the speech that is not solely communicative—for example, its sound, its appearance, or its location. An objective standard for evaluating claimed aesthetic judgments is therefore essential; for without one, courts have no reliable means of assessing the genuineness of such claims.

> For example, in evaluating the ordinance before us in this case, the City might be pursuing either of two objectives, motivated by two very different judgments. One objective might be the elimination of "visual clutter," attributable in whole or in part to signs posted on public property. The aesthetic judgment underlying this objective would be that the clutter created by these signs offends the community's desire for an orderly, visually pleasing environment. A second objective might simply be the elimination of the messages typically carried by the signs. In that case, the aesthetic judgment would be

[71]Ibid., 277–78.
[72]Ibid., 276. Quoting *Schneider v. State,* 308 U.S. 147 (1939), 160.

that the signs' messages are themselves displeasing. The first objective is lawful, of course, but the second is not. Yet the City might easily mask the second objective by asserting the first and declaring that signs constitute visual clutter. In short, we must avoid unquestioned acceptance of the City's bare declaration of an aesthetic objective lest we fail in our duty to prevent unlawful trespasses upon First Amendment protections.[73]

The justice quoted the opening statement of Costonis's article on aesthetics,

Aesthetic policy, as currently formulated and implemented at the federal, state, and local levels, often partakes more of high farce than of the rule of law. Its purposes are seldom accurately or candidly portrayed, let alone understood, by its most vehement champions. Its diversion to dubious or flatly deplorable social ends undermines the credit that it may merit when soundly conceived and executed. Its indiscriminate, often quixotic demands have overwhelmed legal institutions, which all too frequently have compromised the integrity of legislative, administrative, and judicial processes in the name of "beauty."[74]

Considering the conundrum surrounding the issue, it seems appropriate to examine the fundamental meaning of the terms *aesthetic* and *beauty*.

IN THE EYE OF THE BEHOLDER

Of the diverse interests involved in the field of city planning, only the urban designer has the specific interest and capability of deliberately furthering the city aesthetic. But like architects and others involved in the fine arts, urban designers frequently feel rather ill at ease with such terms as "aesthetics" or "beauty." Most would agree that art is less concerned with beauty as an end than with creative expression, whether it be a painter's discernment of his subject or an architect's view of the social character and function of the client or user. Artistic perception may produce a Mona Lisa, Meret Oppenheim's surrealist *Fur-covered cup saucer and spoon,* the Parthenon, or Robert Venturi's *Bill-Ding-Board*. Indeed, architect Venturi only half facetiously embraces the epithet of "U & O," or "ugly and ordinary," in describing his own work.[75] Art and aesthetic pleasure are distinct: beauty is not a requisite of art, nor is art a requisite of beauty, although the two are commonly associated and mutually compatible.

Despite the concept of urban design as artistic expression, the other city planning disciplines—and, indeed, society as a whole—look to and de-

[73]Note 5, 822–24.
[74]Ibid., footnote 4.
[75]Robert Venturi, Denise Scott Brown, and Steven Izenour, *Learning from Las Vegas* (Cambridge: M.I.T. Press, 1972), 84.

pend upon environmental design professionals for their perceived ability to set standards of "good taste" in community aesthetics. In the public environment, artistic creativity may be aspired to, but beauty and function are more popular if less rigorous criteria by which urban design is judged. Certainly it can be reasonably argued that in a democracy, popular taste in public aesthetics should not be offended.

Discomfort with such words as aesthetics, beauty, and ugliness is not limited to designers and artists. When legal minds accustomed to precision deal with questions involving these amorphous terms, they often become mired in a semantic morass. The word *aesthetic* is itself probably the most puzzling. Said one court: "Just what is meant by the use of the term 'aesthetic' is not entirely clear, but apparently it is intended to designate thereby matters which are evident to sight only, as distinguished from those discerned through smell and hearing."[76] Dukeminier notes that "while it is difficult to determine what is the primary offense of much land use, the simulation of blindness affords a simple rule-of-thumb: if a use is offensive to persons with sight but not offensive to a blind man in a similar position, the use is primarily offensive aesthetically."[77] However, in neither the *Oxford English Dictionary* nor in *Webster's Third New International Dictionary* is there any specific mention of visual quality in the definition of aesthetics. Although architecture and urban design as part of the physical world are undeniably visual, professionals would claim environmental aesthetics to encompass the full realm of senses besides the visual alone. In *Design of Cities,* Philadelphia urban designer Edmund Bacon writes, "Architecture is the articulation of space so as to produce in the participator a definite space experience in relation to previous and anticipated spaces. . . . This is architecture, not to look at, but to be in. It draws us into its depth and involves us in an experience shared by all the people who are moving about in it. . . . So it is, or should be, with the city. The designer's problem is not to create facades or architectural mass but to create an all-encompassing experience, to engender involvement."[78] Bacon's claim of total sensuous experience in architecture is substantiated in the Greek origin of the word, *aisthesis,* or "sense perception."

The task of appraising the aesthetic merit of art and design—the judgment between the beautiful and the ugly—is a complex and contentious one that environmental designers and even professional art critics, much less lawyers, should properly approach with trepidation. Wrote a Florida judge in 1953,

---

[76]*Sundeen v. Rogers,* 141 A. 142 (N.H., 1928), 144.
[77]Dukeminier, "Zoning for Aesthetic Objectives," 223.
[78]Edmund N. Bacon, *Design of Cities* (1967; reprint, New York: Viking, 1974), 21–23.

One difficulty to be encountered if we should recognize that the police power may be exercised to solely promote or protect aesthetic qualities is that such qualities are not capable of being tested by any known standard. The word "aesthetic" was first used by Baumgarten about 1750, to designate the science of sensuous knowledge, the goal of which is beauty, in contrast with logic, whose goal is truth.[79]

Whereas the hallmarks of law are logic and reason, the standards of aesthetic judgment are based on other criteria.

The Early History of Aesthetics

Since its first mention in the eighteenth-century writings of Alexander Gottlieb Baumgartner, aesthetics has been defined as the philosophical study of beauty. According to the disciples of Pythagoras, beauty was presumed an intrinsic, objective quality that could be described in terms of abstract mathematical ratios and proportions. Following this classical tradition, the early European rationalists, under the influence of mathematician-philosophers like Descartes, sought a conceptual understanding of beauty in logic and mathematics. By the end of the eighteenth century, after Kant's *Critique of Judgement,* beauty became a focus of German idealism. From this viewpoint, the approach to aesthetics gradually evolved into a largely metaphysical and transcendental quest for universal a priori principles of beauty.

Nevertheless, even Kant renounced absolutes derived from intellectual deduction in the evaluation of aesthetics. He concluded that aesthetic judgment is determined neither from knowledge nor by logic but rather by taste and subjective, albeit disinterested, feelings of pleasure or displeasure. This basis led to a philosophical exploration of the sensory or preceptual qualities of cognition that underlie aesthetic judgment. Kant's conception of the judgment of taste is cited in translation by the Italian art critic, Lionello Venturi:

Taste, which judges whether a work is beautiful or not, has the pretension that its judgment is universal, without being able to furnish the rational demonstration of the rightness of its judgment. For this reason one cannot give any objective rule of taste. Every judgment derived from this source is aesthetic: in other words, its determining cause is the feeling of the subject, not a concept of the object. The search for a principle of taste, which shall be the universal standard of beauty by means of determined concepts, is a vain fa-

[79]*Merritt v. Peters,* 65 So. 2d 861 (Fla., 1953), 863–64.

tigue, because that which is sought is impossible and contradictory in itself. There is not a science of beauty but only a criticism of it. . . . [80]

Thus, over time, aesthetics gradually evolved from an analysis of beauty as an objective concept to the study of aesthetics in terms of a subject's perception and response.

The Romantic epoch of the eighteenth century assigned to beauty the attribute of being an absolute and inherent social virtue. This view is manifest, for example, in the poetry of John Keats. In his *Ode to a Grecian Urn,* Keats intoned, "'Beauty is truth, truth beauty'—that is all/Ye know on earth, and all ye need to know." From this vantage, regulations aimed at beauty require no justification other than beauty itself—"art for art's sake."

Later subjective theories maintain that aesthetics is not an inherent property of an object, as suggested by both the Romantics and the rationalists, but is dependent on the beholder's perception. This assumption remains the basis for most modern analyses of aesthetics. The dichotomy between objective and subjective theories of aesthetics can be compared to the determination of a priori standards of beauty in an object versus the empirical study of perception and response of a subject.

Empiricism and Contemporary Aesthetic Analysis

Contemporary studies of aesthetics characteristically focus on the experiential quality of an observer's perception and response. The empirical study of aesthetics is exemplified in art criticism by such early works as John Dewey's *Art as Experience* and by more recent analyses, such as Rudolf Arnheim's *Art and Visual Perception.* In contrast to the preoccupation with the definition of beauty that characterized aesthetic inquiry, the empirical perspective is closely associated with the psychological and social sciences emergent during the nineteenth century. It attempts to evaluate art using scientific methodology, stressing natural instincts of perception, psychophysiological responses to form and other sensual qualities, and the relationship of art to the cultural attributes of society.

An early example of this sort of analysis is Gustav T. Fechner's nineteenth-century *Vorschule der Aesthetik.*[81] Fechner rejected rationalized, metaphysical deductions "from above" and conceived instead a theory of experimental or biometric aesthetics, whereby aesthetics is approached "from below" with statistical studies of individual aesthetic preferences and associations of basic, standardized objects. In *Aesthetic Measure,*[82]

---

[80]Lionello Venturi, *History of Art Criticism,* trans. Charles Marriott (1936; reprint, New York: Dutton, 1964), 190–91.

[81]Gustav T. Fechner, *Vorschule der Aesthetik* (Leipzig: Breitkopf & Hartel, 1876).

[82]George D. Birkhoff, *Aesthetic Measure* (Cambridge: Harvard U. Press, 1933).

published in 1933, George D. Birkhoff derived psychological and mathematical formulae and indices based on critical and popular responses to visual compositions involving varying degrees of order and complexity. Still other psychological approaches to aesthetics were conceived in empathic theory by Friedrich T. Vischer, in psychoanalysis by Sigmund Freud and Carl Jung, and in gestalt psychology by Kurt Koffka.

More recently, empirical techniques of evaluation have also been applied to studies of natural and urban environmental aesthetics not derived from artistic creation. These include investigations in environmental perception by Elwood L. Shafer, Jr., John F. Hamilton, Jr., and Elizabeth A. Schmidt in 1969[83] and by Stephen Kaplan, Rachel Kaplan, and John S. Wendt in 1972.[84] In the first study, campers in the Adirondacks were shown a random sample of landscape photographs and were asked to rank the scenic value of the pictures in order of preference. A predictive model was then formulated from the derived data, and the test repeated with another set of photographs, some new and some from the original set. In the follow-up test, the results of five of six surveys coincided with the predictive model, indicating that a substantial norm existed in regard to popular response to landscape aesthetics. In the second study, which also focused on consensual response to aesthetic experience, a group of college students was asked to rank photographs of various natural and urban scenic components in terms of preference and complexity. Although these studies dealt mainly with viewer reaction to landscape rather than urban scenes, similar empirical investigations could be undertaken on art and environmental design. Such studies in perceptual response would quantify the "I don't know anything about art, but I know what I like" reaction to aesthetics and design.

Other empirical analyses of environmental aesthetics differ from the Shafer and Kaplan studies in that they focus on the physical or visual attributes of the aesthetic object itself rather than on surveys of perceptual responses to it. Typical of these is a 1969 study by Luna B. Leopold, who devised a method to quantify the aesthetic value of rivers, focusing on sites in the Hells Canyon area of Idaho.[85] Leopold itemized a list of forty-six characteristics in the categories of physical factors, biological and water qualities, and human use and interest. On the assumption that uniqueness is a function of aesthetic quality, ratios were assigned to each characteristic to reflect its degree of distinction, with the resultant summation establishing a measure of aesthetic value for each given site. A similar empirical system to evaluate landscape aesthetics was devised by Frederic O. Sargent in

[83]Elwood L. Shafer, Jr., John F. Hamilton, Jr., and Elizabeth A. Schmidt, "Natural Landscape Preferences: A Predictive Model," *Journal of Leisure Research* 1 (1969).

[84]Stephen Kaplan, Rachel Kaplan, and John S. Wendt, "Rated Preference and Complexity for Natural and Urban Visual Material," *Perception and Psychophysics* 12 (1972), 354.

[85]Luna B. Leopold, *Quantitative Comparison of Some Aesthetic Factors Among Rivers,* Geological Survey Circular 620 (Washington, D.C.: U.S. Dept. of the Interior, 1969).

1966,[86] in which scenery was rated in terms of distance to horizon and by the variety of such features as hills, fields, forests, water, farms, and distant villages. Multiple factors were evaluated according to objective measurements, with separate judgments made for such considerations as eyesores and specific points of interest.

In citing these empirical studies in environmental perception, an article in the *Michigan Law Review*[87] also points to the precise reasoning characteristic of professional architectural criticism. It cites an analysis by critic Henry Russell Hitchcock that identifies specific, perceivable attributes in evaluating architectural design. In his primer *Experiencing Architecture,*[88] Steen Eiler Rasmussen likewise describes such specific, perceivable qualities in building design. Like the empirical studies of Leopold and Sargent, the premise of such scholarly guides for perceptual understanding and critical evaluation of architecture is that aesthetic quality is inherent in the aesthetic object itself rather than a product of subjective response—a premise recalling that held by the Pythagoreans and the early rationalists.

Over time, the nature of aesthetic judgment has gradually evolved from a philosophic search for a priori concepts to applications of scientific methodology. In *The Basis of Criticism in the Arts,* Stephen C. Pepper categorizes modern aesthetic judgment into several types, emphasizing the characteristic common to them all: "It is an empirical method. Anything that rests on an *a priori,* or upon claims of self-evidence, or upon uncorroborated authority; anything offered without evidence or with claims beyond a reasonable probability on the basis of the evidence, in short, anything dogmatic is rejected." In an attitude reminiscent of Justice Holmes's judicial empiricism in *Pennsylvania Coal,* Pepper notes that the empirical approach to art criticism is "based on facts." However, he cautions that "empirical judgments . . . [cannot] claim to be certain, but only probable to a degree justified by the evidence."[89]

First of four criticisms analyzed by Pepper is mechanism, which defines aesthetics as "objectified pleasure," as suggested by George Santayana in *The Sense of Beauty.* This view understands perception of a pleasurable object to be mechanistically "correlated with physiological activities located in the human body,"[90] as colors and other sensations evoke human response. Second is contextualistic criticism that perceives "the aesthetic field

[86]Frederic O. Sargent, "A Scenery Classification System," *Journal of Soil and Water Conservation* 21 (1966), 26.

[87]*Michigan L. Rev.,* "Beyond the Eye of the Beholder: Aesthetics and Objectivity," 71 (1973), 1443.

[88]Steen Eiler Rasmussen, *Experiencing Architecture* (Cambridge: M.I.T. Press, 1962).

[89]Stephen C. Pepper, *The Basis of Criticism In the Arts* (Cambridge: Harvard U. Press, 1949), 17–18.

[90]Ibid., 41–42.

[to be the] voluntary vivid intuitions of quality."[91] The emphasis of contextualism is on experience: "The more vivid the experience and the more extensive and rich its quality, the greater its aesthetic value."[92] Third is organistic criticism, derived from Bernard Bosanquet's *Three Lectures on Aesthetic,* that considers a work of art ideally as an integrated, coherent whole, of which intuition of quality is only one aspect.[93] Fourth is formistic criticism derived from "perceptions satisfying in themselves to the normal man."[94] Aesthetic value of a work of art is measured by its conformity to a norm and ultimately to the culture of which it is an expression. Each of these empirical approaches according to Pepper assumes a commonality in perceptual response:

> In mechanistic criticism . . . we can count on a good deal of uniformity in men's judgments about pleasures in things because of the considerable degree of similarity in men's physiological make-up and behavior. In contextualism there was likewise an anticipation of a pretty fair agreement within any cultural epoch about the quality of the final funded perception of a work of art. And in organicism a stable determinate judgment is predicted of any fully integrated work. Any one of these views would admit that a judgment that diverged markedly from the anticipated judgment in the light of human experience might be called abnormal. . . .
>
> Formism, however, stresses the fact of the normal, seeks to isolate it, and to define value in terms of it.[95]

This latter assumption of a norm underlies the prevalent judicial attitude toward aesthetics. One legal writer notes, on the public control of aesthetics, that "the standard of what is offensive to the sight of the man of average sensibility is the basis of the regulation or restriction."[96] Such a consensual measure of beauty may be depreciated by the artistically sophisticated as a rather mediocre standard. Nevertheless, it can also be argued that greater weight is attributed to the response of the "tastemakers," including artists and professional critics who are able to influence popular opinion on art in the long run, however radical or avant-garde their opinions may seem at first.

Critical conceptions of artistic value and popular notions of the aesthetic or beautiful must be distinguished. In judging the latter, certainly "average sensibilities" and "conventional good taste" are dominant—and

[91]Ibid., 56.
[92]Ibid., 57.
[93]Ibid., 74–95.
[94]Ibid., 107.
[95]Ibid., 96–97.
[96]David J. Miller, "Aesthetic Zoning: An Answer to Billboard Blight," *Syracuse L. Rev.* 19 (Fall 1967), 94.

even democratic—measures. This empirical approach might yield, for example, the conclusions that pop music enjoys a greater following than the twelve-tone compositions of Arnold Schoenberg, that more people prefer the folk-style paintings of Norman Rockwell to the surrealist creations of Marcel Duchamp, and that the suburban, ersatz Cape Cod colonial appeals to a larger housing market than does Robert Venturi's house designs of his "ugly and ordinary" genre. In each paired comparison, the first is typically regarded as pleasurable by the lay public despite its perhaps questionable critical value, whereas the second is generally considered art, though it may not be popularly conceived as beautiful.

With conventional good taste as the standard, it is hardly surprising that the primary function of architecture and urban design is popularly construed to be the creation of a living environment that is pleasurable to the ordinary person. But from a creative standpoint, does this consensual view not compromise individual artistic expression and yield only mediocrity? Furthermore, from the perspective of law, does it not offend the First Amendment? Certainly art is capable of beauty. At the other extreme, some art can be so intellectually or emotionally demanding of its beholder as to constitute a nuisance to those seeking only the soothing massage of the beautiful. The medieval paintings of Hieronymus Bosch, for instance, are deliberate representations of grotesque suffering. However, while one can turn away from a painting, architecture, particularly public or urban design, is omnipresent. With the same empirical tools used to determine consensual concepts of beauty, a compelling argument can also be made that to be held captive in a physical environment evoking intense response, however articulate, can be oppressive and even conceivably psychopathic. Intellectual appreciation of artistic creativity is one thing; the common and natural craving for beauty and comfort another.

Another aspect of aesthetics was suggested by John Costonis, who argues that the "traditional visual beauty rationale" for regulation should be supplanted by an understanding of the need of human communities to ensure "cultural stability" through control of environmental change. He itemizes three "fallacies" that have been the traditional basis for aesthetic regulation: that of relying on "sensory" data resulting from an empirical evaluation of the viewer's response; of seeking "formal" qualities that define some rational standards of objective beauty; and the fallacy of requiring "semantic" or contextual appropriateness to the existing physical environment.[97] Costonis is most perceptive and persuasive in his analysis of a rationale for aesthetic regulation. However, if cultural stability were indeed to become the legal basis for aesthetic regulation as he suggests, the public policy that would result would doubtlessly be a conservative one, resistant

---

[97]Costonis, "Law and Aesthetics," 392–409.

to any change that would upset the environmental continuity and cultural "stability-identity" of a community.

Even if it were assumed that the public need to regulate environmental design were imperative enough to override artistic and constitutional objections for any reason, whether "visual beauty" or "cultural stability," the mechanism for regulation is still fraught with difficulties. Williams points out that any judgment on matters of aesthetics presents problems of "extreme polycentricity" that defy the articulation of meaningful standards to guide administrative decision making and provide for consistency in adjudication. In defining polycentricity, he writes,

> Polycentric problems arise when three factors coincide: (1) a multiplicity of possible solutions; (2) an interdependency of relevant factors so that the outcome as to one feature of the problem will affect the outcome as to other features; and (3) a multiplicity of relevant factors that makes it difficult to trace one solution's superiority to any particular attribute or combination of attributes.
>
> The problems of articulating aesthetic standards represents perhaps the extreme case of polycentricity. The number of potential designs is infinite; the choice as to any single factor, say materials, has an impact on all other factors; and one cannot identify any nonaesthetic features that will even begin to consistently justify the application of any aesthetic concept.[98]

Williams cites design evaluation of architecture as a primary case in point, and this specific problem is discussed in chapter 10, in the examination of attempts by communities to devise preestablished standards for the design review of architecture.

Aesthetics and the Courts

In at least one memorable instance, a bureau of the federal government saw fit to take on the task of aesthetic evaluation. In a famous 1928 case, customs officials sought—happily, without success—to claim that Constantin Brancusi's abstract, polished bronze sculpture "Bird in Flight" was not a work of art but rather "a manufacture of metal" and hence subject to the levy of an import duty. In ruling on *Brancusi v. United States,* the customs court considered the testimony of two government witnesses who "had experience in art and sculpture, who were, in fact, under the accepted definition, sculptors. These pronounced the importation to be neither a work of art nor sculpture."[99] The court rejected their testimony, saying: "Whether or not we are in sympathy with these newer ideas and the schools

---

[98]Williams, "Problems of Aesthetic Regulation," 18–19.
[99]*Brancusi v. United States,* T.D. 43063, 54 Treas. Dec. 428 (1928), 429.

which represent them, we think the fact of their existence and their influence upon the art world as recognized by the courts must be considered."[100] The decision thus rejected a rule set a dozen years earlier by the Court of Customs Appeals in *United States v. Olivotti & Co.*, in which a "representational test" was established by which sculpture qualified as art only insofar as it imitated natural objects, chiefly the human form.[101]

The problem of aesthetic judgment can confound the judiciary as well as the legislative and administrative branches. If, following the empirical approach, the criteria for public controls is public consensus on the aesthetic value of architectural proposals, then it may be reasonable to heed Williams's suggestion that it is inappropriate for judges to rule on aesthetic control legislation, "since it is legislators, not judges, whose function it is to divine the will of the majority."[102] If, however, elected officials (who presumably represent the will of the majority) rather than judges (who are charged to uphold constitutional guarantees, including minority rights) were to determine regulations governing design, then the rights of the minority—whether the property rights of an owner or the expressive freedom of an artist—would become subservient to the will and artistic preferences of the majority.

In considering *Bleistein v. Donaldson Lithography Co.*, a 1903 case on copyright law, Justice Holmes avoided judgment on aesthetics altogether, ruling instead solely on the legal question. His opinion, however, contained a strong defense of artistic expression.

> It would be dangerous undertaking for persons trained only to the law to constitute themselves final judges of the worth of pictorial illustrations, outside of the narrowest and most obvious limits. At the one extreme some works of genius would be sure to miss appreciation. Their very novelty would make them repulsive until the public had learned the new language in which their author spoke. It may be more than doubted, for instance, whether the etchings of Goya or the paintings of Manet would have been sure of protection when seen for the first time.[103]

Holmes's counsel to the judiciary to show forbearance in matters of art was apparently lost on the Virginia lower court that decided *Eustice v. Binford*.[104] In this 1969 case, Brockhurst C. Eustice, an architect, bought land in a subdivision in Arlington County known as Rivercrest and began construction of his own home. The design consisted of twin two-story cubes connected by a passageway and sheathed with cedar siding. To achieve max-

---

[100]Ibid., 431.
[101]T.D. 36309, 30 Treas. Dec. 586, 7 Ct. Cust. Appls. 46 (1916), 588.
[102]Williams, "Problems of Aesthetic Regulation," 6.
[103]188 U.S. 239 (1903), 251.
[104]Note 30.

imum privacy, the house was oriented inward with no windows facing the street. The situation was complicated by the fact that the deed to the land specified architectural review by a committee in the subdivision to ensure "quality of workmanship and material, exterior decoration, harmony of exterior design with existing structures, and location with respect to topography and finish grade elevation." However, all original members had resigned, the committee had never functioned, and no house in the subdivision had ever been subject to review.

When the Eustice house was almost fully constructed, John Q. Binford, Eustice's next-door neighbor, filed for an injunction to prevent completion. Charging that Eustice's house was ugly and resembled "two orange crates," Binford said, "It doesn't look like a house at all."[105] His wife echoed, "We feel it just ruins the neighborhood." Another neighbor agreed that in order "to retain the very pleasant beautiful nature of Rivercrest . . . the only remedy I can see is to tear it down."[106] Expert appraisal testimony on the effect of the house on the value of neighboring properties was conflicting and inconclusive.

With no review board at hand, Judge Charles Russell apparently felt that his ability to judge on legal issues extended to an ability to act as architectural critic. He visited the site to view the house and subsequently issued a permanent injunction to prevent its completion. Russell found the Eustice design as "not harmonious" with other houses in the subdivision and was at variance with a "mutual compact, binding on all lots, for good or ill, to a scheme of relative uniformity."[107] He chose to ignore such issues as the lack of uniformity in enforcement of the covenant, the investment already made by Eustice in his house, his rights of private property, or his prerogative as an individual not to conform. Eustice's appeal to the state high court found that bench equally divided, and rehearing was denied.[108]

Turnbull characterizes *Eustice* as "one of the most outrageous cases of judicial meddling and misconstruction of residential covenants," noting in particular the court's "grievous . . . rewriting of the covenant to include the standard of 'relative uniformity'—a term that contains gross internal contradictions . . . not appear[ing] to have been contemplated by the covenant at all."[109] Even where community regulation of architectural design is accepted, the *Eustice* case stands out as an aberration, for unlike the architectural review cases to be discussed in chapter 10, in *Eustice,* no community review board was involved in considering the merits or deficiencies of Eustice's design. Judge Russell simply devolved the role of architectural

---

[105] John Neary, "A Cube House vs. the Squares," *Life* (Nov. 14, 1969), 83–86.
[106] Ibid., 86.
[107] Turnbull, "Aesthetic Zoning," 240.
[108] *Eustice v. Binford,* 181 S.E. 2d 634 (1971).
[109] Turnbull, "Aesthetic Zoning," 239–40.

critic and censor upon himself. Not least, the judge seemed oblivious to Eustice's possible rights of architectural expression under the First Amendment.

The court order also raises obvious questions concerning the just-compensation provision of the Fifth Amendment, especially considering the decidedly draconian measure of proscribing a house that was almost fully constructed. Said the Minnesota court seven years prior to *Eustice:* "It is settled that purely aesthetic considerations do not form a sound basis for nullifying or destroying definite or valuable interests in property without compensation therefore to the owner."[110] Apparently Russell did not understand that principle to have been quite settled. The impropriety of his decision was exacerbated by the fact that Eustice has met all previously known requirements under enforcement, and that the restriction was imposed as a consequence of litigation "after the event," in violation of Hayek's constitutional principle that rules should be known beforehand. A citizen's right to use his property in good faith, said a New Jersey court in 1956, "should not depend upon the outcome of litigation after the event in which a provision, which he apparently fully meets, assumes a new and different significance by a process of refined interpretation."[111]

The *Eustice* case has added significance in that Eustice was a practicing architect designing his own home. In an article on "Architecture, Aesthetic Zoning, and the First Amendment," Bruce Rubin suggests that "a tract housing development designed solely to serve economic goals might be a legitimate object of aesthetic zoning regulation, while a home planned by an architect for his own use might not."[112] The contention of self-expression on the part of the architect is then unquestionable, since his work is untainted by any possible argument that commercial interest is undeserving of full First Amendment protection—not that the rights of an owner engaging an architect to design on his behalf should be afforded less.

In 1972, a Michigan judge warned, in *Sun Oil Company v. City of Madison Heights,*

> We will all live to rue the day that public officials are permitted to meddle in private affairs or aesthetic considerations since as the majority opinion states each person has his own yardstick for the evaluation of matters aesthetic. We should not open this door which could very well lead to a situation of a most highly regulated society in the world, at the whim and caprice of individual officials without any proper measure for a limitation on such individual values rather than values prescribed by law.[113]

[110]*Olsen v. City of Minneapolis,* 115 N.W. 2d 734 (Minn., 1962), 741.
[111]*Jantausch v. Borough of Verona,* 124 A. 2d 14 (N.J. Sup'r., 1956), 22.
[112]Rubin, "Architecture, Aesthetic Zoning," 181.
[113]Note 20, 531.

Considering the Supreme Court ruling in *Erznoznik* that the First Amendment protects the exhibition of films depicting nudity on a drive-in theater screen open to public view, and in ruling in *Schad* that the same protection is afforded nude dancing in stores despite its prohibition by zoning, surely architectural expression deserves the same degree of constitutional protection against discretionary proscription.

However, how far can self-expression go under the First Amendment without becoming a public nuisance? Williams himself suggests:

> Substantively . . . the legislation could authorize the board to veto only designs that it found to be without serious artistic value or blatantly offensive to community standards. A legislative mandate to an architectural review board, phrased in these terms, would provide comparatively manageable standards for the board to apply and for courts to review. Evidence that critics overwhelmingly found the design without genuine artistic purpose would support a finding that it lacked artistic value. A board's finding that the design was blatantly offensive to community standards would seem intelligibly reviewable by a court that had the design before it. For example, a design taking the form of crude and obvious sexual symbolism executed on a large scale would seem to fall below the standard.[114]

But even this standard is subject to varying interpretations. For instance, a casual stroll through virtually any public art museum shows that nudity has been a constant theme in every period of western art, from the classics to the present day. Sculptural depiction of nudes can be found as a recurrent decorative motif throughout the history of western architecture. Yet conceivably some communities might find a Botticelli or a Rodin sculpture in an open setting so prurient as to warrant censorship.

The issue is not confined to questions of aesthetic theory and esoteric museum criticism. In Beverly Hills, the wife of Arabian Sheik Mohammed S.A. al Fassi expressed amazement at the public furor caused by the exterior redecoration of their newly purchased, Renaissance-style mansion. Of the repainting of a dozen nude human statues from a formerly white color to flesh tone, she asked, "What's the difference between a painted statue and an unpainted one?"[115] Yet architect Stanley Tigerman, wise to the ways of this society, earned kudos from a professional journal for his wit in designing a house that had genitalia as its planar theme.[116] The line between the acceptable and the "blatantly offensive" can be very fine indeed.

[114]Williams, "Problems of Aesthetic Regulation," 33.

[115]Robert Lindsey, "Beverly Hills Upset by Unusual Decor of Saudis' Mansion," *New York Times,* Apr. 23, 1978, 22.

[116]Walter F. Wagner, Jr., "Stanley Tigerman on Being Just a Little Less Serious . . . " *Architectural Record* 160, no. 4 (Sept. 1976), 111, 113.

PRESAGING THINGS TO COME

Several events affecting national policy and the federal courts in particular have recently taken place that may well presage a trend in the manner in which the federal judiciary will treat questions concerning the First Amendment. By all indications, the case of *City of Renton v. Playtime Theatres, Inc.*, decided early in 1986, is only a precursor of a much more rigorous attitude that the Supreme Court will likely take in the future against individual expression and other liberties that offend public sensitivities. Although land use, aesthetics, and design expression are not at issue in any of these events, any erosion of First Amendment guarantees may eventually affect land-use regulation of aesthetics and design as well.

Four cases decided a half-year after the *Renton* case show a growing abhorrence of a majority of the justices toward what they consider offensive, immoral, or deviant behavior. The most spectacular of the cases was *Bowers, Attorney General of Georgia v. Hardwick,*[117] an action challenging the validity of a state statute criminalizing sodomy, in which the Supreme Court ruled that the Constitution does not confer a fundamental right upon homosexuals to engage in sodomy, even at home and among consenting adults. The 5–4 decision apparently reverses an early trend of the Court to protect the personal lives of individuals in the privacy of the home against intrusions by the state. The majority opinion written by Byron White, a justice not known for extremism, is notable for its moralistic and traditionalist invocation of the "ancient roots" of proscriptions against homosexuality.

During the same term, the Court held, in *Posadas de Puerto Rico Associates, dba Cordado Holiday Inn v. Tourism Company of Puerto Rico,*[118] that a Puerto Rico enactment that legalized casino gambling in order to promote tourism but that also prohibited the advertising of gambling to the Puerto Rican public did not constitute a breach of the First Amendment. In *Bethel School District No. 403 v. Fraser,*[119] the high Court gave narrow interpretation to the First Amendment in upholding the disciplining of a public high school student for his use of elaborate, graphic, and explicit sexual metaphors in a speech before a student assembly. Likewise, in a case that at least partially related to land use, the Supreme Court reversed a New York Court of Appeals ruling that held a state statute to be violative of First Amendment rights in authorizing the closure of an "adult" bookstore.[120] The store had been found a public health nuisance as the site of illicit sexual activities, including prostitution solicitation, despite arguments

---

[117] _____ U.S. _____ (1986), 54 U.S.L.W. 4919.
[118] _____ U.S. _____ (1986), 54 U.S.L.W. 4956.
[119] _____ U.S. _____ (1986), 54 U.S.L.W. 5054.
[120] _____ U.S. _____ (1986), 54 U.S.L.W. 5060.

that the public health law was intended to apply only to houses of prostitution and that closure of the bookstore would constitute interference with First Amendment rights.

What is remarkable about these cases is not so much the stance of the justices—although the *Bowers* case certainly seems extraordinary—but the unequivocal nature of the sudden outpouring of decisions regarding what had formerly been seen by the Court as a complex issue with compelling arguments on both sides. The past tendency of the Court at least to equivocate on First Amendment issues may have given way to a current conservative ideology, whereas in the 1960s the direction of the Court had been toward political liberalism.

Perhaps the Supreme Court is merely reflecting the tenor of the times. In the same month that the Court was handing down the foresaid decisions, the Department of Justice under Attorney General Edwin Meese issued the *Final Report of the Attorney General's Commission on Pornography,* which strongly attacked the proliferation of pornographic material, stating among its findings that there exists a causal link between violent pornography and sexual crime—a conclusion diametrically opposed to that reached by the President's Commission on Obscenity and Pornography sixteen years earlier. While the 1970 commission had recommended improved sex education in schools, the 1986 commission suggests more stringent prohibitions and enforcement against obscenity and more severe penalties for offenders.

Perhaps of more lasting significance is the confirmation of William Rehnquist as Chief Justice of the Supreme Court and of Circuit Judge Antonin Scalia as Associate Justice. Both jurists are known for their conservative ideological leanings in past decisions. (The distinction between *ideological* and *political* conservatism and *judicial* conservatism should again be noted.) Rehnquist is considered by his liberal critics as the justice most consistent in ruling against civil liberties (as distinguished from private rights of property). In addition to his appointment of justices to the Supreme Court during his two terms as president, Ronald Reagan has also managed to appoint a major number of judges to lifetime tenure on the lower federal bench.

Considered separately, none of these events of the summer of 1986—neither the Supreme Court decisions, the report on pornography, nor the President's judicial appointments—seems especially momentous. But taken together, they show an evident future of ideological conservatism on the federal bench—just, it might be added, as the courts had earlier demonstrated a liberal bias in the 1960s. Issues related to public regulation of land use, aesthetics, and design have not been specifically a part of these events. Nonetheless, with community coherence and design conformity as conservative ideals, and with First Amendment guarantees a lesser priority, these events logically portend significant directions in land use, aesthetic, and design regulations, at least in consideration of the purview of the federal courts.

The application of design and aesthetic controls is dependent on community and even prevailing national standards and the judicial weighing of these interests against First Amendment guarantees, both of which can change with time. In 1908 an appeals court in Maryland sought to justify an act limiting the height of buildings about the base of the Washington Monument in Baltimore by citing that "the primary object of the law is protection from fire."[121] The real motivation behind the police-power regulation was, in actuality, to further the aesthetic quality of urban design. This sort of rationalization was, as we have seen, typical of the time. Said the court in rendering its decision in *Cochran v. Preston,*

> It may be that, in the development of a higher civilization, the culture and refinement of the people has reached the point where the educational value of the fine arts, as expressed and embodied in architectural symmetry and harmony, is so well recognized as to give sanction, under some circumstances, to the exercise of this power, even for such purposes.[122]

Whether or not that "higher civilization" has been achieved over this century can be roundly debated. Less subject to argument is the evident trend toward regulation on the basis of aesthetics for its own sake.

LATE DEVELOPMENTS

In three related cases decided on November 10, 1986,[123] the Colorado Supreme Court found that where an electric utility company condemns power-line easements over private land, the property owner is entitled not only to an award for the property rights actually taken, but also to additional monetary damages to compensate for the decreased value of the remaining property caused by the unsightliness of the power lines. This landmark recognition of the monetary value of the aesthetic aspects of real property adds further credence to the legal and economic substance of aesthetic considerations. The finding has significant implications not only to the discussion in this chapter but also to that in chapter 12, concerning the public condemnation of aesthetic and design easements over private property for purposes of urban design and planning.

[121]*Cochran v. Preston,* 70 A. 113 (Md., 1908), 115.
[122]Ibid., 114.
[123]*La Plata Electric Association, Inc. v. Cummins,* 728 P. 2d 696 (Colo., 1986); *Bement v. Empire Electric Association, Inc.,* 728 P. 2d 706 (Colo., 1986); *Herring v. Platte River Power Authority,* 728 P. 2d 709 (Colo., 1986).

Chapter 10

A Question of Taste

In a free economy like that of the United States, market forces and pluralist enterprise are at least as determinative of the aesthetic quality of urban land development as are public building and design. As a consequence, the governmental role in urban design and aesthetics is frequently accomplished more through regulation of private development than through actual public works. One of the most direct forms that public regulation can take is the local process of official board review of the architectural design of proposed private development.

Regulation of architectural design by a local design review board is a relatively new but expanding practice. A survey conducted in 1968 by the American Institute of Architects (AIA) of existing review boards found that, of the 101 responding boards of 221 polled, most had been in operation less than ten years, and three quarters had been in existence less than twenty years.[1] Typically created by ordinance as an entity apart from the planning commission and board of adjustment, the board of architectural review is customarily required to have at least the majority of its membership composed of environmental design professionals. According to the AIA survey, 97 percent of board members are architects who are typically prominent local citizens appointed by the city council, usually to serve with little or no remuneration. As do the other official committees, the architectural review board wields substantial power. Even those whose ostensible

---

[1] American Institute of Architects, *Design Review Boards: A Handbook for Communities* (Washington, D.C.: AIA, 1974), 7, 9.

function is advisory possess effective authority to withhold building permission since, barring exceptional circumstances, a local legislative body is more apt to follow than ignore the recommendations of its own panel of expert advisers.

Whereas private review of subdivision developments is often made possible by covenant, public regulation of architectural design typically relies on the police power associated with zoning. As already discussed, communities that can tie aesthetic regulation to a strong and credible supporting objective such as historic preservation have found the courts to be generally sympathetic. In communities unable to claim such a supporting motive, the avowed purpose of design regulation is typically to preserve the existing aesthetic character of the area in order to maintain such general aspect of the public welfare as the local economy and property values.

THE CASES

Architectural review boards are capable of exercising considerable discretion in their task of evaluating whether the design of a proposed development is sufficiently appropriate to the appearance of a community to warrant issuance of a building permit. Such a conclusion was reached in *Reid v. Architectural Board of Review of the City of Cleveland Heights,*[2] a well-known case decided by an Ohio appeals court in 1963.

Donna S. Reid had engaged an architect to design for her a house on a lot located in an attractive wooded area of the affluent suburb of Cleveland Heights. Other houses in the neighborhood were held by the court to be "in the main, dignified, stately and conventional structures, two and one-half stories high."[3] Her architect's proposed design, conceded by a board member to have been "in a class cost-wise with those in the neighborhood,"[4] consisted of a low, single-story complex of twenty modules, each ten feet high and twelve feet square, loosely arranged to form a U-shaped plan laid out to wind through a grove of trees. About 60 percent of the wall space of the house was to be of glass opening onto an enclosed garden; the remainder was to be constructed of cement panels. The house, a garage of similar modular design, and their accessory garden walls, trellises, and courts were to form a series of interior and exterior spaces, all under a canopy of trees and shielded from the street by a ten-foot-high garden wall. The design called for the front structure of the house and garage to be integrated into the wall, extending completely around the garden area. According to the court, since the wall was to be the same height as the house and was without windows, from all appearances the design was for just a

[2]192 N.E. 2d 74 (Ohio App., 1963).
[3]Ibid., 77.
[4]Ibid., 79.

high wall with no indication of what lay behind it and no identification that it would be a structure for people to live in.

When Mrs. Reid applied for permission to build, the architectural review board refused, stating that the project "[did] not maintain the high character of community development in that it [did] not conform to the character of the houses in the area."[5] Mrs. Reid challenged the denial, but the court upheld the board's determination. It cited the board's purpose, as specified by the ordinance: to protect property; to maintain a high character of community development; and to protect real estate from impairment and destruction of value. The court said that the criteria and standards employed by the board in regulating design, use of material, finished grade lines, and orientation were matters of "proper architectural principles" to be adjudged by a board of "highly trained experts in the field of architecture."[6] It found that although aesthetics played a part in the ruling of the board, other factors also influenced its decision. These factors included such considerations as the nonconforming character of a single-story house in a multistory neighborhood, the radical design, the exterior wall, which might appear to enclose a commercial building, the failure of the project to preserve the high character and property values of the neighborhood, and the detrimental effect of the project on future development.

A vigorous dissent against the ruling was entered by Judge J. J. P. Corrigan:

> Should the appellant be required to sacrifice her choice of architectural plan for her property under the official municipal juggernaut of conformity in this case? Should her aesthetic sensibilities in connection with her selection of design for her proposed home be stifled because of the apparent belief in this community of the group as a source of creativity? Is she to sublimate herself in this group and suffer the frustration of individual creative aspirations? Is her artistic spirit to be imprisoned by the apparent beneficence of community life in Cleveland Heights? This member of the court thinks not.[7]

It has been suggested that had Mrs. Reid mustered the perseverance and resources, she might well have won on appeal. However, as David M. Gooder, a lawyer, observed, "Mrs. Reid did not appeal the decision. She undoubtedly decided to build the house where its unique qualities would be appreciated."[8] But if the events of a subsequent case in Missouri is any indication, an appeal to the Ohio high court could just as easily have failed.

Seven years after the *Reid* case, the Missouri Supreme Court was con-

[5]Ibid., 78.
[6]Ibid., 77.
[7]Ibid., 81.
[8]David M. Gooder, "Brakes for the Beauty Bus," in *Junkyards, Geraniums, and Jurisprudence: Aesthetics and the Law* (Chicago: American Bar Association, 1967), 130.

fronted with a similar situation and came to a like conclusion. The setting for *State ex rel. Stoyanoff v. Berkeley*[9] was the suburban city of Ladue, one of the more exclusive residential communities of metropolitan St. Louis. An applicant for a building permit had challenged the authority of the city's architectural board of review to deny construction of a house of contemporary design in an area of traditional-style homes. The board had been established by local ordinance to approve plans and specifications for proposed buildings on condition that they "conform to certain minimum architectural standards of appearance and conformity with surrounding structures, and that unsightly, grotesque and unsuitable structures, detrimental to the stability of value and the welfare of surrounding property, structures and residents, and to the general welfare and happiness of the community, be avoided, and that appropriate standards of beauty and conformity be fostered and encouraged."[10] The court record described the residence proposed by the applicant to be "of a pyramid shape, with a flat top, and with triangular shaped windows or doors at one or more corners."[11]

Court testimony included a claim by the mayor of Ladue that the proposed house was "a monstrosity of grotesque design, which would seriously impair the value of property in the neighborhood."[12] To support this claim, an affidavit was introduced, in which a residential developer alleged that the design of the proposed house would "clash" with the other houses in the neighborhood and would have a detrimental effect on property values. A second affidavit of a city planning and engineering consultant included photographs showing existing area homes to be of traditional Colonial, French Provincial, and English Tudor design. The consultant's affidavit affirmed that regulations similar to the Ladue ordinances were typical of suburban cities in the region and throughout the country for the purpose of ensuring customary architectural requirements in appearance and design of residences, general conformity with the style and design of surrounding structures, and proper architectural development of the community, along with the provision that application of standards include board determination of any adverse effect on surrounding property values.[13]

In response, the lawyers for the applicant claimed that, although the proposed residence was unusual in design, it nonetheless complied with all existing building and zoning regulations of the city. They attacked the ordinances as being "unconstitutional in that they are vague and provide no standard nor uniform rule by which to guide the architectural board." Their petition further alleged that the city acted in excess of statutory authority

[9]458 S.W. 2d 305 (Mo., 1970).
[10]Ibid., 306–7.
[11]Ibid., 308.
[12]Ibid., 307.
[13]Ibid.

in enacting ordinances which "attempt to allow respondent to impose aesthetic standards for buildings in the City of Ladue."[14] They contended that nothing in the state enabling legislation provided for an architectural board, that the local ordinances were invalid and unconstitutional as an unreasonable and arbitrary exercise of the police power, and that they constituted an unlawful delegation of legislative authority to the board. However, the court rejected these arguments, and citing such cases as *Stover,*[15] *Weiland,*[16] *Reid,* and *Hartke,*[17] it upheld the ordinances and the findings of the board.

In this ruling, the Missouri court expressly overruled a decision by a lower state court nine years earlier in *State ex rel. Magidson v. Henze.*[18] In that 1961 case, the court held invalid a University City ordinance establishing an architectural control commission. The commission had denied an application to build four houses that fell slightly below the minimum size requirement for the area and substantially below the size of existing neighborhood homes. The court held the ordinance void as an improper delegation of authority and as an invalid imposition of aesthetic standards on landowners.

In reversing the finding in *Magidson,* the Missouri Supreme Court in *Stoyanoff* averred that the lower court had failed to consider the effect of an applicable section in the enabling act that provided for regulations to promote "the general welfare."[19] The high court emphasized the statutory provision that

> Such regulations shall be made with reasonable consideration, among other things, to the character of the district and its peculiar suitability for particular uses, and with a view to conserving the values of buildings and encouraging the most appropriate use of land throughout such municipality.[20]

As for standards to guide discretion, the court said,

> Here . . . the procedures are for public hearings with notice to the applicant, not only by the Architectural Board but also by the City Council on appeal on the factual issues to be determined under the ordinance. An applicant's rights are safeguarded in this respect, and thus distinguished is the ordinance which was condemned in State ex rel. Magidson v. Henze.[21]

[14]Ibid.
[15]*People v. Stover,* 191 N.E. 2d 272 (N.Y., 1963).
[16]*State ex rel. Saveland Park Holding Corp. v. Wieland,* 69 N.W. 2d 217 (Wisc., 1955).
[17]*Oregon City v. Hartke,* 400 P. 2d 255 (Ore., 1965).
[18]342 S.W. 2d 261 (Mo. App., 1961).
[19]Note 9, 309.
[20]Ibid., 308. Quoting R.S. Mo., 1959, V.A.M.S., Sect. 89.040.
[21]Note 9, 311–12.

In essence, the court held that board discretion need not be bound by definitive, preconceived standards but could instead be moderated by board conformance to proper administrative procedures, an approach suggested by Kenneth Davis, an authority on administrative law.[22]

As a result of the *Stoyanoff* decision, Ronald R. McMillin of the *Missouri Law Review* worried that "judicial recognition that municipalities may regulate exterior building design opens a Pandora's box of problems with which the courts are likely to be faced as architectural control boards spread."[23] In particular, he suggested that to give the term "general welfare," on which the police power is based, "too broad a meaning would seemingly make the three preceding terms of 'health, safety, and public morals' superfluous."[24]

He also pointed out a fact that the Missouri court apparently chose not to mention: that the applicant for the building permit, Dimiter Stoyanoff, was a registered architect in the state and that the proposed residence was for his own use. As suggested by Bruce A. Rubin, there could be no doubt that Stoyanoff's design constituted artistic self-expression, whose eligibility for First Amendment protection was untainted by any possible commercial motive.[25]

In a 1969 article, Harvard law professor Frank Michelman hypothesizes a close analogy and poses a query as follows:

> What A does is to build a deck house in B's neighborhood, which so far is populated only by Tudor-style, Georgian-style, and New England Colonial-style homes. Can it really be said that by buying into such a neighborhood, B somehow staked out a claim not to be exposed to contemporary architecture?[26]

If the courts were correct in their rulings on *Reid* and *Stoyanoff,* then apparently in Ohio and Missouri such a preemptive claim is indeed valid. To pursue this logic further, might not a house of traditional design be properly excluded from a neighborhood composed of buildings of contemporary design? Or indeed could the residents of an area of ersatz Elizabethan houses forbid the building of Colonial-style architecture in the vicinity?

Not all state courts agree with the conclusions reached in the *Reid* and

[22]Kenneth Culp Davis, *Administrative Law Treatise* (St. Paul: West, 1958). See also Davis, *Discretionary Justice* (1969; reprint, Westport, C.T.: Greenwood).

[23]Ronald R. McMillin, "Community-Wide Architectural Controls in Missouri," *Missouri L. Rev.* 36 (1971), 426-27.

[24]Ibid., 426.

[25]Bruce A. Rubin, "Architecture, Aesthetic Zoning, and the First Amendment," *Stanford L. Rev.* 28 (November 1975), 181.

[26]Frank Michelman, "Toward a Practical Standard for Aesthetic Regulation," *Prac. Lawyer* 15 (Feb., 1969), 41.

Stoyanoff cases, however. In 1970, the Connecticut court ruled in *DeMaria v. Enfield Planning and Zoning Commission*[27] that a building permit had been denied improperly on aesthetic considerations only. The commission had found the proposed apartment project "aesthetically displeasing and inappropriate" for the reason that it did "not present a satisfactory image of what the Commission believes apartments should convey to the Town." The court rejected this rationale, stating: "Certainly, vague and undefined aesthetic considerations alone are insufficient to support the invocation of the police power, which is the source of all zoning authority."[28]

AUTHORITY FOR LOCAL DESIGN REVIEW

Two years before *DeMaria,* a New Jersey court, in *Piscitelli v. Township Committee of the Township of Scotch Plains,*[29] ruled that a local ordinance establishing an architectural review board was invalid in that the township could not delegate its statutory grant of power to an architectural commission. It noted that the state statute directly empowering the board of adjustment to hear and decide special exceptions could not be altered in any way by the municipal governing body. The court stated that the ordinance "usurps the power of the board of adjustment and vests unbridled discretion in the Architectural Review Board. There is no authority in [the state statutes] for the enactment of an Architectural Review Board, the purported ordinance is an invalid exercise of municipal power."[30]

The argument that localities lack specific authority to regulate the exterior design of buildings must, however, take into consideration the governing legislation of each particular state, which can vary significantly. As Robert M. Anderson notes in his compendium, *American Law of Zoning:* "Absent a specific delegation of power to regulate exterior design, a municipality might rely upon its constitutional or legislative home-rule powers for enacting authority."[31] For instance, in Ohio, the location of the *Reid* case, municipalities enjoy broad powers of self-government under the state constitution. In Missouri and New Jersey, by contrast, state delegation of authority to municipalities is less sweeping and more subject to varied construction by the courts, as evidenced by *Magidson* and *Stoyanoff* in Missouri and the *Piscitelli* case in New Jersey. Even without specific state enabling legislation, courts have ruled that localities possess sufficient competence to carry out design review. In 1977 an Arizona appellate court

[27]271 A. 2d 105 (Conn., 1970).
[28]Ibid., 108.
[29]248 A. 2d 274 (N.J. Sup'r., 1968).
[30]Ibid., 279.
[31]Robert M. Anderson, *American Law of Zoning* (Rochester, N.Y.: Lawyers Cooperative, 3rd ed. 1986), vol. 2, sect. 9. 78, 349.

found that "the general weight of recent precedent" was sufficient to uphold "the overall authority of communities to regulate matters of aesthetics and design through the zoning power and to create boards of architectural review."[32]

In New Hampshire, the state supreme court reached back into history to find a basis for aesthetic control. In 1970, in *Piper v. Meredith,*[33] the court reversed lower decisions that held that a town, in imposing height restrictions upon construction along a scenic lake shore, had not followed proper legislative procedure for the adoption of a zoning ordinance. In exempting the town from the procedures prescribed under state law, the court cited a common-law authority granted to New Hampshire towns in 1791, which empowered towns in the colony "to make and agree upon Such necessary Rules, orders and By Laws for the Directing Managing and ordering the Prudential affairs of Such Town as they Shall Judge most conducting to the Peace, Welfare, interest & good order of the Town And the Inhabitants thereof."[34]

The question of legislative authorization for design review can be a persistent one, since the Standard Acts on which most states model their land development control laws do not make an express delegation of design review authority. As law professor George Lefcoe comments, "The truly curious aspect of this process is why some courts imply it and others do not."[35]

Where there is no specific legal authority for design review, many local officials at one time or another have exacted concessions from recalcitrant developers by subtle manipulation of bureaucratic red tape. A proven tactic is for the officials to insist, on the one hand, on full administrative procedure if a developer shows reluctance to comply with tough or even unreasonable public regulations, and on the other to offer expeditious treatment to reward him if he accedes. Under the pressure of mounting interest expenses on construction financing as well as other costs, a developer with an application outstanding might just as soon dedicate a roadway, remove a nonconforming sign, or agree to a design restriction—even though not strictly required by law—rather than put up with the cost of nit-picking bureaucratic delays. Officials must, however, avoid the appearance of illegitimate and discriminatory procrastination and must take care not to provoke a developer into taking legal action. Nevertheless, the time and expense involved in initiating a lawsuit—even one that the developer would

[32]*City of Scottsdale v. Arizona Sign Association, Inc.,* 564 P. 2d 922 (Ariz. App., 1977), 923.

[33]266 A. 2d 103 (N.H., 1970).

[34]N.H. R.S.A., Ch. 31, Sect. 39. See 5 Laws of N.H. 587, 591–92; also 2 Laws of N.H. 340, 341–42.

[35]American Institute of Architects, *Design Review Boards,* 30.

surely win if it reached court—would only postpone a proposed project further and add to its cost. At this point, a city confronted with the prospect of waging a losing court fight that could set a precedent against its practices would likely back off and settle, but only after further delay. Notwithstanding avenues recently opened in civil rights and antitrust law that are advantageous to the developer (as discussed in chapter 6), the truism that you can't fight City Hall still applies. Shrewd official exploitation of the nuisance factor of governmental red tape can ensure developer cooperation with local policy. As Richard F. Babcock notes in his book, *The Zoning Game,*

> Many cities have been applying architectural controls to single-family houses for forty years and have avoided a court test of their validity throughout this entire period. It is only rarely that the prospective builder of a single-family house has enough strength of architectural convictions that he is willing to incur the wrath of his neighbors and the time and expense of a long lawsuit rather than modify the design of the residence he proposes to build.[36]

Babcock quotes a lawyer's comments on the workings of a planning commission that are equally applicable to the operations of design review boards.

> If they ever start taking us to court—we do a lot of things down at the Planning Commission we can't do under the law. But we don't tell them that. We put restrictions on them and say you have to have a setback of 100 feet here and so forth—usually you can work it out with them if you're pleasant and they realize you're interested in keeping the value of the land up. This is what you'd call the leverage function of a local zoning ordinance. So we've been really frightened that if they ever really start taking us to court, we're sunk.[37]

With reference to architectural review and in light of the *Reid* and *Stoyanoff* cases, the commentary may be unduly pessimistic, for in the games of politics, negotiation, intimidation, compromise, and legal brinkmanship, the public board is seldom at a total disadvantage.

In practice, of course, the relationship between architectural review boards and architects and their clients is not always one of confrontation. Despite the cases cited, in which disagreement erupted into litigation, the norm is for boards and developers to negotiate and settle their differences without resorting to court action. With the public boards as well as most developers having a stake in the community, the ideal is for attainment of a harmonious accord. As a whole, review boards find it in their communities' best interest to avoid legal problems by exercising reasonable flexibility.

[36]Richard F. Babcock, *The Zoning Game* (Madison: U. of Wisconsin Press, 1966), 98.
[37]Ibid., 90.

THE NEED FOR STANDARDS

Despite the apparent incongruity with which courts have upheld discretionary review, courts have also been wont to emphasize a principle made familiar in earlier discussion on Hayek's interpretation of the Rule of Law: that administrative discretion in design review, like any police-power regulation, must be moderated by the application of reasonable, predefined standards. Said the Supreme Court in 1966 in *Giacco v. Pennsylvania,*

> It is established that a law fails to meet the requirements of the Due Process Clause if it is so vague and standardless that it leaves the public uncertain as to the conduct it prohibits or leaves judges and jurors free to decide, without any legally fixed standards, what is prohibited and what is not in each particular case.[38]

From this standpoint, a common failing of local design regulations has been their inadequacy to channel administrative discretion, a flaw that H. Rutherford Turnbull III suggests falls within the high Court's "void-for-vagueness" proscription.[39] Even while upholding the discretionary judgment of the Cleveland Heights review board, the court in *Reid* cited (in a rather contradictory aside) a notation in *Ohio Jurisprudence* that states: "The discretion conferred on administrative agencies must not be unconfined and vagrant but must be canalized within banks that keep it from overflowing."[40] In much the same language, the *American Law Reports* likewise stresses the importance of standards.

> The rule is generally accepted that the legislature must ordinarily lay down some standards sufficient to canalize the administrative discretion so as to avoid committing decisions affecting the rights of property owners to the purely arbitrary choice of the administrator.[41]

While emphasizing this point, the *Reports* also concedes the need to use discretion to avoid unworkable and inflexible plans. It specifically approves allowances where the legislature acts in an administrative capacity and where there is provision for judicial review.

[38]382 U.S. 399 (1966), 402-3.

[39]H. Rutherford Turnbull III, "Aesthetic Zoning," *Wake Forest L. Rev.* 7 (1971), 237.

[40]1 *Ohio Jurisprudence 2d* 431, Adm. L. & Proc., Sect. 28, as quoted in Note 2, 77. Revised 2 *Ohio Jurisprudence 3d* 162 (1977) Adm. L., Sect. 24. "Although it is a well-recognized principle that board discretion is vested in administrative bodies, the discretion conferred on administrative agencies must not be unconfined and vagrant but must be channeled within banks that keep it from overflowing."

[41]58 *American Law Reports 2d* 1087. See the concurring opinion of Justice Benjamin N. Cardozo in *A.L.A. Schechter Poultry Corp. v. United States,* 295 U.S. 495 (1935), 551.

In general, it may be said that there is a growing tendency to sustain delegations of zoning authority guided only by general policy standards, experience having shown that any attempt to limit the administrative decisions to matters of detail as to which precise standards can be laid down results only in creating an inflexible and unworkable zoning plan with resultant pressures on the legislative body for frequent amendments leading to the evils of spot zoning.[42]

Though there is little denying this "growing tendency" made precedent in *Reid* and *Stoyanoff* of permitting broad discretion in architectural review, the requirement for standards is well established in case law. In 1947, in *City of West Palm Beach v. State ex rel. Duffey,*[43] the Florida court struck down a municipal ordinance regulating architectural design for the reason that the regulation lacked certainty and for leaving exaction to "the whim or caprice of the administrative agency." The ordinance required that "the completed appearance of every new building or structure must substantially equal that of adjacent buildings or structures in said subdivision in appearance, square foot area and height."[44]

Although it might be argued that the *Duffey* decision is dated and outmoded in outlook, several decisions contemporary with *Reid* and *Stoyanoff* continued to maintain the Florida position. One of the best known of these is the 1968 case of *Pacesetter Homes, Inc. v. Village of Olympia Fields,* in which an Illinois appellate court voided an architectural design regulation prohibiting "excessive similarity, dissimilarity or inappropriateness in exterior design and appearance of property."[45]

The ordinance set the standard "in relation to any other structure existing or for which a permit has been issued within a distance of 1,000 feet of the proposed site, or in relation to the characteristics of building design generally prevailing in the area . . . "[46] Several building elements were subject to review: the facade, openings and breaks in the facade, cubical content, floor area, roof line, height, construction, material, and site relationship. In addition, the "quality" of the architectural design and any "inappropriateness" in relation to the context of the neighborhood were also required to be taken into account.

Though widely held by commentators to be considerable in its detail—certainly in comparison with the ordinance upheld in *Reid* and *Stoyanoff*—the regulation was nonetheless held invalid by the court for its failure to prescribe adequate standards to control the actions of the village architectural advisory committee and for conferring too broad a discretion on the body. In a reversal of the West Palm Beach requirement for similarity in

[42]Ibid.
[43]30 So. 2d 491 (Fla., 1947).
[44]Ibid., 492.
[45]244 N.E. 2d 369 (Ill. App., 1968), 37.
[46]Ibid.

appearance, the building application at issue was disallowed because the proposed construction was found to be architecturally similar to other buildings in the area.

Ten years after *Pacesetter,* a New Jersey court, in *Morristown Road Associates v. Mayor and Common Council and the Planning Board of the Borough of Bernardsville,* used similar reasoning to invalidate a zoning amendment establishing an advisory design review committee and setting forth design standards for review of site plans. The amendment had been adopted for the purpose of ensuring that "proposed structures shall be related harmoniously to the terrain and to existing buildings in the vicinity that have a visual relationship to the proposed buildings."[47] Although the ordinance included an extensive description of site and building design considerations, the standards were found by the court to be "so broad and vague as to be incapable of being objectively applied, thereby permitting arbitrary action . . . in the review of site plan applications."[48]

Despite pleas by the borough that the standards were "as precise as the subject matter of the regulations permits," the court agreed with the developer's assertion that the standards invited "arbitrary determination and unbridled discretion on the part of the reviewing agency."[49] The court quoted McQuillin's *Municipal Corporations* as follows:

> As other ordinances, zoning ordinances are required to be reasonably definite and certain in terms so that they may be capable of being understood. The boundaries or limits of zones or district must be clearly and definitely fixed, and the restriction on property rights in the several zones must be declared as a rule of law in the ordinance and not left to the uncertainty of proof by extrinsic evidence. The rule of certainty and definiteness of zoning ordinances verges on or is identical with the rule that they must establish a clear rule or standard to operate uniformly and govern their administration, in order that arbitrariness and discrimination in administrative interpretation and application be avoided.[50]

The restrictions were required to be capable of being understood and complied with by the property owner seeking to meet its provisions. The court noted that the right of a landowner to use his property should not depend on the "outcome of litigation after the event"[51] that could alter the significance of requirements that had already been fulfilled.

The court cited both the *Duffey* and *Pacesetter* decisions with ap-

[47]394 A. 2d 157 (N.J. Sup'r., 1978), 162–63.
[48]Ibid., 158.
[49]Ibid., 160.
[50]Eugene McQuillin, *The Law of Municipal Corporations* (Chicago: Callaghan, 3rd. ed., 1976), vol. 8, sect. 25.59, 141.
[51]Note 47, 161. Quoting *Jantausch v. Borough of Verona,* 124 A. 2d 14 (N.J. Sup'r., 1956), 22.

proval. As for *Wieland* and other decisions in which design review had been upheld, the court noted that the sufficiency of controls in these cases was founded "upon the overall controlling requirement that the proposed construction not cause a depreciation of property values,"[52] a tacit approval of an economic basis for regulation apparently not adequately addressed in the borough's rationale for regulation.

Regarding the regulation at hand, the court focused on the inadequacy of such terms used in the ordinance as "harmonious," "displeasing," or "appropriate" in meeting the test of certainty and definiteness required of zoning regulations. The court found the ordinance's basic criterion of "harmony" with existing structures and terrain to be "conceptual," subject to "whim, caprice or subjective considerations," and vesting the design review committee and planning board with "too broad a discretion." The court concluded,

> The ordinance also offers no workable guidelines to one seeking approval of plans, rendering it almost impossible for an applicant to conform his plans to its requirements and making the utilization of his property dependent upon the subjective reactions of members of an administrative agency as to the harmoniousness of a proposed structure to the existing development. This deficiency likewise precludes the measurement of the reasonableness of a design approval or disapproval, thereby preventing a reviewing court from effectively determining when a decision has been arbitrary or capricious. The portions of the subject ordinance which dictate standards for architectural design must therefore be invalidated as impermissibly vague and indefinite.[53]

It is an anomaly that on the one hand predetermined, evaluative design standards are aspired to and even made requisite by law. Yet even apparently scrupulous attempts to delineate design standards and criteria have failed to pass court scrutiny for reason of being "void for vagueness." On the other hand, though free discretion in design review can reasonably be construed as violating reasonable certainty, in several of the cases examined, such discretionary review has enjoyed court approval.

Dolores Dalton writes of the Olympia Fields ordinance struck down in *Pacesetter:* "It is difficult to imagine a more specific set of standards, yet the court held that the ordinance conferred uncontrolled discretion on the Committee. The court invalidated the ordinance on unlawful delegation ground."[54] Dalton compares this outcome with *Stoyanoff,* in which an ordinance was upheld that allowed for determination by a board of professional architects, based only on "proper architectural standards in appearance and

---

[52]Note 47, 162.
[53]Ibid., 163.
[54]Dolores Ann Dalton, "San Francisco's Residential Rezoning: Architectural Controls in Central City Neighborhoods," *U. of San Francisco L. Rev.* 13 (Summer 1979), 964.

design . . . and general conformity with the style and design of surrounding structures."[55] In *Pacesetter* as well as in *Morristown Road,* the suggested criteria contained in the ordinances were rejected by the courts as being conceptual, vague, and investing too broad a discretion on review. It is certainly arguable that the terms—including "excessive similarity," "harmony," and "displeasing monotony"—are indeed qualitative and subject to interpretation rather than precise determination, and that despite their enumeration in the ordinances, they were no more definitive or exacting than the terms used in consideration of *Stoyanoff* and *Reid.*

In 1974, the American Institute of Architects commissioned law professor George Lefcoe to make a study of practice of architectural design review. Though Lefcoe argues in the paper that protection of property values is not an unequivocally sound basis for regulation, he nevertheless points out that the ordinance in *Pacesetter* failed to mention this economic reason for regulation, a deficiency which conceivably may have been as mortally damaging to the Olympia Fields ordinance as to the Bernardsville regulation. He also points out the lack of a provision allowing neighboring property owners an opportunity to challenge approval administratively.

Lefcoe's most notable comment on the case, however, addresses the perceived vagueness of the ordinance. In an analysis equally applicable to the Bernardsville regulation, he writes,

> Another distinguishing feature of the ordinance was its nitpicking detail. How an ordinance that is too explicit violates the constitutional stricture against vagueness is hard to comprehend. The very basis of an attack predicated on a lack of sufficiently clear and precise standards is undercut by an ordinance as explicit as the one in *Pacesetter.* Alternately, though, such detail may stifle innovation in design, and hence could be subject to challenge as inhibiting freedom of expression and the design professional's right to work.[56]

Lefcoe suggests that conceivably a review board "may simply nitpick the developer's proposal, withhold approval, and by dilatory tactics force him to abandon his plans."[57] If sued, the board could claim that it would have approved any number of alternatives if the developer had only proposed such an acceptable scheme. Under this sort of ploy, Lefcoe suggests, a developer would be stymied unless he could force the board virtually to propose an acceptable design itself, or if he can convince a court of the board's pernicious intent.

[55]Note 9, 310–11.
[56]American Institute of Architects, *Design Review Boards,* 24.
[57]Ibid., 16.

EXCLUSIONARY MOTIVE?

Particularly when more costly processes and methods of design and construction are mandated, architectural review can also be construed as being exclusionary, even though exclusion is a potential characteristic of virtually any form of urban planning control. Cautions Lefcoe,

> Because of the open-endedness of design review, it could be used as an easy subterfuge to block unwanted housing for low- and moderate-income people, or to hamstring development geared for interracial occupancy. Furthermore, design review is a way to increase development costs just in order to insure that all new housing in a community must bear "snob appeal" price tags. If such abuses were tolerated, they would undermine the legal basis for design review and discredit the entire concept.[58]

In proposing a model design review ordinance by local government, Lefcoe enumerates and describes several options on the purview of review. One of these choices specifically exempts housing developments from design examination, thus removing the possibility of social exclusion based on race or economics. However, he also includes the observation that government-assisted low-income housing may be precisely the type of building development that "would benefit from design scrutiny . . . [since] there is no reason why these programs need suffer from inferior design."[59]

Lefcoe further suggests that exclusion may have played a part in both the *Duffey* and *Magidson* decisions in which design regulation was overturned. According to his analysis, one reason why the presiding court in each instance may have invalidated the regulation at issue was that in both cases, had the review processes been approved, the result would have been the exclusion of smaller, less costly housing from neighborhoods built up with more expensive homes. In comparing *Magidson* with *Stoyanoff,* Lefcoe points to the "snob" implication of design review in the earlier case, which would have had "the effect of keeping moderately priced housing out of an exclusive suburb."[60] He distinguishes the socially discriminatory effect of the University City ordinance to *Stoyanoff,* in which the cost of the proposed design nullified the possibility of economically motivated exclusion. In Ladue, denial of Stoyanoff's permit was based apparently on aesthetic grounds, not social discrimination.

The charge of exclusion can, of course, be leveled at any form of land-use control, leveled at architectural review, and even at planning itself,

---

[58]Ibid., 15.
[59]Ibid., 43.
[60]Ibid., 31.

which has been associated with exclusion since its inception. Beyond vigilance on the part of the courts to guard against it, the threat of exclusion can be defeated best at its source by shifting regulatory authority from the local to the regional level—a change involving comprehensive and drastic reform of the entire land-use control structure rather than architectural review alone.

ENFORCING STYLISTIC PREFERENCES
THROUGH THE POLICE POWER

While some communities have adopted regulations requiring new buildings to be in design harmony with existing structures, numerous others have enacted ordinances actually specifying certain stylistic preferences. Typically, the styles favored are traditional, even where a genuine historic basis for the specific style in the area is insubstantial or even imaginary. John Delafons, an English observer of American land-use controls comments on these ordinances:

> Some of them are quite ludicrous, such as the "no-look-alike" and "must-look-alike" regulations which attempt to enforce or prohibit variety, and those which speak in terms of style, such as the comic-opera zoning ordinance of Coral Gables, Florida, which requires that "all buildings shall be Spanish, Venetian, Italian, or other Mediterranean or similar harmonious type architecture."[61]

These stylistic standards and others that prescribe conformity in such considerations as material and color can be faulted from a legal perspective as an impediment of free expression and from a design standpoint as being more an inhibitor of inventive and interesting design than an assurance of design quality. Writes Lefcoe, "These standards direct the attention of design committees to the superficialities of style instead of to the basic aspects of design that are likely to affect community life."[62]

But even while ridiculing ordinances that promote "comic opera" conformity to eclectic architectural styles, Delafons concedes,

> It must be admitted that they do often secure a degree of coherence and conformity in a community which is rather delightful in America because it is so rare. Coming into Santa Barbara, California, one is immediately struck by the cohesion of style and the absence of the usual crudities of downtown. In fact, almost the entire city was rebuilt after the earthquake of 1925, and an architectural Board of Review enforced compliance with the "Monterey"

[61]John Delafons, *Land-Use Controls in the United States* (1962; reprint, Cambridge: M.I.T. Press, 1969), 60.
[62]American Institute of Architects, *Design Review Boards*, 13.

style through the issue of over 2,000 building permits in eight months. The result is one of the most attractive towns in America.[63]

Undeniably there is a gap between established conventions of popular taste regarding such matters as domestic architecture and the designer's creed of seeking innovation and creativity in architectural expression. Notwithstanding the designer's role as "tastemaker," the public propensity toward conservatism and tradition in environmental design, especially regarding single-family housing, is strong indeed. As John Costonis observes, people tend to want "cultural stability-identity" in their environment, whether to maintain historic architecture or recreate familiar if somewhat counterfeit surroundings. He notes that "associational harmony, not visual beauty, is what community groups primarily seek from aesthetic regulation."[64]

However much their neighborhoods are historically and regionally incongruous, or stifle creative expression, that many American homeowners prefer neighborhoods composed of such traditional-style houses as New England Colonial, French Provincial, English Tudor, and Mediterranean to the exclusion of contemporary design is less the result of aesthetic judgment than a reflection of the sociopsychological need for cultural stability. From this viewpoint, even Mrs. Reid's proposed modern design, a one-story atrium house hidden from public view by a rather innocuous wall, was unacceptable—not so much from its invisibility from the street as from its implied threat to the cultural stability of the surrounding community.

It is ironic that the term "proper architectural principles," which was cited in the ordinance, constituted the rationale justifying the actions of the Cleveland Heights review board in the *Reid* case. Arguably, the values advocated by the board were not "proper architectural principles," as taught in most schools of architecture or evidenced by the types of projects cited by professional organizations and journals, but were the popular values held by neighboring homeowners.

The AIA Headquarters Controversy

One reason that courts have upheld the findings of architectural review boards has undoubtedly been their natural inclination to rely on the professional judgment of the architects who compose most review boards. However, even in situations where imitative traditionalism in architecture is not at issue, and where members of the review board as well as the designer of the proposed project are architects of the highest professional repute, the

[63]Delafons, *Land-Use Control,* 60–61.
[64]John J. Costonis, "Law and Aesthetics: A Critique and a Reformulation of the Dilemmas," *Michigan L. Rev.* 80 (1982), 424.

process of discretionary design review has resulted in considerable problems. One such example can be seen in the furor that surrounded the design of the national headquarters of the American Institute of Architects in Washington. Although the dispute did not result in legal action, the circumstances and events that occurred illustrate the faults and weakness of design review under the police power.

For years the AIA had housed its national headquarters in the Octagon, a historic brick house constructed in the late eighteenth century by William Thornton at a corner site near the center of the capital district. As the institute grew, new facilities beyond this landmark and its additions became necessary, and in 1967 a competition was held for the design of a new office headquarters to be located behind Thornton's Octagon.

The winning design selected by the AIA jury of nationally known architects was submitted by the architectural firm of Mitchell-Giurgola. At the time, Romaldo Giurgola was chairman of the Division of Architecture at Columbia University; Ehrman B. Mitchell, Jr., later rose to the presidency of the institute itself. A modification of the winning design was submitted subsequently to the Washington Fine Arts Commission, the board of architectural experts appointed by the President to review designs for historic areas of the capital.

The proposal was rejected. Said Gordon Bunshaft, a member of the commission and senior design partner of the architectural firm of Skidmore, Owings and Merrill: "The design concept is totally out of scale with the existing buildings on the site. This new building would make the existing buildings and garden look like a toy."[65] Mitchell-Giurgola submitted several modified designs to the commission only to have each scheme turned down. Mitchell said, "We feel that we are being asked for facade architecture."[66] His partner, Giurgola, criticized the commission: "I deplore their outdated concern with architecture as a monument."[67] Finally, the winning architects resigned and another firm was commissioned to design the project in a different idiom, albeit contemporary and not traditional.

The resulting debate involved several of the most prominent design professionals in the country. Besides Mitchell-Giurgola and members of the Fine Arts Commission, architects in the leadership of the institute as well as those on the blue-ribbon jury that decided on the Mitchell-Giurgola entry took part. Willis N. Mills, chairman of the AIA headquarters committee, saw a difference in design philosophy regarding the relationship between architecture and community design as the basis of the dispute:

[65]*Progressive Architecture*, "A.I.A. Headquarters: Headquarters for Architecture?" 48, no. 12 (Dec. 1967), 136.
[66]Ibid., 140.
[67]Ibid., 136.

Listening to both sides of this controversy, I believe the disagreement arises from the basic approach to the problem. Mitchell-Giurgola sees this as a challenge to mix the new and the old with proper respect for each other. They therefore seek to create a "place," in Giurgola's term, a single composition where the form of the new building finds its genesis and inspiration in the old. Both are related in a powerful manner to the central garden, which becomes the focus of each. This philosophy is entirely consistent with the original competition program and is an attitude commended by the jury.

The Fine Arts Commission, on the other hand, takes the position of a preservationist. Here is an important building with its Georgian garden. It is a pleasant, tranquil spot, which should not be disturbed. Therefore, anything that intrudes should go away. This explains their first recommendation of leaving the present garden and headquarters building intact and finding new required space in the adjacent Lemon Building. Short of this, any new building (in the view of the FAC) should be anonymous and try to be as invisible as possible.[68]

Ada Louise Huxtable, architecture critic of the *New York Times,* gave a more pointed account:

The AIA's reaction was either chicken or preposterous. Whatever the design's shortcomings may have been, and whatever the Commission's reservations may have been, the scheme was conscientious, concerned, and able, not a speculator's destructive, free-wheeling horror. In retrospect, the Fine Arts Commission seems to have been guilty of an overbearing misinterpretation of its role for an extraordinary and dubious imposition of its own taste. On these grounds, the AIA should, and could, have stood firm, without compromising its belief in the review board function. It could, in fact, have helped to clarify that function constructively and appropriately, and aided in the proper definition of review board responsibilities. It is understandable that at this point Mitchell-Giurgola resigned.[69]

Huxtable's criticism went beyond aesthetic assessment of the Giurgola-Mitchell proposal and of the final design subsequently performed by another firm. She also castigated the attitude of both the institute and the commission: Of the AIA, she wrote,

There seems to be little question that some of the leadership and membership was uncomfortable with the quite unconventional Mitchell-Giurgola design, which was an outstandingly creative answer to the difficult problem of blending scale and style. It dealt in sophisticated subtleties, using what was at that

[68]Ibid., 140.
[69]Ada Louise Huxtable, *Kicked a Building Lately?* (New York: Quadrangle, 1976), 173–74.

time, but has ceased to be, an offbeat vocabulary, clothed modestly in compatible brick.[70]

She criticized the completed design of the new headquarters in language not unlike that used earlier by Bunshaft in condemning the Mitchell-Giurgola solution.

> Its insistent, dominating horizontal bands of precast concrete destroy rather than preserve scale. The design is brutally insensitive to Thornton's far more delicate detail. The Octagon has lost presence; it now looks like a toy. The Octagon garden, while almost the same size as before in square feet, is unbelievably diminished by too much paving and too few trees and the heavy-handed, looming presence behind it.[71]

Design Warfare

The dispute between proponents of the Mitchell-Giurgola scheme and defenders of the design ultimately approved by Fine Arts Commission actually had deeper, more philosophical roots than such objective arguments concerning each proposal's comparable design merit as suggested by Huxtable or on differences between "preservation" or "place" as identified by Willis Mills, chairman of the headquarters committee. At the time of the imbroglio in the 1960s, design theory, as taught in virtually every collegiate school of architecture in the country and as represented on the Fine Arts Commission, was under the influence of modernism and such modernist European architects as Le Corbusier, Walter Gropius, Marcel Breuer, and Mies van der Rohe, the wellsprings of the International Style of modern design.

These pioneers of international modernism developed—together with their counterparts in painting, Pablo Picasso and Piet Mondrian—the pure, stark, cubist form of visual expression, devoid of ornamentation, that dominated the era of postindustrialization in the 1920s. In urban design, their work is exemplified by the grand, idealistic treatises of Le Corbusier. In his influential manifesto, *The City of Tomorrow,* Le Corbusier proposed his sweeping geometry for "A Contemporary City for Three Million People," a concept on which he later elaborated in *The Radiant City.* The originators of modernism, a latter-day derivative of the same Cartesian rationalism that characterized Renaissance design, seemed to covet the absolute control of urban design once exercised by such planners as Sixtus and Haussmann. In his proposed Voisin Plan for Paris, for example, Le Corbu-

[70]Ibid., 173.
[71]Ibid., 174.

sier's solution for the problems of the city was to tear down the city center and start over.

According to one of their critics, architect Robert Stern, the proponents of modernism seek "to construct a man-made world in accordance with ideal formal and social images."[72] Their a priori concepts of social design deal with pure, prototypical solutions in an abstract and universal context. In Stern's view, modernists are "exclusive," intolerant of pluralism and of historic forms, even classical and Renaissance forms, the historical origins of their own rational perspective.

The work of Romaldo Giurgola, by contrast, is identified as that of postmodernism, a reactionary movement in design theory originating about the time of the AIA headquarters affair and reaching preeminance in the 1980s. This approach is characterized by Stern and others who favor it as being "inclusive" of pluralism, for purportedly rejecting any "global" ambitions in design and planning, which they ascribe to the "exclusive" attitude of the modernists. The inclusiveness of postmodernism encompasses a renewed appreciation of historic forms and design concepts, including the decorative details of beaux-arts neoclassicism rejected earlier by the modernists. In his treatise *Complexity and Contradiction in Architecture,* Robert Venturi, the leading theorist of postmodernism, argues for the values of complex pluralism, history, and decoration in architecture. In response to the modernist dictum "Less is more," Venturi retorts, "Less is a bore."[73] Writing with Denise Scott Brown and Steven Izenour in *Learning from Las Vegas,* Venturi complains of the stifling of pluralism in design review.

> Any artist could [tell] the lawmakers that you cannot legislate beauty and that attempts to do so by the use of experts will result not only in gross injustice but in an ugly deadness in the environment.
> Beauty escapes in the pursuit of safety, which promotes a simplistic sameness over a varied vitality.[74]

Whereas the AIA headquarters design proposed by Mitchell-Giurgola is identified as postmodern, the work of commission member Gordon Bunshaft exemplifies the International Style. Perhaps only coincidentally, the design for the institute building that was ultimately approved by the commission was provided by The Architects Collaborative (TAC), a firm guided

---

[72]Robert A. M. Stern, *New Directions in American Architecture* (New York: Braziller, 1969), 8.

[73]Robert Venturi, *Complexity and Contradiction in Architecture* (1966; reprint, New York: Museum of Modern Art, 1977), 16–17.

[74]Robert Venturi, Denise Scott Brown, and Steven Izenour, *Learning from Las Vegas* (Cambridge: M.I.T. Press, 1972), 189.

in approach by the philosophy of Walter Gropius, founder of the Bauhaus school and a progenitor of the International Style.

Considering the modernity and appearance of the approved TAC design, it is certainly arguable whether the Fine Arts Commission was truly concerned with preservation in rejecting the Mitchell-Giurgola proposal, or whether the preservationist argument actually supported the membership's preference for a modernist design by one of its own kind. It seems evident from their designs and writings that the founders of modernism had no great philosophical commitment to the preservation ethic, as witness the professions of Le Corbusier and the case of *Penn Central Transportation Co. v. New York City,* in which Marcel Breuer, also of Bauhaus fame, demonstrated no preservationist's compunction in his schemes for the dismemberment of the beaux-arts design of Grand Central Station. (See chapter 6 for a discussion of the case.)

In comparing the alleged merits or failings of various architectural styles it becomes apparent that the diversity and divergence of architectural philosophies make it virtually impossible to establish a definitive design standard of "proper design principles" to guide discretionary evaluation. Focusing on the ongoing disagreement between the neoclassicists and post-modernists on the one hand and the modernists on the other, John J. Costonis writes,

> The Hundred Years' War still raging between neoclassicists and post-modernists in one camp and modernists in the other, exemplifies similar, if far broader, disagreements over the ideal appearance of the city as a whole. The neoclassicists, who favored Beaux Arts urban design and architectural styles, held sway in the late nineteenth and early twentieth centuries but were driven from the field by the modernists in the following half-century. Regrouped under the post modernist banner, however, latter-day neoclassicists have counterattacked. They endorse elaborate ornamentation, masonry construction, uniform street walls, buildings fit snugly within larger urban compositions, and the eclectic embrace of traditional architectural styles. Modernists, in contrast, champion monumental buildings standing aloof from their surroundings, irregular street walls, lean ornamentation, and a wide variety of building materials and technologies.[75]

Costonis cites the intensity of aesthetic disagreements between the doyens of design and design criticism.

> To Ada Louise Huxtable, the New York Public Library is "one of the last of the great nineteenth century buildings"; to Lewis Mumford, it reverberates with the "hollow echoes of expiring breath." The uniform street walls, cornices, and building facades of Baron Haussmann's Paris, which so delight

---

[75]Costonis, "Law and Aesthetics," 404.

tourists and Parisians alike, caused Camillo Sitte intense pain. "Why," he groaned, "must the straightedge and the compass be the all powerful masters of city building?" New York City's gridiron street system, a product of its 1811 Official Street Plan, is disdained by many urbanists as a monument to execrable planning and greedy real estate speculation. Paul Goldberger, on the other hand, extols its "neat, tight, ramrod-straight views that stretch from river to river." Le Corbusier adds that it is a "model of wisdom and greatness of vision." In Edith Wharton's eyes, the city's brownstones, the pride of a number of its designated historic districts, are loathsome buildings clad in "chocolate-coloured coating of the most hideous stone ever quarried [and set within a] cramped horizontal gridiron of a town . . . hide-bound in its deadly uniformity of mean ugliness."[76]

As in any area of artistic expression, it seems apparent that absolute concepts of correctness or incorrectness are inappropriate.

But however significant the distinction between the two design philosophies represented in the AIA headquarters affair may appear to architects, to the lawyer and layman the difference seems rather esoteric. As lawyer H. P. Kucera remarked in 1960: "Aesthetics should not concern itself with the distinction between the smell of a rose and smell of a lily, but certainly should concern itself between the smell of a rose and the smell of a barnyard."[77] Surely to judge between the Mitchell-Giurgola proposal and the scheme finally constructed is to differentiate between a lily and a rose.

In its rejection of the Mitchell-Giurgola design, the Fine Arts Commission would have been well served to have been informed of the Rhode Island court's earlier admonishment in *Hayes v. Smith*. The police power can require a project architect only to take reasonable account of the context of the surroundings and to make his design proposal compatible, "even if not so compatible as the commission [deems] advisable."[78]

Venturi, Scott Brown, and Izenour write,

> The courts have ruled that beauty is an urban amenity to be sought through the police powers, review boards, and other regulatory measures; but they have omitted to set the standards by which beauty may be defined or the processes through which it may be equitably judged to be present. Local authorities have reacted by appointing "experts" (usually local architects) who use their own discretion in assigning beauty or lack of it to the works of others. The limits set on capriciousness, authoritarianism, or venality in such

[76]Ibid., 403–4.

[77]H. P. Kucera, "The Legal Aspects of Aesthetics in Zoning," *Institute of Planning and Zoning* 1 (1960), 48–49. Quoted in respondent's brief, *Oregon City v. Hartke,* note 17. See *Harvard L. Rev.* 79 (1966), 1321.

[78]167 A. 2d 546 (R.I., 1961), 550.

a system are those internal to the individual review board members. This is rule by man rather than rule by law.[79]

There is no legitimacy, of course, for the police power to favor one design philosophy or architectural preference over the next. Lefcoe comments:

> To the extent that design review systems deny to design professionals the essential choices that they must make to maintain their own integrity, these systems may be adjudged to infringe cherished prerogatives that are readily analogous to the rights expressly protected by the First Amendment.[80]

Where rejection of a certain design by a public review board has been upheld by a court, the assumption has been that architecture as art is guided by established aesthetic principles subscribed to by the architectural profession at large. The court in *Reid*, for instance, defended the review process on the assumption that a board of "highly trained experts in the field of architecture" could make definitive aesthetic judgments based on "proper architectural principles." The apparent feeling was that even if courts and the lay public could not judge on design aesthetics, "highly trained" architects could interpret and agree on "proper architectural principles" well enough to use them as a definitive standard for aesthetic judgment. This Pythagorean assumption of absolute principles and standards in architectural judgment is based on an illusion of definitive expertise in matters of aesthetics. Philip Selznick points to such deference as "the retreat to technology"[81] and Alan Altschuler similarly refers to the apparent invulnerability of expertness in the layman's eyes.[82] However, given the human nature of all professionals, expertness can just as easily be a cloak for dogma and subjectivity as a basis for disinterested objectivity. The chauvinism that seems virtually endemic to great architects toward their own design philosophies and their intolerance of competing ideas is summarized by Costonis.

> With the principal exception of Washington, D.C. . . . the design of American cities is the product of cultural, political, legal, and economic forces that embrace pluralism. . . . The premise that America can have the unified design philosophies or cityscapes of the past while remaining faithful to its own pluralistic traditions is naive, objectionable, or both. Democracy and aesthetic orthodoxy are antithetical. Regrettably, this antithesis has generally been ignored by the Le Corbusiers, Wrights, Gropiuses, and other leading architectural propagandists, by many design critics, and by many members of the

[79]Venturi *et al.*, *Learning from Las Vegas*, 189.

[80]American Institute of Architects, *Design Review Boards*, 17.

[81]Philip Selznick, *Leadership in Administration* (New York: Harper & Row, 1957), 74.

[82]Alan A. Altschuler, *The City Planning Process: A Political Analysis* (1965; reprint, Ithaca: Cornell U. Press, 1969), 334 ff.

preservation movement. The lip service that they pay to the values of plural-ism is belied by their desire to impose personal design preferences on society as autocratically as did the despots of the past.[83]

It should be added that the modernist architects mentioned by Costonis are not the only ones guilty of design chauvinism. As Tom Wolfe amply documents in his popular analysis of contemporary architecture, *From Bau-haus to Our House*,[84] the proponents of postmodernism—inclusive though they may claim to be—show the same sort of disdain for modernism as modernists before them displayed toward the beaux-arts neoclassicism of the past.

The Question of Project-by-Project Review

In situations like the AIA affair and cases like *Stoyanoff* and *Eustice* where the project architect is a licensed professional, another question can be raised concerning the reasonableness of aesthetic review on a project-by-project basis. Even assuming that aesthetics in the public eye is reasonably subject to police-power controls, in the case of building design, the regis-tered architect has already been certified by the state as qualified to practice his profession, by having passed standardized tests including those presum-ably ascertaining his competence in design. Certification notwithstanding, where design review is practiced, the architect may find his aesthetic judg-ment questioned again and again on a project-by-project basis by peer pro-fessionals with public certification not different from his own except for local appointment. This scrutiny is in addition to inspections to ensure com-pliance with building and zoning codes. Writes Lefcoe,

> Would lawyers or doctors tolerate a mandatory system of review prior to the handling of each of their cases? In fact, once professionals are duly licensed, the only controls over professional conduct are at the extremes of malpractice. These standards are often said to be, if anything, too lenient in maintaining professionals' discretion. Why, then, should architects, planners, and other design professionals be asked to submit their work for public approval? Does society have a greater interest in its buildings than in the processes of decision by which lives are risked under the surgeon's knife?[85]

While questions can exist concerning the content and format of the registration examinations and on the criteria for findings of "design compe-tence or incompetence," such testing of professional skills along predeter-mined lines and without the context of a particular application seems less

---

[83]Costonis, "Law and Aesthetics," 368.
[84]Tom Wolfe, *From Bauhaus to Our House* (New York: Farrar Straus & Giroux, 1981).
[85]American Institute of Architects, *Design Review Boards*, 17.

threatening to the rights of private property and free expression than project-by-project review, while still maintaining a measure of public design
control. Of course, if the qualifying exam were to measure aesthetic judgment alone, then the question would be raised concerning the constitutional
propriety of restricting public artistic expression to those who have passed
a test.

THE FIRST AMENDMENT REEXAMINED

Is adherence of private development to "proper architectural principles" by itself such a compelling public interest as to motivate communities to undertake design regulation? On the one hand is the right of free
artistic expression; on the other is the obligation of the public to further the
community's urban design policy and its right not to be held a captive audience. In the Supreme Court's decision in *Rowan*[86] permitting regulation
of unsolicited mailings, the point is made that the public is entitled to some
sanctuary from unwanted expression. It would seem that the later *Erznoznik*[87] ruling allowing the depiction of nudity in movies shown at a drive-in
theater effectively weakened this right. However, concerning architectural
expression, Annette B. Kolis finds that such is not the case. She writes,

> Under *Erznoznik,* the case against architectural design controls would be rela-
> tively clear were it not for two qualifying footnotes in the opinion. The Court
> distinguished the rights of unwilling viewers which were not at issue from the
> rights of the theater owners which were under consideration, further noting,
> "We are not concerned in this case with a properly drawn zoning ordinance
> restricting the location of drive-in theaters or with a nondiscriminatory nui-
> sance ordinance designed to protect the privacy of persons in their homes
> from the visual and audible intrusions of such theaters."
>
> Consequently, as long as an ordinance does not restrict expression solely
> "because of its message, its ideas, its subject matter, or its content," a nar-
> rowly tailored ordinance protecting homeowners against offensive "visual in-
> trusions" will be valid after *Erznoznik.*[88]

Justices with such diverse political philosophies as William Douglas
and William Rehnquist have voted on the side of controls at one time or
another. With reference to the right of the public to be free from annoying
forms of expression, Douglas said in his *Pollack* dissent, "The right to be

---

[86]*Rowan v. United States Post Office,* 397 U.S. 728 (1970).

[87]*Erznoznik v. City of Jacksonville,* 422 U.S. 205 (1975).

[88]Annette B. Kolis, "Architectural Expression: Police Power and the First Amendment,"
Urban L. Ann. 16 (1979), 294–95.

let alone is indeed the beginning of all freedom."[89] In such cases as *Erznoznik* and *Metromedia,* Rehnquist likewise dissented in favor of regulation. Although minority opinions, such judicial dissents are not without significance. Of course, the specific focus of these Supreme Court cases was on First Amendment concerns other than architectural controls. As the majority observed in *Metromedia:* "Each method of communicating ideas is 'a law unto itself' and that law must reflect the 'differing natures, values, abuses and dangers' of each method."[90] There is no predicting which direction the high Court would take should the issue of architectural design regulation ever come before it.

In *Linmark Associates, Inc. v. Township of Willingboro,* a 1977 First Amendment decision that struck down a local ordinance prohibiting the display of "for sale" and "sold" signs on real estate, the Supreme Court seemed to suggest four criteria, gleaned from previous rulings, that should be met in public regulation of aesthetics. First is "whether the ordinance 'leave[s] open ample alternative channels for communication.'"[91] In architectural design regulation, no other art or communication form can realistically substitute for architectural expression. Second, though an ordinance may "promote aesthetic values or any other value," the regulation must be "unrelated to the suppression of free expression."[92] Since an architect or a development owner, especially of a proposed custom-designed home, can make a substantial plea that his freedom of architectural expression would be denied by design restrictions, this sort of regulation would be difficult to justify.

Third, the Court cited *Erznoznik* in limiting regulations to those that "restrict a mode of communication that 'intrudes on the privacy of the home, . . . [and] makes it impractical for the unwilling viewer or auditor to avoid exposure.'"[93] Again it can be well argued that the design of a building, especially a single-family home, would be less intrusive than the giant outdoor cinema screen allowed by the Court in *Erznoznik*. Last, in an observation easily applied to architecture, the Court found that "the proscription applies only to one mode of communication, therefore, does not transform this into a 'time, place, or manner' case."[94]

In identifying the three latter criteria, law professors Daniel R. Mandelker and Roger A. Cunningham make the following observations,

[89]*Public Utilities Commission of the District of Columbia v. Pollack,* 343 U.S. 451 (1952), 467.
[90]*Metromedia, Inc. v. City of San Diego,* 453 U.S. 490 (1981), 501.
[91]431 U.S. 85 (1977).
[92]Ibid., 93. Citing *United States v. O'Brien,* 391 U.S. 367 (1968), 377.
[93]Ibid., 94.
[94]Ibid., 94.

Clearly the aesthetic values sought to be promoted by architectural controls are not "unrelated to the suppression of free expression." Indeed, their very purpose is to suppress free architectural expression at variance with the values of the local governing body or the architectural review board which administers the architectural controls. It is hard to imagine any architectural style so intrusive "on the privacy of the home[s]" of neighbors as to justify restriction of the freedom of architectural expression. Architectural control ordinances that completely ban certain types of architecture certainly do more than merely regulate the place or manner of expression. Moreover, the fact that an architect and his client might be able to build somewhere else in a municipality may not be enough to validate architectural controls, for "[o]ne is not to have the exercise of his liberty of expression in appropriate places abridged on the plea that it may be exercised in some other place."[95]

Architects serving on design review boards would probably reject the suggestion that they are stifling the originality and creativity of their fellow professionals. They would argue that the purpose of architectural review is simply to encourage and promote greater sympathy in new design and construction for the existing context of the surrounding built environment—a reasonable design value and objective quite consistent with contemporary orthodoxy in design theory. Members might point to an observation made by Costonis: "Buildings that are regarded as outstanding architecture when considered in isolation may be offensive in particular settings."[96] The responsibility of the architect to consider the design impact of his proposed development upon the context of the existing environment is expressed in Brent C. Brolin's 1976 dissertation, *The Failure of Modern Architecture.*

> If the guide lines for the building's appearance are to be set more strictly by its visual context or the social value of its iconography, our understanding of "originality" must change. Originality, or creativity, has become synonymous with "new" and "different," and designing to fit in rather to stand out seems a terrifying sacrifice of the designer's ego. It is not. It only represents a change in the ground rules: the prevailing aesthetic of the place is substituted for the architect's aesthetic. Instead of being guided by his own narrowly defined "modern" ideas of what is visually pleasing, the architect substitutes another, probably equally narrow set of visual guidelines; he designs to fit in with the existing visual context or to respect the preferences of the clients who are to use the building.
>
> This does not mean that architects should necessarily produce facsimiles of historical relics, although the average traditional building in a traditional context often looks better than an average modern building in the same tradi-

[95]Daniel R. Mandelker and Roger A. Cunningham, *Planning and Control of Land Development* (Indianapolis: Bobbs-Merrill, 1979), 920.
[96]Costonis, "Law and Aesthetics," 408.

tional context. Some modern buildings do fit in with their surroundings with sacrificing their modernity . . . but unfortunately these are exceptions. Only occasionally does a modern building accept the fact of its context rather than try to shock by its modernity.[97]

Despite the reasonableness of Brolin's suggestion that buildings might conform to the design context of their surroundings in terms of form, proportion, scale, material, and color without becoming imitative or counterfeit in detail and without forfeiting their contemporaneity, the question remains of what the public can or should do if an owner and an architect disagree with a review board's determination that their proposed new construction fails to meet such criteria. This circumstance existed in the controversy surrounding the design of the AIA headquarters building. Even if a developer chooses deliberately to ignore the community's architectural tastes and urban design objectives, no matter how worthy, is the public board within the bounds of the First Amendment to require conformance under a police-power stricture? Given the choice in black-and-white terms, planning attorney and author Richard Babcock apparently believes not. He bases his conclusion on his attitude toward artistic creativity as much as legal grounds in writing,

> I, for one, would accept the consequences of individual choice—with all its risks—rather than permit a consensus to have the force of law. If it follows that I must defend the most tasteless developer as well as a Frank Lloyd Wright, I accept that burden. Neither I nor my contemporaries should have the power to deny the next generation the right to judge whether our efforts had grace or were ugly. . . . The one indispensible ingredient of man-made beauty is the absolute dominance of a single man over the majority. . . . If government is going to regulate design in the name of aesthetics we risk either a cultural dictatorship or, if we insist on a democratic decision-making process, then we are bound to substitute taste for beauty . . . and taste, as Picasso observed, is the enemy of creativeness.[98]

If, from the standpoint of law, a case can be made that regulation of architectural design through board review offends the First Amendment, and, from the viewpoint of art, that it inhibits or destroys creative expression and innovation, is design review of sufficient benefit to community planning and urban design to justify the practice? If one were to adopt a strict view that diversity of expression and organic urban form development are ends to be sought as the most appropriate and beneficial to a pluralist,

[97]Brent C. Brolin, *The Failure of Modern Architecture* (New York: Van Nostrand Reinhold, 1976), 112.

[98]Richard F. Babcock, "Billboards, Glass Houses, and the Law," *Harper's* 232, no. 1391 (April 1966), 30.

free-enterprise society, the obvious answer to the question is no. Observers of city development and design from Lewis Mumford to Jane Jacobs have indeed argued in favor of organic urban development and diversity in the physical composition and visual form of communities. Writes Mumford,

> Organic planning does not begin with a preconceived goal: it moves from need to need, from opportunity to opportunity, in a series of adaptation that themselves become increasingly coherent and purposeful, so that they generate a complex, final design, hardly less unified than a pre-formed geometric pattern.[99]

On the imposition of rationalism in Renaissance planning, he writes,

> As soon as baroque order became widespread, uniform, and absolute, when neither contrast nor evasion was possible, its weaknesses lay revealed. Clarification gave place to regimentation, openness to emptiness, greatness to grandiosity. The solo voice of the planner might be amplified many volumes; but it could never take the place of all the singers in a civic chorus, each holding his own part, while following the contrapuntal score.[100]

The fundamental impact of communal design on the nature of society as a whole is revealed by the importance attached to it by the political despot. Costonis notes that, as part of his quest to impose the Nazi order on society, Adolf Hitler sought "to canonize the architectural traditions of Imperial Rome and to banish the Bauhaus School from the Third Reich." Against such attempts to dictate formal aesthetic order is the pluralist diversity of individual creative expression. Costonis writes: "Aesthetic formalism's most persuasive adversary . . . has been the exuberance of human creativity, which refuses to be immobilized by the rules or traditions of earlier times."[101]

Even contemporary urban design can face the same threat of numbing uniformity in design where rational order through architectural controls is too stringently imposed. In *The Death and Life of Great American Cities,* Jacobs makes an argument that virtually vitiates zoning itself.

> In seeking visual order, cities are able to choose among three broad alternatives, two of which are hopeless and one of which is hopeful. They can aim for areas of homogeneity which look homogeneous, and get results depressing and disorienting. They can aim for areas of homogeneity which try not to look homogeneous, and get results of vulgarity and dishonesty. Or they can

---

[99]Lewis Mumford, *The City in History* (New York: Harcourt, Brace & World, 1961), 302.
[100]Ibid., 350.
[101]Costonis, "Law and Aesthetics," 410.

aim for areas of great diversity and, because real differences are thereby expressed, can get results which, at worse, are merely interesting, and at best can be delightful.[102]

The fundamental focus of design review should not, after all, be so much on the evaluation of individual building design but on whether a proposed design contributes to or detracts from the urban design context of the community environment as a whole. In ages past, adherence of individual buildings to common community norms in architectural design resulted largely from regional constraints in terms of culture, environment, climate, and the availability of construction materials and technologies. In present times, shared knowledge and universal availability of building materials and methodologies throughout the country have put an end to such organically imposed local conformity in building styles. Today, design coherence in a community is usually the result of a more conscious community act, whether brought about by the volition or coercion of developers and their architects.

SEARCHING FOR STANDARDS

To eliminate the potential vagary of discretionary design review of architecture, courts have insisted on legally acceptable standards. As the New Jersey Superior Court stated in *Morristown Road,*

> Because of the subjective elements which can be involved in matters of architectural design, the necessity for clear and definite standards is particularly applicable to ordinances which seek to control this aspect of construction. The formulation of such standards has been described as the "most troublesome problem encountered in municipal attempts to control architectural design." As design controls are enforced by administrative agencies, the prerequisite of definiteness will only be met when the standards sufficiently confine the process of administrative decision and provide a court with an understandable criterion for review.[103]

While rejecting the architectural design standards enacted by the borough of Bernardsville as inadequate, the court cited Anderson's *American Law of Zoning*[104] in acknowledging the extreme difficulty of the task that it sets for communities intending to impose architectural controls.

Notwithstanding attempts to apply sociopsychological, economic, and other criteria to justify and guide official design review, the difficult search

[102]Jane Jacobs, *The Death and Life of Great American Cities* (N.Y.: Random House 1961), 229.

[103]Note 47, 161.

[104]Anderson, *Law of Zoning.*

for standards is exacerbated by the nature of architecture as artistic expression. Just as design legislation and set formulae cannot substitute for architectural creativity, so design judgment defies the measurable specificity demanded by the law. As art critic Lionello Venturi sees it: "There is not a science of beauty but only a criticism of it."[105] Huxtable puts the issue in the following terms:

> The problem with law and the design of amenities and any attempt to deal with the quality of the design involved is that such judgments cannot be quantified—they are unavoidably subjective, although responsible judgment rests on a very specific set of standards and their interpretations. . . . A textbook could be written . . . but there seems to be no way to translate such language into the measurable specifics required by law.[106]

John W. Wade, in his 1977 analysis *Architecture, Problems, and Purposes,* points out that modern architectural criticism as practiced by such professional critics as design professors is made in response to a "gestalt."[107] Deriving from the maxim of modern architecture generally attributed to Louis Sullivan, "form follows function," the gestalt perception of contemporary design judgment conceives architecture as an integrated totality. The aesthetic quality of a building is regarded as a part of a holistic composition, not as an element that can be abstracted and considered separately. This gestalt conception makes narrow consideration of the aesthetic quality of a building's exterior virtually meaningless from a critical standpoint. Compounded by the ethereal nature of aesthetics itself, this view makes even more difficult the judicial demand for definitiveness and precision in prescribing standards in architectural aesthetics.

The propensity of architects to judge design as a gestalt and of lawyers and judges to favor judgment based on precisely defined standards leads not only to special difficulty for official design review but is symptomatic of a basic disparity between the approaches of the design and legal professions. Like all disciplines, architecture and law each have distinctive values, methodologies, and semantic practices peculiar to themselves. In contrast to the law, which places high esteem on accepted doctrine and historic precedent, architecture assigns its highest premiums to originality and innovation. Whereas in law the judicial ethic is impartiality, often in architecture, as in other media of artistic expression, the more creative and established

[105]Lionello Venturi, *History of Art Criticism,* trans. Charles Marriott (1936; reprint, New York: Dutton, 1964), 190–91.

[106]Ada Louise Huxtable, personal letter, March 28, 1978. Quoted by Clifford L. Weaver and Richard F. Babcock, *City Zoning: The Once and Future Frontier* (Chicago and Washington: Planners Press, 1979), 301.

[107]John W. Wade, *Architecture, Problems, and Purposes* (New York: John Wiley, 1977), 15.

the individual, the stronger his convictions in a certain design philosophy. Moreover, members of review boards are generally quite ignorant of the limitations imposed over their actions by the First Amendment. By appointing distinguished design professionals to review boards, the public may find itself, whether deliberately or unwittingly, lending a particular design ideology its police power.

Whereas legal thinking has precision and definitiveness as its standards, architecture as artistic expression is judged on more ethereal, intangible criteria that defy explicit definition. The difference between the two is particularly evident in considering the judicial response to the precision (or lack of it) in the design standards at bar in the *Pacesetter* and *Morristown Road* cases. In all likelihood, it would also be revealed were the law to scrutinize the discretionary reasoning process used by the architectural review boards in evaluating the design proposals in *Reid* and *Stoyanoff*.

With their own training and professional life steeped in the legal approach, judges are accustomed to demanding definitiveness and precision in representations by lawyers, whether in factual evidence, legal arguments, public legislation, or in the judicial opinions of their colleagues. Not surprisingly, legal thinking is probably at its weakest in dealing with other disciplinary processes totally alien to its own, hence the propensity of some courts to defer judgments on such consideration as architectural aesthetics to professional architects sitting on boards of review. When courts do exert their influence on design controls, the precise standards they demand are in the explicit idiom of law, and often seem incompatible with the nature of the creative design process.

Lawyer James L. Bross cited Wade in tracing the absence of a common ground for communication between law and design to the classroom.

> Architectural teaching differs from law teaching in other respects which are critical in their implications for design review. In comparison to law professors who purportedly apply Occam's Razor to cut down unsupported generalities to precise terms, teachers of architecture "respond to the 'Gestalt,' the perceived totality of the project being presented." Because architecture teachers respond to the "Gestalt," there is considerable flexibility in the weighting of critical values applied. . . . ["I]n the judgment process there is no explicit weighting of the judgmental values. There is no explicit proportioning of importance among the many issues that architectural criticism addresses."
>
> Thus, the existing system of architectural education fails to properly articulate substantive standards to balance the competing values in design review. This system also falls short of the legal procedural requirements that decisions be made with "articulate consistency," and with discretion properly structured to insure fair, regular and consistent decisions. "Design criticism has tended to be random and disordered."[108]

---

[108]James L. Bross, "Taking Design Review Beyond the Beauty Part: Aesthetics in Perspective," *Environmental Law* 9 (Winter 1979), 226–27.

REQUIRING ADMINISTRATIVE PROCEDURE
IN DESIGN REVIEW

The difficulty of articulating standards for architectural review that would afford free design expression yet satisfy the requirement of law for precise, predefined criteria has led legal commentators to point to the apparent incongruity and futility of the task. With recognition that creative, high-quality design cannot be attained through mechanical application of legislative standards, many observers have concluded that design regulation must ultimately depend on knowledge and considered judgment. Jesse J. Dukeminier writes,

> What we need . . . to solve a value problem is not an illusion of an absolute standard but decision-makers whose technical training and knowledge of human beings are sufficiently extensive to qualify them to pass judgment on the particular problem and to develop rational techniques for implementing our generalized, flexible, relativistic community values.[109]

Kenneth Culp Davis shares Dukeminier's view but is more specific in his recommendations. In his authoritative *Administrative Law Treatise,* he writes,

> The problem is not whether we want to prevent arbitrariness but how to do it. Putting some words into a statute that a court can call a legislative standard is not a very good protection against arbitrariness. The protections that are effective are hearings with procedural safeguards, legislative supervision, and judicial review.[110]

In searching for a principle to guide discretion, he cites the New Jersey court in its 1952 decision in *Ward v. Scott.* Said that court,

> It is settled that the Legislature may not vest unbridled or arbitrary power in the administrative agency but must furnish a reasonably adequate standard to guide it. But the exigencies of modern government have increasingly dictated the use of general rather than minutely detailed standards in regulatory enactments under the police power. Thus, the Board of Public Utility Commissioners has been guided by simple standards of "public convenience and necessity" and "just and reasonable." . . . [W]e find that the Legislature has not in any sense granted uncontrolled power to the administrative agency.[111]

---

[109]J. J. Dukeminier, Jr., "Zoning for Aesthetic Objectives: A Reappraisal," *Law and Contemporary Problems* 20 (1955), 229.

[110]Davis, *Administrative Law Treatise,* sect. 2. 08, 108.

[111]93 A. 2d 385 (N.J., 1952), 388–89.

In *Discretionary Justice* Davis concludes, "The hope lies, I think, not in better statutory standards, but in earlier and more elaborate administrative rule-making and in better structuring and checking of discretionary power."[112]

Davis's ideas are picked up by Lefcoe, who points to the particular difficulty of attempting predetermined standards in architectural review and suggests the solution lies not in the application of standards but in improved administrative procedure in the conduct of board business. He writes, "As for design review, if what courts fear is favoritism or a lack of predictability for architects and developers, the best way to meet these concerns is not by elaborate formulas in statutes or ordinances but in administrative systems so structured as to minimize precisely these risks."[113] Lefcoe continues by making three specific suggestions:

> Conflicts of interest are assiduously avoided by precluding board members from judging matters in which they have an interest and by allowing applicants to challenge board members whom they believe to be biased. Predictability is attained by the granting of reliable preliminary opinions in advance of formal rulings and the preservation of a record of the board's actions. Consistency of treatment among landowners can be measured by scrutinizing the work of a particular commission over time.[114]

First of these suggestions is that any party with substantial interest in a design proposal be allowed the opportunity to challenge review-board members they believe to be biased and incapable of impartial judgment. Obviously, the fairness of the review process can be compromised if evaluation is made by board officials who are, for example, associates or adversaries of the applicant, whether in design philosophy or in business competition.

Second is the proposed adoption of the judicial practice of opinion writing to the design review process. The idea is favored by architect Robert Venturi and his associates, who argue that review boards should be held accountable for their decisions. Like judges, who are also given great discretionary power, review boards should state the reasons for their decisions in written opinions. This, according to Venturi and his associates, is "a great protection."[115] Their view is also shared by Davis, who reasons,

> Statement of findings and reasons will not assure fairness of the decision, but it will pull in that direction. A member who merely votes yes or no, with

[112]Davis, *Discretionary Justice,* 219.
[113]American Institute of Architects, *Design Review Boards,* 14.
[114]Ibid, 50.
[115]Venturi *et. al, Learning from Las Vegas,* 188.

no findings or reasons, may in human fashion give in to motions or whims. Subjecting his findings and reasons to the view of outside critics—and inside critics—may cause him to try to make his action appear rational, and the easiest way to appear rational is usually to be rational.[116]

In dissenting from the majority in the *Reid* case, Judge Corrigan showed implicit dissatisfaction with the reason given by a review-board member for rejecting Mrs. Reid's proposed design, to wit: "We don't like the appearance of that house in this neighborhood."[117] As in the law, the practice of opinion writing by review-board members would open their actions to the same kind of scrutiny to which the design itself is subject, thus providing an appropriate degree of protection against arbitrary decision making by the public body. Certainly a requirement of review boards to furnish written evaluations and opinions to support their findings publicly would increase the likelihood of substantive professionalism in design judgment.

Finally, with a well-maintained and open record of past board decisions and written opinions, Lefcoe suggests, a procedural model for future board actions can borrow from "common law tradition itself" by deriving principles empirically from precedent decisions.[118] This idea was proposed by Davis, who writes: "Building law through adjudication is a sound and necessary process; the great bulk of American law is the product of that process."[119]

However, not all observers agree that a common-law model would provide meaningful standards upon which to base future adjudications on matters of aesthetics. In his commentary on subjectivity, expression, and aesthetic regulation, Stephen Williams not only maintains that the "polycentric" nature of aesthetic questions makes difficult legislative articulation of aesthetic standards to guide administrative decision, but writes:

> An agency, by a sequence of adjudications, will rarely be able to construct meaningful "common law" standards against which subsequent decisions may be measured for consistency; and procedural devices, such as a right to a hearing or to judicial review, will rarely play any meaningful role in legitimizing the agency's decision.[120]

The reason for this problem, according to Williams, is that aesthetic questions entail three considerations: a multiplicity of solutions; an interdepen-

---

[116]Davis, *Discretionary Justice,* 131.

[117]Note 2, 79.

[118]American Institute of Architects, *Design Review Boards,* 14.

[119]Davis, *Discretionary Justice,* 55.

[120]Stephen F. Williams, "Subjectivity, Expression, and Privacy: Problems of Aesthetic Regulation," *Minnesota L. Rev.* 62 (November 1977), 19.

dency of relevant factors; and difficulty in tracing one solution's superiority over another because of the multiplicity of factors. This polycentric nature of aesthetic questions causes the number of potential designs to be infinite, and, in Williams's opinion, beyond any "common law" standard.

There is no diminishing the complexity of aesthetic questions and the difficulty of abstracting meaningful standards from common law–style procedure. However, a suggestion by Davis may aid in mitigating the problem. He writes:

> Seeing all around a complex subject is not a prerequisite to making a sound rule, because a rule need not be in the form of an abstract generalization; a rule can be limited to resolving one or more hypothetical cases, without generalizing. . . .
>
> An agency which uses three tools for making law—adjudication, rules in the form of generalizations, and rules in the form of hypotheticals—is much better equipped to serve the public interest than an agency which limits itself to the first two of the three tools.[121]

Lefcoe applies Davis's concept of using "hypotheticals" to the process of architectural design review:

> An administrative board can take the essential ingredients of cases it has decided, and convert them into hypotheticals for its annual report. After stating the facts in the examples it has chosen, the board can next explain the problem raised by the facts, and indicate its answer to the problem. Finally, the board should supply reasons for its positions. In this way, guidelines will be evolved which do not tie the board's hands as much as general pronouncements might.[122]

It might furthermore be kept in mind that the American system of precedent case law indeed makes no attempt at generalization or even periodic abstraction; and in fact, in consideration of a case at bar, any precedent can be regarded somewhat as a de facto "hypothetical" from which a governing rule can be derived.

Accordingly, notwithstanding the complex, polycentric nature of aesthetic questions, a definitive and open process of design evaluation, including written opinions, a recording of precedent decisions, and a periodic, public review of past actions can yield principles to structure the exercise of discretion in board review and clarify board actions before interested parties, the public, and the courts. From this empirical process can emerge principles that might afford the "fair certainty" associated by Hayek with the Rule of Law as well as freedom for creative architectural expression so

---

[121]Davis, *Discretionary Justice*, 60–61.
[122]American Institute of Architects, *Design Review Boards*, 14.

difficult to reconcile with more definitive design standards. In fact, it has been pointed out that Hayek's concept itself probably originated in the English common-law process of precedent rather than in American constitutional law.

In proposing a model ordinance for local design review, Lefcoe further suggests a rule to delimit board interference with a development proposal.

> [The suggested ordinance] seeks to embody something analogous to a distinction familiar to lawyers between a *de novo* and a "reasonableness" review. When a court hears a dispute *de novo,* it makes all factual determinations afresh. On a "reasonableness" standard the reviewing court only ascertains whether those primarily responsible for the decision have taken all necessary considerations into account. This distinction has a counterpart in grading systems that differentiate between pass-fail work and honors. It is not the function of the review board under this model to compel all projects to receive an "honors" rating. Their authority is solely to make sure that certain items have been treated passably well. When boards attempt to do more than that, they inevitably find themselves substituting their personal views for those of the architect.[123]

Davis further amplifies the distinction between a check and *de novo* review.

> Paradoxically, the principle of check is often at its best when it is limited to correction of arbitrariness or illegality, and it may be relatively ineffective when it includes de novo review. This is because of the important fact, sometimes overlooked, that a de novo determination may itself introduce arbitrariness or illegality for the first time and not be checked, whereas a check may be limited to the one objective of eliminating arbitrariness or illegality, so that almost all final action is subject to a check for arbitrariness or illegality. The recognized superiority of a check to a de novo determination is one of the main reasons that the mainstay of judicial review of administrative action is a review of limited scope, not de novo review, although in some circumstances de novo review may be desirable.[124]

BRENNAN'S RULE

In addition to these suggested reforms in review procedures is a requirement advocated by Supreme Court Justice William J. Brennan, Jr., that if adopted would lend both legitimacy and substance to any form of aesthetic regulation. Brennan made these recommendations not once but twice, first in 1981 in his concurrence with the court in *Metromedia, Inc. v. City of San Diego* and again in 1984 in his dissent from the majority in

---

[123]Ibid., 38.
[124]Davis, *Discretionary Justice,* 142–43.

Members of the City Council of the City of Los Angeles v. Taxpayers for Vincent. In *Metromedia,* the Justice wrote,

> Of course, it is not for a court to impose its own notion of beauty on San Diego. But before deferring to a city's judgment, a court must be convinced that the city is seriously and comprehensively addressing aesthetic concerns with respect to its environment. Here, San Diego has failed to demonstrate a comprehensive coordinated effort in its commercial and industrial areas to address other obvious contributors to an unattractive environment. In this sense the ordinance is underinclusive. Of course, this is not to say that the city must address all aesthetic problems at the same time, or none at all. Indeed, from a planning point of view, attacking the problem incrementally and sequentially may represent the most sensible solution. On the other hand, if billboards alone are banned and no further steps are contemplated or likely, the commitment of the city to improving its physical environment is placed in doubt. By showing a comprehensive commitment to making its physical environment in commercial and industrial areas more attractive, and by allowing only narrowly tailored exceptions, if any, San Diego could demonstrate that its interest in creating an aesthetically pleasing environment is genuine and substantial. This is a requirement where, as here, there is an infringement of important constitutional consequence.[125]

In other words, Brennan suggests that a court would—and should—approve a municipality's regulation of aesthetic considerations only on the condition that the community demonstrate a "comprehensive coordinated effort" at addressing the overall problem of environmental aesthetics. The inference is that aesthetic regulation, including design review of private development, should be predicated on a demonstrated comprehensive commitment by local government to community attractiveness. Logically, any public effort to beautify the community must entail a plan of urban design, regardless of the ultimate course of action chosen.

In the *Vincent* case three years following *Metromedia,* Brennan was even more explicit. He wrote,

> In cases like this, where a total ban is imposed on a particularly valuable method of communication, a court should require the government to provide tangible proof of the legitimacy and substantiality of its aesthetic objective. Justifications for such restrictions articulated by the government should be critically examined to determine whether the government has committed itself to addressing the identified aesthetic problem.
>
> In my view, such statements of aesthetic objectives should be accepted as substantial and unrelated to the suppression of speech only if the government demonstrates that it is pursuing an identified objective seriously and comprehensively and in ways that are unrelated to the restriction of speech. Without

[125]453 U.S. 490 (1981), 531–33.

such a demonstration, I would invalidate the restriction as violative of the First Amendment. By requiring this type of showing, courts can ensure that governmental regulation of the aesthetic environment remains within the constraints established by the First Amendment. First, we would have a reasonably reliable indication that it is not the content or communicative aspect of speech that the government finds unaesthetic. Second, when a restriction of speech is part of a comprehensive and seriously pursued program to promote an aesthetic objective, we have a more reliable indication of the government's own assessment of the substantiality of its objective. And finally, when an aesthetic objective is pursued on more than one front, we have a better basis upon which to ascertain its precise nature and thereby determine whether the means selected are the least restrictive ones for achieving the objective.[126]

In his substantive analysis of the issue, Brennan admits to a limitation to the approach he suggests but points out that, under the First Amendment, some displeasing use of individual freedoms must be tolerated. He notes,

It is theoretically, though remotely, possible that a form of speech could be so distinctively unaesthetic that a comprehensive program aimed at eliminating the eyesore it causes would apply only to the unpleasant form of speech. Under the approach I suggest, such a program would be invalid because it would only restrict speech, and the community, therefore, would have to tolerate the displeasing form of speech. This is no doubt a disadvantage of the approach. But at least when the form of speech that is restricted constitutes an important medium of communication and when the restriction would effect a total ban on the use of that medium, that is the price we must pay to protect our First Amendment liberties from those who would use aesthetics alone as a cloak to abridge them.[127]

Daniel Mandelker, among others, has asserted that Brennan's stricture is much too severe when applied to public regulation of outdoor advertising.[128] The argument is that police-power regulation of billboards, as in *Metromedia,* or of political posters, as in *Vincent,* should not be hobbled by a need to prove a comprehensive and substantive community commitment to achieve an aesthetic objective; that is, that the constitutionality of billboard and junkyard regulation has been sufficiently well established through modern developments in case law. Nevertheless, municipalities and their planning officials—not to mention members of design review boards

---

[126]466 U.S. 789 (1984), 827–29.
[127]Ibid., 829.
[128]See, e.g., Daniel R. Mandelker, "Sign Regulation," (lecture and discussion), *Fifth Annual Zoning Institute,* American Institute of Certified Planners, San Francisco, October 29, 1985.

as well as judges—might do well to consider Brennan's approach, at least as applied to regulation of building design.

Brennan's rule, by requiring the community to demonstrate a comprehensive plan and program, of which design review could be a part, could produce a standard by which private design could be measured. The design of any private development could be evaluated in terms of its compatibility with the plan and whether it advances or detracts from the stated community objective in design. A requirement for a community to have such a plan should scarcely be regarded as an impediment to the design review process, for indeed its existence would invariably strengthen the legitimacy and substance of review. Clear articulation of a community's policy goals in urban design would increase the likelihood that a requirement for private development to conform to a community's urban design objectives would be sustained on substantive grounds and not on the confused premises of some past decisions.

In conclusion, it seems appropriate that architectural design review should be considered less in terms of individual buildings and more in context of the urban design of a community as a whole. Considering the counsel of scholars and jurists from Hayek to Brennan, it is only reasonable that a prerequisite for design regulation and review be adoption of a public policy and plan that specify in advance the precise urban design objectives and standards that the community is committed to enforce and against which the design of private development can be gauged without prejudice or arbitrariness. In the next chapter, we shall examine the efforts of two major cities, New York and San Francisco, in establishing such substantive objectives and standards for urban design.

Chapter 11

Designing the Invisible Web:
New York City
and San Francisco

With their attention focused on the design quality of individual buildings, regulating communities and their architectural review boards have frequently lost sight of the underlying purpose of design regulation. It is not so much the merits or deficiencies of individual building designs that should weigh in the balance as the relationship of the proposed project to the design context of the whole community. Or, put in another way, the focus should be on urban design. From this standpoint, design review should correctly confine itself to narrow consideration of one essential criterion: whether the design of any proposed development can be considered such a potential nuisance as to subvert the public welfare by detracting from the stated goals and policies of the community in terms of design character, harmony, and beauty. Following Hayek's Rule of Law, those policies must be established and made certain before the fact in order to give substance to the design review process.

Smaller suburban communities, in regulating architectural design, have commonly provided qualitative standards that are generally descriptive of style and context and have relied on discretionary, ad hoc administrative review of individual development initiatives. As foregoing discussion has made evident, this practice has not been without its difficulties and improprieties. Wrote Jesse Dukeminier in 1955,

> It seems to me that something more is needed than a case-by-case exception to the general rule, something approaching more closely to a systematic theory of planning which will cover the presently widely accepted doctrines as well

as develop new ones to replace those which are now causing us trouble. . . . we need a body of meaningful postulates and propositions, the efficacy of which is verifiable by case results and evaluated by community goals.[1]

The absence of a predetermined and definitive community policy on design makes it difficult for review boards to evaluate development proposals consistently and systematically and for courts to assess the legal substance of the review process itself.

As discussed in chapter 10, Supreme Court Justice William J. Brennan, Jr., argues that a community's commitment to a comprehensive and coordinated effort aimed at environmental attractiveness should be a prerequisite to its public regulation of aesthetics. Any such public commitment to community beauty should logically begin with a comprehensive community plan for urban design. A plan that confirms a community's policy and articulates its goals in environmental design would not only legitimize aesthetic regulation but could also provide a substantive basis for systematic controls.

In recent years, the planning administrations of some large urban municipalities, notably New York City and San Francisco, have attempted to address the issues of community appearance and design by just such comprehensive planning approaches to design regulation. By formulating definitive public policies on urban design as well as articulating and enforcing building standards based on those policies, these city governments have endeavored to coordinate development toward affirmative planning objectives, thus minimizing the perception of piecemeal and negative regulation. Predetermined, explicit standards and quantitative criteria not subject to discretionary interpretation are followed to reduce inconsistencies in enforcement and to lessen the possibility of being ruled "void for vagueness."

Whether a result of the past tendency for development pressure to be greatest at the suburban fringe of metropolitan centers, or a consequence of the capacity for zoning to protect residential values, the practice of planning controls has focused, until recently, on suburban rather than urban issues. Since *Euclid v. Ambler* in 1926, the vast majority of zoning cases have occurred in the suburbs and not in center cities. With redevelopment pressure increasing at the urban core over the last twenty years, however, a change is becoming evident. Using principles of land-use zoning and building regulations developed in the last half century, planning administrations of large cities have become increasingly aggressive in managing the three-dimensional design development of their cities. These municipalities have found the legal basis for their design controls in the established black-letter

[1]J. J. Dukeminier, Jr., "Zoning for Aesthetic Objectives: A Reappraisal," *Law and Contemporary Problems* 20 (1955), 237.

law of American land-use regulation. While zoning is generally considered to be the first widely used police-power regulation in the United States applicable to urban design, other regulatory concepts originating in the early twentieth century have also contributed to the basis of contemporary methods of control.

The Supreme Court case supporting the ability of a city to limit building height through the police power actually predated the *Euclid* decision by nearly two decades. In *Welch v. Swasey*,[2] the high Court in 1909 upheld two Massachusetts statutes that regulated building height in Boston. Though fire protection was considered the primary reason for the statutes, the purpose of preserving "architectural symmetry and regular skylines"[3] was also recognized. The Court commented that although aesthetic factors were considered in addition to the other facts of the case, this concern for aesthetics did not make the Court's decision invalid.[4] This sort of rationale with regard to aesthetics was, of course, typical of the period. In 1927, the year following *Euclid,* the Court further agreed in *Gorieb v. Fox*[5] that a requirement for buildings to set back from property lines was a reasonable application of the police power. Together, these early decisions affirming the validity of zoning, height, and setback requirements provided the foundation for newer methods of control.

In more recent years, courts have specifically affirmed the ability of government to regulate the architecture of private developments in the interest of urban design. In the 1969 case *City of St. Paul v. Chicago, St. Paul, Minneapolis and Omaha Railway Company,* a federal circuit court upheld codes imposed by the city of St. Paul to govern building heights for the urban design concept "that the area in front of the mall would be kept clear of obstructions—that the part would remain and provide sort of a front door for the Capitol Center downtown project as well as generally the central business district."[6] In 1974, the Illinois court in *LaSalle National Bank v. City of Evanston* affirmed the power of the city to enforce a 350-foot maximum zone to effect "a gradual tapering of building heights toward an open lakefront and park area."[7] The reasons given in these cases are cited by law professor Stephen Williams as examples of judicial enforcement of the design principle of urban "legibility,"[8] as suggested by the late urban design teacher Kevin Lynch in his study, *Image of the City.*[9] By "legi-

---

[2]214 U.S. 91 (1909).
[3]Ibid., 104.
[4]Ibid., 108.
[5]274 U.S. 603 (1927).
[6]413 F. 2d 762 (1969), 769.
[7]312 N.E. 2d 625 (Ill., 1974), 634.
[8]Stephen F. Williams, "Subjectivity, Expression, and Privacy: Problems of Aesthetic Regulation," *Minnesota L. Rev.* 62 (November 1977), 35, 39.
[9]Kevin Lynch, *The Image of the City* (1960; reprint, Cambridge: M.I.T. Press, 1979), 2.

bility," Lynch meant the structuring of districts, nodes, landmarks, edges, and pathways that identify the city environment as a clear and easily perceived overall pattern.

Some state environmental policy acts, the courts have found, afford local government still further legal grounds to effect urban design. A determination of poor aesthetic effect, such as obstruction of a view by a proposed building or poor adaptation of the structure to the topgraphic configurations or design context of the site, can be sufficient grounds to deny a design proposal permission to develop. One instance in which architectural and urban design controls were effectively imposed for essentially aesthetic reasons is the 1978 case *Polygon Corporation v. City of Seattle,*[10] in which a projected building design's failure to meet the aims of the state environmental policy act was grounds for denial of a building permit. Among the adverse environmental impacts cited were such urban design considerations as view obstruction, excessive bulk and relative scale, increases in traffic and noise, and shadow effect.

The need to follow state environmental requirements also played a major role in *Russian Hill Improvement Association v. Board of Permit Appeals and William C. Haas & Co.*[11] In this 1975 case, neighborhood opponents of a proposed high-rise apartment project in San Francisco successfully convinced a state appellate court that the proposal in question had been approved in violation of the California Environmental Quality Act,[12] which requires public input in consideration of any anticipated adverse environmental impact. A later appeal to the federal circuit court in *William C. Haas & Co. v. City and County of San Francisco*[13] was of no avail, notwithstanding the undisputed claim that the height limitation, down-zoned during the interim from the 300 feet allowable to only 40 feet, would diminish the value of the property from the approximately two million dollars invested by Haas to only a hundred thousand dollars. The case against the high-rise project was notably strengthened by the adoption of a city-wide urban design plan at the time the proposal was first made. Said the federal court, "The land use controls were part of a comprehensive plan for the development of the City to preserve aesthetic values and other general welfare interests of the inhabitants."[14] As for the diminution in value of Haas's property, the court cited the 1915 nuisance case *Hadacheck v. Sebastian,*[15] in which the high Court ruled that a reduction of land value from $800,000 to $60,000 as a result of a municipal ordinance did not constitute a taking. Haas's neighbors, the circuit court said, were subject to

---

[10]578 P. 2d 1309 (Wash., 1978).
[11]118 Cal. Rptr. 490 (App., 1975).
[12]Cal. Pub. Res. Code, Sects. 21100 *et seq.,* Sects. 21005 *et seq.*
[13]605 F. 2d 1117 (1979).
[14]Ibid., 1121.
[15]239 U.S. 394 (1915).

the same restriction against high-rise development; the fact that the Haas company suffered more because of the large amount of land it held was immaterial.

In addition to these cases, standard arguments for urban design might also invoke such well-known Supreme Court decisions as *Berman v. Parker,*[16] in which community beauty was found to be justification for the exercise of eminent domain for the purpose of urban renewal. Said the unanimous Court in that 1954 decision: "The concept of public welfare is broad and inclusive. The values it represents are spiritual as well as physical, aesthetic as well as monetary."[17] Again in *Vincent,* the Supreme Court in 1984 upheld a district court "in its conclusions of law [that] characterized the esthetic and economic interests in improving the beauty of the City 'by eliminating clutter and visual blight' as 'legitimate and compelling.' "[18] Where the burden placed on property owners is mitigated by the transfer of development rights, the *Penn Central*[19] ruling is also certain to be included as an argument supporting the reasonableness of regulation. Perhaps only coincidentally, all the cases arose from public planning efforts in major metropolitan centers, an indication of the growing concern of central cities to control their design and aesthetic qualities.

INCENTIVE AND SPECIAL DISTRICT ZONING: NEW YORK CITY

In the same way that suburban communities have used zoning incentives such as additional unit allowances and commercial use permits to make well-designed planned unit developments attractive to residential builders, cities are offering such inducements as bonus floor-area ratio (FAR) allowances and other forms of regulatory relaxation to encourage urban developers to comply voluntarily to optional design standards and to provide additional public amenities. This incentive approach to urban design control, which tacitly acknowledges regulation exceeding the normal constitutional limits of the police power, is being used in combination with other recent methods of planning regulation to give to zoning, particularly in New York City, a dimension of design control never envisioned in the 1920s. Though New York's program of urban design and architectural regulation has not been without its problems, the experiences and results of this innovation in planning controls are well worth examining.

Early use of bonus FARs was embodied in the city's 1961 zoning resolution, which permitted an increase in the interior space of a building in exchange for the provision of a pedestrian mall modeled after the "tower-

[16]348 U.S. 26 (1954).
[17]Ibid., 33.
[18]466 U.S. 789 (1984), 795.
[19]*Penn Central Transportation Co. v. New York City,* 438 U.S. 104 (1978).

in-a-plaza" paradigm inspired by Mies van der Rohe and Philip Johnson's Seagram Building on Park Avenue. Although the plaza bonus proved extremely popular with developers and was widely employed, its consequences in urban design were dubious and subject to considerable criticism. Since no specific design guidelines were set forth, developers tended to construct plazas that set their buildings apart from their surroundings in the apparent belief that such isolation lent prestige and monumentality to their developments, or simply to avoid maintenance and liability problems. As John J. Costonis observes, this approach resulted in "scores of 'bargain-basement Mies buildings'—cheap, bland imitations of the original; disruption of formerly uniform street walls by redundant, windswept plazas; and buildings that are discordant in scale and bulk with their neighbors and with the streets on which they front."[20] The cumulative effect of this isolation of buildings was an urban design lacking in activity and human interest. Ada Louise Huxtable of the *New York Times* faulted the zoning for being

> the definitive factor in driving out the small enterprises, the shops, restaurants, and services, that make New York a decent or pleasurable place in which to live and work [and replacing them with] a cold parade of standard business structures set back aimlessly from the street on blank plazas that ignore each other.[21]

In the latter half of the 1960s, however, an urban design group was formed as part of the New York City planning commission staff under the administration of Jonathan Barnett. With the introduction of professional insight, the design deficiency of the plaza incentive was recognized, and the city began to improve and systematize the use of zoning incentives. The planning commission created special zoning districts for the purpose of establishing a more reasoned and coordinated policy of urban design.[22] Of the many special districts eventually designated, the earliest ones are still the best known.

The first to be created was the Special Theatre District, which was formed to preserve and enhance the famous but deteriorating show district near Broadway. Zoning regulations in the district include a list of some forty existing area theatres, none of which may be razed without special permission from the city. Restoration of these listed structures is encouraged by FAR bonuses of up to 20 percent, which are transferable to other lots proposed for new development or enlargement. In the district, new construction projects that include a new theater can receive a similar 20

[20]John J. Costonis, "Law and Aesthetics: A Critique and a Reformulation of the Dilemmas," *Michigan L. Rev.* 80 (1982), 370.

[21]Ada Louise Huxtable, "Thinking Man's Zoning," *New York Times,* March 7, 1971.

[22]New York, N.Y., Zoning Resolution (1982); New York City Department of City Planning, *Midtown Development* (1981), and *Midtown Zoning* (1982).

percent bonus; in some circumstances, the increase of the permissible FAR of a lot can be as great as 44 percent. Besides theaters, urban design amenities such as a "through-block gallerias," which provide continuous, covered pedestrian walkways connecting parallel east-west streets, are also eligible for bonuses in floor-area ratio.

To maintain and promote the character of the cultural complex surrounding the Lincoln Center for the Performing Arts, a Lincoln Square Special District was also established. To this end, "use-group" restrictions have been imposed to stimulate development of restaurant, specialty retail stores, and other uses that would remain open during the evening hours of the center's operation. To ensure design harmony of architectural development, a mandatory requirement for building arcades has been imposed along Broadway. For the same purpose and to develop continuity of activities along this frontage, buildings must adhere to a uniform "street wall" line up to a height of 85 feet. As in many other special districts in midtown, FAR bonuses are awarded for such urban design amenities as pedestrian malls and covered plazas.

Developers in the Greenwich Street District of lower Manhattan can likewise receive additional FAR allowances and permission to exceed the maximum 40 percent tower coverage in exchange for the optional provision of planning features beyond those mandated by law. Development contributions can take the form of circulation and design elements, such as subway stations, shopping facilities, pedestrian plazas, arcades, and bridges, as well as payments into a subway improvement fund. A map and manual contain a fixed schedule of FAR bonuses available "as of right" for each specific contribution, thus reducing the need for discretionary administration.

The Special Fifth Avenue District was created for the purpose of forestalling the gradual displacement of the street's famous retail trade by more lucrative office rentals. Zoning regulations reserve the lower floors for commercial retail use and restrict such retail office uses as banks and travel agencies. Continuity of the window-shopping promenade traditional to Fifth Avenue and of the street wall frontage of building facades is being maintained through a mandatory requirement that structures be built to the lot line and be a minimum of 85 feet high. At one time, setback requirements distinguished between the east and west sides of the avenue, but more recent regulations place a uniform 125-foot height maximum on the lot-line facade.

Along Fifth Avenue, the city attempted for the first time anywhere to break from traditional segregated land-use zoning by encouraging a mix of residential with retail and office use. Of all the design considerations eligible for additional floor-area allowances—plazas, through-block connections, covered pedestrian spaces, and landscaped terraces—the FAR bonuses granted for the inclusion of residential use in commercial buildings proved the most controversial.

Since the early 1960s, planners have frequently advocated mixed land use as an alternative to single-use zoning. Probably the most notable was Jane Jacobs, long a leading critic and theorist on the social implications of urban form, who listed mixed use as one of the basic conditions necessary to achieve the "exuberant diversity" which she argues is essential for a healthy and vibrant urban community. In her seminal work *The Death and Life of Great American Cities,* she wrote, "The district, and indeed as many of its internal parts as possible, must serve more than one primary function; preferably more than two."[23]

To observers like Jacobs, the syndrome of virtually all central business districts of American cities to be largely bereft of people and activity at the close of the working day could be blamed primarily on the strict segregation of land-use types implicit in Euclidean zoning. According to Jacobs, introducing residences into commercial zones would not only infuse vitality into urban areas deserted after working hours but would also increase the efficient use of the urban service infrastructure—shops, restaurants, and police and fire stations. Indeed, when one considers the source of life and activity in historic city centers, whether in America or abroad, much of it seems directly attributable to mixed land use, typically brought about by the location of the living quarters of merchants, tradesmen, and their families above their own shops and workplaces at the street level. Thus, mixed-use zoning with a residential component would really amount to a *re*introduction of housing to the city center. Jacobs's theory also suggested that a residential population would deter crime; the presence of the residents in a commercial zone would ensure that there would be "eyes in the street."[24]

In the 1970s, in response to this thinking, a zoning incentive was provided in the Fifth Avenue District that permitted an increase of up to 20 percent in the allowable floor area of new buildings, with the stipulation that the extra space be devoted to residential or hotel uses. Although the regulation was initially well received and a mix of land uses was generated, the size and number of gargantuan buildings that resulted from the bonus provision and other allowances eventually became subject to great public criticism. Finally in 1982, popular reaction led to the expunging of the bonus allowance from the zone.

While the concept of mixed-use zoning was never faulted, criticism of the excessiveness of building size resulting from the combined use of FAR bonuses and transfer of development rights (TDR) is hardly arguable. In

---

[23]Jane Jacobs, *The Death and Life of Great American Cities* (New York: Random House, 1961), 152.
[24]Ibid., 33 ff.

several cases, the allowable floor area of certain buildings was inflated to as much as 50 percent over original zoning. In the Theatre and Fifth Avenue areas, the addition of theater, retail, and residential space has only aggravated the problems of density and congestion that plague midtown Manhattan. In lower Manhattan, the development of the behemoth World Trade Center has also exacerbated problems of local traffic and transit, notwithstanding the provision of additional circulation facilities. Indeed, with a building occupancy equal to the population of a medium-size city, the twin 110-story towers have reportedly so taxed the municipal sewage system that, after its opening, thousands of gallons of raw effluent were allegedly spilled daily into the Hudson River.[25]

Even from a purely visual standpoint, it can be argued that inordinately large buildings contribute little to the quality of city design. The plaza provided by the Chase Manhattan Bank as relief from the narrow streets of New York's financial district offered scant compensation for the visual destruction of the vertical theme of lower Manhattan's skyline, which until the introduction of the bank's up-ended shoebox silhouette in the 1960s was dominated by a symphony of slender towers and ornate spires. Also, notwithstanding the *Penn Central* decision enjoining construction over Grand Central Terminal, the once-imposing Park Avenue perspective of the New York Central Tower built in 1929 had already been substantially diminished some fifteen years prior to the litigation by the construction of the Pan Am Building that looms over the railroad tower. It was the appearance of such gigantic structures along Fifth Avenue that finally led to the demise of the bonus provision in that district.

To the frustration of the urban designers and planners charged with the task of conceiving and writing the regulations, developers and their architects have shown considerable skill in circumventing the intent of the rules for economic advantage while still obeying the letter of the law. Prior to the recision of the bonus provision in the Fifth Avenue District, Roberta Brandes Gratz wrote of a typical development, the Olympic Tower, that received lucrative extra floors for which "the city got a pedestrian arcade few pedestrians know exist, interior retail space left unrented, an interior [mini-park] public area with a waterfall that rarely runs and lights that are seldom lit."[26] Not only were such minimally useful public spaces rewarded, but every other conceivable loophole had likewise been used to reap more and more FAR benefits. Gratz quoted Beverly Moss Spatt, former member of the city planning commission and onetime chairman of the city's landmark commission: "We've reached the point where the tradeoffs are of

[25]Glen Collins, "Notes on a Revolutionary Dinosaur," *New York Times Magazine,* August 6, 1972, 20.

[26]Roberta Brandes Gratz, "New York's Zoning Predicament," *Planning* (December 1979), 25.

minimal public gain compared to what the city is giving away. . . . The builder never loses, and the public only sometimes benefits."[27] Until regulations were tightened, some developers transferred buildable space to narrow cross streets where large buildings were purportedly prohibited. Others followed Breuer's suggested development of Grand Central Terminal by stacking tall, narrow "sliver building" additions in piggy-back fashion over smaller, existing brownstone or other older structures of landmark quality to maximize use of buildable air space. (See chapter 8 for further discussion of "facadism.") But, however easy it may be to find fault with developers, much of the problem lies with the constructed web of planning controls. As the *New York Times* editorialized: "The developers are not to blame; they simply play the game they know. It is the job of the city's planners to control and direct building patterns sensibly; they seem to have defaulted."[28] Costonis writes,

> Incentive zoning has become "Frankenstein zoning" in a number of cities. In New York City, for example, it has sanctioned buildings that outstrip even the bulky, light- and air-blocking slabs that frightened the City into adopting zoning in 1916. It has transformed reasonably predictable and impartial zoning procedures into a bazaar, whose wheeler-dealers include the handful of shrewd developers' lawyers who actually understand what is written—and not written—in the code; a planning staff overly eager to design developers' buildings or to select favored architects for the job; developers willing to go along in return for outsized zoning dispensations; and mayors panicked by fears of municipal bankruptcy and developer-authorized threats to "take their buildings to Houston." Off to the side, the public is demoralized by a "system" that has spun out of control, and puzzled by "amenities" that are unused, unwanted, or if attractive, would have been built without zoning bonus. Whether the buildings constructed under that system are "better architecture" than those that would have been built without it is conjectural at best. That many of them fail to respect their urban design context is clear.[29]

With experience, special-district and incentive zoning in New York City has undergone many changes to improve its planning and design effectiveness and to rectify its faults. A study by William H. Whyte entitled *The Social Life of Small Urban Spaces*[30] played a significant role in the modification of regulations governing the provision and design of open plazas and covered pedestrian spaces favored by later zoning. In particular, the huge increases in building size that resulted from FAR bonus provisions and from

---

[27]Ibid.

[28]*New York Times* editorial, "A Building Booms in the Wrong Place," February 5, 1979.

[29]Costonis, "Law and Aesthetics," 363–64.

[30]William H. Whyte, *The Social Life of Small Urban Spaces* (Washington, D.C.: Conservation Foundation, 1980).

TDR came under fire. Consequently, incentives once generously dispensed to encourage development have been diminished and guidelines substantially tightened in other districts in addition to Fifth Avenue.

More recent attention has focused on midtown Manhattan west of Sixth Avenue, a stagnating area left behind in the rush to develop the more prestigious and economically secure East Side. Designated a growth district, as distinguished from the stabilization district to the east, the West Side is now zoned to encourage development with base FARs as high as 18 along the north-south avenues. Interspersed in both districts are preservation areas designated to protect the old brownstones located on midblocks to the east and the theatres located on side streets to the west. In addition to regulatory incentives, encouragement for development in the West Side growth district has also taken the form of capital improvements and tax concessions.

In lower Manhattan, zoning regulations in the special districts of Battery Park City and Manhattan Landing have been conceived in terms of the areas as a whole rather than on a building-by-building or site-by-site basis. For these two districts, a panoply of rules is being used that define varying building heights, front building wall lines, minimum distances between buildings, and sun and shadow standards. The purpose of these regulations is to guide new development toward such urban design attributes as design continuity with existing streets, visual corridors created by building planes and open space, and visual permeability through such devices as open ground floors. The invisible web of these regulations leaves little to the piecemeal determination of individual developers responding to regulations governing their particular properties, an approach that has resulted more in fragmentary design of separate sites than in truly unified urban design. In lower Manhattan, urban design has been thought of more as the design and articulation of urban space than the modeling of discrete architectural forms.

The wide use of bonus incentives and special-district zoning to achieve urban design objectives has unavoidably contributed to the complexity of the New York City zoning law. There now exist over thirty special districts or subdistricts in the city. The city's zoning resolution is some 700 pages long, nearly three times the length of the San Francisco code and about ten times as long as Chicago's. Barnett cites a planning staff study conducted in 1977 of changes made since the comprehensive revision adopted in 1961, which showed that the law had expanded from 937 to 2,131 sections over the period, with almost three fourths of the provisions being altered in some fashion. Of the new sections, 16 percent have themselves been amended together with the addition of some 1,200 map changes.[31]

---

[31]Jonathan Barnett, *Urban Design as Public Policy* (New York: McGraw-Hill, 1974), 100–1.

The very complexity and variability of New York's incentive and special district zoning resulted until the early 1980s in what Barnett calls the "negotiation syndrome."[32] Originally, the implicit intent was to follow Hayek's admonitions: to develop regulations that would be largely automatic in execution and confer incentives "as of right," to reduce ad hoc determination to a minimum. However, because of the complexity of the design and development issues in the administration of special permits, negotiation between developers and the city became inevitable. In terms reminiscent of Hayek, Barnett notes that the special permit procedure allowed "the city government considerable discretion, which makes it difficult for the public to be certain that it knows what is going on."[33] Moreover, as developers gained better understanding of the procedure, they were able to manipulate the process to their advantage, notwithstanding its unwieldy nature and the time involved. Barnett writes,

> If a developer can buy a piece of property at a price that anticipates one level of development and, through negotiation, can change the zoning category to permit a larger or more valuable form of development, you can be sure the developer will try to do it. Changing land value is, of course, the traditional way in which money is made in real estate.[34]

Barnett cites an instance in which a developer was almost successful in persuading the planning commission to allow a public space—for which a bonus had already been granted—to be rented as a department store. He comments that "if the prime office tenant hadn't objected strenuously, the commission might well have gone ahead with the amendment."[35] Negotiated exceptions and modifications to the height and setback regulation as well as permitted infractions of the sky-exposure plane were also not uncommon.

Such criticism has led to a renewed attempt at a system of more predetermined regulation that would be less subject to the vagaries of ostensible compliance and negotiation. In particular, the problem has been to devise rules governing height and bulk that can establish firm standards to avoid negotiation yet provide sufficient flexibility to permit architectural freedom and creativity. The zoning amendment adopted in 1982 includes a "daylight evaluation chart," a device first used in Britain and designed to measure the amount of daylight that a proposed building will block from the street. An architect would be free to determine the configuration of a structure as long as no more than 25 percent of the sky was obstructed. "Daylight compensation rules" have also been compiled that use a combination of

---

[32]Ibid., 100–2.
[33]Ibid., 79.
[34]Ibid., 100.
[35]Ibid., 101.

diagrams, tables, and formulas to the same end. Although the system has been criticized for its complexity, it is hoped that flexibility will result from the capability of the system to accommodate various design solutions to the problem of daylight encroachment. Despite the sophistication and apparent intricacy of the system, which involves computer analysis of daylight retention, the new regulations signal a return to the original zoning concerns for air and light around buildings and a prohibition of overwhelming building bulk and shadow. Writes Barnett of preparations for the zoning changes:

> In midtown Manhattan at least, the Planning Commission is prepared to go back to a rule-book system where no negotiation would be either necessary or possible. The system is less restrictive than the regulations ostensibly on the books when all the special exceptions were being granted, but more stringent than many of the exceptions. The new rules are a return to a traditional zoning approach in which light and air for neighboring buildings were the primary factors, although the building line and retail continuity provisions prevent a return to the front-yard, side-yard mentality that characterized many of the buildings that took advantage of the plaza bonus.[36]

In considering any system of incentive zoning, a question remains concerning the basis of the original police-power restrictions on height and bulk. If contractual negotiations involving FAR allowances can vary regulating contraints, is this not a tacit admission of the arbitrary basis of the original limitations? Modification of the regulation is even more questionable where the public benefit derived does not relieve the specific problems associated with a particular building's height and bulk, since the original size limitations have their basic justification in such regulation.

Barnett notes that the New York zoning incentives were made possible by a "near miracle."

> The bonus incentives in the New York law were introduced in partial compensation for a cut in the allowable size of buildings that in some cases amounted to as much as 50 percent. The passage of this zoning revision was a near miracle: one of the few cases where local real estate interests have agreed to a substantial decrease in zoned density.[37]

Caution Weaver and Babcock in the same vein,

> It must be trumpeted that [incentive zoning] will not work in most cities unless the political climate permits a substantial reduction in what is presently allowed as a matter of right. As one disgruntled planning director put it, "the

[36]Ibid., 111.
[37]Ibid., 72.

basic allowable densities were so great that nobody bothered with the bonus."[38]

Nor can incentive zoning work where the locational benefits of a regulated site are not great enough to convince the developer that these advantages outweigh those of an alternative location where land prices and regulatory burdens are less costly. Both New York City and San Francisco, which is the subject of following discussion, are densely constructed cities with virtually no undeveloped land area remaining to accommodate continuing growth. In the less insular and constricted surroundings that generally typify many of the rapidly growing cities of the sunbelt region, there is considerably more land upon which to expand horizontally and consequently less incentive to reach out vertically, as in Manhattan. In such environments, height and bulk incentives would tend to be much less effective as an urban design control.

Despite pitfalls in the uses of incentive and special-district zoning, planning administration in New York City should be credited for the imaginative use of new techniques and for the innovative synthesis of district land-use and urban design controls. If extent of use is any measure, then the incentive zoning is immensely successful since almost all major commercial developments in the city's central business district in recent years have received some bonus considerations in exchange for urban design amenities. Certainly there has been no more vivid demonstration of the invisible web than in the application of precise and definitive police-power rules as an implement for urban design in New York City zoning.

COMPREHENSIVE URBAN DESIGN AND PLANNING CONTROLS: SAN FRANCISCO

Another city that is notable for its leadership and creativity in directing development into reasoned patterns of urban design is San Francisco. Through the 1970s and again in 1985, the city revised its planning code extensively in response to the policy recommendations of two major urban design studies, *The Urban Design Plan*[39] of 1971 and *The Downtown Plan*[40] completed in 1983. Both plans attracted great national attention for their innovative conception as well as for the specificity and rigor of their result-

---

[38]Clifford L. Weaver and Richard F. Babcock, *City Zoning: The Once and Future Frontier* (Chicago and Washington, D.C.: Planners Press, 1979), 58–59.

[39]City and County of San Francisco, Department of City Planning, *The Urban Design Plan for the Comprehensive Plan of San Francisco* (1971).

[40]City and County of San Francisco, Department of City Planning, *The Downtown Plan* (1983).

ing legislation. The former won acclaim as the first modern planning analysis of any major American municipality to assess comprehensively the urban form and character of the city as a whole. The latter, which focused in greater detail on the function and design of the city center, gained both renown and notoriety for the stringent limitations it placed on downtown office development and for the unusual requirements imposed on approved projects for the purpose of moderating the social and environmental impact of development.

THE URBAN DESIGN PLAN OF 1971

The earlier, citywide *Urban Design Plan* was developed under a state mandate requiring all California cities to prepare a general master plan to include elements concerning several major issues affected by change, such as land use, housing, circulation, safety, recreation and open space, public facilities, economic development, conservation, noise, scenic highways, and seismic safety. Although urban design was not a specific state requirement, the amount of public attention directed to the urban design element of the San Francisco plan led Peter S. Svirsky, a lawyer on the city planning staff, to observe, "One senses that some people have thought of it as the whole master plan."[41]

The Urban Design Plan identified principles and policies of urban design with special reference to the physical pattern and visual character peculiar to San Francisco. It included considerations ranging in scale from the sweeping to the minute—from recommendations that the shape, height, scale, and color of large new developments be adapted to complement the hill and water vistas of the city and bay to design studies aimed at conserving the form and detail of the city's traditional bay-window facades. With responsibility for an area only one-eighth the size of greater New York, the authors of the plan were able to take both broader and more specific views, studying first the composition and texture of the city as a totality, then the environment and character of entire districts, and finally the consistency of individual development proposals in relation to the whole. The intent of the plan was to establish design criteria to ensure that new development would be in harmony with the physical context of established surroundings and to preserve the natural contours, delicate urban scale, and scenic views of the city.

Through the 1970s, *The Urban Design Plan* was translated from the conceptual language of study and design into the specific mandates of the

---

[41]Peter S. Svirsky, "San Francisco Limits the Buildings to See the Sky," *Planning* 39, no. 1 (Jan. 1973), 9.

city's planning code and zoning maps.[42] Although the boundaries of the original land-use zones of the city remained largely unchanged, the resulting code followed the recommendations of the plan to impose new regulations to control building height and bulk within the various districts. In the central business district, the code permitted building heights from 300 feet at the periphery to a maximum of 700 feet at the core. Structures in other districts were allowed up to 200 or 240 feet in height at certain locations to emphasize topographic features or to conform to existing building forms. In most of the city, however, buildings became subject to a height limitation of no more than 40 or 50 feet. Under the code, the bulk of buildings has been moderated by limitations on maximum plan dimensions in terms of length and diagonal measurements in relation to height, with special dimensional conversions devised to accommodate the sloping sites characteristic of the city.

More than any other municipal zoning, the code revisions generated from *The Urban Design Plan* have spun an invisible web of building regulations that reaches far beyond normal height and bulk zoning to dictate virtually all but the final design of architectural development. To implement the plan recommendations calling for the preservation of the physical context of existing, low-density residential neighborhoods, for example, amendments to the code have imposed unusually strict and detailed guidelines governing the design of new construction. The law, for instance, specifies the use of bay windows, a distinctive feature of San Francisco architecture, by requiring building overhangs to be articulated by multiangled glazed units that continue the bay-window tradition. Buildings over 35 feet wide must be divided visually to maintain the rowhouse character of most blocks in the city.

To achieve visual modulation of building facades, the code also requires that building heights be stepped, that the depth of building walls be varied, and that pedestrian entries be provided for every 25 feet of property frontage. Blank ground-floor facades are discouraged by requirements for visually interesting architectural details such as windows, doors, landscaping, and other features. Garage doors cannot compose more than 30 percent of a building's frontage. Front-yard setbacks of new buildings must equal the average setback of adjacent yards, with at least 20 percent of the resulting space devoted to planting. A similar averaging system is also applied to back-yard setbacks to preserve open space in the interiors of residential blocks. Off-street parking and building equipment mounted on rooftops are required by the code to be screened from public view, garage doors must

---

[42]City and County of San Francisco, *City Planning Code* (1979), Sects. 105-6 (1978) (Maps) and Art. 2.5

screen off carports, and trees must be planted on sidewalks in front of new residential developments.

Perhaps more than the residents of any other major city, San Franciscans have long been active in efforts to preserve the distinctive character and special visual charm of their city. In reaction to the construction of large-scale developments that dominate and overwhelm the finely textured skyline or interrupt the sweeping vistas of the city and bay, a number of citizens have mobilized efforts to curb developments perceived to be excessive in height or bulk. Acting individually or in organized groups, they have pursued an aggressive pattern of litigation, voter initiatives, and public hearing and review under municipal code and state environmental impact and referendum provisions to thwart the development of such high-rise structures. Originally, in certain districts such as Russian Hill and Nob Hill, tower designs were allowed in the 1971 plan to accentuate land forms at certain locations, but public antipathy toward high-rise development prompted withdrawal of the idea. The code limits building heights to 35 or 65 feet throughout most residential areas of the city, and is a reflection of the popular aversion to development. Even where higher structures are permitted, conditional use approval is required of any building proposed to be over 40 feet high.

THE DOWNTOWN PLAN OF 1983

Under the administration of planning director Dean L. Macris, the San Francisco city planning department in 1983 issued *The Downtown Plan,* which two years later was enacted into law by a 6–5 vote of the governing board of supervisors.[43] More specific and detailed than the earlier *Urban Design Plan,* the new plan and code revisions address, virtually block by block and building by building, the visual character and function of the nucleus of San Francisco. In addition to its principal focus on urban design, the plan also takes into consideration such associated comprehensive planning concerns as overall urban densities, economic development, jobs, circulation, and housing. Code provisions derived from the plan are supplemented by related legislation that links downtown office construction to exactions designed to mitigate the effect of such development on the city. Attempts have also been made to rectify some of the problems experienced in enforcing the 1971 plan by modifying and adding to the code.

The design objective, as stated in the plan, is to ensure that new development in the urban core will preserve and enhance the visual image of San Francisco as "a white city spread over the hills" with a texture of "small-scale buildings covering the hills on a grid street pattern, punctuated by

---

[43]City and County of San Francisco, Downtown Ordinance 414–85, File 223–84–4, Sept. 17, 1985, effective Oct. 17, 1985.

green spaces and occasional larger significant structures.[44] The regulations enacted to preserve the aesthetic quality and character of the city are specific to the extent of providing detailed rules governing development in virtually every block of the downtown. As Sam Hall Kaplan, urban design critic for the *Los Angeles Times,* puts it, the *Downtown Plan* "all but dictates the actual architectural drawings for buildings."[45]

As enacted into code, *The Downtown Plan* not only retains nearly all the major provisions recommended in the original 1983 policy proposal, but makes restrictions and requirements governing development even more stringent in several points. Even before its enactment into code, the plan had become a seminal model widely studied in the disciplines of urban design, city planning, and planning law.

Perhaps the most controversial provisions of the new planning ordinance are the severe restrictions enacted to attenuate the effect of the tremendous market pressure for downtown office building construction. Between 1965 and 1981, office space in the center city more than doubled to some 55 million square feet, with new office construction between 1981 and 1985 averaging about 3.5 million square feet each year. In a move bitterly debated as too restrictive by developers and too permissive by environmentalists and conservationists, the board of supervisors has limited office building construction to no more than 2.85 million square feet over three years. The average annual allotment of 950,000 square feet will permit the construction of only about two or three medium-size office buildings per year where the market demand would sustain several times as many structures. The reasoning behind this radical restriction is based on socioeconomic planning projections concerning the economic base of the city, employment, and overall municipal and metropolitan growth as much as on such traditional urban design considerations as building and population density, traffic congestion, conservation, aesthetics, public safety, and the like.

Although the restriction is arguably exclusionary and almost certain not to lower already high commercial rents, which in 1985 averaged about $35 per square foot, one rationale for the restriction on new office buildings is that the pressure to develop office space capable of returning high profits is causing the displacement of small businesses as well as lower- and moderate-income populations that can ill afford new, more expensive quarters. That market development of the downtown would "Manhattanize" San Francisco into a conglomeration of overpowering, high-rise skyscrapers and would destroy the fine old buildings and the small-scale charm of the existing city is only one part of the argument.

---

[44]City and County of San Francisco, *Downtown Plan,* 105, 83.

[45]Sam Hall Kaplan, "San Francisco Reveals Vast Building Plan," *Los Angeles Times,* August 26, 1983.

In addition to the sweeping curtailment of office-space development, and in specific response to the public outcry against the construction of such tall, massive skyscrapers as the bronze-hued Bank of America Building and pyramidal, needle-shaped Transamerica Building that were allowed under the previous regulations, the authors of *The Downtown Plan* have made substantial reductions in the permissible size and height of those buildings actually approved for construction in the city center. Under the 1985 ordinance, the allowable size of office buildings in the city's burgeoning financial district has been lowered from a FAR of 14 permitted by the previous code to a maximum FAR of only 9. In the retail district around Union Square and to the west where many tourist hotels, restaurants, and visitor attractions are located, allowable floor areas have been similarly reduced. Permissible building heights at the core of the city's business district have also been lowered from the maximum of 700 feet stipulated by the 1971 plan and code to a new maximum of only 550 feet, with most future towers limited to 400 feet in height.

With the likelihood that market-generated development will fill the very limits of allowable building "envelopes," San Francisco planners more than most others are at pains to weave the invisible web of urban design regulations with special care, for their ministrations can virtually design not only the city environment as a whole but—with unprecedented specificity— the individual, privately owned buildings that compose it. As an article in *Time* magazine said,

> More problematic than the cap [on office space] development itself will be administering it. Vast power will devolve on the planning director. Of ten buildings proposed next year, say, how to choose which two or three get the go-ahead? How to prevent favoritism and influence buying? Macris says he may assemble a panel of nationally well-known architects to do the judging for the city. The mandarin bureaucracy grows.[46]

And so with these regulations will grow the discretionary prerogatives of reviewers in this ultimate form of design review under the police power.

Just as market forces and early sky exposure plane regulations in New York City produced an aggregation of stepped, pyramidal building forms, the market and the 1971 plan and code in San Francisco have fostered a peculiar "benching" of the city skyline. The austere, rectilinear forms of International Style high-rise buildings have combined with the market tendency of developers to build to the maximum of height and bulk restrictions, producing an urban silhouette of boxy, high-rise building tops, particularly in districts where the height allowance was below 400 feet. As Kaplan points

---

[46]Kurt Andersen and Jane Ferguson, "Outlawing the Modern Skyscraper," *Time* 126, no. 3 (July 22, 1985), 56.

out: "The city's modern skyline of box-topped competing edifices have all the charm of a display of refrigerators in a wholesale warehouse."[47] To prevent this boxy urban form from proliferating—and with, perhaps, a not altogether unbiased nod toward the more decorative preferences of post-modernism—*The Downtown Plan* and code revisions include new controls devised to encourage a wider range of building heights within a district and a greater variety of tapering building forms.

The 1985 regulations governing architectural design contain charts prescribing graduated bulk-to-height ratios that distinguish among four elements of a high-rise building: the base, the lower tower, the upper tower, and the upper-tower extension. In basic terms, the code requires graduated reductions in bulk to create a more slender high-rise form. For example, an optional upper-tower extension that allows an exception of up to 10 percent of the districted height limit may be permitted if the bulk of the upper tower is reduced, effecting a narrower high-rise silhouette and a more sculptured skyline terminus. Vertical building embellishments such as towers, spires, cupolas, belfries, and domes are favored by the new code.

The design of the base and lower tower of a high-rise building is likewise tightly monitored to ensure visual continuity of predominant street walls and harmony with existing streetscapes. A chart is included in the new code specifying setbacks and the amount of spatial separation required between towers. In the city center, greater articulation of building surfaces is also encouraged by a relaxation of previous restrictions to allow for such nonstructural ornamentation as deep-set or bay windows, pilasters, belt courses, and cornices. The use of dark opaque glass is discouraged by the new regulations as is using highly reflective or mirrored glazing. These specifications governing architectural decoration and fenestration not only promote designs reminiscent of older, prewar buildings about the city but give virtual code endorsement to the current fashion of postmodernism. As Macris is quoted as saying: "We think it is time for a departure from the International Style."[48]

The Downtown Plan is conceptually imbued with measures aimed at enhancing the vitality and efficiency of the center city. Provisions that effect "vertical" mixed use are integral in many of its stipulations. To encourage housing to be mixed in with center-city activities, the plan permits buildings in some commercial districts to include moderate-income residential space in excess of allowable floor area, provided height and bulk limitations are otherwise observed. To include development of facilities that would generate pedestrian activities at street level, ground-floor space devoted to circulation, restaurants, retail sales, and personal services in commercial buildings of the downtown area is not counted in computing FAR allotments.

[47]Kaplan, "San Francisco Reveals Plan."
[48]Anderson and Ferguson, "Outlawing the Skyscraper."

Whereas ground-level convenience retail stores that serve office workers and downtown residents are encouraged in all commercial areas, major shopping facilities are not favored in nonretail districts. Such use is discouraged to ensure the concentrated vitality of the central shopping districts, where building usage is reserved mostly for retail stores, restaurants, bars, and similar functions. To provide an attractive environment for passers-by, the plan suggests that building walls facing pedestrian walkways not be blank but have windows, displays, or other points of visual interest.

Developers of downtown commercial buildings are also required to provide open space at a ratio of one square foot to every fifty square feet of office space constructed. The open space must be supplied either at the project site or within nine hundred feet of it. The design of the required space, whether a plaza, terrace, mall, arcade, galleria, atrium, garden, or park, is subject to review of its design quality and practical use to the public. Landscaping is also required on developed street fronts, with trees of approved species and size installed at a minimum spacing along the public walkway. In addition, the code requires 1 percent of the construction cost of downtown buildings to be allocated for works of art that will be prominently displayed at the development site. The code further distinguishes between plazas and seating areas required as amenities for office and retail developments and the recreational function of public parks. It requires sponsors of downtown office space to contribute to a special downtown park fund at a fee of $2 for every square foot of gross floor area developed for office use.

To make the street level of the central business district more hospitable to the pedestrian, the new code incorporates innovative "bioclimatic" provisions regulating ambient wind velocities and direct sunlight access. The code requires buildings to be shaped, or baffles provided, to ensure that ground-level wind currents during daytime hours do not exceed a speed equivalent of 11 miles per hour in pedestrian traffic areas or 7 miles per hour in public seating areas more than 10 percent of the time year-round. For the same purpose, the maximum heights of street walls and sun access angles are specified along designated streets to allow direct sunlight access to public sidewalks. The degree to which shadows are allowed to fall on public spaces is also regulated in the design and shape of new buildings in commercial districts.

A principal concern of *The Downtown Plan* is the preservation of the many historic and architecturally significant buildings and districts that contribute to San Francisco's reputation as a city of outstanding beauty and physical coherence. To this end, the new ordinance established six conservation districts in the downtown, the largest of which encompasses much of the retail and business heart of the city. In these districts, design criteria to be observed in new construction and redevelopment are even more stringent than the already strict standards enforced elsewhere in the city. Such aspects of design as architectural massing, composition, scale, and materials—even components of facade articulation and ornamentation—are subject to scrutiny to ensure their compatibility with the design of surrounding structures.

The new code section on historic preservation includes an inventory and rating of more than 400 buildings of the 1,700-odd structures that compose downtown San Francisco. The rated buildings, which must be at least forty years old, are divided into four classes. These categories include "significant" buildings that are to be retained essentially intact because of their excellence in design or importance to their surroundings; significant buildings that, because of their depth or relationship to other structures, can be added to without detracting from their design quality; "contributory" buildings that rate highly in design excellence but are located outside a designated conservation district; and contributory buildings that enhance the context of their surrounding conservation districts. Specific regulations are provided to preserve each class of rated structures, with transfer of development rights permitted to compensate for the restrictions on redevelopment.

To preserve the urban design context of older buildings in the urban core, where pressure for construction of office space is the greatest, the new ordinance follows the plan's policy recommendation of shifting commercial office development by means of TDR and rezoning from the north side to the south side of Market Street, the principal downtown thoroughfare dividing the city's gridiron scheme. (South of Market Street, the grid is oriented northeast to southwest, in accordance with Spanish colonial law; the gridiron north of Market follows the standard north-south orientation of the 1785 survey system.) The largely underdeveloped Embarcadero region was rezoned as a special redevelopment district to become an extension of the downtown office district, with its growth to be stimulated by development rights transferred from the historic districts of the city. Perhaps in view of New York's experience, where TDR and incentive zoning resulted in excessive building heights, the San Francisco plan and code specifically stipulates that regardless of increases in permissible floor-area ratios resulting from TDR, buildings in the Embarcadero district must still conform to other district limitations governing height, bulk, setbacks, sunlight access, and separation between towers.

Since 1968, the code had awarded bonus FAR allowances to encourage developers to provide certain architectural features, including pedestrian plazas, additional circulation space, transportation access, and observation decks. Unfortunately, as in New York City, the outcome of incentive zoning in San Francisco has not been altogether successful. As Richard Hedman of the city planning department observed, the provisions resulted in "too many bare plazas," new arcades "that many people go out of their way to avoid using," and a streetscape of a "growing 'no-man's-land': new, tidy, crisp, and boring."[49] As a result of this less than successful experience with bonus zoning, the new code has abolished the incentive provision entirely.

One of the most controversial aspects of the city's 1985 planning regulations is the "linkage" provisions that require sponsors of new downtown development to contribute to various community programs or improvements to moderate the effects of development. Some of the stipulations are for physical amenities traditional to urban design, such as contributions to the downtown park fund. Others are remarkable in that the purposes for their imposition are for socioeconomic considerations not generally associated with urban design in a narrow sense, although very much a concern of comprehensive city planning. The new code, for example, requires developers of office space over 100,000 square feet to anticipate employment problems related to added city development by establishing local employment programs and by providing employment brokerage services for the actual lifetime of their projects.[50]

Even more unusual are code provisions aimed at addressing the scarcity of adequate child-care services in the city, especially for children of low- and moderate-income workers employed in commercial developments in the city center. The code requires developers of downtown office space to provide child-care facilities as well as child-care services for the life of their buildings, either on site for projects over 100,000 square feet, or for smaller developments, within a radius of two blocks, possibly in concert with other developers.[51] Alternatively, sponsors of new office developments may contribute to a special fund at a fee of one dollar per square foot of gross office space, with proceeds going to provide affordable and easy access to quality, nonprofit child care.[52]

In addition to linkage provisions in the new planning code, the city has also enacted two companion ordinances that tie development of office space to contributions toward affordable housing and public transit. Like the exactions imposed by the code, the intent of these ordinances is to mitigate the effect of market-propelled development of commercially lucrative office space in the city.

As large-scale office developments continue to attract more workers to the city, the supply of housing has not kept pace with demand. The resulting shortage has made housing costs in San Francisco the highest of any city in the country. Competition for available dwelling units has placed an inordinate pressure on low- and moderate-income households in particular and

---

[49]Richard Hedman, "A Skyline Paved with Good Intentions," *Planning* 47, no. 8 (Aug. 1981), 15.
[50]City and County of San Francisco, Downtown Ordinance, Sect. 164.
[51]Ibid., Sect. 165.
[52]Ibid., Sect. 315.

has forced workers to commute long distances on already congested highways and transit systems, thus affecting adversely the overall quality of life throughout the city. Problems created by the nation's highest rate of gentrification have been exacerbated as older residential structures, particularly hotels converted into low-cost apartments and rooming houses, have been demolished and their low-income tenants, many of them aged, displaced to make way for new, more profitable commercial developments. Because the income generated from low- and moderate-cost housing is insufficient to attract new construction, development of affordable housing cannot be anticipated through market determination.

So that commercial office development will not further reduce the availability of affordable housing, the board of supervisors in 1985 enacted into code a provision requiring developers of downtown office projects to construct or sponsor the development of good-quality housing affordable to low- and moderate-income households. The resulting Office Affordable Housing Production Program is a modified extension of a similar program, initiated in 1981, that required developers of office buildings to furnish some form of affordable housing, whether new or renovated, on or off site, for a population generally equivalent in number to the occupants of their commercial developments who reside in the city.

The new program requires affordable housing units (as defined by code) to be provided in accordance with a formulated proportion of office space developed. If an office-building sponsor chooses to construct the housing itself, 62 percent of the units must be affordable. In lieu of undertaking the construction itself, a developer may elect to pay a subsidy fee of $5.34 for every square foot of gross office space developed, or to furnish a combination of construction and fee to the amount of some $14,000 per unit. Stipulations governing the program are explicit and extensive, reflecting revisions included to rectify problems encountered in the course of administering the earlier housing support program.

A similar ordinance requires sponsors of city center office buildings to help pay for the additional burden placed on public transit because of increased downtown development. The enactment imposes a transit impact development fee of up to $5 per square foot of office space development, with proceeds earmarked to cover all capital and operating expenses incurred in providing additional public transit service made necessary by new commercial development downtown.[53] This developer subsidy of urban mass transit is made in conjunction with planning strategies to alleviate traffic congestion in the center city by encouraging ridership of public transit and increasing the efficiency of automobile commuting about the city. As in the cases of employment and child care, sponsors of large-scale office

[53]City and County of San Francisco, Transit Impact Development Fee, Ordinance 224–81, File 159–80, adding Chapter 38 to the San Francisco Administrative Code.

developments are required by code to prepare a transportation management program and to provide on-site transportation brokerage services for the lifetime of their projects.[54]

In addition to formulating the plan and ordinances to regulate downtown development, planning officials are also moving to implement similar controls to guide development in other areas of the city. San Francisco, like New York, is well known for the special character and charm of its many diverse districts and neighborhoods. Some of the districts reflect a variety of different ethnic and life-style characteristics, not only in the composition of their resident populations, but in the distinctive urban environment created by their neighborhood commercial functions, the retail stores, restaurants, area services and industries, and sometimes even the architecture. Many neighborhoods, especially those bordering the downtown, are exemplary of Jane Jacobs's theories of urban form and function, with an abundance of small-scale older buildings, full population densities, a rich mixture of residential and commercial uses, and functionally articulated, pedestrian-oriented streets. By considering these districts apart from downtown, a distinction is clearly drawn between the essentially mixed-use, residential character of these urban communities and the commercial nature of the downtown area.

In 1985, only a few months before enactment of *The Downtown Plan* into code, the planning commission adopted interim zoning for neighborhood commercial mixed-use districts. The resolutions, covering regulations governing four general districts, sixteen individual districts, and some two hundred and twenty identifiable neighborhoods about the city, is aimed at preserving not only the physical fabric of each district's urban design and aesthetic quality but the integrity of every residential neighborhood. The planning controls are designed to encourage retention and development of housing, to regulate the conversion of existing housing to commercial use, and to ensure that the market propensity to start and expand profitable eating and drinking establishments does not supplant service functions vital to residential populations, such as grocery and drug stores. As is predictable in San Francisco, citizen participation and advocacy have been essential in formulating planning policy and development controls for these various districts and neighborhoods.

Plans and regulations for some individual districts have already been adopted while formulation of the controls for others is in process. Historic-district zoning is expected for Chinatown, under which any redevelopment will be strictly limited to protect the distinctive physical character and ethnic charm of this community and also to maintain the area's bioclimatic environment. The district will be divided into two subdistricts, one for specialty retail and the other for residential/commercial uses. Existing city regula-

---

[54]City and County of San Francisco, Downtown Ordinance, Sect. 163.

tions prohibiting the demolition of residential hotels, which compose two-thirds of Chinatown's housing stock, will be further extended in the district.

Planning regulations governing other districts will likewise place priority on maintaining and increasing the supply of housing. Along Van Ness Avenue, for example, developers will be obligated to furnish three square feet of housing for every square foot of new commercial space. Regulations aimed at protecting existing residential use against commercial encroachment have also been enacted for the mixed-use district north of Market Street. South of Market, district regulations are to encourage the mixing of light industry, home and business services, cultural arts, neighborhood retail stores, community service, and artisan/artist live-work functions.

As might be expected, *The Downtown Plan* and its resulting code revisions have elicited a variety of responses. Paul Goldberger, architecture critic for the *New York Times,* is one of several observers who have commented favorably on the plan, which he calls "intelligent and sensitive"—"one of the most complete prescriptions for growth any American downtown has been given."[55] Complaints range from owners and developers, who charge that the regulations infringe severely upon their property rights, to the criticism of environmentalists, who contend that the controls do not go far enough. Legal challenges to code provisions and regulations related to the plan, such as the transit impact development fee, are in process or expected to occur.

Several commentators are more specific in their criticism of the plan. Tim Redmond and David Goldsmith, for example, aver in a *San Francisco Bay Guardian* article that a basic assumption behind the plan is flawed. Citing a study by economist David Birch of the Massachusetts Institute of Technology, they claim that economic projections made in the environmental impact reports on the plan are inaccurate, in that new jobs actually created by the development of additional downtown office space have amounted to only 10 percent of the number originally anticipated. They cite figures showing that whereas businesses with fewer than a hundred employees have created more jobs, larger companies—presumably the clientele who can afford the high rents demanded of new downtown construction—have actually posted losses in their number of employees, resulting in a net loss of jobs about the city. In conclusion, Redmond and Goldsmith claim that the city's apparent policy of favoring costly new downtown development to accommodate large corporate employers should be realigned to encourage the growth of small local businesses.[56]

In addition, criticism has been leveled at other aspects of the plan and

[55]Paul Goldberger, as quoted by Gerald D. Adams, "A Last Ditch Effort to Save Downtown San Francisco," *Planning* 50, no. 2 (Feb. 1984), 5.

[56]Tim Redmond and David Goldsmith, "The End of the High-Rise Jobs Myth," *San Francisco Bay Guardian;* reprinted in *Planning* 52, no. 4 (April 1986), 18.

its related legislation. Community housing advocates argue that the demand for housing has been underestimated, that a minimum percentage of low-income units as opposed to middle-income units should be stipulated, and that the in lieu housing subsidy fee amounts to only one half of what is actually needed to provide adequate housing.[57] Other critics claim that merely shifting building development to south of Market does nothing to abate unwarranted office construction and would all but obliterate the blue-collar, light industrial area of the city. They further argue that problems of municipal transportation and congestion are not realistically addressed. An observation by Chester Hartman, an authority on San Francisco growth, that the 1983 plan failed to take into account the real danger of a cata-strophic earthquake before the end of the century was soon followed, per-haps coincidentally, by an addendum to the policy plan that included a major section on seismic safety.[58]

Even as ordinances implementing the policies of *The Downtown Plan* are being enacted, citizen groups opposed to development have continued in their efforts to forestall growth that they deem detrimental to the quality of life in San Francisco. Two months after the original downtown plan proposal was released, voters rejected by a margin of just over a single percentage point an initiative that would have drastically curbed high-rise construction in the city. And again, in November 1985, two months after the plan was adopted into code, a similar initiative was placed before the electorate and was rejected. However, in June 1984, for the fifth time in about a dozen years, a proposition limiting building heights came before the voters and for the first time was approved. If the measure survives antici-pated legal challenges, it will prohibit development over 40 feet high that would cast a "substantial" shadow over municipally owned parks. The ap-parent trend of these initiatives indicates continuing voter concern over the issues of high-rise development and urban design in San Francisco and por-tends the imposition of development controls with or without the benefits of a more formal plan.

Beyond the city plans and recent voter initiatives, other aspects of plan-ning regulation are worthy of note in considering urban form controls in San Francisco. Some regulations derive from state authority. California's "general plan"[59] requirement of cities and counties, for example, provides local government with authority to enact "specific plans" as a means for general plan implementation in designated areas. A regulatory device as much as a plan, a specific plan can include regulations, programs, and pro-posed legislation affecting urban design and can be used in place of or in conjunction with zoning to manage various urban design concerns, includ-

[57]W. Dennis Keating, "Linking Downtown Development to Broader Community Goals," *Journal of the American Inst. of Planners* 52, no. 2 (Spring 1986), 135–6.

[58]Chester Hartman, "Viewpoint," *Planning* 50, no. 2 (May 1984), 42.

[59]Cal. Gov. Code, Sect. 65300 *et seq.*, Sect. 65450 *et seq.*

ing land use and facilities, roads and transportation, population and building density, water and sanitation, conservation, and open space.

Another state provision for control is the requirement of the 1970 Environmental Quality Act[60] (EQA) that an applicant for development permission must first file an environmental impact report. As noted earlier, such a report is mandated if a proposed project may have a detrimental effect on the surrounding environment. In San Francisco, only a very few minor types of development are exempt from this report requirement. As demonstrated in the *Haas* case, the California EQA offers a powerful regulatory tool for urban design. It also provides environmental advocacy groups, from such neighborhood organizations as the Russian Hill Association to more widely based groups, such as San Franciscans for Reasonable Growth, considerable leverage in monitoring and challenging official municipal approval of development projects.

More, perhaps, than in any other major city in the country, the regulatory climate to be weathered by developers in San Francisco is a formidable one. Although municipal regulations are already strictly enforced, public planning officials possess considerable regulatory discretion to impose further requirements on developers. Variances, which were earlier shown to be frequently if improperly used to gain flexibility favorable to developers, are specifically limited by the San Francisco code. A section mandates as follows:

> No variance shall be granted in whole or in part which would have an effect substantially equivalent to a reclassification of property; or which would permit any use, any height or bulk of a building or structure, or any type of sign not expressly permitted by the provisions of the Code . . . or which would grant a privilege for which conditional use procedure is provided . . . or which would change a definition in this Code.''[61]

By specifically forbidding abrogation of the minimum requirements of the written code, this provision seems to underscore strict compliance to Hayek's prescription of predetermined regulation.

On the other hand, however, the municipal code accords great discretionary power to public regulators. In a provision unique to the San Francisco code, the city planning commission can initiate discretionary review of development proposals that may have an extensive and detrimental effect on the surroundings, even though the project may fulfill the literal requirements of the planning code.[62] As in the case of challenges based on environ-

---

[60]Note 12.

[61]City and County of San Francisco, *City Planning Code,* Sect. 305 (a).

[62]San Francisco Municipal Code, Part III, Sect. 26. See San Francisco City Attorney Opinion No. 845 (1954) and Opinion No. 79-29 (1979). Also see Lynn E. Pio, Administrative Secretary, San Francisco Department of City Planning, "Memorandum to Members of the City Planning Commission: Discretionary Review Procedures," January 28, 1976.

mental impact grounds, discretionary review is often initiated by popular opposition to a proposed development. In *Haas*, both state environmental quality and municipal code provisions were factors in the court's decisions, as was the city's urban design plan, which provided guidelines for the area in question.

The revisions to the planning code derived from *The Downtown Plan* extend still further the possibility of discretionary administration concerning the design of architecture and site development in particular. The new ordinance specifies review procedures by the planning commission of construction projects proposed for the city's commercial districts and provides for appeals to the board of permit appeals.[63] It outlines the procedures for obtaining development permission, including public hearings, recommendation by the planning director, planning commission approval, and compliance with the state's Environmental Quality Act. Included as subjects of possible review are requests by developers for exceptions from regulations governing building height and bulk, open space, upper-tower extensions, parking, and bioclimatic design stipulations.

Especially notable is a list of architectural and site-design considerations for which the ordinance permits "additional requirements" to be imposed. The list includes the following:

1. Building siting, orientation, massing and facade treatment, including proportion, scale, setbacks, materials, cornice, parapet and fenestration treatment, and design of building tops.
2. Aspects of the project affecting views and view corridors, shadowing of sidewalks and open spaces, openness of the street to the sky, ground level wind current, and maintenance of predominant streetwalls in the immediate vicinity.
3. Aspects of the project affecting parking, traffic circulation and transit operation and loading points.
4. Aspects of the project affecting its energy consumption.
5. Aspects of the project related to pedestrian activity, such as placement of entrances, street scale, visual richness, location of retail uses, and pedestrian circulation, and location and design of open space features.
6. Aspects of the project affecting public spaces adjacent to the project, such as the location and type of street trees and landscaping, sidewalk paving material, and the design and location of street furniture.
7. Aspects of the project relating to quality of the living environment of residential units, including housing unit size and the provisions of open space for residents.
8. Aspects of the design of the project which have significant adverse environmental consequences.
9. Aspects of the project that affect its compliance with the provisions of

[63]City and County of San Francisco, Downtown Ordinance, Sect. 309.

[sections of the code] regarding new construction and alterations in conservation districts.

10. Other aspects of the project for which modifications are justified because of its unique or unusual location, environment, topography or other circumstances.[64]

As suggested in the preceding chapter, any community that wishes to carry out architectural design review should set forth a detailed plan clearly defining the goals and objectives in urban design that provide the rationale for regulation, and specify the necessary guidelines and standards upon which it plans to evaluate the architectural design of private developments. Certainly, the suggestion made by Justice Brennan in the *Metromedia* and *Vincent* cases that a comprehensive and coordinated community commitment to further environmental beauty and design be demonstrated as a prior condition for aesthetic regulation is a requirement that has been substantively met by the San Francisco urban design plans.

As Kenneth Davis[65] would be quick to point out, a degree of discretion is doubtless a necessity in administering the complex controls of the urban design and downtown plans, although in considering the detail and stringency of the design and development regulations of the newly revised planning code, the listing of considerations subject to review under this section seems somewhat redundant—even superfluous. Rather than itemizing, it might be just as reasonable to note in the code that review is authorized to ensure that the objectives and policies specified in the master plan or the purposes of the code are achieved. In view of the competitive climate imposed on downtown commercial development by the three-year limitation on office construction, developers applying for construction permits are already under considerable pressure to comply with the demands of most architectural design restrictions.

REFLECTIONS

Urban designers who seek design controls for their own communities patterned after those used in San Francisco and New York City should be aware of an underlying premise of both regulations: the market incentive for development in these cities is overwhelming. Both cities enjoy—if that is the word—a buyer's market for development that few municipalities can match. For all communities, urban design regulation has substantial implications in terms of economic planning policy. If a city restricts development beyond what the market can bear, developers may decide to relocate their

---

[64]Ibid., Sect. 309 (b).
[65]Kenneth Culp Davis, *Discretionary Justice* (1969; reprint, Westport, C.T.: Greenwood, 1980).

projects to communities where the costs imposed by planning and building regulations are less burdensome. In short, as seen in earlier discussion, even the best-conceived urban design and planning controls can have an exclusionary effect. When many cities are actively competing for development and the jobs and revenue it can bring, local governing bodies are often reluctant to impose development controls. For often legitimate, if short-sighted, economic reasons, cities cannot always afford the "luxury" of even well-designed planning and urban design regulations that might discourage development. Some even offer ad hoc exceptions to existing rules in order to entice developers. At the very least, as experiences in San Francisco have shown, city planning officials can expect political pressure from such pro-development interests as the local chamber of commerce and construction and real estate concerns.

Municipal planning officials should likewise be aware of the mid 1980s experience of some sunbelt cities; earlier development, fueled by flowing petroleum resources, led to catastrophic economic problems later as a result of overbuilding.

Planning in San Francisco, like planning in New York City, finds its basis for control in the police power, the archetype of the invisible web. Allan B. Jacobs, director of city planning in San Francisco when the 1971 urban design plan was drawn, compares planning control under legislative regulation to planning in Boston in the mid 1960s. Planning in Boston was largely implemented under the concept of the "capital web," a theory developed by David A. Crane, then planning director of Boston.[66] Crane's thesis had grown, in turn, out of Edward J. Logue's practice as redevelopment director of manipulating public captial investments as instruments for planning. Jacobs writes,

> The Boston plan has a strong orientation toward public projects and improvements. It places some dependency upon a "capital web" to shape the city and to influence future development. It was prepared in an era of large and expensive federally funded redevelopment projects by the staff of the Boston Redevelopment Authority. Direct public design or control of projects could thus be anticipated. The San Francisco plan was oriented more to citywide policies and principles than to the design specifics of public works. It was concerned with the process of all development and with moderating private development, which the planners could not design themselves. An orientation toward influence and legislation, matters that could be controlled by the San Francisco planners, is therefore understandable.[67]

[66]David A. Crane, "The City Symbolic," *Journal of the American Inst. of Planners* (Nov. 1960), 280, 285–86; "The Public Art of City Building," *Annals of the American Acad. of Political and Social Science* (March 1964), 92.

[67]Allan B. Jacobs, *Making City Planning Work* (Washington, D.C., and Chicago: American Planning Association, 1978), 222–23.

Significantly, urban design through public regulation assumes particular relevance at times like the present, when investment capital is lacking for public improvements at an urban scale.

To implement successfully plans and codes like San Francisco's and New York's, where authority derives more from the police power than from capital expenditures, public planners and urban designers must be schooled sufficiently in the ways of the law to be capable of spinning an invisible web that is both legally sound and conducive to superior urban design. As the experience in these two cities has shown, inadequate consideration or faulty urban-design controls can result in inferior urban design as much as in legal difficulty. The pyramidal wedding-cake forms of the New York City skyline, the boxy towers of San Francisco, the lifeless plazas and public arcades of both cities and, for that matter, the monotonous gridiron plan of most American cities are testament to woven webs of planning law whose effect on urban form was either unanticipated or flawed.

It would be folly, of course, to believe that good, imaginative design can ever be attributed to regulation alone. Public regulations, including incentives, can encourage and perhaps foster but cannot substitute for design creativity. Cities contemplating design controls fashioned after those used in New York City and San Francisco should note the critics of design regulation. Weaver and Babcock quote one observer of New York and its zoning,

> The regulations are getting to be so esoteric and so arcane that it's beyond the ken of all but maybe six or seven people. Now they say there must be a drinking fountain and it shall be no lower than one foot, six inches in height. The next step is to stipulate how far the water will arc and at what temperature. . . . I understand the theory behind it but the regulations are getting so arithmetic that many good architects find that the regulations bind them. . . . You return to the old cliche: Can you quantify good design?[68]

Urban designers must also be aware of the implications of public design controls in terms of overall planning policy. The urban renewal powers of government upheld by the Supreme Court in *Berman v. Parker* suggest a lesson. In that 1954 case, the District of Columbia redevelopment agency and planning commission were successful in arguing the necessity and constitutionality of acquiring unblighted and nonslum properties as well as blighted ones for the purpose of carrying out an integrated and comprehensive urban redevelopment operation. However, the subsequent history of the federal program ultimately proved the process of wholesale renewal and design, through perhaps legal, to be a questionable one that was destructive of many community values in the areas of its operation. In the program's later years, it was found best for renewal operations to strive to accommo-

[68]Weaver and Babcock, *City Zoning,* 62.

date functions and populations already existing in the locality rather than remove them for the sake of an integrated plan. Put in more theoretical terms, it was found beneficial to preserve the fruits of organic urban development rather than to sacrifice them in exchange for a rational plan, however efficient or beautiful.

So it should be with urban design controls. Even in such situations where government authority cannot be denied, the planner and urban designer must be sensitive to the policy and design implications of exercising that power. Urban design, more than architecture, should be more than a designer's rationalized conception of a city beautiful, radiant, or efficient. A democratic city must reflect all the people who live in it, their individual lives and preferences, however untidy and lacking in values that the planner might personally approve. To this end, the urban designer must know where design and control must end and where the organic process of pluralistic determination must be allowed free rein. The invisible web should provide only a structural framework and not be seen as total design.

Nonetheless, reasonable innovation in urban-design controls is needed if an alternative to only minimal modulation of market determination of urban development is sought. Even while rejecting the application of TDR in the 1976 case of *Fred F. French Investing Company, Inc. v. City of New York,* the New York Court of Appeals gave pointed recognition of the need for ingenuity in planning controls.

> It would be a misreading of the discussion above to conclude that the court is insensitive to the inescapable need for government to devise methods, other than by outright appropriation of the fee, to meet urgent environmental needs of a densely concentrated urban population. It would be equally simplistic to ignore modern recognition of the principle that no property has value except as the community contributes to that value. . . .
>
> The legislative and administrative efforts to solve the zoning and landmark problem in modern society demonstrate the presence of ingenuity. That ingenuity further pursued will in all likelihood achieve the goals without placing an impossible or unsuitable burden on the individual property owner, the public fisc, or the general taxpayer. These efforts are entitled to and will undoubtedly receive every encouragement. The task is difficult but not beyond management. The end is essential but the means must nevertheless conform to constitutional standards.[69]

As W. Paul Gormley observed in a 1965 article on aesthetics as a constitutional basis for planning controls,

> Obviously, the courts in the United States have adopted a changed attitude as to private property rights in relation to community planning during the last

[69]350 N.E. 2d 381 (1976), 389.

half century. The aesthetic needs of our major cities now predominate, and the implication of such a social-functional approach seems fairly obvious. Citizens and cities alike must evaluate the interest of the community in protecting existing property rights as against the community interest of rebuilding and rehabilitating marginal and gray areas, in addition to such normal governmental functions as slum clearance and the protection of the health, welfare, safety and morals of the population. The need for urban redevelopment and city planning, therefore, becomes involved with legal doctrines promulgated at a period in history when cities barely existed, let alone city planning.[70]

In a modern free society, the social ideal does not exist in static absolutes, but in a dynamic and ever-fluid balance between public controls and pluralist economic determination, each vigorously advocating its legitimate ends and values in the forum provided by the law. The same dichotomy exists also in the ideal urban design: a city whose beauty and efficiency bespeak the vision and influence of the planner and urban designer yet whose vitality, diversity, and vigor are the inimitable products of a pluralist and free society.

[70]W. Paul Gormley, "Urban Redevelopment to Further Aesthetic Considerations: The Changing Constitutional Concepts of Police Power and Eminent Domain," *North Dakota L. Rev.* 41 (1965), 317, 18.

PART VI

BEYOND THE POLICE POWER

Chapter 12

Paying for the Power to Plan

In 1954, a decision was reached by the United States Supreme Court that would significantly expand the power of government to engage in compulsory urban design and lay the foundation for a program that would reshape America's city centers as not contemplated since the City Beautiful movement of the turn of the century. In the celebrated case of *Berman v. Parker,*[1] the principal objective of government was to compel transfer of private real property to temporary public control. The public purpose in the forced taking was to consolidate diverse private holdings of land and buildings for the purpose of redevelopment and to attach contractual agreements or deed restrictions to the acquired property that would spell out specific terms for the design and use of the assembled property in its resale or lease to private developers. Such mandatory transfers and detailed covenants prescribing redevelopment and use were at the heart of the federal Urban Renewal program of the 1950s and 1960s,[2] certainly the most ambitious and far-reaching undertaking in slum clearance and urban design in recent history.

That the area at issue in *Berman,* a slum in Washington, D.C., was badly in need of renewal was not debated. Rather, the central question was whether a nonslum property in the area, a local department store, could lawfully be seized for the purpose of creating an integrated scheme of urban

---

[1]348 U.S. 26 (1954).

[2]42 U.S.C. 1450 *et seq.,* Slum Clearance and Urban Renewal, Pub. L. 560 (83rd. Cong.), 68 Stat. 622, Title III of the Housing Act of 1954, amending Title I of the Housing Act of 1949, Pub. L. 171 (81st Cong.), 63 Stat. 413, 414.

design. Upon reaching its famous conclusion that the furtherance of community beauty is a legitimate public purpose and valid grounds for eminent
domain proceedings, the Supreme Court answered the question in the affirmative, stating:

> If owner after owner were permitted to resist these redevelopment programs
> on the ground that his particular property was not being used against the
> public interest, integrated plans for redevelopment would suffer greatly. The
> argument pressed on us is, indeed, a plea to substitute the landowner's stan-
> dard of the public need for the standard prescribed by Congress. But as we
> have already stated, community redevelopment programs need not, by force
> of the Constitution, be on a piecemeal basis—lot by lot, building by building.[3]

Berman v. Parker foreshadowed a new application of the power of
eminent domain as well as a new era of active federal involvement in affirmative urban design. But even beyond *Berman* and Urban Renewal, the potential for use of eminent domain as an alternative basis for innovative new
means of planning and urban design controls still awaits exploration.

EMINENT DOMAIN AND COMPENSABLE REGULATION

Historically, urban design controls in the United States have followed
two main avenues. The first is the police power, whose variations, such as
zoning and building height and bulk regulations, have already been thoroughly discussed. As a reactive and "negative" control, the police power
of zoning is essentially an instrument of long-term public policy aimed at
guiding pluralistic and incremental market development of urban land. Its
authority is limited under the Constitution to considerations related to the
"public health, safety, and welfare," "public necessity," and "reasonableness." To be effective as an urban-design control, the police power requires a competitive market for development that would override any disincentive posed by regulation. Such a market exists in San Francisco, for
example, but may be absent in less prosperous cities. The second course
involves the power of eminent domain, by which authority the administrators of Urban Renewal were capable of expropriating or condemning property in fee to attach convenants to control development, use, and design.
The power of eminent domain contrasts with the police power as a means
for positive or initiative planning control. Its use in such project-oriented
programs as Urban Renewal assumes a strong fisc as well as a public commitment to invest in physical development and design.

An ancient prerogative of sovereignty, the power of eminent domain
is believed to have been first articulated by the Dutch legal scholar Hugo

[3]Note 1, 35.

Grotius in 1625 in his dictum *Res subditorum sub eminenti dominio esse civitatis:* that the property of subjects is under the eminent dominion of the state.[4] The power of government is not expressly granted by the Constitution but is implicit in the Fifth Amendment proviso, "nor shall private property be taken for public use, without just compensation."[5] Cases much earlier than *Berman* have sanctioned the power of government and its assigns to compel surrender of private property for public use or for a public purpose. In 1868, for instance, the Massachusetts court in *Dingley v. City of Boston*[6] upheld public condemnation of private land in order to construct improvements to alleviate unhealthy drainage conditions about the city. Likewise, the Supreme Court in 1896 ruled in *United States v. Gettysburg Electric Railway Company*[7] to permit public acquisition of private land for use as a national military park. Through such decisions, the practice of eminent domain with just compensation has become well established as a source of public planning authority.[8]

A favorite law school analogy compares private rights in property to a "bundle of sticks" with each stick representing an individual right. Assuming Blackstone's ideal of property as the "sole and despotic dominion" of the individual, ownership in fee would assign the entire bundle to the private landowner. In practice, however, several sticks can be taken from the bundle without compensation through public regulation. The community's prerogative to eliminate nuisance activities from private land, the power of government to levy property taxes, and its ability to enforce preventive zoning measures in the interest of the public welfare are common examples of sticks that can be withdrawn from private possession by the public. This diminution of rights is limited by the Fifth Amendment, under which, in the words of Oliver Wendell Holmes in *Pennsylvania Coal Company v. Mahon,* "When it reaches a certain magnitude, in most if not in all cases,

---

[4]Hugonis Grotii, *De Jure Belli et Pacis,* trans. William Whewell (1625; reprint, Cambridge: University Press, 1889), *lib.* III, *cap.* XX, sect. VII, 326.

[5]Grotius also required that the exercise of eminent domain be conditioned on public utility and compensation. *Sed ut id fiat ex vi supereminentis dominii, primum requiritur utilitas publica; deinde, ut si fieri potest compensatio fiat ei qui suum amisit, ex communi.* Ibid., *lib.* II, *cap.* XIV, sect. VII, 118–19.

[6]100 Mass. 544 (1868).

[7]160 U.S. 668 (1896).

[8]Note, however, that an owner who feels that government action has effectively deprived him of property value may be able to collect compensation by initiating "inverse condemnation" proceedings. See, e.g., *United States v. Causby,* 328 U.S. 256 (1946), in which the owner of a chicken farm was awarded compensation because the glide path of aircraft using a neighboring airfield leased by the government was found to effect a virtual "taking" of his property. Noise from frequent, low flights over the farm not only disturbed the farmer's home but also caused some of his chickens to kill themselves by flying into the walls of their coops in fright.

there must be an exercise of eminent domain and compensation to sustain the act."[9]

Though the police power and eminent domain are traditionally considered discrete authorities, legal scholars suggest a middle or third alternative that combines qualities of both. In searching for legal means to preserve open space in metropolitan areas, University of Pennsylvania law professors Jan Z. Krasnowiecki and James C. N. Paul write,

> We began by analyzing conventional techniques under the police and eminent domain powers, conclude that they are either inadequate or too expensive for these purposes, and suggest that it is time to stop viewing police power and eminent domain as two mutually distinct, independent and exclusive ways to secure the result desired.[10]

Traditional invocation of public authority in American planning has been described as an "either-or" and "all-or-nothing" proposition. Daniel R. Mandelker is cited as deploring "the American dualism of police power (no compensation)—eminent domain (full compensation)."[11] Taking much the same viewpoint, Richard F. Babcock points out that under the police power of zoning, either the city wins and a proposed development is absolutely prevented, or the city loses and the development proceeds regardless of its impact on the community.[12] Likewise, in considering the exercise of eminent domain, the Court in *Berman* was confronted with an apparently black or white choice: either permit Urban Renewal through expropriation in fee or disallow condemnation and prevent the public improvement. In the context of zoning, Babcock writes: "As attorney for community or developer in a lawsuit, I have often wished for some judicial technique to impose an easement on the property which would limit the use to that intended by the municipality and for which limitation the village would pay."[13] In much the same way, planning critic William H. Whyte observes of eminent domain as a method of conserving open space: "But we do not need to buy up the land to save it. There is a middle way. Through the ancient device of the easement, we can acquire from owner a right in his property—the right that it remain open and undeveloped."[14]

It is significant that the process of eminent domain can be used to expropriate not only fee simple, or all the sticks in a private bundle, but just

[9]260 U.S. 393 (1922), 413.

[10]Jan Z. Krasnowiecki and James C. N. Paul, "The Preservation of Open Space in Metropolitan Areas," *U. of Pennsylvania L. Rev.* 110 (1961).

[11]Daniel R. Mandelker, as quoted by Fred. P. Bosselman, "The Third Alternative in Zoning Litigation," *Zoning Digest* 17, no. 3 (1965), 78.

[12]Richard F. Babcock, *The Zoning Game* (Madison: U. of Wisconsin Press, 1969), 168.

[13]Ibid., 169.

[14]William H. Whyte, *The Last Landscape* (Garden City, N.Y.: Doubleday, 1968), 79.

the sticks or rights necessary to permit the public purpose to be accomplished. In other words, condemnation can be partial, with public acquisition of only those specific property interests required of the task at hand. Compensable regulation might be used to carry out such regulations as the imposition of an especially restrictive land-use rule, the taking of a scenic easement, or the enforcement of a design control that exceeds the constitutional limits of the police power. The amount of compensation would be determined by the difference between the value of the property under the most stringent police-power regulation and its value under the new restriction imposed under eminent domain. In suggesting this technique of compensable regulation as a method of gaining social control of urban space, Charles M. Haar writes: "Compensation allows greater, more intimate, and additional individual controls. There is a growing recognition that the money lubricant needs to be added to the machinery of land use controls in order to achieve greater flexibility."[15] Compensation would not only allow greater flexibility and range in controls for planners but would further provide greater equity for affected property owners. Writes Fred P. Bosselman,

> The run-of-the-mill zoning case involves no intangible civil rights, such as freedom of speech, but only a man's right not to have the value of his property unreasonably depreciated. This property right, unlike most other constitutional rights, can be translated into cash. In perhaps four out of five of the zoning disputes now won by the builder, he could have been compensated without allowing him to construct the building he desired. He could have been paid damages.[16]

THE HISTORIC PATH OF EMINENT DOMAIN CONTROLS

Though half forgotten, the legal foundations of this third or middle alternative for planning control are not new. The roots can be traced to the same early era when such established police-power controls as building height and setback regulations and zoning first originated. One might compare the development of the police power and the power of eminent domain to two parallel yet distinct pathways, both leading to public planning controls. Both are marked with similar milestones denoting their evolution in case law.

In 1903, six years before ruling in *Welch v. Swasey*[17] to uphold the police-power regulation of building heights, the Supreme Court in *William*

---

[15]Charles M. Haar, "The Social Control of Urban Space," in *Cities and Space: the Future Use of Urban Land,* ed. Lowdon Wingo, Jr. (Baltimore: Johns Hopkins Press, 1963), 217.

[16]Bosselman, "The Third Alternative," 74.

[17]214 U.S. 91 (1909).

v. Parker[18] approved a pair of Massachusetts rulings that found eminent domain to be a valid method of limiting building heights "to preserve the architectural symmetry of Copley Square" in Boston. Said the state court in *Attorney General v. Williams,*[19]

> We hold that the statute gives rights in the nature of an easement over lands facing Copley Square, which easement is annexed to the square for the benefit of the public for whose use and enjoyment Copley Square was laid out, and that these rights are similar in their nature to rights in highways, in great ponds, and in the navigable waters of the commonwealth.[20]

Likewise in 1923, four years prior to the Supreme Court ruling in *Gorieb v. Fox*[21] that approved a regulation for buildings to be set back from the property line, the Missouri high court in *Kansas City v. Liebi*[22] authorized a municipal ordinance that also established building setbacks, with provisions for compensation.

Just as police-power zoning is based on the precedent case of *Euclid v. Ambler,*[23] so zoning under the power of eminent domain has an analogous precedent in case law. Almost a half century after *Euclid* had well established zoning under the police power, the Missouri court, in *City of Kansas City v. Kindle,* ruled to uphold zoning through eminent domain. The 1969 case involved the rezoning of an area containing multifamily occupancy to permit only single-family homes, an action that would have caused some property owners financial loss. The court commented,

> Zoning with compensation is a joint exercise of the power of eminent domain and the police power. It is zoning with extraordinary consideration for the property owners involved for it compensates those whose property rights are taken in the process, whereas in conventional zoning the individual who suffers hardship because of special circumstances receives no compensation.[24]

The municipal motive in providing compensation in eminent domain proceedings does not necessarily stem from altruism, however, for the paying of damages can substantially increase the public authority beyond the constitutional limits of the police power. Obviously, the range of the pathway of compensable regulation can far outdistance police-power controls, with

[18]188 U.S. 491 (1903).
[19]55 N.E. 77 (Mass., 1899), 59 N.E. 812 (Mass., 1901).
[20]Ibid., 55 N.E. 79.
[21]274 U.S. 603 (1927).
[22]252 S.W. 404 (Mo., 1923).
[23]272 U.S. 365 (1926).
[24]446 S.W. 2d 807 (Mo., 1969), 813.

the only limitations being the public willingness and ability to pay. W. Paul Gormley observes,

> Such a practice will assure "just" compensation; but the power of government to seize property for aesthetic reasons will thereby become almost unlimited. A public use, in the traditional sense, no longer need be proven. Consequently, at least one conclusion is inescapable; the award of compensation renders the taking legal.[25]

While admitting the legality of this method of extending the public authority, Gormley cautions that the combining of characteristics of eminent domain with the police power through compensation can seriously erode individual rights in property. However, it can also be argued that the reality of limits in the public fisc would prohibit extensive misuse.

Although municipal acquisition of design-control interest in private property is probably feasible in most states under existing eminent domain laws, specific state enabling legislation does exist. A 1915 Minnesota law explicitly provides for planning controls based on the power of eminent domain.[26] Upon petition of 50 percent of the affected landowners, cities of the first class in the state may establish "restricted residence districts"[27] that would prohibit the building, alteration, or repair of certain building types. The statute states,

> The council shall first, after causing the probable costs of the proceedings, if abandoned, to be deposited or secured by the petitioners, designate the restricted residence district *and shall have power to acquire by eminent domain the right to exercise the powers granted* [emphasis added] by [statute] by proceedings hereinafter defined, and when such proceedings shall have been completed, the right to exercise such powers shall be invested in the city.[28]

It should be noted that the object of condemnation in the law is neither title nor an easement in the traditional sense, but "the right to exercise the powers granted," namely, the ability to exercise control over development. In this broad provision, the early Minnesota act differs from most subsequent enabling legislative provisions, which ordinarily refer to a specific acquired interest in property, such as a restrictive easement. Still the 1915 act withstood its first challenge four years after its passage in the case of

[25]W. Paul Gormley, "Urban Development to Further Aesthetic Considerations: The Changing Constitutional Concepts of Police Power and Eminent Domain," *North Dakota L. Rev.* 41, no. 3 (1965), 332.
[26]Minn. Laws, 1915, Ch. 128, Sect. 2.
[27]Minn. Stat. Ann., Sect. 462.12.
[28]Ibid., Sect. 462.13.

State ex rel. Twin City Building and Investment Co. v. Houghton,[29] although only upon reversal. At first, the Minnesota court divided 3-2 against enforcement of the statute to prevent the construction of an apartment building in a designated residential district. The court did not rule directly on the validity of this "ingeniously drastic statute" but said: "It is not believed that the public welfare can be promoted by such legislation."[30] In his dissent, Justice Andrew Holt retorted, "It is about time that courts recognize the aesthetic as a factor in the affairs of life."[31] After rehearing, the majority shifted in favor of the statute's validity, and Holt had the opportunity to affirm his view.[32] In its concern for zoned land use, the second *Houghton* case invoked the planning power of eminent domain in much the same manner that *Euclid* would later invoke the police power.

Much of the controversy in *Houghton* focused on the term "public use" as used in the Fifth Amendment and in the Minnesota state constitution. The first court disallowed an interpretation of the term that would permit compensable regulation, stating,

> By the condemnation which the statute provides neither the city nor the general public gets a physical use of the condemned premises. . . . The so-called use is negative; it prevents an otherwise lawful use by the owner and in no other way is it a use at all.[33]

In a reversal of this attitude, the second court said,

> The notion of what is public use changes from time to time. Public use expands with the new needs created by the advance of civilization and the modern tendency of the people to crowd into large cities. Such a taking as here proposed could not possibly have been thought a taking for public use at the time of the adoption of our Constitution when the state was practically a wilderness without a single city worthy of the name. The term "public use" is flexible, and cannot be limited to the public use known at the time of the forming of the Constitution.
>
> What constitutes a public use at the time it is sought to exercise the power of eminent domain is the test. The Constitution is as it was when adopted; but, when it employs terms which change in definition as conditions change, it refers to them in the sense in which they are meant when the protection of the Constitution is sought.[34]

---

[29]174 N.W. 885 (Minn., 1919).
[30]Ibid., 888, 887.
[31]Ibid., 888.
[32]176 N.W. 159 (Minn., 1920).
[33]Note 29, 887.
[34]Note 32, 161. Quoting *Stewart v. Great Northern Ry. Co.,* 68 N.W. 208 (Minn., 1896), 209.

As *Houghton* exemplifies, interpretation of the term "public use" as the basis for exercising eminent domain has undergone the same intensive scrutiny as the term "public necessity," applied to police power. In both contexts, the applicability of the concept has expanded substantially as a result of the ever-increasing exigencies of the public welfare. In 1922, the Supreme Court in *Joslin Manufacturing Company v. City of Providence* stated,

> That the necessity and expediency of taking of property for public use is a legislative and not a judicial question is not open to discussion. Neither is it any longer open to question in this court that the legislative may confer upon a municipality the authority to determine such necessity for itself.
>
> The question is purely political, does not require a hearing, and is not the subject of judicial inquiry.[35]

By the time of the *Berman* and *Kindle* cases, the term "public use" had been broadened from actual physical "use by the public" to encompass concepts of "public purpose," "public benefit," and "public advantage."[36] As Gormley observes,

> The power of eminent domain contains a two-fold limitation; just compensation must be paid, and the property cannot be taken unless it is seized for a public use. In fact, the concept has been stretched to such an extreme position that the requirements of public use no longer exists; and seizure is justified if only the public purpose test has been met.[37]

CONDEMNING CONTROL EASEMENTS

Since the early adoption and use of the eminent domain act in Minnesota, other states have passed legislation specifically to enable condemnation of partial interest in land for the purpose of compensable regulation. The interest acquired is alternatively called "development rights," "interests less than fee simple," "restrictions," "covenants," "air rights," "scenic easements," "conservation easements," or "protective easements." It states,

> Without limitation of the definition of "lands" herein, the commissioner may acquire, or approve grants to assist a local unit to acquire . . . an interest or right consisting, in whole or in part, of *a restriction on the use of land by*

[35]262 U.S. 668 (1922), 678.
[36]Philip Nichols, *The Law of Eminent Domain* (1909; reprint, New York: Bender, 1983), vol. 2A, sect. 7.02, 7.23–7.43.
[37]Gormley, "Urban Development," 320.

others including owners of other interests therein [emphasis added]; such interest or right sometimes known as a "conservation easement."[38]

The preservation of historic and other landmark buildings is a function for which compensable regulation has prime applicability. The New York City landmark preservation law allows the public to acquire specified interest in historic buildings for preservation. The interest may be

> any right or interest in or title to an improvement parcel or any part thereof,
> including but not limited to, fee title and *scenic or other easements* [emphasis
> added], the acquisition of which by the city is determined by the commission
> to be necessary and appropriate.[39]

To preserve the beauty and integrity of the urban design character around the state house and other nearby governmental properties at the state capital of Annapolis, the Maryland code specifically permits the state to acquire, through condemnation if necessary, "architectural easements" to prevent private owners from undertaking development that, in the judgment of the board of public works, "would be detrimental to the architectural and scenic beauty of the property and of the specified area."[40]

Beyond its use in landmark preservation, the acquisition of easements to control or restrict development bordering scenic rural highways is probably the most common application of condemnation of less-than-fee interest in land. This technique has been employed to regulate agricultural and low-density residential use, to prohibit other building uses, billboards, and junkyards, and to prevent the destruction of trees and other vegetation on privately owned land, that scenic beauty may be maintained to an extent not otherwise possible. The provision of compensation virtually negates most arguments opposing similar regulation based on the police power.

The state with the greatest experience in the use of scenic easements is Wisconsin. In planning its segment of the Great River Road, which follows the Mississippi from Lake of the Woods in Canada to New Orleans, the state instituted a program of acquiring easements that would enforce the preservation of the natural beauty along the roadway without displacing the farmlands adjacent to the right-of-way. The idea was that this acquisition of partial interest would enable the existing land uses to be maintained and would also permit substantial public savings in acquisitions in fee—a basic rationale for any such venture in compensable regulation. In 1966, in *Kamrowski v. State,* the Wisconsin Supreme Court upheld this method of

[38]N.J. Stat. Ann., Sect. 13: 8A–12.
[39]New York, N.Y., Admin. Code, Ch. 8–A, Sect. 207–1.0b.
[40]Md. Ann. Code, Art 78A, Sect. 14c.

control. It rejected the plaintiff's contention that public enjoyment of scenic beauty along a roadway is not a public use required for exercise of eminent domain, concurring instead with the lower court's finding that "the 'occupancy' is visual."[41] The court succinctly summarized the basic argument for compensated controls as follows:

> Whatever may be the law with respect to zoning restrictions based upon aesthetic considerations, a stronger argument can be made in support of the power to take property, in return for just compensation, in order to fulfill aesthetic concepts, than for imposition of police power restrictions for such purposes.[42]

The National Park Service has also had some experience in the use of scenic easements to preserve natural beauty along highways. In developing the Blue Ridge Parkway in Virginia and North Carolina and the Natchez Trace Parkway in Tennessee, Alabama, and Mississippi, the Park Service originally expected to use scenic easements extensively to preserve scenic beauty along the routes. However, because of difficulties in obtaining injunctive authority to prevent property owners from engaging in such violations of the compensated restrictions as the cutting down of trees, the Park Service eventually discontinued acquiring easements and instead settled for fee acquisitions of smaller areas of land. Despite this experience, several states, besides Wisconsin, that participated in the Great River Road project have authorized acquisition of scenic easements adjacent to federally funded highways. Since 1964 and the construction of the Blue Ridge and Natchez Trace Parkways, the use of scenic easements has apparently improved, and a number of federal parkways have used easements to preserve natural scenery, notably at the Ozarks Riverways, Cumberland Gap, Harper's Ferry, Manassas, Piscataway near Mount Vernon, and the George Washington National Park in Virginia.

Despite its notable approval of scenic easements, the court in *Kamrowski* also pointed to a limitation on the flexibility of controls gained through compensation, a limitation not far removed from a restriction that binds the police power. Compensation, the court implied, does not obviate the need for the "fair certainty" that Hayek prescribed as a requirement of the Rule of Law. The nature and extent of acquired rights in property must be explicitly defined. The court said,

> More importantly, however, we consider that the concept of preserving a scenic corridor along a parkway, with its emphasis upon maintaining a rural

---

[41]142 N.W. 2d 793 (Wisc., 1966), 797.
[42]Ibid.

scene and preventing unsightly uses is sufficiently definite so that the legislature may be said to have made a meaningful decision in terms of public purposes, *and to have fixed a standard which sufficiently guides the commission in performing its task* [emphasis added].[43]

In other words, both the rights taken and the price to the public must be specific and clear. Haar refers to "the money lubricant . . . to achieve greater flexibility." Flexibility gained through compensation must be understood as only an increase in range over the police power, not a blanket acquisition of autocratic ad hoc discretionary power. As in the case of police-power zoning, clear standards are necessary for controls secured through eminent domain. A lack of sufficient guidelines can invalidate otherwise reasonable controls acquired through condemnation.

In the 1922 case of *Pontiac Improvement Co. v. Board of Commissioners of Cleveland Metropolitan Park Dist.,* the Ohio court recognized the public right to condemn less-than-fee interest in land but ruled against condemnation in the case, which it ruled "void for vagueness." Said the court,

> In this case, the rights and privileges which are sought to be secured are not certain, and their exercise by the board would be entirely indefinite. The right to regulate and control, the right to prevent certain things, such as the erection of fences, walls, structures, etc., when conferred upon the park board, is not of such a character as to inform the owner of the property as to what has been taken away from him or what uses it would be safe for him to make of his property in the future.[44]

Just as police-power regulations should aim at clarity and be founded on a comprehensive plan, controls obtained through eminent domain must follow the same stricture, notwithstanding the greater range made possible through compensation. Krasnowiecki and Paul make the following summary of the flexibility in controls derived through eminent domain:

> The point of all this is that there are strong indications in the law of restrictive covenants that flexible restrictions, depending for their definition on the exercise of somebody's discretion, will not be enforced by the courts unless there is a definite community scheme applicable to a described area which can supply a standard against which the exercises of discretion involved can be measured.[45]

[43]Ibid.
[44]135 N.E. 635 (1922), 640.
[45]Krasnowiecki and Paul, "Preservation of Open Space," 194.

APPLICATION OF COMPENSABLE REGULATION

In a 1961 article, "The Preservation of Open Space in Metropolitan Areas,"[46] Professors Krasnowiecki and Paul propose a technique of land reservation through compensation that would supersede the police-power method of official mapping. The principle that they suggest could have diverse applications in urban design and planning control besides open-space preservation, ranging from land-use restrictions to architectural controls. Compensation would permit regulation to be more restrictive than police-power measures yet also provide equity for owners of regulated property. Rather than the norm of outright purchase of fee or of easements, however, Krasnowiecki and Paul advocate a system of financial guarantees.

According to the scheme, at the time an area is selected for preservation or future development as public open space, affected properties would be assessed to ascertain their fee value at that date. Property owners would then be guaranteed receipt of the full assessed value of their properties upon sale. If the property was sold for less than its assessed value, the public would pay the owner the difference as compensation. To prevent the possibility of fraudulently depreciated sales to take unfair advantage of the guarantee, sale prices would be arrived at through administered public sales. The proposal includes other detailed considerations, such as adjustments for changes in monetary values between the time of assessment and actual sale.

The authors believe that the scheme, though largely conceptual, offers advantages over condemnation of development rights for its avoidance of a concentration of compensation costs in the initial period of regulation. The proposal also overcomes possible overevaluation of development values sometimes attendant to less-than-fee acquisitions, since assessments, guarantees, and sales are all in terms of fee values. The fact that only one assessment of initial property values is necessary is believed to be a considerable administrative advantage. It would obviate the need for assessors to determine the actual value of alienated property interests, which could involve complex speculation on the extent and the effect of controls. Furthermore, the guarantee of assessed value at the initiation of controls would allow any appreciation of properties to reduce or negate the expense of compensation, while permitting the private owner to profit from speculative increases in value above the guarantee.

In an article Krasnowiecki later wrote with Ann Louise Strong, a lawyer and planning professor at the University of Pennsylvania who had also collaborated on the scheme, they admit that the guarantee system "has been

[46]Ibid.

attacked for its complexity in administration."[47] However, it should also be recognized that any system of controls that strives for equity is bound to be more complicated than the decrees issued under the police power or wholesale acquisitions of fee title through traditional condemnation.

A more serious problem that Krasnowiecki and Paul recognize and that any such innovative concept of controls would face is not legal but rather political and social in nature. They write,

> One may expect misunderstanding or hostility as a reaction to proposals which envision broadened government ownership or control of land, for it may be one thing to reserve open space of immediate development of some traditional public facility, but it is quite another matter to reserve it—at public expense but without public possession—simply to promote aesthetics and to control the forces of private development now and for the indefinite future. Notwithstanding precedent in the redevelopment field, this technique of land use control may appear to many to be a radical departure.[48]

Indeed, when Ann Strong and John C. Keene, also a lawyer and a professor of planning at Pennsylvania, led a sponsored effort in 1968 to institute a similarly creative scheme of compensable regulation, public reaction resulted in the ultimate rejection of their proposal. Their scheme, *The Plan and Program for the Brandywine*,[49] included a panoply of public works and planning programs designed to combine rational development of the rural region of the Brandywine Creek in eastern Pennsylvania with preservation of the natural resources of the watershed. With early awareness that distrust of its innovative management techniques would make public acceptance of the plan difficult, the planners decided to forego the eminent domain powers that were originally contemplated in hopes that negotiated purchase of conservation easements would be sufficient to secure the required restrictions on private development. Compensation to owners of regulated land was to range up to 90 percent of fee value, depending on the property and the easement required. Because of the experimental and unique nature of the program, compensation funds would not have come from local revenues, as would be the norm, but from state and federal sources as well as from private foundations underwriting the plan. Though the program held great benefits for the region and would later be described

---

[47]Jan Z. Krasnowiecki and Ann L. Strong, "Compensable Regulations for Open Space," *Journal of the American Institute of Planners* (May 1963), 94.

[48]Krasnowiecki and Paul, "Preservation of Open Space," 209.

[49]Institute for Environmental Studies. *The Plan and Program for the Brandywine* (Philadelphia: Institute for Environmental Studies, Regional Science Research Institute, U.S. Geological Survey, 1968).

by one commentator as "an almost perfect plan,"[50] it was nonetheless rejected by the Brandywine community.

In a post-mortem analysis of the plan and its rejection, Keene and Strong point to the subscription of local officials to "the Jeffersonian principle that government governs best which governs least,"[51] and the local perception of property in terms of Blackstone's ideals. They write,

> Many Brandywine residents think of property as a concrete, tangible thing. It is a specific piece of land, a home, a sacred enclave completely subject to the owner. To them, the "bundle of rights" concepts of property is hypertheoretical and unacceptable. It has implications that seem somehow subversive of the established order. They do not accept the fact that the township supervisors, through the use of zoning and subdivision regulations, are empowered to limit significantly the ways in which landowners may use their land. For these people, ownership is virtually an absolute right to do with the land as one wishes and anything diminishing that right is at least wrong and probably unconstitutional. Certainly, the originally proposed use of eminent domain was anathema to many as a matter of principle.[52]

The residents apparently felt that conservation easements amounted to joint ownership of land with the government rather than regulation with compensation. Keene and Strong commented: "The very idea of sharing ownership with a government agency was to some as distasteful as sharing one's wife with the township engineer."[53] The authors also saw a disparity in perception of the plan's intent in paying compensation. Whereas the planners believed that compensation would be a fair solution to the constitutional problem of police-power implementation of a plan, area residents saw compensated controls only as an usurpation of their private property rights. Charles M. Haar identifies a view that "a 'little' government control may do as much violence to principles as laissez faire, and even more to principles of equality, than would a 'lot'."[54] The "little" sharing of property rights with government seemed repugnant to opponents of the Brandywine program, perhaps even more than would police-power zoning measures or even condemnation of fee title.

The rejection of the Brandywine plan should not be lightly dismissed

[50]Peter Thompson, "Brandywine Basin: Defeat of an Almost Perfect Plan," *Land-Use Controls Quarterly* 3, no. 2 (1969), 29.

[51]John C. Keene and Ann Louise Strong, "The Brandywine Plan," *Journal of the American Institute of Planners* 36, no. 1 (Jan. 1970), 55.

[52]Ibid., 56.

[53]Ibid.

[54]Charles M. Haar, *Law and Land,* (Cambridge: Harvard U. Press and M.I.T. Press, 1964), 252.

by urban planners and designers as the action of an ignorant, rural populace. In any city or suburb where innovative urban design or planning is attempted, the political and social forces at work at Brandywine would likely be present also. From their experience, Keene and Strong offer advice to proponents of any innovative technique of planning control, whether in environmental management or urban design. First, they advocate, sufficient time must be allowed to educate and win the endorsement of the constituency; second, positive inducements must be apparent to counter the spectre of negative restrictions; third, the strangeness of the program must be dispelled by proceeding initially at a small and experimental scale; and finally, the objectives and processes of the program must remain flexibile and not appear overwhelming. The authors observe that the Brandywine project, "with its heavy baggage of legal, hydrological, financial and research goals, was probably overloaded."[55]

Whatever the sociopolitical difficulties encountered in the implementation of compensable land-use regulation, there has been a revitalized interest in this technique of public planning in the second half of the twentieth century. This renewed attention contrasts to the neglect accorded compensable regulation from the mid 1920s to the 1950s. During this early period, the widening path of zoning and building regulation under the police power virtually obliterated any trace of the alternate route of compensable regulation, even though the foundations of both had been laid during the same era. In 1936, Edward Bassett, a pioneer of police-power zoning said,

> No effective zoning plan could be accomplished by the exercise of eminent domain. If there were some diminution of the full use of property, the city would need to pay the loss to the private owner. This would mean a laborious and expensive proceeding for almost every parcel of land. Since the City could not afford to pay this cost out of public funds, but would need to assess the awards on the property benefited, the cost of the process would be enormous. The restrictions would consist of public easements of a permanent nature. But as every living organism grows and changes, these easements would have to be changed from time to time by successive applications of condemnation. The method would be clumsy and ineffective. Some states in their zoning enabling acts have tried to provide for the employment of eminent domain in whole or part, but the attempts have never been successful.[56]

Even as late as 1968, Robert M. Anderson, author of the treatise *American Law of Zoning,* wrote of the 1915 Minnesota act providing for planning control under eminent domain,

[55]Keene and Strong, "Brandywine Plan," 58.
[56]Edward M. Bassett, *Zoning* (NewYork: Russell Sage, 1936), 27.

This technique for limiting the use of land through the creation of residential districts, piecemeal and at the instance of residents, was approved by the courts, but it was a practical failure. Its objectives were limited, its machinery was cumbersome, and it was expensive. The failure of this early attempt to zone through eminent domain prompted adverse comment, and little use was made of this power until urban redevelopment became an important tool in the implementation of community plans.

It seems unlikely that efforts to employ the power of eminent domain to restrict land use played any significant role in the early development of comprehensive zoning other than the negative one of demonstrating that this tool was not adequate.[57]

While the subordinate role of compensable regulation must be attributed at least in part to the seeming economy of the police power, which places no apparent burden on the public fisc, the difficulty encountered in implementing compensable regulation is not so much its financial demands, legality, or complexity. Rather, as the Brandywine experience shows, it is the natural tendency of people to fear and reject anything new that contravenes accustomed practices, particularly when it involves unfamiliar public restraints affecting the value of their property. In Great Britain, where compensated regulation of land development is the norm, this method of control is accepted with no more misgivings than is zoning under the police power in the United States.

Although compensable land-use regulation enjoys little more than experimental status in contemporary American planning, its potential has been well recognized in the search for more flexible, far-reaching, and equitable methods of development controls. The 1976 *Model Land Development Code*[58] of the American Law Institute, the most extensive attempt at comprehensive reform since the original Standard Enabling Acts, includes the acquisition of less-than-fee interest in land as an integral part of its suggested provisions for public land acquisition. If adopted, the fifth article of the code would authorize a local land planning agency to exercise eminent domain, if necessary to achieve a variety of planning objectives. These objectives may include environmental protection, historic and recreational open-space preservation, development of public facilities, and prevention of natural disasters. Two purposes for which acquisition of interest may have specific urban design applicability are separately enumerated in the code. The first is preserving and improving landmark buildings and preservation districts. The second is "facilitating development or conserva-

[57]Robert M. Anderson, *American Law of Zoning* (Rochester, N.Y.: Lawyers Cooperative, 1968), vol. 1, sect. 3.05, 82.

[58]American Law Institute, *A Model Land Development Code Complete Text and Commentary* (Philadelphia: American Law Institute, 1976).

tion of a specially planned area designated by the local government if the acquisition is consistent with a precise plan.''[59] This language seems expressly suited to implementing an urban design plan through compensable acquisition of design interest in private property.

PUBLIC RECAPTURE OF COMPENSATION COSTS

By practical necessity, a principal consideration in any contemplated use of compensable land-use regulation is the public cost of the compensation itself. In the scheme suggested by Krasnowiecki and Paul, the cost of compensation is an integral consideration in the concept; in the Brandywine case, because of the innovative nature of the program, the planners were able to enlist sources outside the local community to cover the cost of compensation—a luxury that seldom is afforded. Considering the complexity of the legal and economic issues involved, it may be appropriate to examine in historic and general terms the basis for public recoupment of compensation expenditures.

In an 1829 federal case, *Chesapeake and Ohio Canal Co. v. Key,* just compensation was interpreted to be "a compensation that would be just in regard to the public as well as in regard to the individual."[60] In 1955, another federal court reiterated the constitutional obligation to protect the public interest as well as the private individual.

> On the one hand it contemplates that the monies paid into the common Treasury by the taxpayers shall be jealously guarded as a public trust against unfounded and unjust claims. On the other, it guarantees that the Government, having regard for the rights and welfare of its citizens and respect for the restraints on its authority, shall deal fairly and equitably with each of them.[61]

This dual obligation was a factor in the three historic urban renewal projects discussed in chapter 1: the rebuilding of Rome; the reconstruction of London after the Great Fire; and Haussmann's redesign of Paris during the Second Empire. The ambitious scope of the last project was diminished for lack of foresight; no prudent consideration had been made of the ramifications of compensation for public acquisition of private property. In a study of the history of the development of Paris, Jean Bastie wrote:

> The Council of State, the Supreme Court of Appeal and the expropriation committees were over generous to the landowners. Expropriations meant

[59]Ibid., sect. 5-106, 182.
[60]*Chesapeake and Ohio Canal Co. v. Key,* 5 Fed. Cas. 563 (No. 2,649) (C.C.D.C., 1829), 564.
[61]*United States v. One Parcel of Land,* 131 F. Supp. 443 (1955), 445.

overnight fortunes for many owners, the more so as they recovered that part of their land not required for public services, which has gained considerably in value. But the higher than expected cost of the expropriations and of the works prevented Haussmann from constructing at least a third of the roads he had planned.[62]

Two distinct aspects of compensation had been slighted in the redevelopment of Paris. First, compensations paid for expropriated properties were excessive. Second, though less apparent, increases in the value of neighboring real estate caused by the public improvement, including rises in the value of properties of which a portion had been acquired and paid for from public funds, were not recovered by the state. In the earlier reconstruction of Rome, the Pope had recognized the windfall appreciation in the value of neighboring properties caused by his planning project and laid claim to the gain as being caused by public action. Writes Lewis Mumford,

> Pope Sixtus IV in 1480 wisely met this [cost of city redevelopment] by imposing an extra charge on property owners who profited by improvements made in their neighborhood. Unfortunately, this sound procedure, like his other remarkable innovations—the condemning of private land for such public purposes as street widening—was not taken up seriously by the municipalities till the end of the nineteenth century.[63]

Actually, condemnation of private property for public purposes and the accounting of benefits accorded to individual properties by such public enterprises were considered in England during the rebuilding of London under Charles II. Steen Eiler Rasmussen writes,

> Much can be learnt from the way in which the project was intended to be carried out. As was promised in the King's proclamation, the rights of the owners before the fire were to be respected and no one wished to make any alteration in them. It was, however, evident that some changes must take place and that it must be possible for the City to buy ground which, on account of its situation, formed an obstacle in the way of a favourable project. Where this was the case, an impartial jury was appointed to judge its value and the town had to pay the private owner. At the same time it became evident that the plan was to the advantage of many of the landlords, and consequently they had to pay to the community which had occasioned the rise in values.[64]

---

[62]Jean Bastie, "The Paris Area—Growth and Organization," *Urbanization in France* (Paris: International Federation for Housing and Planning, Centre de Recherche d'Urbanisme 1968), 46.

[63]Lewis Mumford, *The City in History* (New York: Harcourt, Brace and World, Harbinger 1961), 393.

[64]Steen Eiler Rasmussen, *London: The Unique City* (Cambridge: M.I.T. Press, 1934, ed. 1967), 119.

Where a public planning program is successful in creating social benefits, a distinction can be drawn in apportioning its cost between those "general" benefits that are enjoyed by the community as a whole and "special" benefits that accrue to particular property owners in the program area. In the first instance, the cost to the public is normally met through general revenues assessed from the entire community; in the second case, the cost may be distributed to the beneficiary landowners in proportion to the special advantage received. If the desirability and market value of particular properties at a project location are significantly enhanced as a result of public expenditures for a new roadway access, for example, or for an urban design program, it is appropriate for the public to lay claim to the special values that it has created that are over and above the advantages enjoyed and paid for by the community at large.

Where individual landowners stand to reap a windfall at public expense, there are three basic approaches to reducing or recapturing the public expenditure, including compensation paid for a regulatory program. The first is to set off special benefits from awards for compensation or damages; the second is to impose special tax assessments on properties deriving special benefits; the third is to recoup benefits through a tax on increases in property value caused by the program.

When a program, as for design controls, imposes a restriction or seizes an easement that lessens the value of an individual property, just compensation is due. But if the program succeeds in its objective of area-wide improvement through stringent, compensable regulation of all land in the vicinity, then the value of all properties in the area is often increased, notwithstanding the restriction. (This rationale is, after all, a proven principle behind all Euclidean zoning.) In such an instance, the increase in value of a regulated property that is caused by the program can properly be set off against the compensation required for the restriction. Charles Haar writes of an analogous situation:

> Frequently, the same piece of property may be both benefited and damaged by an improvement, a fact which, if not considered in fixing the award, results in unfairness. The classic case is the taking of part of a farm on the outskirts of the city for a highway. The public pays for the land taken and also for damages to the remaining property because of the severance. Then the road is built, making subdivision or commercial development feasible, so that the value of the remaining land is in fact increased, not diminished. This has led to the rule in some states that benefits accruing to property may be deducted from any award made for damages.[65]

In considering a similar situation in which compensation was due for land taken for a highway, the Supreme Court in *Bauman v. Ross* said,

[65]Haar, *Law and Land,* 282.

When part only of a parcel is taken for a highway, the value of that part is not the sole measure of the compensation or damages to be paid to the owner, but the incidental injury or benefit to the part not taken is also considered. When the part not taken is left in such shape or condition as to be in itself of less value than before, the owner is entitled to additional damages on that account. *When, on the other hand, the part which he retains is specially and directly increased in value by the public improvement, the damages to the whole parcel by the appropriation of part of it are lessened* [emphasis added].[66]

However logical and persuasive this argument, it should be emphasized that the complexity of practical issues surrounding the setting off of benefits is not diminished. Such questions as the distinction between "general" and "special" benefits and the valuation of property "before and after" a public program are often subject to controversy. Moreover, it should be noted that whereas Haar and the Court in the *Bauman* case both made reference to partial takings, the interest assumed in each case is fee title. There is considerably less experience when an interest is only a "design easement" or a planning restriction on land. The intangible quality of a design restriction, the speculative nature of a program's effects on property values, and the effect of external factors on those values are formidable questions of law, land economics, and real estate appraisal that must be addressed in determining the amount of compensation and benefit set-off in each situation. In addition to convincing the judiciary, there is also the problem of gaining community acceptance of any scheme utilizing compensation and set-off.

The second approach of special assessments to recapture public expenditures is more established and commonly accepted. By this method, the cost of a public undertaking that especially enhances the value of a particular property can be charged to the owner. The origins of this technique of public finance can be traced in old English law to an act of 1662 that authorized any excess cost for the widening of streets in Westminster to be recovered through assessments on properties in proportion to the benefits received. After the Great Fire, the act was amended to permit recapture of the public expense of repairs and improvements by making it lawful "to impose any reasonable tax upon all houses within the said city or liberties thereof, in proportion to the benefits they shall receive thereby."[67] The language of the 1667 act was later transported virtually word for word to the New World. A provincial act in 1691 allowed special assessments to be adopted to finance public works in the colonial settlement of New York. In discussing these historic laws, Edwin R. A. Seligman, a writer on taxation, noted that even earlier provisions to recapture the cost of public "better-

---

[66]167 U.S. 548 (1897), 574.
[67]19 Chas. 2, Ch. 3, Sect. 20 (1967). Amending 13 and 14 Chas. 2, Ch. 2, Sect. 29 (1662).

ments" existed in New Amsterdam, and that Dutch precedents for such assessments date to the sixteenth century.[68] Seligman also observed that the practice of special assessments is today more popularly employed in the United States than in Europe.

The Kansas City ordinance at issue in the *Liebi* case of 1923 provided that the cost of compensation to owners of regulated properties be raised in the area benefiting from the control. The court described the enactment as stating "that damage caused by the enforcement of the ordinance should be paid for by special assessment upon real property situated within the benefit district."[69] Just as the amount of compensation paid for regulation can vary from property to property in proportion to the easement taken or the restriction imposed, a special assessment can be levied in proportion to the special benefit received by each individual property within a program district. Assessments can be imposed on all property receiving benefits in an affected area, regardless of whether a property is involved in a regulatory taking. It is a commonly accepted method of recovering the cost of public improvements whose benefits fall especially on particular properties. As Philip Nichols notes in his authoritative treatise *The Law of Eminent Domain,*

> It is . . . almost everywhere held that an owner whose land has been taken for a public improvement is not exempt from a betterment assessment upon his remaining land based upon the benefit arising from the improvement for which his land was taken, even if the effect of the assessment is to swallow up his whole claim for compensation.[70]

Nevertheless, it is also prudent to heed the observations of such critics of compensable regulation as Bassett and Anderson, who note that a system requiring assessments of individual properties to recover the costs of restrictive easements would likely be complex and cumbersome.

The cost of compensable regulation might also be recovered through the comparatively new method of tax increment financing. This third means of recapture consists of levying a tax on incremental increases in land value caused by a publicly funded program. The technique makes possible public projects that otherwise would be difficult to implement because of high "front end" costs and benefits that accrue over a long term. Since the mid 1960s and the reduction of federal resources for such expensive local undertakings as urban redevelopment, tax increment financing has seen increasingly wide application as an alternative means for cities to fund capital im-

---

[68]Edwin R. A. Seligman, *Essays in Taxation* (1895; reprint, New York: Macmillan, 1928), 433–36.

[69]Note 22, 406. Citing Kansas City, Mo., Ordinance No. 39946, Sect. 5.

[70]Nichols, *Law of Eminent Domain,* vol. 3, sect. 8.2(1), 8–86.

provements. In California, for instance, the method has been available since 1952 but has been used extensively only since the drying up of federal funds.[71] Today, a vast majority of states have adopted legislation enabling the law.

In a designated program area where land values are expected to rise as a result of public investment, assessed valuations are "frozen" when the project is established, to determine the tax base already extant and not attributable to the undertaking. The frozen base then remains a revenue source for all previously existing ad valorem taxes. Thereafter, any appreciation of value that can be ascribed to the project and not to property improvements made by the owner is subject to a value increment tax, the proceeds of which are earmarked to retire the debts incurred by the public program. Unlike the special assessment, which is based on the cost of a public program, the value increment tax is related only to the benefit actually realized.

Describing as a "halfway house between the property tax and a user charge,"[72] the increment tax is advantageous in the equity that it provides both the public and the private owner. On the one hand, it allows communities to recapture the "unearned increment"[73] of increases in private land values that are a product of broad social factors of growth rather than the efforts of the individual owner. On the other, because the tax is levied on values in excess of the base determination, it avoids taxation of appreciation gained before the public program was enacted. Furthermore, the tax on actual increases in value places the burden of speculation on the benefits of a public program more fairly on the public, not on the private owner. As Dick Netzer, an authority on the economics of the property tax, notes, the land-value increment tax is more equitable than the special assessment to recoup the cost of a public improvement program, since "the tax is made only when and if land values do actually rise in response to the improvement, not in the cheerful expectation or desperate hope that land values may rise sometime in the future."[74] Because the tax is tied to the performance of a public investment, it is also capable of returning part of any speculative gains back to the public. If combined with a system of value guarantees, as suggested by Krasnowiecki and Paul, the tax could be levied on profits realized in sale of property that exceed the guaranteed value, making it an effective supplemental capital gains levy.

[71]Cal. Const., Art. 16, Sect. 16 (West's Supp. 1984) and Cal. Health & Safety Code, Sect. 33670.

[72]Dick Netzer, *Economics of the Property Tax* (Washington, D.C.: Brookings Institution, 1966), 213.

[73]Edwin H. Spengler, "The Taxation of Urban Land-Value Increments," *Journal of Land & Public Utility Economics* 17, no. 1 (Feb. 1941), 55.

[74]Netzer, *Economics of the Property Tax,* 213.

In addition to the system of value guarantees suggested by Krasnowiecki and Paul as well as other methods of compensable planning control and cost recapture are more recent innovations, such as the "windfall for wipeouts" technique devised by Donald G. Hagman and Dean J. Misczynski.[75] As noted in chapter 6, this method would place a tax on windfall rises of private values that are created by public planning action, to recover compensation made for value wipeouts caused by planning activities elsewhere.

BRITAIN REVISITED: PLANNING REGULATION AND COMPENSATION

In light of the consideration given in the early chapters to the English roots of American property and land-use law, it seems fitting to note the system of land-development regulation that has evolved in Great Britain. British planning controls today are based not on the police power, as in the United States, but on compensation. In this century public authority over land use and development in Britain has been acquired through a national program of expropriation of private development rights in land with compensation made to the owner.

There is a curious consistency between the idea of compensation and the nature of British society, which has survived in spite of radical evolutions in social ideology. It seems quite appropriate that a society that produced Blackstone, who wrote on the sanctity of private property, should require that compensation be returned to the owner to atone for the intrusion of government on the use of property. Ironically, however, Britain has since evolved from the era of Blackstone to become a nation considerably more receptive to social controls than are its former American colonies. The British concept of compensation has likewise adapted to accommodate the shift toward greater social authority; their system of compensable land-use regulation has, in fact, permitted far greater planning controls by the state than can be contemplated under the more limited American scheme traditionally based on the police power.

The epitome of compensable land-use regulation is embodied in the British Town and Country Planning Act of 1947.[76] Introduced by the socialist-oriented Labour Party, which governed Britain after the Second World War, the act was the principal tool used to carry out the *Greater London Plan, 1944,* and its companion, the *County of London Plan* of 1943 devised by Sir Patrick Abercrombie.[77] The conceptual basis for Abercrombie's plan

[75]Donald G. Hagman and Dean J. Misczynski, eds., *Windfall for Wipeouts: Land Value Capture and Compensation* (Washington: Planners Press, 1978).

[76]10 and 11 Geo. 6, Ch. 51 (1947).

[77]Patrick Abercrombie, *Greater London Plan, 1944* (London: HMSO, 1945). Patrick Abercrombie and John H. Forshaw, *County of London Plan* (London: Macmillan, 1943).

was the book *Garden Cities of Tomorrow,* written by Sir Ebenezer Howard at the turn of the century.[78]

Howard proposed that the overcrowding and squalor that had plagued England's central cities since the Industrial Revolution could be alleviated by directing the population expansion of the cities to small, self-sufficient "new towns" located as satellite communities within wide "green belts" of agricultural land surrounding the urban centers. Howard, a remarkable clerk-turned-planner, demonstrated the efficacy of his scheme by constructing, at his own initiative and without government assistance, the new garden cities of Letchworth and Welwyn outside London. Within a half-century, the idea of green belts and new towns had become the basis of official British urban-development policy and perhaps the most influential planning concept in the world.

Two studies were made by the British government during the war, the 1940 *Report of the Royal Commission on the Distribution of the Industrial Population,* known as the Barlow Report, and the 1942 *Report of the Committee on Utilisation of Land in Rural Areas,* known as the Scott Report.[79] These reports adopted the essence of Howard's concept of decentralization as the national policy for post-war urban reconstruction and became the official doctrines behind Abercrombie's plans.

A critical problem of the garden city concept was that of regulating land development, particularly the preservation of the agricultural green belts, where development was to be virtually prohibited. The natural course of urban growth is to expand into the less developed areas surrounding the central cities. Farm land becomes more valuable, not for its agricultural use but because of its potential for development. This economic tendency was recognized in the 1942 *Report of the Committee on Compensation and Betterment,* commonly known as the Uthwatt Report.[80] The report suggested that land value could be divided into two separate elements: first, the value attributed to its existing use, and second, the value of its potential for development into more profitable uses.

Following the general recommendations of the Uthwatt Committee, the Town and Country Planning Act of 1947 expropriated the second component of land value—the potential for development—from all land throughout England and Wales. This compulsory acquisition of development values by government effectively precluded conversion of privately held land to more intensive use and made real Howard's vision of urban

[78]Ebenezer Howard, *Garden Cities of Tomorrow* (1902; reprint, Cambridge: M.I.T. Press, 1965).

[79]Royal Commission on the Distribution of the Industrial Population, *Report* (Barlow Report) (London: HMSO, 1940), Cmnd. 6153. Committee on Utilisation of Land in Rural Areas, *Report,* (Scott Report) (London: HMSO, 1942), Cmnd. 6378.

[80]Expert Committee on Compensation and Betterment, *Final Report* (Uthwatt Report) (London: HMSO, 1942), Cmnd. 6386.

green belts. In exchange for compensation, the owners of land were forced to relinquish all future rights to develop, the act restricting land use to those existing prior to its enforcement. As a result of the legislation, any development proposal in Britain must first obtain "planning permission," not under the authority of the police power as in the United States, but through the right of state-acquired interest in property. The 1947 act defined "development" comprehensively as "the carrying out of building, engineering, mining or other operations in, on, over or under land, or the making of any material change in the use of any building or other land."[81]

Sir Desmond Heap, a leading authority on British land planning law, wrote as follows:

> The 1947 Act . . . contained some of the most drastic and far-reaching provisions ever enacted affecting the ownership of land . . . and the liberty of an owner to develop and use his land as he thinks fit. Indeed, after [enforcement of the act], ownership of land, generally speaking, carries with it nothing more than the bare right to go on using it for its existing purposes. The owner has no right to develop it, that is to say, he has no right to build upon it and no right even to change its use.[82]

The socialization of all development rights throughout England, Wales, and later Scotland conferred upon the British government virtually unlimited authority to plan and control development. Not only did the system of compensation make possible the establishment of green belts and new towns, it has also enabled the enforcement of public plans for urban design. Legislation subsequent to 1947 provided for definitive and systematic design control in urban areas selected for intensive change. In so-called urban "action areas," for example, development would typically be required to adhere to urban design schemes prepared by government planning authorities. Guidelines for urban design could take the form of detailed architectural plans and elevation drawings and even perspective sketches illustrating the design intent of the public planners. Before the granting of planning permission, the use and exterior appearance of proposed buildings would be subject to approval to ensure design compliance with official plans.

With the nationalization of all development value in land, planning authority in Britain is centralized. Thus, "local plans" concerning action areas, districts within a jurisdiction, or such special subjects as recreation or conservation are required to conform to broader, regional "structure plans" which in turn must be consistent with national planning goals and policies. Also in contrast with American practice, appeals from planning

---

[81]Town and Country Planning Act of 1947, note 76, Sect. 12(2).

[82]Desmond Heap, *An Outline of Planning Law* (London: Sweet and Maxwell, 1978), 13.

decisions are directed not to the courts but through the administrative hierarchy, from the local and regional jurisdictions up to the central authority at the national level, which is now the Secretary of State for the Environment.

The 1947 act set aside a fund of 300 million pounds to settle claims of landowners whose development rights had been expropriated. To offset in part the public cost of this compensation, the act authorized the assessment of "development charges" to landowners successful in obtaining permission to develop. The development charges were used to recover the "betterment" or increase in land value attributable to the grant of planning permission.

Though apparently simple and reasonable in theory, the system of compensation and betterment proved complex and unwieldy in practice and was plagued with substantial administrative difficulties. As a result, many of the provisions of the 1947 Town and Country Planning Act were eventually repealed, including the idea of value based on existing use and the requirement for development charges. In addition to practical problems, the political winds that in 1947 had blown in favor of nationalization were to shift over time. The Labour government with its socialist leanings was replaced on subsequent occasions by the Conservatives, who favored private rights and opposed the wholesale expropriation of development values, a concept at the very heart of the 1947 act. But although many of the provisions of the original legislation have been rescinded, the ideal of green belts and new towns has continued as the basis of British urban policy, and compensable regulation has remained the conceptual foundation of British land planning controls.

The invisible web of compensated planning regulation has never been thoroughly explored in the United States as it has in Great Britain. Certainly from the standpoint of planning, the concept has advantages. Payment of compensation has allowed the British to further the range of public planning controls considerably. If American planning were to make similar recompense for regulatory authority exceeding the constitutional limits of the police power, the public power to plan and control private development in the United States would likewise be enhanced. Moreover, in theory, the idea of compensation seems ideologically well suited to American society, where fundamental values are attached even more strongly than in Britain to the concept of private property. If applied to architectural design review, for example, compensation would permit the enforcement of stringent public design policies while also providing equity to the private owner—in financial if not in First Amendment terms.

However, it can also be argued that the extended public authority that compensation makes possible would still be offensive to the American ideals of individual freedom and private enterprise. Though compensation may seem consistent with American respect for private property, the concurrent increase of public control over land development and urban design may be regarded with suspicion by Americans—not necessarily from Brandywine—who are jealous of their private and "inalienable" constitutional rights. To them, compensation is insufficient to sweeten the bitter taste of "paid socialism." The question is not one of law or public policy so much as ideological suitability and cultural acceptance.

The advantages of urban design through public regulation, or any form of city planning, can be advanced only at some sacrifice of individual rights. Accordingly, the design and appearance of a city is implicitly determined in the weighing of ideological as well as economic costs against social and design benefits: whether the degree of urban design control obtainable through compensable regulation is worth the trade-off of private prerogatives and if so, to what extent regulation beyond the police power can be tolerated by property owners in the community, even with compensation. As Heap observed in the 1947 British planning act: "Planning at its best must, if it is to be effective, come very near to being a sort of benevolent despotism. At its worst, it could, of course, develop into an objectionable dictatorship."[83]

The issue involves not only property rights but also such attendant freedoms as the economic liberty to engage in private enterprise on the land as well as the freedom of individual expression in architectural design. The degree of individual freedom (and its obverse, the degree of regulation) is reflected in city form somewhere on a continuum from rational, centralized urban design, as mandated by public planners, to uncoordinated, organic urban growth, as spawned by market forces and unfettered private development.

American planners may cast envious eyes upon the authority and discretion exercised by their British counterparts. However, theoretical and ideological considerations aside, it should be recognized that the British model is not without practical weaknesses. British planning legislation is forbiddingly complex and subject to almost annual revision. The idea of compensation has necessarily introduced considerable financial complications. Moreover, it can be argued that the restrictive character of British planning regulation has been a disincentive for constructive land development and economic enterprise. The centralized system of administration, while reasonable in theory, has created an awesome bureaucracy. Though workable in a small and relatively homogeneous society like Britain, a similarly central administration applied to a large and heterogeneous country like the United States would hardly be tolerable if attempted at a national level.

Thus, even if American planners were to emulate the British web of compensated regulation, the system could not be transposed without con-

[83]Ibid., x.

siderable mutation. It is particularly significant that administrative authority in Britain has always enjoyed greater discretion and flexibility than in America. The Constitution as well as the master plan, as conceived in the *Fasano* case, both prescribe the characteristic of "fair certainty." It has been pointed out, for example, that Parliament can repeal even the Magna Carta at its discretion; the American Constitution cannot be altered except through comparatively tortuous means.

Regardless of compensation, it cannot be expected that public planning in the United States can ever attain the degree of discretionary authority that is exercised by planners in Great Britain. As shown in the chapter 10 discussion of architectural design review and such cases as *Duffey, Pacesetter Homes,* and *Morristown Road Associates,* specificity and standards are required in the United States for police regulations to be sustained. The courts in *Kamrowski* and *Pontiac* make the same demand of restrictions imposed through condemnation of less-than-fee interest in land. The rights acquired and the restriction levied must necessarily be explicit and defined in advance, not left to ad hoc discretion.

Although compensable regulation as practiced in Britain need not be considered as a substitute for traditional police-power controls in American planning, it can nevertheless be a substantial tool in more limited applications. Compensation may be useful and necessary to extend public authority where regulation would exceed the constitutional bounds of the police power, as in the preservation of the scenic environment along the Great River Road in Wisconsin. It is notably suitable to specific, focused applications of architectural and urban design controls where restrictions over such aspects of buildings as use, form, height, and open space—and conceivably even over such considerations as materials, detail, and color—can be explicitly defined in advance by drawings and specification. Within a broad scheme such as the San Francisco urban design plan, compensable regulation can be an effective supplemental authority to ensure enforcement of selective design objectives beyond the regulatory capability of the police power.

Chapter **13**

The Web of Fiscal Policy and Taxation

Beyond the police power and the power of eminent domain, the effects of fiscal and tax policy on urban planning and development can hardly be overstated. Following the Jeffersonian ideal that government governs best when it governs least, the federal branch has traditionally been averse to wielding its police power, largely reserving the exercise of this direct authority to state and local governments. Instead, especially since the Roosevelt administration, the primary source of power for the national government has been the federal fisc. Significantly, the use of economic power as an instrument of urban planning has assumed a distinctly free-enterprise tenor in the United States.

In societies less capitalistic than the United States, city planning is commonly initiated by the central government acting directly in a regulatory, financial, or proprietary capacity. In contrast, federal planning intervention in America has characteristically shunned direct involvement, where possible, in favor of economic incentives and disincentives that encourage local or private activity to fulfill the national policy objective. Even during recent Democratic administrations when the government's role in urban affairs has generally been prominent, federal involvement has consistently demonstrated the peculiarly American penchant for oblique national intervention, thus preserving at least the appearance of voluntary participation by the private sector and the local community. Befitting a society in which the ideal remains private or local initiative free from federal interference, economic incentives—however compelling—allow at least the option of nonparticipation and hence ostensible freedom of choice.

The economic carrot-and-stick approach is not necessarily less persuasive or effectual than are more direct controls. Offering incentives is, however, sometimes less immediate and definitive in effect and more appropriate for accomplishing long-range policy goals than specific project objectives. This approach also has a greater propensity for producing unintended or unanticipated side effects. By the same token, incentives that are directed at objectives other than planning can have considerable impact on urban planning and land-development issues, whether incidental or accidental.

An example of federal intervention through financial incentives that has resulted in significant expansion of community planning in America, as well as growth of the planning profession itself, was the federal 701 program for local planning assistance.[1] Named after a section in the Housing Act of 1954, 701 offered grants that generally covered two-thirds of the cost of planning as an inducement for local communities to plan. Unfortunately, although Section 701 is generally credited for being the financial wellspring that made local planning commonplace in the United States, the program has been discontinued by the Reagan administration, under its policy of cutting back on domestic expenditures and, not incidentally, of reducing federal involvement at the local level.

FEDERAL SUBSIDY

Patterns of urban development and design are significantly shaped by what planner and urban designer David A. Crane has described as the "capital web."[2] The network is extensive, encompassing not only publicly owned transportation and utility systems but the full array of urban development elements, including urban design and landscape, public buildings, and subsidized housing. The traditional ethic attached to private ownership in America has tended to restrain wholesale government participation in the urban real estate market, where private ownership of developable property under local zoning regulation is the preferred norm.

Since federal activity in urban affairs reached its post-Depression peak in the 1960s, however, government expenditures affecting city development have steadily declined. Funding for capital improvements once carried out under such federal programs as Urban Renewal and Model Cities, together

[1]40 U.S.C. 461, Housing Act of 1954, Title VII, Sect. 701, Pub. L. 560 (83rd Cong.), 68 Stat. 640.

[2]David A. Crane, "The City Symbolic," *Journal of the American Inst. of Planners* 26, no. 4 (Nov. 1960), 285–86.

with appropriations for the many federal housing-assistance programs implemented by the Johnson administration, have been discontinued. Under subsequent Republican administrations, funding for various federal grant programs promoting urban redevelopment have been reduced and amalgamated into the Community Development Block Grants program. Unlike the programs it replaced, which were oriented under federal direction to specific urban problems and needs, the block grants program allows greater local discretion and flexibility in the disbursement of federal funds. Under Ronald Reagan, who is committed ideologically to the ideals of greater local and individual self-sufficiency and generally opposed to heavy spending on social programs, federal aid to cities for capital improvements has been curtailed even more.

In an effort to reduce deficit spending, which in 1986 totaled about $200 billion per year, President Reagan signed the Balanced Budget and Emergency Deficit Control Act,[3] popularly known as the Gramm-Rudman-Hollings Act after its congressional sponsors. The act provided for annual deficit reductions over five years to the amount of $171.9 billion in fiscal 1986, $144 billion in 1987, $108 billion in 1988, $72 billion in 1989, and $36 billion in 1990, to arrive at a balanced budget by 1991.

A key provision in the act was that if Congress failed to meet the specified annual budget cuts, the Comptroller General would act to reduce the budget automatically, apportioning cuts equally between domestic and defense programs. Seen by many as a congressional act of desperation to control runaway federal spending while observing the President's pledge not to raise taxes, the Gramm-Rudman-Hollings Act was labeled "a bad idea whose time has come,"[4] since it forced Congress to meet its responsibility of resolving difficult and contentious funding priorities within the budget— a task it has still failed to do.

For all the furor surrounding this radical act, the Supreme Court declared the legislation unconstitutional in July 1986, noting that it would place responsibility for execution in the hands of an executive officer who is subject to removal only by the Congress, a stipulation causing an unconstitutional intrusion by the legislature into the executive function. While the Gramm-Rudman-Hollings act was found to be constitutionally defective, there is no mistaking the intent of both President Reagan and the Congress to effect substantial budget reductions that will most certainly cause severe changes in urban programs. In reading the following discussion, and notwithstanding the fate of Gramm-Rudman-Hollings, the policy effects of anticipated cuts in federal fiscal resources for existing programs should be kept in mind.

[3]2 U.S.C. 901, Pub. L. 99–177, 99 Stat. 1038.
[4]Otto Friedrich, "A Bad Idea Whose Time Has Come," *Time* (Feb. 3, 1986), 81.

Housing

Unlike other countries in which publicly owned housing is the more common form of housing assistance, the United States, in a manner that will be seen as typical, has chosen to extend public housing aid indirectly through the conduit of free enterprise. The first federal agency organized to administer this aid was the Federal Housing Administration (FHA), which was formed during the Depression and which still operates as a branch of the greatly expanded Department of Housing and Urban Development. The FHA was not created to own or administer public housing; rather, its function is to operate mortgage guarantee programs that underwrite private development of housing. It is largely to the credit of the FHA that terms for financing individual home ownership are more favorable in the United States than almost anywhere else in the world. The result has been the benefit of widespread home ownership and a pattern of housing and community development marked with the indelible imprint of FHA rules and regulations.

Prior to the creation of the FHA, home purchase loans were difficult to obtain, and then only under extremely unfavorable terms for the borrower, with high interest rates, large down payments, short periods for repayment, and the constant danger of foreclosure. With no guarantee of repayment, risks were also high for lenders, making them reluctant to approve home loans. The FHA made mortgage conditions considerably more attractive for borrower and lender alike by stipulating uniformly favorable loan terms for the borrower together with mortgage insurance that would insure the lender's risk in the event of default.

The proliferation of detached single-family tract housing in this country can be directly attributed to the FHA. Although later programs also made mortgage insurance available for multifamily cooperative and condominium housing, the initial subsidy of essentially single-family homes, coupled with the traditional preference of Americans for this low-density housing type, has virtually underwritten the development of the single-family residential suburb as a distinctive element of American urban form.

The influence of the program on housing and community design has extended beyond the apparently simple financial incentive. The FHA's *Minimum Property Standards*[5] for home construction, which must be followed in order to qualify for its loan guarantees, are detailed and specific. By specifying allowable materials, construction techniques, and minimum siting requirements, the standards have virtually set the national format for detached tract housing design. In the mass production of economical development housing units, the FHA minimum construction standards—for ex-

---

[5]U.S. Department of Housing and Urban Development, *Minimum Property Standards for One and Two Family Dwellings* (Washington, D.C.: USGPO, 1982).

ample, stipulating the narrowest distance between buildings and the minimum spacing of wood studs in frame wall construction—have in fact become the standard for most residential development in the country, regardless of whether the particular project is required to meet FHA requirements. Because of the volume and scale of housing developments with federally guaranteed financing, these standards for individual house design have in concert determined the design of the total suburban community. The invisible web of FHA standards for finance eligibility has been the greatest single impetus and determinant of suburban house and community design in America, far greater in influence than the most ambitious architect, developer, or city planner.

For many years, however, most of the government's successes at promoting the benefits of home ownership were confined to the middle class. The President's Committee on Urban Housing, chaired by Edgar F. Kaiser, said in its 1968 report, "The most successful housing programs were not aimed at the poor at all, but rather were designed to help the middle class obtain mortgage financing. The nation has been slow to recognize unequivocally the necessity for subsidy if the poor are to be adequately housed."[6]

Implicitly, the FHA favored development of the suburbs where, not coincidentally, the population was and still is predominantly middle class and white. Until the race riots that marked the "urban crisis" of the 1960s awakened the national consciousness and conscience, the FHA did little to ameliorate the plight of the disadvantaged dwellers of the older inner city. The National Commission on Urban Problems, commonly known as the Douglas Commission after its chairman, Senator Paul H. Douglas, observed in its final report, *Building the American City,*

> The main weakness of FHA from a social point of view has not been in what it has done, but in what it has failed to do—in its relative neglect of the inner cities and of the poor, and especially Negro poor. Believing firmly that the poor were bad credit risks and that the presence of Negroes tended to lower real estate values, FHA has generally regarded loans to such groups as "economically unsound." Until recently, therefore, FHA benefits have been confined almost exclusively to the middle class, and primarily only to the middle section of the middle class. The poor and those on the fringes of poverty have been almost completely excluded. These and the lower middle class, together constituting the 40 percent of the population whose housing needs are greatest, received only 11 percent of FHA mortgages.
>
> This tendency to neglect the poor has been reinforced and partially extended by the FHA tendency to shun the central cities and concentrate on the suburbs. The experience of members of the Commission and others convinced us that up until the summer of 1967, FHA almost never insured mortgages

---

[6]President's Committee on Urban Housing (Kaiser Committee), *A Decent Home* (Washington, D.C.: USGPO, 1968), 54.

on homes in slum districts, and did so very seldom in the "gray areas" which surrounded them. Even middle class residential districts in the central cities were suspect, since there was always the prospect that they, too, might turn as Negroes and poor whites continued to pour into the cities, and as middle and upper-middle income whites continued to move out.

The result was a general, even if unwritten, agreement between lending institutions and FHA that most of the areas inside the central cities did not have a favorable economic future, and that their property values were likely to decline. . . .

There was evidence of a tacit agreement among all groups—lending institutions, fire insurance companies, and FHA—to block off certain areas of cities within "red lines," and not to loan or insure within them. The net result, of course, was that the slums and the areas surrounding them went downhill farther and faster than before.

For many years FHA operated with the conventional racial prejudice characteristic of many middle class real estate men. The agency's original personnel was primarily recruited from this group in the 1930's. Until 1948, when restrictive covenants or written agreements not to sell to Negroes were declared unconstitutional by the Supreme Court, FHA actually encouraged its borrowers to give such guarantees and was a powerful enforcer of the covenants. The FHA definition of a sound neighborhood was a "homogeneous" one—one that was racially segregated.[7]

Since the urban crisis and the civil rights movement of the 1960s, the government has rectified many of its earlier failings in housing policy. Under the Department of Housing and Urban Development, formed in 1965, federal housing assistance has been extended to the urban poor, particularly the minorities. While FHA programs benefiting the middle class and the suburbs still remain, they have been augmented by other programs aimed specifically at providing housing assistance to low-income city dwellers.

During the Johnson administration, a multitude of federal assistance programs for low-income housing was established under the Department of Housing and Urban Development. To supplement public housing assistance, which was first authorized by the United States Housing Act in 1937,[8] various housing subsidy programs were created during the 1960s to help people with low or moderate incomes to obtain suitable housing, whether existing, new, or rehabilitated single or multifamily units. Some of the major HUD programs were Section 202 housing for the elderly or handicapped; Section 221 (d) (3) below-market interest rate loan program for low-income rental housing; rent supplements to assist low-income families afford suitable housing beyond a percentage of their income; Section 235

[7]National Commission on Urban Problems (Douglas Commission), *Building the American City* (Washington, D.C.: USGPO, 1968), 100–1.
[8]42 U.S.C. 1437–1437n, Pub. L. 412 (75th Cong.) (1937) 50 Stat. 888.

mortgage assistance for low-income home ownership; and Section 236 mortgage aid for low-income rental housing.

Under subsequent administrations, however, and especially under President Reagan, federal appropriations for housing aid have been substantially reduced; increasingly, available assistance is couched in the open market and in local administration. At this time, the principal legislative vehicle for low-income housing assistance takes the form of amendments made since 1974 to the 1937 Housing Act.

Under Section 8 of the act as amended,[9] federal housing assistance for low- and moderate-income families has consisted of two complementary policy elements. The first side of the policy equation is to increase the supply of housing suitable for low-income occupancy by availing state and local governments of federal financial aid to support new construction or substantial rehabilitation of qualified low-cost, privately owned units. The second part is to distribute financial assistance directly to low-income aid recipients to enable them to participate as consumers in the expanded private low-cost housing market.

The first part of the policy equation to increase the availability of good quality housing for low-income families is presently exemplified by the Rental Housing Rehabilitation and Development program,[10] or HoDAG, which was enacted in 1983 to replace the New Construction and Substantial Rehabilitation provisions of Section 8. The program makes funds available, in areas suffering shortages in decent and affordable housing, to applicant state or local government agencies so that they may assist in the production of privately owned rental housing of suitable quality. The grants provide subsidies of up to 50 percent for the development of new or rehabilitated multifamily projects, of which at least 20 percent must be reserved for households with incomes falling below 80 percent of the area median. The Reagan administration has followed the precedent of the Community Development Block Grants program by delegating the responsibility for HoDAG supervision to the local government grantees, unlike Section 8, which was administered directly by HUD.

Whereas HoDAG is similar to the Section 8 New Construction program in promoting the production of new or substantially rehabilitated rental apartments, there are several major differences that reveal the particular bent of the Reagan ideology. The earlier program mainly provided housing assistance to very poor families with incomes of only 25 to 30 percent of the area median; HoDAG projects serve mostly households of somewhat more comfortable means. Only 20 percent of the units must be set aside for

[9]Note 8, as amended in 42 U.S.C. 1437f subsequent to Housing and Community Development Act of 1974, Pub. L. 93–383, Title II, 88 Stat. 633, 653, 662.

[10]42 U.S.C. 1437o, Housing and Urban-Rural Recovery Act of 1983, Pub. L. 98–181, Title III, Sect. 301, 97 Stat. 1155, 1196.

lower-income families, and these may have incomes of up to 80 percent of the area median. Also, unlike the continuing commitment of the Section 8 program, HoDAG assistance is a one-time grant aimed at providing leverage to obtain further project funding from other sources. Although more localities may well qualify for funds by meeting or exceeding program requirements, such as by providing for more than the minimum proportion of low-income clients and assisting more large families with children, fewer low-income families are actually served. This is because total funding available for the HoDAG program is considerably less than that granted earlier programs, making competition for assistance substantially greater.

Ideologically, the preference of the Reagan administration is to promote home ownership and the self-sufficiency and stewardship that being a homeowner often engenders, rather than to encourage continuing dependency on rentals. Under an Urban Homesteading program enacted in 1974,[11] unoccupied and deteriorated city homes under federal ownership can be transferred through local authorities to private home ownership. Homesteaders who agree to repair, maintain, and live in the units for a minimum of three years are able to receive full title to their units at no cost. With the success of homesteading one- to four-family units, the government is now experimenting with the homesteading of multifamily dwellings, including the "privatization" of multifamily public housing projects.[12]

The second half of the equation to help low-income families afford decent housing consists of rent payments made directly to eligible aid recipients or their landlords. Each family qualifying for assistance is subsidized the cost of approved housing in excess of its own contribution of a stipulated portion—formerly 25 but now 30 percent—of its income.[13] In addition to housing produced by the rehabilitation and new construction programs, direct payments are also available to help low-income families meet the cost of renting existing privately-owned housing. Unlike most assistance programs, which are tied to specific projects or units, the existing housing program involves the issuance of certificates or vouchers that aid recipients can use as payment toward the rent of any approved low-cost housing of their choice.

Broached as early as 1937 and attempted in prototypal form in the Rent Supplements program and under Section 23 of the U.S. Housing Act as amended in 1965, the idea of direct rent-subsidy payments has enjoyed increasing popularity over recent years. Largely because it offers apparent public economy by foregoing large government outlays for housing production and other capital improvements, the use of direct housing payments

---

[11]12 U.S.C. 1706e, 1974 Act, Title VIII, Sect. 810, 88 Stat. 734.

[12]50 FR 14987. See also Sheri L. Singer, "Public Housing Sale," *Planning* (Sept. 1985), 28.

[13]40 FR 15542 (1975).

has been favored by the Reagan administration over other forms of housing assistance. In 1970, the federal government launched an extensive nation-wide demonstration, the Experimental Housing Allowance Program,[14] to test the system. This demonstration led to the use of voucher payments as a fundamental element of the Existing Housing component of the Section 8 program established by the Housing and Community Development Act of 1974.[15] In 1983, Section 8 was further amended with a provision for yet another Voucher Demonstration program[16] in anticipation of greater reliance on the system as the primary form of future federal low-income housing assistance.

The use of direct housing payments received a substantial boost in 1982 after the Commission on Housing appointed by President Reagan judged this form of assistance to be more economical and effective than production-oriented programs under Section 8. In their report, the commission recommended that the use of direct housing payments be expanded and that housing production efforts be subsumed as an element of the Community Development Block Grants program.[17]

Following the commission's advice, the administration's policy on low-income housing is to expand upon the voucher system while cutting back on programs that subsidize the development of low-cost units. This approach would effectively focus on only the consumer-oriented demand side of housing policy, deemphasizing the production-oriented supply-side complement to the equation.

Critics of this singular market-oriented approach point out, however, that the true root of the nation's low-income housing problems lies in the inadequate stock of affordable units, particularly in the older city centers where the low-income population predominates. They argue that the administration's preoccupation with market determination—of privatization of public housing, and of promoting ostensible consumer choice by arming aid recipients with vouchers to fend for themselves in a tight housing market—does little to solve the basic problem of an inadequate supply of suitable low-cost housing.[18] The arguments against the use of housing vouchers alone are summarized by Grace Milgram:

> The idea of providing some form of rental payment to or on behalf of families for use in the existing housing stock rather than building new units for them

[14]Housing and Urban Development Act of 1970, Pub. L. 91–609, Title V, Sect. 504, 84 Stat. 1770, 1786.

[15]Note 9, and 43 FR 61246 (1978).

[16]Note 10, Sect. 207, 97 Stat. 1181.

[17]President's Commission on Housing, *Report of the President's Commission on Housing* (Washington, D.C.: USGPO, 1982).

[18]See, e.g., Floyd Lapp, "Viewpoint," *Planning* 51, no. 7 (July 1985), 42.

. . . [has] been considered and rejected over the years, partially because of a perceived need to add to the stock of standard quality housing and partially because of a prevalent fear that increasing effective demand for housing without directly adding to supply would force up rents, not only for recipients of aid but for all low-income renters. There was also concern that abandonment of all new construction would lead to a situation in which public funds were used to pay landlords of substandard or even slum housing unless costly regulations could be strictly enforced. When rent payment programs were adopted, as in Section 23 and rent supplements, they were only one part of an array of programs in which new construction continued as a major element.[19]

It is unreasonable to believe that housing vouchers as a factor can supplement demand enough to fuel market production, particularly in deteriorated urban slums where investments would be considered high risk at best. In view of the government's reduced appropriations for all housing programs, the critics question the private sector's ability, without government support, to meet the need for decent housing for very low-income families. Conceptually, at least, past programs have attempted to address the supply problem by fulfilling both sides of the equation. In implementing the rental rehabilitation program under Section 8, for example, only one voucher or certificate was supposed to be issued for every low-cost housing unit made available, so that the number of approved units and the number of households eligible for occupancy would theoretically be kept current. With increasing reductions in government assistance new or renovated low-cost housing, however, the likelihood of striking this balance is becoming more and more remote.

While the prognosis for the very low income dweller of the urban slum is rather bleak under present federal housing policy, prospects for a fortunate few with moderately low incomes is somewhat better. Publicly assisted development of housing for such families has placed subsidized units in developing areas of the city which had previously been the domain of the middle class. Under HoDAG, the clients of housing assistance, including minorities, are being dispersed in new or substantially renovated developments throughout the city. This placement of some lower-income households in privately owned developments within middle-class communities is intended to relieve some of the stigma attached to concentrated, low-income "project" housing. Nevertheless, until this society and its government return their attention to urban slums and the needs of the very poor, the task of providing adequate housing for everyone remains undone.

[19]Grace Milgram, "Housing the Urban Poor: Urban Housing Assistance Programs" in *Housing: A Reader,* Congressional Research Service, Library of Congress (Washington, D.C.: USGPO, 1983), 134.

New Communities in America: An Unfulfilled Promise

It would be difficult to discuss federal policy on urban design and housing over the last half century without making at least some reference to the HUD Urban Renewal and New Communities programs. Although both programs are no longer in effect, their impact on urban design has been substantial. The federal Urban Renewal program has left an indelible imprint on the physical design of many major city centers, whereas the New Communities program, though not as widespread in effect as Urban Renewal, demonstrated significant federal effort and potential in community development and design.

The conceptual origins of modern American communities can be traced to the efforts of such pioneers as Clarence Stein and Henry Wright in the 1920s and such early community housing projects as Sunnyside Gardens, New York, and Radburn, New Jersey. The work of Ebenezer Howard and Patrick Abercrombie in Britain were, of course, also well known in this country as were the inspirational examples of British garden cities and new towns. With the growing acceptance of cooperative and condominium ownership and planned unit development in the 1960s, new communities such as Columbia, Maryland, and Reston, Virginia, emerged through private development without special government assistance. Federal involvement began in earnest under Title VII of the Housing and Urban Development Act of 1970 on Urban Growth and New Community Development.[20]

In some ways, Title VII can be considered a progressive outgrowth of the government's participation in housing through the FHA. But unlike the FHA, which even today considers home financing essentially on an individual or small-project basis, the New Communities program demonstrated a more sophisticated attitude in its treatment of housing as an essential but limited part of total residential community development. The program integrated housing as a consideration within a broader community planning agenda encompassing such concerns as area economics, employment, commercial activity, public facilities and infrastructure, transportation, education, culture, and recreation.

However, despite its progressive approach to housing and community development, Title VII retained the traditional American approach to low-profile federalism and intervention through economic incentives. Though the development of new communities would seem logically to derive from national or regional planning priorities, as in Britain and other countries, American development has instead been based essentially on free market determination, with federal participation invoked only upon voluntary application by private developers for optional public financing assistance.

---

[20]42 U.S.C. 4511, Pub. L. 91-609 (1970), Title VII, 84 Stat. 1791, superseding 42 U.S.C. 3901, New Communities Act of 1968, Pub. L. 90–448, Title IV, 82 Stat. 513.

This approach assigns the initiative to the private sector and an essentially reactive role to government, making the process comparable to FHA participation in housing, albeit for projects of a far larger scale.

Several fundamental characteristics distinguish American new-town development from that in Great Britain. Whereas the placement and growth of British new towns have been the result of national planning policy, the location and development of American new communities have been privately determined by the regional market. Moreover, the British have been able to ensure an adequate economic base for each new town by requiring private industries petitioning for planning permission to locate in accordance with public planning priorities. Private developers of American new communities, on the other hand, have had to rely largely upon private means to induce supportive industries and activities to locate at their sites. The result is that the American developments are generally less self-sufficient economically than their British counterparts and more dependent upon their relationship with neighboring metropolitan areas.

Title VII authorized federal grants, loans, and financial guarantees to be made to qualified development projects. The furnishing of minimal public facilities and such services as streets, utilities, schools, clinics, and fire and police posed a formidable problem for developers, since no sales revenues could be expected until these essential but costly capital improvements had been provided. Title VII program also authorized technical assistance, specifically for required social planning, to ensure adequate and smooth integration of diverse social, racial, and economic groups. Unfortunately, with the government's resources diverted by the war in Vietnam and later because of a flagging economy, actual appropriations for new community projects fell short of original expectations, and the program did not fulfill its anticipated potential.

In addition to inadequate government assistance, poor management on the part of developers and bad luck with the prevailing economy have caused many new developments to falter. The problem of attracting primary industries to establish an economic base and the need for massive front-end expenditures in order to create a viable community from the ground up have often proved insurmountable. Even New York, which attempted the most ambitious state program in new community development, saw its development agency, the Urban Development Corporation,[21] end in failure. Opponents of public participation in large-scale domestic enterprises, such as the development of new communities, have claimed with some irony that Columbia, Maryland, and Irvine Ranch, California, perhaps the most successful new communities, have been developed without special federal aid.

In terms of imparting human scale and residential character to commu-

---

[21]N.Y. Unconsol. Laws, Sect. 6251 *et seq.* (McKinney's).

nity design, the degree of success seems historically to have been in inverse proportion to the degree of design participation by government. In any event, some critics charge that the attention given to new towns has amounted to little more than a redesign of suburbia and a diversion of attention from the more urgent problems of the inner city. In fact, federally supported new communities have also been developed in urban areas, as evidenced by such "new-towns-in-town" as Cedar Riverside in Minneapolis and Roosevelt Island in New York City.

Urban Renewal: Gone But Not Forgotten

Whereas the New Communities program tended to focus on suburban housing development, the Urban Renewal program stressed the physical redevelopment of the decayed sectors of the center cities. First established as the urban redevelopment program by the Housing Act of 1949,[22] the program was later modified and expanded under the name of Urban Renewal by the Housing Act of 1954[23] for community improvement through slum clearance and new construction. Following the norm of other federal aid programs, participation was predicated upon voluntary application by urban communities that met specified program requirements.

The impact of the Urban Renewal program on American urban design has been unmatched since the City Beautiful movement of the 1900s, bringing new awareness to urban design as a field bridging architecture and city planning. However, during its life, the program was also severely criticized for its narrow focus on only the visible aspects of urban decay, for the limited scope of its project-by-project approach, and for its failure to address adequately fundamental social and economic issues as part of a comprehensive policy basis for physical renewal.

Most of all, the program was faulted for failing to meet the original intent of introducing active citizen participation into the community renewal process. Instead, commercial and development interests that stood to gain directly from capital outlays in construction and physical improvements virtually dominated the planning process to the exclusion and detriment of neighborhood residents and small business operators, who were frequently displaced. Thus, while many American city centers and local commercial interests benefited from the urban design projects that the program made possible, a high price was exacted from the inhabitants of the renewal areas, many of whom belonged to the low-income and minorities groups the program was originally supposed to assist. Political scientist

[22]Housing Act of 1949, Title I, Slum Clearance and Community Development and Redevelopment, Pub. L. 171 (81st Cong.), 63 Stat. 413, 414.

[23]42 U.S.C. 1450, Housing Act of 1954, Title III, Slum Clearance and Urban Renewal, Pub. L. 560 (83rd Cong.), 68 Stat. 622.

Harold Wolman observed that the concern for slum clearance "was not about the deprivations suffered by their inhabitants, but rather about the affront to aesthetic sensibilities caused by these blights on the urban landscape."[24]

While the 1954 ruling by the Supreme Court in *Berman v. Parker* was widely regarded as a victory for Urban Renewal, in hindsight the power granted by the court may have been too great for the program's own good. Because the decision upholding "integrated plans for redevelopment"[25] allowed wholesale acquisition of properties in the renewal area regardless of their functional status, renewal agencies were not constrained to accommodate existing social or economic conditions, however benign. Buildings and activities, situated in areas slated for renewal but not contributing to the blight, were nonetheless swept away. Sometimes entire districts encompassing socially viable if poor communities were destroyed for the sake of achieving a seemingly rational urban design goal, much in the style of the grand Renaissance schemes of Europe. Because of the *Berman v. Parker* decision, there was no legal compulsion for social sensitivity in planning and design; as a result, the program gained a reputation for a heavy-handed bulldozer approach to slum removal and reconstruction.

From the standpoint of design, the centralized public authority essential to Urban Renewal's policy of integrated redevelopment found expression in the holistic rationalism of the International Style, an idiom of modern architecture characterized by an all-encompassing global approach to community revitalization. Urban Renewal, in its sweeping rationality of "integrated redevelopment," yielded urban designs of a civic scale and monumentality reminiscent of earlier European ages, intolerant of pluralism or organic determination in either community or design.

With little aid from the Urban Renewal program to ameliorate the poor living conditions of the inner-city ghettos, unrest among low-income and racial minority slum dwellers eventually erupted into the riots and firebombings that marked the urban crisis of the 1960s. These events, coupled with criticism by observers and scholars of Urban Renewal, impelled a shift in emphasis from reconstruction focused on monumental civic design to rehabilitation of residential neighborhoods of the inner city.

One result of this reevaluation and reform of the government's domestic policies and programs was the Demonstration Cities and Metropolitan Development Act of 1966, which created the Model Cities program.[26] Unlike Urban Renewal, the Model Cities program was directed more at fulfilling the broad range of social and economic needs of the urban poor

---

[24]Harold Wolman, *Politics of Federal Housing* (New York: Dodd, Mead, 1971), 28.

[25]348 U.S. 26 (1954), 35.

[26]42 U.S.C. 3301, 3334, Demonstration Cities and Metropolitan Development Act of 1966, Pub. L. 89–754, 80 Stat. 1255, 1262.

by providing a wide variety of social services—job training, employment programs, and child care—as well as improving the physical condition of the community. To avoid some of the mistakes of Urban Renewal, far greater attention was given in Model Cities to the planning process itself. A fundamental aspect of the program was to provide opportunities for extensive participation by all members of the model community in determining program directions and priorities through the process of advocacy planning.

Federal Aid to Cities Since the 1960s

As noted earlier in this chapter, many of the federal urban assistance and redevelopment programs conducted by the Johnson administration, such as Urban Renewal and Model Cities, were consolidated by subsequent Republican administrations into the Community Development Block Grants (CDBG) program.[27] While the block grants are intended to ameliorate blighted conditions in urban areas and to assist persons of low and moderate income, local administrators are allowed far greater discretion and flexibility in the actual use and allocation of federal funds than under the previous "categorical" aid programs. Federal revenue-sharing with local governments through block grants reflects the conservative belief of many Republicans that much of the policy and fiscal power assumed by federal bureaucracies under earlier Democratic administrations should be decentralized and invested instead in state and local governments.

Initially authorized under Title I of the Housing and Community Development Act of 1974, the Community Development Block Grants program allocates funds to states and localities principally on a "formula" basis, with all metropolitan cities and urban counties automatically qualifying for "formula entitlement" funding. Metropolitan cities are the central cities of designated Metropolitan Statistical Areas (MSAs), formerly Standard Metropolitan Statistical Areas (SMSAs), or other cities within MSAs having populations over 50,000. Funding eligibility is based on a community's census statistics, including population, overcrowded housing, and poverty.

In addition to entitlement allocations, nonentitlement block grants are provided to small cities under the administration of either the states or HUD on a competitive basis. The Secretary of Housing and Urban Devel-

[27]42 U.S.C. 5301, Housing and Community Development Act of 1974, Pub. L. 93-383, Title I, 88 Stat 633. The seven grant programs amalgamated under the CDBG program were Urban Renewal (including the Neighborhood Redevelopment Program), Model Cities, Water and Sewer, Open Space Land, Neighborhood Facilities, Rehabilitation Loans, and Public Facilities Loans.

opment is also able to award block grants from a discretionary fund to needy communities not eligible for either entitlement or small city funding.

In 1977, under President Carter, the Community Development Block Grants program introduced by the Nixon and Ford administrations was supplemented with the Urban Development Action Grants (UDAG) program aimed specifically at assisting cities and urban counties experiencing severe physical and economic distress.[28] Unlike CDBG, which provides federal funds to all qualified cities regardless of their economic or physical well-being, UDAG is intended to aid communities in special need. The program is geared toward reclaiming city neighborhoods suffering from excessive housing blight and abandonment and revitalizing urban communities experiencing population outmigration and a stagnating or declining tax base. UDAG funding is specifically intended to help such communities take advantage of opportunities to attract private investment.

Under the Reagan administration, however, funding for CDBG and UDAG has been substantially reduced. Even more than other recent Republican presidents, Reagan is a proponent of market determination. During his first term, he proposed as the centerpiece of his administration's urban policy an aid concept known as Enterprise Zones (EZs). First introduced in Britain under the Conservative government of Prime Minister Margaret H. Thatcher, Enterprise Zones employ tax-reduction incentives and relief from prevailing administrative regulations rather than outright financial grants to encourage private investment in depressed urban areas.

The administration's proposed Enterprise Zone Tax Act of 1982[29] would have provided such incentives as federal income tax credits, exemption from capital gains taxes on new investments, and federal industrial revenue bonds to finance small-business projects, and would have relaxed nonstatutory federal regulatory requirements at the request of state and local governments, which themselves would have been encouraged to offer comparable tax and regulatory relief. Critics of the bill, however, question the cost efficiency of Enterprise Zones compared with UDAGs, which the Reagan administration would discontinue.[30] Critics are skeptical of the proposed incentives' effectiveness to lure new investments, suggesting that even where investments do occur, the likelihood would be for existing businesses outside a zone to relocate in an EZ rather than for actual new ventures to be created. They point out that, especially in comparison with an earlier EZ

---

[28]42 U.S.C. 5318, Urban Development Action Grants, Housing and Community Development Act of 1977, Pub. L. 95–128, 91 Stat. 1125, amending Housing and Community Development Act of 1974, Title I, Sect. 119, 88 Stat. 633.

[29]H.R. 6009, S. 2298 (1982).

[30]See, e.g., Robert Mier, "Enterprise Zones: A Long Shot," *Planning* 48, no. 4 (April 1982), 10. Also see David A. Wenzel, "UDAGs Are Better," *Planning* 48, no. 4 (April 1982), 14.

proposal made by Republican House member Jack F. Kemp and Democratic Representative Robert Garcia,[31] the tax incentives proposed in the administration's bill would serve more to benefit businesses new to the zone rather than businesses already in place, thus encouraging the sale of the latter to larger, outside concerns that could take better advantage of the tax provisions.

In any event, nothwithstanding consideration of EZs in the Congress and the passage of some form of EZ legislation by several states, federal interest in Enterprise Zones has diminished perceptibly since 1982, especially in light of the present desire to reduce the federal deficit. The administration's lack of commitment to Enterprise Zones—and indeed to any affirmative urban aid program—was made apparent in Reagan's failure to mention EZs or any other positive urban tax-assistance program in his tax-reform plan unveiled in 1985. The implication of this plan, the House and Senate versions, and of taxes in general on urban policy will be the topic of discussion later in this chapter.

Federal Aid for Urban Transportation

Considering the pivotal role played by transit and circulation systems in the determination of urban form, it would seem derelict indeed to discuss the effect of law on city development without mentioning federal legislation on urban transportation. To even the most casual observer, it is apparent that with very few exceptions, urban passenger transportation in postwar America has been based essentially on the private automobile rather than on public mass transit. Other than in San Francisco, Washington, D.C., Atlanta, and Miami, where rapid-transit rail lines have been constructed since the 1960s, most urban passenger rail systems date back well before the Second World War, primarily in the older cities of the northeast. Despite substantial federal aid for all forms of urban mass transit in the 1970s and some increase in public patronage of the resulting improved systems, since the war Americans have become increasingly dependent on the private automobile as the primary means of transportation, particularly in newly developed urban areas.

Given most people's natural preference for private automobiles over shared mass transit, and the ability of the American economy to deliver automobiles at a volume and cost to satisfy market demand, it would be rather presumptuous to attribute the car-oriented nature of American urban development primarily to legislation rather than to attribute legislation to popular social preference. Nonetheless, by providing the necessary infra-

---

[31]Urban Jobs and Enterprise Zone Act of 1981 (Kemp-Garcia Plan), H.R. 3824, S. 1310. See also H.R. 7563, S. 2823 (1980).

structure of public roads and highways, federal legislation on transportation has played a major role in making the private automobile the principal means of transportation, in cities as well as rural and suburban areas. The Federal-Aid Highway Act of 1956, which authorized funding for the federal Interstate Highway System, was the watershed legislation.[32] Contemplated since the Second World War, when it was known as the National System of Interstate and Defense Highways, the Interstate Highway System now spans the nation in a forty-four-thousand-mile network of high-speed, limited-access roadways linking the major cities, and is the largest public works project ever undertaken in American history. The system's urban interchanges—the arterial connections and perimeter beltways—compose the backbone of express highways that serve automobile circulation in most metropolitan areas, giving the automobile the best possible public infrastructure with which to function as an effective means of mass urban transportation.

Whether the highway system is the optimum mode for urban transportation is, however, subject to question. After the 1973 oil embargo imposed by the petroleum-producing nations and the consequential widespread realization of the nonrenewable nature of fossil fuels, Congress took steps to promote the greater fuel efficiencies that are possible through use of mass transit. The Federal-Aid Highway Act of 1973[33] for the first time allowed the highway trust funds derived from the federal tax on gasoline to be diverted to uses other than the construction of highways. As the Interstate System nears completion, these funds could be allocated to improving mass transportation systems.

Congress also appropriated federal funds specifically for urban mass transit. The National Mass Transportation Assistance Act of 1974[34] provided matching grants that covered 80 percent of the cost of capital improvements in local transit, such as the upgrading of rail facilities and the purchase of buses. Significantly, it also underwrote public ridership of mass transit directly by providing funds subsidizing 50 percent of the operating expense of municipally owned mass transit systems. The Federal Public Transportation Act of 1982[35] specifically earmarked for public transit an amount from the highway trust fund equaling one cent of a five-cent increase of the tax on each gallon of gasoline. Although the infusion of federal funds has resulted in improved urban mass transportation services and

[32]23 U.S.C. 101 *et seq.,* Federal-Aid Highway Act of 1956, Pub. L. 627 (84th Cong.), 70 Stat. 374.

[33]Pub. L. 93–87, 87 Stat. 250.

[34]49 U.S.C. 1601 *et seq.* Pub. L. 93–503, Title I, 88 Stat. 1566, amending Urban Mass Transportation Act of 1964, Pub. L. 88–365, 78 Stat. 302.

[35]Pub. L. 97–424, Surface Transportation Assistance Act of 1982, Title III, 96 Stat. 2097, 2140.

increased ridership, budget cuts by the Reagan administration have curtailed further advances under federal sponsorship. Today, reliance on the automobile as the primary means of transportation in the United States remains as prevalent as ever, and the urban freeway and its interchanges are a much more pervasive and dominant element of American urban design than passenger mass transit systems, particularly in new and developing urban regions.

TAX POLICY AND THE BUILT ENVIRONMENT

Apropos of a society founded on capitalism, a principal means for public control of private enterprise in the United States is tax policy. Wrote Jerome P. Pickard: "Any tax system is an instrument of public policy, and cannot avoid this role; although neutrality is frequently stated as a goal, in the very nature of things any specific tax has an incidence which varies among taxpayers or objects taxed."[36]

Taxation has two distinct but equally important functions. The first is undertaken regardless of the nature of a society: to raise revenue to pay for the machinery of government and to finance the expense of community undertakings, whether urban renewal, aid to the needy, or the maintenance of a strong military. The second purpose of taxation is as an instrument of public policy: to encourage or discourage certain social or economic practices by the imposition or relaxation of tax levies. There are many examples of taxation as an instrument of policy. A levy on tobacco to discourage smoking; an import tariff to protect domestic industries by increasing the consumer cost of competitively priced foreign goods; a low income tax rate on gains realized from the disposal of capital investments to encourage economic enterprise—each exemplifies a tax policy application. Whereas more socialistic governments might impose direct prohibitions or demands, in contrast, tax policy is useful in capitalist societies, for it provides ostensible freedom of choice as well as a powerful incentive for private activity to conform to the government's policy objectives.

The Real Property Tax

The antecedents for taxing real property are historical. Obligations tied to land tenure formed the basis of feudal society, to cite an early example. During that period, wealth was measured in terms of land, and thus taxation on wealth meant taxation of real property. Although now one can be wealthy without owning any real property whatsoever, the ad valorem tax

---

[36] Jerome P. Pickard, *Changing Land Use as Affected by Taxation* (Washington, D.C.: Urban Land Institute, 1962), 24.

on property remains. Even Adam Smith, eighteenth-century proponent of capitalism, viewed a levy on property as justifiable. Today the real property tax is the principal source of revenue for local governments, paying for municipal services whether or not related to property.

The policy benefits of real property taxation as practiced in the United States, however, have been questionable. Because the bulk of the tax is levied upon the value of improvements on the land rather than on the value of the land itself, any development, however beneficial, would subject the owner to an increased tax burden. Thus, the property tax has actually served to penalize constructive development and to encourage nonproductive land speculation. As Orlando E. Delogu wrote,

> The extent of the failure to recognize the relationship between the power to tax and land use objectives is best evidenced by the almost total lack of coordination in municipal government between property tax assessment policy and land use planning policy.[37]

Delogu pointed out that local tax assessors generally place priority on revenue needs and accordingly tend to value land not at its present use value but rather at its potential value under hypothetical greatest-capacity use. He cited the example that agricultural or open land in the path of future subdivision development is often assessed as land capable of residential use years before the area is actually ripe for such development. As a result of such practices in assessment, the tax burden on agricultural or open land acts upon the owner to sell or subdivide simply to pay the tax, even though both he and the local planning agency may have preferred to retain the land in its open or agricultural state. Delogu continued,

> The past and present disappearance of many rich agricultural areas and scenic open-space or wooded areas near growing urban and suburban complexes can be attributed in part to these assessment practices. The irony of the situation is made complete when we recognize that the community may (now or in the future) be spending a portion of its tax revenue to acquire land for park and open-space purposes, which the land use planner has recommended. In this situation there is not only a failure to use the power to tax positively to achieve land use control objectives but taxing policy is actually at cross purposes with and serves to defeat land use objectives.[38]

Assessment practices have also poorly served renewal of the inner city and the interests of its inhabitants. In 1972, I participated in an investigation directed by John Keene of the University of Pennsylvania on the urban

---

[37]Orlando E. Delogu, "The Taxing Power as a Land Use Control Device," *Denver L. Rev.* 45 (1968), 280.

[38]Ibid., 281.

policy implications of the real property tax, using the city of Philadelphia as the case study.[39] Despite a Pennsylvania state constitutional provision that all tax levies be uniform, and the policy of the Philadelphia Board of Revision of Taxes to establish assessed values at 65 to 69 percent of fair-market value, the city's Department of Finance admitted,

> Taxable properties are not being uniformly assessed. Analysis of sales showed that assessed value in one ward was 39.5 percent of market value, while another [was] 66.3 percent. These two wards represent the extremes, but all wards show significant variations.[40]

The burden of the inequity was shown to fall most heavily upon the central sections of the city, notably on residential areas inhabited by low-income blacks. Systematic investigation of tax wards showed the ratio of tax assessments to sales values to have been considerably higher in these areas than in other parts of the city.

A similar study of tax assessment practices in Boston by Oliver Oldman and Henry Aaron found a pattern not unlike that uncovered in Philadelphia. Wrote the investigators,

> In general, ratios are lower for high-priced properties than for low-priced properties . . . Single family residences are assessed at the lowest ratio in any region and in the jurisdiction as a whole. . . . The relative overassessment of the central city has been a common finding of assessment-sales ratio studies. . . . Political power rests in the periphery, sometimes referred to as the "bedroom" communities, because that is where houses are located and the voters live.[41]

The conclusions drawn of these studies substantiate an assertion made by Pickard, that "within metropolitan areas, property taxation tends to be heaviest in central cities and older core communities, where the real estate market is weak and there are many problems of neighborhood obsolescence; property taxes are often lightest in well-to-do suburbs of medium age."[42]

---

[39]John C. Keene, ed., *Policy Implications of the Real Property Tax* (Philadelphia: Institute for Environmental Studies, U. of Pennsylvania, 1972).

[40]Richard T. Lai, "Effect of Property Taxation in Residential Rehabilitation in the Older Center City: General Considerations," in *Policy Implications of the Real Property Tax,* John C. Keene, ed. (Philadelphia: Institute for Environmental Studies, U. of Pennsylvania, 1972), 58, 64. Quoting *Report on Real Property Assessments and Real Estate Tax Revenue,* Office of the Director of Finance, City of Philadelphia, 1971.

[41]Oliver Oldman and Henry Aaron, "Assessment-Sales Ratios Under the Boston Property Tax," *National Tax Journal* 18, no. 1 (1965), 38–39, 41, 43.

[42]Jerome P. Pickard, *Taxation and Land Use in Metropolitan and Urban America* (Washington, D.C.: Urban Land Institute, 1966), 11.

The higher tax levies in the slum areas of the city magnify the adverse impact of property taxation on rehabilitation in areas which need investments in improvements the most. Effectively, the administration of the tax places an additional burden on the poor, since the heavier assessment ultimately increases the cost of their housing, whether rented or owner-occupied. The high tax in the center city can also repel settlement by higher income groups who can afford renovation. Property-tax expert Dick Netzer writes that "an effective city rebuilding strategy requires that the central cities encourage more private expenditure for housing, and this may in turn require that housing be much cheaper in the central city than in the suburbs."[43] Higher tax rates would only add to the disincentives.

The detrimental effect of the property tax on the built American environment is subtle but pervasive. It discourages any improvements that might raise the value of property. As Martin Meyerson and Edward C. Banfield noted:

> The most serious defect of the real property tax is that it discourages new investment. As it stands, the tax offers property owners no incentive to tear down old houses, office buildings, stores, and factories and build better ones in their places. On the contrary, it actually penalizes efforts at modernization; a new building is at a tax disadvantage as compared to an old one.[44]

Even modest building renovations are penalized, including rehabilitation of the dilapidated dwellings of the poor. In the words of Pickard, "Present city property tax policies place a premium on neglect and discourage owners from renewal rehabilitation, or adequate maintenance of property."[45] During the 1960s, when federal assistance was available to help bring slum housing up to the minimum health and safety standards required by code, some observers alleged that owners might actually reject such aid for fear that the improvements would cause the local assessor to raise their property valuation and tax levy.[46]

In cities both large and small, one of the most prevalent aspects of community blight is the proliferation of underused and vacant properties, often in various states of neglect and disrepair. A primary cause for this abuse of urban land is speculation abetted by low taxes on unimproved property. Taken in aggregate, such speculation on land has been a primary

[43]Dick Netzer, *Impact of the Property Tax: Its Economic Implication for Urban Problems* (Washington, D.C.: USGPO, 1968), 22.

[44]Martin Meyerson and Edward C. Banfield, *Boston: The Job Ahead* (Cambridge: Harvard U. Press, 1966), 28.

[45]Pickard, *Taxation and Land Use,* 10.

[46]Lai, "Effect of Property Taxation," 66. See also George Sternlieb, *The Tenement Landlord,* (New Brunswick, N.J.: Rutgers, 1966), 214–17.

contributor to haphazard, "leap-frog" development and inefficient urban
sprawl.

The Seagram Case

The policy implications of the real property tax have effect beyond
housing and land planning to encompass commercial urban development
and ultimately the design quality of the city as a whole. At the high end of
the financial ladder, the consequence of assessing architectural improvements was made evident in 1963 in the case of *Joseph E. Seagram & Sons,
Inc. v. New York Tax Commissioner*. The appellant in the suit had constructed as its Manhattan headquarters the Seagram Building, a monumental and unusually expensive structure designed by architects Mies van
der Rohe and Philip Johnson. Considered a landmark of modern architecture, the 38-story bronze-and-glass tower was, in the words of the court,
"world-renowned for its striking and imposing beauty."[47]

Though the great cost of the building could not be justified by rental
income alone, even including Seagram's own tenancy, the quality of the
design and construction was a premium to the corporation's public image.
Using this reasoning in considering the high prestige and cost attached to
the building, the city refused to assess the property based on capitalized net
income of total rental space, though this formula was the usual method of
assessing commercial properties. Instead, the city computed the tax based
on replacement cost less depreciation, thus resulting in a considerably
higher real estate tax.

In a 4–3 decision, the New York Court of Appeals agreed with a lower
court finding that where a building is designed more for "prestige and advertising value" than rental income, "the actual building construction cost
. . . is some evidence of value."[48] The court upheld the higher tax assessment, stating,

> This does not mean that advertising or prestige or publicity value is erro-
> neously taxed as realty value. It certainly does not mean that a corporate
> sponsor of esthetics is being penalized for contributing to the metropolis a
> monumental and magnificent structure.[49]

Regardless of this claim, the effect was the same. Real estate tax is normally
the greatest single expense in maintaining commercial office buildings in
New York City and less than ten years after the ruling, Seagram, Inc., sold

[47]200 N.E. 2d 447 (N.Y., 1964), 448.
[48]Ibid.
[49]Ibid.

its namesake building. Said a *New York Times* editorial of the upheld appellate court decision,

> If the ruling stands, no sensible investor will put up a quality building, knowing that he will pay outrageously for the privilege. No realtor in his right mind will proceed with anything but minimum standard construction and maximum plot coverage. . . . Who would make such a gesture and risk producing a superior or "prestige" structure when he will be punished for it? If a way is being sought to condemn the city to perpetual architectural mediocrity, the Tax Commission has found it.[50]

The architectural community was even more incensed. Complained an editorial in the *Architectural Forum,*

> Who are these judges to set the New York architectural standard at the lowest going? . . . Make no mistake, if this outrageous decision is permitted to stand, its effects on our three-dimensional cities will not be superficial, but disastrous. The power to tax architecture on its quality is the power to prevent it.[51]

Certainly such experiences are unlikely to encourage other developers to invest in design quality, the cumulative effect being a built urban environment of tax-imposed shabbiness and mediocrity. While the court decision was widely denounced, the fault lay not so much in myopic judge-made public policy as in the invisible web of revenue law on property taxation, which impelled the issue and the eventual ruling. Instead of venting its anger on the courts, the architectural community would have done better to support legislative reform of the tax.

Delogu criticized the system of property taxation that penalized Seagram, Inc., in more general terms. He wrote,

> Another aspect of local government tax policy which has a negative effect on local land use objectives is the practice of immediately raising the assessed value and thus raising the property tax on properties which have recently completed improvements. These improvements may have been made as a matter of personal or civic pride, in response to the enforcement of a building or housing code, or as part of a neighborhood rehabilitation program. Whatever the motivation, the fact is that a desired land use objective, *viz.,* the care, maintenance, and improvement of real property, is less likely to occur because an immediate and direct penalty attaches. The greater the extent to which the land use objective is sought to be advanced (the higher the value of the improvement), the greater is the penalty.[52]

---

[50]*New York Times* editorial, "A Penalty on Quality," May 21, 1963, 36.

[51]*Architectural Forum* editorial, "How to Ban Architecture," 118, no. 5 (May 1963), 97.

[52]Delogu, "Taxing Power," 281.

Actually, the *Seagram* case seems to be a deviation from the rule in New York. Although many other cities offer tax abatement to attract desired economic development, New York provides tax relief as an incentive and compensation for public restrictions on redevelopment in order to preserve designated historic and architectural landmarks. Because the city has more than its share of tax-exempt properties, such as churches, governmental buildings, nonprofit organizations, and diplomatic missions, those properties that cannot claim exempt status are left with a disproportionate tax burden.

Property Tax Reform

Because many of the problems associated with the property tax stem from the practice of assessing the full value of a property to include improvements, reformers have frequently suggested that the tax would be more neutral in its effect if assessments were based on land value alone, without consideration of developed values. The premise of this approach is that increases in the value of a site are generally attributable to societal activity in the vicinity and therefore is logically more subject to public recapture, whereas improvements on the site can be ascribed to the owner's efforts and investments. The concept, first suggested by the nineteenth-century economist Henry George,[53] is based on the reasoning that site-value assessment would shift the tax penalty from constructive development of a property to speculative possession of idle or underutilized land, thus discouraging the latter. In comparing the usual tax, which places a preponderance of the levy on improvements with a tax on land value only, Mary Rawson summarized the policy implications as follows:

> The tax on improvements evidently contributes to the shortage of housing and to the deterioration of our cities by its inhibiting effect on building and capital investment. The tax on land, through its tendency to lower land prices, lowers the real cost of housing. By providing a stimulus to the efficient use of land, it encourages rebuilding in central areas and it checks the practice of holding land in a vacant or ill-used state.[54]

Although site-value taxation has been used in other countries, such as Australia and New Zealand, in only rare instances, notably in Hawaii and Pittsburgh, has this practice been attempted in the United States. However, even in Pittsburgh, the county and school district levies that constitute a considerable proportion of the tax remain tied to full property values,

[53]Henry George, *Progress and Poverty* (1879; reprint, New York: Robert Schalkenbach Foundation, 1966), 433 ff.
[54]Mary Rawson, *Property Taxation and Urban Development* (Washington, D.C.: Urban Land Institute, 1961), 11.

thereby diluting the effect of reform. Nonetheless, in hearings before the National Commission on Urban Problems in the 1960s, Pittsburgh mayor Joseph M. Barr stated that the site-value tax "has generally helped to encourage the improvement of real estate, especially the building of large commercial office structures. I also believe this system has been particularly fair and beneficial to homeowners."[55] In its final report, the commission said,

> The "social" argument for taxation of land value and, perhaps even more specifically, of increases in land value, is: since such values result largely from social and governmental factors, rather [than] from actions by the property owners, it is entirely proper for government to capture through taxation a significant part of the economic benefits that flow in the first instance to private landowners.[56]

As stated earlier, no tax can be really neutral, and the commission recognized this fact. Arguably, site-value taxation could promote overdevelopment, particularly in urban centers where land values are the highest. Nonetheless, the commission concluded that the benefits of site-value taxation far outweigh its limitations, certainly in comparison to the existing system. It advised that the executive branch direct a study be made "by which Federal taxation might be used to recoup for public purposes a materially increased portion of increases in land value," and that the states consider "higher taxes upon land values or land-value increments."[57]

These recommendations were not enough to satisfy some individuals on the commission. In a supplement included in the 1968 report, these commission members wrote:

> We regret, however, that the Commission as a whole did not see fit to endorse some wider applications of the Pittsburgh plan, which taxes the gifts of nature—such as land—at twice the rate that it taxes the products of men's labor and saving. For this would further diminish the burdens on effort, and hence stimulate improvements. We believe Pittsburgh was on the right track when it introduced this differential tax system.[58]

Because the supply of land is fixed, speculative holding of this commodity from the development market can virtually guarantee unearned profits. Douglas and his colleagues unleashed an unusually bitter attack on land speculators who stood to benefit from the property tax:

---

[55]National Commission on Urban Problems (Douglas Commission), *Hearings* 1 (Washington, D.C.: USGPO, 1968), 313.
[56]National Commission on Urban Problems *Building the American City*, 388.
[57]Ibid., 394.
[58]Ibid., 395.

The owners of the land can go to Hawaii and rest languidly on the beaches or make prolonged safaris into the inmost regions of Africa. They may study Shakespearian literature at Stratford on Avon, or Zen Buddhism in Japan, or ponder urban problems in Washington. They can go up in space capsules or down a hole in the ground. They will become richer and richer without toil or sweat. For, as Doctor Johnson once remarked in another connection, here are "riches beyond the dreams of avarice."[59]

The focus of the attack was not fully justifiable, however. For in the American free-enterprise system, it must be expected that individuals bent on capitalist gain will seek any legally sanctioned means to make profit. The fault lies with the system that allows and even encourages investment in socially counterproductive speculation.

The property tax has also been criticized for the manner in which its acquired revenues have been dispersed. In many communities, much of the income from the tax is used to finance public education. In California, in the 1971 case of *Serrano v. Priest,*[60] and in New Jersey's 1973 case *Robinson v. Cahill,*[61] the courts found that property taxation produces inequities in public education; affluent school districts can afford a low tax rate and still provide better schools than poorer districts, taxing at a higher rate, can. However, when the same issue came before the Supreme Court in the 1973 case *San Antonio Independent School District v. Rodriguez,*[62] the high Court upheld the property tax as a lawful method of financing public education, reasoning that the equal-protection clause of the federal Constitution infers no guarantee of equal opportunity in education.

The property tax as presently administered in most jurisdictions is regressive and penalizes the poor most severely. Not only do they live in the urban areas that receive the highest tax assessments, but they must also spend a greater portion of their income on housing, which is then subject to taxation. Even the middle class with fixed or moderately rising incomes can be hard hit, since property taxes have commonly been known to increase much more rapidly than the rate of inflation, thus forcing relinquishment of homes that the occupants can no longer afford. Furthermore, as pointed out by the New Jersey court in *Southern Burlington County N.A.A.C.P. v. Township of Mount Laurel,*[63] the property tax encourages communities seeking to reduce the tax burden of financing public education and other social services to exclude the principal clients of such services—families with young children and low- or moderate-income groups.

For all the problems associated with the property tax, it is ironic to

---

[59]Ibid., 396.
[60]487 P. 2d 1241 (Cal., 1971).
[61]303 A. 2d 273 (N.J., 1973).
[62]411 U.S. 1 (1973).
[63]336 A. 2d 713 (N.J., 1975).

note that the property tax is a weak source of revenue compared to the income tax. However, the negative effects of property tax can be adjusted to support reasoned planning policies and objectives.

THE FEDERAL INCOME TAX

As suggested earlier, taxation as an instrument of public policy is a distinctive characteristic of government in a capitalist society. Indeed, in the United States, the primary source of both revenue and policy power for the federal government is the income tax.

Beyond its certainty—an attribute the old saying has taxes sharing with death—at least four other characteristics distinguish the federal levy. First and foremost is the immeasurable impact of federal revenue policy on the social and economic condition of every American, whether rich or poor, or whether the consequences be good or bad, planned or unintended. Second is the bewildering complexity of a code that can confound even experts, whether accountants, lawyers, judges, or public officials. Third, the fact that any tax provision has as many champions as it has detractors—that one individual's sustenance is another's poison—has infused federal tax policy more than any other public issue with the politics of special interests. Fourth is the propensity for the tax law to change, not only from one administration to the next but indeed from one year to another. This last characteristic is especially pertinent now that the federal tax code has undergone one of its most extensive revisions since its inception in 1913.[64]

The impact of the invisible web of federal revenue law is complex and pervasive. In terms of urban development and planning alone, its considerations are well beyond the scope of this chapter. This brief synopsis can point to only a few of the most evident policy consequences of the tax in very general terms and without attempting to address details or specifics.

As the president credited for advocating the present reform and guiding it into legislation, Ronald Reagan has held to the conservative principle that the national economy, and hence American society as a whole, can best be served by encouraging private investment through provision of advantageous tax incentives aimed at the wealthy who are financially capable of investing. One premise on which the president's approach to tax policy is based is that economic expansion, fueled by private investment and coupled with reductions in government spending on social programs, can effectively reduce the federal deficit without raising taxes. In contrast, liberal lawmakers typically prefer a more progressive policy of taxation that would reduce the deficit and pay for programs to benefit society and aid the less fortunate by imposing higher levies on the well-to-do.

[64]United States Constitution, 16th Amendment (1913), Internal Revenue Code, 26 U.S.C., as amended subsequent to Pub. L. 591 (1954), 68A Stat.

Philosophy aside, the Tax Reform Act of 1986,[65] like any piece of major legislation, represents both combination and compromise among a multitude of practical political and economic concerns. Its passage followed more than two years of study and negotiation by the executive and legislative branches of government as well as intensive lobbying by private special-interest groups concerned about how tax reform might affect them. In addition to the president's own proposal,[66] reform plans were submitted by individual legislators,[67] by the Treasury Department,[68] and by both houses of Congress.[69] The final act was signed into law on October 22, 1986, to become effective for the 1987 tax year.

One of the most notable differences between the new and previous codes is the tax rate. Under the new law, the rate for individuals has been reduced, especially for the very poor, who will pay no income tax at all, but also for the well-to-do. In place of the fourteen tax brackets for married taxpayers under the old law, the new code has only two rates of 15 and 28 percent. Families with very high incomes, however, are subject to a "marginal" rate (on every dollar earned above a specified amount) of 33 percent because of provisions that phase out the 15 percent rate and personal exemptions as income rise. Nonetheless, even that top rate is lower than the previous ceiling of 50 percent and substantially below the top rate of 70 percent that existed when President Reagan took office in 1981. Likewise, the top corporate tax rate has also been reduced from 46 percent under the old law to 34 percent.

To balance the lowering of tax rates—to keep the reform "revenue neutral" so that there will be neither a great increase nor decrease in overall federal tax revenues—many deductions to declared income or tax shelters allowed under the old law have been reduced or eliminated. As entrepreneurs and investors modify their practices for their own economic advantage under the new tax code, their behavior will profoundly affect the urban real estate market and city development, including urban design, housing, and preservation. Accordingly, whether for good or ill, the invisible web of

[65]Tax Reform Act of 1986, Pub. L. 99–514, 100 Stat. 2085.

[66]*The President's Tax Proposals to the Congress for Fairness, Growth, and Simplicity* (Washington, D.C.: USGPO, 1985).

[67]Fair and Simple Tax Act of 1985 (Kemp-Kasten Bill), H.R. 777, S. 325; Fair Tax Act of 1985 (Bradley-Gebhardt Bill), S. 409, H.R. 800.

[68]Department of the Treasury, *Tax Report for Fairness, Simplicity, and Economic Growth* (Washington, D.C.: USGPO, 1984).

[69]Tax Reform Act of 1985, H.R. 3838, passed by House, Dec. 17, 1985. (See Text of H.R. 3838 and Report by the House Ways and Means Committee, also Joint Committee on Taxation, Summary of H.R. 3838 as reported by the House Ways and Means Committee, Dec. 7, 1985). Tax Reform Act of 1986, H.R. 3838, passed by Senate, June 24, 1986. (See Text of H.R. 3838 and Report by the Senate Finance Committee, also Joint Committee on Taxation, Summary of H.R. 3838 as reported by the Senate Finance Committee, June 5, 1986.) Compromise bill passed by House on Sept. 25, 1986, and by Senate on Sept. 27, 1986.

the federal tax code is a determinant of urban policy sine qua non, demanding the attention of the urban planner and designer as much as the capitalist or legislator.

But despite the policy intent of reform, experience has shown that virtually any revenue measure can cause side effects unintended by the policy makers. These side effects occur as the market responds to the tax incentives in ways unanticipated by lawmakers and policy analysts. Since the Tax Reform Act was conceived largely on the basis of past experience, and because its own policy effects are still somewhat speculative and subject to final empirical determination and adjustment, it is fitting to examine at least in cursory fashion the experience of past tax policies that have led to the present reform.

Capital Gains

Since the earliest days of the Republic, Americans have placed great stock in Adam Smith's thesis that private investments of capital serve to benefit society as a whole by expanding the economy, creating both goods and jobs, and generating taxable as well as disposable income. Hence, to give special encouragement to this fundamental activity of capital investment, federal tax law since 1921 had allowed the proceeds or capital gains realized from the sale or investment holdings to be given preferential treatment.[70] Before its reform, the law permitted 60 percent of the gain realized from the sale of long-term investments to be exempt from taxation, thus resulting in a considerably lower levy on capital gains. Under the new code, however, capital gains are given no special advantage and are taxed the same as other income.

The problem with the capital-gains provision from an urban planning standpoint was that the lower tax levy encouraged not only investment in economically regenerative ventures, such as manufacturing and construction, but also unproductive speculation on commodities, including underused real estate. The favorable treatment of gains realized from the disposal of real estate not held primarily for sale tended to promote speculation and to discourage constructive improvement of property. Any substantial improvement could endanger the preferred capital-gains status of the property upon its sale by exposing it to the higher rate levied upon ordinary income. In other words, like the ad valorem property tax, the capital-gains provision actually penalized productive development or redevelopment and rewarded inactivity. Though aimed at the investor rather than the developer, the tax offered no encouragement for the latter to develop or improve his holdings, thereby sanctioning underutilization and neglect of land and existing buildings and promoting patterns of wasteful leap-frog development. The 1986

[70]Revenue Act of 1921, Pub. L. 98 (67th. Cong.), 42 Stat. 227, 232.

tax act effectively ended this disincentive by rescinding the special preference given to capital gains.

Depreciation and Tax Shelters

Other aspects of federal revenue law have made real estate especially
attractive to the investor seeking to shelter his income from taxation. Investments in income-producing real estate, such as buildings used for business
or rent, have enjoyed the advantage of depreciation, whereby the full cost
of an investment in other than nondepreciable land could be recovered by
writing off the amount over a prescribed period of time. Before the tax
reform, the time required to write off a building was typically nineteen
years, with the additional advantage of provisions that allowed accelerated
rates of depreciation during the early years of an investment. Under the
new code, however, the time required for depreciation has been extended
to twenty-seven-and-one-half years for residential real estate and thirty-one-
and-one-half years for nonresidential real estate, with the investment depreciated in equal, or "straight-line," increments.

Arguably, the premise that buildings depreciate in worth to no more
than the value of the land they sit on is a fiction, since most buildings kept
in reasonable repair (with maintenance itself a deductible business expense)
actually tend to appreciate in value. The fiction was moreover exposed by
the fact that, after an owner had depreciated a property to the extent of its
full yield of tax benefits, he could then sell it—typically at a capital gain
and without making improvements—and the new owner could then repeat
the depreciation process all over again, reaping the same tax benefits as his
predecessor did.

Significantly, investors in real estate have also managed until now to
retain a powerful tax advantage that had been denied virtually all other
forms of investment. Since the 1970s, investors in most fields have been
prohibited from making deductions from taxable income in excess of the
amount for which they are personally liable, or "at risk." Previously, each
participant in a limited-partnership syndicate (so called because of the limitation on the partners' liability) could, for example, invest ten thousand
dollars in a venture and sign a nonrecourse promissory note (for which he
would not be personally liable) for ninety thousand dollars. He would then
be eligible to claim depreciation on the full sum total of one hundred thousand dollars even though his actual commitment is only ten thousand. In
using nonrecourse borrowing to gain leverage, an investor could reap depreciation deductions that could exceed his actual investment liability. It
was not necessary for a venture to be profitable—indeed, it could be deliberately managed at a loss—in order to obtain tax deductions several times
the initial expendable investment. By using this strategy, a canny investor
could lawfully reduce the tax obligation on even a substantial income virtu-

ally to zero. Legislation passed in 1976 and 1978 put a stop to this tax sheltering practice in most fields of investing other than real estate. The 1986 tax code eliminates this tax-shelter advantage of "passive" limited-partnership participation in real estate also, subjecting investments in real estate to the same "at risk" limitation governing other types of investments.

In addition to depreciation, new investments, in certain elements of a building, such as elevators, could be separately eligible for investment tax credits. These credits, amounting to 10 percent of the cost of the component, were usually advantageous over deductions in that they could be subtracted directly from taxes owed rather than from taxable income. Like accelerated depreciation, the investment tax credit has been repealed by the 1986 code.

The tax provisions for not-at-risk real-estate syndication, accelerated depreciation, and investment credit provided investors with an incentive to seek loss-structured tax shelters rather than income-producing enterprises. The result of this tax characteristic was a spate of overconstruction and a still present surplus of vacant commercial and office buildings in many urban centers, particularly in the sunbelt states. Overbuilding occurred because investors could still benefit from loss-oriented tax shelters despite their lack of tenants and a negative cash flow. From a socioeconomic standpoint, the boom-and-bust cycle in construction caused by questionable tax policy has adversely affected local economic and social stability, and a high vacancy rate in buildings contributes neither to sound real estate values nor to vital urban design.

The process of depreciation also provided no inherent incentive for conscientious maintenance and renewal of income property and indeed tended to foster the "milking" of deteriorating real estate investments for their tax benefits. As economist Jerome Rothenberg wrote in 1967, "Gains—whether income flows or capital gains—do not depend on adequate maintenance of the property. On the contrary, systematic neglect of maintenance increases the amount of gains."[71] Rothenberg's observation is shared by Richard E. Slitor, who wrote in 1968,

> The old-fashioned motives of careful stewardship, conservation, and rational long-range management of investment are apparently subordinated in the tax shelter operation which often characterizes multiple-unit rental housing development, luxury as well as slum.[72]

Even since Slitor's report to the Douglas Commission on the federal income tax in relation to housing, the tax-shelter motive has been the root cause of

---

[71]Jerome Rothenberg, *Economic Evaluation of Urban Renewal* (Washington: Brookings, 1976), 50.

[72]Richard E. Slitor, *The Federal Income Tax in Relation to Housing* (Washington: USGPO, 1968), 38.

many condominium conversions. In these conversions, which have affected luxury rentals perhaps even more than low-income housing, a landlord would convert his investment in rental apartments into condominium sales after the tax-shelter benefits of the property had been exhausted, thus causing displacement of those tenants unwilling or unable to buy.

Although some reforms were instituted before 1986, federal income tax policy did little to further sound urban development and planning policy, notwithstanding its immeasurable potential to do so. As Donald Hagman observed,

> All of these tax avoidance schemes that affect decisions to hold or develop land seldom dovetail with local plans and regulations to shape development. The tax considerations may be inducements that overpower the ability of local governments to control development.[73]

Land development enterprises will be affected more than most other types of businesses by the 1986 tax reform because past development practices depended heavily on tax shelter incentives that have now been abolished. The act will more reasonably promote profit-motivated economic behavior instead of loss-oriented investment in tax shelters. With this policy change, the value of many office and apartment developments, especially in overbuilt urban areas, will fall as the tax benefits disappear. As a consequence, construction activity will also slow down. Conversely, however, the reduction in development will cause rents to rise as the availability of building space declines, especially as developers attempt to compensate for lost tax benefits.

Harnessing Income Tax Policy

To encourage private purchase of bonds that are issued by state and local governments to finance capital projects and programs, the 1986 Tax Reform Act continues the past policy of exempting from federal income taxation the interest received from municipal bonds. The incentive is necessary since such bonds yield a relatively low return and cannot compete with higher-yielding commercial issues. The law makes a distinction between "industrial development bonds" that are used to pay for governmental operations and those used to finance "private activities." Whereas the former is accorded tax-exempt status without qualification, private activities must conform to specific rules governing "exempt facilities" in order to be granted the tax preference.

The new code is less generous than its predecessor in its listing of activi-

---

[73]Donald G. Hagman, *Urban Planning and Land Development Control Law* (St. Paul: West, 1971), 365.

ties that qualify for exempt-facilities status. Of those that do qualify, many if not all are elements integral to city planning and design: airports; docks and wharves; mass commuting facilities; multifamily residential rental projects; and facilities for water supply, sewage and solid waste disposal, electric energy or gas supply, hazardous waste disposal, district heating and cooling, and air- and water-pollution control. Types of projects previously allowed tax-free bonding but omitted from the new code include facilities for sports, conventions, or trade shows, and parking, although parking facilities are still permitted if attached to an exempt facility. The deletion of these municipal functions, as well as elimination or tighter restrictions on facilities ancillary to exempt activities—hotels, office buildings, retail shops, food services, and industrial facilities connected to mass urban transportation complexes—will make funding for many types of traditional urban design programs more difficult and expensive to obtain.

Among the projects remaining eligible for advantageous tax-exempt municipal bonds is multifamily low-income rental housing. In addition to this incentive and to supplement governmental housing subsidies, the old code offered an array of inducements to attract the investor. Not only were opportunities for syndication and rapid depreciation available but also special incentives specifically designed to stimulate investment in low-income housing. For example, expenditures incurred in rehabilitating existing low-income rental units could be depreciated over an amortization period of only sixty months. Though the 1986 act eliminated most of these incentives, they have been replaced by tax credits that will return over a ten-year period 70 percent of the present value of qualified new construction or rehabilitation expenditures on low-income housing that does not receive federal financing assistance. Other qualified low-income housing will be eligible for a similar 30 percent credit.

Tax credits were also provided to encourage use of renewable energy resources such as solar energy. The residential energy tax credit, which reimbursed 40 percent of up to ten thousand dollars of the cost of a residential renewable energy system, was one of several tax credits that played a major role in the development and use of renewable energy resource systems. However, interest in alternative sources of energy has dwindled, and the 1986 tax act has allowed the residential energy credit to expire.

As noted in chapter 8, recent high interest and activity in the preservation and adaptive reuse of older and historic buildings is largely attributable to a tax policy that has reimbursed owners part of the cost of rehabilitation. Enacted by the Tax Act of 1981,[74] the credit subsidized the renewal of old buildings on an ascending three-tier scale, covering 15 percent of the expense of renovating nonresidential structures that are at least thirty years old, 20 percent for those over forty years, and 25 percent of certified his-

[74]Economic Recovery Tax Act of 1981, Pub. L. 97–34, 95 Stat. 172.

toric structures, including residential buildings. In 1980, before the credit was established, 614 restorations of certified historic structures were recorded. In 1984, after the credit was authorized, the number of projects had increased to 3,214.[75] As former Atlanta budget and planning commissioner Leon Eplan is quoted: "Very few federal actions, including urban renewal or block grant programs, have had as positive an impact on private investment in the cities as the 1981 tax act."[76]

Even though President Reagan expressed great pride in the success of his adminstration's 1981 rehabilitation tax credit in promoting high-quality, private redevelopment and revitalization of the older center city, his original federal tax code reform proposal would have discontinued this incentive. However, Congress prevailed in retaining the measure, although it replaced the three-tier credit with a less generous two-tier version that provides a 10 percent credit for buildings constructed before 1936 and 20 percent for the rehabilitation of certified historic structures.

The Home as a Tax Shelter

The tax incentives for home ownership have been so successful and the beneficiaries so numerous and politically powerful that, despite apprehension in the residential real estate and development industry regarding the effect of tax reform, the new revenue code will continue most of the considerable advantages of home ownership. Interest on home mortgages, including loans on second homes, will remain deductible from taxable income, as will payments on state and local property taxes.

Although elimination of the capital-gain tax denies homeowners a lower tax rate on gains realized from the sale of their homes, other provisions remain that allow them to avoid taxation on the sale of their principal residence. If, within two years either before or after the sale, they purchase a replacement home costing more than the sale price of the first, the tax on the gain is "rolled over" or postponed until the profit is actually withdrawn, no matter how many times the replacement process occurs. The accumulated capital gains from such home sales can indeed escape taxation altogether, for after the age of 55, the homeowner is entitled to a once-in-a-lifetime tax exclusion of up to one hundred twenty-five thousand dollars on these gains.

In contrast to its continued support of home ownership, the revised tax law will affect the home rental market adversely, both for the renter and the investor. Some 60 percent of all multifamily housing developments

[75]Kurt Andersen and Madeleine Nash,"New Gilded Age Grandeur," *Time* 126, no. 9 (Sept. 2, 1985), 46–47.
[76]Robert Guskind, "Tax Reform Blues," *Planning* 51, no. 7 (July 1985), 9.

are financed by syndicated tax shelters. With elimination of many of the tax benefits, such as accelerated depreciation, that were enjoyed by housing syndicates in the past, there will be no tax incentive for investment in private rental housing. With less investment, fewer rental housing units will be built, and a tighter and more expensive market for renters will result. As previously noted, however, the new tax code continues the federal policy of encouraging investment in low-income housing, by replacing previous incentives with a tax credit for investments in low-income rental housing.

The tax advantages of ownership over rental, together with the general accessibility of favorable home mortgage loans made possible by the FHA, have been significant factors in the development and expansion of the American suburb. In spite of the expansion of inner-city condominium development, the typical middle-income home buyer with a family continues to demonstrate a strong preference for traditional, detached single-family houses at the urban fringe. Hence, any incentive to buy has tended to expand the pattern of single-family suburban decentralization of the city.

The effects of the Tax Reform Act of 1986 will be felt for many years by all participants in urban land development, from developers, architects, realtors, builders, construction trades, and suppliers to potential investors and consumers of housing and commercial land development. Likewise, the interests of urban designers, city planners, and planning and development lawyers—not to mention cities and city dwellers—will be affected as well. Indeed, while the restructuring of the invisible web of the federal internal revenue code will effect immense changes on city development, planning, and design, the consequences of this reform will reach beyond urban planning issues alone into every facet of American life, making explicit the relationship between government and free enterprise in the United States.

Ronald Reagan's avowed philosophy has been to remove the artificial influence of tax avoidance considerations and leave more to market determination. Until the consequences of the 1986 tax act have been determined empirically by the collective behavior of the American people, the jury is still out as to how successful the president, the Congress, the policy and tax analysts, and the special interests have been in engineering this reform. Some of the problems brought about by past tax policies, such as overbuilding to gain a tax benefit rather than to meet a need, will likely be eliminated or curtailed. But other problems, some unforeseen, may just as likely arise. For example, if investments in real estate are made less attractive by abolition or reduction of their tax advantages, real estate sales and development would also drop and rents of available units would rise, at least until future market demand prompts reinvestment. Some Cassandras are predicting that elimination of such previous tax provisions as accelerated depreciation and the investment tax credit will bring about recession as investment and entrepreneurial risk-taking decline. Certainly, Reagan's reform is bold and entails some risk. Because his tax policy is based conceptually on the market, it contrasts in principle with previous reforms, which have characteristically been tied to traditional adjustments in regulation.

As professionals, city planners and designers must be certain that their administrations and client communities are well informed and take full advantage of every available government incentive and subsidy program. Moreover, federal fiscal policy and taxation should be regarded by those committed to improving the quality of urban life as a political forum in which they must strive to advocate policies that would advance the best interests of all who live and work in the city and to guard against measures that would do harm. Indeed it is hardly an exaggeration to say that the invisible web of federal fiscal and tax legislation can have as compelling and pervasive an effect on urban planning and housing considerations as all local zoning regulations combined.

PART VII

CLOSING REMARKS

Chapter 14

Synthesis

In exploring the historic and practical association that has existed between the law and urban design from feudal times to the present, this book has delved into a vast diversity—some might say a disparity—of topics. There are those considerations that deal with long-lasting, broad, philosophical principles; others concern the minutiae of contemporary events and practices that are continually evolving. Some aspects are matters of fact, whereas others reflect more the conclusions and opinions of the author. It is far too late in these closing remarks to broach new topics or to argue new ideas. Nonetheless, as an architect and planner who has both practiced and taught in these professions, I may be forgiven for reiterating, as in the classroom, some of the principal concepts that I would like to leave with the reader.

First, it must be reemphasized that, to whatever degree practicable, the rules and restrictions of public regulation of urban design and planning, as in any field, should be established and well defined before the event. This principle, possibly more than any other, distinguishes a free society governed by the Rule of Law from a dictatorship subject to the ad hoc discretionary judgment of a ruler, however wise and benevolent. The arguments supporting this thesis come not only from Hayek, the Constitution, and a vast majority of jurists and legal scholars but also from a common sense of fairness and reasonableness: that the rules of any game should be made certain in advance and be known by all participants before play commences. Certainly the principle imposes limitations on the actions of public regulators—notably city planners, urban designers, and members of architectural design review boards—but the restriction also establishes the line between control of private architecture by the owner and its regulation by the public, as well as between a free society and the totalitarianism of arbitrary rule.

The second principle, an extension or derivation of the first, comes from the observations made by Supreme Court Justice William J. Brennan, Jr., in the *Metromedia*[1] and *Vincent*[2] cases with regard to outdoor advertising. As applied to design review of private land development, it suggests that for any review or control of architecture to be constitutionally valid, a community "commitment" and "comprehensive coordinated effort"[3] toward environmental beauty and design must be convincingly demonstrated as a prior condition to regulation.

This prerequisite can be reasonably met, as in New York City and San Francisco, by the formal adoption by the local planning commission and legislature of a community plan that defines, in full context and in appropriate written and graphic terms, the regulating community's policy objectives in urban design. These goals should further be translated into substantive design criteria and guidelines that, when enacted into code, can enable private development to implement the public's design policy through simple compliance with the law. The documented criteria, whether rigorous or permissive, would delimit and guide administrative discretion through its provision of a clear reference standard by which the design proposals for individual private developments can be impartially evaluated in architectural review or by the courts in exercising judicial oversight.

The existence of a predefined and clear community design plan is so fundamental in my opinion that, like Justice Brennan, I maintain that any deficiency in such a policy statement should render void any form of design regulation—especially architectural design review—as lacking in an adequate legislative standard. (I differ, however, with the justice's holding that billboard regulation based on aesthetic and nuisance considerations should also be struck down if a comprehensive community commitment is not made evident, since there is ample precedent in case law to substantiate such regulation.) A community design plan would also serve to make design review less a piecemeal and negative reaction to private development initiatives and more a part of an affirmative public process toward purposeful community design.

In considering questions of design, the judiciary has not infrequently relied on the expert opinion of design professionals serving on local boards of architectural review. While such deference on seemingly technical issues

[1]*Metromedia, Inc. v. City of San Diego,* 453 U.S. 490 (1981).
[2]*Members of the City Council of the City of Los Angeles v. Taxpayers for Vincent,* 466 U.S. 789 (1984).
[3]Note 1, 531-32.

may appear reasonable, it has sometimes worked to the detriment of design creativity and First Amendment guarantees, since many aspects of design are more philosophical or expressive than technical. Rather than effectively delegating their authority and responsibility to the boards, the courts should instead base their deliberations on the requirement and content of a substantive community design plan, which should be clearly articulated in terms that laymen in design—whether property owners, neighbors, lawyers, or judges—can fully comprehend, without struggling with obfuscating design jargon.

The third concept borrows from the teachings of law professors Kenneth Culp Davis and George Lefcoe, who argue for proper administrative procedures where rigorous a priori guidelines and rules are unworkable, and where common sense dictates the exercise of reasonable administrative discretion. Their admonitions include the right of applicants who come before a design review board to challenge board members whom they can substantively prove are biased for such reasons as business competition or design philosophy. They should also be allowed the prerogative of appeal, not redundant de novo proceedings concerning design considerations by a second panel of design professionals, but on procedural grounds before professionals trained in law or administration. Perhaps most important, applicants as well as their opposition should be entitled to written opinions from the review board that adequately explain and justify the reasoning of its decisions. Written documentation would properly subject the actions of review boards to the same open scrutiny as the design proposal of the applicants, and the accumulated record of written design opinions could lead to de facto "common law" design-review policies that would provide substantive guidelines, in addition to the community's urban design plan, to aid in the impartial evaluation of subsequent design proposals placed before the board.

The fourth consideration, which requires a somewhat more extensive discourse, concerns the contrast between organic determination of urban development and the deliberate design of rationalism. This discussion was included not so much for its introductory function but for the valuable lessons that history and experience can offer the present in determining the future. The lesson has particular relevance to the city planner contemplating the drafting of urban design controls.

Many urban designers have been trained in the tradition of architecture which tends to view urban design largely in terms of project design of a grander scale and greater complexity. However, in a pluralist, free-enterprise society such as the United States, realistic opportunities for urban designers to approach projects of a truly urban dimension with the rational, unified control customarily assumed for projects of a smaller physical scale and lesser social complexity are few and far between. Certainly, since the prolific mid-century era of Urban Renewal, when planners enjoyed the largesse of an activist federal government (whose involvement indirectly nurtured urban design as a field), such opportunities have declined substantially. Over the years, federal generosity and participation have turned to frugality and reticence, and development entrepreneurs with vision and brilliance are unfortunately all too rare. Consequently, the traditional "global" approach to city planning, modeled after the "exclusive" methodology of Le Corbusier and following the rationalist tradition of Sixtus and Haussmann, can often lead only to unfulfillment and frustration.

More to the issue, the urban designer must be fundamentally aware that the design character of a community is inextricably identified with the implemental processes involved in its attainment. The rational approach to city design that assumes virtually total control on the part of the urban designer or his sponsor (usually the governing body of the community) typically results in an urban design idiom of a perfection and scale more expressive of a unitary and absolutist society than a free-enterprise system in which pluralism, however untidy and seemingly disorganized, prevails in both design and social function.

Such leading writers as Lewis Mumford and Jane Jacobs have long taught the design community that, notwithstanding the less apparent design coherence resulting from pluralist determination, organic city building can yield spontaneous qualities of human-scale beauty, diversity and vitality in life, and other manifestations of democracy and freedom that unified rationality and absolute control in urban design can seldom imitate. In addition, such social analysts as Herbert Gans have convincingly demonstrated that the centralized and remote authority of modern-day rationalism, as espoused by the Urban Renewal program, has produced imposing and monumental civic centers too often at unacceptable social costs to the original, target-area community.[4]

From this viewpoint, it seems reasonable to adopt an approach to urban design theory and planning controls consistent with Friedrich Hayek's teachings: that in a free-enterprise democracy, the proper role of the public planner and urban designer is to design only the legal framework that guides pluralistic urban land development, and to modulate organic city growth rather than attempt to control all aspects of community design. Mumford and Jacobs tell us that the finest fruits of healthy and vibrant urban design depend on pluralism for their fertilization. Accordingly, the city and its components should be seen less as physical artifacts subject to rational design determination than as organisms that can only be influenced and guided. To put an ironic twist on the modernist aphorism "less is more," the lesser the control, the greater the level of spontaneity and vitality in organic, pluralist urban development.

[4]Herbert J. Gans, *The Urban Villagers* (1962; reprint, New York: Macmillan, Free Press, 1982).

What, then, of the urban design plans and codes for San Francisco, which are as strict as any conceived for a major city in America? Do these controls go too far in regulating toward a centrally conceived, rationalist goal in urban design? Arguably so. But the stringency of the San Francisco urban design controls is balanced by a market for urban land development that is as distended and potentially rampant as in any expanding metropolitan area of the country. A forceful argument is made in the city's plans and ordinances themselves that rigorous regulation is required to check the overwhelming market for development and to turn the potential for detriment and chaos into social, economic, and design advantage. Still, planning director Macris's remark that "it is time for a departure from the International Style"[5] betrays a questionable public policy of favoring one design philosophy over another.

The appropriate degree of regulation and the question of whether it imposes too much centralized rationalism in planning or is too permissive in allowing pluralism to degenerate into unplanned chaos are issues that cannot be decided by an absolute and static standard. Rather, they are dependent on prevailing economic conditions and social considerations, not to mention the political climate existing in the community. Justice Holmes's admonition in the *Pennsylvania Coal*[6] case to look at the "particular facts" is very appropriate to city planning. Thus, the intensity of controls suitable for San Francisco or New York may be entirely inappropriate for other communities, or even for the same community at a different time and under changed circumstances, economic or otherwise.

From this consideration derives the fifth principle that an urban design plan, like all other elements of a community's comprehensive general plan, must be subject to periodic public review and occasional complete revision to adjust to changing circumstances and evolving perceptions and values. Continuous planning evaluation of the real-world effect of an urban design plan and its implementing land-use legislation would prevent these instruments from becoming out-of-date vestiges of static, end-state planning, without relevance or conscientious enforcement.

Although drafted by professionals, the policy underlying the plan must have the support of the community, including a consensus of both residents and development interests. If particular viewpoints or philosophies, whether on social, economic, design, or stylistic issues, are represented in the plan, there should be ample opportunity for those with differing views to debate the policy and to effect possible revision and amendments. In this regard, all parties should be allowed the right to present testimony, including the opinions of their own experts. Open hearings would not only edu-

---

[5]Kurt Anderson and Jane Ferguson, "Outlawing the Modern Skyscraper," *Time* 126, no. 3 (July 22, 1985), 56.

[6]*Pennsylvania Coal Company v. Mahon,* 260 U.S. 393 (1922), p. 413.

cate and invite public participation in the formulation of urban design policy affecting the appearance, function, and design of the community, but on a more individual level, they would afford private land owners the opportunity to debate regulations that, if adopted, may restrict the use and design development of their particular properties. This approach would not differ substantially from the public hearing requirement of other components of a general land-use plan, of which the urban design element should be an integral part.

The sixth consideration concerns the potential of virtually all land planning controls, no matter how meritorious their ends, to effect some form of exclusion. Although treatment of this complex and divisive issue has been limited in this work, it has still been shown that social exclusion has been a characteristic—sometimes even a desired, if unacknowledged, purpose—of planning since its inception. The dark propensity for planning regulation to exclude segments of society has many manifestations, including discrimination against those of low or moderate income through minimum zoning requirements; limiting the number of people who can move to a suburb through unduly restrictive land-use requirements; prohibiting unwanted industry through environmental and natural-resource planning; and censoring nonconforming design creativity through architectural design review. Public planners and designers must work to mitigate the exclusionary effects of their control strategies, and they must remain aware of their professional responsibility, legal obligation, and even moral duty to protect those who have no voice in local decision making against parochial interests, even of their immediate client community.

A root cause of parochialism in planning, of course, can be traced to the Standard Acts that underlie most state enabling laws on planning and zoning. Under these anachronistic legislative models, most planning authority is delegated to local rather than to regional levels of government. To address this issue in a fundamental way, urban designers and other city planners should strive to reform state enabling legislation on planning and zoning.

The seventh premise of this book is that readers should look beyond the confines of traditional past practices and disciplinary perspectives to examine and harness *all* the various social forces that affect the physical form and social character of urban development. The specific focus of this book, of course, has been the influence of the law on urban design and planning. Especially at a time when Washington is loath to spend federal resources on local programs, it seems at least expedient for urban designers to direct attention away from traditional design and coordination of capital projects and toward urban design through the public regulation of private developments. But beyond regulation through zoning, planners should also look to other public authorities that affect urban design and development, specifically to the options of compensable regulation, eminent domain, public subsidy, and tax policy. Largely because of the inertia of past practice and because fiscal and tax policies are mostly beyond the ready manipulation of local planning officials, these public authorities have not been taken full advantage of as instruments for planning and urban design. However, now that cuts in the federal budget and federal tax reform are stripping much of the initiative effect of fiscal and tax policies on urban planning—and, ironically, because of these reductions—there appears to be heightened awareness of the policy implications of these public authorities on the form and development of cities.

The eighth consideration is a critical summary of defects that have been found, over the last half century of practical application, to characterize planning regulation under the Standard Acts. The list of shortcomings is provided to reinforce awareness of the weaknesses of the existing system of controls and to impart sensitivity to its deficiencies.

First, the present system of zoning relies almost totally on the police power. Typically, there is little or no consideration of alternative sources of public authority such as compensable regulation, eminent domain, subsidy, and tax policy. Second, despite growing integration of socioeconomic considerations in planning, zoning administration is still steeped mainly in physical planning. As a result, the critical socioeconomic implications of community growth and planning are all too often lost or given only passing thought. Third, even in consideration of physical planning alone, zoning administration is concerned only with the public regulation of the use and development of private property. Rarely is zoning integrated with the planning and scheduling of public infrastructure and capital improvements, whether roadways and other transportation systems, schools and other public buildings, community open space, utility systems, intercommunity transportation terminals, and other physical facilities—much less coordinated with such public-service functions as public safety, education, health, and subsidized housing.

The fourth shortcoming of planning regulation is that its administration is fragmented even within a governing body. The Standard Acts apportioned authority for community planning and zoning to three separate entities; the local legislature, the planning commission, and the board of adjustment, thus opening the door to a possible lack of coordination and even to internal conflicts. Many communities have a fourth governing body, the board of architectural review. Fifth, the appointed membership of all local boards vested with planning authority, including the elected membership of the local city council or county board, is composed mostly of amateurs. The result is that, for better or worse, planning administration is typically more responsive to political considerations than to professional values. Sixth, partly because of the nonprofessional background of appointed officials in the past, and partly because of weaknesses inherent in the Standard Acts, the implemental character of zoning has frequently been confused, by the public and even by some officials, with the policymaking function of planning. However, planning has increased in professionalism over the last few decades, owing to the better training and use of staff planners, and this confusion has diminished appreciably.

The seventh weakness is an underlying problem of the Standard Acts. Instituted in the 1920s, the Standard Acts were based on the premise of end-state planning, with insufficient flexibility to adapt to change and opportunity. Most innovations in planning, including planned unit development, transfer of development rights, performance zoning, and compensable regulation, are aimed at increasing flexibility in planning regulation by investing more authority in administrative discretion. The eighth criticism is that the Standard Enabling Acts, by investing planning authority in local rather than in regional or state government, has failed to provide an effective administrative hierarchy with regional responsibility and authority. The result has been competition and exclusion, with local communities planning and zoning to advance their own parochial self-interests, even at the expense of their neighbors. Like the problem of flexibility, reform of this characteristic will require structural changes in the basic system.

Last in this list of nine shortcomings is related to the immediately preceding note. The absence of a regional hierarchy in planning administration forces too much reliance on the legal system for appeals, thereby burdening the courts and relegating critical questions of planning to a judiciary that may or may not be knowledgeable on planning matters. Most reforms suggest that, as a part of increased administrative discretion in planning under stringent procedural guidelines, planning administrations should be permitted to exercise a greater appellate function, in line with a regional hierarchy and under the watchful oversight of a learned judiciary.

Finally, though the perspective and language of this book are deeply immersed in the traditions of law, I would like to believe, as an architect and planner rather than a lawyer, that this work can be considered a practical study in urban design, if in a somewhat unusual and unaccustomed sense. Having practiced and taught in various aspects of architecture as well as in planning, I see law as a practical extension of both disciplines, and have sought, in this work, to break the disciplinary barriers that separate the professions. Admittedly, such melding is not an easy task for such dichotomous perspectives as design and law. As one might observe, a designer perceives a work as compromised if it has been done before; a lawyer sees a work as compromised if it has not. Still, an interdisciplinary perspective can open new doors to creative planning controls and urban design.

As one imbued with both the design values of architecture and the social priorities of planning, I revel in the egalitarian notion that urban design offers the benefits and delights of environmental design to all members of a community, rich or poor. Nonetheless, my advocacy for the values of urban design is tempered with the realization that in a democracy like the United States, social ideals are hardly ever to be found in absolutes. Instead, just as the ancient Chinese found the holistic harmony of Tao embodied in a dynamic yin-yang tension of opposite but complementary forces, a modern democracy's ideals exist in a dynamic, ever-changing balance between apparently conflicting ends: conservatism and liberalism; self-interest and altruism; public regulation and private enterprise; centralized planning and pluralist determination; and rational city design and organic urban development. The Constitution guarantees all Americans freedom to participate in the process and to advocate positions—even extreme ones—for one extreme will invariably provoke a reaction toward the other, in the ebb and flow of a shifting, fluid balance.

Thus, unlike a totalitarian society in which rational and simplistic determination is the rule, a democracy is characterized by seeming ambiguities, in which freedom finds itself in the dynamic relationship between opposing ideas. These conflicting forces include, on the one hand, those who consider pluralist and independent determination both a virtuous means and a desirable end, and on the other, those who seek the social benefit possible through community cooperation and reasonable, centralized authority. The same dichotomy is apparent in the issue of free design expression in architecture versus public regulation of design through imposition of standards and design review, or in a larger context, of free expression and use of land in private development versus community goals in urban design. One untempered by the other would result in design anarchy at one extreme and dictatorship and environmental sterility at the other. Indeed, any static resolution of this dilemma would in itself diminish the greatest values and strengths of American society.

Under the aegis of the Constitution, the American system of adversary case law—itself rooted in the empirical origins of medieval common law—guarantees the advocacy of a diversity of social ends and ideals. The resulting pluralistic diversity of goals and ideas is an essence of the organic process of urban development, which in turn has been shown to be the appropriate foundation and design expression of a democratic, free-enterprise society. To recall an observation from the opening paragraph of the introduction, law and urban design exist in a cultural symbiosis, at once expressing and molding the very nature of social man, and determining each other as attributes of his civilization.

Bibliography

Abercrombie, Patrick. *Greater London Plan, 1944.* London: His Majesty's Stationery Office, 1945.

Abercrombie, Patrick, and John H. Forshaw. *County of London Plan.* London: Macmillan & Co., 1943.

Adams, Gerald D. "A Last Ditch Effort to Save Downtown San Francisco." *Planning* 50, no. 2 February 1984, 4.

Advisory Commission on Intergovernmental Relations. *Building Codes: A Program for Intergovernmental Reform.* Washington, D.C.: USGPO, 1966.

Agnor, William H. "Beauty Begins a Comeback: Aesthetic Consideration in Zoning." *Journal of Public Law* 11, no. 2 (1962), 260–84.

AIA Journal. "Award of Merit: Wurster, Bernardi & Emmons." 46, no. 1 (July 1966), 46–47.

AIA Journal. "Lever's Landmark Status Upheld: Demolition Threat Deserted." April 1983, 17.

Albertson, Robert J. *Zoning for Aesthetics.* Master's thesis, University of Pennsylvania, 1955.

Altschuler, Alan A. *The City Planning Process: A Political Analysis.* 1965. Reprint. Ithaca, N.Y.: Cornell University Press, 1969.

American Institute of Architects, Committee on Design. *Design Review Boards: A Handbook for Communities.* Washington, D.C.: American Institute of Architects, 1974.

American Insurance Association. *National Building Code.* New York: AInA, 1976 (revised periodically).

American Law Institute. *A Model Land Development Code: Tentative Draft No. 1.* Philadelphia: ALI, 1968.

435

American Law Institute. *A Model Land Development Code: Complete Text and Commentary.* Philadelphia: ALI, 1976.

Amsterdam, Anthony G. "The Void-for-Vagueness Doctrine in the Supreme Court," *University of Pennsylvania Law Review* 109, no. 1 (1960) 67–116.

Andersen, Ralph, and Associates. *Redevelopment and Tax Increment Financing by Cities and Counties in California.* Pasadena: Southern California Executive Directors Association, 1976.

Andersen, Kurt, and Jane Ferguson. "Outlawing the Modern Skyscraper." *Time* 126, no. 3, July 22, 1985, 56.

Anderson, Martin. *The Federal Bulldozer: A Critical Analysis of Urban Renewal, 1949–62.* Cambridge: M.I.T. Press, 1964.

Anderson, Robert M., "Architectural Controls." *Syracuse Law Review* 12, no. 1 (1960–1961), 26–49.

———."The Board of Zoning Appeals—Villain or Victim?" *Syracuse Law Review* 13, no. 3 (1962), 353–88.

———. *American Law of Zoning.* Rochester, N.Y.: Lawyers Cooperative, 1968.

Architecture. "New Federal Legislation to Restrict Billboards Proposed." 75, no. 1, January 1986, 18.

Architectural Forum, editorial. "How to Ban Architecture." 118, no. 5, May 1963, 97.

Arnheim, Rudolf. *Art and Visual Perception.* 1954. Reprint. Berkeley and Los Angeles: University of California Press, 1974.

Attorney General's Commission on Pornography. Final Report. Washington, D.C.: United States Government Printing Office, 1986.

Babcock, Richard F. "The Unhappy State of Zoning Administration in Illinois." *University of Chicago Law Review* 26, no. 4 (1959), 509–41.

———. "Billboards, Glass Houses, and the Law." *Harper's* 232, no. 1391, April 1966, 20–33.

———. *The Zoning Game.* Madison: University of Wisconsin Press, 1966.

———. "Zoning." In *The Practice of Local Government Planning.* Edited by Frank S. So, Israel Stollman, Frank Beal, et al. Washington, D.C.: International City Management Association, 1979.

———. "Eastlake v. Forest City Enterprises." *Land Use Law and Zoning Digest* 28, no. 8 (1976), 3–4.

Bacon, Edmund N. *Design of Cities.* 1967. Reprint. New York: Viking, 1974.

Barnett, Jonathan. *Urban Design as Public Policy.* New York: McGraw-Hill, 1974.

———. *An Introduction to Urban Design.* New York: Harper & Row, 1982.

Barrett, Robert. "Still Fighting: Mom of 'Evicted' Baby Says She Won't Call off Her Battle with Sun City." *Arizona Republic* (Northwest edition), July 7, 1986.

Bassett, Edward M. *Zoning.* New York: Russell Sage Foundation, 1936.

Bassett, Edward M., and Frank B. Williams. "Model Laws for Planning Cities, Counties and States." 17, vii *Harvard City Planning Studies* (1935).

Bastie, Jean, "The Paris Area—Growth and Organization." In *Urbanization and Planning in France.* Paris: International Federation for Housing and Planning, Centre de Recherche d'Urbanisme, 1968.

Baumgarten, Alexander G. *Reflections on Poetry.* Translated by Karl Aschenbrenner and William B. Holther. Berkeley and Los Angeles: University of California Press, 1954.

Beard, Charles A. *An Economic Interpretation of the Constitution of the United States.* 1913. Reprint. New York: Macmillan Co., 1960.

Beardsley, Monroe C. *Aesthetics from Classical Greece to the Present.* New York: Macmillan Co., 1966.

Bentham, Jeremy. *Theory of Legislation.* Translated by R. Hildreth. 1780. Reprint. London: Kegan Paul, Trench, Trubner and Co., 1911.

———. *An Introduction to the Principles of Morals and Legislation.* Edited by J. H. Burns and H.L.A. Hart. 1780. Reprint. London: University of London, Athlone Press, 1973.

Bergs, Robert A. "Aesthetics as Justification for the Exercise of the Police Power or Eminent Domain." *George Washington Law Review* 23, no. 6 (1955), 730-50.

Birkbeck, Morris. *Notes on a Journey in America.* 1817. Ann Arbor: University Microfilms, 1966.

Birkhoff, George D. *Aesthetic Measure.* Cambridge: Harvard University Press, 1933.

Blackstone, William. *Commentaries on the Laws of England.* 1765-1769. Reprint. London: Dawsons, 1966.

Blucher, Walter H. "Is Zoning Wagging the Dog?" In *Planning 1955.* Chicago: American Society of Planning Officials, 1956.

Blumberg, Grace. "Legal Methods of Historic Preservation." *Buffalo Law Review* 19, no. 3 (1970), 611-39.

Blumenfeld, Hans, "The Role of Design." *Journal of the American Institute of Planners* 33, no. 5, September 1967, 307-10.

Bosanquet, Bernard. *Three Lectures on Aesthetic.* 1915. Reprint. New York: Bobbs-Merrill, 1963.

Bosselman, Fred P. "The Third Alternative in Zoning Litigation." *Zoning Digest* 17, no. 3 (1965), 73-80.

———. "Regulations of Signs in the Post-McLuhan Age, or—Can Billboards Be Beautiful?" *Land Use Control Quarterly* 2, no. 3 (1968), 14-20.

Bosselman, Fred, and David Callies. *The Quiet Revolution in Land Use Control.* Washington, D.C.: United States Government Printing Office, 1971.

Bosselman, Fred, David Callies, and John Banta. *The Taking Issue.* Washington, D.C.: United States Government Printing Office, 1973.

Bowen, Catherine Drinker. *The Lion and the Throne.* Boston: Little, Brown & Co., Atlantic Monthly Press, 1956.

Branch, Melville C. *Continuous City Planning.* Planning Advisory Service Report no. 290. Chicago: American Society of Planning Officials, 1973.

Break, George F., and Joseph A. Pechman. *Federal Tax Reform: The Impossible Dream?* Washington, D.C.: Brookings Institution, 1975.

Brolin, Brent C. *The Failure of Modern Architecture.* New York: Van Nostrand Reinhold Co., 1976.

Bross, James L. "Taking Design Review Beyond the Beauty Part: Aesthetics in Perspective." *Environmental Law* 9 (Winter 1979). 211-40.

Bryden, David P. "The Impact of Variances: A Study of Statewide Zoning." *Minnesota Law Review* 61 (May 1977), 769-840.

Bufford, Samuel. "Beyond the Eye of the Beholder: A New Majority of Jurisdictions Authorize Aesthetic Regulation." *University of Missouri at Kansas City Law Review* 48 (1980), 125-66.

Building Officials and Code Administrators, International. *Basic Building Code.* Chicago: BOCA (revised periodically).

——. *Basic Housing Code.* Chicago: BOCA (revised periodically).

Butler, Stuart B. *Enterprise Zones: Greenlining the Inner Cities.* New York: Universe Books, 1981.

Canter, David, and Peter Stringer. *Environmental Interaction.* New York: International Universities Press, 1975.

Carnegie, Andrew. Autobiography. New York: Houghton Mifflin Co., 1920.

Cartwright, Timothy J. "Problems, Solutions and Strategies: A Contribution to the Theory and Practice of Planning." *Journal of the American Institute of Planners* 39, no. 3, May 1973, 179–87.

Chapin, F. Stuart, Jr. *Urban Land Use Planning.* Urbana: University of Illinois Press, 1965.

Clay, Philip L. "The Rediscovery of City Neighborhoods: Reinvestment by Long-time Residents and Newcomers." In *Back to the City: Issues in Neighborhood Renovation.* Edited by Shirley B. Laska and Daphne Spain. New York: Pergamon Press, 1980.

Coke, Edward. *The First Part of the Institutes of the Laws of England, or a Commentary Upon Littleton.* 1628. Reprint. London: Clark, Saunders, and Benning, Maxwell, Sweet, et al, 1832.

——. *The Second Part of the Institutes of the Laws of England.* 1642. Reprint. London: E. and R. Bronke, Bell-Yard, New Temple Bar, 1797.

Collins, George R., and Christiane C. Collins. *Camillo Sitte and the Birth of Modern City Planning.* New York: Random House, 1965.

Collins, Glen. "Notes on a Revolutionary Dinosaur." *New York Times Magazine* August 6, 1972, 12.

Columbia Law Review. "The Police Power, Eminent Domain, and the Preservation of Historic Property." 63, no. 4 (1963), 708.

——. "Zoning, Aesthetics, and the First Amendment." 64 (1964).

Commission on Obscenity and Pornography. *Report.* Washington, D.C.: United States Government Printing Office, 1970.

Committee on Administrative Tribunals and Inquiries. Oliver Franks, Chairman. *Report* (The Franks Report). London: Her Majesty's Stationery Office, Cmnd. 218, 1957.

Committee on Utilisation of Land in Rural Areas. *Report* (The Scott Report). London: His Majesty's Stationery Office, Cmnd. 6378, 1942.

Conti, John V. "Preserving the Past." *Wall Street Journal* August 10, 1970.

Cook, Robert S., Jr. *Zoning for Downtown Urban Design.* Lexington, M.A.: D. C. Heath & Co., 1980.

Costonis, John J. "The Chicago Plan: Incentive Zoning and the Preservation of Urban Landmarks." *Harvard Law Review* 85, no. 3 (1972), 574–634.

——. *Space Adrift.* Urbana: University of Illinois Press, 1974.

——. "Law and Aesthetics: A Critique and a Reformulation of the Dilemma." *Michigan Law Review* 80, no. 3 (1982), 355–461.

Cowan, H. Bronson. *A Graphic Summary of Municipal Improvement and Finance as Affected by the Untaxing of Improvements and the Taxation of Land Values.* New York: International Research Committee on Real Estate Taxation, 1958.

Crane, David A. "The City Symbolic." *Journal of the American Institute of Planners* 26, no. 4, November 1960, 280–92.

———. "The Public Art of City Building." *Annals of the American Academy of Political and Social Science* 352, March 1964, 84–94.

Cribbet, John E. "Changing Concepts of the Law of Land Use." *Iowa Law Review* 50, no. 2 (1965), 245–78.

Cunningham, Robert L., ed. *Liberty and the Rule of Law.* College Station: Texas A.&M. University Press, 1979.

Cunningham, Roger A. "Scenic Easements in the Highway Beautification Program." *Denver Law Review* 45, no. 2 (1968), 167–266.

Dalton, Dolores A. "San Francisco's Residential Rezoning: Architectural Controls in Central City Neighborhoods." *University of San Francisco Law Review* 13 (Summer 1979), 945–70.

Daniels, Lee A. "City Finds Gentrification Beneficial." *New York Times* March 23, 1984.

Davidoff, Paul. "Advocacy and Pluralism in Planning." *Journal of the American Institute of Planners* 31, no. 4, November 1965, 331–38.

Davis, Douglas. "Raiders of the Lost Arch." *Newsweek* 107, no. 3, January 20, 1986, 66.

Davis, Kenneth C. *Administrative Law Treatise.* St. Paul: West Publishing Co., 1958.

———. *Discretionary Justice.* 1969. Louisiana State University Press. Reprint. Westport, C.T.: Greenwood Press, 1980.

Delafons, John. *Land-Use Controls in the United States.* 1962. Reprint. Cambridge: M.I.T. Press, 1969.

Delogu, Orlando E. "The Taxing Power as a Land Use Control Device." *Denver Law Review* 45, no. 2 (1968), 279–95.

Department of the Treasury. *Tax Reform for Fairness, Simplicity, and Economic Growth.* Washington, D.C.: United States Government Printing Office, 1984.

Descartes, Rene, "Discourse on the Method of Rightly Conducting the Reason." In *The Philosophical Works of Descartes.* Translated by E. S. Haldane and C.T. R. Ross. Cambridge: University Press, 1934.

Dewey, John. *Art as Experience.* New York: Minton, Balch, 1934.

Dicey, Albert Venn. *Introduction to the Study of the Law of the Constitution.* 1885. Reprint. London: Macmillan & Co., 1956.

Dillon, John Forrest. *Commentaries on the Law of Municipal Corporations.* 5th edition. Boston: Little Brown & Co., 1911.

Donovan, Thomas B. "Zoning: Variance Administration in Alameda County." *California Law Review* 50, no. 1 (1962), 101.

Dukeminier, Jesse, Jr. "Zoning for Aesthetic Objectives: A Reappraisal." *Law and Contemporary Problems* 20 (1955).

Dukeminier, Jesse, Jr., and Clyde L. Stapleton. "The Zoning Board of Adjustment: A Case Study of Misrule." *Kentucky Law Journal* 50, no. 2 (1962), 273–350.

Dunham, Allison. "Griggs v. Allegheny County in Perspective: Thirty Years of Supreme Court Expropriation Law." *Supreme Court Review* (1962), 63–106.

———. "Property, City Planning, and Liberty." In *Law and Land.* Edited by Charles M. Haar. Cambridge: Harvard University Press, M. I. T. Press, 1964.

Dunham, Allison, and Fred P. Bosselman. "The Reporters' Reply." *Land-Use Controls Ann.* (1971), 113.

Epstein, David G. *Brasilia, Plan and Reality.* Berkeley and Los Angeles: University of California Press, 1973.

Evanson, Norma. *Le Corbusier: The Machine and the Grand Design.* New York: George Braziller, 1969.

Expert Committee on Compensation and Betterment. *Report* (The Uthwatt Report). London: His Majesty's Stationery Office, Cmnd. 6386, 1942.

Fechner, Gustav T. *Vorschule der Aesthetik.* 1876. Reprint. Leipzig: Breitkopf & Hartel, 1897.

Field, Charles G. *Building Regulatory Practices and the Courts.* Washington, D.C.: Federal Trade Commission, 1980.

Field, Charles G., and Steven R. Rivkin. *The Building Code Burden.* Lexington, M.A.: D.C. Heath & Co., 1975.

Freund, Ernst. *The Police Power.* Chicago: Callaghan, 1904.

Frieden, Bernard J. *The Environmental Protection Hustle.* Cambridge: M. I. T. Press, 1979.

Friedrich, Otto. "A Bad Idea Whose Time Has Come." *Time* 127, no. 5, February 3, 1986, 81.

Fuller, Lon L. "Adjudication and the Rule of Law." In *Proceedings of the American Society of International Law.* Fifty-fourth Annual Meeting of the American Society of International Law, April 28, 1960, Washington, D.C. Vol. 54.

Fulton, William. "The City Takes its Cut." *Planning* 47, no. 9, September 1981, 23.

Gallion, Arthur B., and Simon Eisner. *The Urban Pattern: City Planning and Design.* 1950. D. Van Nostrand. Reprint. New York: Van Nostrand Reinhold Co., 1980.

Gans, Herbert J. *The Urban Villagers.* 1962. Reprint. New York: Macmillan Co., Free Press, 1982.

Geneslaw, Robert, and George M. Raymond. "Ramapo Dropping its Famed Point System." *Planning* 49, no. 6, June 1983, 8.

George, Henry. *Progress and Poverty.* 1879. Reprint. New York: Robert Schalkenbach Foundation, 1966.

Ghent, William J. *Our Benevolent Feudalism.* New York: Macmillan Co., 1902.

Godschalk, David R., David J. Brower, et al. *Constitutional Issues of Growth Management.* Chicago and Washington, D.C.: Planners Press, 1977.

Goldberger, Paul. "In Perpetuum." *Architectural Record* 174, no. 5, mid April 1986, 112.

Gooder, David M. "Brakes for the Beauty Bus." In *Junkyards, Geraniums, and Jurisprudence: Aesthetics and the Law.* City: American Bar Association, 1967.

Gormley, W. Paul. "Urban Redevelopment to Further Aesthetic Considerations: The Changing Constitutional Concepts of Police Power and Eminent Domain." *North Dakota Law Review* 41, no. 316 (1965), 316–32.

Gratz, Roberta Brandes. "New York's Zoning Predicament." *Planning* 45, no. 12, December 1979, 24.

Greer, Scott. *Urban Renewal and American Cities.* Indianapolis: Bobbs-Merrill, 1965.

Greiff, Constance M., ed. *Lost America: From the Atlantic to the Mississippi.* Princeton, N.J.: Pyne Press, 1971.

———. *Lost America: From the Mississippi to the Pacific.* Princeton, N.J.: Pyne Press, 1972.

Grotii, Hugonis. *De Jure Belli et Pacis.* Translated by William Whewell. 1625. Reprint. Cambridge: University Press, 1889.

Guenther, Robert. "Gentrification of Inner Cities Loses Much of Former Vigor." *Wall Street Journal* December 31, 1984.

Guskind, Robert. "Tax Reform Blues." *Planning* 51, no. 7, July 1985, 7–13.

Haar, Charles M. "The Master Plan: An Impermanent Constitution." *Law and Contemporary Problems* 20, no. 3 (1955), 353–418.

———. "In Accordance with a Comprehensive Plan." *Harvard Law Review* 68, no. 7 (1955), 1154–75.

———. "The Social Control of Urban Space." In *Cities and Space: The Future Use of Urban Land.* Edited by Lowdon Wingo, Jr. Baltimore: Johns Hopkins Press, for Resources for the Future, Inc., 1963.

Haar, Charles M., ed. *Law and Land.* Cambridge: Harvard University Press and M. I. T. Press, 1964.

Hagman, Donald G., and Dean J. Misczynski, eds. *Windfalls for Wipeouts: Land Value Capture and Compensation.* Chicago and Washington, D.C.: Planners Press, 1978.

Hagman, Donald G. "Reporter's Comments on Village of Belle Terre v. Borass." *Land Use Law & Zoning Digest* 26, no. 6 (1974), 3–4.

———. "Commentary." *Land Use Law & Zoning Digest* 26, no. 6 (1974), 10–11.

———. *Urban Planning and Land Development Control Law.* St. Paul: West Publishing Co., 1971.

Hall, Edward T. *The Hidden Dimension.* New York: Doubleday, 1966.

Hall, Peter. *The World Cities.* New York: McGraw-Hill, World University Library, 1966.

Halsbury's Laws of England. 4th ed. "Town and Country Planning." Edited by Lord Hailsham of St. Marylebone. Vol. 46. 1984.

Hamilton, Walton H. "Property—According to Locke." *Yale Law Journal* 41, no. 6 (1932), 864–80.

Hartman, Chester. "Viewpoint." *Planning* 50, no. 5, May 1984, 42.

———. *The Transformation of San Francisco.* Totowa, N.J.: Rowman and Allanheld, 1984.

Harvard Law Review. "Administrative Discretion in Zoning." 82, no. 3 (1969), 668–85.

Hawkins, Benjamin M. "The Impact of the Enterprise Zone on Urban Areas." *Growth and Change* 15, no. 1, January 1984, 35–40.

Hayek, Friedrich A. *The Road to Serfdom.* 1944. Reprint. Chicago: University of Chicago Press, 1960.

Heap, Desmond. *The Encyclopedia of Planning Law and Practice.* London: Sweet and Maxwell, 1959 (revised periodically).

———. *An Outline of Planning Law.* London: Sweet and Maxwell, 1978.

Hedman, Richard. "A Skyline Paved with Good Intentions." *Planning* 47, no. 8, August 1981, 12.

Heeter, David G. "Toward a More Effective Land-Use Guidance System." *Land-Use Controls Quarterly* 4, no. 1 (1970), 8.

Heeter, David G., and Frank Bangs. "Local Planning and Development Control: One Bad Apple Spoils the Barrel." *Land-Use Controls Ann.* (1971), 27.

Herber, Lewis. *Crisis in our Cities.* Englewood Cliffs, N.J.: Prentice-Hall, 1965.

Hines, Thomas S. *Burnham of Chicago.* New York: Oxford University Press, 1974.

Hitchcock, Henry Russell. "Frank Lloyd Wright—Model in the Exhibition." In *Modern Architecture International Exhibition.* New York: Museum of Modern Art, 1932.

Hitchcock, Henry Russell, and Philip C. Johnson. *The International Style.* 1932. Reprint. New York: W. W. Norton & Co., 1966.

Hofstadter, Richard. *Social Darwinism in American Thought.* 1944. Reprint. New York: George Braziller, 1969.

Holdsworth, William S. *A History of English Law.* 1903. Methuen & Co. Reprint. London: Sweet and Maxwell, 1966.

Holmes, Oliver Wendell. *Holmes-Pollock Letters.* Edited by Mark D. Howe. 1941. Reprint. Cambridge: Harvard University Press, 1961.

Hopf, Peter S. *Designer's Guide to OSHA.* New York: McGraw-Hill, 1975.

Horowitz, Louis J., and Boyden Sparkes. "The Towers of New York." *Saturday Evening Post* 208, no. 39, March 28, 1936, 20.

Howard, A. E. Dick, ed. *Magna Carta, Text and Commentary.* Charlottesville: University Press of Virginia, 1964.

Howard, Ebenezer. *Garden Cities of Tomorrow.* 1902, Reprint: Cambridge: M. I. T. Press, 1965.

Howe, Frederic C. "In Defence of the American City." *Scribner's* 51, no. 4 (April 1912), 484–90.

Hsu, Evelyn. "'Sunshine Ordinance' Is the First Growth Limit to Pass in S.F." *San Francisco Chronicle* June 7, 1984.

Huxtable, Ada L. "Thinking Man's Zoning," *New York Times* March 7, 1971.

——. *Kicked a Building Lately?* New York: Quadrangle Books, 1976.

Institute for Environmental Studies. *The Plan and Program for the Brandywine.* Philadelphia: Institute for Environmental Studies, Regional Science Research Institute, U.S. Geological Survey, 1968.

Jacobs, Allan B. *Making City Planning Work.* Washington, D.C., and Chicago: American Planning Association, 1978.

Jacobs, Jane. *The Death and Life of Great American Cities.* New York: Random House, 1961.

Jaffe, Martin. "A Commentary on Solar Access: Less Theory, More Practice." *Solar Law Reporter* 2 (1980).

James, William. *Pragmatism.* Cambridge: Harvard University Press, 1975.

Jencks, Charles A. *The Language of Post-Modern Architecture.* New York: Rizzoli International Publications, 1981.

Johnson, Stephen B. "State Approaches to Solar Legislation: A Survey." *Solar Law Reporter* 1, no. 5 (1979), 55–137.

Kanner, Gideon. "Comment." *Land Use Law & Zoning Digest* 33, no. 5, May 1981, 8–10.

Kant, Immanuel. *The Critique of Judgment.* Translated by James C. Meredith. 1952. Reprint. Oxford: Clarendon, 1964.

Kaplan, Sam Hall. "San Francisco Reveals Vast Building Plan." *Los Angeles Times* August 26, 1983.

Kaplan, Stephen, Rachel Kaplan, and John Wendt. "Rated Preference and Complexity for Natural and Urban Visual Material." *Preception and Psychophysics* 12, no. 4 (1972), 354–56.

Keating, W. Dennis. "Linking Downtown Development to Broader Community Goals." *Journal of the American Institute of Planners* 52, no. 2, Spring 1986, 133.

Keene, John C., ed. *Policy Implications of the Real Property Tax.* Philadelphia: Institute for Environmental Studies, University of Pennsylvania, 1972.

Keene, John C., and Ann Louise Strong. "The Brandywine Plan." *Journal of the American Institute of Planners* 36, no. 1, January 1970, 50–58.

Kelly, Eric Damien. "Q & A: Municipal Liability," *Planning* 51, no. 2, February 1985, 17.

Kendig, Lane. *Performance Zoning.* Washington, D.C.: American Planning Association, 1980.

Kidney, Walter C. *The Architecture of Choice: Eclecticism in America 1880–1930.* New York: George Braziller, 1974.

King, Martin J. "Rex Non Protest Peccare??? The Decline and Fall of the Public Use Limitation on Eminent Domain." *Dickinson Law Review* 76, (Winter 1972), 266–81.

Knowles, Ralph L. "The Solar Envelope." *Solar Law Reporter* 2 (1980).

———. *Sun Rhythm Form.* Cambridge: M. I. T. Press, 1981.

Kochner, A. L., and Howard Dearstyne, *Colonial Williamsburg.* Williamsburg, V.A.: Colonial Williamsburg, 1949.

Kolis, Annette B. "Architectural Expression: Police Power and the First Amendment." *Urban Law Ann.* 16 (1979).

Krasnowiecki, Jan Z., and James C. N. Paul. "The Preservation of Open Space in Metropolitan Areas." *University of Pennsylvania Law Review* 110 (1961), 179.

Krasnowiecki, Jan Z. "Planned Unit Development: A Challenge to Established Theory and Practice of Land Use Control." *University of Pennsylvania Law Review* 114, no. 1 (1965), 47–97.

Krasnowiecki, Jan Z., and Ann Louise Strong. "Compensable Regulations for Open Space." *Journal of the American Institute of Planners* 29, no. 2, May 1963, 87–97.

Krye, Kenneth K., Jr. "Historic Preservation Cases: A Collection," *Wake Forest Law Review* 12, no. 1 (1976), 227–74.

Kucera, H. P. "The Legal Aspects of Aesthetics in Zoning." In *Institute on Planning and Zoning* 1 (1960), 21.

Kucirek, Joseph C., and J. H. Beuscher, "Wisconsin's Official Map Law." *Wisconsin Law Review* (March 1957), 176–221.

Lai, Richard T. "Effect of Property Taxation in Residential Rehabilitation in the Older Center City: General Considerations." In *Policy Implications of the Real Property Tax.* Edited by John C. Keene. Philadelphia: Institute for Environmental Studies, University of Pennsylvania, 1972.

Lane, Barbara Miller. *Architecture and Politics in Germany, 1918–1945.* Cambridge: Harvard University Press, 1968.

Lapp, Floyd. "Viewpoint." *Planning* 51, no. 7, July 1985, 42.

LeCorbusier. *Toward a New Architecture*. Translated by Frederick Etchells. 1927. Reprint. New York: Praeger, 1974.

———. *The City of Tomorrow*. Translated by Frederick Etchells. 1929. Reprint. Cambridge: M.I.T. Press, 1971.

———. *The Radiant City*. Translated by Pamela Knight et al. 1933. Reprint. New York: Orion, 1964.

LeGates, Richard T., and Chester Hartman. "The Anatomy of Displacement in the United States." In *Gentrification of the City*. Edited by Neil Smith and Peter Williams. Boston: Allen & Unwin, 1986.

Leopold, Luna B. *Quantitative Comparison of Some Aesthetic Factors Among Rivers*. Geological Survey Circular 620. Washington, D.C.: United States Department of the Interior, 1969.

Light, Charles P., Jr. "Aesthetics in Zoning." *Minnesota Law Review* 14 (January 1930), 109–23.

Lindsey, Robert. "Beverly Hills Upset by Unusual Decor of Saudis' Mansion." *New York Times,* April 23, 1978.

Lloyd, Dennis. *The Idea of Law*. 1964, Reprint. Baltimore: Penguin Books, 1970.

Locke, John. *The Second Treatise of Civil Government*. Edited by J. W. Gough. 1690. Reprint. Oxford: Basil Blackwell, 1948.

Longhini, Gregory, and Vivian Kahn. "Ballot Box Zoning." *Planning* 51, no. 5, May 1985, 11–13.

Los Angeles, City of. *Solar Envelope Zoning: Application to the City Planning Process, Los Angeles Study*. Golden, C.O.: Solar Energy Research Institute, SERI/SP-98156-1, June 1980.

Lynch, Kevin. *The Image of the City*. 1960. Reprint. Cambridge: M.I.T. Press, 1979.

———. *What Time is This Place?* Cambridge: M.I.T. Press, 1972.

Maitland, Frederic W. *Collected Papers*. Edited by H. A. L. Fisher. 1911. Cambridge University Press. Reprint. Buffalo, N.Y.: Hein, 1981.

———. *Domesday Book and Beyond*. Cambridge: Little Brown & Co., 1897.

Mandelker, Daniel R. "Judicial Review of Land Development Controls under the ALI Model Code." *Land-Use Controls Ann.* 1971, 101.

Mandelker, Daniel R., and Roger A. Cunningham. *Planning and Control of Land Development*. Indianapolis: Bobbs-Merrill, 1979.

Marcuse, Peter. "Abandonment, Gentrification, and Displacement: The Linkages in New York City." In *Gentrification of the City*. Edited by Neil Smith and Peter Williams. Boston: Allen & Unwin, 1986.

Mason, Alpheus T. *Brandeis: A Free Man's Life*. New York: Viking, 1946.

———. *William Howard Taft: Chief Justice*. New York: Simon & Schuster, 1964.

McElroy, Joseph J. "You Don't Have to Be Big to Like Performance Zoning." *Planning* 51, no. 5, May 1985, 16–19.

McKee, Sally J. "Solar Access Rights," *Urban Law Ann.* 23 (1982) 437–55.

McMillin, Ronald R. "Community-Wide Architectural Controls in Missouri." *Missouri Law Review* 36 (1971).

McQuillin, Eugene. *The Law of Municipal Corporations*. 1904. Reprint. Willmette, I.L.: Callaghan, 1981.

Megarry, R. E. "Compensation for the Compulsory Acquisition of Land in England." In *Law and Land*. Edited by Charles M. Haar. Cambridge: Harvard University Press and M.I.T. Press, 1964.

Merriam, Dwight H., Jane R. Rosenberg, and C. Luther Propst. "Governmental Liability under the Civil Rights Act of 1871 (42 U.S.C. 1983) and the Antitrust Laws." American Institute of Certified Planners, *Fifth Annual Zoning Institute,* San Francisco, 1985. Hartford, C.T.: Robinson & Cole.

Merriam, Dwight. "Caught in the Takings Muddle, Legally, We've Been Had." *Planning* August 1985, 23.

Meyerson, Martin, and Edward C. Banfield. *Boston: The Job Ahead.* Cambridge: Harvard University Press, 1966.

Michelman, Frank. "Toward a Practical Standard for Aesthetic Regulation," *Practical Lawyer* 15 (February 1969), 36–42.

Michigan Law Review. "Beyond the Eye of the Beholder: Aesthetics and Objectivity." 71, no. 7 (1973), 1438–63.

Mier, Robert. "Enterprise Zones: A Long Shot." *Planning* 48, no. 4, April 1982, 10.

Milgram, Grace. "Housing the Urban Poor: Urban Housing Assistance Programs." Congressional Research Service, Library of Congress. Washington, D.C.: United States Government Printing Office, 1983.

Miller, David J. "Aesthetic Zoning: An Answer to Billboard Blight." *Syracuse Law Review* 19, (Fall 1967), 87–94.

Milner, James B. "The Development Plan and Master Plans: Comparisons." In *Law and Land.* Edited by Charles M. Haar. Cambridge: Harvard University Press and M.I.T. Press, 1964.

Minard, Lawrence. "Wave of the Past? Or Wave of the Future?" *Forbes* 124, no. 7, October 1, 1979, 45.

Ministry of Housing and Local Government. *Development Plans: A Manual on Form and Content.* London: Her Majesty's Stationery Office, 1969.

Moore, Charles. *Daniel H. Burnham, Architect, Planner of Cities.* Boston and New York: Houghton Mifflin, 1921.

Morrison, Hugh. *Louis Sullivan.* 1935. Reprint. Westport, C.T.: Greenwood Press, 1971.

Moynihan, Cornelius J. *Introduction to the Law of Real Property.* St. Paul: West Publishing Co., 1962.

Mumford, Lewis. *The Culture of Cities.* New York: Harcourt, Brace & Co., 1938.

———. *The City in History.* New York: Harcourt, Brace & World, Harbinger, 1961.

Nathan, Richard P., Paul R. Dommel, Sarah F. Liebschutz, et al. *Block Grants for Community Development.* Washington, D.C.: United States Government Printing Office and Brookings Institution, 1977.

National Commission on Urban Problems (Douglas Commission). *Building the American City.* Washington, D.C.: United States Government Printing Office, 1968.

———. *Hearings* 1. Washington, D.C.: United States Government Printing Office, 1968.

National Institute of Building Sciences. *Greater Use of Innovative Building Materials and Construction Techniques Could Reduce Housing Costs.* Washington, D.C.: United States General Accounting Office, 1982.

National Institute of Building Sciences. *A Study of the Regulations and Codes Impacting the Building Process.* (1979).

National Trust for Historic Preservation. *A Guide to State Historic Preservation Programs.* Edited by Betts Abel. Washington, D.C.: Preservation Press, 1976.

——. *Directory of American Preservation Commissions.* Edited by Stephen N. Dennis. Compiled by Andrea Zizzi. Washington, D.C.: Preservation Press, 1981.

——. *Tax Incentives for Historic Preservation.* Edited by Gregory E. Andrews. Washington, D.C.: Preservation Press, 1980.

Neary, John. "A Cube House vs. the Squares." *Life* 67, no. 20, November 14, 1969, 83.

Netter, Edith, ed. *Land Use Law: Issues for the Eighties.* Chicago and Washington, D.C.: Planners Press, 1981.

Netzer, Dick. *Economics of the Property Tax.* Washington, D.C.: Brookings Institution, 1966.

——. *Impact of the Property Tax: Its Economic Implication for Urban Problems.* National Commission on Urban Problems. Washington, D.C.: United States Government Printing Office, 1968.

Neutra, Richard. " 'Practical' Cities Must not Be Full of Irritation." *The American City* April 1954, 122.

Newton, Norman T. *Design on the Land.* Cambridge: Harvard University Press, Belknap, 1971.

New York City, Department of City Planning. *Midtown Development.* New York: Department of City Planning, 1981.

——. *Midtown Zoning.* New York: Department of City Planning, 1982.

New York Times, editorial. "A Penalty on Quality." May 21, 1963.

Nichols, Philip. *The Law of Eminent Domain.* 1909. Reprint. New York: Bender, 1983.

Northwestern University Law Review. "Aesthetic Control of Land Use: A House Built Upon the Sand?" 59, no. 3 (1964), 372–94.

O'Hearn, Patrick J. "Reclaiming the Urban Environment: The San Francisco Urban Design Plan." *Ecology Law Quarterly* 3 (1973).

O'Leary, Jeremiah D., Jr., "On Being an Incrementalist during a Revolution." *Land-Use Controls Ann.* (1971), 43.

Oldman, Oliver, and Henry Aaron. "Assessment-Sales Ratios under the Boston Property Tax." *National Tax Journal* 18, no. 1 (1965), 36–49.

Olmstead, Frederick Law, Jr. "The Scope and Results of City Planning in Europe." *Hearing Before the Committee on the District of Columbia.* Senate Document no. 422, 61st Congress, 2nd. Session, March 11, 1910, 69.

Orgel, Lewis. *Valuation under the Law of Eminent Domain.* Charlottesville: Michie Co. Law Publishing, 1953.

Osborn, Frederic J. *Green-Belt Cities.* New York: Schocken Books, 1969.

Page, Clint, and Penelope Cluff, eds. *Negotiating for Amenities.* Washington, D.C.; Partners for Livable Places, 1982.

Peattie, Lisa R. "Reflections on Advocacy Planning." *Journal of the American Institute of Planners* 34, no. 2, March 1968, 80.

Pepper, Stephen C. *The Basis of Criticism In the Arts.* Cambridge: Harvard University Press, 1949.

Philadelphia, City of, Office of the Director of Finance. *Report on Real Property Assessments and Real Estate Tax Revenue.* Philadelphia: Office of the Director of Finance, 1971.

Philbrick, Francis S. "Changing Conceptions of Property in Law." *University of Pennsylvania Law Review* 86, no. 7 (1938), 691–732.

Pickard, Jerome P. *Changing Land Use as Affected by Taxation.* Research monograph no. 6. Washington, D.C.: Urban Land Institute, 1962.
——. *Taxation and Land Use in Metropolitan and Urban America.* Research monograph no. 12. Washington, D.C.: Urban Land Institute, 1966.
Pinkerton, Linda. "Aesthetics and the Single Building Landmark." *Tulsa Law Journal* 15, no. 3 (1980), 610–43.
Planning. "Offshore Leasing." 50, no. 5, May 1984, 33.
Platt, Rutherford H. "Feudal Origins of Open Space Law." *Land-Use Controls Quarterly* 4, no. 4 (1970), 27–41.
Pollack, Mark. "The Property Tax and Rehabilitation in Philadelphia: A Detailed Analysis." In *Policy Implications of the Real Property Tax.* Edited by John C. Keene. Philadelphia: Institute for Environmental Studies, University of Pennsylvania, 1972.
Pomeroy, Hugh R. "Losing the Effectiveness of Zoning Through Leakage." *Planning and Civic Comment* October 1941, 8.
Powell, Richard R. *Powell on Real Property.* 1949. Reprint. New York: Matthew Bender, 1981. (With Patrick J. Rohan)
President's Commission on Housing. *The Report of the President's Commission on Housing.* Washington, D.C.: United States Government Printing Office, 1982.
President's Committee on Urban Housing. *A Decent Home.* Washington, D.C.: United States Government Printing Office, 1968.
Progressive Architecture. "A.I.A. Headquarters: Headquarters for Architecture?" 48, no. 12, December 1967, 136–40.
Proshansky, Harold M., William H. Ittelson, and Leanne G. Rivlin, eds. *Environmental Psychology: Man and His Physical Setting.* New York: Holt, Rinehart, and Winston, 1970.
Public Administration Times. "Coastal Management at Issue in Congress." 8, no. 17, September 1, 1985.
——. "Tax Credits Spur Historic Preservation." 9, no. 4, February 15, 1986, 8.
Rasmussen, Steen E. *Experiencing Architecture.* Cambridge: M.I.T. Press, 1962.
——. *London: The Unique City.* 1934. Reprint. Cambridge: M.I.T. Press, 1967.
Rawson, Mary. "Property Taxation and Urban Development." Research monograph no. 4. Washington, D.C.: Urban Land Institute, 1961.
Redmond, Tim, and David Goldsmith. "The End of the High-Rise Jobs Myth." *San Francisco Bay Guardian.* 1985. Reprinted in *Planning* 52, April 1986, 18.
Reilly, William K., ed. *The Use of Land: A Citizens' Policy Guide to Urban Growth.* New York: Thomas Y. Crowell, 1973.
Reps, John W. *The Making of Urban America.* Princeton, N.J.: Princeton University Press, 1965.
——. "Requiem for Zoning." In *Planning 1964.* Chicago: American Society of Planning Officials, 1965.
——. *Town Planning in Frontier America.* 1965. Reprint. Princeton, N.J.: Princeton University Press, 1971.
Rhyne, Charles S. *Survey of the Law of Building Codes.* Washington, D.C.: American Institute of Architects and the National Association of Home Builders, 1960.
Rider, Robert W. "Transition from Land Use to Policy Planning: Lessons Learned." *Journal of the American Institute of Planners* 44, no. 1, January 1978, 25.

Rodwin, Lloyd. *The British New Towns Policy.* Cambridge: Harvard University Press, 1956.

Rothenberg, Jerome. *Economic Evaluation of Urban Renewal.* Washington, D.C.: Brookings Institution, 1976.

Royal Commission on the Distribution of the Industrial Population. *Report* (The Barlow Report). London: His Majesty's Stationery Office, 1940 Cmnd. 6153.

Rubin, Bruce A. "Architecture, Aesthetic Zoning, and the First Amendment." *Stanford Law Review* 28 (November 1975), 179–201.

Saalman, Howard. *Haussmann: Paris Transformed.* New York: George Braziller, 1971.

Saarinen, Eliel. *The City.* Cambridge: M.I.T. Press, 1943.

Sampson, Roy J., Martin T. Farris, and David L. Shrock. *Domestic Transportation: Practice, Theory, and Policy.* Boston: Houghton Mifflin, 1985.

San Francisco, City and County of, Department of City Planning. *The Urban Design Plan for the Comprehensive Plan of San Francisco.* 1971.

———. *Residential Design Guidelines.* 1979.

———. *Guiding Downtown Development.* 1982.

———. *The Downtown Plan.* 1983.

———. *Proposed Amendments to the Downtown Plan.* 1984.

Sanders, Welford. *Zero Lot Line Development.* Planning Advisory Service Report no. 367. Chicago and Washington, D.C.: American Planning Association, 1982.

Sanderson, Richard L. *Codes and Code Administration.* Chicago: Building Officials Conference of America, 1969.

Santayana, George. *The Sense of Beauty.* London: Adam and Charles Black, 1896.

Sargent, Fredric O. "A Scenery Classification System. *Journal of Soil and Water Conservation* 21 (Jan.-Feb. 1966), 26–27.

Sayre, Paul. "Aesthetics and Property Values: Does Zoning Promote the Public Welfare?" *American Bar Association Journal* 35 (June 1949), 471.

Schmertz, Mildred F. "Boston's Historic Faneuil Hall Marketplace." *Architectural Record* 162, no. 8, December 1977, 116–27.

Schussheim, Morton J. "The Rental Housing Development Grant Program: Some Early Observations." Washington, D.C.: Congressional Research Service, Library of Congress, November 21, 1985.

———. "The Reagan 1987 Budget and the Homeless." Congressional Research Service, Library of Congress, March 20, 1986.

Sedgwick, Theodore. *A Treatise on the Rules which Govern the Interpretation and Construction of Statutory and Constitutional Law.* 1857. Baker Voorhis. Reprint. Littleton, C.O.: Fred B. Rothman & Co., 1980.

Seligman, Edwin R. A. *Essays in Taxation.* 1895. Reprint. New York: Macmillan Co., 1928.

Selznick, Philip. *Leadership in Administration.* New York: Harper & Row, 1957.

Shafer, Elwood L., Jr., John F. Hamilton, Jr., and Elizabeth A. Schmidt. "Natural Landscape Preferences: A Predictive Model." *Journal of Leisure Research* 1 (1969).

Shipman, Sally. "Viewpoint." *Planning* 50, no. 8, August 1984, 42.

Short, Robert. *Dada & Surrealism.* New York: Mayflower, 1980.

Shultz, Earle, and Walter Simmons. *Offices in the Sky.* Indianapolis: Bobbs-Merrill, 1959.

Singer, Sheri L. "Public Housing Sale." *Planning* 50, no. 9, September 1985, 28.

Slitor, Richard E. *The Federal Income Tax in Relation to Housing.* Washington, D.C.: United States Government Printing Office, 1968.

Smith, Adam. *An Inquiry into the Nature and Causes of the Wealth of Nations.* 1776. Reprint. Chicago: University of Chicago Press, 1976.

Southern Building Code Congress. *Southern Standard Building Code.* Birmingham, A.L.: SBCC (revised periodically).

———. *Southern Standard Housing Code.* Birmingham, A.L.: SBCC (revised periodically).

Speer, Albert. *Inside the Third Reich.* New York: Macmillan Co., 1970.

Spencer, Herbert. *Social Statics.* London: Chapman, 1851.

Spengler, Edwin H. "The Taxation of Urban Land-Value Increments." *Journal of Land & Public Utility Economics* 17, no. 1, February 1941, 54.

Spreiregen, Paul D. *Urban Design: The Architecture of Towns and Cities.* New York: McGraw-Hill, 1965.

Stein, Clarence. *Toward New Towns for America.* 1950. Reprint. New York: Reinhold Co., 1957.

Stern, Robert A. *New Directions in American Architecture.* New York: George Braziller, 1969.

Sternlieb, George. *The Tenement Landlord.* New Brunswick, N.J.: Rutgers University Press, 1966.

Stevens, Mark, Gerald C. Lubenow, Maggie Malone, et al. "Putting on a Good Face, Saving Old Facades is a Controversial Compromise." *Newsweek* 106, no. 14, September 30, 1985, 76.

Svirsky, Peter S. "San Francisco Limits the Buildings to See the Sky." *Planning* 39, no. 1, January 1973, 9.

Tawney, Richard H. *The Acquisitive Society.* New York: Harcourt Brace, 1920.

Thompson, Peter. "Brandywine Basin: Defeat of an Almost Perfect Plan." *Land-Use Controls Quarterly* 3, no. 2 (1969), 29–38.

Time. "New Gilded Age Grandeur." September 2, 1985, 46.

Toll, Seymour I. *Zoned American.* New York: Grossman, 1969.

Toynbee, Arnold. "Lectures on the Industrial Revolution of the Eighteenth Century in England." London: Longman Green & Co., 1908.

Trimble, Gerald M. "Tax Increment Financing for Redevelopment: California Experience is Good." *Journal of Housing* 31, no. 10, November 1974, 458.

Tunnard, Christopher, and Henry H. Reed. *The American Skyline.* Boston: Houghton Mifflin, 1955.

Turnbull, H. Rutherford, III. "Aesthetic Zoning." *Wake Forest Law Review* 7, no. 2 (1971), 230–53.

U.S. Bureau of Budget. *Evaluation, Review, and Coordination of Federal Assistance Programs and Budgets.* Circular no. A-95, July 24, 1969.

U.S. Congress. Joint Economic Committee, Subcommittee on Urban Affairs. *Industrialized Housing.* Washington, D.C.: United States Government Printing Office, 1969.

U.S. Department of Housing and Urban Development. *Minimum Property Standards for Multifamily Housing.* Washington, D.C.: United States Government Printing Office, 1979.

———. *Minimum Property Standards for One and Two Family Dwellings*. Washington, D.C.: United States Government Printing Office, 1982.

U.S. News and World Report. "Why New Towns Are Running Into Trouble." 77, no. 11, September 9, 1974, 60.

Van Alstyne, Arvo. "Taking or Damaging by Police Power: The Search for Inverse Condemnation Criteria." *Southern California Law Review* 44 (Fall 1971), 1–73.

Veiller, Lawrence. *A Model Housing Law*. New York: Russell Sage Foundation, 1914.

Venturi, Lionello. *History of Art Criticism*. Translated by Charles Marriott. 1936. Reprint. New York: Dutton, 1964.

Venturi, Robert. "A Bill-Ding-Board Involving Movies, Relics, and Space." *Architectural Forum* 128, no. 3, April 1968, 76.

———. *Complexity and Contradiction in Architecture*. 1966. Reprint. New York: Museum of Modern Art, 1977.

Venturi, Robert, Denise S. Brown, and Steven Izenour. *Learning from Las Vegas*. Cambridge: M.I.T. Press, 1972.

Wade, John W. *Architecture, Problems, and Purposes*. New York: John Wiley & Sons, 1977.

Wagman, Robert M. "Protecting Solar Access: Preventing a Potential Problem." *Golden Gate University Law Review* 7 (1977), 765–809.

Wagner, Walter F., Jr. "Stanley Tigerman on Being Just a Little Less Serious . . ." *Architectural Record* 160, no. 4, September 1976, 111.

Wall Street Journal. "Senate House Bills Remain Apart on Top Rates, Fate of Some Deductions." June 25, 1986.

Weaver, Clifford L., and Richard F. Babcock. *City Zoning: The Once and Future Frontier*. Chicago and Washington, D.C.: Planners Press, 1979.

Weber, Max. *The Protestant Ethic and the Spirit of Capitalism*. Translated by Talcott Parsons. 1904. Reprint. New York: Charles Scribner's Sons, 1958.

———. *On Law in Economy and Society*. Edited and translated by Max Rheinstein. 1925. Reprint. New York: Simon & Schuster, Clarion, 1954.

Wenzel, David A. "UDAGs Are Better." *Planning* 48, no. 4, April 1982, 14.

Wermeil, Steven. "Supreme Court Puts off Zoning Question for 'Another Day' Causing Confusion." *Wall Street Journal* July 1, 1985.

Werth, Joel. "Tapping Developers." *Planning* 50, no. 1, January 1984, 21.

West, Jack. "Four Applicants Seek to Create Age-Limit Zones." *Arizona Republic* (Northwest ed.), July 7, 1986.

Whitehill, Walter M. "The Right of Cities to Be Beautiful." In *With Heritage So Rich, Special Committee on Historic Preservation*. U.S. Conference of Mayors. New York: Random House, 1966.

Whiting, Charles C. "Twin Cities Metro Council: Heading for a Fall?" *Planning* 50, no. 3, March 1984, 4.

Whyte, William H., Jr. *The Social Life of Small Urban Spaces*. Washington, D.C.: Conservation Foundation, 1980.

———. *The Last Landscape*. Garden City, N.Y.: Doubleday, 1968.

Wilcox, Charles J. "Aesthetic Considerations in Land Use Planning." *Albany Law Review* 35, no. 1 (1970), 126–47.

Williams, George A. "Fine Points of the San Francisco Plan." *Planning* 50, no. 2, February 1984, 12.

Williams, Stephen F. "Subjectivity, Expression, and Privacy: Problems of Aesthetic Regulation." *Minnesota Law Review* 62 (November 1977), 1–58.

Wilson, James Q., ed. *Urban Renewal: The Record and the Controversy.* Cambridge: M.I.T. Press, 1966.

Wolfe, Tom. *From Bauhaus to Our House.* New York: Farrar Straus & Giroux, 1980.

Wolman, Harold. *Politics of Federal Housing.* New York: Dodd, Mead & Co, 1971.

Index

References to footnotes are indicated by *n*.

$$
\begin{array}{r}
80 \\
12 \\
\hline
160 \\
80 \\
\hline
960 \\
960 \\
\hline
1920
\end{array}
$$